THE PSYCHOLOGICAL ASSESSMENT OF CHILDREN

JAMES O. PALMER, PH.D

ASSOCIATE CLINICAL PROFESSOR
DEPARTMENT OF PSYCHIATRY
AND
STAFF PSYCHOLOGIST, CHILDREN'S DIVISION
THE NEUROPSYCHIATRIC INSTITUTE
THE UNIVERSITY OF CALIFORNIA
AT LOS ANGELES

JOHN WILEY & SONS, INC.

NEW YORK · LONDON · SYDNEY · TORONTO

Library of Congress Catalogue Card Number: 70-101976

SBN 471   65772   7

Printed in the United States of America

10   9   8   7   6

THE PSYCHOLOGICAL
ASSESSMENT OF CHILDREN

This book is dedicated with respect and affection to

JEAN WALKER MacFARLANE, PH.D.,

Professor Emeritus, The University of California,
whose scientific and humane interest in children
is a model for all of her students and colleagues

PREFACE

The dilemmas of an author are perhaps of little concern to the reader, unless their intrusions into the book are disruptive. This book reflects my dilemma, as is indicated by the title of Chapter 1, "The Scientist-Clinician." Although this is explained and discussed in the text, I did face at least one general problem, which pervades the whole book and which should be mentioned here.

There exists a question of the degree to which a book on clinical assessment should cover either scientific facts and theories or the techniques of assessment per se. It was my original intention merely to write down what I tell my students as I supervise their clinical work with children. To put these thoughts into print has been a long and laborious task, chiefly because what I try to instill in my students is that they must think about what they are doing. Thus, technical tasks, such as how to score an intelligence test or even the Rorschach Technique, are, in my opinion, something the student can read in a manual and practice on his own. The correction of the student's technical work is a minor aspect of supervision. Since, in most instances, these tasks are well covered in manuals, they are given only passing reference and consideration in this book. Similarly, it is to be expected that the student clinician will have had a general background in the behavioral sciences with respect to both fact and theory. Thus, references to scientific facts and theory in this book may seem superficial to readers who are more deeply involved in these matters.

In my experience, the most crucial aspect of clinical training for beginning students is to learn how to relate fact and theory to their clinical work and, in writing this book, I have emphasized their import to the student. However, many facts have only been hinted at or have been even omitted, and much theoretical material may have been ignored or given such short shrift as to disappoint some readers. At the same time, it has been necessary to probe enough of the details of technique and procedure to illustrate their scientific basis and their relation to fact and theory. At other points, I found it necessary to propose possible theoretical constructs. I hope the student will recognize these as "proposals" and will not think them established and univocally accepted but, instead, will consider them as rough models for theory constructions. I intended to illustrate how many of the problems of the clinical process have to be thought through in as logical fashion as possible.

Thus, the peculiarities and errors in this book are my own. However, they have been minimized by the assistance of several colleagues who were kind enough to advise me on many points. I am particularly grateful to Paul Carlson, who helped to formulate the general outline, to Leila Beckwith, who read and criticized the final manuscripts, and to Justin Call and Martha Bernal, for their criticisms and comments on parts of Chapter 18. Dorothy Brown and Randy Langer were the students who worked diligently on the many technical aspects of putting this book together. Vivien Lucas was the patient and enduring typist. But, most of all, I thank my wife, Minerva. This book could never have been completed without her constant encouragement and support.

JAMES O. PALMER

CONTENTS

LIST OF CASES

LIST OF FIGURES AND PLATES

THE PSYCHOLOGICAL
ASSESSMENT OF CHILDREN

THE HYPOTHESES OF ASSESSMENT

Chapter 1

THE SCIENTIST-CLINICIAN:
AN INTRODUCTION

A. A DEFINITION AND ITS IMPLICATIONS

Psychological assessment is the use of scientific knowledge and methods in order to study the behavioral problems of an individual child. The overall purpose of this book is to demonstrate how this knowledge and these methods may be applied to the individual case. An examination of the implications of this definition may serve to clarify this purpose.

The chief reason for considering this definition in some detail is that for many psychologists it poses a major dilemma—that of the "scientist-clinician." On the one hand, a child's behavior usually requires clinical attention because that behavior is socially disruptive. Assessment thus has a social purpose and context, which places a social obligation on the psychologists. A scientist, on the other hand, has as his prime concern the formulation of general laws, rather than the study of individual cases. Nor can the scientist be limited by social demands and purposes.

Since the clinical psychologist must learn how to function as practitioner *and* scientist, an examination of the purposes both of assessment and of science might make a resolution of this dilemma possible. These considerations provide the rationale for the organization of this book.

B. THE PURPOSE OF AN ASSESSMENT

By definition, the purpose of an assessment is "to study" behavior. In this sense, an assessment has the same goal as any scientific investigation. However, the problems that confront a clinical psychologist differ in several important respects. The "pure" scientist is relatively free to select and define those general problems which attract his interest and whet his curiosity. The clinician however, receives his problem from those who are concerned with the behavior of the child: parents, teachers, physicians, or other responsible authorities. These social authorities define the problem, in effect, at least initially. What is most significant is that they delegate to the psychologist the responsibility for "studying the child's behavior." It is this social obligation which most sharply distinguishes the problems that face the scientist-clinician.

Because clinical concepts and operations are most clearly understood by reference to clinical data, the reader will find illustrative clinical case material utilized throughout this book. The nature of the problems to be solved in assessment and the social obligation placed on the clinician are epitomized in what is known in clinical parlance as the "presenting problems." Here are some examples:

CASE 1

Peter, age six, is described as "hyperactive." Twice he has been "expelled" from kindergarten because he constantly runs around the room and yard, disregarding the teacher's requests and instructions and interfering with the activities of other children. Even more seriously, he sometimes leaves the school grounds and wanders about the streets. At home, also, he is constantly "on the go," disobedient, into everything, always demanding. He talks constantly but his speech is "babyish," his vocabulary limited, and his enunciation poor. He sleeps only in brief naps and is often awake and out of bed at night. The school refuses to accept him in the first grade. His mother believes he is "brain damaged" and has taken him to several neurologists, who give her equivocal answers but no positive findings. His father believes firm discipline is the answer but finds punishment to be of little effect. Desperate, the parents turn to the psychological clinic asking, "What's wrong with Peter? What should we do?"

CASE 2

Karen, age ten, is one of the best behaved girls in the fifth grade. Her school work is superior and always very neat, except that her handwriting is quite cramped and tiny. However, she always seems frightened. She jumps with a start when spoken to and responds in such a low voice that the teacher finds it necessary to keep encouraging her to "speak up." Extremely shy, she has no friends and would spend every recess in the bathroom if permitted to do so. Her feelings are so easily hurt that she will burst into tears at almost nothing— yet she never complains. Her mother, who has been aware of Karen's shyness for several years, is very worried about her, but her father tends to dismiss the problem. Karen has also suffered from occasional repetitive nightmares and chronic constipation. It was the latter symptom that brought Karen and her mother to the psychologist. The family pediatrician had advised them that he found no physical causes for Karen's constipation and was of the opinion that it was a part of her overall personality difficulty.

CASE 3

Ted, age 13, has an eight-year history of classroom disturbance. Now in the ninth grade, his behavior is almost intolerable. He whispers and giggles constantly and makes gestures which seem sexually suggestive, sending the class into gales of laughter. Even after he is excluded from the room, it may take the rest of the hour to settle the class. When reprimanded, Ted becomes contrite and promises to reform. He is seldom directly hostile; in fact, he is usually good natured and always eager for attention and praise. His schoolwork is mediocre; "inattentive," "careless work habits," "doesn't stop to think," say his teachers. Despite his classroom antics, other children do not choose him as a friend. He participates actively in all athletics but is a poor player and a "poor sport," jeering at others, complaining about the rules, and "horsing around," breaking up the game. The boy's vice-principal strongly advised Ted's mother to seek psychological help.

CASE 4

Roberta, age 16, is repeating the tenth grade but probably will not pass because she frequently cuts classes; sometimes she leaves the school grounds for several hours. Sullen and defiant, she responds to any adult overture, either discipline or sympathy, with a sneer. In her dress and make-up she overdoes the latest teenage fads; several times this semester, the girls' vice-principal has sent her home to change her clothes because she violates the standards set by the student body council. Her seductive manners command the attention of the boys, but they tease her and are not attracted to her. Her acne has been particularly severe recently. She is friendly with several girls who have poor reputations and records of serious delinquency, but Roberta is not known to have engaged in any illegal behavior other than truancy. Roberta's mother, when she was finally contacted by the school, disowned any responsibility for Roberta's behavior, saying that Roberta was completely out of her control and would not obey anything she said. Consequently, Roberta has been referred to the Juvenile Court; the Court requests psychological assessment.

These cases are presented as only a tiny sample of the personal and social problems which require assessment. The central point illustrated in these clinical vignettes is that they are situations of desperation, both for the child and for those responsible for the child. In each instance, the parents, school, physician or court ask, "What is wrong with this child?" and, what is even more important, "What is to be done?"

Since these are personal and social problems, the parents usually try to answer them on the basis of their own knowledge and experience. Normally, parents accept responsibility for the child's behavior and, as will be discussed in subsequent chapters, many parents are loathe to admit they may have failed and have to seek help. At least they see the fact that the child is disturbing to them, and usually by the time they decide to seek psychological help, they also perceive that the child is himself disturbed. Moreover, they have often taken measures to correct the situation. Peter's father spanked him daily. Karen's mother tried inviting other children over to their home (which embarrassed Karen further) and doctored her constipation with patent medicines. The vice-principal lectured Ted endlessly, and his parents stood over him while he did his homework. Roberta's mother had tried restricting and denying her privileges and money; one teacher had made extra efforts to befriend her, but to no avail.

Usually school authorities also try a variety of educational techniques and arrangements for the child before they seek outside advice. When parents and school turn to courts, the child may be subjected to a series of legal warnings and remedies in an effort to alter the child's behavior. Assistance with these problems is still sought from the minister, priest, or rabbi, who attempt to reply with a combination of religious law, moral dictum, and humane wisdom. Increasingly, these problems have been referred to the physician, especially the pediatrician, who seeks answers in terms of the physical health and development of the child.

Sometimes (perhaps more often than psychologists may imagine) parents are able to solve these problems on their own. Or the teacher, judge, minister, or pediatrician—in combination with one another and with parents—are able to help the child without further specific knowledge. Usually it is only after all efforts to alter the child's behavior have been ineffective that the parents and other authorities turn to the psychologist with the question, "What is to be done with this child?"

Although the ultimate question is "What is to be done?" the initial question "What is wrong with this child?" must be answered first. In fact, it is usually because no one has undertsood the cause of the child's disturbance that the methods of handling and changing his behavior were ineffective. Thus, *the essential purpose of a psychological assessment is to determine the nature and extent of the disturbance in order to select and formulate the mode(s) of behavioral change.* Note that this statement presumes that there *are* different modes of treatment, different ways of altering behavior, different milieus in which the child may be placed. If one presumes that *all* behavioral problems can be handled by a single form of treatment, for example, by psychoanalysis, by operant conditioning, by nondirective counseling, or by foster home placement, then there is no need for assessment. In fact, the orthodox adherents of some of these "schools" of behavior change have seen no necessity for assessment. However, in this book it is assumed that there are many different ways of altering the child's behavior and environment. Commonly children's problems call for a combination of approaches.

This statement of the rationale for assessment thus would seem to imply a relationship between "what is wrong" and "what is to be done," so that if the problem were defined carefully enough, the remedy would be obvious. Unfortunately, the relationships between the problems of childhood and methods of behavioral change are far from clear, as will be discussed in detail in Part V. However, the contention of this rationale is that, by defining the problem by means of a thorough assessment, it is at least easier to examine the potentialities of various approaches to behavioral change. Most of all, a thorough assessment provides the data for planning treatment so that a general mode of behavioral change can be made specific to the child, his family, and their difficulties.

C. THE UTILIZATION OF SCIENTIFIC KNOWLEDGE AND METHODS

This second key phrase in the definition of assessment leads to a consideration of the relationship between these clinical goals of assessment and the goals of science. Such consideration is necessary because the goals of society are not necessarily the goals of the scientist. The "pure" scientist has as his goal the expansion of knowledge, especially in terms of general laws. His motivation is his own scientific curiosity. He is relatively disinterested in the practical, immediate questions of individual behavior, except as they may provide some hints or leads to the broader, theoretical questions which he is exploring. As a citizen, he may be cognizant of the importance of the social-personal question; however, as a scientist, this may seem irrelevant.

Although the goals of the clinical psychologist cannot be limited to those of the "pure" scientist, the task of seeking answers to the questions posed by personal problems of the individual child is often an intriguing challenge to his scientific curiosity. However, this type of scientific satisfaction is only a token if the knowledge gained from the case in question cannot be used as a basis for understanding of future cases. Often the clinical psychologist's appetite for research is whetted as he gains new knowledge from an individual case or is able to make new hypotheses. It is in this sense that the goals of "pure" and "applied" science converge. Of course, the clinical psychologist receives his greatest personal satisfaction whenever his assessment aids the child, and he can find long-range satisfactions in helping the community to think scientifically and humanely about children.

The social responsibility of assessing disturbed children places severe demands on the psychologist's scientific knowledge and acumen. This responsibility becomes even more awesome when the problems presented by the child extend beyond the available knowledge and techniques. Despite the extensive surge of research on child development and behavior over the past decade, many of the common behavioral and social disturbances presented by children remain more a matter of "expert opinion" than of scientific knowledge. For example, there is very little research as yet on any of the patterns of behavior illustrated in Cases 1–4 above. For the most part, there is little more than accumulated clinical hypotheses (and biases) about such prevalent phenomena as school phobias, adolescent sexual promiscuity, or even that much discussed but little researched annoyance, enuresis. More alarming is the ignorance about suicide in children, although among adolescents it is currently one of the major causes of death. Research has not yet determined why children attempt to kill themselves, let alone provided any reliable technique of predicting the possibility of suicide.

In view of these social responsibilities and the relative paucity of research findings, every clinical psychologist must ask: How is it possible to make assessments of the individual child which are at all valid and significant? The answer proposed and elaborated on in this book lies in the clinician's development and utilization of three equally important and interacting scientific assets. The *first* is a comprehensive and integrated knowledge of fact and theory from the behavioral sciences. The *second* basic scientific tool which the clinical psychologist can bring to bear on the clinical question is the ability to observe behavior carefully and accurately. His training in methods of collecting, sampling, and collating behavioral data brings skills not possessed by the layman or other professionals. His knowledge and skill need to be combined with yet a *third* faculty fundamental to all scientists: the ability to reason logically, both deductively and inductively.

As to the first asset, even though "general" psychology (as distinct from applied psychology) is not primarily concerned with the problems presented by an individual child, the general laws that have been developed about learning, perception, motivation, and other psychological functions do provide the basic core of knowledge for the work of the scientist-clinician. Very often, when the clinician seeks to understand a new and complicated problem in the personal life of an individual child, his chief resource is his knowledge of these scientific laws. Even more directly pertinent are research studies in developmental psychology. Insofar as these clinical questions involve social as well as personal problems— and to some extent there is a social aspect to all personal problems—social psychology, sociology, anthropology, and even history and economics are fundamental to the basic knowledge of the clinical psychologist.

Unfortunately, in practice, the clinical psychologist too often goes through the motions of an assessment with little recognition that the data that he is gathering are, in fact, related to or made comprehensible by the seemingly abstruse theories or research studies he learned about in graduate school. In a survey of the attitudes of clinical psychologists, Wildman and Wildman (1967) report that a majority appear to operate without much reference to any one definite theory of personality. It would seem unlikely that clinicians ignore theory altogether, but rather that they use a variety of theories—without making their theorizing explicit. The student most often needs an integration of this background in behavioral science with the clinical tasks and techniques of assessment. A complete analysis and integration of this general knowledge is beyond the scope of this book. To attempt to state even the principal relationships between clinical assessment of children and the rest of psychology and the behavioral sciences is an admittedly ambitious undertaking. Yet, the techniques of assessment and its procedures are not understandable nor applicable without at least a recognition of these principles. Part I of this book is intended as an outline, painted with a broad brush, of the basic hypotheses underlying assessment, drawing on general psychology, on developmental psychology in particular, and on the social sciences.

However, these "theoretical considerations" are intended chiefly as a review and reminder, since it is to be hoped the student already possesses much of this background knowledge. In the long run, the focus of this book is on the *utilization* of assessment. Thus, only passing references will be made to the pertinent research and theories chiefly to illustrate how they can and must be used by the clinician.

As to the second of the clinician's assets derived from his scientific training, Part II of this book is concerned with methods of systematic collection, recording, and analysis of data. The methods of a scientific investigation should be logically derived from the theoretical framework within which the scientist is operating. As will be discussed in further detail in Chapter 6, one of the main difficulties for the scientist-clinician is that the techniques of assessment have sprung from a variety of seemingly unrelated theories, many of which were never made explicit in the first place and which have often since been replaced by other concepts. Whether such a variety of theories can be integrated is doubtful, but at least an attempt will be made in this book to relate the rationale behind the most commonly used techniques to the general theoretical framework of child development discussed in these initial chapters.

Although the scientist's theory may focus his attention on certain kinds of data, he must not be blinded in his observations by his theory. One of the cardinal rules of scientific method is that no datum, however exceptional or "accidental," may be ignored even though seemingly inexplicable or extraneous to the theory. In fact, such observations are the test

of the comprehensiveness of the theory, which may have to be extended or revised. Moreover, the history of science is replete with instances in which discoveries were initiated by accidental or incidental observations. Scientific discovery often begins with naturalistic exploration. Although such exploratory investigations more often begin with hunches than with explicit theory, and data collection is seldom completely random, discovery often depends on what initially appears to be miscellaneous observations. As a scientific procedure, a clinical assessment is more analagous to such naturalistic exploration than to statistical surveys or to systematic experimentation. Thus, the clinical scientist has to be as observant of the exception as he is cognizant of what is "lawful" or "expected." Often it is through the presence of an exception to the rule, or the absence of what is expected, that the clinician begins to find some explanation for the question, "What is wrong with this child?"

It is with this background knowledge of the general science of human behavior that the clinical student is able to begin to accumulate knowledge about the individual. This study of an individual often seems initially to be altogether different, involving not only new procedures but, what is even more strange, a new kind of data than is collected in more general scientific studies. In contrast to the two or three "controlled" variables of the usual experimental study, an assessment involves a wide variety of detailed data about many different variables all at once. Sometimes the beginning student is almost overwhelmed by this wealth of information. Moreover, in experimental investigations, the fact that there are many instances of the same kind of behavior makes it relatively easy to analyze the data and draw conclusions. In contrast, a clinical assessment consists of many bits and pieces of data, only a few of which fall obviously into the same category, and which may seem at first to defy analysis. In fact, to the beginning student a case history and a handful of responses to a few "tests" may not even seem to be "data"—in the sense of the term as he learned it in general psychology. That these seemingly discrete pieces of information and responses are indeed "data" may be more easily recognized and accepted as the student learns how to find communalities and interrelationships among them. In order to assist the student in recognizing and using clinical data, the main evidence offered in support of many of the concepts discussed in this book will be life histories and responses of individual children—rather than citations of experimental or actuarial studies.

One other aspect of clinical observation that should be noted at the outset is that the attitudes and feelings of the observer are intimately involved. Particularly in work with children, it is often quite difficult to remain entirely emotionally neutral and "unbiased"— even if such neutrality is desirable. "Observer bias" has, of course, long been recognized in many fields of science, and has been regarded as a largely extraneous but almost unavoidable variable in the study of human behavior by human scientists. Yet, in clinical studies, this "observer bias" can be used, in fact needs to be used, as part of the observation, but the psychologist must first be aware of them within himself. His preparation for the clinical assessment of children should include an assessment of himself. Such self-recognition thus enables the psychologist to recognize similar feelings and attitudes in others in an objective, nondefensive, fashion.

As to the third asset of the clinician's scientific heritage, it is in studying human behavior in general that the psychologist learns to reason deductively, by checking hypotheses against the data provided from observations. Such deductive reasoning is often required in clinical assessment when the clinician is called upon to investigate possible reasons for a child's behavior. However, this behavior often poses questions for which there are no ready hypotheses. Frequently, the data seem relatively meaningless and inexplicable. The clinician, like the naturalist, then must learn to construct hypotheses, to think *inductively*, or, to use the more usual clinical term, to "interpret" his data. Such inductively determined interpretations then become the "working" hypotheses for treatment. It should be noted that deductively formed conclusions also are seldom complete, that the behavior of the individual child seldom exactly fits a general law, and that the conclusions so drawn are, in effect, also working hypotheses.

Moreover, the clinician, like any other scientist, should not and cannot limit himself exclusively to purely formal logic. As the physicist Robert Oppenheimer pointed out in his address to the American Psychological Association (1956), scientific thought and discovery often involve the use of analogy, which is an equally traditional form of logic. Argument by analogy often enables the clinician to derive meaning and form for his data, and

thus to begin to formulate hypotheses about them. Last but not least, the scientist-clinician depends on a thought process common to all science: intuition. This "aha!" experience, as Helmholtz labeled it over a century ago, remains the essential element for creative insight necessary to all scientific discovery.

D. WHAT IS A "BEHAVIOR PROBLEM?"—A DEVELOPMENTAL DEFINITION FOR "PSYCHOPATHOLOGY"

The third aspect to be considered in this definition of assessment is the term "behavioral problem." As was indicated above, this "problem" is initially defined socially by the complaints of the parents or others responsible for the child. However, there is often the question of whether these complaints and concerns are justified. Is there "something wrong with this child" or are the parents unduly alarmed? In the cases cited above, most laymen and probably most psychologists would agree that a parent should be concerned about the child's behavior. The fact that either a parent or child is subjectively distraught in itself constitutes a problem. In effect, the parent or other social authority requests that the psychologist further define the nature of this problem. This request is typically phrased by the common question: "Is *that* normal?"

Before considering the scientific criteria for defining behavior problems, a brief historical aside concerning concepts about personal distress may be in order, for these attitudes out of the past continue to affect how people regard assessment and the relief of behavioral disturbances. Scientific psychology itself dates back only a little over a century, and the history of clinical psychology can be counted in decades. According to Kanner (1962), scientists gave little recognition to psychological disturbances in children much before the twentieth century. Moreover, it is only in the latter half of this century that the clinical psychologist has been considered as a possible resource for problems of personal distress.

Up until about the nineteenth century, the mind of a child, if children were deemed to possess a mind, was considered to be so ephemeral as to be understood only by the poet. When it was recognized that the child was disturbed, he was thought to be "accursed" and the priest was called upon to exorcise the "devils"—or a magic potion or talisman was secretly sought from the local witch. Much more often, the child who demonstrated what would now be considered a psychological problem was thought "willful" and disobedient. Where such a "headstrong" child could not be managed by the parents, legal authorities stepped in and the child's socially disturbing behavior was deemed criminal and subject to legal punishments, which were often quite harsh. These century-old concepts have never been completely discarded and, far more than psychologists like to think, continue to be used in our modern society. At times they even enter into the attitudes of psychologists. The legal concepts have been considerably modified to take into account psychological concepts about childrens' behavior. Yet, such legal concepts as "delinquent," "insane," and "incorrigible" are in current use, even among psychologists. Many legal authorities and others continue to regard psychologists' explanations of childrens' behavior as attempts to excuse the disturbance to society. When psychologists become righteously defensive and disregard the socially disrupting effects of childrens' behavior, they only serve to justify the view that they do not believe in "discipline."

Nor have witchcraft and magic been completely abandoned. In this past decade, some ancient panaceas for human misery have been reintroduced, for example, Rauwolfia as a legal tranquilizer for adults and cannibis (marihuana) as an illegal magical escape for adolescents. Many parents become impatient with scientific deliberations over their distresses and fear that the psychologist will blame them. Frequently they regard their childrens' behavior as a curse for their own sins and wish that the psychologist could provide some magical invocation to sweep away their guilt. At times, under the pressure of such clients, psychologists have been known to cut short their scientific assessments and respond to the clients request that they "play God" and provide immediate relief by providing them with some advice or decision without further investigation.

The first attempts at scientifically understanding behavioral disturbances were made by physicians around the end of the eighteenth century. As scientific medicine began to show some promise of ameliorating physical ailments, people began to look to the physician for relief of psychological distress also. In the nineteenth century diseases began to be categorized, using symptom patterns and, when physicians began to assess and treat behavioral disorders, they naturally used the conceptual framework with which they were then familiar. Moreover, since most of their patients were adults, these diagnostic terms referred to adult symptoms. As physicians, they concentrated on those behaviors which appeared to be associated with physiological disturbances, and they tended to assume a physiological basis for others, even when no disease process was obvious. The newly born science of psychology was just then developing out of philosophy and was concerned chiefly with the general nature of the mind. "Mental disease" thus became the province of a branch of medicine, that is, psychiatry. As psychiatry developed, many physicians began to recognize that they were dealing with psychological rather than primarily physiological phenomena. The theories of such psychiatrists as Freud, Bleuler, Jung, and Adolph Meyer—to name only a few—were primarily psychological, even though these theories often had a biological reference point. Freud frequently referred to himself as a psychologist. Nevertheless, the basic disease schema and its terminology have remained as the conceptual framework in psychiatry.

As psychologists turned their attention to behavioral disorders, they too adopted this available medical model of "mental illness." Thus, Hathaway and McKinley (1943) used the current Kraepelin nosology for the MMPI. The original criterion upon which attempts were made to validate the Rorschach Technique was the "diagnosis" of psychiatric and neurological diseases. Psychologists continue to investigate a set of behavior disorders labeled "schizophrenia." Their research adds to the psychological knowledge about the behavioral disorders covered by this medical label, but few if any of these investigators question the medical model underlying their studies.

As evidence accumulates concerning the behavioral nature of these so-called "diseases," the adequacy of this disease model has come to be doubted. For example, the psychiatrist Szass (1961) challenged what he termed "the myth of mental illness." Szass was soon joined by psychologists, such as Albee (1966). In essence, they argue that this medical model fails to account adequately for the fact that much of the behavior subsumed under these medical concepts is not primarily physiological but is, in essence, learned behavior. The fact that most psychiatrists have used chiefly a psychological treatment, that is, psychotherapy, lends some support to Szass' argument. Many psychologists began to substitute the term "behavioral change" for "psychotherapy" or "treatment." Szass and others also argue that these behavioral disorders should no longer remain chiefly in the medical domain. At this writing, behavioral problems are being handled in a variety of settings, often without medical involvement. Nevertheless, the major responsibility for relief of personal distress and socially disturbing behavior often remains assigned to and claimed by the medical profession. This debate continues and probably will increase in intensity.

The inadequacies of the disease model are most marked when it is applied to children's behavior. First, it has long been recognized that children do not demonstrate many of the symptoms usually associated with the disease syndromes used to categorize behavior disorders among adults. In the psychiatric literature there has been considerable disagreement about what patterns of symptoms in childhood should be included in even the broader categories of psychoses and neuroses. When the term schizophrenia was first applied to children, many psychiatrists thought it was inappropriate, since these children did not commonly demonstrate such classic symptoms as hallucinations, delusion, or confused thought processes. Thus, the term schizophrenia when used to describe children's behavior was modified considerably; the classic symptoms were no longer the main criteria and, instead, greater emphasis was given to the child's lack of affective spontaniety and to his failure to relate to others. As the term childhood schizophrenia finally evolved, it referred chiefly to a difficulty in interpersonal relationships, which is a purely psychological phenomena. Incidentally, this change in the concept of schizophrenia during childhood has led to considerable research about the nature of adult schizophrenia and that concept has also been altered.

Second, children present many symptoms that are not included in the medical categories used to describe adult "diseases," such as enuresis, school failures, and speech disorders. The American Psychiatric Association's Manual for Diagnostic Classification (1952) lists only seven classifications for emotional disorders among children (aside from "mental deficiency"). None are as well delineated as the ones that are applied to adults. Most are of the all-inclusive type, such as "Behavioral

Disorders of Childhood." Thus it is often difficult to conceive of these categories as "diseases." Third, the symptoms that children manifest often seem relatively less stable than those suffered by adults. Although observers may agree that the child shows various signs of disturbance in general over a period of years, the symptoms often change. During one child's life, he may suffer a variety of "illnesses." For example, he may have "colic" as an infant,* subsequently be enuretic, then demonstrate a school phobia on entering school; later he may have an "alexia" when he tries to learn to read, and afterward be a "behavior problem," becoming a "delinquent" or "psychopath" as an adolescent. Although such series of symptoms are often interrelated and, as will be discussed throughout this book, consist of an accumulation of developmental difficulties, such a shifting set of symptoms makes it difficult to adhere to the disease model.

Fourth, in applying the adult disease model to children's behavior problems, one of the greatest difficulties lies in differentiating "normal" and "abnormal." For example, a person who has difficulty in distinguishing reality from fantasy, who uses neologisms, who is often quite illogical, who appears unaware of social amenities, who occasionally exhibits himself sexually, and who is unable to perform any useful work would certainly be regarded as "abnormal" and "mentally ill" if he were an adult, but it is questionable whether these terms are applicable if he were only four years old. The behavior of many normal eight-year-old children is decidedly "compulsive" at times, and much of the behavior of a normal adolescent might be described as "manic." Yet, the repetitive behavior so characteristic of eight-year-olds and the rapid changes of mood and the impulsiveness of adolescence are "normal" for these respective age groups; the use of these terms from the disease model to describe such behavior creates an unnecessary and misleading pathological bias.

In summary, the basic fallacy of the disease model is that in using this model, there is a tendency to gloss over the constantly accumulating mass of evidence that these disturbances of childhood—and for the most part, also among adults—are learned, social interactions rather than physiological disturbances. The

---

* Contrary to popular notion, this layman's term does not denote any particular physiological disorder but, instead, a generalized infantile reaction to stress and discomfort.

disease model does not account for this learning process in a developing child.

Such a bias toward psychopathology is created when the problem is placed in the dichotomy of "normal" versus "abnormal." The problem to be assessed is more effectively and pertinently conceptualized by reformulating the question: *To what extent and in what ways is the child's development deterred?* This question focuses on development, and the child's difficulties are thus seen in the perspective of changes accompanying his growth. In order to clarify what is meant by this developmental model, the next two chapters of this section are devoted to a discussion of "the laws of growth" and "varieties of learning." One of the important reasons for adopting this developmental point of view in assessing children's behavior is that the purpose of assessment is to determine the possibilities of changing that behavior. The very fact that the child's patterns of behavior are not yet completely determined usually increases the possibility of change. This possibility is furthered since growth often continues despite the barriers of stresses and impediments. In fact, at times the child's growth may be hastened or strengthened by stress, if it is not too overwhelming and if opportunities exist for surmounting impediments. In contrast, the alteration of adult patterns of behavior often involves changing long-established habit patterns, both the extinction of chronically reinforced attitudes and the learning of new methods, at a time of life when the individual normally does not accumulate new habits.

Admittedly in shifting from the disease model to an undisguised use of a psychological model based on development, it is not easy and perhaps not altogether necessary to discard the familiar terms associated with the old model. Some of these terms do describe definite psychological mechanisms. The central point is the shift in conceptual framework. Perhaps the most noticeable change in terms is the use in this book of the term assessment itself. Assessment of development is not the same as "diagnosis," which implies a pathology. Even the hybrid term psychodiagnosis is not appropriate, for it usually implies that a "psychopathology" is present. Both terms are used chiefly to describe a disturbance in a mature organism, and do not allow for the concept of growth. The term assessment is also broader than "testing," or "examination," or even "evaluation" for it includes all of these. "Tests," as will be seen, are only one form of data collection. "Examination" has the implication of being routine, of lacking the planned and thoughtful data collection process of assessment. Assessment involves not only a planned, purposeful "examination" pertinent to the clinical question at hand, but also analysis of the data, an "evaluation" of results. However, this term "evaluation" does at times carry with it the sense of social "value judgment," which the scientist might consider inimical to objective analysis of data. As will be seen, the clinician often cannot avoid the consideration of social values, for these social judgments usually play some part on the child's functioning. However, such value judgments form part of the data, not of the analysis of it.

Chapter 2

A DEVELOPMENTAL HYPOTHESIS

A. THE NATURE OF GROWTH

A child often seems to grow in spurts, to be far behind or advanced "for his age" in comparison to his peers; he may never go through a certain "stage," or he may continue with behavior other children have long outgrown. A child may seem unaware of some fact or be quite the incapable of a specific act one day and then, suddenly and almost miraculously, recognize that fact or perform that act. In assessing the individual child, it is necessary, of course, to recognize what these variations mean; are they random, chance events or do they follow some recognized scientific laws? The term "random" implies that the order of nature is unknown, and the phrase "scientific law" merely means that an order in nature has been conceptualized, on the basis of fact and logic. Assessment of the individual child has evolved from and been made possible by the scientific accumulation of facts about development, studies of the interrelationships between such facts, and finally, evolvement of higher order constructs or "laws." Over the past century, many facets of child development have been studied in detail, and a plethora of theories advanced—far more than can be covered in this chapter. In order to make more explicit the meaning of a developmental framework, it may suffice

to review two familiar and well-accepted generalizations about development, particularly because they set the guidelines for assessment.

The first principle is that the child's functioning develops from diffuse, gross, overall reactions to increasingly coordinated and finely differentiated functions.* This principle of diffusion-to-differentiation is initially manifested in the child's perceptual-motor development. The newborn, lying on his back, flails both his arms and legs and arches his back if stroked on his stomach or in response to a sudden noise; he shows no sign of focusing his eyes on objects, and it is often necessary to place the nipple in his mouth to feed him. However, within a very few weeks, he makes definite grasps at objects over his head, follows moving objects with his eyes, and searches actively for his mother's nipple when held to

---

* To be precise, two growth processes may be distinguished: a whole-to-differentiation process, in which the child learns to separate out particular perceptions, thoughts, or feelings from very global or generalized impressions, and a diffuse-to-integrated process, in which the child learns to control his reactions to such impressions more specifically and effectively. This distinction will be discussed in more detail in Section IV, using the terms "input" and "output." However, since these processes constantly interact on one another and thus may be considered as a set of interactions, it is possible to discuss them as one in this introductory section.

the breast. Within only a few more months, the infant, first supported in a sitting position, then able to sit on his own, makes increasing strides in observing and reaching for his world. Scales for assessment of behavioral development during the first year of life are based on this differentiation of perceptual-motor functioning (Cattell, 1940, Gesell, 1940). This principle is demonstrated in all subsequent functioning, locomotion, speech, toilet training, and learning of other socially imposed demands, preschool interpersonal and group relationships, acquisition of formal training in intellectual and motor skills at school and on the playground, and later the adolescent's groping for social and sexual maturation. To cite only a few commonplace examples, the child stands before he walks, intones sentences before he uses words, is more likely to explore a nursery school room, its objects, and inhabitants in seemingly aimless fashion before adopting specific play and companions; he can draw a circle before he can draw a square and a square before a diamond (see the Stanford-Binet, age levels II, IV, and VII). On the Rorschach inkblots, preschool children respond chiefly to the whole blot, often ignoring or confusing even the main details, but by age 8 the children are much more cautious about making such overall generalizations and more aware of the irregularities in the form.

Even to the beginning student of child development, this principle of diffusion-to-differentiation may seem so obvious as to require only passing mention. Unfortunately, this basic principle is too often ignored and violated by the authorities responsible for training the child—and sometimes is forgotten even by the clinical psychologist. The classic example, of course, is in toilet training. In the early decades of this century, soon after psychologists became acutely aware of the miracles of conditioning, they began to advise mothers that routine habits of defecation and urination not only could but should be instilled in the child at the earliest possible age. Since it is quite possible to establish such conditioned reflexes quite early, mothers began to boast that their baby could follow a toilet routine and control the relatively small muscles of the anal sphincter, even before the child had mastered control of the larger muscles systems needed to sit securely on a toilet. Moreover, this social stress, one of the first major interchanges between the child and his social group (his parents in this instance), was imposed before the child learned the first major technique of interpersonal exchange: speech. Subsequently, psychologists discovered that such premature conditioning of relatively complex behavior too often led to undesirable side effects, to overgeneralized attitudes about emotional control, and even to compulsive habits.

On the other hand, this whole-to-differentiation principle is the basis for several changes in educational techniques over the past several decades. In arithmetic, many children are now taught the "principle of numbers" and mathematical relationships in the first years of grade school — a topic formerly reserved for college students if taught at all — and they later learn the specific skills of addition, subtraction, multiplication, and division. Similarly, children now learn other languages by speaking them before they work out the details of grammar.

Before discussing and illustrating further the utilization in assessment of this whole-to-differentiation principle of development, it is necessary to consider a second overall pattern. The unfolding of behavior from wholes to parts does not proceed at an evenly regulated pace and, to comprehend and use it, the rates of growth must be taken into account. The age at which children develop certain specific skills in motor activity, in intellectual tasks, and in emotional and social controls has been a frequent subject of study in the field of child development. A knowledge of these research studies is often vital in the interpretations of data from an individual child. However, these studies of growth rates of specific skills are seldom interrelated, except in major longitudinal studies. The fact that the differentiation process of each skill does have unique features makes any generalization hazardous. To provide a schematic background for the subsequent consideration of specific assessment of the different functions of the ego, it may be helpful to disregard these differences for the moment and to posit a hypothetical single developmental curve.

The generalization that applies to most growth curves may be summed up as an "accumulation-integration" process, or more precisely as "accelerated accumulation-crisis-integration." As is shown in many studies of learning of various kinds, a child usually accumulates many basic aspects of a skill at an increasingly accelerated rate, but not at all evenly, to a point where he seems to cease to learn further. Then during the so-called "plateau" of the learning curve, it has been observed that he goes over, repeatedly practices, or, to use a term from psychoanalytic therapy, "works through" and integrates what he has learned, polishing off the skill and eliminating conflicting habits and attitudes, before rising to new heights on the learning curve and perfecting the skill he is learning.

By combining these two "laws" of development, it is thus possible to project some order in the constantly changing life of the child. This combination is illustrated in diagrammatic form by the hypothetical curve of the rate of development of the ego shown in Figure 1. During the first six years of life, the infant* is developing extremely rapidly, accumulating a variety of ego functions and subfunctions or details. He acquires in this brief period most of the major tools and techniques of ego functioning. He develops the major part of his muscular controls, begins to think logically, assimilates the basic mores of his culture, and he passes through the major formative stages of "psychosexual" development. At no other time in his life will the child learn so much and so rapidly. The variability of this rate of ego development is also more extreme than at any other point in the child's life. Almost no preschool child seems to develop at a steady rate, and the differences

---

* In the ensuing discussion, the term "infant" is used more broadly than is common in developmental psychology and includes all the preschool years as distinct from the central period of childhood or "latency," ages 6–12.

between children during these years are often extreme. Nor do all the ego functions develop evenly; a child may be quite advanced in language development but be slow in motor proficiencies, or he may be quick to develop controls over his affect but remain socially overdependent. Data from all longitudinal studies confirm this variability. It is for this reason that predictions from infant behavior to later childhood or adolescence have little validity, no matter how refined the measurements. Admittedly this very generalized curve does not indicate the variations within these three stages, such as the rapid spurts of growth between ages four and six.

Somewhere around age six, the overall rate of the child's development becomes less precipitious, and while it does not actually form a flat plateau, the curve is not as steep. Moreover, during this central period of childhood, the variability both between children and within the individual child is less extreme. At this time, the child develops more evenly, in not quite as many leaps and bounds. The reason is that he is no longer accumulating so many new functions. Although he learns some new skills at school, the latency child does not develop new basic functions. Instead, he is integrating and practicing the previously learned functions.

With the onset of puberty, the curve of development again rises sharply, at least for a brief period, while the child struggles to develop methods to cope with new physiological stress and to learn new social behavior,

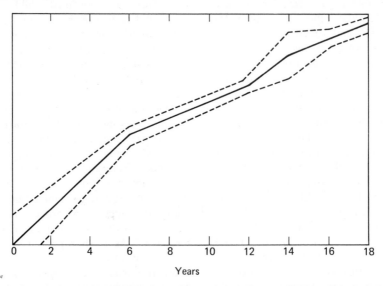

FIGURE 1. Normal rate of development of ego functions (dotted lines indicate variability).

in order to meet the demands for achieving the final steps of adulthood. Again, the variability in the rate of development is obvious even to the casual observer. Adolescents are precociously adults one moment and infantile the next. Asked the age of her son, one mother replied, quite accurately, "He's 12 going on 17!" The data available on late adolescence suggest that as the child enters into young adulthood, the curve again slacks off and the variability in development is again less extreme. However, the pace of development still varies considerably in the last years of high school and the early years of college or young adult life. These last steps of adolescence are also usually integrative.

These shifts from one stage of development to another are critical periods in the child's life, during which he changes his social milieu as well as his pace of development. On entering school, he not only begins a regime of practiced learning, he also takes the first step toward breaking family ties and loosening the heretofore relatively complete dependency on his parents. The anxieties arising from such separation need to be allayed and resolved before the child can proceed to the status of schoolchild. Moreover, such separation anxiety is repeated at pubescence, as the adolescent struggles for independence and for identification with his peer group. The final critical period of shift and separation occurs as the adolescent leaves the parental nest altogether and becomes a young adult.

The main reason for restating these principles of development is to emphasize the fact that change and crisis are a normal and necessary part of childhood. This is not to say that extremes of behavior, of stultifying tension, or of utter lack of control, often analogous to adult emotional and social distrurbances, are not signs of emotional and social disturbance in childhood. Such extremes cannot be dismissed as "something the child will outgrow" (Work and Call, 1965). The chief signs of "abnormality" in childhood are the absence of growth, the failure to change, and the retreats from the critical shifts from one stage of childhood to the next. *Unmanageable stress during childhood is manifested chiefly in disruptions of the growth process.*

Psychological assessment of a child thus begins with assessment of the nature and rate of his development and proceeds to an investigation of possible factors that may be deterring (or overaccelerating) his growth.

The principal biological and cultural factors that delimit growth will be discussed subsequently in this chapter. However, *psychological* assessment is not concerned primarily with the biological or social environments per se, but rather *with the learning processes* of the human organism in a defined culture. Thus, before examining the factors affecting growth and learning, it may be helpful to consider briefly the relationships between assessment and the theories of learning.

B. ASSESSMENT AND LEARNING

In assessment of children, a knowledge of the facts and theories of human learning processes is essential. The plural "theories" needs to be emphasized because no one learning theory has been promulgated which is complete and comprehensive enough to cover the complexities of the developing life pattern of an individual child. In assessment, one needs to be aware that, as Tolman (1952) in his classic paper has pointed out, there are "many kinds of learning." Learning during infancy, for example, consists largely of simple conditioning, of repetitive stamping in and stamping out of response patterns. The accumulation of habit patterns of varying strengths arising from a complexity of drives occurs throughout childhood. Learning through one single traumatic conditioning is so often reported in emotional disturbances that the clinician often looks for such an incident. Such a single vivid experience may be generalized to other experiences or it may be a culminating event, triggering other behavior.

The question of how a child has learned is thus essential to every assessment. Most, if not all, of our assessment tools deal with learned behavior almost exclusively. The behavior they sample is learned even if the intent is to make inferences from such learned behavior about "native potential," "inherited traits," or "brain damage." For example, an I.Q. test consists of graded series of learned achievements from which the assessor may attempt inferences about the learning potential of the child. Similarly, responses to projective techniques consist of attempts to fit learned responses to unstructured stimuli. Much of case-history taking is also aimed at the question of *how* a child has learned and adapted.

Nevertheless, learning theories derived

from comparative research often seem to be unrelated to the task of assessment. As was mentioned above, the hiatus between learning theory and clinical assessment is to a great measure an artifact, resulting from a failure in the training of clinical psychologists. However, it is also true that the term "learning theory" and the research studies on learning have traditionally focused on only one question about learning and that is *how* the child learns. However, the assessing clinician must be concerned with several other equally important questions of learning. Thinking in developmenal terms, the clinician also needs to know *when* the child learns; *when,* in the developmental sequence, may be a more important question than how. *When* may also be thought of as "under what circumstances", that is, when in a sequence of the child's experience. *Why* the child is learning is only vaguely included in traditional "learning theory" (which is still grappling theoretically with the problems of motivation), but in clinical assessment the drives, motivations, avoidances, rewards, etc. need to be spelled out. Often these motivations are central to the child's rehabilitation. The question of *what* is learned is considered to be of little or no import in traditional "learning theory." Yet, the content of learning is central to the study of human behavior. Parents, school authorities, and society at large are upset by the "bad" habit the child has learned or the "good" habit he has failed to learned, and although they may ask, "However did he learn that!" they do not really care about the method by which the child learns or even how it becomes unlearned. Moreover, traditional learning theory does not differentiate between learning various types of tasks. For example, there may well be a difference between learning to handle sexual excitement by vomiting as opposed to fire-setting, or, more important, the learning of more socially and personally acceptable patterns. Perhaps the extinguishing of fire-setting (whatever the motivation) does involve the same learning processes as in the control of vomiting — but this is not known.

Central to the clinical inquiry and yet also relatively ignored by the traditional learning theorist is the question of *who* is learning. Interested almost solely in the general problem of learning processes per se, the comparative psychologist has not been concerned with individual differences in learning. Yet, there is considerable evidence from educational as well as clinical psychology that individuals differ widely not only in overall learning ability but in their ability to utilize various learning processes. Some children and adults condition more easily than others; some generalize quickly, others not at all. What is more important is the fact that new learning by the child does not take place on an empty slate. Each task, habit, or attitude is learned by a child who already has an accumulation of other learned tasks, habits, and attitudes, to say nothing of his unsatisfied drives and frustrations, or his conflicting emotional investments. It might be difficult, for example, to teach a starving child to use a fork!

An equally important corollary of this question of *who* is learning is the question *from whom* is the child learning? Increasingly, psychologists, especially clinical and social psychologists, are becoming aware that learning does not take place completely inside the child. Rather, most learned behavior occurs in a social setting as part of a social interaction. In most instances some adult or peer acts as teacher to the child, and how well the child learns is dependent in part on his relationship to this instructor or group of instructors. Very often the motivating force is the child's dependency, both physical and emotional, upon the adult, or the approval and status in his peer group. Even the natural curiosity of the child needs to be stimulated or at least encouraged by adult authority. Nor does the relationship necessarily have to be "positive"; children learn from those they fear or dislike or are rebelling against, although the question of "what" they learn in such relationships again arises. Thus, some children learn how *not to learn* at school, to spite their ambitious parents. A close examination of how some children avoid learning is often quite revealing, for it takes an active effort on the child's part to avoid paying attention to the teacher and the class.

C. BIOLOGICAL DETERMINANTS OF DEVELOPMENT

It is widely accepted that the outer limits of learned behavior are set by the child's physiological structure, which itself is limited by genetic factors, congenital events during the fetal period, and the forces of physiological maturation which proceed through adolescence. Equally recognized is the fact that within these limits there is a great deal of variability of behavior — the result of an interaction of sociocultural stress—and of accumulated, individual experience upon this physiological organism. It would be presumptuous, however, to assume that these determinants play an equal or even proportionate role in every child's life pattern. Thus, it may be helpful to consider the relevancy of each of these determinants of development to the task of assessment.

1. *The Relation of Genetic Determinants of Development to Assessment*

At the beginnings of scientific psychology, when the first systematic studies of behavior were being conducted, the scientific world of the nineteenth century was in a philosophic ferment over the discovery of the evolution of the species. It is noteworthy that Darwin was also interested in the development of behavior in the human species and included his observations of childhood development in his theory of evolution. The new science of psychology was further influenced at the turn of the century by the advent of the Mendelian theory of genetic transmission of physiological traits. Thus it was natural that the concept of inherited psychological traits appeared to be promising, even though this concept was based chiefly on speculation or on very simple and indefensible research. This concept, as a major explanation of human behavior, was even more acceptable, since until the early part of the twentieth century, no other major theories had been conceived. As Freud began developing his psychoanalytic theory, he also accepted the general concept of inherited traits or "instincts." The new concept of learned behavior, beginning in Pavlov's laboratories and spreading to the United States after World War I, became the major alternative and from the contrasts between these two theories came the many "nature-nurture" studies of the succeeding decades. Despite this increased understanding of the role played by postnatal learning in development, the interest in and acceptance of the concept of inherited behavioral traits has never completely waned and has, indeed, received new research impetus over the past decade (Jackson, 1964).

At one time, the genetic inheritance of traits was the major consideration in clinical assessment of children. When "mental disorder," particularly mental retardation (or "feeblemindedness" as it was then known), was thought inherited, the only answer was preventive—sterilization. At one California hospital alone, between 1920 and 1950, nearly all retarded patients were sterilized. As psychologists began to recognize the multiple causes of behavior, including intellectual retardation, and the possibilities of other therapies and rehabilitation measures, the use of sterilization became quite restricted. Today most psychologists agree that the genetic inheritance of physiological structure is only one of the many complexities determining behavior and child development. The nineteenth-century rule that "structure determines functioning" has been modified to "structure interacts with stress to determine functioning." Moreover, with the intensely increased mobility of the world population, the pockets of generations of inbred peoples are fast disappearing. Liverant (1960), in an incisive and critical review of genetic factors in intellectual development, points out that geneticists are far more skeptical of the inheritance of complex behavior than are some psychologists!

Currently in assessment, inheritance of traits rarely becomes a major variable. While most psychologists might be tempted to regard the extremes of behavior, especially in intellectual functioning, as possibly genetic, they are cautious about the logical error of arguing that whenever other determinants cannot be established, a trait is therefore inherited. Instead, objective data are required before any conclusion can be drawn, and when the data are sparse or unreliable, then the psychologist can only report that no conclusion is supported. One main reason that clinical psychologists are slow to attribute behavioral disturbances, even in infants, to inherited traits, is that there are no exact methods for assessing this factor. Most of our psychological tests are basically measures of learned achievements or reactions. Observers of infants during their first few months of life often do note obvious signs of nascent emotional and intellectual behavior which are remarkably similar to the more fully developed traits in their parents. Even so, it is difficult to attribute even this behavior entirely to inheritance. The possibility both of conditioning during these first days of life and of congenital influences needs to be considered.

Although the direct genetic inheritance of behavioral traits remains largely unknown and thus unassessable, there is considerably more evidence concerning the genetic transmittal of physiological features such as bone development, overall body shape, pigmentation, etc., and susceptibility to diseases such as diabetes or hemophilia. Such inherited structures and susceptibilities do have psychological effects insofar as they result in limitations on bodily function and thus deter the learning of skills and cause social embarrassment and anxiety. Therefore it is necessary for the psychologist to possess at least passing knowledge of physiological inheritance and to help the patient take it into account. Although the possible inheritance of behavioral traits continues to be used defensively as an excuse by some parents, undesirable physiological traits are just as often considered "skeletons in the family closet," to be kept hidden or even ignored and forgotten. The following case illustrates how these attitudes can distort family relationships and child development.

CASE 5

Martha, age nine, was totally deafened by encephalitis at age five months. Although she had attended a school for the deaf for approximately two years, she had not developed any intelligible speech. However, she had learned rudimentary finger symbols and was fairly adept at making her wants known by gestures. Communication with her was difficult but up until about six months prior to being referred to the Guidance Clinic, she had been relatively tractable, responding compliantly to adult restrictions and requests, eager for attention and eager to learn. Over the past six months, she had become increasingly restless, irritable, and naughty. Most provocative to the school, where she lived, was her overt sexual curiosity, accompanied by open masturbation and attempts to involve other children in sexual play. Then school authorities began to notice Martha's development of secondary sexual features, her rounding breasts and pubic hair. Stains on Martha's clothes and linen suggested that her menses may have begun.

Initially, in the interview with Martha's mother, she desperately advanced various explanations for Martha's behavior: some of the older children must have initiated Martha into sex play; Martha had always been homesick and, after a brief illness several months ago

during which she stayed home, she was even more reluctant to leave her family; or, finally, maybe this behavior was another residual effect of the encephalitis. When the interviewer reminded her of the school's report about Martha's physical development, Martha's mother began to weep and then admitted that she, her two older daughters, and her mother and her maternal aunts had all begun to menstruate quite prematurely. She herself had come from an old-fashioned prudish family and had received no information from anyone regarding this development. When about Martha's age, she only sensed that all sexual functioning was a taboo topic and so suffered silently in fear and shame, believing something dreadful was wrong with her. Only after many months did an elderly servant discover her misery and take pity on her and present the facts to her mother. Even then, her mother's cold impersonal instructions on feminine hygiene were of little comfort.

Later, when faced with the same problem in her older two daughters, she was able, with considerable anxiety, to explain haltingly the facts of menstruation shortly before they experienced their first menses. In the face of the difficulty of communicating with Martha, she despaired and made no attempt, hoping that perhaps Martha's menses might not begin until Martha was somewhat older and able to understand more easily. She continued to regard this familial trait as a kind of "curse," since sexual impulses were aroused before the child was socially able to handle them. Indeed, she was so ashamed that she had never even mentioned the fact to her own husband! The interviewer was the first person with whom she had been able to discuss her feelings on the subject. Having so explored her own feelings, she accepted a program arranged in cooperation with the school nurse and one of Martha's favorite teachers in which the three of them together were able to help Martha understand what was happening to her and to control her behavior.

2. The Relationships of Congenital Determinants of Development to Assessment

Dating from antiquity, the idea has persisted in many cultures that events impinging on a pregnant woman could "mark her child for life." Pregnant women were protected from scenes of violence; sexual intercourse during pregnancy is still frequently tabooed; touching or wearing certain talismans or repeating specific incantations was encouraged, and special diets and regimes of exercise were prescribed — all intended to affect the future character as well as the health of the child. Although such taboos and totems are often unfounded superstitions, scientific evidence has gradually been accumulated concerning the effects of both biological and psychological stress on fetal development. For example, the effects on the child of certain diseases such as measles suffered by the pregnant mother are known and the deleterious effects of various toxins have been established. Moreover, several studies have shown that anxieties or stress endured by the mother may affect her pregnancy. Zemlich and Watson (1953), for example, discovered that those primipera women who had strong feelings of rejection toward the unborn child suffered excessive and continued bleeding, nausea, etc., more often than did mothers who accepted the pregnancy. The occurrence of miscarriages during emotional stress is commonly noted by both physicians and laymen. In reading case histories, one is often struck by the number of miscarriages and difficult pregnancies reported by emotionally disturbed women or by the frequency with which mothers of premature or otherwise poorly developed babies are described as emotionally disturbed. Yet, there is little research on the possible effects of the mother's emotional condition during pregnancy on the subsequent development of her child and this aspect of congenital determinant of development remains speculative.

The defects in development usually attributed to congenital stress are primarily physiological and secondarily psychological. Most important to psychological functioning are those trauma during fetal development to either the sensory-motor or the central nervous system. Similar trauma may occur from injuries at birth, when the anxieties and tensions of the mother may also result in somatic accidents seriously affecting the child. In contrast to genetically determined physiological defects, these congenital deterrants to future development are both more definable and more within the realm of possible prevention. With more research on the relationship between maternal tensions and the course of pregnancy and gestation, assessment and treatment of the anxious pregnant mother may become more possible and more frequent.

As with hereditary factors, the most important aspects of congenital determinants to assessment are the personal emotional attitudes held by the child and his parents. Adjusting to and overcoming handicaps which start before or at birth are often difficult for both the disabled child and his family. Although few such families are entirely free from some feelings of continued fear, resentment, and guilt, the children who are referred to psychological assessment are only a small minority of the handicapped. Very probably there are at least an equal number who are not so overwhelmed by their emotional attitudes as to need psychological attention. A few years ago this writer participated in a nationwide survey of congenitally brain-damaged children who had lived continuously at home and attended day-care educational and rehabilitation centers (Cain and Levine, 1961). A large majority of these children and their parents showed no marked emotional disturbance, even though many of the children were severely handicapped. On the other hand, there are many congenitally damaged children in clinics and hospitals who are the object of overanxious, ambivalent concern by their parents and who do develop emotional disturbance. Often this results in or is demonstrated in more disability than can be accounted for physiologically, as can be illustrated by the following two cases.

CASE 6

Mandie, age seven, was born six weeks prematurely; both of her knee sockets, her hip sockets, and the roof of her mouth had failed to develop completely and she suffered double hernias. During the first four years of her life, she endured six major operations, and half of her body was almost continuously encased in a cast. The usual motoric exploration of her environment had been denied her. Her speech then consisted of hollow grunts, intelligible only to her mother, although Mandie responded to speech with wrapt attention and often with appropriate reactions. Repair of her palate was the final surgical correction. Thereafter, with intensive rehabilitation work and speech therapy, both at the hospital and at home, she made rapid progress. By age 7, she could walk without crutches, albeit with an unsteady balance and a halting gait, and her speech, hollow and slow, was understandable to everyone. Her responses on I.Q. tests indicated above average to superior intelligence.

Placement in a regular first grade class at public school was recommended. Mandie and her mother seemed overjoyed and celebrated by a shopping spree in which they purchased matching mother-daughter outfits.

Scarcely six months later, Mandie was referred again for psychological study. Her achievement at school was far below what had been expected. Previously a bubbling, happy, and compliant child, she had become listless, irritable, and inattentive. Frequently she was absent from school with brief, minor, undiagnosed complaints. Although completely toilet trained soon after her body casts were removed, she had had a series of daytime soiling "accidents," which were the final reason for suspending her from school.

Mandie's mother, Mrs. B., appeared sorely disappointed and wept as she sought some explanation for this turn of events. "I had so hoped everything would work out wonderfully for her," she said. "I've tried my best, done everything, spent every minute and every cent just for her. She's been my whole life these past seven years." She explained that her husband had deserted her shortly before Mandie's birth, leaving her almost destitute and alone. "It was horrible — I almost went out of my mind." In a subsequent interview, she confessed that she had known her husband only briefly, that Mandie was conceived before their marriage, which she now believed he had entered into only because of his guilt over the pregnancy. The pregnancy and marriage had been angrily disapproved by her parents, and she had rebelled and left home at age 17. Over the past seven years she had been able to work only at odd hours, since Mandie had to be taken to the clinic almost daily, and only because she had some personal funds, "my savings for my college education," was she able to support herself and Mandie. "When Mandie started school," she said, "I'd hoped I could get a better job or even go back to school myself." However, she did not immediately seek full-time employment; "I didn't know whether Mandie might still need me at home." Gradually her fears were more than realized, as Mandie complained of weakness and seemed disinterested in school.

Mandie claimed to want to go to school but was not as disappointed as her mother. She recited her physical complaints and even complained about her disability. Although she had never actually complained about school, she averred that the work was "too hard." (The speech drills in prior years had been much more intensive and tiring than public school classes.) Finally, she launched into a tirade against another disabled classmate, a girl she considered to be the teacher's favorite. Mandie's responses to the projective tests were full of anger, frustration, and depression. Her fantasies indicated considerable ambivalence toward maternal figures, portrayed as evil witches who made constant bizarre demands on their victims and held them captive by unknown magic, only to be released by the "good fairy" or, in her most elaborate tale, "a handsome prince appeared from the sky to claim the heroine as his daughter."

CASE 7

Willis, age twelve had been blind from birth, because of a "retrolineal fibroplasia," the result of overuse of oxygen at his birth.* Both of his grandfathers were physicians; one was the director of the hospital where he was born. From the time of his birth, his mother, a professor of education, abandoned her career and "sacrificed" her life to seeking care for Willis. With constantly conflicting counsel from the grandfathers, she brought Willis to the attention of most of the major medical and educational centers for the blind in the United States and Europe, but was never satisfied. Willis never remained in any school longer than six months. He was a major "behavior problem," excessively demanding, destructive, restless, and inattentive. His father, an outstanding professional tennis star ("a tennis bum," his wife called him — in front of Willis) remained uninvolved in his wife's desperate search for an answer to Willis' disability. When Willis was six, his parents divorced and Willis' father obtained custody of his two older daughters. Willis then became his mother's sole companion.

At age 12, Willis was blatantly psychotic. He chattered away in almost meaningless sentences, rocking back and forth in the chair. Reports from various schools for the blind and private tutors indicated that at one time he appeared to have superior intelligence, was curious about everything, eager to learn, and was rapidly becoming proficient at reading Braille. Willis now could not respond to tests and scarcely could be drawn away from his

---

* This iatrogenic disorder has now been eradicated as a result of the discovery of the effect of this practice.

personal world of fantasy into even momentary conversation. His confused outpouring of words suggested an admixture of overwhelming depression, loneliness, and despairing rage, uttered in a high-pitched, flat singsong.

His mother, a tense, tight-lipped woman, recited Willis' history in a monotone, with precise details of dates, places, and names in chronological order. She was well aware of Willis' present condition, citing the psychiatric diagnosis. She reported that Willis had received "extensive psychiatric care," mentioning the names of several well-known psychoanalysts, but it was evident that he had never remained in treatment for more than three months. When she was asked about her present situation, her composure faded and she began to weep. During the past year she and Willis had floated from one hotel to another across the world until she had run out of money. She had exhausted a large fortune and was now penniless and in debt. She could find no employment in her profession, and there was no one to care for Willis if she did take a job. She was entirely separated from all friends and family. Moreover, she felt she was in danger of becoming an alcoholic, as drinking was the only answer she had found for her own depression. She knew that Willis probably should be hospitalized but could not bear to part from him. Twice in the past month, she had made plans to kill him and herself. With some encouragement from the psychologist, she accepted arrangements to admit both Willis and herself to a public mental hospital. Four months later, she was able to leave the hospital, although Willis remained there, unimproved. She obtained a sales job, supporting herself, and returned to the clinic for an extended period of psychotherapy.

In both of these cases, the intense compensatory "sacrifice" of the mother overshadowed and determined the course of the child's congenital disability and consequent development. Only drastic intervention kept Willis and his mother from complete tragedy, and Willis had become more disabled psychologically than physically. Mandie and her mother needed only a brief period of counseling before Mandie could continue on the spectacular course of development she had manifested since age four.

Admittedly, these two cases are gross deviations from the usual course of development of children with congenital handicaps. Yet, far too often similar parental emotional reactions and interrelationships with the child interfere with the most expert rehabilitation and educational efforts. The import of the disability can only be assessed in the perspective of all other life factors.

3. *The Relevance of Physiological Maturation to Psychological Assessment*

Although genetics and congenital events set the limits on the physiological environment of the child, the most important biological factor relevant to his psychological assessment is the continued, progressive maturation of his physiological structure and its functioning. The study of the relationships between this physiological maturation and the development of psychological functions has long been a major scientific interest and effort, especially in developmental psychology. Although it is not possible to review this research in this volume, knowledge of these studies is very important to the clinical psychologist, for it is from a familiarity with this research that the psychologist is able to relate the biological and psychological growth of the individual child. There are, however, several general conclusions from this body of research which need to be mentioned. First, although the relationship between biological and psychological development is far from a perfect correlation, the overall trend is quite similar in both (as illustrated in Figure 1). Second, these general parallels between biological and psychological growth suggest the possibility of an underlying general "growth" or maturational factor. However such a growth factor may be conceptualized, there can be little doubt that the main phenomenon distinguishing childhood from maturity is this fact of a continually growing and developing organism. Third, with some rare exceptions (see Case 5), this biological development proceeds without interruption and in relatively regular order. Although a child may not mature psychologically, his biological development is not halted. Thus, although a child may remain intellectually or emotionally retarded, he nevertheless develops physiologically into an adult. This fact is sometimes ignored, especially in the assessment of retarded children. One of the conflicts for any adolescent is that he has to deal with biological maturity. This conflict can be particularly acute for the emotionally immature or intellectually retarded child.

Although lags or accelerations in biological development may not be as devastating and disabling as some of the trauma occurring during the fetal stage or at gestation, such variations in postnatal biological development are much more common and probably have much more effect on psychological development than is commonly recognized in clinical assessment. For example, the child who is developing biologically slowly may not be capable of performing the skills expected of him by his environment. As will be discussed in Chapter 3, these skills include motor functions, perceptual and intellectual functioning, and affective control and expression as well. Similarly, the child whose physiological maturation is accelerated may find himself forced to handle biological stress which he is as yet psychologically unprepared to handle — as illustrated in Case 5 above.

Among the various aspects of biological development which should be taken into account in a psychological assessment of a child are: (a) the development of neurological functioning, (b) neuro-muscular development, (c) skeletal development, (d) the physiological aspects of sexual development, and (e) the history of the physical trauma or diseases which the child may have suffered. As regards postnatal neurological development, the aspect most relevant to assessment is the setting-in of the neuro-electric rhythm known as the Alpha rhythm, which usually is completed around age six. Prior to that time, the child experiences mild but normal neuro-electrical disrhythmias which in part account for some of his erratic and variable functioning. Such neuro-electric dysfunction may be manifested in hyperactivity, poor attention, restlessness, and inability to sleep, or in sluggishness, apathy, and extra need for rest — as well as in overt convulsive seizures. When such symptoms persist, neurological assessment is in order, even though there be other psychological and environmental stresses that may also be disturbing to the child. On the other hand, both psychologists and neurologists have become cognizant that neuro-electric rhythm may be interrupted by such stress as psychological tension and anxiety (Ulett and Gleser, 1952). Whether such stresses can deter the development of the Alpha rhythm in childhood is not established, but the possibility of an interaction between this neurological development and psychological factors often needs to be entertained in assessment of children.

Neuro-muscular development is both biological and psychological. It consists of the development of a coordinated pattern of neurological reactions involving the muscular system, including such behavior as walking, use of arms and hands, eye movements, and speech muscles — all essential to various psychological development. This neuro-muscular development, more than any other biological maturation, is then dependent upon the psychological excercise of the functions involved. Thus, if a child is prevented from walking, talking, or other movements, etc., his neuro-muscular development may also be delayed; yet it will proceed quite rapidly once the child is permitted to exercise these functions. The presence of a neuro-muscular disability is obvious in the child with cerebral palsy or muscular deformans but may be less obvious in the awkward, poorly coordinated child who is failing to learn to read. Neurological assessment is thus also warranted in such cases, and the possibility of an interaction between retarded neuro-muscular development and psychological stresses must be considered.

The possibility that skeletal development affects psychological development has long been considered by psychologists and has been a major concept for such theorists as Kretchmer and Sheldon in their studies of body build and temperament. The psychoanalytic theorist, Adler, also considered skeletal development a major variable in his study of compensatory neuroses. Although these studies and theories may seem antiquated and lacking in scientific support, they do form the background to the current concepts regarding "body image" as an important factor in the child's development. It is important for the clinical psychologist to consider the child's skeletal development and its possible relationships to both the development of various psychological skills and to the child's personal identity. These relationships will be discussed in greater detail in Chapter 3. Suffice it to say that skeletal development is a rough index of the overall biological development of the child. Although it is quite possible that the child whose skeletal development is retarded may nevertheless develop normally in other respects, such slow skeletal development is often part of an overall retardation in biological growth. Moreover, the small-sized child, especially boys, often feel and act psychologically young, and withdraw from social situations in which they have to compete with children whose skeletal development is normal. Similarly, the child whose skeletal development is far advanced may feel out of place. Girls, particularly, tend to feel ungainly and unfeminine if their height and bone structure is out of proportion to their age norms.

The frequency of extreme variations in physiological sexual growth is not clearly established, but such variations are probably fairly common. Because of the social taboos on discussing sexual functioning in general, and childhood sexuality in particular, the variations in sexual development are difficult to investigate. A major exception is the studies of sexual growth emanating from the Institute of Child Development at Berkeley (Shuttleworth, 1949). Parental reports are probably not accurate, since parents — particularly of psychologically disturbed children — are often poor observers of their child's development and are apt to be ignorant of or to distort facts about sexual development. Quite frequently, these facts are not disclosed until afer the assessment, during the therapeutic sessions with the parent or child. Of course, it is very difficult to judge sexual development other than on the basis of such evidence as the appearance of pubic hair in boys or the development of feminine figure and the onset of menses in girls. Occasionally during therapeutic interviews, children do mention sexual sensations prior to puberty and adolescents and adults will recall such sensations. It is quite possible that sexual curiosity and sexual play also are coordinated with the development of sexual physiology, but there are so many possible extraneous stimulations that it is difficult to ascertain which is biological and which is external. Psychological manifestations and concomitants of sexual development will be discussed in more detail in Chapter 3. The important fact is that, although sexual maturation reaches its peak at puberty, it begins early in infancy and gradually increases through childhood, affecting all of the individual's development. Thus, although the child is able to delay direct satisfaction of his sexual impulses until long after puberty, the stress of the biological sexual urge is a factor to be considered at all stages of development.

The physiological diseases and trauma which the child may suffer are not actually part of his growth, but they so often form a crucial factor in the background of his psychological development that a history of these biological events is usually an essential part of an assessment. Very often, prolonged illness or a series of minor illnesses can deter psychological as well as biological development. Diseases or injuries which debilitate the child's whole system often slow growth. Even when a child is only slightly restricted by a disability, such as a limp or a mild heart condition, it is quite possible for him to regard himself as inadequate and for this feeling to be generalized to other functions, causing difficulty in learning skills that would not otherwise exist. The child's psychological development is, of course, even more retarded if the parents overemphasize the disability and reinforce his dependency on them. In considering the import of such illnesses or injuries, one should take into account not only the severity of the trauma but also the amount of time during which the child is restricted, for it is when a child is held back from learning over a period of time that psychological development is most deterred. Thus, for example, one child may become critically ill with pneumonia almost to the verge of death, but if this illness occupies only a few weeks of a child's life — and has no physiological sequalae — it is unlikely that this event in itself would have major psychological effects. On the other hand, should the child suffer a constant nose and throat infection over a period of three or four years, requiring daily medication, rest, and restriction of his activities, it is more possible that his psychological development would be deterred. Although diseases and injuries may be devastating at any time in the child's life, it is also important in an assessment to note the ages at which the child suffers such trauma. There may be more psychological injury for example, just when the child is learning to walk or talk, or the year he enters school, or at puberty. In addition, there are some diseases that seem to develop along with the child's body, such as diabetes, which may become critical only in adolescence but which probably slow and deter the child's development long before there are clinical manifestations of the disease. This writer once treated a seven-year-old child who was depressed, hypochondriacal, and compulsive. Among his symptoms was a stiff gait and a seemingly mechanical way of handling objects. When the psychotherapy was initiated, a medical examination revealed no signs of any disease or physiological disability and the child's muscular behavior was thought to be part of his psychological tension. Three years later, the child's depression and much of his compulsiveness had disappeared but his muscular stiffness had increased and he began to complain of pains in his joints. At this time medical examination revealed clear signs of the onset of a juvenile arthritis.

This interaction between the maturational process and other determinants has been illustrated in all of the cases cited so far. Martha's early sexual development, probably genetically determined, would have been disturbing to her and the family even if she had not been deaf. This accident of premature sexual functioning occurred not at the normal change into puberty but at a point when she should have experienced a relative emotional quiescence, allowing her to establish sexual peer relationships, accumulate educational skills, etc. Mandie's growth in infancy was deterred by her physiological handicap but, once the surgical reparations were complete, her rehabilitation was made possible by this maturational process. What deterred Mandie was not the handicap per se, but the fact that she was ill prepared for the normal separation from her mother which entry into school requires. Note that despite the absence of her father, Mandie showed "ambivalence" toward her mother and dreamed of a rescuing prince. Willis' psychotic behavior masked his development; considerable further observation would have been required to understand his fragmented development. One might guess, however, that his mother might not have been so easily persuaded to give up her intense struggle on economic grounds alone; an unmentioned fact in her relationship with Willis was his approaching adolescence.

Chapter 3

❧

SOCIAL AND PERSONAL
DETERMINANTS OF DEVELOPMENT

A. SOCIAL DETERMINANTS

The child's sociocultural "inheritance," like his physiological genetic "inheritance," has its beginnings many generations before his birth. Whole sets of predetermined attitudes and expectations await the child at birth and may even determine whether he will be born at all! For example, if he is conceived out of wedlock, abortion may be considered or attempted (even though abortion be also taboo) —since the guilt surrounding illicit, premarital sexual relationships is often intense. Moreover, even if the parents are subsequently married, they often continue to feel guilty and resentful toward the child who forced them into a marriage they felt unprepared to accept; frequently in such instances the grudge against the child is increased by secretly blaming all further marital dissension on him, creating a scapegoat of the child who consequently becomes emotionally disturbed. Such a pattern of attitudes is wholly culturally determined. In contrast, among some primitive tribes, conception of a child is taken as evidence that the putative father is ready for marriage, and the pregnancy of the unmarried girl is celebrated! Moreover, even in Western culture, it must be admitted, the marriage ceremony does not

necessarily imbue a couple with realistic parental attitudes. The "curse" on the child born "out of wedlock" remains almost as intense today in our culture as it did in "Victorian" days, despite our "broadmindedness." Although governmental statistics suggest that childbirth out of wedlock is not at all uncommon (there are no statistics on premarital conception but most authorities agree it is even more widespread), only occasionally are these facts given public recognition, usually only by a reformer's outrage and without suggestions for remedy. Intentional abortion (the technical medical term is still "criminal" abortion!) remains largely outlawed; almost no one even thinks of suggesting that the "illegitimate" child be accepted and supported, although in many other cultures automatic provision is made for care of the child, such as avuncular adoption of both child and mother, without prejudice against either. Moreover, this cultural attitude toward "legitimacy" of birth is reflected commonly in assessment procedures, for example the date of the parents' marriage is rarely collected as routine "face sheet" data and seldom mentioned in case history interview, unless reported by the parents as a concern to them; even then it is rarely discussed as a significant item in case conferences. Similarly, the taboo on abortion

25

is so strong that, although many authorities privately consider that attempts at self-abortion by the mother may well be a source of injury to the unborn child and a possible cause of mental retardation, there is little or no research on this topic.

Similar, but less intensely, tabooed attitudes also exist regarding such factors as the racial and religious background of the parents, the age of the parents (case histories often casually mention that the mother was "too young" or "into middle age," as if there were only certain age limits within which a woman could be an effective mother), or the number of children that is supposed to be a proper size family. That a child should come from parents of similar cultural backgrounds, have been conceived after a respectable period of marriage, be born when the mother is neither too young nor too old, and be a member of a sib-ship that is neither too small nor too large, all are too often accepted as "fact" rather than as a cultural norm. Seldom is recognition given to the possibility that variations from this norm may have advantages as well as create problems or that the child whose birth meets these norms may have a restricted view of society.

Over the past decade, there have been increasing numbers of studies of maternal attitudes during pregnancy and at childbirth, of the effects of feeding and weaning practices, of maternal attitudes toward infants during the first year of life, of toilet training practices and of many other aspects of the infant's responses and of parental reactions and demands (Caldwell, 1964). All of these studies have shown clearly that socialization begins at birth and continues at a rapid pace. Again, however, many of these studies are concerned with "effective" attitudes toward child-rearing, but few objectively study these practices as socialization per se. The "facts" presented by these studies, which often seem conflicting, suggest chiefly that different parental attitudes and practices of infant care probably create the basis for different personalities. However, even in our relatively heterogenous culture, with its avowed credo of individual differences, conformity has a higher value than variation. The standards preached by manuals on childbearing often influence psychologists as well as parents. Mothers who are anxious about childbirth and experience prolonged and painful labor, mothers who do not want to breast feed the child (or do want to), mothers who hover over the baby (or fail to hover over it), mothers who toilet train the baby "too soon" (or "too late"), all may be implicitly considered inadequate — and this list of "sins" in the orthodoxy of child-rearing is far from complete. However, not every mother who is anxious about childbirth necessarily has overall poor relationship with the child, nor does toilet training before age one or after age three in itself predict "anal" personality traits. As will be discussed further, these experiences must be evaluated in the light of the total personal experience of the child. While these events are often important hallmarks in the socialization of the child, which the psychologist should investigate and assess, the psychologist should also be able to recognize them as *variations on culturally determined values.*

Recognition of the social values of the culture of the child (including also the social values of the investigators) is thus essential to assessment of the child's development. All cultures take advantage of the accelerated learning curve of infancy and insist that mothers instill into the child the values of the culture from the beginning of life. For example, that "cleanliness is next to godliness" is learned by most American babies from the day of birth on, for unlike most other babies in the world they are bathed religiously every day, no matter the effect on their skin, digestion, psychological comfort, or the patience of the mother. Nor is there any proof that daily bathing is vital to health. In some cultures babies are made to cry, since it is thought good for their lungs. In Western culture, the mother sings, "Hush, little baby, don't you cry." In some cultures, babies are masturbated by their mothers to pacify them, while in Western culture babies are conditioned against touching their genitals by such strong disapproval, that they often learn sexual pleasure is taboo before they learn speech.

During the first five to six years of life, an intense socialization is conducted by the family, abetted by other social institutions such as the nursery school. During this period, the child learns the cultural values regarding food and elimination of bodily wastes; he learns a vocabulary and grammar and most of its implications; he learns social values regarding expression of anger, aggression, ambition, pleasure, pain, and most other emotions. He learns about the roles assigned to the sexes and to many other social groups. There is considerable evidence that at least the fact of racial prejudice, if not all of its implications, is well-known by most five year olds of both the dominant and minority groups (Trager and Yarrow, 1952).

In the years between infancy and puberty, the child is encouraged to practice these social lessons continually in play, in work, and in formal schooling. In a circle around the adult, the children listen to legends of Washington or of Kamehameha, or to the sayings of Confucious or of Emily Post. In both China and America, where scholarship and intellectual achievement are highly valued, it is considered even more serious for the child to fail to learn to be polite than to fail to learn to read; the bright child who is impudent is chastized as a "smart alec" and given a status below the compliant but poor scholar. Moreover, teachers are selected and retained more for their compliance to social values than for their scholarship. The teacher who dresses oddly or wears a beard is more offensive to the community than the child who fails to conform. Indeed, "socialization" rather than attainment of intellectual skills had become an openly acclaimed emphasis of public education in much of America — until the competition of the Soviet Union with the event of the "Sputnik." Even so, both competing countries utilize as much classroom time instilling their respective values as on purely intellectual tasks. Moreover, the formal instruction in intellectual skills also is based on a cultural value system. In modern Western culture, both in the United States and the USSR, reading, writing, and arithmetic are taught because they are essential to production in highly technical and competitive societies. Later, the sciences are emphasized for the same reason. Learning for the sake of learning or science to satisfy curiosity are values of a past era — even though there is now the leisure for such pleasures. "Dawdling" curiosity is seldom encouraged. Appreciation of the arts or artistic creativity are considered educational "trimmings," so that even when a child shows potential talent he is rarely encouraged to do more than develop it as a hobby. Art of any kind is so seldom seen as a possible career that it is a wonder there are either inspired painters or good jazz saxophonists. The effects of some of these cultural values on education are, of course,

recognized by many educational leaders, and experimental schools, such as the Montessori system, are being designed to fit the child's education to his particular needs, but these attempts remain experimental and very limited in scope.

The assessing psychologist must therefore constantly take into account these values in education. When Johnny fails to learn to read but has a "high I.Q.," the psychologist must consider not only such factors as the educational method being used or Johnny's unconscious rebellion against parental (and societal) values, but also the possibility that Johnny's intellect may be invested elsewhere and that reading per se has secondary value to him. It is debatable whether physicists, sculptors, oil drillers, and accountants necessarily should have the verbal competency needed by political scientists, advertising men, secretaries, and clinical psychologists. It should be noted further that many intelligence tests reflect cultural values by sampling primarily verbal skills or at least requiring verbalized responses. In assessing the child's potential for creativity, the psychologist can use "I.Q." as only one item of data.

Thus, before the onset of puberty the child in most cultures has learned the values and practiced most of the behavior demanded by his society. During adolescence, two further basic social lessons are learned: (1) the rules of mating and (2) the independent practice of social behavior. Before or about the time of puberty, most children learn the "facts of life," the physiological facts about sexual functioning and much of the culture's mythology concerning them. Except in the middle and upper classes of modern urban Western culture, most children have observed sexual acts in animals and even in humans and have experimented in sexual play. Even when the anxious middle class American parent asks, "How shall I tell my children about sex?" he does not mean the physiological facts, for he usually admits that "they probably know already," but he wants to know how to instruct them in the social rules.

What the parent — and sometimes the educator and psychologist — forgets is that in most cultures these social rules are not transmitted by adults, but by peers. In primitive cultures this training in sexual behavior was quite formalized; among the Iroquois, the adolescent boy was sent to an isolated "long house" to be instructed by other teenagers;

in certain Pacific Island tribes, pubescent boys are sent to separate islands. Girls are commonly isolated also, to be instructed by older sisters, or specially designated priestesses or other single women, how to dress, how to react to courtship, how to protect their virginity — or how to seduce men. In modern Western culture, this instruction in mating behavior is less formal but definitely is primarily conducted by the peer group itself, albeit with the grudging approval and secret incitement of the adult society. However, it is more often the adults rather than the peers who are most concerned if an adolescent is disinterested in or resistant to learning these rules.

The goal of a culture's socialization is, of course, the relatively independent adult who "knows his place" in his society without question or supervision. Although the child has learned much of society's demands before puberty, he has until then been under adult guidance. In each society there exist various institutionalized methods for shifting from adult supervision of behavior to self-discipline during adolescence. In primitive societies this process was formalized in "puberty" rites, during which the young American Indian, for example, proved his manhood by his ability to withstand isolation and the elements and by his prowess as a hunter and warrior. In more recent cultures, these puberty rites became religious rites, for example in the Christian Confirmation or the Jewish Bar Mitzvah. In the latter ceremony, the Jewish father solemnly declares that he is no longer responsible for the sins of the child and that henceforth the son must bear his own guilt. Analogous preparations were made for the girl to take up her duties as a wife and mother. In Western society, this final process of socialization is much more complex and prolonged, but no less formal, including such ceremonies as school graduations, gang and fraternity initiations and the "first date." Moreover, partly because our culture is so highly complex, this stage of socialization is initiated, with increasing frequency, almost before puberty (with "social" dancing in the sixth grade) and extended into the mid-twenties (when many young adults are still students).

The complexity of the modern world and the consequent extended demands of the culture on the child for socialization create many stresses on development. Although most students of clinical psychology appear to have at least a passing acquaintance with these cultural stresses, the import of cultural factors to the assessment of development is often not clear. Since all children in the same culture face similar stresses, it might seem possible to disregard cultural determinants and focus instead entirely on the variations of individual perceptions and experience. Perhaps if one were to assess children in an isolated and stable society, social stress as a determinant of development might be relatively ignored. The anthropologists of a generation ago (Kardiner, 1939; Linton, 1945), who demonstrated how culture determines personality, were comparing relatively closed societies. Even class and caste as determinants of personal identity (for example Davis and Warner) appear to be gradually breaking down under the pressure of the "outer-directed" open-ended society of today (Reissman et al., 1950).

Both the social scientists and the general public agree that American society provides the child today with fewer and fewer well established societal identifications. The "extended" family, the clan or "kith and kin" with its "name" and membership and implications of support and guidance, has almost disappeared in the United States; one can no longer depend on "relatives." The presence of an aunt, uncle, cousin, or even grandparent residing in the home has a far different meaning to the child today than it did a generation or so ago. Moreover, with the rising divorce rate there are an increasing number of children who are growing up with shifting and multiple parents. Even the larger social "units" are less definite; there is at least a promise that being born Negro in the United States will lose some of its caste limitations within this generation, and consequently so will being born white. Similarly, class identifications, rich and poor, seem to be amalgamating into one middle-class — both in the United States and in the USSR — thus forming a classless society quite different than that dreamed of by Karl Marx. Sociologists and psychologists now write of the individual's search for identity in a society which no longer offers definite social-unit boundaries for the individual identification.

Even a synopsis of these many evolving social changes is beyond the scope of this book. At best, a few of those changes can be mentioned as illustrations of the considerations one must make in assessing the development of a child growing up in the latter half of the twentieth century in the United States and comparable societies. Among these changes, the most obvious are the vast scientific and technological advances. Diseases and starvation, which until recently killed or crippled up to 50% of the population before the age of six, now are being rapidly eliminated. With only minimum medical care and preventive measures, the child today is protected from the intense worries about health which plagued even the most recent past generations. Moreover, aside from automobile accidents, the child is much more protected than ever before from environmental accidents and calamities. Illness and death as a childhood fear thus has less basis in reality, and is less frequently a "presenting complaint" than a few decades ago. When life entails a great deal of hard physical work, illness is often the only valid excuse from constant labor. Although psychosomatic dysfunctions continue to be a major complaint among children, "enjoying poor health" is less respected today, even among middle-aged women, and the nature of functional illnesses is different; the "grand hysterie" and "fainting spells" of the Victorian era described by Charcot have given way to functional, systemic reactions, such as asthma and childhood ulcers.

The result of the reductions of these threats to life has been not only to lessen fear but to promote growth. Not only are fewer children damaged during pregnancy and childbirth, but babies are both larger and more vigorous than ever before and they grow faster and larger. They are fed better and their bodies, unhampered by the necessity for combatting disease, instead are fitted for increased activity. As a result, the "body image" is changing; being small is more than ever a "trauma" to a boy, and being large is threatening to girls. In addition, the psychologist's standards of perceptual and motor acuity may need continued revision. The chances of death during adulthood have also lessened and children have the promise of a much longer life-span. As a consequence, it has been possible to extend adolescence a bit longer. A young girl can delay marriage if she is assured there is less chance she will die in childbirth. A young man can spend more of his life in school.

The main prevailing cataclysmic threat to life today is that of nuclear war and extermination. Children are made very aware of this

danger through all public media or through air raid drills. Both scientific and lay authorities are of the opinion that this threat has contributed to a "let's have fun — tomorrow we may die" attitude among many adolescents, if less overtly in the adult population whose unspoken feelings they mirror. Violence and destruction, while actually less common in everyday life than in prior generations (despite news paper stories), remain a popular theme in public legend and private fantasy. "An A-bomb going off" has become almost a "popular" response to several Rorschach ink blots. Yet, while this nightmare of nuclear holocaust hangs over the world, the possibility of elimination of war has never been so publicly considered and so close to realization. Children learn both the imminence of global destruction *and* the hope of lasting peace.

The reduction of these life threats has permitted an increasing focus on psychological and social stress. In less technically developed societies, the "neuroses" of modern society are considerably less obvious; starving and diseased peoples who are exhausted by physical labor do not appear fazed by psychological problems, except when driven to mass psychotic disturbances by their hardships (Benedict and Jacks, 1954). In Western cultures, "mental illness", that is, psychological dysfunctioning, has been declared the major "health" problem of this generation by all authorities, including President John F. Kennedy — just before his death at the hands of a deranged man. The referral of a child for psychological assessment, once considered by parents as an insult to their integrity and a matter of shame, no longer carries quite as much opprobrium. An increasing number of adults and children possess considerable information about psychological functioning and are "psychologically minded," a factor which is changing the atmosphere in which assessment takes place.

Another effect of the scientific and technological advances of the present era on the psychological development of children has been the intense impetus to intellectual growth. The scientific complexity of modern civilization places a high value on intellectual achievement and a demand for intensified and prolonged education of the child. Very likely within a decade of this writing, children will face not only the demand already present for a greater number of school years, but of more per year and hours per week, in order to keep up with the increased amount of knowledge required of them. As never before, children are complaining about homework and the lack of time to play. Parents and schools are consequently much more concerned with the child's academic achievement and learning ability. "Slow in school" is by far the most common and desperate complaint made about the child.

Moreover, there is some evidence that the overall level of intelligence is increasing, at least for such intellectual activities as information, social comprehension, speed of learning, and perhaps even the ability to think abstractly. No doubt television and other mass media greatly add to the child's information as well as his fantasy. As a result, the standardization of IQ tests grow more rapidly out of date. The Stanford-Binet, revised twice since its origin in 1917, still contains such anachronisms as a thimble and a picture of a man sawing wood! Schools are often puzzled to find that the mean IQ of their pupils is 10 to 15 points above the average on tests standardized only a decade ago.

A second major social change affecting the psychological development of children is the rapid growth of the world's population. Although the *rate* of increase in the United States has slowed down and is less than many parts of the world, the actual number of births continues to be vastly greater than in prior decades. Statistics indicate that this growth in the United States is not from increased family size, but is a result of the greater number of children who survive. Thus, the child today is less likely to experience the death of a sibling or even a parent. He is also less likely to have a mother who is frequently pregnant.

As a result, children today grow up in a much more crowded world. Their homes are likely to be somewhat smaller and less private than in the prior generation, at least among the middle-class. Their schools are much larger but are nevertheless more crowded— as are their playgrounds. Open places to play are vanishing in many urban and suburban areas, and the automobile has almost pushed the bicycle off the streets. In crowded apartment houses and suburban housing developments, the child's need for physical activity and noise-making is often repressed, if not diverted. Similarly, in a crowded classroom he

has to learn to be quiet and study on his own while other children receive the teacher's attention, even though as a healthier child his energy and activity level may be greater. He has to learn to "get along with other children" as never before because there are fewer places for privacy and isolation and more children to "get along with." The pressure for conformity to both adult and peer standards remains intense, even though these standards are relatively less rigid and more evanescent. As with the technological stresses, the population increase focuses the attention of the child and his caretakers onto problems of human interrelationships as never before. The self-contained "introverted" child, no matter how contented he may be, is often considered "maladjusted" by teachers or even by parents, while the out-going "extrovert" may be forgiven his transgressions, even if he is under considerable tension.

A third major social pressure on the child is the mobility of his society. Not only does he live in a highly technical and over-crowded world, but he and the people about him are frequently on the move. He is likely to change residences within a city several times and to move from one city to another at least once during his childhood. In these moves he must "adjust" to new neighborhoods, new playmates, and new schools, and his parents and sibs are meeting similar changes. Nor is this mobility restricted to one socioeconomic level; even in census tracts containing privately owned, single-family dwellings, ownership has been discovered to change at least once in five years in 50% of the properties. Under these circumstances, neither neighborhood, school, nor peer groups can offer stable values with which the child can identify. Family life may also be interrupted; as father moves from job to job, he may not always be able to take his family with him. Personal belongings, toys and dolls, and pets, all so important to the child, may disappear as the family moves.

In prior generations and cultures, the individual's identity was set for him by the mores of a relatively small and stable group from which he rarely moved and his "neurosis" consisted of a conflict between these social values and satisfaction of his own needs. The child today floats in an ever-changing "lonely crowd" (Reisman et al., 1950), with which he may have only passing contact or conflict but which offers little personal emotional support or sense of "belonging." His struggle thus is less likely to be *against* society but *for* recognition. Often he seems a "rebel without a cause" (Lindner, 1944); his acts appear meaningless, unwarranted "bids for attention," whether in adolescent delinquency or in infant asthma.

The following two cases may serve to illustrate some of these social stresses. Note that, although these two youths come from altogether different backgrounds, the social pressures are quite parallel.

CASE 8

Jimmy B., a 15-year-old Negro boy, was brought in for psychological assessment from Juvenile Hall, where he was awaiting trial for assault and battery on a policeman during a civil rights demonstration. His act of violence had been in contradiction to the "nonviolence" discipline of the demonstrating group, and they had not requested that he be released on bail. Moreover, he was well known to police and school authorities both because of his previous aggressive behavior toward authority and because until recently he had been one of the "most promising" boys in his school. School records showed Jimmy's scores on achievement tests to be two to three years above grade placement and his IQ was 134. (The average at his high school was below 100.) Yet, during the past year he had done little school work either in class or at home and at the time of his arrest he had not attended school for several weeks and was facing failure in all subjects. Once a star athlete, he had been dropped from all sports because of poor attendance at both practice and competition games and because of his inadequate academic record. Quick of temper, he was often the center of altercations on the school grounds and usually reacted to school authorities either with sullen silence or sneering retort. He was not known to be a member of any school clique or neighborhood gang, although a majority of his classmates had such affiliations, but appeared to be a "lone wolf" with no close friends of either sex.

Jimmy was born in a Negro ghetto in Chicago, shortly before his mother's 16th bitrhday. She had left her rural Mississippi home the previous year but had found no permanent employment. She was unmarried and Jimmy knew nothing of his putative father, other than that he was allegedly white.

City welfare funds and several "boyfriends" were their only source of income for almost three years, until Mrs. B's first marriage. This first permanent father owned a coffee shop in a small "down-state" city, where Jimmy lived for the next three years. His mother, now 19, tired of working as a waitress and restless in the doldrums of the smaller city, left her husband and, taking Jimmy, joined her parents who had moved to Detroit. From age six to eight, Jimmy was cared for by his grandmother, who had six children of her own — all younger than his mother. Jimmy remembered this period as a "happy" time, with "regular meals and a regular family." He had used his mother's maiden name as his family name and so identified himself with his grandparents, even to calling them "Mom" and "Dad" in imitation of his mother, whom he addressed by her first name. Jimmy had attended school two years when his mother married again. The boy hated his new father for taking him from his grandparents' home and moving him to a new school. In turn, the new father felt rebuffed in his friendly overtures to the boy and was often unnecessarily harsh in his discipline. During the next four years, the family lived in many different small apartments and Jimmy changed schools twice more. Jimmy also "hated" his sister, born to his mother when Jim was nine.

After four very unhappy years, Jimmy's mother returned again to her parents, now in Los Angeles. However, the grandparents' home no longer proved to be what Jim had hoped. With three of their children, Jimmy, his sister, and mother, they were crowded in the two-bedroom flat of a housing development. All of the adults worked, usually at different hours; although there was usually one or another adult at home, no one assumed direct responsibility for Jim. However, according to his mother, "Jim never gave us any trouble." No one in Jim's family had completed high school, but his grandfather was very proud of Jim's scholastic achievement, and frequently advised him to "stick to his books" as the only way to get ahead. When Jim's uncle, two years his senior, became active in a militant organization dedicated to civil rights for Negroes, Jim joined him. Together they picketed markets demanding jobs for Negroes, demonstrated at the school board for desegregated schools, and passed out leaflets demanding desegregated housing.

Jim's face glowed as he spoke avidly about "Freedom Now."

CASE 9

Wayne L., also 15 but white, was failing at high school. However, Wayne's school work had been mediocre at best throughout his elementary school years. Although Wayne's IQ of 95 was within the "normal range," the mean IQ at his school was 117. In temperament, Wayne was a placid, good-natured boy who seemed eager to please adults but who irritated them, especially his father, by his awkward and childlike ineptitude in everything he did. Like Jimmy B., Wayne was also an isolate, but not altogether by his own choosing; he shyly sought companionship from his peers, who considered him a "spaz" (a derogatory term derived from *spastic*), but Wayne seemed almost to enjoy their teasing.

When Wayne was born, his father, although 30 years old, was an undergraduate at a small state college, struggling to obtain higher education following military service in World War II. Indeed, it seemed to Wayne that his father was always studying and could never be interrupted. Because Mr. L. also had to work to eke out a marginal standard of living for his family, he could not complete his A.B. until Wayne was four. Then Mr. L. moved his family to a larger city where he worked for a year as an assistant manager in a supermarket. Discontented with a financially unrewarding and intellectually boring job, Mr. L. decided to return to the university to obtain a teacher's credential. Mrs. L. wearied of the family's very restricted economic existence and was angry at her husband's refusal to "settle down" at a job after years of "sacrifice" for his education. After considerable bitter marital dissension, the L's separated and Wayne and his mother moved to another city to live with Mrs. L's parents.

Unlike Jimmy's relatively young grandparents, Wayne's grandparents were elderly; Mrs. L was their youngest daughter. Wayne, who had learned to be quiet in the "crackerbox" married students' dormitory apartment while his father studied, had little trouble continuing to be quiet when Grandma was ill or Grandpa napped, or mother came home from her job as a secretary with a headache. When Wayne was nine his father remarried and his mother agreed to return him to his father so that she could accept a better job

in an overseas government post. Wayne had completed the third grade. A year later, Mr. L, now a teacher, changed jobs and Wayne changed schools once more. The school recommended that Wayne repeat the second semester of the fourth grade, but Mr. L's pride was offended and he decided instead to tutor Wayne at home, to help him "keep up with his class." Two years later, after Mr. L obtained his master's degree, he found an administrative position; he was then able to buy a new home for his family in a new suburb, where no schools had yet been built. Wayne traveled eight miles on a school bus to attend a crowded junior high, which operated on a "double session" basis each day; leaving home at 6:45 A.M., he returned at 3:00 P.M. At home, Wayne spent many hours "glued to the TV" while his stepmother, with whom he "got along well," was occupied with the care of his infant step-sister. Now that Mr. L was about to complete his doctorate in education, he was very embarrassed by Wayne's academic failure and threatened to send him to a special boarding school for backward students. As Wayne discussed this proposal, he became tearful and admitted he seriously contemplated suicide.

Although Jimmy and Wayne were quite different personalities and came from diverse socioeconomic strata, the social stresses which shaped their development were strikingly similar. Both boys were frequently moved to new locales and new schools. Both were out of step in their schools, intellectually and socially. Both had experienced severe disruption of the structure of their family. Both lacked any person or social group with which they could identify — until Jimmy joined the civil rights movement. Both seemed to experience considerable violent anger; Jimmy outward toward society, and Wayne toward himself in his threat of suicide.

Some of the implications for assessment of these social stresses on child development may be summarized as follows.

1. The standardization of many of our assessment procedures and information is rapidly becoming less and less meaningful. Technological improvements in health and the standard of living are creating new and changing norms in children's psychological growth, especially with regard to activity levels and intellectual development.

2. As a consequence, the assessor today is

evaluating children who will probably live longer, have more leisure, and need longer and more complex formal education. Thus emotional spontaneity and intellectual curiosity will need to be fostered.

3. The nature of children's anxieties, as derived from their environment and culture, is changing. There is less personal threat to his life, although he may experience a vague impersonal sense of impending nuclear doom. The child struggles less and less against the structures of social institutions, but instead is a rebel without a cause in a search for identity. Assessment of children's emotional development may thus have to shift from merely looking at personal and familial interactions to a recognition of the broader scheme of shifting social settings and the child's sense of "belonging."

4. Assessment per se is becoming a social institution. With older, established value systems fading, parents turn to the psychologist as an "expert," seeking "the right way" to rear the child. In an increasing number of cases, the parents' voice conflicts over changing values and shifting social stresses, and these adult conflicts are mirrored in distorted fashion in the child. Moreover, self-revelation is probably less restricted when an individual seeks "identity." On the other hand, as parents and children become more "psychologically minded," there is a greater tendency to give "socially acceptable" responses to tests and interviews (Edwards, 1957).

5. Assessment is directly affected by these social stresses by the very fact that the assessor is also a member of the society, subject to the same shifting values. Moreover, he is assigned a role as an official shaman. The prototype of the child psychologist comes from the middle to upper middle classes; even though he may have intellectual doubts and rebellious attitudes concerning his background, he is likely to function in conformity with the values of his social group. Moreover, his conformity is reinforced by his clients, the bulk of whom come from the same social strata. Appreciation of one's own social assumptions and social stresses is often more difficult for the beginning student than an understanding of the position of clients from other social backgrounds. The student should observe whether he expects of all of his clients the same values of intellectual achievement, social ambition, personal habits, personal attachments, sexual behavior, etc. as he does of himself. If so, his assessment of the child may be skewed and incomplete, if not invalid.

B. PERSONAL EXPERIENCE AS A DETERMINANT OF DEVELOPMENT

While these biological and social stresses shape the basic framework of the child's development, the stresses affecting his unique modes of functioning, which set him apart from other children in his culture, are his personal experiences during these formative years. By far, the most influential of all the child's experiences are those arising from his relationships within his family. As is implied in the above discussion, whatever may be the child's biological inheritance or the conditions of his birth, and whatever the cultural stresses, the effect of such stress is determined by and filtered through the attitudes and reactions of the family. Although, in general, the family as a social institution strives to instill cultural mores and values in the child, and transmits methods of dealing with social stress, the most important aspect of the family interaction upon the child derives from the structure of the family itself, the nature of the interactions between family members, and the roles assigned and lived out by the child and the other family members. Although the family has always constituted the central influence on the child, with the gradual dissolution of other cultural memberships from which the child can form an identity, the family assumes even a greater role in the child's identification process.

The force of family influence lies, of course, in the dependence of the child upon his parents for satisfaction of his needs, not only his biological needs for food, shelter, and comfort but, of at least equal import, the satisfaction of the child's emotional needs. It is chiefly through the reward and deprivation of the parents' love and approval that the parent is able to influence the child's behavior and ultimately shape his identity. The manner in which these satisfactions are given depends in no small degree on the child's position within the family constellation and on the roles assigned to him or played by him within the family for their common satisfactions. Most parents make at least perfunctory efforts to satisfy the child's needs — and where these efforts are *merely* perfunctory, the child feels deprived. In return, each family places on the child certain demands — demands to satisfy their needs and to prevent the child from interfering too greatly in his dependent state with the satisfaction of their needs. Many factors determine the roles assigned the child in the family, such as: the parent's identification of and with the child as being like or unlike themselves or one of their sibs or parents; the parent's preconceived hopes or fears for the child; the parent's attitudes toward the first, middle, or last born; the parent's preoccupation with the child because of his particular demands or, obversely, a relative neglect of his needs because of the demands of his sibs. A very important factor is the parent's ambivalence toward having any children at all and thus toward the birth of this child in particular. Such ambivalence depends on such factors as the age of the parents, the maturity with which they can handle their own dependency needs, and the compatibility of the marriage. Many of these parental attitudes are formed before the birth of the child (see above), but are revised in the first years of his life depending on further events, for example, if the child becomes a burden by being chronically ill, a poor eater, hyperactive, or hypersensitive. The birth of younger siblings or the reaction of older sibs may also alter the family's concept of a particular child.

Both tradition and the personal desires of each parent for a child of a certain sex influence attitudes toward the child. The premium given male children in many cultures makes parents hope for boys, for whom they have high expectations. Thus, the firstborn male in a generation may be highly valued and have a great deal to have to live up to. In contrast, the girl may be a relative disappointment, even though everyone denies it. Very often, many of these attitudes toward the unborn child are reflected in the name that his parents select. If named after a relative, the child becomes associated in the mind of the parents, and then in his own self-image, with the relative and the attitudes toward that relative. Even where there is no such direct association, the choice of the name usually turns out to have some personal associations, not only for the parent selecting the name but for the other parent also. Bizarre name combinations have been noted to be much more frequent among institutionalized psychotic adults. The child's own reaction to his name is often a good clue to his own self image as, for example, in the following case.

CASE 10

Dana, age 11, was the youngest of four daughters. Her oldest sister, Dorothy, age 23, was named after their mother but was nicknamed Dolly. Her second sister, Doris, age 21, was named atfer her paternal grandmother, and was called "Sis." Deanna, age 19, was named after a movie actress, but insisted on being called "Lee" — her middle name. Dana's parents denied that they had any particular reason for selecting her name; "We just liked it." One of her father's favorite jokes, which Dana dreaded to hear him repeat, was that they had about run out of girls' names beginning with D and if they had had another girl, he'd have said "Damnation" and she would have been called that. He had made it clear in many other ways also that they had sorely hoped for a boy when Dana was born. It seemed quite probable that Dana might well have been named after her father, Dan, for throughout her infancy she was called "Danny Boy" by him and her sisters, although her mother demurred, and referred to her instead as "my little Dane . . . because she was blonde and the rest of us are so dark."

The age difference between Dana and her sisters was occasioned by the fact that the mother had had considerable difficulty in childbirth with all three of the older girls and was extremely reluctant to have another child. However, she felt very pressured to bear a son, not only by her husband but by both his parents and hers, who still maintained many of their European traditions. Once the decision was made, however, she resigned herself to it. Mrs. D remembered being more relaxed and happy during this pregnancy and was determined to enjoy this, her last child. However, the delivery was extremely difficult, requiring surgery, and Mrs. D made a very slow recovery. When she learned that she had given birth to a girl, she felt she had failed her husband and their parents, and became markedly depressed. Shortly after she returned home, she made a suicide attempt and was hospitalized again for several months. Thereafter she remained a rather grim, quiet, and withdrawn woman. Nevertheless, with Dana she tired to rally her spirits, determined to devote herself to caring for this last child. Moreover, Dana required considerable care; she seemed "allergic" to most everything. She was a poor eater and often vomited back the carefully prepared special formulas. She slept poorly and was often "colicky." She was a frail child, and although her health was relatively good after the first year of her life, her mother remained anxious and overprotective. However, she was also a beautiful child, with delicate features, deep brown eyes, and blonde curls. Her father overcame his disappointment and "adored her" as did her sisters. During her preschool years, "We called her 'our princess' and spoiled her terribly." However, the older sisters formed a coterie of their own, and as they entered adolescence they had less time for Dana. Dana, who had "worshipped" her sisters, was fascinated by their teenage activities but felt rejected by them and would come weeping to her mother when their door was closed in her face. When Dana was five, her father suffered a financial failure and went into bankruptcy. Although the family did not lose their home and continued to have at least a marginal income, their previously comfortable standard of living was sharply reduced. To economize, Mrs. D carefully saved leftover food from each meal and began to remodel the older sisters' dresses to fit Dana. Already sensitive about food and vain about her appearance, she complained bitterly, whereupon Lee labeled her 'little leftover,' an epithet which would send Dana into a weeping tantrum.

At school, Dana suffered again over her name. To distinguish her from a boy in her class also named Dana, the children started calling "Dick," an abbreviation of her last name. Dana silently accepted this new name, but was even more uncomfortable, for as she said later she regarded it as a "phoney." Only a short time before, she had realized that her father had changed his patronym from Dreyfus to Dickson to avoid antisemitic discrimination in his business. Because of her slight build and her mother's constant admonitions to be careful about her health, Dana felt unable to compete in the physically active play of her peers. She withdrew, sitting hunched over on a bench in the schoolyard. In conference with her mother, one of the teachers happened to remark on Dana's slumped posture. Mrs. D became exceedingly anxious because throughout her own childhood her mother had hauled her from doctor to doctor, seeking correction

of her slight curvature of the spine. In recalling this condition, Mrs. D remembered with revived embarrassment being hospitalized and, at age 14, while immobilized in traction, being examined by a series of young doctors. Despite these experiences, Mrs. D unconsciously repeated her own mother's behavior, and began taking Dana to orthopedic specialists, each of whom advised her that Dana had nothing wrong with her spine. Dana became increasingly resistant to these medical examinations and finally refused all further appointments.

Shortly after Dana's tenth birthday, a series of events markedly changed the D's family constellation. In rapid succession, both of her older sisters married and left home. Dana was very excited about her sisters' romances and weddings, but could not understand her parents' resistance to these events; both parents felt the girls were too young and should have gone on to college. For the next several months, Dana tried to become very close to Lee, was always in her room, asked many favors of her, and talked endlessly about Lee's boyfriends and Lee's activities. However, Lee brushed Dana aside and complained to her parents that Dana was becoming a nuisance. When it was discovered that Lee was illegitimately pregnant, the parents tried to keep the fact a secret from Dana and avoided all discussion of it with her, even though she was fully aware of it. However, she had only a vague idea of sexual functioning for the topic was taboo in the family. Dana became increasingly morose, withdrew into her room, and would talk to no one. The same week that Lee ran away from home, her mother went to the hospital for a hysterectomy, another event which was not previously discussed with Dana. Three days later Dana tried to commit suicide by swallowing a handful of sleeping pills.

In the hospital, Dana sat immobilized in a corner on the floor, facing the wall, wrapped up in a large sweater which belonged to Lee. She refused to talk to anyone and would not respond to her name, but when questioned, said her name was "Ella," "because E follows D." Much later, when she began to talk with her psychotherapist, she admitted that she associated "Ella" with "Cinderella." She allowed nurses to lead her to meals or to the bathroom or to bed, but became violently combative when they tried to remove her sweater, and completely resisted medical examination. It took her several months to accept the daily, patient attempts of her psychotherapist to get her to discuss her problems. Then she began to pour out her intensely guilty feelings, to the effect that she regarded herself as the cause of all of her family's troubles. Shortly thereafter, she was able to return home and to go back to school, but continued in outpatient psychotherapy for several years.

Although this case history illustrates how a child's identity may be affected by the preconceived attitudes of parents, by the nature of changes in the family constellation, and by the personification of these attitudes in the names given the child, it is far from complete in at least one major aspect. What needs to be spelled out is the actual nature of the emotional relationships within the family. This history suggests that the family may well have used Dana as a scapegoat, but the interrelationship with her mother and with her father is only barely hinted at in this recitation of events. For example, the possible effects of the mother's original ambivalence toward Dana's conception and birth on their subsequent relationship required further investigation. The data presented above suggest that both parents may have tried to cover their disappointment over her sex by making extra efforts to care for her and demonstrate their affection for her. How Dana reacted to her father's attentions, for example, and the possible effect they had on her self-concept are not recorded. Having a name associated with her father may have intensified her relationship with him, but probably in very ambivalent fashion, thus confusing her further as to her identity. How these relationships were perceived both by the child and by the parents became a key question in the assessment.

The nature of these affectional relationships and their effect on the personality development of the child have, of course, been the central concern and contribution of psychoanalytic theory. In this and the previous chapter, passing reference has been made to some of the developmental concepts of psychoanalysis. At this point, it may be helpful to consider very briefly some of the contributions — and limitations — of psychoanalysis as a developmental theory. Psychoanalysis as a theory has evolved from the simple biological theory of instincts of Freud's earliest writings to a much more complex social theory of personal development. Psychoanalytic theory now includes *inter*personal as well as *intra*personal development. "Sexuality," even childhood sexuality, includes, in psychoanalytic theory, not only the biological drive per se, but all the social and interpersonal associations that go with it. The tie that binds child to parent and parent to child contains an affectional bond of remarkable intensity. This affectional bond is related to physical care and protection of the child but, as can be easily demonstrated both in the overt behavior and in the fantasy of the child, it also is related to the sensual or sexual life of the child. In behavioral terms, the "sexuality" of this bond is established in many small ways, which demonstrate the attitudes of the parent and establish the attitudes of the child.

If the child experiences eating as a pleasure, over and above satisfaction and relief of his hunger, such pleasure is derived not only from the sensual satiation of a full stomach, but also from the comfort and warmth of being fed. When the mother is anxious, angry, or even just impersonal, the child often reacts with disappointment. Feeding may also be a means whereby the mother seeks to alleviate anxiety in the child or even to "seduce him." The mother-child relationship is also "eroticized" by such "oral" activities as kissing, biting, cooing, talking, and singing. Through these pleasurable rewards, the child becomes attached to and identified with the mother. Psychoanalysts use the term "incorporation" to describe this aspect of the emotional relationship between mother and child. As the psychoanalysts have pointed out, these activities are an essential part of the normal mother-child relationship. It is only when the child's needs for such affectional stimulation are chronically frustrated, or when the mother persists in infantilizing the child by continuing such behavior throughout childhood to an extreme degree, that the child's development may be deterred and disturbed (see, the Case of the T family in *The Experience of Anxiety*, Goldstein and Palmer, 1963).

Similar interpersonal interactions constitute the data behind Freud's other stages of "psychosexual development" of the child and their implications for parent-child relationship. The relationship between mother and child becomes compounded when the mother begins to demand that the "pleasure" which the child finds in relieving the tension of his bowels and bladder be regulated through toilet training. Just as the feeding relationship becomes generalized to many other interactions between them, the toilet training is usually a *prototype* of the subsequent demands of the mother for the child to conform to her wishes. If this first disciplining of the child turns into a battle, the ensuing parental demands for conformity are frequently also fraught with dissension and resistance. Data on the attitudes toward and procedures used in toilet training are thus often important clues to the development of the mother-child relationship.

The stage which Freud regarded as the climax of infant psychosexual development, is, of course, the "Oedipal" stage. Perhaps no other single concept in developmental psychology has received so much widespread attention and controversy. Often this concept has been blindly accepted or just as blindly rejected with little attention to the phenomena which it seeks to explain, or to the corrolaries and implications of the concept, and, least of all, to the behavioral data necessary to establish its import to the development in an individual child or to the general development of all children. Even if it were possible to encapsulate here the discussion of and evidence for this theoretical concept, which has occupied whole volumes (Mullahy, 1948), such is not the intent of those paragraphs. However, insofar as the main purpose of this chapter is to illustrate the relationship between theory and practice in the applied task of assessment, a brief examination of this most famous of all developmental constructs may thus be in order.

Before examining this particular construct in detail, a brief aside is necessary regarding the rules for using any such abstraction. First, before using any hypothetical construct, it is necessary to understand the theory thoroughly and precisely, its purposes and limitations. A second rule is that the purpose of such theory is to *predict,* not necessarily future behavior, but the existence of other behavior, either past or present, which may otherwise escape the notice of the investigator or appear inconsistent or inconsequential. The third rule for clinical use of hypotheses is that the clinician should not demand infallibility of the hypothesis for all cases but should, on the contrary, be prepared to accept a "null hypothesis" in some cases. Thus, there may be times when there is little evidence

available or where the import of the hypothesis is inconsequential. (The complete absence of any behavior relating to the hypothesis, however, would suggest the possibility of either inadequate data gathering or an extraordinary situation.) It may be noted that acceptance of the null hypothesis in a clinical case is somewhat different than in a research experiment, for the clinician is not primarily interested in the general "proof" or "disproof" of a hypothesis, but in its utility in the exploration of the single case. Acceptance of the null hypothesis in one case does not necessarily limit the usefulness of the construct in the next case, although, of course, should a construct be rarely applicable, it might easily fall into disuse.

The phenomenon called Oedipal complex refers to the intense and basically erotic attraction by the child to the parent of the opposite sex. That most children form such relationships, which in some instances last for many years, has long been observed by both laymen and poets, most notably Sophocles and possibly even earlier in Egyptian legend. However, little of this phenomenon to which Freud referred is directly observable behavior. Rather, what Freud discussed is an elaborate *fantasy,* a fantasy which Freud maintained is derived not from any special stimuli in the parental behavior, but arises chiefly from the child's own biological impulses. In line with the general developmental hypothesis of generalized to specific functioning, this attachment may be considered to be a specification of a formerly diffuse erotic impulse or drive, the attachment being formed to the parent or parental figure of the opposite sex, with whom the child has had opportunity to form such an attachment. According to psychoanalytic theory, the *fantasy* of possessing the parent of the opposite sex arises inevitably in the child's imagination, no matter what his overt behavior. However, the child may show little or no overt attachment or may even avoid or reject that parent because of the taboo on incest and the hypothesized corrollary that there arises the fantasy of a retaliation in the form of "castration."

Of what practical use, then, is a construct such as the Oedipal complex? First, its purpose and limits: Originally, the construct had as its purpose chiefly the understanding of adult behavior, specifically of the syndrome labeled hysteria. The fact that Freud generalized from the data obtained from the free associations of emotionally disturbed adult women to other adult behavior, abnormal and normal, and then to child development, often without providing much other evidence, has been one of the questionable aspects of his theory. However, the construction of scientific laws from the observance of seemingly exceptional and heretofore unrelated phenomena is far from unusual. The immediate question is: what predictions or discoveries about this particular child's development can be made using the Oedipal construct? The psychoanalytic answer is that a prolonged or intense preoccupation with this fantasy may result in a wide variety of childhood behavioral disturbances, particularly if the Oedipal attachment and its fears become generalized for the child into other situations. Particularly, one might expect the child to placate the parent of the same sex, to manifest fears of destruction, to be unable to develop other social attachments outside the family, and very possibly to regress to more infantile behavior. It should be noted, in this regard, that this one psychoanalytic concept cannot be used in isolation from other parts of psychoanalytic theory, and that this is only part of an overall theory of childhood sexuality.

How, then, might the clinician explore the possibility that an "Oedipal complex" underlies a developmental disturbance? What kind of evidence is necessary and how may it be sought? Here, again, the clinician must be aware of the specifics of the theory. The construct concerns a *fantasy*, and a fantasy often hidden from direct observation of manifest behavior. Freud specifies that the existence of this complex is usually observable only or mostly from the child's fantasy productions and dreams, and then more often than not in "disguised" or symbolic form. The clinical value of such evidence in the child's fantasy lies not only in "explaining" the symptom, but more in focusing the clinician's attention on the behavior of the child — and of the parent —in the parent-child relationship which otherwise might escape his attention. Both child and parent, insofar as the parent may exacerbate the child's fantasy, would, according to Freudian theory, attempt to cover any manifestation of this attachment. Thus, the parent may be unaware of and fail to report ways in which his behavior or the nature of the family situation or other events may serve to prolong the child's normal Oedipal attachment into a "complex." For example, the parents

might not think to report that the child is in the habit of "playing" in the parental bed every morning, or if they do think such a fact to be important, they may be too embarrassed to mention it. They may not notice that their son always makes a wide circle around the room when his father is sitting there, or that he anticipates punishment from his father in unwarranted fashion; they may think it only cute that the daughter always seeks her father out to take her to the bathroom or to tuck her into bed. Moreover, they very likely would hotly and defensively deny that such behavior was at all important or unusual. In gathering data concerning a possible Oedipal disturbance, the clinician must keep in mind another specification of the theory, namely, the concept of repression.

What are some of the limitations of this construct? Recognition that it derives from and has its greatest usefulness in conceptualization about pathological states, rather than normal behavior, has already been mentioned as a limitation. However, the greatest disadvantage is the absence of any definite norms or standardization of evidence. Even if it be granted that an Oedipal attachment occurs for every child, the theory never specifies exactly at what point the normal becomes pathological. Only rough ground rules and "clinical judgment" define the difference between a normal "conflict" and a pathological "complex." Nor are there data concerning the normal variations of the age at which a child might be expected to have "resolved" such a conflict. Thus, if such fantasy attachments are to be expected in all children somewhere between the ages of three and six, to consider the attachment as a "complex" might require evidence of a considerably intense conflict. Or, if the child were chronologically older than six, but generally retarded in his development, one might have to seek further evidence to see whether the Oedipal conflict were the source of the developmental retardation or just one part of it. All in all, such a construct becomes a powerful tool in assessment only when the data about the personal experience of the child are carefully and thoughtfully gathered. The use of this construct to organize the data is illustrated in many cases throughout this volume, as in, for example, Case 10 in this chapter and Case 47 in Chapter 17.

The pattern and sequence of personal, idiosyncratic experiences are often the key to the understanding of the development of the child. By the term "idiosyncratic" is meant those events and circumstances in the child's life after his birth, aside from the normal maturational stresses and beyond the conflicts of his social group. Chiefly these "personal experiences" occur as part of his family relationships, the personal rewards and frustrations which he experiences and learns to expect, and they shape his *personal* (as differentiated from his *social*) identity. Many other events and persons may also condition the child's view of himself, such as physical illness, injury or strength, achievements or failures in school or on the playground, friendships or enmities with peers or teachers, etc., but usually the child's ability to cope with such experiences is derived in large part from those he has already had during his preschool years in interaction with his family. These interpersonal interactions between the infant and his mother, father, and peers set the stage for his first steps in leaving the nest and coping with stresses beyond the home, at school and on the playground. Nor does the influence of these relationships stop as the child enters school, for as he struggles to cope with extrafamilial stresses, the family's encouragement and support, or criticism and rejection, of his behavior continue to be his central criteria and motivation, as long as he remains dependent on his family. Even in late adolescence, when the young adult is seeking to divest himself of the last vestiges of such influence and dependency, the desire for a final parental "blessing" is seldom more than thinly disguised, no matter how outwardly rebellious the adolescent may appear.

Chapter 4

❧

THE EGO AS THE
OBJECT OF ASSESSMENT

In Chapter 3 some of the main forces that shape the development of the child were outlined: the physical body which houses him (and "is" him in a sense), the familial and social environment which grants him a social identity, and the history of personal events which forms the continuity of his self. As will be discussed below, all of these become gradually internalized into his total personality. Although information about these factors is essential in every individual case, such data serve primarily to "explain" the child's state of development. They neither describe nor predict the actual behavior of the child. The first objective in an assessment is to describe the behavior of the child, his abilities, his achievement, and his potentialities for coping with his social and physiological environments. Only with objective evidence about the child's ongoing behavior is it possible to begin to hypothesize about the possible antecedents to or consequences of his development.

That the objective of assessment is to describe behavior may seem such a simple truth as not to warrant further consideration. Yet, in many instances, psychologists become so concerned with the stresses on the child as to

gloss over his actual functioning. Moreover, psychologists too often actually confuse the external stresses with the behavior itself, and speak of the stress (or assumed stress) as if it were the behavior! This error is typified by the term "organicity." Psychologists commonly report that they have administered "tests of organicity" or "brain damage," even though they have not actually examined the brain — nor any other organ. With slightly more precision, they may speak of "signs" of brain damage but this is more than a problem in preciseness of language, for such assessors also frequently fail to describe exactly what behavior the child did manifest. The functioning behavior per se needs to be reported because it may have more than one possible antecedent. For example, while certain behavior is often found to be associated with disturbances in the central nervous system, many of the same symptoms are also found in emotional disturbances. At times, psychologists also dwell on the social and interpersonal stresses on the child as if they were describing the child's behavior. Such statements as "he is a deprived child" or "he has an overprotective mother" do not describe behavior. Neither can such facts (or conclu-

40

sions) be related to the developmental problem at hand until the details of the current functioning of the child are known.

A. *The Functions of the Ego.**

Any assessment should begin with a study of the development of the "ego." However, ego is a rather vague concept, difficult to describe even in general terms and not a "unit" of behavior which can be observed or measured per se. The various aspects or functions of the ego need to be defined in as operational a fashion as possible, so that they may be related to specific measurements or other samples of behavior. Without commitment to any one theory of personality, the ego may be conceived as consisting of six functions as shown in Figure 2. These functions are not at all discrete, but overlap one

* Several similar terms such as *personality* or *self* might be used to indicate the overall functioning of the child, but these terms have different connotations, as will be discussed subsequently. Ego, as it is used here, is the most commonly accepted term.

with the other, especially as the child develops. The order in which these functions are arranged around the central core of "identity" is admittedly debatable. The circles are overlaped to indicate that the interrelationships between these functions vary considerably from individual to individual. For purposes of clinical assessment, the arrangement of this circle of functions is of little practical importance. However, in assessing the individual case, it is essential to describe how these functions are interrelated.

The development of these functions over the total period of childhood will be considered in the balance of this and the succeeding chapter. At this point, each may be defined briefly. "Motor" refers to the variety of muscular skills that the child develops, and to the sensory receptions that are interrelated with these skills, helping the child to regulate his movements (chiefly kinesthetic, tactile, and visual). Included under this heading are the kinesthetic aspects of other kinds of functions, such as speech, gestures, and motoric

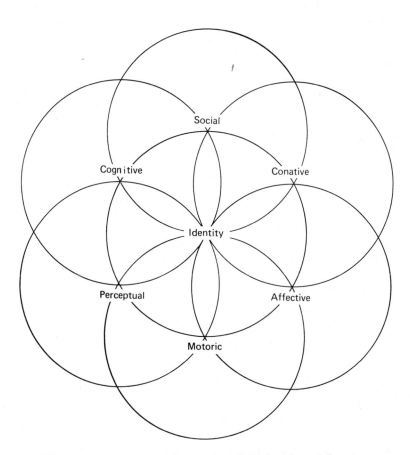

FIGURE 2. Schematic representation of the functions of the ego.

expression of affect. As will be seen, this function of the ego is far more discrete and more important during the developmental years than during adult life. "Perceptual" refers to the child's ability to discriminate and interrelate the stimulations he receives through his sensory organs (other than in motor reactions); to see, hear, and touch in such a fashion that what he is sensing forms objects to him, with distinct shapes, colors, textures, and sometimes sounds. Again, this ego function is more obvious in infancy and early childhood; perception in adult years is so much a part of cognitive function that it is noticeable only when it does not function effectively, as in some types of central nervous system disorders.

"Cognition" is an admittedly old-fashioned term for "intelligence," but the latter term is so often associated with — and thus delimited by—the IQ tests, that it may be helpful to return to the older and somewhat more inclusive term. By cognition is meant the ability to compare and contrast the objects perceived, to abstract and generalize about them, and thus to comprehend and put meaning to them. Cognition includes the ability to remember what is once perceived, to hold perceptions as ideas to be considered after the sensation has faded. This rubric includes the perception and comprehension of social situations, emotional expressions, and feelings, as well as the perception and understanding of physical objects and the physical environment. Last but certainly not least, cognition includes constructive and creative thought, the generation of new concepts and ideas (see the discussion of cognitive output in Chapter 12).

The term "affect" designates the feeling, moods, temperaments, and emotions that the child experiences. This function might also be labeled "sensory" in that it involves visceral, tactile, and kinesthetic sensations, plus tension, pain, and even tumescence and satiation. As will be seen, it is often difficult to distinguish the affective aspects of ego functioning from the conative or motivational drives or from the socializing functions of the ego. Although placed on the opposite side of the circle (Figure 2), affective functioning, as every clinician readily realizes, constantly interacts with and overlaps the cognitive.

By "conative" is meant both the physiological needs of the child and those social drives and motivations which are internalized.

Often these drives are affectively loaded and are confused with the "emotions"; but far more frequently than clinicians may consider, the child may have little or no feeling attached to his drives, especially when his need-gratifications are met satisfactorily. In such instances, the child's affects may be more attached to his perceptions or to his intellectual activities or social functionings. The chief difference between conation and the social functioning of the ego is that conation includes only those social drives which are internalized, that is, which the child perceives and experiences as part of himself.

Under the heading "Social" are those behavioral activities which the child performs as a part of the social milieu in which he exists and in which he participates. Included in these social functions of the ego are the child's attempts to conform to social pressures and norms, to interact with others, to communicate, to affect his social milieu, and to obtain need-gratifications from others. The overlap between social functioning and other ego functions is very considerable; yet, during childhood, social activity may — or may not — be accompanied by affect, or be a part of the child's motivations, or even be intellectually apprehended. For the young child, social activity, which is interrelated with and expressed through his motor activities, is more likely to be perceived than cognitively understood.

To use the term "identity" to indicate the overall interrelating of these functions is to tread on tender theoretical grounds. Some personologists refer to "identity" in the adult as "character formation," but in the child such character formation remains incomplete. However, as used here, identity refers chiefly to the child's ability to distinguish himself from the environment, especially from other people, to characterize himself, and to assess his own functioning, his own needs, and his own place in society. It is in this sense of self-perception that identity can be thought of as the core of the ego.

B. SENSORY-MOTOR DEVELOPMENT

Muscular activity of the fetus precedes birth and is the first sign of life. At birth and for a brief period thereafter, gross uncoordinated muscular and sensory activity is about the only visible behavior of the neonate. Otherwise, during the first few weeks of life, the infant is for all intents and purposes sans affective, cognitive or social behavior. Several coordinated reflexes are present — the startle, the grasp, orienting reflexes, visual tracking and fixation, and uditory localization, according to recent studies of neonates. The most important coordinated muscular activity is the sucking reflex, seemingly an innate behavior which allows the infant to feed and thus sustain life. However, studies (Call, 1964) have suggested that even this reflex is not quite as automatic and innate as has been supposed. Breathing also usually has to be given a start, with the traditional pat by the obstetrician or midwife.

These elementary muscular activities, while relatively but not entirely independent of environmental stimuli, soon become part of a sensory-motor network. Nevertheless seemingly random, exploratory movement continues to be a predominate part of the child's behavior throughout his infancy, his childhood, and even his adolescence. Wiggling, wriggling, fiddling, turning, twisting, kicking, throwing, jumping, convulsing, all are a continuing part of the behavior of children of all ages. Alternated with this muscular activity are periods of rest and sleep. Almost from birth, children appear to differ in the amount and type of activity and rest they require. Whether their activity level is something "constitutional," genetically or congenitally determined, is uncertain, nor is there much known about the effects of environmental stress and learning on the development of activity levels. However, either hyper or hypoactivity, either constant restlessness or inertness, may be a sign of either emotional or physiological disturbance as will be detailed subsequently (see particularly Chapters 12 and 16). But it may be necessary to have some estimate of the usual activity level of the individual child in order to evaluate whether or not his activity at any one time is for him either excessive or below par.

That this exploratory reaching-out soon becomes purposive has been well detailed by Piaget (1954). Much of this activity is actually sensory, tactile exploration (see the following section of this chapter). However, Piaget also emphasizes that the infant begins to learn about his world through kinesthetic sensations. He discovers himself as moving and through moving, in a kind of Cartesian, "I move, therefore I am." This muscular activity becomes the seeds of intelligence and later of socialization and identity formation. The measurement of infant intelligence thus consists of graduations of motor activity — developing from random reactivity to grasping, holding and pulling coordination, and purposeful manipulation and operation of objects outside of his own body. This development is illustrated in Figure 3, which shows items from the Cattell Scale of Infant Intelligence and the Vineland Social Maturity Scale.

Thus, the first task of the infant is to gain control over his muscular-skeletal system. Although gaining this control depends on and in part is derived from physiological development (for the central nervous system itself is not yet reacting in a steady alpha rhythm), the development of this activity itself is distinct from physiological growth. As Jones (1949) among others has shown, muscular coordination is only partially related to skeletal development or other indices of physiological development. Learning to hold up the

Cattell:		Vineland: Year O–I
2nd Month	3. Follows rings	2. Balances head
3rd Month	5. Inspects own fingers	3. Grasps objects within reach
4th Month	1. Manipulates fingers	8. Sits unsupported
5th Month	5. Picks up spoon	11. Drinks from cup unassisted
6th Month	3. Manipulates mirror	13. Grasps with thumb and fingers
7th Month	5. Exploits paper	15. Stands alone
8th Month	1. Pulls ring by string	References: Cattell, P. 1940; Doll, E., 1947.
9th Month	3. Rings bell	
10th Month	1. Uncovers toy	
11th Month	2. Secures cube under cup	
12th Month	3. Marks with pencil	

Figure 3. Sample items from the Cattell Infant Intelligence Scale and the Vineland Social Maturity Scale illustrating the measurement of the rate of motor development as a part of cognitive development.

head, to turn over, to creep and crawl, to sit and stand, and to walk proceed very rapidly during the first year to 18 months in such regularity in most children that these behaviors are often regarded as entirely maturational. The many trial and error practice movements which the infant goes through may go unobserved. This motor development during early infancy assumes importance when it is realized how much further motor, intellectual, social, and emotional development depend upon it. For example, much practice of arm to mouth, of finger to finger, and of balancing is required before the infant can begin to feed himself, drink from a cup, or hold a spoon. Control over large muscle systems is necessary before the infant can control throat muscles for speech or the anal sphincter for toilet training.

This muscular control is also obtained in a social interaction, through the handling of the baby by the mother and in response to her encourgement and discipline. There is speculation that such habits as handedness may be determined by the direction in which the mother holds the baby to the breast or lifts him. Call (1967) observed that the mother's confidence and security in holding the infant appears to affect the development of his coordination. When the mother herself is anxious and clumsy with the baby, the infant often seems insecure in his own movements. This writer has often been struck in his observations of infants in a well-baby clinic of how often the activity level of the infant seemed to reflect that of the mother. The busy, moving, active mother often has an active, wriggling baby, while the passive, quiescent mother a more quiet baby. However, there are also many instances where the activity levels of the mother and child were not so consonant or are even in conflict. It often appears that such differences arise when the mother's activity level is extreme, reflecting her anxiety. Thus, when a mother tries to handle her anxiety in obsessive activity, hovering over the baby, constant fiddling with him, and worrying about his motor activity, the baby is fussy, restless, but not well developed in his own motor coordination. Another mother may make more demands for coordinated movements than the baby is capable of, thus stultifying him. Many young mothers feel that they are failing if they cannot get the baby to perform coordinated motor activities

as soon as they think he should. At the other extreme, the depressed withdrawn woman may both fail to play with the baby or otherwise stimulate him, and also be made nervous and annoyed by his activity. Either type of mother may, in their respective fashions, restrict the baby's activity.

Within the first year of life, these motor activities become gradually coordinated with the perceptual intake of stimulus, so that the infant is not responding merely to his own internal sensations. In this process motor activities such as grasping, reaching, holding, manipulating, operating, and retaining, become skills for handling and coping with the environment. The ability to stand erect and walk gives the infant a new visual perspective and enlarges his world. Observe the child learning to walk; he seldom watches his feet, as might an adult learning to dance; instead, he is looking across the room.

An analogous random motor activity of the throat muscles precedes speech. But preceding actual communication through sound is considerable social interaction and communication between mother and child on a purely motor level. The baby discovers that mother responds to wriggles, to stiffening, to holding his breath, to kicks and to grasping, and then to cries, coos, and gurgles. The smile, for example, considered by many authorities as the first definite hallmark of socializing, begins to appear about the second or third month. Repetitive imitation of sounds, intonations, accents, and sentencelike vocalizations preoccupy the one year old. Nor does this motoric production of sounds completely cease once speech is achieved. Making and imitating noises persists throughout childhood and even into adolescence. When unrestricted, the child seems to mouth sounds continuously, chirping, clicking, spluttering, whooping, shouting, humming, whistling, singing, and chanting unintelligible and almost meaningless noises. Some of this noise making is a reinforcement process in which the child repeats sounds he has heard in order to remember and learn them, and some is a creative act, an expression of fantasy. Insofar as these nonsense sounds amuse or annoy others, when they are funny noises or sounds of derision or hostility, they serve as nonlanguage communication. However, they also seem to constitute a motoric exercise, a continuous vital assertion of the self and a release of inner tension, as witness the music popularly enjoyed by adolescents.

This acquisition of motor skills and the coordination of perceptual and motor activities continue to be major activities of the preschool child. As they become achievements in the eyes of adults and peers and are rewarded or envied, these skills become social acts. Some of these acts such as self-feeding or bowel control are demanded of the child. Toilet training, as the psychoanalysts have emphasized, is a classic example of this socialization of and through motor control. That eye and throat movements and other muscular activity accompany thinking in the child has been repeatedly observed by investigators of children's cognitive processes. These muscular activities are part of the way the child learns to think. It is also true that cognitive activity requires a control over motor activity. Interesting in this respect is the research on the Rorschach movement response (Meltzoff, et al, 1953) which shows that projection of movement onto the inkblot can be significantly increased by cessation or interruption of motor activity.

Thus, the motor control and coordination gained during the preschool years are basic to the child's school tasks of reading, writing, and logical thinking. Not only does the child have to learn to make the very fine eye and finger coordinations required for literacy, he has to learn how to sit still for long periods of time in a classroom and to interrupt and cease motor activity so that he can think abstractly, and bring to mind the movement he has experienced. Most important, the motor activity must become internalized cognitive activity.

Throughout these school years, the child continues to develop refined motor skills. With increased accuracy he runs, skips rope, bounces and catches balls, strikes with his fist and with bats, draws, whistles, spits, and performs many other purposeful and random acts. Again, acquisition of these skills is related to his social maturation. His level of achievement draws the accolades or the derision of his peers and elders. Here, social-sexual differences begin to appear regarding motor activity. The "little lady" is not supposed to achieve as extensively in these acts as is the boy. No wonder that girls achieve in their studies somewhat better than boys in the elementary grades, or that among boys

there is a zero correlation between achievement in sports and grade average (Start, 1961).

The so-called "awkward" age of pubescence does not seem to refer as much to the teenager's motor activity as to his social behavior, and social self-consciousness. Often the adolescent seems to become much more aware of the social meaning of his movements, but also becomes much more poised, graceful, and skillful. His walk takes on rhythm even before it is put to music in dancing. Girls are embarrassed by their elders and peers who now regard what was previously considered an innocent sprawl as "not ladylike" or "suggestive." The girl acquires postures that the boys understand as seductive, and the boys learn to walk and stand and perform feats that will attract girls. Athletic competition, already regarded as the epitome of virility, takes on even more seriousness, and the boy who cannot compete must find substitute achievements. Rhythmical activity, not only in dancing but in all forms of music and in sports, takes on extra import for the adolescent. Acquired at this age are many skills involving the use and operation of tools and machines, especially the automobile. Hayakawa (1957) has speculated that the power of the car extends and replaces the motor prowess of the man. When teenagers talk about cars, they are chiefly interested in power, speed, and manueverability, rather than in the adult concern with economy, comfort, or social prestige.

Thus, an investigation of the child's coordination and control is often part of the assessment of his development. However, it is not easy to separate motor behavior from perceptual activities, and most "tests" involve both of these variables. Direct observation of the child at play or in other social situations provides the most objective data, but is not often available to the officebound psychologist. However, the psychologist should learn to observe the child's motor activities and skills as they appear during his contacts with the child in the examining room or playroom, that is, how the child sits, moves, handles test materials, etc. Interviews with the child provide a subjective report of the his attitudes and perceptions of his motor activities. Most children like to talk about their play and to boast of their motor prowess. Thus, the latency boy who avoids this topic or who describes only sedentary play may be suffering from some handicap, social, emotional, or possibly physiological.

The assessment of motor development, and of motor handicaps is detailed in Chapter 12. Suffice it to say, motor development varies considerably from child to child, depending upon inheritance, rates of physiological maturation, nutrition, and the stimulation and opportunities offered by the environment. Thus, this development may be deterred by many conditions, including genetic and congenital defects, injuries and diseases, and emotional and social deprivations. In many instances, failures in motor development involve several or all of these conditions. Investigation of a motor handicap often requires a detailed and thorough history. Recently, attention has focused on the more subtle failures in motor development, which often go unnoticed. However, a thorough psychological assessment is also necessary of motor behavior of children suffering such gross and obvious defects as cerebral palsy or muscular dystrophy. The degree and nature of the motor handicap cannot be assumed by looking at the crippled child, nor can one depend only on the subjective reports from parents. Not only is it necessary to assess the degree of impairment, but even more important is an evaluation of its possible effects on other aspects of the child's development. For example, a child suffering from cerebral palsy may be slowed in his perceptual and cognitive development because he cannot kinesthetically explore objects or gain other basic knowledge of them through touch and manipulation. Moreover, his motivations may lag as he finds himself incapacitated, and he comes to regard himself as inadequate. Such motivational attitudes may then be affected by the responses of others to his handicap, for example, the overprotection of parents or rejection by peers. The presence of more subtle motor handicaps, especially of lags in motor development, may go unnoticed during the preschool years and come to light only when the child is unable to perform the more complex and coordinated motor tasks underlying reading or when he fails to control his motor activity on entering school.

Obversely, disturbances of motor behavior are often indications of generalized emotional and social imbalances. Slowed-down motor behavior is one symptom of depression, even in infants. Repetitive gestures, sounds, or movements may be part of a child's obsessive fears, or even of autism. Excessive rocking, clinging, twirling, and tiptoe walking are considered by many authorities as symptoms of childhood schizophrenia, but these behaviors can also be observed at moments among normal children below age six (Liebowitz, Palmer & Colbert, 1961). Hyperactivity, too, is usually indicative of some disturbance of development. It may arise from some disease or endoctrine disbalance, such as a thyroid disorder, but more frequently such hyperactivity is a reaction formation, a desperate attempt to compensate for feelings of inadequacy either in intellectual or social spheres or in motor skills themselves. The frequency with which children use random motor activity as a defensive measure against anxiety attests to its import in the child's life. The uneasy guilt-ridden teenager also feels constantly restless, has to be "on the go" and "do something, anything" to rid himself of his anxiety.

C. PERCEPTUAL DEVELOPMENT

Perception and motor behavior are so interrelated that it is often difficult to conceive of them as separate functions. However, over the past decades, a body of research has been amassed which clearly establishes both that a person's motor responses do not always reflect the nature of his perceptions, and that perception does not always lead to an immediate motor response. Yet, since it is admittedly difficult to assess perception separately from a motoric or verbal response, this distinction is sometimes blurred in clinical assessment. It is in the study of the developing child that this becomes especially important. Although some interaction between these two ego systems begins shortly after birth, it is not until almost age nine that the average child can coordinate them sufficiently to reproduce even the simple line figure of the Bender-Gestalt Test (Koppitz, 1963). Coordination of increasingly more complex configurations with a variety of motoric patterns continues to be an essential part of the developmental process throughout childhood. A failure to accomplish this perceptual-motor coordination leads to serious developmental difficulties in all aspects of ego functioning.

Although perception is derived from sensory stimulation, the psychological act of perception is to be differentiated from the physiological phenomenon of neural excitement. Again, this is a developmental distinction. In the neonate, there appears to be little perceptual behavior other than sensory intake. At most, eye movements and head-turning are partially under control. However, what begins as passive sensory receptivity evolves rapidly into differentiated recognition and even an ordering of sensations, which is how perception is usually defined. Perception may further be distinguished from cognition, in that it covers only the awareness of sensations, and the differentiation and ordering of stimuli, but not comprehension, meaning, abstraction, or other facets of intelligence. The importance of these distinctions to assessment will be seen when various handicaps and symptoms of perceptual disturbance in development are considered.

The development of perceptual discrimination closely parallels the differentiation process in motor activity. At birth and for several weeks thereafter, tactile sensations seem to be the most predominate sensory mode. The infant is more sensitive to touch, temperature, and kinesthetic stimuli than to light or sound. He can sleep in the light amid noise but will awaken if he is too cold or warm or if stroked. He is most sensitive to changes in the position of his body and to the tonus of his viscera. He does not appear to distinguish the sensations of his own physiological environment from that outside of his body.*

At first, these primitive sensations give the child little or no cues for perceptual organization. Yet, they form the basis of later intellectual, affectional, and motivational behavior patterns. Touching his own toes, rocking his body — which results in kinesthetic sensations — and listening to his own sounds are his initial experiences. Up and down and around becomes meaningful as he becomes able to lift his own head and hold it erect,

and later to sit and then stand. The warmth, the softness, and perhaps even the odor of his mother's body blends in with his own bodily sensations but gradually become distinct to him. He soon discriminates her touch, her grasp, and her voice. Visual discriminations, however, require the development of the motor ability to focus his eyes on an object; the neonate stares and stares and turns his head and stares some more.

The infant's sensations also acquire affective, motivational, and social meaning for him. Certain sensations "satisfy" him, give him pleasure, frighten him, or are perceived as painful. But not all sensations commonly thought by adults to be uncomfortable are necessarily perceived in that way by the child. He may actually be more alert and quite "happy" when slightly hungry. Being thrown in the air by his father does not necessarily frighten him, but may bring gales of laughter. In fact, an infant often appears to seek new sensations. The extension of the infant's sensory-perception experience is, of course, abetted by his parents, who feed, cuddle, stroke, and coo to him. Rocking and singing to the baby, holding him, and hovering over him form the basis of his initial social relationships. The importance of this stimulation to his later social development has been demonstrated by the observations of orphaned children by Renee Spitz (1946) and Goldfarb (1955), and of infant monkeys by Harlow (1958). Without such sensory stimulation by the parent, both the human and the anthropoid infant may become listless and less motivated to explore the environment on his own.

As the infant becomes motorically sure of himself, he unceasingly explores his environment, alerted by every sound and sight. As soon as he can crawl, he tries to touch and grasp everything, putting it to his mouth, which seems to be a particularly sensitive zone. He seems to "see" through the ends of his fingers and his lips and tongue. As soon as he can speak he wants everything identified. His unbounded curiosity becomes a concern to adults who must rescue him from hazards. They may also become annoyed by the child's demands to touch, handle, and see everything, and they may try to curtail his perceptual explorations with sharp orders of "No, don't touch," whether or not he might hurt himself or whether or not adult property is endangered. Yet, visual exploration alone does not

---

* The reader may have already noted that throughout this book the child's body is considered an "environment" from which he receives stimulation with which he must cope, as if his body were distinct from a "self" doing the coping. While this distinction is proposed partly for heuristic purposes, it should be noted that the discrimination between his body and external environments is one of the perceptual tasks of the developing child. As will be detailed further, the child also learns to identify himself in more ways than purely physiological and to separate his body from a "self."

quite satisfy the child's curiosity throughout his development. The school-age child and the adolescent too are never quite content until they have put their hands on whatever they see. The softness, hardness, the viscosity, the warmth and coldness, the weight and motility of an object are just as important to the exploring child as the visual shape and color. The child apparently first learns shape perception through handling objects. Color as a defining part of an object and discrimination of colors appear later in infancy than form perception.

Visual discrimination develops apace with other perceptions. The child sees things and reaches for them. He hears sounds and looks around him. As his seeing, hearing, and reaching become coordinated, his awareness of spatial relationships develops. His hearing, of course, is most essential to his development of speech. The infant must learn not only to discriminate and imitate discrete sounds but intonations and language structure as well. One measurement of an infant's alertness is his attention to sound, including the sound of his own voice. Thus, on infant IQ tests the baby is asked to repeat words and word combinations.

The refinement of perception continues at a rapid pace throughout infancy and even into the school and adolescent years, albeit less noticeably. After the child has learned the motor act of holding a crayon, he begins to try to reproduce forms. He not only learns to pedal his tricycle but to steer it through space. Catching a ball involves a complex visual-motor coordination. The relationships between the development of perceptual ability and of language are now widely recognized. Since difficulty in language development is so often a clinical complaint, and a sign of other difficulties in development, it is important to recognize the complexities involved. In such cases, the tendency is to look first for distortions in the child's associative process, in his ability to put together the words he had heard or read. Perceptual differentiations have to be accurate and discriminate if the associations involved in word identifications are to be made. Teachers of foreign languages are now discovering that learning of new languages is impeded if the basic phonic components of the new language cannot be distinguished (Ervin-Tripp, 1966). Sometimes children who appear to be otherwise intelligent may have speech or reading

difficulties arising chiefly from defective auditory discrimination.

Thus, the child who is "ready" for school must have already developed the ability to discriminate between simple forms and between simple sounds. He must also be able to make some groupings of visual and of auditory stimuli, to see and hear things that are identifiable as "different" or "the same." Thus, on the Stanford-Binet, at age four, he must "put his finger on the thing in the picture that is not the same as the other things." The Columbia Mental Maturity Test and the Leiter International Scale use such discrimination and grouping as the sole measure of intelligence (requiring very complex discriminations and associations at the higher levels). Reading requires both letter and letter-grouping discrimination. The child who has difficulty in making perceptual groupings may well have difficulty in conceptualization of numbers, so that no matter how well he succeeds in memorizing multiplication tables, arithmetic will be a meaningless exercise to him and mathematics will be completely incomprehensible.

In addition to being basic to the child's intellectual development, his perceptual development is also closely tied to his social and emotional growth. Much of the infant's relationship with his mother, which is his initial social, interpersonal relationship, consists of tactile, kinesthetic, and other sensory stimulations. Throughout the period of infancy and on into childhood, it is vital that the child receive sensory demonstrations of comfort and affection, since they apparently form the basis for later social trust in others when physical contact may not be present. The child finally learns that love is possible without direct sensory stimulation, having been satisfied and then weaned from it. Even more important, the petting and fondling of the child forms a foundation for his subsequent adult erotic experiences. Of course, the sensual stimulation that the child experiences in his "erogenous zones," as the Freudians have labeled those sensitive parts of the body, are not usually thought of by psychologists as "perceptions." Yet, the child does *perceive* affection and satisfaction and love through being kissed and fondled. Slaps and spankings and loud voices and facial expressions convey anger to him, while other expressions convey tenderness, sorrow, or pain.

Genital sensations, including tumescence, can be observed early in life. In most cultures, the child learns to associate these sensations with taboos before he discovers any other meaning to them. However, despite the taboos, these sexual sensations become a part of his perception of himself because these perceptions are from within the child's own body. Although the taboos against childhood sexual play do teach him to control himself publicly, they also heighten the child's curiosity. Even in cultures where there are few taboos against childhood sexual play, sexual stimulation appears associated with curiosity. The child peeks in prohibited places, the bathroom or parents' bedroom, often without quite knowing what he is looking for. And sometimes the taboos against peeping may be generalized in the child's mind, creating a suppression of all visual curiosity. "See no evil, hear no evil, speak no evil," the child is admonished, and if this warning is heavily reinforced, it may be widely generalized so that the child may be unsure of what is "evil."

Disturbance in perceptual development may thus be associated with disturbances in emotional and social development as well as the more commonly recognized and too often presumed defects in the sensory organs or in the central nervous system. In fact, the child who cannot perceive the words on the page, or hear the teacher's instruction, or reproduce forms on paper is as likely to be suffering from guilt feelings about seeing or hearing as from visual or auditory defects or poor neural synaptic contacts. Anger floods the nervous system and blocks perception far more frequently than cerebral hemorrhages or tumors in the child's brain. Thus, in assessing perceptual development, the psychologist needs evidence about the child's emotional behavior as well as his physical health in order to interpret what he observes in the child's perceptual behavior. As will be discussed further in Chapter 12, it is possible to distinguish some perceptual behavior which is more characteristic of emotional disturbance than of brain damage. Considerable perceptual material is used in assessment, such as the Draw-A-Person, Bender-Gestalt, and other "visual-motor" tests, but interest has focused chiefly on either the content of the drawing (Machover, 1949) or on motor errors.

Perhaps the only major technique that has as its theoretical base the interaction between perception and other aspects of ego functioning is the Rorschach. Since in the United States psychologists have been more concerned about the precision of their instruments and less clear about the theoretical base, many users of the Rorschach have given little more than lip service to the theory of perceptual modes introduced by Herman Rorschach in his original work (1921). This theory and its implications for assessing development will be discussed in further detail in Chapters 7 and 9. Suffice it to say at this point that the possibility that visual modes of perceiving form, movement, shading, and color are related to the child's development of general social and perceptual modes (or, as Rorschach is usually translated, "experience types") is a fascinating but as yet only barely explored hypothesis (Rickers-Oviaskina, 1961; Palmer, 1955).

D. COGNITIVE (INTELLECTUAL) DEVELOPMENT

The assessment of intellectual development has, of course, long been a major item in studying child behavior. It remains today a central factor in assessment, through not, as in the earlier days of clinical work, the only item. Although intellectual achievement is certainly a major factor in the child's ability to meet his world, one reason that psychologists tended to give it a primary importance was the fact that for many decades the only precise instruments for measuring any kind of child development were the "IQ" tests. During the first decades of this century, IQ tests were developed which were highly objective, well standardized, and reliable predictors of other hallmarks of intellectual behavior, chiefly of academic achievement. Yet, despite this precision of measurement, questions continued to plague behavioral scientists: What is being measured? What is intelligence? The debates that raged in the psychological literature on these questions between 1920 and 1940 were largely concerned with what then was called the nature-nurture question. Is intelligence chiefly a genetically predetermined set of faculties, or is it a complex of learned achievements? Although this question has continued to concern psychologists (Liverant, 1960) and remains unsolved if not unsolvable, the debate has largely subsided and has been shelved with the answer of "both." Instead, psychologists have proceeded to consider operationally what they were measuring. "Intelligence is what intelligence tests measure" was the popular tautology in the 1930's. Subsequently there were the factor analytic studies of Spearman in England and Thurston in the United States. While the general results of such factoring has been the discovery of a major overall "G" factor, running across all subtests, with slightly different secondary factors, depending on the content of the scales included in the test, the problem of identifying the factors left much of the definition of intelligence unresolved.

A developmental approach provides, to this author's way of thinking, a more comprehensive definition to the complexities of behavior generally labeled intelligence. The nineteenth century concept of intelligence as a unitary "faculty" is far too narrow. Rather, intelligence is a developing complexity of behaviors, interrelated but seldom quite perfectly integrated. In rough developmental order, it consists of: sensory exploration, perceptual discrimination, retention and recall, associative conceptualization, and judgment and evaluation of the individual's environment (including his internal stimuli). The development of this intellectual complexity is best illustrated in the widening complexity of tasks at each age level in the mental age tests. While it is not correct that intelligence is what tests measure, it is true that the better tests, such as the Binet, derive their validity from the fact that they sample this development fairly accurately. Thus, a test of generalization such as "Similarities" would not discriminate among four year olds (most of whom might fail it), nor would a simple test of perceptual discrimination measure intellectual capacity in nine year olds, most of whom would pass it. A great deal of study has been given to the development of these patterns of intellectual behavior; it is known when certain kinds of intellectual behavior will appear and at what age it begins to be a consistent part of the child's functioning. During infancy, there is an enormously rapid expansion of intellectual functioning, so that by age six nearly all of the facets of intellectual behavior are present, at least in nascent form. During the preschool years, the child constantly explores the environment, comparing and contrasting experiences, naming and conceptu-

alizing, seeking "why" and evaluating what he learns. Yet, during this expansion period, the child's overall intellectual functioning is quite unsteady and unreliable. It often seems that there is so much of the world for the child to grasp that he never quite has the time to integrate and absorb it all. He tries many forms of intellectual functioning, but does not seem to stop to really develop any one securely. Thus, he may practice memorizing and at one moment show a phenomenal memory for some specific piece of information, such as the names of automobiles, but then not remember his own last name. He may quickly form a conceptual map of the trip across town to the nursery school but bumps his head as he crawls out from underneath a table. This acceleration of development without concomitant integration is reflected in the relatively wide variability of IQ scores during infancy, and results in their relatively low predictive validity.

During the later years of childhood, there is a constant working over and practice of the thinking "games" the child has already tried. In a process analogous to his kinesthetic development, the child repetitiously fashions these intellectual "motions" into consistent "skills." This development of skills is, of course, aided, abetted, and directed by the society through formal "education," but continues also in and out of school, in contests with peers, in response to adult pressure and exasperation, and during the child's own musings and private observations. Children seek out and enjoy "intellectual games"; even in societies where the achievement motive is not as extreme as in our own, children are often described as seeking knowledge faster than the teacher-parent, or wise man, can give it. Although the child may say he "hates" school, often it turns out what he hates is the boredom of waiting his turn in overcrowded classrooms, the repetitious drill of something he has already learned, or the repression of his curiosity in favor of some topic or skill for which he is unprepared. "Hating" school also refers to hating school authority, and the traditional resistance of school so much more common 50 to 100 years ago probably represented the child's resistance to the authoritarian school master who drilled the child on dull lessons unrelated to his own curiosity. In our modern schools, which attempt to whet the child's curiosity and to present him with skills and knowledge related to practical everyday events, the majority of children openly avow that they like school or only feign "hating" it.

With the onset of puberty, going to school and the development of intelligence assume more meaning for the child. During the childhood years, intellectual activity seems relatively purposeless to the child. He goes to school because he has to and wants to; although he vaguely realizes that this activity will serve some purpose in the future, for the moment it is mostly an exercise of his own curiosity. During adolescence, the child discovers that intellectual activity has a personal and social purpose. The skills that have been nurtured during childhood now must be applied toward an eventual vocation, toward understanding and dealing with society, and toward an identity as an intellectually capable person. Learning, which heretofore has been fun, now becomes a responsibility. This shift is embodied in the change of relationship at school between the child and teacher when he leaves elementary school and enters high school or even junior high. No longer is he dependent entirely on one teacher in one settled classroom; now he floats from teacher to teacher in shifting groups. At first his courses are planned out for him, but as he proceeds through high school, he must make increasing number of decisions about what he wants to learn. His homework, previously a drill of the day's lessons, now consists of seeking and integrating knowledge on his own, beyond the classroom. At home and in his peer associations, too, an increasing degree of intellectual independence is expected of him. His parents now require him to be less "thoughtless" and to proceed with tasks without extensive repeated instructions. In sports, he has to "use his head," plan activities, and recognize relations without extensive direction.

Despite the excellent research on the development of intelligence, psychologists have only begun to explore the motivational "why" of intellectual development. Perhaps one should ask, as did Frenkel-Brunswik,* "Why does the child fail to learn?" and accept the fact that he usually does. However, it is in looking at this question of failure, at the pathology of intellectual retardation, that it is possible at times to perceive that there is

* Unpublished remarks at a symposium, University of California, 1954.

an affective, conative, and social setting within which the intellect develops. Over the past decade, psychologists have come to realize that when the child is entirely preoccupied with the satisfaction of basic physiological and social needs, he may not be able to explore and absorb his environment intellectually. It is also true that the completely satiated animal or infant may not learn. Observations of infants have shown that they are most alert and exploratory just before meals or when slightly uncomfortable. Similarly, a child may be drowned by competition, but without some competition, his curiosity merely meanders. Social and personal ambition, even if almost overweening, usually heightens intellectual development. Very likely, the child's intellectual growth is also tied in with his sexual development. Even observers who do not necessarily adopt psychoanalytic concepts have recognized the stimulus generalization of sexual curiosity, especially during late infancy. Psychoanalytic theory suggests that the intellectual work of childhood is made possible by the release of energy to the ego upon resolution of the Oedipal complex. Once the child has learned to repress his libidinous and aggressive drives, he can divert and sublimate these drives into school work. The child who is still fighting the psychosexual battles of infancy is disinterested in and unable to devote himself to relatively emotionally neutral, problem-solving tasks.

Intellectual development in our technologically complex and achievement-oriented society possesses a high social value. Every parent desires and sees as a necessity that his child be bright and achieve at school. Currently, as never before, mental deficiency is conceived of as a personal tragedy—usually for the parent more than for the child, for the child initially does not experience much loss. No doubt the high social value currently placed on intellectual achievement and education is quite realistic. In addition to the technical competency necessary for most vocations and professions, there is a need for every citizen in a democracy to be cognizant of the complications of his society, national and international. With these realistic pressures, and with the stamp of institutionalized social prestige on intelligence, parents and society are currently putting ever-increasing pressure on the child for intellectual achievement. Thus, the parent who seeks prestige through his child's achievement, to make up "for what I never got," now has his aim justified, and is more prevalent than ever. Almost vanished is the parent of only a generation ago who said, "I succeeded without education—you don't need it."

Often the question facing the assessor is whether or not the child is developing the intellect to meet these social and parental demands. Moreover, there are considerable indications that the general intellectual level of the population may be rising. For example, in the restandardization of the Shipley-Hartford Scales, this writer (1964) discovered that the mean raw scores were considerably higher than in the original standardization of 20 years before. Educators are recognizing that the average child can absorb and comprehend far more information with increased rapidity than was thought possible two decades ago. Moreover, children are now learning complex intellectual skills at an earlier age, skills previously considered possible for the young adult of superior intelligence. However, although a greater number of youths are now quite capable of higher education and are flooding our colleges, the intellectual requirements for college entrance—or even high school graduation—also continue to spiral upward. Children with average or below average intelligence often become discouraged over school achievement especially the middle class child, as these prestige values on achievement are strongest in the middle class. Feeling themselves a potential failure in the eyes of their parents and teachers, they may try to cope with this pressure with a variety of mechanisms. Some may have the ego strength to reject the parental-teacher pressure, shrug it off, and suffer only momentary self-doubts. Many struggle valiantly to comply, and their anxiety takes the form of somatic complaints (being sick is a legitimate excuse for school failure, whether the illness is feigned or unconsciously suffered). Many fight back with misbehavior at school, becoming a troublemaker in the classroom although a compliant child at home. Often they find surcease in those peer groups among whom school achievement has a negative prestige. Some become increasingly depressed, with falling self-esteem, and finally overtly rebel after puberty.

The psychologist assessing the child's intellectual development must, therefore, be aware of this aura of social prestige and the stimulant of social pressure for achievement. For almost a generation, psychologists have tended to eschew intelligence testing as a routine chore, to be handed over to the teacher or psychometrician. Assessment of emotional functioning via the projective techniques became the more prestigeful task. However, the need for precise and comprehensive assessment of cognitive functioning in children is now greater than ever before. It is essential to distinguish both the child's strengths and weaknesses and to determine which aspects of his intellectual growth may be held back by emotional or social problems, which might be altered to allow further growth. Assessment of intellectual development is also very important because intellectual functioning is often such a hallmark of the child's response to social and emotional frustration, over and above the frustrations entailed in intellectual achievement per se. The interrelationships between intellectual, social, and affective development have been so well recognized over the past decade as almost to blur the distinctions between them. Slow intellectual development and school failure in the early school years are often the initial signs of emotional and social immaturity. The child who is clinging to the dependency state of infancy often resists intellectual growth and does not want to assume responsibility for independent problem-solving tasks. Such children may often appear bright enough, except when put to the test; then they ask the questions, often trying to reverse the tester-testee roles in the assessment situation. They show spurts of idle curiosity, but avoid actual absorption of knowledge or achievement of skills.

Mild or moderate intellectual retardation is also often a common symptom of other emotional disturbances. Intellectual apathy is a common symptom of depression in children as well as in adults. The anxious child has difficulty concentrating, cannot remember facts, makes hasty judgments and faulty intellectual discriminations. Although distortions in thought processes are more difficult to distinguish in the unformed intellectual functioning of the child than in the ideation of the adult psychotic, the persistence beyond the preschool years of tangential, "magical" thinking in a child's problem-solving behavior may be a prodromata of schizophrenia. Similarly, it may be only in subtle signs in his intellectual development that weaknesses in the child's neuro-physiological development are discovered. For all these reasons, assessment of the child's intellectual development requires expert knowledge and skill.

E. AFFECTIVE DEVELOPMENT

Affective behavior has its counterparts or functional expressions in sensationlike experience, in physiological and neurological functioning, in conative behavior, and in social interaction, but none of these exactly defines nor entirely includes emotional experience. Analogous to electricity, emotional experience seems to run through all these other behavioral phenomena, and to be observable and even measurable in terms of them. Yet, the phenomenon labeled affect is relatively independent and discrete from other psychological phenomena. There are indications that affective experience is in itself a necessary function of human existence. Such experiments as Harlow's research (1959) on affectional comfort in baby monkeys or Spitz (1945) and others (Yarrow, 1964) on emotional deprivation in human infants strongly suggests that emotional stimulation may be a need in itself. Moreover, all research and clinical observation indicates clearly that emotional expression cannot be withheld without severe repercussions to the organism's functioning, and may even result in death. Thus, affective experience appears to serve a necessary and independent function for the individual. It gives the meaning to life; it "colors" or "moves" the form of experience—to use an analogy from Rorschach. Thus, sex without affection or eating without pleasure or fighting without anger, while common enough, seem to most people to be somewhat empty. Even learning without curiosity becomes compulsive pedantry. Some affects appear to serve specific functions. Pain and anxiety are signals respectively of physiological and psychological danger. Anger and hostility prepare the individual for defense and offense. Love paves the way for affiliation, reinforcing both dependence and sex. From all of these general considerations, it may be argued that a careful assessment of these affective reinforcing agents is a necessary part of the psychological understanding of the child.

The course of development of affective functioning follows, in general, the same pattern as the other ego functions. Temperament, which is usually defined as a proclivity to certain modes of emotional experiencing, is still considered by many European psychologists to be primarily genetically determined. Insofar as hereditary factors determine the physiological structures through which the emotions operate, this hypothesis may have validity. It seems reasonable to assume that some of the temperamental differences observable in infants almost from the moment of birth may be attributable to constitutional differences, that is, to be based on even slight "normal" differences in endocrine structure, skin sensitivity, visceral or motor reactivity, or even in the structure of the reticular formation of the brain. However, as occurs in other psychological functioning, the impact of environmental stress and the child's learned readjustments to this stress soon becomes so extensive as to mask whatever constitutional determinants may exist. Assessment perforce deals chiefly with these learned patterns of affective behavior.

Whatever affective experience might be attributed to the newborn infant is so generalized as to be indistinguishable. However, within the first few weeks of life, the infant's cries do appear to differ markedly in affective tone and, at least to the mother, to indicate pain, anger, or loneliness. In turn, the infant reacts differently, even before age six months, to angry voices or to affectionate cooing, and soon becomes able to distinguish some facial expressions. For the most part, the neonate's affective discrimination is very gross, and consists largely of a comfort-discomfort dichotomy. Vocalizations that can be interpreted as satisfaction or happiness also are observable early in life. The first smile, usually at about two to three months, is the classic sign of the beginning of affective expression. Laughing usually precedes speech by a few months. Attempts to express affection by returning patting and petting can be observed in the first year of life. Rage is rather obvious in the baby's cries by six months, distinguishable from discomfort and often accompanied by gross motor activity in full blown "temper tantrums."

Since so much of the infant's existence is concerned with his bodily functions, rather than with social interactions, it is understandable that a great deal of his affective experience is derived from or related to his own body. Whether or not certain focal spots of the body are "eroticized" for the infant, as Freud maintained, there is little doubt that the infant finds great pleasure in putting objects to his mouth and sucking on them—a pleasure that persists through much of the child's later life and in formalized fashion on into adulthood in such habits as smoking or chewing gum. At least, affective life appears to start with the mouth as the center of sensitivity or receptivity. Being cuddled and petted also bring expressions to the baby's face which can be interpreted as joyful. Whether the infant experiences sadness or depression in the adult sense is quite doubtful, but there is no doubt that the infant who fails to receive the usual emotional stimulation from the contact of a maternal figure becomes first restless and crying, then apathetic and unresponsive, to the point of failing to eat and even of death.

Preoccupied as the infant appears to be with his own functioning, Freud's assertion that the infant finds pleasure in and is affectively concerned with his bowel and urinary functioning seems a reasonable possibility. This assertion that bowel functioning is pleasurable is, of course, unacceptable to most laymen, since from the time of our bowel training everyone learns to regard these functions as "dirty," as disgusting, and as taboo in public discussion. However, privately, even adults speak of "finding relief" in defecation and, albeit with embarrassment, may admit a pleasure in it. The "joy" of the face of the baby in defecation is readily observable, and throughout infancy most children appear to enjoy going to the toilet and to be preoccupied with the process of elimination, despite the attempts of adults to quash this affective reaction. A good deal of affective interaction does take place between the child and his mother before toilet training is usually attempted. Not only does the baby receive a great deal of emotional support and affection, but the mother probably has begun to negatively condition expressions of rage when she begins to wean the baby—not only from the breast and bottle, but from a total "demand" schedule. Thus, to at least a slight degree, the baby begins to experience some frustration, some moments when his needs are not entirely satisfied. However, prior to toilet training, mothers in our society make little demand on their infants to control pleasurable activities. Although in weaning the baby the mother does impose a delay in gratification, she does not usually prohibit the pleasure involved. Moreover, in weaning, the mother provides the control; no demand is put on the child for self-control and no punishment is involved. In contrast, toilet training is often much more affect-ladened than any prior experience for the child. The resistance and anger that the child experiences is aroused not so much by the delay in gratification but by the demand that the child impose the control on himself. Thus, it is at this time that the child first experiences intense feelings of guilt, of self-recrimination for not living up to parental expectation. Imposition of guilt is, of course, the most common method of toilet training in western culture.

Although the child may have experienced some of these emotions prior to toilet training, the toilet-training situation and the events surrounding it are the prototype of many future social interactions in which the child experiences strong emotions that society demands that he control. Of course, bowel control is not the only restriction imposed on the two year old. The psychological lesson for the child is self-control over affect. He learns that it is required that he himself control and delay pleasure and, with even greater intensity, he begins to learn control over his anger. At the same time he learns bowel control, he is walking and learning to talk. Thus, parents are not only saying, "You must tell me when you need to go pottie," but they are constantly saying, "No!" to many other things, things the baby cannot touch, things he cannot have, and places he cannot go. Parents are asking him to feed himself and to begin to care for his own needs in many little ways. No longer is he "King Baby" whose every want is supplied immediately. His repetitive, "No," muttered even to himself in play, is both a practice of this self-control and a reflection of his anger. Although he has experienced rage many times before, he now begins to differentiate feelings, associate them with specific situations, and even substitute words for motor behavior as a means of expressing affect.

During the "terrible two's" and three's, the infant is considerably concerned with affective experience, not only anger but tenderness as well. He can change rapidly from negativistic resistance to charming affablity. He learns to give out with affection, exchanging kisses at random. His play, especially with a pet or a doll, involves considerable affect and learning of affect expression and control. He takes out his rage on his Teddy Bear, then kisses and cuddles it at the next moment. He projects his feelings and emotions onto others and also reflects the affection and anger between his parents or sibs. Often he will naively and openly express his concern over the feelings of others and the feelings exchanged between them, cutting through the adult repressions and denials of affect. It is puzzling to him that adults cover feelings. Thus, his mother may nag his father in angry fashion but when the three year old asks, "Why are you angry at Daddy?" she may well deny her anger, believing that the child should be protected from it, and in adult fashion hope to keep private her feelings toward her husband.

As the child's psychological existence begins to shift from his bodily functions into relationships with others, he begins to experience new emotions. Guilt and shame follow him from his toilet training into other social situations. He learns cues from mother's face and mother's voice to avoid situations that might lead to these emotions. As he begins to be a social individual with possessions and privileges, he learns covetousness and jealousy. Particularly, he finds he must share mother with father and possibly with siblings. Feelings of murderous envy overwhelm him at times. He may make up daydreams in which the whole world blows up. Then he will be full of temporary phobias of retaliation for his destructive fantasies.

These preschool years are also full of pleasurable excitement. Each new event and situation is greeted with wonderment. Curiosity, though often classified as a drive, also contains the affect so vital to intellectual development. The child continues to find new pleasure in the development of his body, his motor activities, and his speech. Play becomes a drive in itself and playfulness an emotion. Many little things seem funny to him without his knowing quite why. However, humor in the more adult sense usually does not begin to be observable in any quantity until almost the end of infancy. Thus, Terman found that the question "What's funny about that?" to be appropriate on the Binet at the seven-year level. However,

even the five year old attempts to make jokes, and in late infancy children may experience moments of uncontrollable laughter over "nothing at all." All in all, infancy is marked by spontaneity of feelings, both pleasurable and unpleasant.

Authorities have long argued over when the child first experiences and learns fear and anxiety. The behaviorist, Watson, posited fear as an inborn reflex—a notable exception of his overall theory that all behavior is learned through conditioning. Subsequently, his students found that many infants appeared to be without fear, and suggested that what Watson had observed in the newborn was a startle reflex. Infants under age two or three do occasionally react with fear of new objects, places, and people, but these reactions are shortlived and not as extensively demonstrated as in the three to four year old. However, as the infant suffers physical or psychological injury, he does learn to become afraid. The two year old has to be protected from physical and social hazards and kept from climbing into the laps of strangers. By age three, the child begins to learn caution and to display brief bouts of shyness.

If anxiety is distinguished from fear, and defined as the anticipation of danger rather than a direct reaction to a present hazard, then one may say that until the child has built up enough experience to learn of *potential* hazard, he may not experience more than momentary anxiety. At this age, the infant reacts with rage or tears to an immediate stress, not in anticipation of threat. Fortunately the pangs of anxiety are not commonly experienced by infants under two and anxiety states in babies are rare. Some babies, less than two years old, do display expressions and behavior very comparable to adult anxiety. It may well be that such infants have accumulated enough experience of loss, especially of emotional support, that even in the first years of life they learn to anticipate threat from minor clues and thus develop a generalized state of anxiety. It is when the infant begins to shift from a primarily physiological to a more social organism that he first appears to experience any affect near to what is usually called anxiety in adults and older children. For anxiety, though often manifested physiologically, does seem to be chiefly a social affect, developed and aroused in social interactions.

Psychoanalytic theory holds that while the infant may experience threat and react with rage or apathetic withdrawal, true anxiety does not develop until the infant is involved in the primary social relationship of the Oedipal conflict.* The psychoanalytic definition of anxiety contains three specifications: first, anxiety is anticipatory. Although some analysts (Fenichel, 1945) compare anxiety to pain as a "warning signal," it is clear that anxiety, unlike pain, occurs before there is any danger. Second, anxiety is social, involving chiefly fear of loss of love or the expression of anger. Third, anxiety is conflictual. Whereas a child *fears* danger or a threat imposed upon him, he is *anxious* only about the threats which are held over him in reaction to what he wants to do. Thus, a child who is beaten by a sadistic parent with no consistent pattern may be terrorized but does not necessarily experience anxiety as defined here. However, the child who is angry at the parent whom he also loves will experience anxiety lest in the expression of his anger he lose parental love. Or, in the more complicated example of Oedipal conflict, the boy who desires exclusive possession of his mother may be anxious lest he invoke the jealous wrath that he has projected onto his father.

Thus anxiety, as defined above, involves the intellectual ability to conceptualize and abstract, to formulate in fantasy and imagination, and to differentiate affects so that conflicts can be anticipated. There is, of course, little sign of such conceptual ability before age four. Although there is some debate about the ability of intellectually retarded children to experience anxiety, manifestations of anxiety can be observed among the mildly retarded, but the moderately to severely retarded appear incapable of anticipating social dangers or of differentiating conflict.

Whether the Oedipal fantasy is as central in the emotional development of the child as Freud thought, it is a prototype of the internalized situation in which the child first experiences anxiety. The child imagines possessing the parent of the opposite sex and anticipates the anger and retaliation from the parent of the same sex—all in fantasy. Only the affect is real: he *is in love* with his mother; he *is jealous* of his father; he *does fear* castration; he *is anxious.*

Thus, along with an ever-widening scope of motor skills, perceptual differentiations, and cognitive processes, the preschool child accumulates a wealth of affective experiences. Since the child has not as yet developed any defenses or methods of coping with affect, he experiences them as "raw" feelings. Emotions are easily aroused and easily discharged. Sensitive, he wears his feelings on his sleeve. Spontaneous, he expresses directly what he feels in actions and in words.

As he progresses from infancy into childhood, the child learns to cover his feelings, delay expression of affect, and defend himself from overwhelming emotions. The psychoanalysts attribute the change to the "resolution" of the Oedipal conflict, wherein the child abandons his dreams of relation with the parent of the opposite sex, suppresses his sexual desires, and adopts a relatively sexless life. Certainly, by the time he is six, he is under increasing pressure to stop acting like a baby, to hold back his tears, to suppress his boisterous laughter, and to cease expecting to be cuddled constantly. Temper tantrums are no longer tolerated and anger must be held within, if he is to satisfy parental standards in Western culture. The torturous "Why" of his curiosity is now relegated to the control of the classroom. This lesson of control over affect is not learned easily nor quickly. In fact, Western society provides for both the release of affect and the development of initial social controls in the preschool years through nursery school and kindergarten. These preparatory classes serve to teach the child both to "socialize" or to "express" himself through interaction with children and adults other than those upon whom he depends so intensely at home. He has formal lessons in "sharing," in "cooperating," and even in competing without overt expression of anger.

The emotional "latency" of childhood, as Freud so aptly labeled it, is far from complete and sets in gradually. The child remains relatively spontaneous with his peers, but much more shy and reserved in front of adults than his younger sibs. Stoltz and Smith (1959), in a study of children's reaction to frustration, divided the Rosenzweig Picture

---

* That is, as presented by Anna Freud (1946). Noticeably different in this respect are the concepts of Melanie Klein (1932) who posits the appearance of anxiety and guilt during the "oral" phase. However, the phenomena which she describes as anxiety is quite different from that described by Anna Freud.

Frustration Study into those situations involving frustration of the child by an adult and those involving interaction between children. In the child-child situations, children responded to the pictures with far more open expressions of aggression than in the adult-child pictures. However, the child was much less apt to express feelings of hurt to other children than to adults. Loosli-Usteri (1931), investigating the imagination of latency children, speaks of *"le conscience du hazard,"* the awareness of chancing a fantasy, to the Rorschach inkblots. Latency becomes a time for learning to handle and control affect— for the feelings do not actually disappear. Several childhood games involve merely the ability not to flinch, no matter what the insult or hurt. The child who loses his temper is taunted by his peers as a baby. Demonstrations of affection are limited, even with parents, and are accompanied with embarrassment. At eight, a boy is more apt to shake hands on saying good night than to publicly be kissed —though a kiss in the dark from mother as the light is turned off may be acceptable.

With the onset of puberty, the child experiences a new avalanche of affect. Whereas during latency the child seems relatively carefree and insensitive, he now displays moody spells and is sensitive to every emotional nuance. Girls, particularly, seem to be a bundle of feelings at ages 12 to 13. For the junior high school girl, everything "matters." Her parents and her younger sibs find her unbearably "touchy." She is overwhelmed by romanticism and "takes everything to heart." Boys of this age seem to retain much of their practiced masculine indifference to emotional stress, at least outwardly, but they also are less obtuse and more aware of the emotional side of life than they were a few years previously. Increasingly, the teen-age boy finds it necessary to deny and repress feelings, but with greater difficulty.

During adolescence, the child seems to awake from the latency of his middle childhood and reexperience the emotions of infancy with renewed vigor. In folklore, the legend of Sleeping Beauty epitomized this process. In this childhood fantasy, the heroine is driven from the love of her father by the jealous "stepmother" who threatens her life; she becomes the companion of sexless little men, but finally is put to sleep when poisoned by the stepmother-witch. Only the kiss of the adolescent prince reawakens her. In this reawakening, the adolescent again begins to resent parental controls and becomes anxious in the conflict between desired love from the parent and assertion of independence. His anger again flares easily against both parents and peers. He flushes with embarrassment over a social *faux pas* or over the sudden expression of his feelings. He is much more sensitive to the erotic facets of his affectionate feelings. Often he feels guilty for no good reason, as if he had committed some unknown, unmentionable crime, and is quick to feel accused and blamed. Parents, teachers, and policemen find him ready to defend himself on every issue. Struggling with a tangle of emotions, he turns to writing poetry, joining religious and political movements, driving at high speeds, anything and everything to release the tensions and express the feelings he is experiencing. No doubt these effective experiences are aroused and spurred on by the reawakening and resurgence of sexual drives and by the new demands for personal and social independence. But the affective intensity of adolescence is also a struggle in itself. No longer can he repress emotions as he did in latency; now he must learn how to express them in interchange with peers and adults, to use them to obtain love along with sexual satisfactions and to aid in establishing his independent place in society. In all cultures, the rites of puberty stress this achievement of emotional expression and control. Not only are deeds of daring demanded, but so, too, are declarations of feelings. Introspection is almost an obsession for the adolescent; each is a Hamlet in his own right.

Assessment of the child's affective life is thus a goal in itself, for the development of the ability to be aware of the emotional side of life, to express one's own feelings, and to control one's emotions so as to utilize them as an enrichment of all experiences is necessary for the fulfillment of adult life. Indeed, the Declaration of Independence lists as one of the three aims of mankind, "the pursuit of happiness." How well the child is learning and developing this pursuit is a major task of assessment.

The most common problem in affective development lies in this assimilation of emotional controls. Some of this control, as has been implied above, almost seems inherent in the organism's course of development. After a rapid accumulation of affective experience during infancy, the child himself—with the aid of society—seems to need and accept a "latency" period, a period of assimilation. During adolescence, the child often appears to alter between states of affective flooding and withdrawal, of "sturm and drang," sometimes almost in definable cycles. "We just can't understand him," one mother said of her 15-year old son, "Last week he raged at anything we said, never sat still, seemed to be looking for a fight, or some excitement. This week he's the sweet little boy we used to know, busy with his studies, and nothing bothers him."

Most commonly the conflict for the child arises with the controls set by society as a whole and by his parental authorities in particular. Social interdictions on individual emotional behavior appear to have three main, related purposes: first, a society needs to protect the group against mass emotional outbursts that might disrupt the work of the group or lead to precipitous or irrational acts by a large part of the society. Second, a society tries to protect the individual from the same thing, that is from the disrupting effects of overwhelming outbursts of affectively loaded behavior. Third, every society seeks to instill in the child the many institutionalized forms of behavior designed to channel, sublimate, or formalize the expression of affect so that it will not be overly disturbing to either the group or the individual. For example, for the release of anger and hostility (a primary concern of society), there are such childhood activities as hostile, competitive "sports" accompanied by cries of "fight, team fight" or "kill 'em"; there are war games and publicly encouraged fantasies of hostility in "fairy" tales which are full of horror and there are sadistic comic strips and hour after hour of TV violence.

One current social dilemma is whether, in encouraging the child to so fill his fantasy life with hostility and violence, adult authorities are supplying an outlet that will prevent the child from needing to express hostility in action or whether flooding him with these socially supplied examples of violence puts a social stamp of approval on violent behavior. Perhaps the answer lies in the extent to which the child can differentiate between fantasy and reality. However, a massive dosage of social fantasies of violence such as television and comics currently supply often heightens children's fantasies, especially in the preschool age group who are still engaged in absorbing emotions and who do not as yet clearly distinguish fantasy from reality. It is during this age that there are more reports of night terrors after seeing horror movies on TV or fatal accidents resulting from playing out hangings from Westerns. The latency child enjoys thrillers, tortures himself with ghost stories, etc., but constantly reassures himself publicly that these are imaginary, and after age seven or eight begins to give up Cowboy and Indian or war games in favor of socially approved aggressive sports. The effects of social stimulation of hostile fantasy on adolescents is not clear; but again, their excitability is high and they are quite emotionally impressionable. Too many teenagers do seem to interpret these social fantasies as condoning their own impulses to act out hostility.

Of course, the purpose in presenting hostile fantasies and encouraging hostility in games in many societies is to train the child for engaging in war as a young adult. Previous societies did use these institutions to prepare their youth both for the hunt and for war. The butchery of the buffalo or the neighboring tribe had to be trained into the Indian brave with accompanying drum and dance. The heroics of war continue to be exhorted to children in most modern societies. However, it is now necessary to instruct children that total annihilation in nuclear warfare is a horrible possibility to be feared.

In general, however, children are not permitted to become involved in the emotions surrounding death; adults act as if children should be shielded from knowledge of death and have no need to mourn. Children's participation in funerals is minimized or prohibited, and the facts of death and mourning are rarely explained to them. In contrast to the Puritanical ethic of the immediately prior generations, children are now socially encouraged to enjoy life, both by words and by actions of adults. However, the ideals of happiness set forth in magazine advertisements or in movies which portray everyone as having the luxuries of life, and as being without serious emotional conflicts, are often actually depressing to the economically or emotionally poverty-stricken child. He may be able to indulge himself in fantasies of well-being and happiness for the moment only, and then have to face the harsh realities of his deprivations. Romanticism and sexual stimulation are also promoted in public fantasies, in love stories and songs, in dress and adornment, and in music and dancing. Whereas only a generation ago, children were shielded from this sexually tinged emotional stimulation, much of Western culture today readily exposes not only adolescents but also younger children to a barrage of sensual stimulations and affect.

Many of the social values regarding emotional expression have been rapidly changing in Western culture during the twentieth century, accompanied by changes in the amount of stimulation given the child. At the same time, rules and mores restricting emotional expression have been loosened. However, these changes have been neither complete nor consistent. Thus, side by side with the new values put on emotional freedom and expression, the child learns at least to give lip service to the Puritanical mores, which preach repression and denial of feelings. Frequently adolescents express considerable cynicism as to whether there are any genuine feelings at all in today's society.

Furthermore, although Western societies have tended to loosen old and inappropriate restrictions on emotional expression and are stimulating emotional expressiveness, the institutionalized modes of expressing these emotions have also been dropped and this has largely been left to the individual. A great deal of emotional expression and fantasy was previously supplied by organized religion. Mass picnics, communion services, rites of puberty, May Day dances, and even the Fourth of July are institutions almost out of memory in urban America. Even in rural Mexico, the author observed a village fiesta which was staged chiefly for the tourista and sniggered at by the local children! A great deal of entertainment, including sporting events, is made available in the home via TV. There are too few public places for dancing, for adults or adolescents. A high school near the author's home sponsored only two teen-age dances last year because "so few children are interested in public dances." Thus, at present in our society, children are highly stimulated by socially sponsored fantasies of emotional expression. They are given only minimum social rules for emotional control and are left largely to their own individual resources to find expression.

Thus, the conflicts surrounding emotional control have also shifted. Whereas Freud wrote about a Victorian society which stifled emotion and promoted repression, the typical conflict faced by many children today is almost the opposite situation, that is the anxiety of creating their own emotional outlets and controls, with only minimal and inconsistent social standards as guidelines. Many parents are conscious of this conflict and attempt to help their children reach some resolution of it, but they often are even more caught up in these changing social values, since it was during their own childhood that many of these changes began. This parental dilemma is frequently expressed by such statements as, "I don't want my child to suffer like I did under silly rules; I want him to be free to express himself. But I can't let him go wild, and he keeps testing me." It is the constant testing, not of rules but of emotional reactions in others, which is so characteristic of childhood behavior today. This testing is one of the most frequent complaints by parents, not only because it is emotionally fatiguing but because it arouses so much guilt in the parental generation which did not itself resolve these conflicts. Typical is the parental statement, "That child almost makes me want to scream—but, of course, you're not supposed to scream." In a teachers' discussion of corporal punishment, one teacher remarked, "Of course, you are never allowed to spank a child in anger," to which another replied sardonically, "Yes, you can only hit them in cold blood."

"Emotional disturbance" is so much a component in all psychological disturbances that the two terms have almost become synonymous. Severe affective disturbances of psychotic proportion, such as the so-called manic-depressive psychosis or psychotic depressions, were once one of the major reasons for protecting people in institutions, but these terms are seldom used as diagnostic descriptions currently and were almost never applied to children. Very likely, such affective storms were common when our culture practiced severe emotional repression and when the psychodynamic pattern of perfectionism and family ambition, which underlies these symptoms (Gibson, 1958), were more common in our culture. However, cycles of depression and hyper-manic behavior can very often be observed as one feature of children's emotional disturbances, or even in normal children during the transitional phases of childhood. The hyperactive, demanding, boastful, irritable child very often has less noticeable periods when he is withdrawn, sullen, noncommunicative, and expressing feelings of self-doubt or even suicide. Occasionally, like some adults, such a child may be able to verbalize some of his feelings of sadness, inadequacy, rejection, and despondency. More frequently, the child "acts out" these emotions in his behavior, for example, as part of his school failure, in his social isolation from his peers, in a lack of interest in normal play activities, in poor appetite or sleeplessness, or even in semisuicidal behavior or "accident-proneness." Such a child may be masking depression by his frantic and obsessive attempts to be liked by everyone, by efforts to be perfect in his school work, or by an intense preoccupation with some hobby. Acting-out of guilt in violent, destructive— sometimes nearly self-destructive—behavior is a very common part of "Juvenile delinquency." The following case may serve as an example.

Case 11

According to her parents, Mary had always been a "straight A student," "very obedient," and "well behaved," "friendly though modest," and "a bit shy" and "God-fearing." "Suddenly," at age 14, she became excessively defiant of all adult authorities, neglected her school work and cut school, adopted the most extreme adolescent style of dress and language, and became "boy-crazy." By age 16, she was boasting of her sexual adventures so that even her parents were convinced that she was promiscuous. At first, Mary defiantly denied that there was anything wrong with her behavior, insisting that her parents and other adults were unduly repressive and failed to understand teen-age needs. By the third interview, however, she burst into tears, saying that she had always tried to be good but knew that she really was evil and that this was her inevitable fate. An adopted child, she had always felt she really could not live up to her parents' rigid moralistic standards. Although during childhood she had succeeded in meeting their demands, which had become internalized as demands on herself, she was unable to continue to meet these standards under the pressure of puberty. She had many angry feelings toward her adoptive parents but feared to express them because she felt that she might again be deprived of parents. Her behavior was in a sense a substitute, indirect expression of this hostility. Moreover, she hoped that if her parents had some real reason to be angry at her, and if she did something for which she would inevitably be punished, then "God would forgive me" for her greater "sin" of hating her parents.

The absence of affect or inappropriate affective response in the face of stress is as common a symptom of psychologic disturbance in children as it is among adults. In classic diagnostic terms, such behavior is recognized in the "belle indifférence" of hysteria, "affect isolation" of the obsessive-compulsive, or the "bland affect" of schizophrenia. The counterphobic, whistling-in-the-dark attempt to ignore social and personal conflict is epitomized in the "What, me worry!" slogan of *Mad* magazine.* Older children and especially adolescents are often able to maintain an outward cover of affective indifference in a "Who cares?" sneer. Younger children, more dependent on others for emotional support and less experienced in emotional control, are less able to deny their feelings. A pervasive emotional blandness in a very young child may well be part of a very severe emotional disturbance, such as in the syndrome called "childhood autism."

Thus, over the years a child may learn to mask his sensitivity to emotional stimulations, inuring himself against stress, and revealing his anxieties and depression only in behavioral manifestations. By the time he becomes an adult, this reaction may be so generalized a pattern to so many situations that the sources of his conflicts become unclear in his current situation and can be revealed only in recollections of childhood trauma during psychotherapy. However, in childhood, before such a neurotic pattern becomes fully developed, the affective aspects of the child's disturbance are more likely to be directly *reactive* to an ongoing conflictual situation, or to some loss or deprivation in the immediate past. Severe emotional deprivation, especially during infancy, can result in very generalized psychologic disturbance, lasting for many years if not resulting in permanent disability. Yet, the developing child is also emotionally quite resilient, and is able to bounce back from emotional stress a little more readily than adults. Socially, during childhood, demands for emotional de-

* A humor magazine, popular with both children and adults, which in slap-stick fashion spoofs many current social problems.

pendency are more acceptable whereas the adult is under pressure to work and produce more independently. Last, but not least, the biological and social pressures toward continued growth often force the child past emotional trauma, helping him to bypass it temporarily with perhaps only minimal disturbance at the time and giving the impression that the child has "out-grown it" or "gone through a stage." Unfortunately, such unresolved conflict may later appear in adolescent or adult life as a neurotic disability. Such reappearance of reactions to childhood trauma usually occur when the adult meets an emotional stress similar to the earlier trauma. The adult "neurosis" thus reflects the failure to learn to handle affective functioning during childhood.

THE EGO AS THE OBJECT
OF ASSESSMENT, CONTINUED

A. MOTIVATIONAL DEVELOPMENT

As was demonstrated in the previous chapter, it is difficult to discuss affective development without also discussing the drives, needs, and motivations of the child. In fact, the distinction between a drive and the affect accompanying it is sometimes lost because the same term is used to denote both. However, both biological needs and social drives may be accompanied by various degrees and kinds of affect which differ extensively from child to child. Obversely, a child may attach the same affective valence to different drives. Thus, in assessment it is important to distinguish between affect and drive, for affect alone is not necessarily an indication of drive satisfaction or deprivation.

In theoretical discussions of motivation, needs and drives are often treated as if they were relatively constant or repetitive states of the organism, which require intermittent satisfaction but have little or no individual variation. Such classical discussions also distinguish between the biological "need" and the social "drive," as if the motivations or stress arising from within the child's physiology had little or no socialization and as if the child's social drives had no biological origins. Perhaps these distinctions serve a theoretical or heuristic purpose, but in assessment it is difficult

to treat the child's motivations as either entirely biological or social.

The so-called biological needs, for oxygen, water, food, sleep, pain-avoidance, relief from extremes of temperature, and sex appear to vary a great deal in intensity and frequency from child to child, even at birth. Moreover, as will be discussed later, the strength of these needs vary over the child's lifespan, some being crucial for him at one stage of development and others assuming major import for him at another age. Almost from the start of life, all of these needs are "socialized" in one form or other, that is, there are socially approved and tabooed forms of seeking and receiving gratification of these needs. These social modes of gratification then become motivations in themselves. There are even polite ways to breathe; for example, asthmatic breathing annoys and threatens others. The child learns that only certain food and drink are acceptable and must be consumed according to social mores—and at certain times, in selected places. The same is true of sleeping and in the dress and shelter required to avoid temperature extremes. Protection against pain is highly institutionalized, not only in the institution of medicine but in safety rules and in many unwritten taboos. Social regulation of sex is so obvious as to need no comment. Yet, a society has to provide a variety of possibilities and variations for need-gratification if it is to remain adaptive to the needs of its members. If a society prohibits promiscuity and polygamy, it must permit divorce and provide for the care of widows; moreover, such societies usually tolerate some degree of prostitution. A society that taboos dairy products must promote a diet full of fats and alternate sources of calcium. A society that prohibits alcoholic beverages adopts Coca-Cola.

The conditions of group living also create demands on the individual not always directly related to his "biological" needs, though often affecting his biological functioning and, in the long run, deriving from the biological nature of the human species, for example the demand that the child learn to control the elimination of bodily wastes. Strictly speaking, defecation, urination, and perspiration are physiological functions which the body performs without having to seek any gratification outside of itself—as in the search for food or for a sexual partner. Elimination of wastes becomes a "need" only when it has to be delayed and controlled. Other so-called "social" needs, such as affiliation, achievement, and acquisitiveness, appear to have their roots not so much in the physiology of the individual as in the overall biology of the species. For example, the affiliative drive becomes particularly strong in our species which has a very frequent, almost continuous, sexual cycle and in which the young remain dependent on the adults for almost a quarter of the life span. Achievement and acquisitiveness are fostered in a species which is biologically interdependent. Again, each culture dictates the various means by which these needs are met.

Thus each child must learn both the social regulations for need satisfactions and, within these rules, develop the skills to attain gratification. Usually, these social rules involve delay of gratification or the acceptance of substitute gratifications. Assessment is concerned with these learned processes and with the affect resulting from delays in satisfaction or with partial or substitute satisfaction.

The socialization of need gratification takes place in coordination with the development of the skills to meet the means of gratification. It is chiefly when the social lesson is out of phase with the child's development or is inadequately or inconsistently taught that the child experiences conflicts and becomes anxious. Although some social rules are "out of date" and no longer applicable following technological and demographic changes, such meaningless vestigal rules are not so much a problem for the child as for the whole society—even though the protest is often carried by the child in conflict with adult authority.

Need-gratification skills develop in much the same pattern as other psychologic functions. The newborn infant appears to experience his needs directly and immediately. He himself is unable to delay or control them and, if not gratified, reacts with generalized frustration and "rage." Since he is totally dependent on others, chiefly his mother, for need gratification, his need "affiliation" is immediately developed. As he is able to reach and hold, walk and talk, and develop other refined motor skills, he becomes increasingly able to feed himself, pull up his own blanket over him, and get his own drink of water. Thus, he begins avoiding the delay of gratifications caused when his mother cannot immediately meet his needs. In so far as such self-gratification has this reward, he develops a need for achievement. However, since the infant remains able to satisfy his needs only to a small degree, he also seeks to reassure himself that his needs will be met if he is unable to do things for himself. Thus, even in areas where he can meet his own needs independently, he may occasionally demand gratification by his parents, testing their availability.

If the child is assured that parents are available to meet his needs whenever necessary, he is able to progress in the development of the skills leading toward independent gratification. In the normal development of the child, this parental role of both insuring gratification and at the same time fostering independence is not necessarily conflictual but indeed complementary. The child experiences threat only when he feels that he cannot depend either on his parents or on himself to meet his needs satisfactorily and consistently. Some deprived children will make extra strides in developing skills for self-gratification, driven into precocious independence by their anxiety—but always with an underlying feeling of insecurity. More commonly, children who experience inconstant and insecure gratification are poorly motivated in developing self-help skills and remain "infantile." They may even appear intellectually retarded as well as socially and emotionally immature.

In effect, parental love consists of a generalized promise or symbol of need gratification to the dependent child. Thus, the parent offers love as a reward or a reassurance for independent behavior and threatens the withdrawal of love to insure compliance with social demands. Again, these are normal, complementary interactions in normal parent-child relationships, and not necessarily conflictual. In most instances, the parent only has to express momentary disapproval, and then add rewards and reassurance to love as the child complies. Moreover, the normal child perceives this compliance as further evidence of his independence. Acceptance of social controls is also reinforced by the process of identification, which will be discussed more fully later on in this chapter. Suffice it to say at this point that through this process of identifying with the adult, the child accepts these controls as part of himself; he "internalizes" them, so that control becomes a need within him quite similar to his physiological drives. In essence, the child learns to approve and disapprove his own behavior, controlling himself with guilt independently from the actual reinforcement from the parents. As both Mowrer (1950) and Freud have pointed out, this self-reinforcement through guilt is a part of normal child development and is not necessarily conflictual. The child experiences conflict in establishing impulse controls chiefly when (a) the parents' threats of withdrawal of love are more intense and more frequent than the rewards, or (b) the demands for compliance are inconsistent with or beyond the child's skills, or (c) compliance is not sufficiently rewarded with renewed reassurance of love. Similarly, guilt becomes a problem for the child when the parent intimates that the child is "unworthy" of love, that is, he is not demonstrating that he is establishing his own controls.

Most of the child's physiological needs cannot, of course, be long delayed without a threat to his life. His parents and society can require that he wait for food until mealtime, and then that he eat slowly, using the correct feeding instruments and accepting preferred diets and menus—but he has still to be fed regularly. He must defecate in specified places and perhaps delay defecation for brief periods, but such delay may be more than can be expected from a very young child whose motor skills are still being developed. In both instances the child learns that temporary control will be followed by gratification and approval. Moreover, in establishing these controls, the parent is usually more involved in establishing affect control, especially over greed or anger, as was discussed above.

The only major physiological drive that can be delayed relatively indefinitely, and the one that society is most concerned about delaying and controlling until adulthood, is sex. The gradual development of sexual need-gratification skills within the complexity of social institutions and taboos involves a network of social and personal attitudes and feelings, interwoven with interpersonal relationships and affects. Thus, sexual development, in this broad perspective, is quite frequently one of the chief reasons for which children are brought for assessment. Moreover, in other cases, difficulties in sexual development frequently appears, during the process of assessment, to be a major if not the central factor in the child's conflicts. Even when sexual behavior and attitudes prove not to be developmental problems in themselves, sexual gratifications are so delayed and so socially regulated that other concerns and conflicts about other developmental adjustments often become generalized to sexual development. All in all, the way in which the child handles his sexual drive is often a prototype of his overall motivational and affective development.

Despite the importance of the sexual drive in the child's development, almost all that is known about this phenomenon comes from clinical observations. Originally, knowledge of childhood sexuality was derived from the memories of adult patients during psychoanalytic treatment, but in the past decades considerable knowledge has been learned from the assessment and treatment of children also. The absence of any other kind of scientific investigation, either actuarial or experimental, is, of course, chiefly because of the taboo which still exists in our society against open discourse between adults and children regarding sex—even though both adults and children openly discuss this topic among themselves much more freely than in previous generations. The massive denial and resistance with which the scientific community as well as the layman originally met Freud's discovery of "childhood sexuality" has now largely abated, but there is still prevalent in academic psychology a disregard of this phenomenon, and sometimes even a dismissal of it as purely a psychoanalytic concept. Thus, because sexual development is so complicated and because it is often given short shrift, it may be helpful to examine this particular motivational force and its relationship to assessment of children in somewhat greater detail.

In what ways and to what extent is the sexual drive manifest even during childhood? The fact is that, although children do not attain sexual maturity physiologically until puberty, and even somewhat later socially, sensitivity to sexual stimulation is present at birth and the sexual drive as an integral part of the child's overall motivation continues to expand throughout his development. In male newborns, genital tumescence is commonly observed when the infant is excited, even as he struggles for his first breath. Clitoral sensitivity can also be noted in female neonates. However, as is true for most behavioral phenomena during the first years of life, differentiation of this sensation is not immediate. When the child is bathed and diapers are changed and genitals touched, the child will momentarily cease wiggling and his facial expression will seem to express a combination of puzzlement and pleasure. As muscular control is achieved, he or she will be observed to rub the genital area against a pillow or pull at the diapers, even when dry. Manual masturbation may begin whenever the child has achieved sufficient manual dexterity and is part of his exploration of his body. However, during these initial years of life, the infant's needs for food, sleep, and tactile comfort are so constant and predominate that his need for sexual stimulation seems very secondary. Understandably, the child's "pleasure" is derived chiefly from the satisfaction of these other drives, so vital to his rapid physiological development. Whether or not this generalized "pleasure" can properly be labeled "erotic" is questionable, since such psychoanalytic concepts were derived largely from the study of memories, associations, and dreams of adult neurotic patients. It would seem more precise to hypothesize that when these initial nonsexual drives are not satisfied in infancy, it may be difficult for the child to begin to differentiate the less vital sexual drive. Thus, "pleasure" may continue to be indiscriminately experienced and generalized from one drive to the next, or be sought by substituting one drive for the other.

However, in the normal progression of the child's development, the child does not need either to substitute sexual gratifications for unsatisfied "primary" needs of infancy or to "eroticize" other needs. This "eroticizing" of other needs, particularly "oral" and "anal" activities, does appear in adult psychoneuroses, but it occurs only, as Freud was also careful to point out, when social prohibitions on sexual development are excessively and severely instilled. Otherwise, such "eroticizing" appears only incidentally as a part of what Freud called the "psychopathology of everyday life," that is, in the substitutes which the majority of a society accepts for sexual gratification. Thus, when the child's constant vital needs are met, so that he is free to explore and develop other functions, he proceeds to expand and refine his sexual gratification skills, including acceptable substitutes.

Besides the fact that sexual gratification can be delayed, it also differs from other drives in that it is by its very nature ultimately a social act. Although all needs are subject to social rules, in adulthood most of these needs can be satisfied without depending on others and, indeed, society expects adults to obtain need gratifications relatively independently. However, the obverse is true for sexual gratification. Although children are very dependent on others for most needs and learn to become independent, sexually the need for a mate comes to the fore only with puberty and is realized actually in adulthood. However, gradually throughout childhood, the child becomes aware of this interpersonal aspect of sexuality and its social ramifications, preparatory to his eventual social and physiological maturation of his sexual drive during adolescence. At first, the child knows "love" as the gratification of his needs for food and comfort in his dependent relationship upon adults; only gradually does he come to know "love" in the sense of gratification of sexual needs in an interdependent relationship with another adult. Admittedly, "love" is seldom if ever completely defined distinctly one way or the other by either adult or child. Most adults continue to seek some gratification of their needs, other than sexual, from other adults, especially from their mates. And even in infancy, the "eroticization" of interpersonal relationships begins to take place.

If sexual love is a generalized interdependent function in adulthood, it is understandably very generalized in the dependent child who is still learning to discriminate all of his functions and feelings. Thus, in infancy, the child cannot discriminate his sexual pleasure from other need gratifications and, insofar as he has need for sexual love, naturally looks for satisfaction in dependent fashion from the same sources as he receives other gratifications, that is, from his parents. Because his sexual need is fairly generalized and immature, he is easily satisfied by the petting, cuddling, and kissing which his parents provide. Almost as soon as he has learned to locate and discriminate the source of his sexual sensations in his genitalia, he also learns to discriminate between the sexes both physiologically and socially. With mounting sexual curiosity, the child of four to six peeks in on his parents in the bathroom, joins them in bed at every opportunity, and asks embarrassing questions. He also engages excitedly in sexual exploratory play with other children of both sexes. He observes manifestation of adult sexuality between his parents (if not the sexual act itself), feels left out, and jealously seeks the attention of the parent of the opposite sex. All this exciting knowledge is reenacted in play, in playing "house" or in kindergarten love affairs. The four-year-old girl who announces she is going to marry her daddy soon begins to add boy playmates as her prospective mates. At the same time, the child becomes acutely aware of social taboos. Genitalia, he discovers, are the only part of the body *always* covered by clothes. Sexual parts of the body and sexual functions can only be referred to by euphemisms at best and then only in privacy. All of sex, he discovers, is secret— which everyone knows! At the same time, the child discovers that sex is part of personal identity, that a recognition of self includes being a boy or girl, and that certain types of expected social behaviors have a sexual basis. The child uses the parent of the same sex as a model, thus inadvertently reinforcing the sexual aspects of the relationship with the parent of the opposite sex. What is seldom made clear is that the child *needs* to have an an "Oedipal" relationship with parental figures in order to learn how to relate to the opposite sex, that this is a prototype for his future sexual relationships. Moreover, he needs to learn about eroticized interpersonal relationships in a setting where there is no demand upon him to fulfill any sexual obligation beyond his skills and maturation. While the "incest taboo" has other social purposes, it also establishes this parent-child relationship as a learning situation. The taboo is a prohibition: "you must not have sexual relations with parents," but it is also a protection for the child: "You do not have to perform as a sexual adult as yet." More often than not, the chief reason that the "Oedipal *relationship*" becomes a neurotic "Oedipal *conflict*" is that the parents may unwittingly intensify this sexual aspect of the child-parent relationship, often to satisfy some of their own needs. According to psychoanalytic findings, the child learns to handle the affective aspects of sexuality, the jealousy and frustration, by fantasy— particularly the fantasy of the retaliation of "castration." However, if the child experiences a generalized acceptance and "love" in the relationship with his parents, without demands for sexual behavior and with support for controls, then his fantasies and fears subside. All in all, the social taboo in childhood sexuality in essence protects the child by forbidding him to enter into a relationship beyond his ability and thus reassuring him.

Infant sexuality, then, as with other psychological functions, consists of a rapid accumulation of experiences in which the child learns to make very basic biosocial discriminations. By the time he is six, he should learn that he can delay and control his sexual impulses until past puberty. He also needs to learn that these impulses are ultimately part of an intense interpersonal relationship for which he does not yet have the skills.

The development of these social skills will be discussed in more detail in the next section of this chapter; suffice it to say that the children begin this period of "latency" by engaging in a sexual social behavior outside the family circle, practicing and establishing their separate sexual roles, as boys or as girls, without the necessity of intersex involvement. Until a child is sure of this social-sexual role, he is not ready to enter into sexual relationships. Although much of the latency child's sexual interest and activity is repressed— especially in contrast to infancy—his sexual curiosity, especially regarding sexual functioning and skills, is not altogether abated. Once the boy begins to be assured of his masculinity and the girl of her femininity, this curiosity can be expressed. During these central years of childhood this curiosity takes the form of become intellectually aware, for example, learning sexual terms and the "facts of life." Not infrequently in the later years of this period of childhood, ten to 12, this activity includes homosexual play and intense homosexual social relationships, That is, close "buddies" among boys and "crushes" between girls. Such eroticized interpersonal relationships are most likely to occur just before or during the initial stages of the physiological onset of puberty.

A lapse of several years, depending on the species, between the physiological maturation of sexual functioning and actual mating occurs in animals other than man. Thus "adolescence" appears to have biological as well as social roots. Most mammals, especially the anthropoids and other "social" animals, do not mate during the first season of sexual maturity, but engage furiously in the practice of mating rituals.* Human adolescence is more prolonged than in other species, partly because the whole of human childhood and adulthood is also longer, but even more because the human social-sexual relationship is so much more complicated and there is so much more for the adolescent to learn and practice. In contrast to other species, the human adolescent must learn to engage in a continuous sexual relationship (rather than seasonal, as is true of most other species), and in a relationship which is supposed to last until the maturation of the offspring, again much longer than in other mammals. In primitive and feudal societies, where the life-span was much briefer than now and social behavior was much more controlled, adolescence was foreshortened also and formalized in puberty rites and in institutionalized separation of sexes until the mates could be selected by the society.

In more open societies, where selection of a mate is left up to the individual, a great deal of the adolescent's time and energy is engaged in learning about and in preparatory practice for mating. Romantic and sexual daydreams preoccupy the teen-ager's spare moments, in the classroom as well as at bedtime or in front of the TV. He progresses from teasing, pushing, and giggling to holding hands, kissing, fondling, and "petting," frequently proceeding on into premarital intercourse. Marriage may be delayed until the boy has learned skills for independently earning a living, but in the United States, as well as in the U.S.S.R., marriage is gradually being subsidized among college students albeit indirectly and subtly by student grants, and by the fact that wives

also commonly help to support the family while the husband is still learning a trade or profession.

The fact that the adolescent is frustrated by the delay of gratifications and made guilty over the breaking of social taboos is well recognized. However, to a considerable degree, this frustration is compensated for by the fact that the teen-ager is not completely prepared for a continuous sexual relationship and is more than often made anxious if he or she is accidently over-involved. Currently, the social taboos are so loosely applied and so commonly violated that they fail in their original intent, that is to protect the child from too early release of impulses which he has not learned to gratify satisfactorily.

The more serious "sexual" conflicts of adolescence do not usually arise from repression of the sexual impulses per se, but more often from the problem of attaining personal and sexual identity or from eroticized aspects of dependency needs. As was mentioned previously, during the adolescent resurgence of impulses, many of the lessons of infancy and early childhood are retested. The conflicts involved in these learning experiences are also often revived. The child's efforts to establish a sexual identity, a problem which had been laid aside after infancy, now again becomes of primary importance to him. He has to prove himself a man over again, with even greater intensity. His errors embarrass him and his failures depress him. Similarly, the young girl has to give up her sexual neutrality of latency and accept the fact of her femininity which appears with her first menses and her feminine figure. Currently, the achievement of an adult feminine role is particularly stressful, since the social role for women is in transition, with the old traditional passive-receptive role no longer accepted but with no new role as yet accepted by society.

Also during adolescence, the child is struggling to divest himself of the last remnants of dependency on adults for need gratification in general, a struggle rife with conflict since he not only seeks independence but hates to give up the irresponsibility of childhood. Insofar as this dependency was "eroticized" in earlier years, it may appear in adolescence primarily as a sexual conflict. If a child is still seeking to maintain dependency on the parents for other need gratifications, he may avoid and repress sexual activities in adolescence—or he may plunge headlong into premature sexual

---

* Kinsey, an entomologist, seems to have ignored this zoological fact in his classic study (1948) of the sexual behavior of humans, for he maintained that human sexual problems would be ameliorated if mating began immediately with the onset of puberty!

promiscuity in an effort to find the insufficient parental love in hetero- or homosexual relationships. Similarly, no little of the parent-child conflict so common at this age stems from a revival of the infantile "Oedipal" relationship; young ladies who were once "daddy's little girl" now reverse the field and become strangely critical of their father's habits and ideas—while at the same time acting toward him in a teasing and seductive manner. Toward mother, teen-age girls are even more intensely ambivalent, belligerently seeking conflict with them, all the while imitating them and seeking solace and comfort from them. To parents, this is often bewildering and they too often respond by attempting not only to reinforce the controls of childhood, but to grasp the child even tighter to their bosoms. In such instances, the child experiences a double load of guilt, both over the tabooed sexual attachment to the parent and over the anger at the parent for reinforcing the dependency aspects of their relationship.

As was indicated in the above discussion of the development of the child's sexual drives, the child has many other motivations to learn to handle and sex per se does not actually become of major concern to the child until puberty. For example, the child's physiological growth constitutes a need in itself which pervades much of his behavior and pushes him past many obstacles. Curiosity, as part of his cognitive functioning, with roots in both motor and perceptual stimulation, in sensation, and the sexual drive, becomes a drive in itself. Many of the needs listed in Murray's (1938) need-press schemata have roots in childhood. For example, N affiliation starts with the child's dependency on the mother for all other need gratification, and remains a strong need in most children throughout infancy and much of childhood. N achievement starts with the development of motor skills and soon becomes basic to the child's search for identity. Murray's Thematic Apperception Test has therefore become the classic instrument for assessing need-gratification development (see Chapters 9 and 14).

Aggression as a need also seems to be associated with the child's need to grow, to exercise, to defend against pain, to search for sensory stimulation, and to fend against frustration of all other needs. This concept of aggressiveness as a pushing out into and, at times, against the world should be distinguished by the assessor from the affective state of anger and the accumulated generalized anger called hostility. Anger and hostility are often expressed aggressively but just as often in a passive negative manner. The confusion of these concepts comes from the fact that aggression, even without anger, is often socially disapproved and repressed, as aggression may incite anger in others. In this way, children may come to associate aggression with anger and thus fear that their own aggression will be interpreted as an offense and an expression of anger. However, in our society, competitiveness is promoted and many relatively nonhostile channels are provided for satisfying this aggressivity. The child learns to channel aggression into personal achievement. Children are expected to enter into aggressive games. Many aggressive fantasies are permitted and intellectual competition is fostered. However, the child who is very fearful lest his anger overwhelm him and bring down retaliation on his head may attempt to repress all aggressive behavior even to the point of withdrawing from purely intellectual challenges, and thus appear retarded. Aggressiveness and sexual needs are often intertwined, sometimes even equated, in the child's mind. Sexual behavior often contains as much aggressive as it does passive and tender behavior. Moreover, in our society almost equally strong taboos on overt expression of both needs are instilled in the child during infancy. The vulgar terms for sexual acts which he learns in secret from his peers he finds also are used by peers and adults to express intense aggressive hostility. Thus, even though sex per se may not be as hush-hush as it was a generation or two ago, it still contains a taboo association with aggressiveness. In many instances, the so-called "sexual" problems of adolescence turn out to be more concerned with expressions of aggression and rebellion. The adolescent may withdraw from normal social-sexual behavior for fear of appearing aggressive or, obversely, he may become sexually promiscuous as a means of establishing an aggressive male (or female) role while simultaneously rebelling against parents and society at large.

As may be evident from this discussion, the motivation that is most central and relatively specific to childhood is the drive toward independence, that is, relative independence from others in gaining other need gratifications. Since this drive is an integral part of all other need gratifications in childhood, it may not seem at first glance to be a "drive" in itself. However, this achievement of independent need gratification is an essential part of motivational functioning during childhood. While yet a child, his needs have to be, and usually are, supplied for him, but he is under constant pressure both from society and within himself to become progressively more independent. The social pressures toward adult independence are obvious. However, the drive toward independence also has its biological roots in the child's overall drive toward growth. Even in the infant, who is completely dependent, the striving toward independence is manifested in his struggle to gain control over motor functioning in his first efforts at having a will of his own as he learns to say "No!" and in his social mastery at the toilet. He is driven from the "Oedipal" relationship to seek his affiliative and sexual gratification on his own among his peers. He accepts education as a means of gaining intellectual independence. During adolescence, as the child approaches adulthood, independence obviously becomes an autonomous need, for as an adult it is vital. In many societies, the adult who remains chiefly dependent on others for need gratification may be totally rejected and in danger of his life. Even a "welfare state" is unable to supply all of an adult's needs or protect him from all hazards. Evidence from history suggests that, socially and personally, youths and adults will fight for independence against all odds, disregarding other needs.

For most individuals, this gradual progression toward independence contains some of the most pleasurable and rewarding experiences of childhood—and some of the most intense anxiety and conflict. Much of the pain in growing up comes from the temporary failures in attempts at independent need gratification, in the frustration and embarrassment at having to depend on others. As was mentioned above, the central conflict comes from giving up the security of having needs supplied by parents, a conflict endured by all children, which is only finally resolved in adolescence, as the child gains final confidence in himself. This conflict becomes a most intense deterrent to the child's growth if his dependence is fostered either by neglect—so that he fears he will never be able to satisfy his own needs—or through overprotection—so that he begins to feel that only parents can supply needs.

Since adult independence rests on the development of need-gratification skills, assessment of the motivational development of the individual child is focused chiefly on the learning of these skills. Although children, as well as adults, probably vary considerably in the strength of their drives, the intensity of the motivation per se is seldom the question in assessment. Indeed, no adequate measures of drive intensity have been developed—partly because until the individual has developed need-gratification skills, it is almost impossible to distinguish the child's struggle to attain these skills from the drive itself; only when as an adult he is able to gratify his own needs can the strength of his motivations be estimated meaningfully. Even the strength of his drive toward independence can be estimated only indirectly, that is, the intensity of the child's struggle to develop and need-gratification skills is a measure of his drive for independence.

In a majority of cases, the central question is: "How well is the child developing need-gratification skills?" or "What is the strength of his drive toward independence?" For if his drive toward independence is not fostered or is thwarted or blocked, he may fail to progress in all other functions. If the conflict over independence becomes too intense, the child may seek to avoid the anxiety by regressing to a more infantile state of dependency. Much, if not all, of "psychopathology" in childhood is derived from this conflict. The refusal to enter into the struggle for independence is an essential feature—if not entirely the essence of childhood schizophrenia, and many of the bizarre behaviors of the schizophrenic child appear to be attempts to magically invoke need gratification altogether independently, while simultaneously rejecting the necessary skills. Observations of the histories of such children often suggest that the child may have experienced need gratifications from parents in a mechanical "magical" fashion, with little or no human contact or emotion, and without relation to his struggle for independence. In the so-called "behavior disorders" of childhood, the child's symptoms very often appear to be attempts, direct or indirect, to test out independent need gratification, particularly to see if it is socially acceptable and effective. Even in reactive depressions, when the child has actually experienced a severe loss or deprivation, the very fact that he is depressed rather than angry derives from his realization that he cannot independently gratify his own needs.

B. SOCIAL BEHAVIOR AS A FUNCTION OF THE EGO

The role of social and cultural forces in shaping behavior and development of the child has already been discussed in Chapter 3. In that chapter, these social factors were viewed as external stresses or determinants. As was frequently mentioned, these social stresses gradually become "internalized," so that the child begins to experience these pressures as internal motivations, as part of himself, rather than as external stress. What remains to be discussed at this point are several related questions: How does this socialization process take place? How does the child come to experience these social values and mores as the "right" way to behave, as part of his own ego? Under what circumstances and through what processes does the child incorporate these social attitudes into his personal identity and what effect do they have on his self-concept? How is the adoption of this social conscience coordinated with or in conflict with his drive toward independent need gratification? How is this process interrelated with other developmental processes? These questions need to be understood and assessed before the level of any particular child's social development can be estimated or symptoms of social dislocation can be diagnosed.

As was discussed in Chapter 3, preparations for the child's socialization begin before his birth. These consist of the many social institutions, formal and informal, which society has developed chiefly for the purpose of transmitting these values to the child. Schools, churches, playgrounds, peer groups, childrens' literature, advertisements: all aim both direct and subtle messages to the child indicating that society expects him not only to behave in a certain way but, in essence, to be a certain kind of person. The original and chief transmitter of these values is, of course, the parents and family. Indeed, the development of the child's socialization is so closely tied in with the values held and transmitted by the parents that assessment per force usually includes some data regarding the parents' social attitudes and behavior. To a very great extent, the degree to which the child develops an internalized conscience depends upon several factors: (1) the kind of conscience developed by the parent; (2) the degree to which the parent has internalized social values as part of his own identity; (3) the degree to which the parent is at peace or in conflict with these internalized values; (4) the degree to which the parent bows in conformity to or rebels against external social forces and rules; and (4) the manner in which the parent through word and action conveys these values and conflicts to the child, both directly and subtly.

Very commonly, parents begin planning the transmission of these values when they first contemplate having children. Even the adolescent girl or boy occasionally thinks out loud, "When I have children, I want them to learn to behave (in such and such fashion)." Very often such statements concern methods of discipline or allowances for freedom, but at the same time these fantasies convey social attitudes. Young parents usually begin by perceiving children as essentially projections of themselves and their values, their hopes and ambitions. They hope for a boy or a girl, not only because a child of one sex or the other will expand or compliment their own sexual identity, but also because they have some image of what a boy should be like or how girls behave. Thus, they may look forward to having sons because sons, in previous traditionalist societies and to a great extent today, publicly carry out society's goals and work. Or, they may wish for a daughter because they fear the aggressive behavior of boys and believe girls to be more conforming. If they themselves have acquiesced to social pressures only with considerable resistance and conflict, they may dread having any children at all, lest they be unable to control the child and thus have their own conflicts unmasked.

Even though the mother may not be conscious of her own attitudes, she conveys them to the child from the moment of his birth in her tone of voice, her handling of the baby, her schedule of feeding and bathing and toileting him, her tenderness or roughness, etc. If she places a high value on "discipline," she may begin by sticking to schedules rigidly trying to avoid responding to the baby's demands, clucking sternly when he cries in anger; if she is convinced that cleanliness is next to godliness, she may react with disgust to his excrement. If she is consciously or unconsciously a rebel, she may neglect the baby, just to avoid conforming to society's rules for child care. If she is torn between career and children, she may unconsciously convey her resentment either in half-hearted care of the baby or in an overprotective smothering as compensation for her guilt. Infants reared in public creches and orphanage nurseries by impersonal attendants, even though they receive adequate physical attention, have been found to grow lacking a sense of humaneness and trust in others, and grossly insecure in interpersonal relationships —even if they do not immediately become psychotic. (Yarrow, 1964; A. Freud and Burlingham, 1944). Even before he is one year old, the baby may learn, through conditioning, that an expression of anger results in rejection, or that he can threaten his mother by holding his breath, or just nobody cares. Since the infant is completely dependent on his parents for need gratifications, the manner in which these needs are met becomes the reinforcing agent in this social conditioning. If the mother frequently allows the baby's feeding to be interrupted by other things, the baby soon realizes he comes second in his mother's attention; or vice versa, if she allows nothing to interrupt her attention to him, he becomes "king" in his world, until a second child enters the picture.

In the beginning, the child's social world consists almost entirely of himself and his mother. Indeed, there is considerable evidence to suggest that the infant does not discriminate between himself and others and experiences his mother as an extension of himself. In psychoanalytic terms, the infant "incorporates" the mother in the feeding situation. Melanie Klein (1932) has particularly emphasized the relation between this "incorporation" and the first steps in the formation of the super-ego or conscience. More recently, observers of infants have come to realize that although this "oral" relationship with the mother is probably the primary or at least a very important part of his initial social experience, the child also needs tactile stimulation and sleep patterns, which are also conditioned by the mother's behavior.

Although the infant is at first a passive receiver of social stimulation, he soon begins to make active, aggressive demands on his social world. Even before he has much motor development, his cries become differentiated, thus communicating his needs to his mother. As soon as he can sit up, as he visually explores, and then as he stands, crawls, and walks, his social world greatly expands not only in increased interaction with his mother but with other family members as well. Shortly thereafter, parents begin to teach him what he can explore, see, and touch, and thus to convey their value of possessions and their relationships to people. He may learn that mother prizes property— or that possessions are not as important as people. He begins to sense whom he can approach with impunity, who is cold and warm, and even whom his mother likes, dislikes, fears, or is angry with. Even before he learns to speak, he hears and understands "No!" —and learns whether and when "No" means "absolutely not," "watch out," or just "oh, dear!" As has already been discussed, this aggressive social interaction between mother and child is epitomized in the toilet-training situation. In this and similar social training, the important fact is that the child begins to discriminate fully between his own needs and the demands of society.

However, at this stage, even though he is constantly conditioned and is "incorporating" social values with his milk, so to speak, he experiences these social demands as *external* and separate from himself. He may echo his parents' statements, "*You* a bad boy!" but he seldom says, "*I* bad!" He learns to fear punishment or deprivation, or to expect rewards, and so conforms to parental demands, but these values are not as yet his own. He reacts chiefly on the basis of praise and punishment, but guilt in the sense of self-admonition is only embryonic in infancy. The fantasies of the four to five year old are characterized by phobias of external punishment or by magically obtained rewards from Santa Claus figures. *Thus the infant's super-ego is chiefly external.*

During the latency years, a gradual but marked change takes place in the nature of the child's conscience. Increasingly he does what he "should" do without having to be told or punished. He begins to find reward in his own achievements. Much of his play with his peers is concerned with rules and rule setting. Among eight year olds, half the recess period at school may be taken up with the rules for the game. Social values and mores are accepted as absolutes, and variations either in the child's own behavior or in the behavior of others is perceived by the child as a threat. When a mother says to a three year old, "Aren't you ashamed!" he may cry because of his mother's disapproval, but an eight year old who has committed a transgression hangs his head in shame and embarrassment before anyone mentions it. Mothers learn to become aware of the child's misbehavior because he looks guilty!

Exactly how this internalization of social values and demands takes place has, in this writer's opinion, never been clearly established. It is a long-range process, with some signs of internalization in the latter years of infancy, and extends throughout childhood on into adolescence. Indeed, many otherwise "mature" adults seem to operate largely on the basis of an external conscience, on the basis of a fear of punishment, or on the expectation of reward rather than on self-regulation and self-attainments. This internalization can be explained at least partially on the basis of social conditioning. that is, as "autonomous" habits, wherein the child has learned to carry out social demands before the conditioning reward or punishment occurs. Certainly, despite the latency child's concern with self-regulation, his self-control is seldom sufficient and continued reinforcement from the parents and teachers is required.

However, explanation of socialization based entirely on conditioning seems, in this writer's opinion, incomplete. It explains *how* social learning takes place, but does not account for *when*. On the basis of conditioning alone, one would expect more signs of personal guilt and shame earlier in childhood, without the marked distinction between infancy and latency. Moreover, conditioning alone does not account for the qualitative change in the child's super-ego. For the child's conscience is not merely an automatic habit formation and not just a well-conditioned fear of external punishment. Some factor other than simple habit formation seems present, for the child is learning to punish and reward himself.

In psychoanalytic theory, this qualitative change in the child's super-ego is attributed to changes in the internal sexual dynamics of the child at the onset of latency.* According to psychoanalytic theory, the child begins to internalize parental and social demands as a part of the "resolution" of the Oedipal situation. In essence, the psychoanalytic theory

hypothesizes that the child, being motivated by an *internal* biological force (sex) responds with an internalized fantasy level (the Oedipal fantasy) and, in turn, fantasies a punishment (castration). This internal fantasy of punishment arouses and forms the basis of most guilt feelings, according to Freudian theory. Furthermore, to escape and compensate for this guilt, the child begins to identify with the parent of the same sex, and by the process of generalization, with the values of society.

If one takes the somewhat broader developmental point of view, as has been discussed throughout the previous and present chapters, this psychoanalytic statement may be considered as describing a prototype of many changes taking place in and about the child at the conclusion of infancy. It describes what has already been stated above about the child's cognitive development, that he has developed the ability to conceptualize on a fantasy level, can imagine what might happen, and can generalize from one situation to another; latency is a period for practicing this cognitive activity and relating it to social skills, which enable him both to control his impulses and to find gratification through and in these skills. He is now more capable of delaying impulses, especially his needs for erotic affection, for which he can now substitute nonerotic friendships. The internalization of social values may thus be viewed as part of the child's overall drive toward independence, wherein he is seeking and practicing skills which will ultimately make him independent of his parents. The embarrassment, shame, and guilt which the latency child experiences when he misbehaves is, according to this view, a special form of anxiety. During infancy the child has experienced anxiety chiefly when his environment failed to satisfy his needs; in latency, he becomes anxious when, in his striving toward independence, he fails himself. As long as he depends on others, he can blame them; when he hopes to do things on his own, he blames himself.

With the onset of puberty, this still new and barely established internalized super-ego is sorely tested. The upsurge of sexual impulses creates a severe strain on the child's self-control and is a constant source of embarrassment and guilt to many junior high school children. However, this struggle of the teenager to control his sexual impulses is only one part, albeit a central factor, of the changes

---

* It should be noted that psychoanalytic theory does not deny the importance of social conditioning, for Freud often referred to conditioning as a *method* of learning but, instead, sees this conditioning as occurring and depending upon the child's psychosexual development.

in his struggle for independence. During latency, he sought independence by imitating and emulating adult behavior. His conformity to social rules was the means for attaining self-control and social recognition. However, this identification with the adult only partially satisfies the child's independence strivings. After he attains social skills through conforming and identifying, he begins to feel rebellious, to seek more extensive independence, which mere conformity does not permit. With these social skills, he can try his own wings, formulate rules for himself, and rebel against parental dictates. Parents at this point often despair at the seemingly negativistic behavior of their once well-mannered and well-behaved child. He or she adopts unconventional dress, language, tastes, and attitudes. However, the teenager rebels chiefly on the edges, that is, against superficial conventions. seldom against the basic rules of society. Moreover, the rebellion is directed only against the parental generation's mores, and the teen-ager is overly conventional with respect to his own peer group. Often his "rebellion" actually is provided for in social institutions. He joins an "illegal" high school "fraternity," becomes a "surfer," or identifies with a rebellious adult social movement. His clothes, his haircut, and even his assertion of independence are advertised as acceptable in every adult magazine and TV commercial. In American culture, as Margaret Mead emphasizes in her book, *And Keep Your Powder Dry* (1942), this adolescent "rebellion" is expected and encouraged as a national virtue. It is an expected behavior as part of the preparation of an independent citizen in a democratic society. In more tradition-bound, autocratic societies, this rebellion of youth, if tolerated at all, is allowed only a brief show and then in highly formalized fashion. Only in democratic societies is the drive toward rebellious independence necessary and thus fostered. Moreover, in democratic societies, the individual is expected to chose his own mate, and thus a great deal more freedom of sexual behavior is allowed and even encouraged during adolescence.

The assessment of the child's social development is among the most frequent reasons for referral, for failures in social behavior impinge directly on the parents and school, much more than poor development in motor, perceptual, or even cognitive functioning. If the infant cannot be conditioned, if the la-

tency child does not conform and attempt to control himself, or if the adolescent oversteps the accepted boundaries of rebelliousness, the parent and society take the child's failure as a mark of failure on their own part. When their redoubled efforts continue to fail, they seek help.

In the assessment of social development, as has been emphasized in discussion of assessment of other functions, it is necessary to keep in mind that social development is not independent of these other functions and that failures in the child's social development may derive from and/or result in retardation of other functions. As was already mentioned, the social embarrassment suffered by the child who is slow to develop motorically or who is physically handicapped commonly causes him to withdraw in shyness, or to become antisocial, demanding, and rebellious. A handicapped child may be spurred on to develop his social functioning to the point that he is able to be a leader, or at least to manipulate his environment very successfully. The intellectually slow child is also slow to learn social behavior and social controls. Obversely, the socially immature child waits to be told what to do and what to learn. Affective, motivational, and social development are often indistinguishable aspects of the same process. The development of affective and motivational controls is a social process; social development is motivated by need gratifications and social learning involves—and even requires—considerable affect. As Mowrer (1960) has pointed out, guilt is a powerful social catalyst.

C. THE DEVELOPMENT OF AN IDENTITY

One of the central features of clinical assessment which differentiates it from other scientific approaches to the study of behavior—the actuarial or the experimental (Goldstein and Palmer, 1966), is that rather than studying one facet of behavior across a sample of children or under laboratory situations, the aim of assessment is the study of the interaction of all aspects of behavior within the single individual. Indeed, terms like "the total organism" or "the whole personality" have become shibboleths in clinical psychology, often poorly defined and loosely applied. Allport (1948), in his classic review of the term *personality,* found over 100 different definitions, many of which are still currently used. Most often in clinical parlance, the term *personality* is confused with what has been distinguished above as affective or emotional functioning; quite often in assessment reports, there is a section on intelligence and one on personality—as if intelligence were not part of personality! Yet, as has been quite evident in this discussion, it is difficult to understand any one facet of behavior in isolation; moreover, facets of behavior cannot be viewed as interacting except in terms of an overall concept, that is, a personality. However, for the most theorists, the term personality does not merely refer to a totality of functions. It would not seem sufficient to speak of a moving, sensing, perceiving, comprehending, motivated, and social organism (to sum up the developmental features discussed so far). Most students of personality posit some kind of a "unifying force," and X-factor tying together, possibly regulating and amplifying, all aspects of the individual's beravior. For Freud, this integration was embodied in the child's sexual development; others have posited other genetic bases or have emphasized social integration. Adolph Meyer (1948) and Carl Rogers (in his earlier writings (1942-1951), emphasized the unifying force of biological and social growth. Maslow (1950) thought in terms of the long-range creativity of the individual, using such terms as "self-actualization" or "self-realization." Nearly all of these theorists, in discussing whatever force they posit as unifying the child's behavior, use the concept and often the term, *identity*, a concept also currently central in the theory of existentialism or "experiential" schools of thought.

This term, *identity,* has particular heuristic value for two reasons. First, it focuses attention on how the phenomenon takes place, that is, the ways in which the child comes to perceive himself as a unity. It thus implies and emphasizes a developmental process rather than a single force. Indeed, as will be discussed, all the forces mentioned above enter into this process of attaining an identity. It comes closest to describing how the child himself experiences his own development, consciously and unconsciously.

Second, as was discussed in the conclusion of Chapter 3, the term *identity* focuses attention on one of the primary conflicts of our times. In the historically preceding feudal millenium, there was little need for concern over individual identity. Nearly all of the individual's identity was socially determined at (or even before) his birth, by the class and caste of his family; no mobility or change or choice was allowed, and if the individual concerned himself with his identity, it was to struggle to live up to what was socially expected. If he challenged this socially imposed identity, he was made an outcast or was likely to be killed, for example, by drinking hemlock or burning at the stake. In such cultures, children do not "develop" an identity, but "inherit" it. In assessing a child from one of the so-called "underdeveloped" countries of the world, where remnants of feudalism still exist, this stress of predetermined identity would have to be taken into account. Even in the current American culture, vestiges of this type of identity persist.

Over the past 500, and especially during the past 200, years, the cultural changes represented in the rise and triumph of democracy, science, and technology created a new identity, in which the central factor has been the struggle for personal freedom. By the beginning of this century in this country, most children were taught that a man was a man not for what his father was but for what he himself achieved and accumulated. One had to "achieve" identity in rivalry and competition with one's sibs and peers; the very fight for such achievement was an ingredient of this identity, and the failure to so struggle was considered to be both a personal and a social failure. Most of the theories of personality of the immediate past century echoed this ideology. Psychoanalysis, for example, emphasized the struggle of the child to free himself from the father.* In this country, behaviorism made it clear that any kind of identification was possible through conditioning and learning, although as applied in getting the child to "adjust" through "guidance," this theory went against the tide of the struggle for personal freedom. More significant and lasting were the ideas of Dewey (1938) and Mead (1932) in promulgating greater freedom for the school child to learn at his own pace and according to his own motivations.

In many parts of the world and for the caste-bound Negro and other racial minorities in this country, this struggle for freedom continues to be the major element in personal

---

* Freud began writing before the feminine struggle for freedom developed in Austria!

identity. The battle-cry of "Freedom Now!" has been sounded by the civil rights movement in the United States. As it is defined by the leaders of this movement, this motto centers upon the attainment of a personal identity. The American Negro seeks the same opportunity to achieve and the same individual respect that most other Americans have already gained over the past century. The assessor working with Negro children need to realize that this generation is very involved in this struggle. For the Negro child today, identity means the *right* to be somebody, as opposed to "keeping one's place." However, for a majority of the generation of Americans since World War II, there is a relatively new question of identity (a question that has been particularly brought into focus by the Negro's struggle for personal freedom): Who is this somebody that the individual is free to be? Essentially, this question had been brought up by the social novelists and poets, such as F. Scott Fitzgerald (1925) and John Dos Passos (see particularly his *USA*, 1938, depicting the search for identity in the 1920's), or in such allegories as Huxley's *Brave New World* (1946), or Orwell's *1984* (1950), which depicted the loss of identity in a world of technocracy. Psychologists were made aware of this new question through the writings of such philosopher-psychologists as Eric Fromm, in his *Escape from Freedom* (1947), and then through Sartre and the existential writers, and most recently by Carl Rogers.

Outwardly this question of "Who am I?" manifested itself as a protest against being a cog in a standardized world, like Chaplin in the cinema classic, *The Machine Age,* or typified more recently by the protesting student in the Student Free Speech Movement at the University of California in 1964 who, wore a sign saying, "I am a student; do not fold, spindle, or mutilate!" But this question of identity is not merely a protest against the *Man in the Grey Flannel Suit* (Wilson, 1955), or the *Organization Man* (Whyte, 1956). The "hippies" the white "freedom fighter," the sampler of LSD, the office manager in the "sensitivity course," all began to ask: "If I'm not this standardized cog, who am I?" "What kind of person am I?" "Why am I doing the things I'm doing?" "How do I relate to others?"

Because this new question of identity is most often voiced by young adults or by adolescents, it may not at first glance seem to have bearing on the assessment of children. However, this adult conflict, often mislabeled a "character neurosis," has its roots in the identity formation during the childhood of this generation which, although it was different from that of previous generations, went relatively unnoticed. At most, the older generation bewailed that more children than ever before seemed not to "care about money" (or to care too much and not want to work), to be uninterested in achieving at school, to ignore set moral values and mores, to cross and ignore lines of social institutions such as race and religion.

It would seem reasonable to suppose that this new question of identity, which is scarcely more than a generation old, will appear with even greater intensity in the coming generations, among the children who will be assessed by the clinicians reading this book. Unfortunately, since the psychologists of this generation have only begun to recognize the question, there is little in the way of scientific background nor of assessment techniques to offer as guidance. However, since the question will probably continue to be central in assessment in the future, it may prove helpful to the student's thinking to review what is known about identity formation in general, at the same time speculating about the formation of this specific question of identity: Who am I?

As was mentioned in Chapter 3 (see Case 10), one of the most important precursors of the child's identity has usually been his name, an identity given him before or at his birth. In the past in Western cultures, his name often had recognized associations and connotations. His surname identified him with a family clan, and he was told by his father or grandfather always to remember that he was a . . . and that whatever he did reflected on that name. His name also reflected the national origin of his ancestors. His given name had family connotations; he was likely to be named after some family member, with a middle name from some other (often lesser regarded) family personage. (It was fairly common practice for a boy to have his mother's maiden name as his middle name, which sometimes added to the boy's struggle in attaining a masculine identity.) Thus, the child was associated in the parent's mind (almost before he drew his first breath) with the mother's brother, the father's mother, or an aging well-to-do uncle. Often the child was consciously or unconsciously expected by his parents (and later by the child himself) to emulate the characteristics of his godparents (both good and bad). Not infrequently the child might later be quite embarrassed by his name, especially if it were uncommon or if it had some untoward meaning to his peer group or to other associates who came from different cultural backgrounds. Teasing about names is still one of the most common forms of exchange of hostilities among grade school children.

Over the past generation, the choosing of names for children has changed considerably. There has been a fairly widespread alteration and change of patronyms, such as respelling, shortening, or complete change of non-English family names. The traditional given names from the Bible or those transmitted from generation to generation are much less commonly given the child. Instead, the mother now is likely to choose some name for the baby which "sounds pretty" and is popular at the moment. Often these given names are new variants of old names, with a touch of originality but not enough to be "off-beat." Thus, instead of three Mary's in a class or four John's, there are several Marilyn's and Johnathan's. Without the mother quite realizing it, the name must be stylish; Karen and Sheila, Sharon and Judith (names unused a generation ago) have replaced Ruth, Hannah, Josephine, and Lillian. Currently, no socially aware mother would name her son Melvin, Alvin, or Homer. Thus, while parents currently avoid names which might be so unusual as to be socially embarrassing to the child, this generation of children is usually given socially common, relatively innocuous—and meaningless—names.

Another familial precursor of personal identity is also changing, that is the child's position in the family constellation. At one time, the fact that the child was the firstborn, middle child, or "baby" of the family was accompanied by rather specific attitudes and values. In the old-fashioned Chinese family, children were not even addressed by name by their parents or sibs, but as "eldest son," "second daughter," etc. In upper class European families, the birth order of the sons determined the profession chosen for them by the family; the oldest son was supposed to follow his father's occupation, inherit most of his estate (and be responsible for his mother's welfare), the second son to become a priest, the third son to be a professional man, etc. To a less rigid degree, this institutionalization of birth order as a part of identity has been followed in the United States, especially in the first generation born here. It was considered that the older children had more family responsibility and should be more conforming, while there was more permission for a younger child to be "wild," to be less achieving, or to leave the family nest at an early age.

However, the underlying rationale for these family attitudes has been greatly altered. First, when mortality in childhood was high, the identity of the child had to be planned; the stability and continuation of the family required not only early training of at least one child to take over the economic and social responsibilities of the adults (who then aged more rapidly than now), but also the early inculcation of values, attitudes and identities for these tasks. Second, the family is no longer so entirely responsible for either the social and vocational training and placement of their children, nor are children so obligated for the eventual care of the parents. Education through high school costs the parents little or nothing in most countries today. Pensions and insurance free the child from the eventual responsibility for their parents.

Perhaps in another sense, birth order may always be one of the underlying factors in the child's identity formation. The oldest child in the family will have had the concept of himself, for at least a short period, of being the "one and only"—and later feel that he is in danger of being replaced. As his mother's first child, he is subject to more of her anxiety initially—and more of the family's expectations in the long run. In contrast, once the mother has gone through childbirth and infant rearing with her first child, she is often less tense and more relaxed with subsequent children. The first born is always in the lead—but not necessarily considered a leader by his sibs. The second and subsequent children never know what it is not to have to "share," but they may form an identity as "second" in terms of the mother's anxieties if not in terms of her affections. Even though they may escape the mistakes the older child makes or the parents make in rearing him, they realize that the older child is in some way "special." Moreover, the second child may grow up to see himself as someone who is the object of envy and who is in danger of being pushed aside by a competitor not of his own choosing. The youngest child in a family has the advantage—and disadvantage—of the role of "baby," of whom little may be required or expected. He may receive an extra portion of mother's attention and affection, but he also may find that his mother continues to treat him as an infant throughout childhood and cling to him as her last child.

Complicating these patterns of identity imposed by the sibling constellation are the attitudes of the parents toward certain family positions which they themselves have experienced. For example, a mother who herself was a middle child may have special feelings, both positive and negative, toward her middle child who in return may identify himself more with mother than with father. Sometimes these identifications are as strong as the sex identification and complicate sexual identification. Similarly, a father who grew up as the oldest child may expect his oldest child, son or daughter, to be like him, an expectation which the child has to take into consideration in his or her identity formation, whether or not the child accepts and incorporates these expectations. Furthermore, these identity pressures from the family constellation are complicated by the differences between sibs in age and sex. The oldest child who is only a year or so older than his next younger sib would have far different identity as a competitive or envious person than if the next younger sib were eight to ten years younger. The intensity of such feelings and identity might be similar, but the quality of the identity as "oldest" would be different. For siblings near in age, the identity of both approaches a twinship; for sibs widely separated, especially when the older child has made some identification with the parents, the older child may see himself in *loco parentis* to his sib. Similarly, there is more than a shade of difference to the identity "I am the oldest boy in a family of girls" from "I am the older brother of a little brother or brothers." Most special is the "little princess" who has only older brothers, or the "spoiled prince" who has several older sisters.

The influence of these family patterns are somewhat neutralized in current family "planning" and child-rearing practices. The modern mother has at least intellectual information about conception, pregnancy, childbirth, and infant care, and fewer superstitions to face about these things than her mother

or grandmother. Thus, her anxieties in these regards may be less as she thinks of her first child. Indeed, such negative feelings as she may project onto the oldest child may be more in terms of his unwarranted arrival before she has a chance to develop a vocational career. Planned parenthood is at least an ideal in our current society; parents attempt to have their children at recommended intervals, of two and a half to three and a half years. Adoption of a child to balance the sexual-age pattern is often considered. However, such planning is more often talked about than practiced. Most children still arrive as "accidents," more or less accepted. To compensate for these inequalities in age and sex patterns, parents often consciously attempt to "love all our children equally," and feel guilty about any of their behavior which inadvertently reveals their underlying biases. By such planning and equalizing, parents may prevent or relieve some of the child's conflicts concerning identity. However, the child who finds he is just one of his parents' loves and concerns may have yet another identity task. If not a special or unique member of a sibship, the child must then establish himself as somebody in his own eyes. If he is not special to his parents, then he is like everyone else, and lacks an identity. To compensate for such feelings, the parent must say, in effect, "I do not love you any more or less, or expect more or less of you, than your sibs, but I love you for different reasons and expect different kinds of things of you, not because of your birth order or sex, but because of your own qualities and behavior." Thus, in essence, a part of the child's identity depends on how he is accepted by others.

With such former indications of acceptance and identity as name, sex, and birth-order somewhat devalued the more basic question of degree to which the child is desired by his parents comes into focus. Case histories of adults and autobiographies both literal and fictional give proof that there have always been children who were at least unexpected "accidents" and unwanted interferences in their parents' lives. As was noted in Chapter 3, such feelings and identifications inevitably arise for the child born or even conceived out of wedlock; for such a child, the implication of his illegitimacy hangs over his head, even though any conflict is consciously denied by the parents. Parents who marry very young and have children while they themselves are still growing out of adolescence into adulthood may unconsciously (or even consciously) regard the child as an imposition. The same may be true in any marriage in which the child arrives before the couple has adjusted to one another. Parents may resent a child who arrives at an inauspicious time in their educational or vocational or economic strivings, or when they are ill, depressed, or "too old to have anymore children." Most serious is the guilt and resentment felt toward the child whom either or both parents planned in order to preserve a marriage that is dissolving. In such an instance, even more than the others mentioned, the child may come to identify himself as a pawn in the parental hostilities, as a person who sticks in the craw of others. In such circumstances, it would be unusual if the child did not at least occasionally wonder in the back of his mind, or feel unconsciously as part of his identity, "Am I an accident, an unwanted person?"

This question of how the child is regarded by his parents may become even more important in childrens' identity formation, not only because other identity factors are being neutralized, but because of changing values regarding parenthood and parental obligations toward children. In most Western societies, parents are supposed to want the children they conceive. (Strangely, only unwed mothers are given any choice!) The parents' social conscience demands that they make children feel wanted and loved, whether or not they really are. These demands are so strong that (in contrast to some other cultures) children who are legitimately conceived are rarely given to other people to rear. Even when this is done, there is so much ambivalence about it that it is often not successful, even though there are many childless couples who seek to adopt children. This ambivalence arises within the parents, for foster and adoptive parents, if given the opportunity, can usually reassure the child. Furthermore, there is a social standard that people should want to be parents. However, unlike prior generations, there are other adult values—and identities—which often have equal or greater value than parenthood. In the past, a man ploughed his fields, worked at his job, conducted his business or profession largely to support his family. Long after the Industrial Revolution, the father's work was in his home or immediately adjacent. Only when under the threat of famine or the promise of great fortune, such as a gold rush, did he leave his family and then with considerable personal trepidation and fear of social censure. The righteous man of the nineteenth century would not think of putting his career above family life. Women, of course, had no destiny except as mothers and wives. However, as career achievement and the accumulation of possessions and wealth gradually became the goals in Western society, these values came into conflict with the demands of the paternal role. More and more fathers came to act—and talk—as if their entire role was their career and money making, and that most of the care of the children was the responsibility of the mother. Although most fathers seem to struggle to maintain some involvement with their children, the careers for men in our society often require so much time and emotional investment that men have little left over when they do attempt to be fathers. As a consequence, not only does the child in such a situation form a closer attachment to the ever-present mother than to the father, but comes—albeit unconsciously—to identify himself as "my mother's child" and as "someone not worthy of father's attention." Where a father's interests and goals are, for the most part, outside of the home, boys may feel a lack of a male model with whom to identify, or at least see masculinity as a matter of emotional distance. Girls may also suffer, for to be feminine requires the admiration and affection of a man, beginning with father. For women, the conflict between education and career on the one hand and motherhood on the other has also complicated the identity formation of the child. In past generations, only in the families of the poor did women have to earn part of the living, and then it was piecework in the cottage or, if out of the home, there was a grandmother or older sister to take care of the children. With the depression of the 1930's and the subsequent need for women in industry during World War II, more middle class women began to be employed outside the home, but still only a relatively small number sought a career other than as housewives. The "feminists" of the beginning of the twentieth century won a moral but empty victory when they established a woman's right to a career, for this right continued to be hobbled by society's demand that the role of being mother had priority over all other feminine roles.

How parents of the latter half of this century will regard having children remains to be seen. One can only speculate as to the values they will instill into the identities of the children whom the readers of this book may be assessing. Very likely some of the attitudes of the past, as discussed above, will continue to prevail. Some men will continue to be too busy achieving and accumulating to be fathers, but there are indications that many men are becoming more and more aware of the distance between themselves and their children and are making at least tentative efforts, during their increased leisure time, to share with their wives the care and discipline of the children. The role of women as mothers shows even greater signs of changing. Perhaps Betty Friedan was at least partly correct in her polemic (1963) against what she labeled the "feminine mystique," a massive pressure by all public media and by many "professionals" for women to conform to an image of being happy but useless housewives. However, employment figures indicate that there is an ever-increasing number of married women working outside the home; they work not only to supplement the family income (often to provide "luxuries" for the family), but often with the open admission that they prefer to be away from the house and children. Usually this admission is accompanied by expressions of guilt similar to those voiced by their working husbands. More and more commonly, both husband and wife believe that a woman should have satisfactions "outside" the home, but neither feels entirely comfortable about it, either between themselves or in the face of public opinion. If more and more mothers do tend to find employment "as soon as the children are old enough," very likely the children's attitudes toward themselves will change. Perhaps there will be more children who feel deserted, unwanted, and therefore unworthy and inadequate. And perhaps more parents will see children, especially second or third children, as interfering with their other aims and interests. However, it is also possible that the once bored and restless housewife can return from a job feeling "fulfilled," more appreciative of her children and husband, and feeling more justified in her demands on them to share in housekeeping activities. Under such circumstances, children and husbands could no longer regard the mother as a servant—or themselves as uninvolved and thus unimportant to the family. Instead, family positions

and duties might become more democratically assigned and distributed. Thus, in assessing the child's feelings or self-importance and identity, it is necessary to investigate the attitudes of the parents, especially of the mother, toward both their parental and extraparental roles. One must also assess the amount of ambivalence and guilt—or possibly freedom —involved in the interaction of these roles with their children.

Although all of these factors set the stage for the formation of the child's identity, they constitute only the background for the many subsequent experiences of the child in which he gains a sense of himself as a person. In the initial phase of infancy—according to classical psychoanalytic theory—babies do not experience themselves as separate identities but as part of their mother, who is their whole world and is thus part of them. However, when the infant does not suffer any undue separation from the mother, when the physiological separation of neonate from the womb is followed by continued body contact and nurturance from the mother, the infant soon becomes satisfied and secure enough to begin to explore himself. A great deal of the sensory-motor activity of the infant (as described above) constitutes in effect the first step of self-recognition. The infant finds that his toes and his nose are part of himself, and different from other objects and people. His cries and his activity affect others, and others address him in tones different than those they use with older children or adults. These first steps in the development of his "body image" are followed by discoveries such as the facts that he can manipulate objects, control his body functions, delay gratifications without being destroyed, and share with and compete with his siblings. All of these experiences seem essential to his sense of identity, for if he is restricted, for example by physical disability or illness, or held back by parents who do not want things touched or who rush to do everything for him, he may begin to feel insecure about himself. If he experiences controls over functions such as toilet training purely as externally imposed conditioning, rather than as a self-rewarding achievement, then he may continue in later life also to expect some stimulus outside of himself as a signal for controlling his behavior. He needs to begin to conceive of himself as an independent unit capable of self-imposed controls rather than as a puppet to be manipulated. His identity is formed through becoming a self-activating person.

The differentiation of the self from other objects and persons in the environment during infancy takes on many forms. It is practiced in play with dolls and toys. The three year old uses his Teddy bear as a mirror, identifying him as "good" or "bad," as "angry" or "happy," creating a character in the image of himself. His identification proceeds in and through his speech, as he learns the personal pronouns. The use of the first person subject is developed last when he finally learns to say "I" and identify this term as himself.

The development of identity during infancy includes, of course, the beginnings of sexual identity, starting with the infant's discovering in the exploration of his body that his genitals give a pleasurable sensation. Very soon he finds that this part of his body is usually something private about himself. In association with urinary control, the taboo on self-exposure is strengthened. These initial steps in identification as a sexual person usually only briefly precede the awareness of sexual differentiation. The "I am a boy" or "I am a girl" may or may not be associated with genital differentiation at first. In prior generations, children learned these sexual distinctions by observing differences in dress, behavior, and expectations long before they had any clear idea of the physiological differences. Now, by the end of infancy most children are aware of the bodily, genital differences as well. With the change of attitudes toward sex, especially toward children's knowledge of it, this fact is perhaps less commonly a mystery. Children are allowed to see the naked infant of the opposite sex and to ask questions. They may even observe their parents in the nude on occasion. They go to the toilet together in nursery school and are less prohibited from bodily exploration of one another during infancy. Very likely their doubts about their sexual identity in this respect and at this age are less than in the previous generations. The heightened importance once put upon this differentiation when it was so hidden may become deemphasized. When sexual differentiation makes less difference but is a natural and accepted fact, the importance of having a "phallus" or the fear of being "castrated" may be lessened.

The formation of identity during infancy, including the child's sexual identity, comes chiefly from the interaction with other members of the family. These social interactions with the family, epitomized in the so-called Oedipal relationship, have already been discussed, especially regarding boys. For girls, as the psychoanalysts point out, this facet of identification is slightly more complicated. Girls maintain their dependency on their mothers as objects for identification sexually and socially, but give up their fantasies of rivalry with their mothers for their father's affection.

Once the child makes the break from inter-family ties and enters the world of peers and adults in school, his identity is furthered by competition, by achievement drives and aspirations, by social expectations and controls. During this period of his life, these other social pressures may be almost more important to him than any sense of sexual identity, especially in the current generation. At one time, if the child could not meet social demands for achievement, he or she could fall back on sexual identification. Boys could disdain academic achievement and depend on being rough and tough males. Girls, who were not expected to be scholars, could choose to be "little ladies" and "mother's helpers." In many other ways, sexual differentiations during latency are changing. Both boys and girls are now expected to achieve at school. Aggressive behavior in school-age boys is much less condoned than in prior generations and, in contrast, is somewhat more permitted in girls. Being an expert in kickball in the third grade is almost as important to a girl as to a boy. School-age children must, therefore, seek some identity in addition to their sexual identity. If possible, they find it in school achievement or in play skills. A great deal of the school child's sense of social importance today is derived in a struggle for social popularity. A concern with social status, which used to be chiefly an adolescent stress, seems now to be appearing at an earlier age, among the grade school children. The latency child appears to be increasingly concerned with who plays with whom, who likes whom, who knows whom, who can beat whom, etc. In part, this childhood emphasis on identity through the social "pecking" order reflects the struggle of the adult to maintain identity in a mass society. Like his parents, the child is a member of the "Lonely Crowd" (Reisman etal., 1950). As was noted in Chapter 3, he lives in a constantly shifting social group; his neighborhood peers are always moving away (or he himself moves), and each year there are fewer and fewer children present in his class who were there in prior years. In contrast to his parents, who more likely had a relatively stable school and neighborhood environment, he has less chance to know where he stands with peers or with adults outside his family. If he is going to "be somebody," it will be on the basis of his own achievement rather than in relation to any set social group. Nevertheless, he also struggles to find where he fits in a shifting social group.

During adolescence, the struggle to attain an identity comes openly to the fore with increased intensity. Seeking to form an identity of his own, the teen-ager denies his ties with his parents and their values but, still lacking security in himself, he seeks support by conformity to peer fads and pressures. The teen-ager's "crazy" acts and "crazy" ideas are often his way of testing out his identity, of seeing if he can do things uniquely or think thoughts of his own. At the same time, an adolescent fears being different or "crazy." If not in the "swing" of things or "in with the crowd," he may feel lonely and depressed even though he has friends with the same problem. If staid, he may feel he has to defend his lack of spontaneity. If shy, he may try playing the clown. If brash, he is also overapologetic. Often the identities of adolescents are so mercurial that on the Rorschach or the MMPI their responses seem "psychotic."

This search for identity requires considerable "ego-strength," that is a sense of security and freedom. Unfortunately, not all adolescents feel free enough or secure enough to test out their own possibilities. Some try to cling to childhood, and attempt to maintain an identity as a child. They depend on parents for their identity. Occasionally adolescents rush into a mock adulthood, pretending that everything is solved. Sometimes the conflict is too much for an adolescent, who then becomes overwhelmed with anxiety and panic. Even children who have seemed placid or stolid in their latency may become depressed or "act out" during adolescence. The majority, however, seem to be able to rise above it all, as if it were a great adventure. They seem to be able to enjoy life and to see themselves as teen-agers having fun. Although they occasionally worry about the future, they do not feel under continuous pressure. Only after a fling of seeming irresponsibility are they able

to gradually accept the strictures of adult responsibility. On the other hand, the adult who never identified himself as an adolescent, who withdrew from his adventure, often feels as if something were missing from his adult identity.

In summary, perhaps the most important fact about identity formation in childhood is that it *is* in formation, that it is developing. In contrast to the identity conflicts of adulthood, which are often neurotic or even psychotic in proportion, the identity struggles of childhood are for the most part a normal process. Similar to the other growth processes discussed earlier, the child's identity development involves times of conflict and the course of this development is commonly erratic. Brief shifts in identity or temporary regressions are not necessarily causes for alarm, especially among adolescents. However, when such shifts and regressions persist, they are indications of severe disturbance in development.

However, in nearly every case, assessment of identity development is a central factor in the overall evaluation of the child's growth. Disturbances of identity are derived from and interrelated with all other facets of the child's development. Therefore, disturbances of identity are often the clue to disturbances and deterrences in other ego functions. The child who is playing extremely different roles at home and at school, for example, may be "acting out" social, motivational, or even perceptual imbalances. If he has a perceptual handicap, he may not suffer at home and thus be able to identify as an "angel," yet be unable to function at school where he is a restless and resistant "devil"; if the handicap is unrecognized, his behavior will appear as a "split" in his personality, both to the parents and the school, and subjectively to the child himself. Obversely, the child who is uncontrollable at home and a model of conformity at school may be working out conflicts over the control of his impulses, using the school as a setting for practicing controls but demanding permission at home to relax controls. If these imbalances in other fazes of his development are not corrected, the child may eventually suffer a more prolonged and definite disturbance in his sense of identity. As the child's identity forms, it becomes a distinctive attitudinal core, affecting and directing all other aspects of the child's behavior. Increasingly as he matures, his behavior becomes more dependent on how he sees himself and how he feels about himself. Thus, disturbances in this development of identity may create disruptions in all other facets of his behavior. The child who feels he does not belong, or feels basically unworthy, or finds "double messages" from parental authorities demanding dual roles, or regards his own body as unacceptable may be so concerned with his identity as to be unable to function effectively in any way. Unable to obtain a clear perception of himself, he is likely to distort perceptions of other people and objects. Lacking a sense of self, he is likely to see himself as unable to control his own motivations or to obtain gratifications for himself. He may even react with motoric clumsiness or regress to using motoric gestures and activities to find himself, much like a normal infant in the first stages of identity development. Such overall intensive disturbances in identity are often labeled "childhood schizophrenia" or, in infants, "infantile autism."

SUMMARY

In this and the preceding chapter, the functions of the ego were considered in the order of their relative development, beginning with those most closely tied in with the child's physiological functioning, that is his motoric and sensory functions, and ending with a discussion of a purely psychological concept, that is the child's sense of identity. The pri-mary object of the organization of this chapter was to emphasize the need to consider all these ego functions and the core of the ego, the child's identity, in a developmental framework. However, a discussion of the ego as the object of assessment might also begin with consideration of this core concept, with subsequent discussions of the various functions through which the child experiences and manifests his developing sense of identity. Such a perspective might be particularly meaningful in reporting an assessment because questions about identity development so often appear as part of the referral. Moreover, even when such questions are not raised, a discussion of any aspect of the ego necessarily includes consideration of that function in relation to the child's concept of himself. The chief reason, then, for focusing on the child's sense of identity in any assessment is that any disruption or deterrence of any particular ego function becomes psychologically meaningful to that particular child only insofar as it affects his identity. As has been mentioned repeatedly and illustrated in several case vignettes, it is quite possible for children to be subjected to considerable stress, physically or socially, without necessarily suffering a psychological disorder. Admittedly, such stresses may create a temporary sense of distress. However, it is when the stresses of life create in the child a permanent feeling of loss, or make him doubt his developing abilities and, most particularly, his worth to others, that a psychological disturbance is created.

Part II

METHODS OF DATA COLLECTION

Chapter 6

THE NATURE AND EVALUATION
OF ASSESSMENT TECHNIQUES

A. THE HYPOTHESES AND THE TECHNIQUES

In any psychological research, the experimenter usually states his hypotheses or problems and then proposes various methods or techniques to test or investigate them. He adopts or invents techniques that directly or indirectly sample the behaviors that he is investigating, presenting as part of his scientific argument some evidence or rationale supporting the relationship between his method and the variables being sampled. If the clinical assessment of the child is to be scientific, then the techniques for data gathering should be related to the "hypotheses." Given the theoretical framework presented in Part I of this volume, one might expect a presentation of techniques which sample the various functions of the ego and measure their development in the child. Unfortunately, the relationships between the techniques commonly used in assessing children and the hypotheses which were outlined in Part I are quite complex and far from being specific. The purpose of this section is to explore these complexities and to attempt to relate these techniques to this particular set of hypotheses.

However, a brief aside on some of the reasons for this gap between hypothesis and technique may be helpful as an introduction to this subsequent discussion. In the first place, for various reasons, few if any of our techniques were constructed as methods of sampling some clearly defined function. Most clinical instruments currently in use were originated over 20 years ago on the basis of practical needs rather than theory. Intelligence tests, for example, were invented before there were theories of intelligence. "Projective techniques" were spawned while psychology was still in the process of defining "dynamics." The rationale behind perceptual-motor tests has only recently been considered. Much of the theory behind clinical techniques has been developed through clinical and research application. In fact, no little of the general theoretical framework presented in Section I was derived from clinical experience using these techniques. As a result, the assessor has the advantage of a wealth of knowledge and theory provided in recent decades of experimental research and clinical experience with these techniques. For example, both the Kraeplinean nosological concepts on which the MMPI was based in 1938 and the "need-press" system of the TAT of 1936 seem very old fashioned and oversimplified today. As will be discussed subsequently, the development of pattern analysis of MMPI profiles during the past decade makes possible a "dynamic" use of this technique in assessing adolescents, and the evolution of "ego psychology" over the past 20 years has greatly enhanced the usefulness of the TAT.

Nevertheless, none of these techniques have been as extensively overhauled as they should be. A totally new or even revised set of techniques updated to meet current knowledge and theory is sorely needed. Moreover, new methods of behavioral changes are being developed that will need new methods of assessment or revision of present techniques. All in all, there should be techniques to test hypotheses, not hypotheses about tests. Without a new or revised set of tools, it is necessary to delineate with precision the nature of the stimuli presented to the child and observe the behavior elicited with increased objectivity. Most important, it is necessary to revise the interpretation of the data derived from these techniques, utilizing the knowledge and theory about child development now available. In so doing, it may be possible to utilize these old tools much more effectively. By translating the findings in terms of more recent theory, it may be possible to perceive new patterns out of such behavior, as have the students of the MMPI.

A second reason for the gap between theory and technique in assessment may lie in the fact that many students today seem unacquainted with the theories behind the techniques which they use. For example, students learn to administer, score, and "interpret" the Rorschach, but seldom read Rorschach's original monograph (1921), and know little of the Jungian theory or of the theories of perception current in Rorschach's time, from which he drew his concepts. Similarly, they are often unaware when they use the TAT of Murray's *Explorations in Personality* (1938). They rarely read Wechsler's original volume (1944) or Bender's monograph (1938). Although some of the theory presented in these studies is now out of date and disputable, much of it remains valid and has been expanded, which has made it part of the conceptual framework used today in clinical psychology. In discussing these techniques in the following chapters, an attempt will be made to note some of these original concepts and to examine them afresh.

A third reason for the seeming lack of relationship between theory and technique lies in the nature of manifest or observable behavior itself. If this writer's theory of ego functions were carried to its logical conclusions in the construction of new assessment techniques, it would seem that we would need different techniques for each function. Ideally, there should be techniques which tap only affect or motivation or cognitive or conative functioning, so that the assessor would not have to dig each out among responses to various techniques. Some techniques have attempted to do this, but with little success. Intelligence tests, for example, propose to measure cognitive abilities, but the motivational aspects of these achievement scales remain enmeshed in every response. Even the latest studies on the Bender have not succeeded in disentangling the motor from the perceptual facets of this behavior (although such a discrimination would aid considerably in differentiating the "expressively" and "receptively" handicapped child). *Most clinical techniques are both multipurpose and multifacet.* They sample a variety of behaviors relatively indiscriminately.

However, the difficulty lies not so much in the techniques themselves, as in the fact that *any* behavioral response is multipurpose and multifacet. Each contains some affect, some perception, some motivation, some intellectual task, some social aspect, and some motoric tension. Perhaps the kinds of techniques needed are those which provide stimuli that would highlight the function to be studied, while diminishing the role of other functions or at least providing means of measuring their effects. At the same time, in order to study the interrelationship and interaction of these functions in the total pattern of the ego, techniques would still be needed to stimulate systematically more than one function. For example, it might be desirable to measure "social intelligence" as well as "culture-free" intelligence, or to assess a child's motivation under conditions of both high and low affect. To assess the development of "identity," it would seem necessary to permit all of these functions to flow freely without definite stimulation. In view of these considerations, it is quite probable that although these techniques should be rebuilt, whatever new techniques are derived may not be very different from those which are now extant. In the long run, the important aspect of clinical techniques is neither their content nor their structure but how we, the users, observe and discriminate and conceptualize the responses that the child gives.

To examine the nature of assessment, it is helpful to distinguish between "methods" and "procedures." This chapter, under the rubric "method," will cover the sampling of behavior and the general methods of analyzing clinical data. The subsequent chapters briefly review the techniques commonly used to sample the child's behavior, their rationale and how they operate. Thus, the term "method" refers to an overall process and "technique" to the specific tools used in the method. Part III will then be concerned with the procedures of applying this method and these techniques.

No matter what techniques are used, there is an overall method of logic in every assessment. A limited sample of the child's behavior and his past history are obtained, using standardized techniques. Then the data are organized according to various methods of scientific analysis. Finally, inferences about the child are drawn from this analysis. Although this logical process may seem almost an assumed routine to most clinicians, a closer examination of this process is warranted in order to understand clearly what can be gained from clinical techniques and how to apply them.

B. THE SAMPLING OF BEHAVIOR IN ASSESSMENT

In research studies, the term "sample" usually refers to the number and variety (that is, demographic characteristics) of the subjects used in the experiment. In assessment, the "sample" in this actuarial sense consists of an N of one — or at most of a family. However, assessment is concerned with the sampling of the different kinds and "levels" of behavior. An assessment samples not only of a number of one kind of response but also a variety of behaviors. As in experimental designs, the way these samples of behavior are selected and collected is also very important. However, in assessment, the usual demographic variables used to describe the sample, such as age, sex, socioeconomic status, and IQ, are not, as in experiments, "ruled out" or "held constant," but become essential variables in the investigation.

The kinds of behavior to be sampled have been roughly outlined in the attempts in Chapters 4 and 5 to give operational definition to the functions of the child's ego. More specific relationships between the kinds of behavior samples by the more common clinical techniques and these ego functions will be discussed in Chapters 7 to 9. At this point, it is necessary to consider the manner in which the child's functions are expressed or demonstrated or, as it is commonly designated by personality theorists, the "level" of ego functioning. Freud designated the "unconscious" and "conscious" as levels of ego functioning, adding a "preconscious" state of awareness. The fact that much of the ego functions on an unconscious or automatic level of awareness may be missed by the casual student of psychoanalysis. There is a tendency by some writers and students to confuse the "unconscious" with what Freud labeled the "id" (which was included in the ego schemata of Chapter 4 as biological motivations). However, Freud makes clear that "id" impulses can be quite conscious at times; in fact, awareness of impulses is one of the aims of psychoanalytic treatment. Similarly, the "super-ego" or social value system also functions for the most part on an "unconscious" level of awareness.

However, it is very difficult to operationally define and utilize Freud's concepts, since whether or not a child is aware of his functioning and is operating on a conscious level is almost impossible to divine even if he is asked. If he denies it, it is difficult to know whether this denial is *suppression* of what the child thinks we would not approve or what he feels anxious or guilty about, or if it is a *repression*, that is, if the motivation or other ego function is actually out of the child's awareness. Without denying the heuristic value of these psychoanalytic concepts in understanding psychotherapuetic processes, it may be more helpful for the purposes of assessment to describe these levels of behavior in terms of how they are observed. Rosenzweig (1950), in classifying psychological tests, posits three "levels" at which tests sample behavior: the "objective," "subjective," and "projective." Although these terms, as Rosenzweig used them, do describe the kinds of behavior that are covered in the terms to be used in this discussion, these terms were introduced to describe the tests rather than the child. Moreover, these terms have been so used and misused in clinical psychology that they have collected positive and negative halos which might confuse the reader. Therefore, it may be helpful to rename these categories to indicate the three levels at which the child's ego functioning is observed: (1) his *manifest* or *overt* behavior; (2) the *subjective* expression of his thoughts or feelings; and (3) his *associative* behavior. It may be noted that this scheme of "levels" of observation does not distinguish between levels of awareness; no assumption is made as to whether the child is conscious of what he is demonstrating in his manifest behavior, in his subjective reports, or in his associations. This question of the child's awareness of himself and his behavior is a separate consideration.

By *manifest* behavior is meant that which is directly observable, what the assessor can see the child do and hear him say. It includes his motor behavior — both utilitarian and random — his expressive gestures and sympathetic reactions, and much of his verbal behavior as well, except when he is talking about himself. For example, "manifest" includes the child's responses to IQ test questions or the number of verbs and adjectives used on the TAT (but not the content of the TAT story itself).

Subjective, then, refers to the child's reports about his own behavior, his opinions of himself, his verbalizations of his feelings, and also his reports of the behavior of others or other people's reports about the child.

By *associative* behavior is meant those illogical, idiosyncratic reactions in which a child appears to reflect (or to use the more popular term, *project*) his personal feelings, motivations, and ideas. Most commonly, associative behavior can be observed when the child is instructed to respond in an associative fashion to the Rorschach Ink Blots or the TAT, or when he is asked what his dreams make him think of. However, associative behavior during interviews is often seen when the child or parent begins a sentence with, for example, "That reminds me . . . ." There is an associative side to a great deal of the child's behavior, but it is often difficult to sample in the few, brief contacts of the usual assessment, at least not as definitively as in the more extensive contacts of psychotherapy.

Associative behavior may be illustrated by the following sequence of events during the assessment of a six-year-old boy who came to the clinic because of his persistent enuresis. Asked to make a drawing of his own choice, he sketched a rocket ship with red flames shooting out of the top (rather than as is usual from the rockets at the bottom); when finished, he volunteered that he could write his name on the drawing and proceeded to make a large letter "P" (the first letter of his name, Peter), but instead of completing it, he continued to make more "P's," all the while shouting, "Pee, Pee, Pee." Excited and flushing, he began to talk about how much he loved his mother, how she "never, never" punished him and how he "never, never" got angry with her, even though the assessor had not asked him about any of this material. However, this set of associations was very brief, thus limiting any analysis of it or inferences from it. What the assessor could note was the fact that in the treatment of other enuretic children, persistent associations have been noted between "pee pee" and excitement, and both angry and sexual feelings about the child's mother.

There are two major reasons why the assessor needs to be definitive about the "level" at which he is observing. First, each level yields somewhat different clues about the child's ego functioning. Some ego functions can be observed easily at one level but are difficult to observe at another. Second, the child's functioning may change, sometimes quite markedly, from level to level. For example, he may demonstrate one type of affect or motivation at one level and show a different, even opposite feeling or drive at another level. It is this variation in behavior from level to level which gives clues regarding the existence of conflicts, defenses, and "dynamics."

1. *Manifest Behavior*

This offers the best observation of the child's developing skills. Thus, in manifest behavior, one can easily observe the child's motor development, his intellectual efficiency, and even his creative abilities, and how he achieves intellectually. The kinds of social coping mechanisms he has developed may be observed on the playground or at home or, if such observations are not feasible, in his relationship with the assessor. Some aspects of his affect are also directly observable, for example, the anger in his voice, the depression written across his face, or the anxiety in the tremor of his hands. Children have a fairly wide variety of expressing their affect in manifest behavior; one may express it in hyperactivity, another in remaining as rigid as a statue. Yet, reading people's faces is far from an exact or reliable way of sampling their affect. Even children may mask their expressions, tone down their voices, or otherwise hide their feelings. Most confusing is the fact that in a single facial expression or gesture the child may be expressing a mixture of feelings. In summary, manifest behavior often yields well-defined clues about the motor, intellectual, social, and to varying degrees, the affective functioning of the child's ego. Manifest behavior may also suggest hypotheses about the child's perceptual functioning and his motivations, but these ego functions are not usually easily observable from manifest behavior.

2. *Subjective Behavior*

A child's feelings about something or someone, his perception of a situation, or his motivations may more easily be discovered by the simple device of asking him. Psychologists have long used subjective reports from their subjects, adult and child, as one sample of the subject's behavior — even though psychologists recognize that both adults and children do not always "tell the truth" about either their behavior or their feelings and opinions. Both questionnaires and interviews are limited by (1) what the subject is *willing* to tell, and (2) what he is *able* to tell about himself. Psychologists have discovered that (1) children are not always good observers of their own behavior and (2) many of their feelings and motivations remain below the level of their awareness. Nevertheless, subjective reports remain one of the mainstays of assessment — if for no other reason than that subjective reports do reveal the perception of the self. The degree to which the child is developing an effective and accurate self-perception may be assessed by contrasting these subjective reports with that behavior which was observed on a manifest level and through his associations. Manifest and associative behavior yield cues about the feelings which he cannot or will not talk about.

However, even under these limitations, many children and adults are more free in discussing themselves than the skeptics would have us believe. Because children are thought not to verbalize as logically and accurately as adults, there is a tendency in the literature on assessment of children to emphasize non-verbal techniques, observation of free play, or associative samples, with little discussion of such subjective techniques as interviews with children or children's questionnaires. In practice, however, clinicians frequently conduct interviews with even quite young children. Moreover, there is more than a grain of truth in the popular notion that children by and large are "naive" or "open-faced" and "tell all." As with adults, whether a child will subjectively report about himself and his family depends a great deal on his trust in the assessor and on the intensity of his need for help. One advantage in using subjective sampling with children is that in contrast with adults they do not have to hide their dependency on others for approval and support. Thus, quite often they will be less defensive in discussing their attitudes and feelings. Moreover, their defenses are not as complex as those of an adult. The most frequent defense of children is negative and embarrassed silence. Such denial is usually so blatant that even the child himself cannot long countenance it. In most instances, a child, if encouraged and supported, will spill over his subjective feelings and volunteer a great deal about himself and his environment. Children's reports about "factual" matters certainly may be distorted either by lack of information or by the intrusion of their own associations. However, children's reports on their home life, on parental behavior, and especially parental affect are not to be dismissed merely because they may not give an accurate chronological account or become confused on dates and places. Thus, sampling of ego functioning on the subjective level in children can yield considerable data concerning affective, conative, perceptual, and even social behavior. Except insofar as one considers the logical aspects of the child's verbalization, or can check the accuracy of his facts and observations, subjective reports add little to assessment of intellectual functioning. The nature of a child's vocalization is, of course, a manifest behavior, giving clues about his motor functioning. But he may also describe and evaluate his motor behavior quite accurately.

3. *Associative Behavior*

Although at one time associative behavior was considered outside the pale of science and considered childish (sic!), since Freud's discovery of the "royal road to the unconscious" via dreams, there has been an expanding recognition of and utilization of associative sampling of behavior in both clinical and other scientific studies of children's functioning. A plethora of techniques has been introduced that is designed to investigate children's fantasies — in addition to the observation of free play. Unfortunately, there has been too little attention paid to the rationale behind many of these techniques or to the logic of the analysis of responses to them. Nevertheless, these projective innovations have enabled the psychologist to sample the alogical ideation, the perceptual functioning, the affect, and the motivations that underlie the child's manifest and subjective behavior.

In understanding what is meant by "associative" or "projective," a word needs to be said about the term "alogical." Actually, associative ideation in the broad sense of the term is the basis for all thinking, as has been recognized by most philosophers and their heirs, the psychologists, since at least the eighteenth century. The rules of "logic" used in Western philosophy are largely attempts to (1) provide means for distinguishing associations that also have a basis in the extrapersonal world from those which are chiefly intrapersonal and (2) provide rules for communication of these extrapersonal associations.* As was discussed in Part I, the intellectual development of the child consists for the most part of learning and applying methods of distinguishing such associations. However, as was also noted, a great deal of this learning about *formal* associative thinking is practiced in the child's fantasy. The child invents, imagines, fantasies, and thus develops "creative" thinking as a necessary background to predicting and comprehending reality. If he is to learn by experience, he has to be able to fantasy what experiences may bring. Thus, although children's associative behavior may be largely alogical, it has in it the seeds of his intellectual development.

Another reason for sampling and understanding the alogical associative processes in children's functioning is that the rules of logic provide only a very limited testing of

reality. Although logical reasoning is necessary for much effective problem-solving behavior, it is not the only effective way of experiencing reality. Affective, conative, and motor functioning are neither experienced nor conducted according to "rules of logic," but are quite as much part of the experiencing of reality as is intellectual functioning. Children usually recognize that the "rules" governing these functions often have little relation to any "logic." Adolescents are quick to spot the blatant inconsistencies of social mores and behavior. There is, of course, a *psycho*-logic to these functions, and children learn psychological coping methods to direct their ego functions. Sampling of this alogical associative behavior in children thus gives the assessor an opportunity to estimate how well the child is learning the psycho-logic of ego functioning. The associative behavior sampled in the child's responses to inkblots, TAT pictures, or drawings provide a wealth of data about the child's motivation and affect, and his skills in coping with them.

C. ANALYSIS OF THE BEHAVIOR SAMPLED

The usefulness of data, in any scientific study, depends a great deal on how it is organized and analyzed. Although the actual procedures of analyzing the data come after the samples of behavior are collected, for the most part the data are not gathered in helter-skelter fashion but in as systematic a fashion as possible to facilitate its analysis. Sometimes the clinician may gain some impressions from random or casual observations of the child. However, such observations are limited in value because in their evaluation, it is often discovered that many other facts and variables are needed in order to draw any conclusions from them. Such casual observation tends to provide data that defy analysis. Thus, for the most part, samples of behavior are most useful if drawn with some methods of analysis in mind.

Any sample of behavior may be analyzed in several different ways, and the assessor should be prepared to use more than one method, even if the specific technique is most commonly analyzed by only one method. Three such methods commonly used in assessment may be distinguished: (1) the "metric"

---

* In contrast, Eastern philosophies are more concerned with intrapersonal experiences and thought, resulting in different rules of "logic." In this regard the Eastern philosophies are more *psycho*-logic.

or "scoring" approach; (2) the analysis of "patterns" of behavior; and (3) the analysis of "themes."

1. *Metric Analysis*

From a strictly scientific point of view, all clinical techniques should have some form of *metric* analysis. In fact, some kind of standardized measuring units are available for most clinical samples of behavior. Some of these scoring systems, like those for observations or for interviews, have never been developed much beyond the experimental stage and are thus unknown to most clinicians. These are apt to be limited to the experimental variables for which they were built. Like most of the scoring systems for the TAT, they tend to be clumsy and require considerable time and effort to apply. Moreover, clinicians seem to have an aversion to metric analysis of their data, as if in some magical fashion they destroy or contaminate their data by calculating scores. This aversion may have arisen because at one time metric analysis was the only respected approach. Since many of the ego functions had not been sampled at all, let alone by techniques with well-developed metric analysis, the task of assessment seemed impossible if one were limited only to those techniques with scores. Also, clinicians were entranced with the newly introduced projective techniques, which, although they often had some rough scoring system, lent themselves more easily to nonmetric methods of analysis.

The advantages of metric analysis of behavioral data are obvious: it provides operational units by which the extent and intensity of any variable can be estimated. Since a great deal of the description of and prediction about ego functioning is in terms of extent (for example, of ability or of defensiveness) and intensity (for example, of anger or depression), some form of metric analysis is invaluable. The chief disadvantage lies in the fact that a separate measure for each variable is necessary (except where two or more variables can be recategorized under some higher level of generalization). Often the trouble with some of the current scales is that they try to measure several variables at once, variables that cannot logically be lumped together. If metric scores were available for every variable needed for a thorough assessment, all the IQ scores, plus all the perceptual

scores, plus scores on each kind of affect and each type of social behavior, etc., the result would be analyzable only by using a computer program — an idea that is being entertained in several quarters. Computer analysis would be required not only because of the mass of scores and "signs," but also because very few of these variables are actually discreet and independent of one another, and any actuarial analysis would have to take into account the intercorrelations between scores.

Another problem in the use of metric analysis is that some guideline is needed to establish when a score has clinical import. What is the "cutting score?" At what point on a scale can it be said that a child is developing satisfactorily? For some types of variables, for example, school achievement, it is easy enough to establish a norm for an age group. Such a norm uses an *extra*personal criterion. However, if *intra*personal dynamic, such as repression, is being assessed, some other kind of criterion would have to be adopted: How much can the child repress without deterring other development? Or, how much does he need to repress in order to avoid being overwhelmed? In clinical work, the psychologist is frequently faced with the fact that quite a few variables have a simple present-not present significance. For example, one suicidal attempt or one grand mal seizure may be clinically "significant." This "cutting-point" problem has been interestingly conceptualized by Fisher (1959) in his "inverted pear" diagram, and critically examined further by Storms (1960). Every clinician who takes note of one inverted drawing on the Bender, of a single Rorschach, or one TAT response should be aware of this problem. The cutting-point problem, of course, increases in the assessment of children since a different cutting point in a scoring system would be needed for each developmental level, if not for each year.

Perhaps the biggest complaint that clinicians voice against metric analysis is that when behavior is "reduced" to a score, one loses the richness of the personality, the dynamics of the interactions between forces in the individual and of his interpersonal relationships. Metric analysis, say its critics, leads quickly to "test-oriented" assessment in which the unique character of the child is ignored. However, metric analysis in itself does not mean being "test-oriented," for one can become enmeshed in one's technique no matter what method of analysis is used. One can lose sight of the child and of the dynamics, etc., if one considers metric analysis the *only* method and does not use it in combination with others. Actually, the difficulty lies not in the metric method itself, but in its misuse, particularly when it comes to drawing inferences from the score or sign. As will be discussed later, metric analysis is most commonly associated with "direct" inferences, although it can be the basis for other types of inference as well.

2. *Pattern Analysis*

In order to avoid some of these difficulties with the metric method, clinicians and other users of tests have turned to analyzing *patterns* of responses. The most commonly recognized pattern analysis has been the profile of scores, for example, on the MMPI or Wechsler tests. In this way the clinician groups sets of scores together and avoids the problem of too many seemingly unrelated scores. Even on the Binet, it is common clinical practice to subdivide the items into patterns and look at success and failure on items involving verbalization, memory, or judgment, for example. On the Rorschach, one needs to regard not only the individual scores but the total "psychogram," the interrelationship between the various kinds of perceptual cues used by the child. Furthermore, Rorschach analysis includes what is known as "sequence" analysis, which means looking through the protocol to note how one response follows another. Such sequential examination of behavior is actually used in practice by many clinicians in analyzing the behavior of the child during play observations or in interviews, although it may not be as formalized or as systematic as on the Rorschach and is not labeled as "sequential."

3. *Thematic Analysis*

Such analysis of sequential patterns leads into what may be called *thematic* analysis, a term associated, of course, with the Thematic Apperception Test. "Thematic" refers to the patterns of behavior or ideation *within* the protocols of test responses or of interview or observation notes, in contrast to the overall pattern of scores or sequence of scores. Such themes consist of summary statements of what the child is doing or saying in any one unit of response or behavior, such as a TAT story, a set of interviewer-child responses in an interview, or interaction between the child and a peer on the playground, as, for example, in the following TAT story (to Picture 1, Murray series — Boy with violin):

"He's trying to study his violin. He doesn't want to — or maybe he does, I don't know. It's his grandfather's violin and his father wants him to play it like he does. So does his mother. He wants to but he's tired of studying it. (What happens?) His mother calls him back in to practice . . . . I guess he comes, 'cause he doesn't want to make his mother cry. (How does he feel then?) He feels bad."

Such a story might be analyzed, along with other stories, into patterns of needs and stress of various kinds, for example, the press for achievement, the need for conformity, the need for play, etc. The theme, however, might be summarized as "ambivalence over conformity with and identification with parents, leading toward guilt feelings in response to maternal depression."

Another example may be taken from an interview with a family: Before the interview began, the two children began a noisy game which did not permit conversation. Neither parent made any move to quiet the children. Finally, the father, red in the face, asked interviewer's permission to interrupt the children! After several attempts, he succeeded in getting them to stop and listen. The children then began complaining to the interviewer that their father never plays with them. Father denied this in a hurt voice and asked for verification from his wife that he spends considerable time with his children. The wife begrudgingly admitted that they watch TV together. Father, more flustered, declared "This isn't the topic," and reminded his wife that they were really there to talk about the boy's enuresis. The sister, age 9, began to giggle pointing at her brother. The son, age 7, looking hurt and embarrassed, flung himself on the floor. Mother tried to comfort the son, glaring at the father. The son then declared angrily that "father is always hurting me." The father again, on the defensive, asked, "When?" "When you're playing with us," retorted the daughter. The "theme" here appears to be one of mutual accusation and control by creation of guilt.

Finally, it is necessary to look at the over-all pattern of themes, the recurrent themes and the idiosyncratic ones. To borrow still other phrases from musical analysis, one can examine *theme and variation,* noting where possible the "leit-motiv," the central patterns of interaction or dynamics within the ego. Such thematic analysis is thus a method of extracting some of the interrelationships between the various ego functions, particularly between the affective, conative, and social. Such thematic analysis can also be conducted to study the perceptual and cognitive reactions to social stress versus personal motivation. It helps to answer such questions as: How well does the child perceive and comprehend when under stress? Or, how well can he perceive and understand the stresses themselves?

D. THE EVALUATION OF TECHNIQUES

Traditionally, the adequacy of a technique is determined in terms of its standardization, reliability, and validity. These determinations require well-designed and conceptualized research. A thorough knowledge of such research, both actuarial and experimental, is without question necessary to the background of the assessor. However, since this volume is directed chiefly to the overall nature, processes, and procedures of assessment, rather than being about techniques per se, a review of the research studies behind each technique is beyond its purview. Moreover, the pertinent question for assessment is how such research results are applied in everyday use. Thus it may be helpful to consider the relationships between such research and assessment.

In considering this question it is necessary to review at least the essential features of these traditional approaches to the evaluation of clinical techniques. These statistical evaluations are, of course, particularly associated with and arose out of the construction of those techniques commonly called "tests." A "test" may be defined as any standardized sample of behavior. Sometimes it is forgotten that other assessment techniques, such as interviews or observational techniques also have questions of standardization, reliability, and validity. "Standardization" usually means three things: first, the sample of behavior is always taken in the same way, using standard instructions, standard stimuli, and a standard or uniform method of analyzing the responses. Second, standardization refers to the established range and variety of responses obtained. On a well-standardized technique, responses can be identified as "normal," "usual," "frequent," "unpopular," "stereotyped," "pathological," "bizarre," "idiosyncratic," "imaginative," etc. Standardization establishes the number of subjects who usually "pass" or "accept" or "fail" or "reject" an item or a set of items. Third, standardization includes a reference population to which the norms are applicable. Most tests are, of course, standardized on a fairly broad range of children, from various socioeconomic backgrounds. Since assessment is concerned with development, a standardization sample needs to be stratified by age, to obtain age norms. Other research studies may compare these norms of the original standardization sample with the responses of other groups of children not included in the original sample or with subsamples of the original. Although studies of individual differences (which are really *group* differences) are not commonly considered to be standardization, in effect they add to the standardization by supplying further norms in terms of differences between groups.

1. *Standardization*

The applicability of standardization to assessment techniques may seem so obvious as not to warrant discussion. The use of standard instructions and stimuli, the knowledge of the range and variety of responses obtained therefrom within the "normal" population, and differences between these responses and those given by other kinds of children constitute the guidelines for drawing inferences about the level of development of the individual child. Such norms are basic to any estimate of the effectiveness of each of the ego functions. At one time, before much was known about "dynamics" or the interaction of ego functions, assessment consisted wholly of these "norms." Currently, psychologists sometimes become so involved in the "psychodynamics" that they tend to forget or ignore the basic normative data, or even deride it as "pigeonholing" the child. For example, if a child who is known to be beset by social and personal stress and to lack affective controls achieves a very low score on a standardized "IQ" test, some clinicians are prone to excuse the child's performance and say "he is not *really* retarded because . . . "; such statements fly in the face of the facts, for by these established standards, the child is, for whatever reason, "retarded" in his intellectual development. Obversely, one may find what at first sight seems to be "pathology," for example, gross distortions on a test of visual motor functioning or repeated themes of Oedipal conflict on the TAT, but it may be forgotten for the moment that the visual motor task is more complex than a child of this age can manage, or that the child is at the age when Oedipal fantasies are at their height.

It is, of course, necessary at times to alter slightly the instructions or even the stimuli of a standardized technique in order to attract a child or to enable him to understand what is wanted. Or, sometimes it may be helpful to "inquire" further about a response the child has made than is called for by the standard procedures. However, such alterations should have a definite rationale and not be just the whim of the assessor. Moreover, the assessor must clearly recognize that he has altered the technique, thus affecting his analyses and inferences from it. Carelessness about and ignorance of the instructions and stimuli are far too often an error of the clinical tyro and are characteristic of amateurish research.

2. *Reliability*

The reliability or consistency of a technique also involves several different questions. The first that might be mentioned deals essentially with how reliably the standardized method of analyzing the technique is used, that is, the reliability of the "scoring." Here the question is: Can several assessors score the test the same way? — this is called *inter*judge reliability. Similarly, there is an *intra*judge reliability: how reliable is any one assessor in his scoring? *

Interjudge reliability is essentially a measure of how well assessors can communicate with one another, for if assessors do not analyze in the same way it is unlikely that

they will make the same inferences. A technique with low or unknown interjudge reliability opens the door to differences in clinical impressions and results. Statements of intrajudge reliability are rare — except where a technique is being used experimentally — for this reliability varies with the assessor. In practice, each assessor should check his own consistency in analyzing his techniques (although few assessors make such a check). For example, every once in awhile an assessor should pull a sample of protocols from his files, have the responses copied with the scores omitted, and then rescore and check the rescoring against the original at least by casual inspection, if not statistically. Such a personal check enables the assessor to know how consistently he himself operates in using his techniques, and to recognize what changes he may be making, whether consciously or inadvertently. Of course, such a personal, intrajudge check reveals only the consistency of scoring. It is still quite possible that there are consistent biases. An assessor should also cooperate with other assessors from time to time in a similar informal interjudge reliability check. The need for such checks from time to time is illustrated by the fact that in a classroom experiment, students who had been "thoroughly" trained in the use of a standard intelligence test for over a year varied as much as five IQ points in scoring the same protocol!

More commonly, reliability refers to the consistency with which the child responds to the stimuli, or in test constructor's terms, the consistency with which the test "pulls" certain responses. Actually, there are two such kinds of test reliability: the "test-retest" correlation which checks consistency of respondents over a specified time, and intratest reliability, commonly measured by the "split-half" or similar test correlations, which give a measure of whether the child responds to similar items in the same manner. In thinking about these kinds of reliability, the assessor must ask himself both what he expects from the child and what he expects from the technique in question. For example, reliability over time in a growing and changing organism, whose "mind is not yet made up," may not be expected to be as great as that in an adult. In fact, if one is interested in rate of development, that is, in changes, techniques which have a high reliability over time may not yield much information! Yet, one might

---

* Similar studies of the interjudge or intrajudge reliability of inferences can be made but are rare. More often such studies are made of clinical judgment in general, rather than of specific techniques.

not gain much information from an item or a technique on which children generally responded randomly over relatively brief periods of time. Similarly, on a technique designed to sample a single trait or dimension, it might be well to have a high split-half reliability, but on a technique designed purposefully to sample the variation of the child's perceptions, split-half or other measures of item reliability are meaningless. As Rosenzweig and his colleagues (1948) discovered in the construction of his Picture Frustration Study, it is quite possible that at the beginning of a test (or interview, or observation), a child may be quite guarded and then become more expansive or self-revealing as he becomes more confident. Obversely, he may begin with naive, open-face admissions of his feelings and attitudes only to become anxious and guarded as he unconsciously realizes he is revealing himself. Such change of test-taking attitudes or "set" may not affect the split-half reliability if the split consists of alternate items. However, children also may vary their set from item to item, following a revealing statement by an innocuous or covering or retracting response. In fact, the inventors of the TAT purposely chose picture stimuli which they believed might be innocuous or less "anxiety-producing" to present to the child subsequent to those pictures believed to be more shocking stimuli. Whether or not these hypotheses about the anxiety-provoking nature of such stimuli are valid, such possibilities make the assessor think twice before accepting interitem correlations as the only measure of reliability.

The question of the internal consistency of a technique becomes slightly different when the technique is designed to sample ego dynamics. Here the reliability question might be phrased: Do the items of the technique pull responses that are generally recognizable as unique to that child, or do the items draw responses from different children which are so similar or "popular" or "socially desirable" that they tell us little about the child other than his conformity to social norms? A brief check on the card pull reliability (of adult patients) on the TAT was made in a classroom demonstration (Palmer, 1952) where naive judges were asked to match stories from different cards by the same subjects; although most subjects were successfully matched above chance, some TAT cards were missed significantly more often than others.

3. *Validity*

Perhaps the most involved question asked about clinical techniques is that of validity. A full discussion of this complex topic cannot be included here, but attention may be drawn to three aspects that have particular pertinence to the practical task of assessment. First, there is the question: Validity of what (Jenkens, 1946)? A validity study should begin with a careful examination of the purposes of the technique, that is, what a technique is designed to sample and measure. Any validity study should begin with a recognition and understanding of its rationale. At the same time, a validation should state clearly the operations that the technique demands of both the subject and the assessor. Validation studies too often appear to be poorly acquainted with the purposes and nature of the technique under study. Sometimes validation studies even ignore the standard administration and scoring of the technique! For example, a few years ago a number of studies appeared purporting to check the validity of the so-called "color shock" on the Rorschach. None of these studies paid any attention to Rorschach's rationale for using color in his inkblots or what he or other Rorschach experts have given as the theoretical base for drawing inferences from the subject's response to color — or in this instance, the failure of the subject to respond. These studies were concerned with whether more signs of shock occurred on colored cards than achromatic cards, and the results did show that such signs of shock were equally present on both. However, whether the shock to achromatic cards means anything different than the shock to color, as maintained by Rorschach theorists, was not even considered by these research studies. Moreover, in some of these studies no inquiry was made to determine whether the subject's response might be based on the color — ignoring the fact that such inquiry is an integral part of the Rorschach operations.

Second, the assessor, in reading validation studies, needs to ask: What *kind* of validity? Cronbach and Meehl (1955) distinguished four types of validity studies: (1) concurrent, (2) predictive, (3) content, and (4) construct validation. As the authors point out, each of these aspects of validity needs to be studied. The assessor needs to know (a) whether the behavior sampled by the technique is similar to other current samples of that kind of behavior, (b) whether and to what degree one can draw inferences from (predict from) this sample of this kind of behavior as to other kinds of behavior in similar or even different situations, (c) whether the sampled behavior is part of the universe of behavior to which the prediction is made, and (d) whether or not the "constructs" or rationale of the technique have been demonstrated as supportable hypotheses in experimental studies. Techniques may be quite valid in some respects and invalid in others. For example, the predictive validity of IQ's obtained from "infant" scales is zero; there is no predictable relation between the IQ obtained on, say, the Cattell at age 6 months, and the IQ obtained on the same child on the Binet at six years. (Nor, as was discussed in Chapter 4, would such predictability be possible from what is known about the development of intelligence.) On the other hand, infant IQ scales do have fair descriptive validity; the infant's responses are valid representations of his current intellectual development, as compared with other infants of the same chronological age. Moreover, there is considerable evidence from the experimental literature on infants that the rationale behind the items included in such scales is valid; the motor tasks and visual discriminations required in these scales correspond to what Piaget has shown to be the "seeds" of intelligence.

The conscientious student who reads the research literature on clinical techniques carefully and with a critical eye is apt to be quite discouraged and disillusioned concerning both the techniques and the research. He will find that many of the major clinical tools are inadequately and haphazardly standardized, possess only questionable reliability of any kind, and have only "face" validity or even that their validity has not been questioned. Moreover, he will discover that many of the reliability and validity studies have been inadequately thought out, poorly designed, and sloppily executed. He may justifiably ask how it is possible to carry on assessment with such tools. Or he may attempt, as do many clinicians, to rationalize away the whole question, to try to declare that these questions of standardization, reliability, and validity have little or no bearing on "dynamic" assessment.

Or, since they seem insoluble, he may go blithely ahead and not worry about it at all. This writer is not content with such arguments and believes it is far better to be painfully aware of the limitations of clinical techniques, constantly demanding of ourselves the required improvements in test construction and research design. Unfortunately, "tool-sharpening" research is currently not considered prestigious.* It may not seem "important" research, that is, not to establish anything "basic" about behavior, but in this writer's opinion, studies of validity often add to our general knowledge about behavior, and even routine studies of reliability or checks on standardization contain kernels of facts about development.

How then can an assessor carry out his studies of the individual child with poorly standardized tools of doubtful reliability and unknown validity? Where such research is lacking, the answer to this question lies in an increased responsibility to examine these tools carefully and thoughtfully. It becomes essential to understand clearly the rationale and constructs underlying the technique, and to know whether such a rationale seems reasonable in the light of experimental research on these constructs (even though the experimental work does not directly refer to the clinical tool). There is added reason to analyze carefully the operations of the technique, to see if these operations at least appear to sample the behavior in question in a uniform, standard manner. As was suggested above, an assessor may spotcheck his consistency as a judge of the behavior sampled. And if he does not have opportunity to conduct formal reliability and validity studies, he must constantly scan his clinical studies, observing as best he can any signs of inadequate reliabilities or of invalid descriptions, inferences, and predictions. The clinician who remains thus critical of his own techniques will be better prepared to make the crucial research studies.

In evaluating the techniques of assessment, psychologists may well begin by reminding themselves that although they aspire to be scientists and strive to be as scientific as possible in their methods and thinking, the techniques they use are far from the accurate scientific instruments they would like them

---

* Such studies seldom are acceptable as doctoral theses and are not considered as worthwhile items in a professor's bibliography.

to be. Rather, these techniques are more comparable to the tools of the artisan. Their accuracy thus depends a greal deal on the skill of the assessor, how expertly he uses them, how well he knows the nature of the material he is working on, that is, the developing ego, and the plans and designs he has in mind as he works. Like the workman's tools, the assessor's techniques are not as central to his product as is his knowledge of child behavior and his skill in using the techniques to study the problem at hand. How these techniques can be put to use, the procedure of assessment, will be discussed in the forthcoming section. At this point, however, review is needed of the general purposes, operations, accuracy, and clinical advantages and disadvantages of some of the most commonly used techniques.

Chapter 7

TECHNIQUES BASED ON
SAMPLES OF MANIFEST BEHAVIOR

Many frequently used techniques are based on the rationale that by sampling directly observable behavior, one may predict that the child will behave similarly in other situations where his behavior is also manifestly observable. As will be seen, manifest behavior may also yield valuable clues regarding other levels of behavior. Inferences from such samples are often simple extrapolations. Included among such techniques are: structured and unstructured observations of the child at play or work, structured tests of intelligence, structured tests of educational achievement, tests of visual-motor reproduction, and tests of determinants of perception.

A. UNSTRUCTURED OBSERVATION

Naturalistic observations were the beginnings of science. Before there were telescopes or even mathematics, scientists observed and recorded the movement of planets and stars while watching them from hilltops; zoology and botany began with expeditions. Similarly, scientists such as Darwin (1877) and Preyer (1881) began watching infants in daily activities. From these observations, hypotheses were drawn, later to be tested in the laboratory or in statistical studies. Both Freud and Piaget were essentially naturalists. In the assessment of individual children and in the study of the general development of children, such naturalistic observation remains a revered and cherished technique, employed widely — if not always very wisely.

The basic elements, or "operations," of such observations are: (a) the setting and its structure and (b) the degree of interaction between the child and the observer. How a child behaves in a hospital ward is likely to differ from how he behaves on a schoolyard, and both may differ from his behavior in and around his own home. The observer should ask himself, "To what degree does the situation impose limits on the child's behavior?" "Does it demand certain tasks of him and obligate him to specified or implied social relationships, or does it allow a relatively free choice of behavior and social interaction?" Whether the observer himself is part of the situation for the child also changes the nature of his reactions and of the observations. When the child realizes his behavior is under observation, he acts differently than when the observer is out of his sight or awareness. Thus, the behavior observed during the administration of other techniques (aside from the child's responses to these techniques) contain a large element of reaction to the assessor and his behavior. The child also reacts to being "put to the test." These elements may be lacking (and other factors present) when, for example, the assessor stands behind a one-way screen and observes the child at play in a nursery schoolyard that is familiar to the child. Therefore it is very necessary in reporting and drawing inferences from such "unstructured" observation to state clearly just how unstructured the situation was, and to define how and where the child was observed.

Sampling of behavior via direct observation also requires that the frequency and length of our observations be specified. Brief, *en passant,* or haphazard observations are apt to yield biased or at least unreliable results. The assessor should plan his observations carefully and, depending on the situation, the child, and the aims of the assessment, he should decide in advance whether he needs to make a series of brief observations, several lengthy observations, or to vary the extent and frequency. Again, these factors must be specified when drawing conclusions from direct observations.

The analysis of such observation is often more "unstructured" than the sample. In clinical practice (as distinct from research studies), the observed behavior is seldom scored or rated in metric fashion. The fairly reliable rating scales constructed in research studies of development have not been adopted in clinical use. However, the careful assessor who makes detailed notes may be able to detect patterns of repeated reactions or sequences of reactions in the child's behavior. If he makes enough observations in a variety of situations, he may be able to demarcate recurrent themes in the child's behavior. If the assessor falls back on some intuitive global impression, his conclusions are also likely to be global and nonspecific.

Because this sample is assumed to consist of "direct" manifest behavior, there may be a temptation to draw only "direct" inferences from it. There is often an aura attached to direct observation of the child which contains the implicit assumption that because one is observing the child *au naturel* rather than via a more formal "test," few or no inferences may be drawn. However, it is still quite possible to use such data inductively, to build hypotheses from it about different aspects of ego functioning. Various hypotheses may be deductively checked out using such unstructured behavior as a criterion. One may want to know, for example, what kind of hypotheses might be drawn about the child's impulse controls from his playground activities. Is the murderous hostility blatant in his fantasy on the TAT represented in his interactions with peers and adult authorities? If so, in what form? With what stimuli?

Perhaps the greatest difficulty in using this technique is that there is no way of firmly establishing the reliability of either samples or judgments. One reason for making a series of observations, rather than depending on just one or two long periods of observation, is that expanding the number of samples or "items" may increase this reliability. Similarly, by using a number of observations, the psychologist may be able to inspect the consistency of his judgments. Nevertheless, the assessor must always keep in mind that in using unstructured observations there is considerable possibility that both his sampling and his analyses of the data may be quite biased. The fact that the reliability over time of this technique is unknown and that reliability of judgment varies greatly from assessor to assessor limits, of course, the validity of the inferences that are drawn. It is possible to gain quite valid insights from a single casual observation, but the confidence in such validity often ranges from overweening pride in one's own intuition to scoffing distrust and disregard of such hunches, valid though they may be. However, insofar as the purposes of the observations are carefully thought out in advance, the operations specific to these purposes, and the data systematically analyzed, the validity of inferences is strengthened.

In considering the validity of conclusions about such "unstructured" observation, it is necessary to remember that while the observation is "direct," there can be no assumption about the level of the child's behavior. Since no direction or structure is laid down for the child, he is free to interact with his environment in a "direct" fashion — or to associate to it. Whether the child is at play or taking "tests" in an office, much of his behavior may be quite "projective" or associative. Thus, his behavior in the sandbox or on the tricycle or even his posture, gestures, and facial expression while taking an IQ test may be as much a matter of "internal" associations and of projection of these associations as they are reactions to the immediate stimuli in the situation or task at hand. If the child's behavior in such situations is largely on the associative level, then inferences from it about his mainifest behavior may be of doubtful validity. For example, if a child starts hitting another child on the playground, he may be reacting aggressively to something the other child has done or threatens to do, and one might be tempted to infer that this represents a sample of how this child reacts when attacked. However, if this were the only sample of the child's social playground behavior, the possibility could not be ruled out that the subject was projecting bottled-up feelings of hostility onto some innocent bystander. In this latter instance, the manifest behavior, hitting, would not depend on a manifest stimuli, and probably would be more frequent and less predictable. Here again, several extended observations may be needed to be able to discern to what extent the child comes onto the playground ready to pick a fight, seeking attention, or feeling depressed and withdrawn, and to what extent and in what fashion he reacts to the situation and the behavior of the people in it. Both aspects and their combination need to be considered in assessing the child's ego-functioning.

Keeping the above precautions and limitations in mind, then observation of the child outside of the office — on the playground, in his home or classroom, or in his daily routine on a hospital ward — can be a very useful adjunct to assessment. Used in conjunction with other techniques, it offers several possibilities that are otherwise unobtainable. First, by obtaining such a sample of the child's behavior when he is not under pressure to perform vis-à-vis the assessor, it is possible to estimate how much of the child's reactions to other techniques represent a "testing set." Comparing the two situations, the extent to which the child is usually anxious, uncontrolled, poorly motivated, or ambitious, etc. can be estimated. Moreover, it may be possible to define more clearly the degree to which the testing situation has promoted these reactions. Thus, the external observation can yield another estimate of the generalizability of inferences from other techniques. However, one must be very careful in using such "manifest" behavior as a criterion for validating other techniques. When the same kind of behavior is observed, both on the playground and during the formal testing in an office, one may be able to conclude that this is a general set the child brings to different situations; when he reacts differently, it may be assumed

at best that in the office he is reacting to the fact that he is being "tested," and that he distinguishes between the pressures of the adult demands for performance and the social pressures of the playground. In either instance, the psychologist will be better able to evaluate the child's responses to the tests. His test responses may also yield further information about the nature of the child's extratest behavior and behavior outside the office. Moreover, in the long run, these correlations between overt behavior and test responses — be they strongly positive, quite negative, or even zero order correlations — yield clues as to interactions between various ego functions and between various levels of behavior. Thus, for example, if a child who has been observed to be quite conforming, passive, and cautious on the playground tells wild tales of violence to the TAT, there is some evidence that his feelings of hostility are more likely to be worked out on the fantasy level than in overt behavior. Or, if the child makes a high score on an intelligence test but obtains low grades in school, where he "goofs off" or plays the role of the stupid clown, questions need to be raised about his feelings of adequacy in social situations, his dependency on others to solve problems intellectually for him, or his resistance to authorities other than the assessor.

B. STRUCTURED TESTS OF INTELLECTUAL ACHIEVEMENT

These thoroughly standardized and reliable tests of intellectual achievement have been so widely used and known for several decades that a general review of their composition and nature would seem almost unnecessary. A detailed inspection of their construction and composition is too extensive for these pages. However, just because these techniques are universally accepted, their basic rationale is seldom clearly stated; their operations are infrequently delineated; their validity is not questioned; nor is their clinical utility evaluated. Hoary as these techniques may be with scientific respectability, it may be helpful to examine these questions about them in order to understand clearly their place in an assessment battery.

1. The rationale underlying IQ tests is that they consist of direct, manifest samples of

highly structured problem-solving behavior. It is assumed that these samples are so similar to problem-solving tasks in other structured situations that one can directly extrapolate to and predict the behavior of the child in these other situations. It may seem that this statement of the rationale of IQ tests is another way of defining intelligence as being "what IQ tests measure" (see Chapter 4); however, the only specification in this rationale about the nature of the intellectual functioning being sampled is that it is structured problem solving. Thus, these samples of intellectual behavior do not include problem solving in unstructured situations, which is yet another kind of cognitive behavior, albeit related to that sampled by IQ tests, but which is more observable in our "associative" techniques. Neither is there any assumption as to whether the child's "true" intelligence, intellectual potential, or learning capacity is being measured, or whether his responses represent, as is more frequently the case, his current intellectual efficiency or level of achievement. These questions may be answered only by inspecting the operations and content of these scales and the nature of the responses of the child in question.

The rationale behind IQ scales is delimited further by the fact that the problem-solving tasks presented to the child are usually arranged in order of increasing difficulty. Moreover, the fact that the child's responses are analyzed by age norms is based on the assumption that as the child grows older his intelligence also grows, that is, that he learns and achieves more effectively. If it can be shown by a series of such examinations (or from other data) that this intellectual growth has been fairly steady over the child's lifetime, then it would seem reasonable to hypothesize that the child's performance *at this time* represents part of an overall growth pattern whether because of an inherent developmental rate or of a constancy in environmental factors or both. Otherwise, these operations limit the psychologist to the statement that this IQ represents the current rate of achievement of the child as compared with other children of the same age.

2. In the operations of an IQ test, the assessor is placed in the position of an authority figure questioning the ability or adequacy of the child. This is such a common situation in Western culture that quite frequently neither the assessor nor the child questions this social aspect of the operations. Moreover, as will be discussed further in subsequent chapters, there are procedures for making the child feel relatively at ease if he does not accept such intellectual challenge. However, it should be noted that in no IQ test are there any formal instructions to the child informing him that his intelligence is being challenged. Sometimes the instructions to certain subtests hint at this when the child is told, for example, "Now I want to see how many words you know," or "Now I am going to test your arithmetic." However, there is an unspoken presumption that if the child were told, "Now I am going to test your intelligence," his anxiety and resistance might well be increased. Perhaps it would be more definitive to say his anxiety would be crystallized, for most children soon become aware that that is exactly what the psychologist is up to even though both the child and assessor usually conform to the social amenity of avoiding any direct statement of the challenge and pretend they are playing intellectual games.

In Western culture, which emphasizes achievement and problem solving, a child has to recognize and accept intellectual challenge by the time he begins school. However, some children, for example, those who are culturally deprived, actually fail to comprehend and accept this social aspect of the IQ operations. They may see the situation as an enjoyable child-adult relationship in which they are receiving attention, but do not comprehend that they are expected to achieve. Or, if they do realize the demand upon them for problem solving, they may just ignore it or respond on a more associative level. Such children play "games" other than the one presented by the IQ test, often frustrating any assessor who hopes to extract an IQ from the child. Such very resistant children are admittedly exceptions. Yet, many children do have at least some twinges of resentment over the implicit assumption that they accept without question a problem-solving, achievement orientation. Perhaps the most important aspect of this social assumption in IQ testing is that it is quite similar to the school situation, where it is also tacitly assumed that the child will accept intellectual challenge. Thus, observations of the child's acceptance or rejection of the demand to achieve on an IQ test may give clues about his attitudes toward intellectual achievement in general.

Allied to this assumption of achievement

orientation in IQ tests are the success-fail patterns created by the way IQ tests operate. These patterns differ from scale to scale. On mental age level scales, such as the Binet or Merrill-Palmer, the child experiences complete success at the basal level and complete failure at the end. On point scales, consisting of several subtests, such as the Wechsler scales or the Arthur Point Scales, complete failure occurs at the conclusion of each subtest, followed by success at the beginning of the next. Although the assessor may mollify the effects of this aspect of IQ scales with certain procedures (see Chapter 11), it is important to note how the achievement-oriented child (or the achievement-resistant child) reacts to this factor. The child's reactions both to the assumption of achievement orientation and to the success-fail operation are clues to the interaction between the cognitive and conative aspects of his ego functioning.

3. The original standardizations of the major IQ scales were, in most instances, quite thorough. However, as was mentioned previously, there have been many rapid social, cultural, and educational changes in American society since these tests were constructed, and they may have seriously altered the norms. Most of the standardization samples did not include Negros or other minority groups. The oldest of these scales, the Stanford-Binet, is the only one that has been statistically revised at approximately 20-year periods, the most recent revision having been carried out in the 1950's.*

Most of the other major techniques used in assessment are at least 15 years old, and some over 30 years; Wechsler Scale for Children (Wechsler, 1949), Columbia Mental Maturity Scale (Burgemeister, et al, 1954), Leiter International Scales (Leiter, 1948), Arthur Point Scales (Arthur, 1947), Cattell Infant Scales (Cattell, 1940), Merrill-Palmer Pre-School Scales (Stutzman, 1931), and the Goodenough Draw-A-Man (Goodenough, 1926). As indicated by Palmer's study (1964) of the Shipley-Hartford Scales for adolescents, it is quite possible that the mental age and

IQ norms for these scales have changed considerably. Thus, inferences from the IQ have to be limited still further to read: This IQ represents the rate of development of intelligence of this child at this age, compared to other children of the same age as of a decade or even 30 years ago!

The size and range of behavior sampled by IQ tests varies widely from test to test. Most contain a great number of items in order to encompass the wide range of abilities called for within the age range for which the scale is intended. However, the number of items actually administered to the individual child is comparatively small! The WISC, with ten to 12 subtests, may present the adolescent with as many as 100 separate problems, but this number is likely to drop to about 50 or less for the average six to eight year old. On the Binet, the average child who passes most items on the mental age scale a year less than his chronological age, and fails all two years past his age level, will have been presented with 48 items (some of which have several subitems). Both the Binet and Wechsler tests have a fairly varied content, sampling different kinds of intellectual behavior and thought processes. However, the Binet remains largely verbal, with very few nonverbal items in the older age scales. Yet, the Binet has the distinct advantage in that it was designed specifically for children, and its items are addressed to children, attract their interest, and hold their attention. The Wechsler Scale for Children, on the other hand, appears to be essentially a revision of one of the adult forms (very comparable to the Army Wechsler used in the military during World War II), scaled down to children and lacking in children's items. The Grace Arthur Performance Scales, originally constructed for assessment of deaf and non-English speaking children, contains only nonverbal items and, except for the Healy Picture Completion (the most old-fashioned of the subtests), appears to be a bit more "culture-free" than either the Wechsler or the Binet — both of which are obviously directed at middle class American children. The Merrill-Palmer, scaled for infants two to six, has the distinct advantage of considerable flexibility in the choice of subtests, so that a subtest inappropriate to the child at hand may be omitted or tests rejected by the child do not count against him (below a basal point). However, the reliability of this scale when so foreshortened is unknown. The other major

---

* Unfortunately, there seems to have been little attempt to revise the content of the Binet. It still contains objects seldom seen by children today, such as a thimble, a man sawing wood on a sawhorse, and a steam locomotive, plus other vestiges of the 1917 original. The Arthur Point Scale with its pictures of ladies in long dresses and high-button shoes, children in knickers, etc., is even more antiquated.

infant scales, the Cattell and Gesell, sample chiefly those functions demonstrated below age two, that is, alertness, attentiveness, motor coordination, imitativeness, visual discrimination, etc. The assessor employing these infant scales should examine carefully the reliability of the individual mental ages, for these vary considerably. For example, the reliability of the Cattell at six months is fairly respectable, but falls greatly at nine months. However, both behavior and growth have been clinically observed to be quite variable at the nine-month level.

Some IQ scales sample only one intellectual activity. These scales, such as the Columbia Mental Maturity or the Peabody Picture Vocabulary (1965), were designed chiefly as tests for specific handicaps, such as cerebral palsy or other speech and motor difficulties. The assessor using these instruments must remember that he is tapping only the single intellectual function. The Leiter International, also a nonverbal scale, employs matching, although it is a bit more complex than the Columbia. The Goodenough Draw-A-Man Scale, which scores the drawing of a man for detail and complexity, may seem to tap chiefly visual motor coordination but it probably involves more complex functions for it is highly correlated with social adjustment as well (Ochs, 1950). IQ's calculated from the Goodenough correlate very respectably with Binet IQ's and even higher with Wechsler Performance Scales (Estes, et al, 1961). It has the distinct advantages of being attractive to children, easily administered and scored, and quite reliable. Also, the same drawing can be used as a "projective" test — even though the instructions differ.*

The above discussion concerning individually administered intelligence tests also applies in general to the so-called group-administered "paper and pencil" intelligence tests, such as the The Lorge-Thorndike, The Thurstone PMA, Iowa, Stanford, California Mental Maturity, Otis, Detroit, and others. These tests are, of course, much more commonly used in the public schools or similar settings where large groups of school age children are assessed and where individual assessment of each child is not possible. Most of these tests, designed chiefly to predict academic success, are almost entirely verbal and heavily dependent on education. The chief exceptions are the Henmon-Nelson (1957–1958) and the Raven Matrices (1956). The latter also is used in individual assessment as a test of perception but has only British norms — stated in percentiles rather than the American IQ. The chief disadvantages of any group-administered test is that the attitudinal set of the child is difficult to estimate. If he succeeds, one may guess that his motivation was fair, that he was striving to achieve; if he fails, there is little way of knowing whether he has an intellectual defect, poor motivation, or simply has not followed directions. Although many of these tests correlate fairly highly with the Binet or Wechsler scales, there is a tendency for the scores on these group tests to overestimate the extremes, that is, children with very low scores on group intelligence scales seem often to obtain slightly higher IQ's on the Binet or Wechsler and, vice versa, those with very superior group test scores, when tested individuals, frequently fall back toward the mean as much as ten to 15 IQ points. Observation of the high-achieving child during the individual test often suggests that he has somewhat more tension in the one-to-one testing relationship than children of less endowment, and is especially discomforted by nonverbal visual-motor tasks (even though his success on these latter tasks is also superior). In contrast, the child with an intellectual handicap or of mediocre talents, especially the immature and dependent child, may be poorly motivated on group tests but, given some encouragement and individual support, may perform much better on individually administered tests, especially on items not involving educational achievement. All in all, these group tests are fairly effective screening devices for measuring the child's intellectual efficiency in public performance, while the individually administered test, more varied in content, is a measure of how the child functions in the one-to-one setting, a measurement that may be more helpful when dealing with questions of extremes of talent.

3. Although metric analysis is built into IQ tests, that is, they have scores standardized on large samples of normal children, analysis is not necessarily limited to the total IQ score or even to scores on the subtests. However, this

---

* It should be noted, however, that if the usual instructions for the "Draw-A-Person" are used, rather than the specific instructions of the Goodenough, the Goodenough norms cannot be applied. The child must be instructed to draw "a whole man and the best man you can draw. Make *all* of him."

metric analysis is usually basic to any other kind of analysis of these techniques. In supervising advanced clinical students, this writer has observed a tendency for the student, once he has become familiar with other, more complex analysis of his materials, to become careless about the mere routine procedures, for example, in giving instructions or asking the test questions or even in scoring and adding up the scores!

Analysis of profiles of subtest scores or patterns of achievement on various kinds of intellectual tasks within the total scale is commonly the next step. Comparison is made between the success on one type of task with failure on another. Mental age scales like the Binet or Merrill-Palmer may be so analyzed as well as the point scales such as the Wechsler or the Grace Arthur. One may compare achievement on, for example, the verbal with nonverbal tasks, or the tests of attention span and attention to detail with tasks involving more complex judgment and logic, or tasks involving learned skills and information with tasks involving comprehension. Such analyses are most helpful in going beyond the assessment of overall level of intellectual development to a more detailed assessment of the child's cognitive functioning and its relationships with other of his ego functions. Thus, the seven-year-old child who on the Binet can repeat digits, copy a diamond, answer questions about a story, but has less than a six year old's vocabulary, cannot make the simplest verbal similarities and is not able to fathom "what's foolish about this picture?" may be doing well or even above average work on tasks involving routine learning of one-to-one concrete associations, but the development of his independent judgment and analysis of a situation may be quite retarded. Another child who can verbalize well about the social reasons for certain behaviors on the WISC "Comprehension" subtest but becomes flustered and fumbles his way incomprehensibly through the social items of the "Picture Arrangement" may be said to understand social situations in the abstract, but once he is involved in them be unable to decide what they mean or how to act. Such analysis of the child's cognitive functioning leads to inferential hypotheses about his other functions, about his conative, social, or affective maturity. From patterns such as the above on the Binet, one might want to test out the hypothesis, for example, that the first child

is too dependent emotionally on others to begin to make independent intellectual judgments, or possibly that severe emotional or physiological handicaps deter more complex thought process. Further evidence bearing on such hypotheses can, of course, be gathered from the quality of his responses to these tests themselves, from the types of failures the child is making, as well as from other techniques designed more to test social and emotional adjustment.

Caution should be observed, however, in analyzing such profiles or patterns of subtests from IQ scales. As has been shown in studies of profile analysis of the adult Wechsler scales (Derner, et al, 1950), the variability of the means of the Wechsler subscales is fairly large and differs considerably from subscale to subscale. Regarding the Wechsler I and the WAIS, Wechsler himself advises that no conclusions be drawn about subscale differences unless the difference is at least four or more standard scores. Even if one observes the precautions that Wechsler and others advise concerning the use of profile analysis on the WAIS, the WISC requires further caution in transposing the analytic method used on an adult scale to analysis of a childrens' test. Not only is it likely that the subtest variabilities are not the same (and the subtest variabilities of the WISC have not been examined as closely as those of the WAIS), but it would be unreasonable to expect that the profiles obtained would have quite the same significance. The patterns of cognitive behavior in the still developing ego of the child may look like those found in more mature adults but, as was discussed on Chapter 4, the patterns in the child's thinking are still more subject to change, and the aim of assessment is the study of those possible changes.

In addition to analyzing the scores on the subtests of various kinds of intelligence tests, it is also well to examine the sequence of successes and failures across tests. Thus, on the Binet, one commonly looks at the range of success, from basal age to total failure. One may more closely examine how failure follows upon success or vice versa. Does the child, having succeeded, become overconfident, or having failed an item, does he usually seem to try harder on the next? Does he become increasingly confident or increasingly discouraged? It should be noted that the subtests within any mental age group are not necessarily arranged in any order of difficulty, but are supposed to be about equal. As Jastak (1950) has shown, the items within the sub-scales of the adult Wechsler I are far from being arranged in an exact order of difficulty and inspection of the WISC suggests that the order of difficulty on this children's scale is also only approximate.*

Erratic patterns of success and failure across subtests, unrelated to content, may suggest lapses in attention or even conscious maling-ering. The bright child may be bored by simple questions, give careless or even non-sense replies, only to become challenged by more difficult items where he can show off his intellectual talents. Such a response pattern may be important to note in making inferences from the test to his behavior in other situa-tions. Perhaps his behavior in the classroom is also marked by boredom, disdain for simple tasks, and utilization of his talents to obtain social approval. One might ask further if such behavior is fostered consciously or uncon-sciously by his parents; might they reward occasional demonstrations of intellectual prowess but demand little in the way of con-tinued intellectual labor?

Thematic analysis of these structured tests of intelligence is also valuable, whether or not the associative content of the child's re-sponses are considered. The themes of intel-lectual processes may be considered as well as ideational themes. In the next step beyond profile or pattern analysis, one examines not only whether the child reasons well but how he reasons. Thus, one might examine items from various subtests, noting when the child attempts analytic judgments or feats of con-centration and how he goes about it. Does he first usually attempt a wholistic approach, then break the task down into details, or does he take it detail by detail, forming intermediate associations? For example, on the Object As-sembly of the WISC, does he see the auto before he assemblies it or only afterwards does he exclaim, "Oh, it's an auto!" Does he, on Vocabulary, give first a generalization and then examples, or does he give several con-crete associations and end up with a general-ization? Is his problem solving usually trial and error or does he sit back and think first? Is his thinking personalized? Does he refer

the question to himself, saying "I'd do thus and thus" or "I've never seen that!" Does he associate the task with some personal experi-ence or object? Does he rush headlong into tasks, scarcely waiting for instructions or, at the other extreme, does he ask for help or sit passively as if waiting for further cues?

Along with these thought processes and behavioral themes in the quality of the child's responses to IQ tests, one also finds many clues in the associative content. Although primarily designed to sample manifest prob-lem-solving achievement, these tests often also provide samples of associative behavior, in the phrasing and choice of wording the child uses on the verbal tests or in the idiosyncratic behavior accompanying his non-verbal responses. Often these associative clues appear when the child is struggling with a problem he cannot quite fathom; sometimes his associations seem to block his problem solving, and he hides behind a "Don't know." On the other hand, the bright child may "free associate" in an imaginative, creative fashion, guessing partially or even completely success-fully. Often the emotionally disturbed child carries his anxieties, fear, and obsessions with him into his problem solving. Many of the items on both the Binet and WISC are con-cerned with social impulse control, for exam-ple, "What is the thing to do if a child much smaller than yourself hits you?" (WISC) or "What should you do if someone hits you without meaning to" (Binet)? Other items contain stimuli that frequently arouse asso-ciation of violence or hostility. For example, on the Binet, pictures of a gun on the Picture Vocabulary, or the "What's foolish?" ques-tions such as "lost both his hands in an acci-dent"; or "the body of Christopher Columbus when he was only twelve years old"; or, on the WISC, "Why are women and children saved first in a shipwreck?" or vocabulary items calling for definitions of "knife," "nitro-glycerine," "affliction," "hari-kari." Even seemingly neutral stimuli, such as the incom-plete man or the mutilated pictures on the Binet, may evoke threatening associations to some children.

As to the kinds of inferences to be drawn from the behavior sampled by these tech-niques, the assessor's attention is usually focused initially on the direct extrapolation from their manifest behavior to other prob-lem-solving situations. Some of the data may also contribute to predictions about his be-

---

* In fact, there appears to be large jumps in the degree of difficulty on items on the WISC, from very easy to rather difficult items with few of intermediate difficulty, particularly on Compre-hension and Vocabulary.

havior in less structured situations, such as his ability to behave rationally and test reality in social and interpersonal relationships or in anxiety-producing situations. However, the clues gained from these structured samples need to be checked out through other techniques which provide more option for independent judgment and more clues about emotional stress reactions. Rather than direct prediction, inductive inferences from the patterns and themes of the child's responses can be made, leading to hypotheses to be cross-validated on other techniques. In turn, hypotheses from other techniques, or from the referral question, may be checked out from the data gathered from these techniques.

To cite a common example, the child's medical history or other evidence may suggest a neurological handicap, and it is possible to examine the data from an IQ test to see how much behavioral evidence there may be for such a hypothesis. In such instances, of course, one can only disprove the null hypothesis. How this null hypothesis is stated determines the kind of conclusion that is logically permissible. If, for example, the statement is "There is no evidence to support this hypothesis," then the statement can be easily disproven by any scrap of evidence. However, the only conclusion that can logically be drawn should be stated as: The data are not inconsistent with or do not rule out the hypothesis. Somewhat stronger is the statement: "There is insufficient evidence to support the hypothesis that . . ." which can be disproven only by demonstration that there is more than sufficient evidence.

C. STRUCTURED TESTS OF EDUCATIONAL ACHIEVEMENT

Techniques designed to assess the child's level of educational achievement are a highly specialized topic, more relevant to educational psychology than to clinical assessment, and a full discussion of these tests is beyond the purview of this book. They are much more commonly administered and interpreted by the school psychologist and are not a usual part of the clinic test battery. However, school achievement is one of the most common referral questions and, in order to assess the ego dysfunctions or other factors that might underlie such school failure, the clinician frequently needs to begin with an assess-

ment of the school achievement per se. Where records of school testing are available, the clinician should be familiar enough with these techniques to understand the scoring, the patterns of scores, and the content of tests, so that he can relate these results with the results of his own assessment of the child. Since school achievement records are not always readily available, the clinician should also be prepared to administer this type of technique himself.

Much of what has been said about the rationale, the factors of set and achievement drive, and the effects of culture regarding intelligence tests also applys to these tests of educational achievement. In addition, in drawing inferences from the child's performance on these tests, the clinician must take into account the child's attitudes toward school achievement. For example, the rebellious adolescent who, to use the old phrase, "Doesn't care if school keeps," may resentfully dawdle his way through such a test even though he has learned the necessary skills.

Like the IQ tests, these techniques usually consist of subtests tapping various academic skills, such as reading comprehension, reading speed, arithmetic skills and reasoning, spelling, grammar, logical analysis, etc. Analysis of the patterns of these subscores often yields further specific information about the child's abilities and underlying attitudes, giving clues to be checked out in further individual assessment. Difficulty in learning to read is a most common reason for referral. Learning to read is, of course, basic to the acquisition of all other academic skills. Difficulties in learning to read are so often associated with the total functioning and maturation of the child that failure in this skill often becomes a question for clinical as well as educational assessment. In such instances, other techniques are usually needed in addition to the reading achievement test, such as tests of perception, assessment of motivation, and of affective controls.

D. STRUCTURED TESTS SAMPLING VISUAL-MOTOR AND PERCEPTUAL FUNCTIONING

1. General considerations

As discussed in Chapter 4, the child's ability to perceptually discriminate, recognize, organize, and reproduce the world about him is a core function of his ego. This ability is basic to his intellectual development and, in the long run, to all other ego functions as well. A large part of the items on infant IQ tests consists of direct sampling of the development of this perceptual acuity and recognition. For example, on the Cattell, there are items such as visual following of a swinging ring held over the supine infant, self-recognition in the mirror, exploration of the bell, copying a line, etc. and, on the Binet, copying a circle, a square, a diamond, the three-figure form board, and copying a string of beads. On the WISC, perceptual functioning is an integral part of most of the nonverbal subtests: perception of detail on the Picture Completion, perceptual organization and reproduction on Block Design, Object Assembly, and Digit Symbol. The Porteus Mazes, Kohs Blocks and Sequin Form Board on the Arthur Scales also sample this ego function.

The rationale behind these samples of visual-motor, perceptual tasks calls for a bit more analogy than the IQ scales. Even the tasks on the IQ scales are not altogether similar to the intellectual tasks toward which the psychologist is extrapolating in his predictions. Although when the child is asked to copy a figure, follow a maze, or match blocks to a form board, it is not his drawing ability or form board skills per se that are being tested but, instead, the perceptual functions that are posited to underlie the tasks. It is hoped that the visual-motor behavior required in copying a geometric figure is analogous to or contains the same elements of perceptual behavior as are involved in reading, driving, sorting out objects or even people, and possibly social events and interactions. Actually this rationale is stated in a negative fashion, that is, if the child makes errors in this test sample of every simple perceptual tasks, he is likely to make similar errors in much more complex perceptual behavior. Since the techniques labeled "perceptual-motor" tasks are often referred to as tests of organic brain damage, it may be well to note that in this rationale, no mention is made of the etiology of possible errors made by the child in performing these tasks. It should be emphasized that although neurophysiological handicaps may be one common deterrent to perceptual motor functioning, they are far from the only cause of such dysfunctioning,

especially in children.

The sample of behavior from these techniques is very small. The Bender contains only eight drawings, the Graham-Kendall 15; the Porteus has 11 mazes; the Seguin contains ten blocks (but is usually administered three times); the Kohs block consists of the reproduction of from eight to ten designs, depending on the form used. The assessor should therefore never depend on any one of these techniques as the sole basis for assessing perceptual functioning but should use more than one separate test and in conjunction with the items on the IQ scales and with the Rorschach.

Metric analysis via standardized scores is possible for all of these tests. Unfortunately, the standardization of the Porteus, Kohs Blocks, Seguin, and other form boards is so out of date as to be lost in antiquity. When using them, therefore, the assessor should err on the side of caution, especially since these original norms were stated in terms of intellectual rather than perceptual growth. Thus, the small errors that count against the child in estimates of intellectual development may not necessarily mean that he has any perceptual motor defect; on the other hand, gross failures on these techniques may be evidence of such defects, if consistent with other evidence.

2. *The Bender-Gestalt and the Graham-Kendall Memory for Designs Tests*

As regards the Bender-Gestalt, although several major attempts have been made to construct scoring methods, none has achieved popular acceptance. The simple scanning or inspection, as introduced by Loretta Bender (1938) and promulgated further by Hutt (1960), remained for many years the chief method of analyzing these figure drawings. However, the norms given by these authorities were far too gross for application by most clinicians and often resulted in unreliable judgments. Koppitz's (1963) normative studies on children ages five to ten provide more precise standards. Furthermore, Koppitz presents studies relating her scores on the Bender to intellectual development and school achievement. Although intellectual and perceptual functioning are so closely related during these ages, Koppitz does not provide a method whereby the perceptual functioning might be distinguished from the intellectual. On the other hand, the Graham-Kendall

Memory for Designs (1948), which has a much simpler scoring system, can be corrected for both age and IQ. However, since the administration of this test involves immediate memory, it is more complex than the simple copying task of the Bender, and it is difficult to determine whether a failure is a result of the child's misperception of the form or a lack of concentration.

Using several such techniques, one may assess the child's performance on a slightly larger scale, with a greater variety of stimuli, and come up with informal patterns. For example, a child who makes no gross errors on the Graham-Kendall and who matches the Seguin blocks to the board without error and within the time limit norms, but who cannot even begin to reproduce the Kohs block designs, would appear to have little difficulty in accurately perceiving simple form but considerable difficulty in the analysis and reconstruction of more complex stimuli. Qualitative inspection of the way the child goes about copying the Bender or Graham-Kendall (1948) figures, placing blocks in form boards, or reproducing the Kohs designs often provides more specific cues about the child's perceptual functioning than the overall scores. For example, one may observe how important the accuracy of perception is to the child. Does he become preoccupied with detail, forgetting the overall Gestalt, or is he content with a rough sketch, ignoring the details? Does he try to patch up his errors with elaborations or to add to the figure some extraneous "inner" perception of his own? Does he have to shift the materials, the design, the paper, and the blocks around for some different perspective?

Although none of these techniques gives any rules about establishing with the child which is top or bottom of a page, this is a very important precaution. If no top or bottom is established, rotations of the Bender Figures (considered the hallmark of brain damage by the inventor of this technique) are, in this writer's experience, quite common among normal junior high school students! However, if the child is asked to "write your name at the top of the page" before beginning to draw, such rotations seldom occur. Nor are there precise instructions about whether the child is to be allowed to turn the page or the drawing, as many children do. In this writer's experience, children frequently turn their paper and their bodies at right angles to the present figure, thus drawing all figures at a 90° angle to the figure although in line with the top of their drawing paper. Other children have to turn their drawing paper around in order to accomplish certain angles. Probably none of their rotations are significant in the sense of those described by Bender (1938) or by Hutt (1960), but they may well be significant to the perceptual motor functioning of the child being observed.

As to the reliability and validity of these techniques, one is rightly disturbed and discouraged upon reading such reports as Goldberg (1965) who found that expert clinicians could not predict brain damage from the Bender above a base rate, or any better than most students or even nonprofessional secretarial assistants! Tamkin (1965) also found the Bender to be nondiscriminating with regard to functional disorders in adults. On the other hand, this technique does seem to have some promise, as was originally intended, in discriminating levels of perceptual motor development in children. Koppitz cross-validated her developmental norms quite successfully and Byrd (1965), in a study of Bender differences between normal and emotionally disturbed and delinquent children, found notable differences, but also remarks, "Maturational effects on reproduction of designs are noted up to age sixteen." The brain damage cutting scores of the Graham-Kendall have been cross-validated (1948), although unfortunately without indication of the base rate of "organicity" of the sample used in this study.

In summary, in using these techniques, the assessor should observe the following precautions: (1) The restricted sampling of each of these techniques requires that more than one be used in order to obtain a wide enough sampling of the child's behavior. The use of several also permits an informal analysis of patterns of scores. (2) Results should be analyzed on the basis of established age norms (or age should be taken into account). (3) The inadequacy of some of these norms and the fact that reliability of the child's performance on most of these techniques is not established require that the assessor err on the side of caution and take as significant only gross deviations from the norm. (4) The lack of clear-cut instructions on some of these techniques requires that the assessor adapt and take into account uniform procedures of his own, and observe and record the operations of the child in carrying out the task. (5) The assessor should not assume that brain damage is the only possible etiology of a child's failures on these techniques nor attempt to predict brain damage from these techniques alone (see chapter 12 for further discussion of this point).

E. UNSTRUCTURED TECHNIQUES SAMPLING PERCEPTUAL BEHAVIOR: THE RORSCHACH TECHNIQUE

Variations in perceptual behavior and their implications for the overall functioning of the ego were the central concern of Herman Rorschach as he presented his theory and findings in his original monograph (1921). Labeled a projective technique in this country, the basic perceptual aspects of the Rorschach have often been underplayed or even grossly ignored. However, Symonds (1949) has forcefully argued that the Rorschach is not truly a projective technique in the same sense as the TAT. In this writer's opinion, also, the sampling of associative behavior on the Rorschach is limited especially in its use with children. The degree to which the behavior sampled on the Rorschach may be called "manifest" is admittedly debatable. As will be seen, the rationale of the Rorschach depends entirely on analogy, and it could be argued that rather than demonstrating perceptual functioning directly, the child projects his modes of perceptual selection onto the inkblot. The chief reason for including the Rorschach as a sampling of manifest behavior is to emphasize its value in assessing perceptual functioning.

Because of the confusing plethora of literature on the Rorschach, much of which fails to deal with Rorschach's original hypotheses, it may be well to restate these basic assumptions as succinctly as possible. In essence, Rorschach posited that: (1) In making perceptual (visual) judgments, people utilize not only the outline or form but other stimuli as well, that is, the color of the stimuli, both chromatic and achromatic; the visual recognition of texture; other aspects of shading or hue, such

as chiascuro; and cues in the stimuli suggesting possible movement. Rorschach was also concerned with how much of the stimuli the person utilizes, (his "location" scores), and how he organizes his percept. (2) Each of these determinants of visual perception has its analogous counterparts (Rorschach is translated as saying "equivalents") in the way people perceive — or, to use Rorschach's term, "experience" — other stimuli, such as social and affective stress. Thus, Rorschach hypothesized that in projecting movement onto an inanimate inkblot, the individual puts some of his own kinesthetic experience into the situation and, analogously, might perceive other situations on the basis of his own prior experiences, sets, attitudes, values, etc. Conversely, since the color of the blot is very much a part of the stimuli, when it determines a person's response, his judgment in other situations would not be a projection but would be "colored" by environmental stress, that is, by the person's interactions with the environment. By similar analogous reasoning, responses determined by texture are associated with sensitivity to environmental nuances, inkblot perspective to taking perspective viewpoint in other situations, and chiascuro to the "clouded sensorium."

In his monograph, Rorschach repeatedly distinguished between *perception* and *response,* but this distinction is often forgotten in the clinical use of this technique. Rorschach made it clear that what he believed he was sampling was how people *perceive,* but not necessarily how they behave or, in his terms, how one *experiences* (Erlebnis) not how one *lives* (Erlebens). Two people may perceive in quite the same manner, but their responses may be quite different or on the other hand, two people may react or behave in the same way but on entirely different perceptual bases. Thus, reasoned Rorschach, it is necessary in studying perception to divorce the perception from the response and ask, as one does in the Rorschach inquiry: How did the person see it and what determined the perception?

Of course, Rorschach did hope to be able to predict from known patterns of perceptual selection to at least broad patterns of social and emotional behavior, such as psychopathological states. Currently, many clinicians continue to try to presage the behavior of the child, to decide how the child is going to act or react to events or stresses by reading the child's inkblot responses. They do not seem discouraged by the mounting research evidence to the effect that prediction from perceptual behavior to other kinds of behavior is a risky plunge into the unknown. Unfortunately, there is only a beginning number of studies that attempt to formulate some of the relationships between perception and behavior, that is, to what degree and in what way one's perception of a situation determines how one will react. Even though most psychologists hold this possibility as self-evident, until the basic details are so determined, users of the Rorschach are on much safer ground if they limit themselves to *explaining* overt behavior rather than attempting blindly to *predict* it. Given this rationale, one may say that this child's delinquent behavior or his schizophrenic behavior is associated with (or to stretch the logic a bit further — is derived from) such and such patterns of perceptual behavior. In some instances, research studies support a statement to the effect that these perceptual patterns are frequently present in persons diagnosed as schizophrenic or who are becoming delinquent, but here also the psychologist must be logically cautious.

When, as too often happens, clinical and research studies using the Rorschach Technique falter, one of the most frequent errors is that despite the fact that precise directions are given in most major texts for administration and scoring of the Rorschach, some clinicians seem to ignore these standard operations — or even worse, to be ignorant of them. Often clinicians who are properly meticulous in reciting the exact instructions or questions on the Binet or Wechsler and who certainly would not attempt to interpret other techniques without scoring them, strangely enough seem to regard the Rorschach as not needing any precision either in instructions or analysis. However, the Rorschach is an unstructured technique only in the respect that the stimuli are purposefully vague enough to allow a variety of responses. The situation needs to be structured for the child, and there is a definite structure for the assessor in conducting a Rorschach examination and in analyzing it.

The set or instructions given the child are quite crucial, for how the child understands the task often determines the nature of his responses. For example, if one merely says "Tell me what this might be" or "What does this look like," the child may struggle to find some acceptable "right" answer even if he has been told "there are no right or wrong answers." If he is not also told, as recommended by Klopfer and Kelly (1942) (page 32), "What *you* see, what it might be for *you*, what it makes *you* think of," he may suppress his idio-syncratic "engrams" and voice only some "popular" response. In using the Rorschach with children, this author recommends the following variant on Klopfer's directions:

"Here are some cards with splotches of ink on them. I want you to look at them carefully and tell me what *you* see in the ink. What kinds of things (emphasizing the plural) can you make out of it? What kinds of things does it suggest to you or even just make you think of? Everyone sees different things on each of these. There are no right or wrong answers. I just want to know your ideas."

Often with children, it is necessary to repeat these instructions on the second or even third card, especially if it is apparent that the child does not fully understand. For younger children it is helpful to make up a sample blot with the child before introducing the first Rorschach card.

The key operation in Rorschach administration is, of course, the "inquiry," for it is in this operation that the essential perceptual question is posed: "What about the inkblot helped you to see . . . ." Again, clinical carelessness in conducting a thorough inquiry is all too common, especially among clinicians who overemphasize the associative-projective aspects in the content of the responses. For if one is only interested in the contentual aspects, then an inquiry only serves to gain further associative elaborations. Conducting an inquiry with children entails some special procedures that are not usually required for adults. With children under age eight or very hyperactive or impatient children, it is most effective to ask about the perceptual determinants immediately after the response is given, before presenting the subsequent blot. The younger or impatient child may reject further consideration of their responses after the administration of the ten cards, considering the test to be over. Or, they tend to deny or completely revise their impressions. Sometimes such a simultaneous inquiry does run the danger of suggesting or promoting the use of the determinants on further responses, but in this writer's experience, this is not a serious impediment. Indeed, the chief problem in conducting a Rorschach inquiry with children is getting them to specify the determinant of their response at all. Even adolescents, to say nothing of younger children, do not always comprehend the usual inquiry questions addressed to adults. Thus, if the child looks puzzled or repeats himself when asked, "What about the inkblot suggests that to you?" the question may be rephrased or the child may be asked, "Well, tell me more about it." This latter question quite often invokes descriptive material about the concept which, in the child's words, contains the determinant. For example, children may use terms such as "icky," "weird-o," or "gooey." However, such terms may have to be explored just a bit further, as the child may be referring to the textural aspects of the test, but he also may be intimating that the concept has some chiascuro aspect for him — or even that it is moving. For example, to Card IV, a six-year-old girl said it was an "icky bear or monster!" After she outlined the form, she was asked, "What's icky about it?" "The way he might grab you. So black and all," she replied. Many children cannot directly verbalize that the textural aspects of the blot determine their response; however, texture may be scored when the child gives a response with quite possible textural aspects and indicates by rubbing the card or pointing to the shading or uses some childhood term as "icky." Rorschach inquiry with preschool children has to be much more concrete and precise. Here one is usually interested in form accuracy, as other determinants are rare and usually appear spontaneously, if at all. One has to be most careful not to suggest to the infant what he might see. Thus, if the child calls Card I "a doggie," he may very well be perceiving the usual canine face; but should one ask "Show me the parts of the doggie," the child might feel he has to make a complete dog even though he did not see it that way, and end up confusing the assessor with a confabulated response. In many situations adults get confabulated responses because of their unconscious imposition upon the child of their perceptual functioning. An inquiry such as "Tell me about the doggie *you* see" will better allow the child to describe such perceptual limits as he possesses. Given such permission, the preschooler normally is quite free in expressing his own ideas. However, as the child enters latency, where variations from reality are more threatening, he is less willing to take a chance, presenting *"la notion du hasard,"* as Loosli-Usteri has aptly labeled it (1931).

The reason for this detailed discussion of standardized administration and careful inquiry of the Rorschach is that the analysis of the child's responses, both metrically and qualitatively, depends on these operations. Since the method of scoring is so well described by Klopfer, et al (1956) and in other standard works, it would be presumptious to review it here. Suffice it to say that in scoring children's Rorschachs', although one may have to depend on children's language and phrasing, it is still necessary to stick closely and objectively to the evidence obtained in the inquiry. For example, most children over the age of four are quite capable of expressing and naming colors or specifying movements if these are part of their percept. Thus, just because the child calls Card VIII a "flower," one cannot presume he is using the color, even if he adds, "It's pretty." One must still inquire, "What makes it pretty?"

Metric analysis of children's Rorschach responses and of patterns of scores has been immensely improved by the advent of the two volumes of Ames, Ilg, and Metraux on children's (1952) and adolescent's Rorschach responses (1959). These volumes provide the age norms and variance, subdivided by sex, which are so necessary in judging the child's perceptual growth as measured by the Rorschach. By using these norms, it is possible to answer such questions as: Is the child utilizing the perceptual cues and organizations which might be expected of him at this age? Is he learning how to respond to the emotional cues and stresses in his environment without undue concern? Is he beginning to internalize his experiences and to form attitudes and concepts of his own upon which to judge further experiences? Are his impulses playing too large — or too little — a part in his judgments? Are his perceptions of the world more dominated by inner tension, clouded by anxiety, or denuded of emotion by repression more than one might expect of the child at this age? A carefully administered, scored, and analyzed Rorschach will often give the assessor many clues toward answering these and similar queries.

The question of the size of the sample of perceptual behavior obtained by the Rorschach Technique is seldom given much concern in the literature, except for passing remarks warning against the use of records with less than 15 to 20 responses. Although among adults, such brief records may be infrequent, many normal children give only one or two responses per card, rejections are far more frequent, and often the child cannot be encouraged to expand. While this small number of responses may actually mirror the limitations of their perceptual experiencing, that is, one and only one response is all they can make to most situations, analysis of the proportion of their responses among the various determinants in such limited records is per force curtailed. Thus, it is not much help to know that the average five year old produces .8 *Fm* responses per record, when one is faced with a record containing three rejections and seven responses, one of which is an *Fm*. This problem of how to evaluate the raw scores in the face of shifting *R* has always plagued Rorschach users; the usual solution has been to transpose them into proportions of the total *R*. Sometime, it is to be hoped, these proportions will be restated as standard scores. Increasing the number of cards used with children might also be advisable. Although an expanded set of inkblots has been developed by Holtzman and his colleagues (1961) for adults, norms on Holtzman's blots for children have not been reported. Sometimes when children do not seem to understand the possibility of giving more than one response per card, one can suggest a second turn through the cards requesting an alternative response per card. However, if this procedure is adopted, notice should be taken that the standard operations are being quite radically altered, especially if one is also using a simultaneous inquiry. Such a second set of alternative responses would then have to be interpreted as the percepts the child makes under pressure and suggestion.

Most of the reliability and validity studies on the Rorschach have dealt exclusively with adults, and the literature on children is relatively sparse. The interscorer reliability for adult records is above question (Ramzy and Pickard, 1949). Adults tend to give much the same kind of responses with comparable patterns of determinant scores when a Rorschach is readministered after brief periods during which there are no known personality changes (Hertz, 1934). Since the stimulus value of the Behn and other sets of inkblots varies so much from Rorschach's ten blots, there is really no comparable form for reliability comparison, nor does the usual split half of items seem applicable to this technique. The gradual unfolding of increasing perceptual complexity and differentiation over the childhood years makes it unreasonable to expect a consistency of a child's Rorschach pattern year after year — although it would seem doubtful that major changes would appear over a few months time, especially after year six. The norms provided by Ames, et al (1952) do reveal these developmental patterns and, in this sense, indicate reliability for the Rorschach with the children.

The fact that these norms are consistent with the general observations about perceptual and emotional behavior, as Ames, et al (op. cit.) have so well illustrated, also gives support to the general validity of this technique. Such clinical observation of the relationships between perceptual development and other aspects of development does not, of course, meet the more stringent demands of independent and uncontaminated validation studies. The great difficulty in conducting such studies lies in the fact that there is no independent criterion. So far, the Rorschach is the only instrument of its kind; therefore studies are needed in which other behavior can also be scored in the same manner as the Rorschach, that is, according to the perceptual determinants that the child seems to be using. However, whether perceptual behavior can be measured and scored from, for example, social interactions, remains to be explored. The construct validation of the Rorschach as used with adults has received increasing attention over the past decade, and there is now a considerable body of evidence to suggest that the theory which Rorschach posited in interpreting the inkblot responses is consistent with other kinds of behavioral observations (Meltzoff, Singer, and Korchin, 1953; Fonda, 1960; Palmer, 1955, 1956, 1957; Palmer and Lustgarten, 1962). Such studies on adult behavior do give the Rorschach user some greater confidence in applying the test to children—but the basic validation work remains to be done.

In summary, since perceptual development is so very basic to the development of all the other functions of the child's ego, the Rorschach technique, with all its limitations and unknowns, continues to occupy a central position in the assessment of children, for it is the only well-established measure of perceptual growth.

TECHNIQUES BASED
ON SUBJECTIVE REPORTS

Asking a person to report on his own behavior, thoughts, and feelings has long been a major technique in psychological assessment. Such subjective reports supply much of the information available concerning the person's attitudes toward his environment and himself. However, assessors are aware that clinical subjects are often very poor and inaccurate observers of their own environment and even less accurate in describing their own behavior. In addition, those who come as patients in a clinical setting often have considerable difficulty in expressing and objectively reporting their own emotional attitudes or evaluating the emotional attitudes of others. When they are attempting to deal with threatening and anxiety-producing data, they are quite apt, as Freud originally pointed out, to suppress or completely repress and forget about data which might make their plight more understandable. Children's subjective reports in particular often seem garbled, full of inaccuracies, and interlarded with wishful thinking. For these reasons, some clinicians regard children's self-reports as too unreliable to warrant consideration. Yet there may be some validity to the old saw that "out of the mouths of babes" come naive truths. Some children do seem much less inhibited in discussing their family affairs and even their own behavior and feelings than do more reserved and repressed adults. On the other hand, it is not uncommon to find children flatly denying facts about their behavior or avoiding any mention of their feelings or fantasies.

Rather than considering such reports as being either true or false, that is, as valid assessments of the actual behavior of the individual, most clinicians utilize these self-reports as sources of data about what the subject thinks of himself, his environment, and his behavior. Whether the subject's view is the same as another observer's is a different question. Indeed, a comparison of the subject's report and reports and observations of others forms yet another kind of datum.

This latter form of data consists usually of interviews and reports from others. While such reports may be considered in some way more objective, it is necessary to keep in mind that they too are essentially subjective. Such reports from others are merely another viewpoint of the child's behavior. Even official school reports or juvenile court documents do not necessarily reflect any more truth about the child than do the child's reports about himself. For example, an eleven year old, hospitalized on a psychiatric ward, seemingly a polite, well-behaved but depressed lad, had been labeled as "unmanageable" by by the Boy's Home where he had been living. As evidence, they cited how he "swung on the gates" after being told not to. In another instance, an immense, obese 14-year-old idiot was brought to the hospital for the retarded, shackled to two deputy sheriffs, and labeled a "sex maniac." Later, it turned out, he had wandered away from home and, not being toilet trained, had urinated publicly in the park! In other instances, of course, what parents and children dismiss as nothing at all turns out on school records or court findings to be serious behavior disturbances. Whatever the validity of these reports, it is important in assessing the child to have as full a picture as possible of how the child's parents, school, and other peers and authorities may see and regard him, for this strongly influences the social roles he may try to play or is allowed to play and impinges as well on his self-image.

In this section, three types of subjective reports are to be considered: (a) unstructured interviews with the child, (b) structured questionnaires used with the child, and (c) reports and observations of others about the child, both structured and unstructured.

A. UNSTRUCTURED INTERVIEWS WITH THE CHILD

The assumption or rationale for open-end interviewing of the child is that through direct, friendly, and encouraging questions, the child will describe *his* view of his environment and of his behavior, revealing his own attitudes and feelings. The validity of this assumption depends, of course, on how the interviews are conducted, as will be discussed in more detail in subsequent chapters on procedures. However, at least three interrelated factors affecting this rationale should be mentioned at this point: (1) the motivations of the assessor, (2) the motivations of the child, and (3) the interpersonal situation or relationship evolved between them.

Although the overall, long-run motivation of the clinician is to aid in the development and welfare of his client, the immediate aim during assessment is frankly *investigatory*. This does not at all mean, of course, that

the interview needs to be conducted in a cold, impersonal, or inquisitional manner. But it does mean that at this initial stage in a clinician's contacts with the child, the clinician has to ask questions and explore feelings and attitudes in a manner which he might not use if he were conducting psychotherapy. There is a cliche in clinical psychology that "therapy begins with the first contact." Probably this is true but, even so, an investigatory attitude on the part of the clinician sets the stage for therapy. Such an investigation is vital to the clinician for it provides the initial data upon which he can formulate his therapuetic hypotheses and goals. And the child, even though he may be unable or unwilling to respond to these questions during an assessment interview, becomes aware that, in the long run, therapy will be dealing with all of his feelings, even those about which he is most anxious. Many of the things the child mentions or the assessor asks about during the assessment interview often do not come up again for discussion until much later in therapy. This "working through" or relearning process of psychotherapy, however, is definitely *not* part of the assessment and should be avoided at this stage, even if the child seems to want to engage in it. Not only would such therapeutic exploration interfere with assessment, but the clinician does not at this point have enough data to know where he is going with therapy. On the other hand, if a thorough assessment is not conducted, including introductory investigatory interviews, future therapy may be seriously impeded or misguided.

For example, an 11-year-old boy volunteered during the initial interview that he slept very restlessly and had bad dreams. The assessor asked about the child's dreams and fears, which the child willingly discussed, and on the basis of this data plus other data from other techniques, hypothesized that the child's sleeplessness was related to his difficulties in controlling his anger. However, the assessor did not explore the child's sleep habits or conditions. Several months later the child revealed that he usually slept with his mother. Surprised, the therapist asked why he had not mentioned this before. "You never asked!" replied the boy. Although the question, "Do you sleep with your mother?" is far from a routine inquiry during assessment, simple questions about sleep habits, for example, "Who puts you to bed?" and "Do you have a bed or a room by yourself?" might well have brought out this important fact, and given a different emphasis to and more detail for the therapeutic hypotheses.

If, as is described in Part IV, the purposes and procedures of the assessment have been clarified with the child before beginning with any technique, the child will be at least somewhat aware of the assessor's aims. He should be informed that the assessor is interested in "what makes children happy — and what makes them unhappy, what they like and do not like, what is easy and what is difficult, etc." Children's reactions to such information in an assessment situation vary widely. Some are so bound up in their own anger and negativism or their own fears that they barely hear such an introduction and pay it little mind. Undoubtedly many children initially are at least mildly threatened with the realization that their hidden anxieties may be unmasked. However, most children usually recover from this initial frank expose of the assessor's intentions and, as rapport becomes more positive, the child actually begins to feel even more at ease in the face of a straightforward, open-faced approach. Nevertheless, the child's own preconceptions about the assessment in general, and about responding in interviews in particular, may not be assuaged even if the assessor explains his purposes. Those children who are experiencing considerable overt anxiety, who have complaints, "problems," or "unhappiness" may be quite eager to find a sympathetic listener. Other children, especially those who have learned through bitter experience to mistrust inquiring adults, may regard the interview as an intrusion on their privacy and "take the Fifth Amendment," refusing to testify against themselves. Some children persist in this defensiveness throughout the assessment, so that about all one learns is the intensity and extent of their defensiveness.

While the child may well be able to block the assessor by diversion or negativism or tears from getting direct statements, these attitudes and other interview behaviors constitute in themselves data about the child. Moreover, since the main aim is to gather data about feelings and attitudes rather than "facts" per se, this interchange between assessor and child, which takes place throughout the assessment but particularly during interviews, constitutes a major source of data. Indeed, this inter-relationship is a technique

in itself, which will be discussed further in a subsequent section of this chapter. Suffice it to say at this point that the interview provides the best vehicle through which to observe and explore this relationship.

As regards the operations of interviewing children, although this section has been labeled "unstructured," the term "open-ended" might be more advisable. Open-ended means that the interview can be adaptable to the responses of the child, and in fact, should follow through with what the child feels free to talk about. However, assessment interviews do need structure in the mind of the assessor, who must be able to gather his data and explore as many facets of the child's world with him as time allows. Thus, the assessor needs to have in mind the questions and areas to be explored, even though he may not necessarily follow any set outline nor phrase questions in a standardized form. Thus, an interviewer may begin with whatever the child mentions in response to the introductory statement of the purpose of the assessment, and explore from there. In any case, the interviewer probably will find it necessary from time to time to change the topic, again in contradistinction to a therapeutic interview, and say, "Now I'd like you to tell me a little about . . . . "

The chief reason for using such interviewing operations is, of course, to obtain as wide a sample as possible of the child's attitudes and feelings regarding many different situations and persons. Usually in one or two hours, a facile interviewer can cover the following general topic areas with the child.

1. The child's view of his complaints, symptoms, and stresses.

2. His view of his current environment; home, peers, school, and current functioning: sleeping, eating, digestion, and elimination habits, and with an adolescent, sexual interests, as well as his feelings about them.

3. His view of his development and his history, including his projections into the future.

Regarding the "complaints," many children are able to give some of their own reasons for coming to the psychologist's office. Their first responses to questions about complaints are frequently tentative and terse, but with encouraging exploration they can expand upon them. The assessor should not be content with a single statement, but should continue to explore for sources of psychologic discomfort other than the one mentioned initially. For example, many children begin by mentioning academic difficulties and dissension with siblings. "I hate school," a ten year old says, or "My sister bugs me. That's the only thing I'm ever unhappy about." However, as the interviewer explores these initial statements, it often turns out that the child has feelings of inadequacy regarding academic achievement, that his parents have high aspirations for him, or that there are conflicts with his parents over homework and spare-time activities which are part of an overall familial dissension. Sometimes a child may initially deny any complaints or stresses. "I dunno," an eight-year-old girl says, "I haven't any problems. I'm happy. My mother just brought me here." However, she was able to discuss some of the things about her behavior which worried her mother, even though she herself maintained that she was unconcerned about them. If the child fails to mention the complaint or difficulties mentioned in the referral, it is customary to ask the child directly about them, again with emphasis on an honest exchange with the child. Quite frequently this writer begins the assessment with a brief interview, saying, "Let me see (looking at the referral note), your pediatrician called me and asked me to see you because you have been having a lot of headaches." Or, "When your mother made this appointment for you to see me she seemed very worried over your school work." However, after exploring the referrant's complaints with the child, the child's own complaints are explored, for example, "Well, those are some of the things that bother your mother or teacher, but what are some of the things that bother *you,* that are important to you?"

Usually, discussion of these complaints leads easily into a description of the child's everyday life, his family and home, his school, and his recreation and other activities. The assessor asks such questions as "Who is in your family? Which ones live at your house? Does anyone else live there? Describe them to me. What do you like best about them? Least about them? . . . etc." Of course, the child may have mentioned these things in stating his complaint but it is often wise to have him repeat, since he may add to the feelings he hinted at earlier. He should be asked what he does with each member of

his family, that is, how he relates to them. He should be asked to describe the family living quarters, and his own corner of the home. To get at his activities, the child may be asked to describe in detail what happened the day before the interview, and how this day was different from most other days. If he describes a weekday, he might also be asked to describe a weekend day. Such a description helps to get at the awakening, the family relationships at the beginning of the day, the school routine, play activities, eating habits and relationships during meals, study habits and evening family relationships and activities, ending with questions about sleep habits. "Who decides when you go to bed? What do you think of before you fall asleep? What kind of dreams do you have? . . . . etc." If not already discussed, the child should be questioned about the routine of his physiological functioning, his appetite, digestion, and elimination habits. When he mentions his play, it is a good idea to inquire further about what he likes to do for fun, when he gets a chance to do what he likes, who he likes to do it with, how does he feel when he is restricted from what he likes to do. Or again: What are the things he has to do that he dislikes? Who makes him do them? Does he have any ways of getting out of such tasks? Etc. Such a discussion may lead easily into methods of punishment and control used by the parents or other adult authorities, and how the child regards such discipline.

A child's view of his own developmental history is often a fascinating and revealing set of data. His chronology is often vague and confused; his sense of time differences is out of kilter by adult standards; and his memory of events emphasizes childhood pleasures and sorrows rather than adult crises. However, it is these very distortions which gives us clues about his feelings, motivations, and behavior. A five year old's excitement and anxiety about the time the toilet bowl overflowed may reveal not only his feelings about self-controls but, depending on his associations of the moment, also give clues about events which are otherwise vague in his memory. In this case, it was the birth of his sister, as he explained, "Mommy wasn't there. She was in the hospital and there was nobody to fix it." When children are initially asked to tell about their lives, they often feign ignorance, but usually a question such as "What is the very first thing you can remember, from the time you were a teeny weeny baby?" sets off a trail of memories, which can gently be encouraged by the interviewer, although he should avoid trying too hard to make the child be exact, or calling attention to the child's apparent inconsistencies. On the other hand, children may be much more accurate regarding family attitudes toward him and among themselves than the fact-citing adult. In the above example, the child was telling something of which the adults may have been unaware, namely, that while his mother was hospitalized with childbirth, he felt insecure and unprotected and afraid that things might get out of control.

B. INTERVIEWS WITH PARENTS

Whereas in interviewing the child the clinician is interested in the child's attitudes, feelings, and associations, and does not pretend that he is getting at other kinds of facts with any validity, the rationale in interviewing parents as a source of data about children is not always as clear-cut. Traditionally, parents were interviewed because clinicians hoped that they would supply factual, objective data. As Wenar (1961) describes the "Ideal Research Mother," the clinician also may hope that "such a mother could, a) faithfully record events, feelings, and interpersonal relations as they happen; b) remember with perfect fidelity; and c) have the power of total recall upon request." Moreover, anyone seeking facts from parental reports would frequently be annoyed, if not surprised, to find several common biases. First, and most obvious, the parent has considerable personal investment, consciously and unconsciously, in the child as representing and reflecting his efforts. Although parents usually accept overtly and intellectually the assessor's investigatory role, they often attempt in many ways to fend off any investigation which they regard as reflecting on their adequacy as parents. In such circumstances, they may water down or even distort the facts, conveniently forgetting certain aspects of the development and rearing of their child or even omitting what others might regard as crucial. Even those parents who may cry *"mea culpa"* and describe what they regard as their failures often appear to do so because they hope that the assessor will forgive them, since they are demonstrating "insight."

Since the parents want help for the child, but do not want to admit to anything but helplessness on their own part, they are also apt to enlarge upon and heavily emphasize those circumstantial pressures on the child which are beyond their own control, especially outside of the home. A clinician should take warning when a parent begins, "Perhaps I haven't been the best parent in the world, but . . . . " and goes on to complain about the school, the neighborhood, the child's health and physique — "despite everything I've tried to do." Such statements are intended not only to defend against self-incrimination, but also to press the psychologist to do something about those features of the child's behavior for which the parent is avoiding responsibility. Furthermore, many parents exaggerate any undesirable behavior in the child which does not directly reflect upon themselves, and minimize anything the child does about which they feel overtly guilty. All this is not to say that parents are solely to "blame" for the child's behavior as other stress and circumstances outside the home often do play a major part in disturbing children's development. Rather, it is to emphasize that parents usually think in terms of "who's to blame," while assessors are trying to consider what kind of stresses are bearing on the child and how he is handling them. Thus, torn between trying not to appear inadequate and yet wanting desperately to obtain help, parents often present very conflicting and confusing pictures of their child and his adjustment.

Next, as Wenar (op. cit.) also points out, even parents of normal children change their attitudes toward their children over the years, which affects their memories of events and the emphasis on their viewpoint about the child. Now that the child is presenting a problem to them, they remember more vividly the difficulties they had with him earlier or the traumas he endured, and it is difficult to assess whether these earlier problems and circumstances actually led to the child's present condition or whether the parents are merely searching for something to blame.

Because of these and other biases in parental motivations during interviews, some clinicians are inclined to discount the use of such interviews as any source at all of facts and to regard them as another, entirely subjective, view. Yet, the parental reports do yield considerable data about their feelings and attitudes, including their own distortions as they have come to impose them on the child. Thus, one may see from these reports the kind of parental world that the child is facing. Such parental attitudes are reflected not only in their view of the facts, but even more in the defensive biases discussed above.

However, if the clinician decides to accept parental reports as another projective technique, he runs the serious risk of having no source whatever of facts. Some clinicians aver that facts per se are not really necessary at all, since the main interest is in feelings, attitudes, and perceptions, and that the assessor's aim is psychological facts — not historical events. However, this is a difficult position to maintain. Despite the importance of the attitudes of both the child and his parents to the understanding of the child's ego development, these purely psychological phenomena are associated with and, indeed, derived from nonsubjective facts, from objective events, experiences, and stress in the child's life. Knowledge of these data of reality is also essential to the assessment for, ultimately, in any form of treatment or rehabilitation, one aim is to assist the child and his parents to test and to assess more effectively and univocally these realities for themselves.

Fortunately, it is possible to use the same data to assess both kinds of facts. This can be accomplished by cross-checking the data from several different sources. In fact, such a cross-check is necessary in order to be able to identify the biases in the parent's and child's accounts. First, the parental and child reports can be checked against one another (and, if each parent is interviewed separately, a third source of data is available). Where all agree on a fact, the assessor has at least some measure of reliability, although the possibility of biases running throughout the family should be kept in mind. Where there are gross inconsistencies, a second step in analysis of the data is necessary, that is, to discover the kinds of biases present in each informant. Here one can refer to the other sources of data: the observations and tests on the child and tests administered to the parents in order to discover what kinds of defenses the parents are prone to utilize. Thus, the Rorschach responses of the child may help tell us how accurately, in how much

detail, and with what kind of distortions the child usually perceives a situation. Or the MMPI profile on the parents can outline the patterns of defenses with which the parents commonly approach situations. By thus cross-comparing the data, one can estimate, for example, that such and such is probably a fact since both the parents and the child report it, but it is likely that the child interprets it as such and such while the parents tend to underrate or over emphasize it in such and such a manner.

Several different kinds of data may be sampled through an interview with the parents: (a) A detailed description of the current behavior of the child is usually essential. This description should include the ways in which the parents have attempted to deal with the child's behavior, and their feelings and attitudes about it. (b) In most cases, the parents can supply considerably more detail about the child's past development, from conception to the present, than can the child. Such a history is vital to assessment, since it provides an estimate of both the rate of the development and some of the past stresses or continuous stresses that may affect the child's current status. (c) In order to understand fully the child's history, at least an outline of both of the parents' background and the marital and family history is essential. The role of this historical material in the present adjustment of the child has been outlined in the previous chapters. One technique for obtaining such material initially is the use of a biographical data sheet which the parents can be asked to fill in before being interviewed, as shown in Figure 4. Such a data sheet orients the parents to the interview and can be used as a basis for discussion.

Although metric methods of analyzing interviewing materials have been constructed (Dollard and Mowrer, 1947), they are seldom used clinically. However, when the child's developmental landmarks are compared with various reported norms, a metric analysis is being used. Thus, whether the child learned to sit up, walk, talk, was weaned from the bottle or breast, was toilet trained, began to speak single words and then sentences, etc., within the period that is common to most children can be established. These norms have been the subject of considerable research in child development and are spelled out in most guidebooks for parents, such as Spock (1946), with at least some hint of the variability,

The following information will be helpful in understanding the answers to the tests which you are taking. Please answer *all* items. Thank you.

1. _____, _____, _____
      Last Name   First Name   Initial

_____
    Street Address   City   Zone   Phone Number

2. *Sex* (circle one): Male   Female

3. *Today's Date:* _____ _____ _____
           month   day   year

4. *Your birthdate:* _____ _____ _____
           month   day   year

5. *Your age:* _____ _____
           years   month

6. *Racial Background* (circle appropriate number):
   '1' Caucasian   '4' Mexican
   '2' Negro   '5' Other (specify)
   '3' Mongolian   _____

7. *Your religion* (circle number):
   '0' None   '3' Jewish
   '1' Catholic   '4' Other (specify)
   '2' Protestant   _____

8. *Your current marital status* (circle appropriate number):
   '0' Single   '4' Separated
   '1' Married   '5' Other (specify)
   '2' Divorced   _____
   '3' Widowed

9. *Childhood family:* Please write in the space below the year of birth and, if not now living, the year of death of your parents, brothers, and sisters: for example, 1880–1942; or if alive, 1920–. If you don't know, please write in "unknown." If you have no brothers or sisters, please write in "none."

   Father:_____

   Mother:_____

   Brothers:_____

   _____

   Sisters:_____

   _____

10. *Marital history:* Please indicate the year of your marriage. If married more than once, write in the years when married and when the marriage ended and how it ended for each marriage. For example: "1948–1952, divorced." Please include your present marriage: for example, "1955–." If you have never married, please write in "unmarried."

   _____

   _____

   _____

11. *Children:* Please write in the first name, sex, and birth year of each of your children. If you have none, please write in "none."
               Name   Sex   Birth year

   _____

   _____

   _____

12. *Head of household:* Who is usually the *main* source of your financial support (circle appropriate number)?
   '1' Myself   '5' My wife
   '2' My father   '6' Someone else
   '3' My mother   (specify)_____
   '4' My husband

13. *Occupation:* Please write in the kind of work you most usually do to earn a living. Please use a "job title," indicating what you do (not merely where you work). If you are retired, what kind of work did you used to do? If you listed someone other than yourself as head of household in item 12, first put down what occupies *most* of your time, such as "housewife" or "student"; then in the spaces that follow, enter the occupation of the person you listed as head of household.
   Your occupation: _____

   Occupation, head of household: _____

14a. *Education:* Please circle the number which shows approximately how much schooling you have completed:
   '1' Post-graduate university studies
   '2' Graduate, college
   '3' Some college (not graduate), or other education beyond high school
   '4' Graduate, high school
   '5' 10th–11th grade
   '6' 7th–9th grade
   '7' Less than 7th grade
   '8' Other (specify) _____

14b. If in item 12 you indicated another person is the main source of your financial support, please circle the number which shows approximately how much education they completed.
   '0' I support myself
   '1' Postgraduate university studies
   '2' Graduate, college
   '3' Some college (not graduate), or other education beyond high school

Figure 4. BIOGRAPHICAL DATA SHEET

'4' Graduate, high school
'5' 10th–11th grade
'6' 7th–9th grade
'7' Less than 7th grade
'8' Other (specify) _____

15. What are the main things for which you seek psychiatric help?

_____

_____

_____

Relatives see at the Psychiatric
Clinic: *Name*   *Birth year*

_____

_____

FIGURE 4.—*Continued*

and of sex differences. However, the case history material becomes most valuable and meaningful when the clinician looks for patterns of behavior and events and long-range trends or themes. As suggested in Chapter 4, the assessor should pay particular attention to the crises or stress periods in the child's development to see how the child and his parents reacted, and then compare this reaction with the next crisis pattern. For example, the manner in which the child reacted to the birth of a sibling might be compared with the way he accepted being separated from the family when he began school. Patterns of family interactions and the roles the child plays with and for various members of the family need to be systematically analyzed. It is often helpful to construct a schematic chart. The following data extracted from a case history illustrate how much a schematic analysis might be drawn up.

CASE 12

Billy V., age eight, was brought to the clinic with the following complaints by his parents: He was doing poorly at school and was not learning to read — although IQ tests at school indicated above average intelligence. Teachers reported that he "is poorly motivated," "demands attention," and "is very immature." His mother complained that Billy "whines," "drags his feet" when demands are made on him, and "always seems to want something." Mr. V stated that Billy was "babied" and overprotected by Mrs. V. and Billy's sisters, ages 14 and 16. It appeared to him that Mrs. V intervened and prevented him from disciplining Billy.

The following "facts" from the interviews with the V's and Billy appeared pertinent.

1. Regarding Mr. V:
   (a) He also was the youngest of three children, and had two older sisters.
   (b) His father died when he was eight years old.
   (c) Mrs. V regarded her mother-in-law to be overprotective of her husband, which he denied.
   (d) Mr. V seldom expressed any anger except at Billy, or in arguments with his wife about Billy.
   (e) Billy was named after his father.

2. Regarding Mrs. V:
   (a) Her younger and only brother had died at age 12 of a lingering illness.
   (b) She had squabbled with her older sisters all of her life.
   (c) She remained very close to her parents whom she visited almost daily.
   (d) Mrs. V had had two miscarriages after the birth of her daughters, before Billy's birth.

3. Regarding Billy:
   (a) Both parents had wished for a boy before Billy's birth.
   (b) Billy's birth was normal but he was "sickly," and a "poor sleeper and a poor eater" for the first two years of his life.
   (c) Much to her despair, Mrs. V did not succeed in toilet training Billy until age three, and he continued to have "accidents" and to wet the bed until age six.
   (d) Billy expressed many fears, especially of "monsters."
   (e) Billy viewed his father as angry and his mother as "nicer."

These facts, among others, suggested the following hypothesis about the pattern of family interactions.

1. Mr. V's relationship with Billy appeared very ambivalent. It seemed likely that he identified with his namesake, but Billy's role in the family probably reminded him of his own overprotected childhood which he wished to deny. Moreover, having lost his own father when he was eight, he might have threatening fantasies about his own role as the father of an eight-year-old son. In any event, he felt pushed out of his role as father to Billy. Last but not least, Billy was the object of all of his overtly expressed anger — including any dissension with his wife.

2. Mrs. V probably identified Billy with her sickly brother, whose death left her the youngest in her family. Her battles with her sisters probably made her feel closer to Billy than to her daughters. Her prior miscarriages probably made Billy even more precious to her. Finally, and of most immediate import, she was reenacting with Billy the prolonged attachment with her own parents.

3. Thus, Billy was infantilized by his mother, and did not have to develop need-gratification skills. Since his mother regarded him as sickly, he probably felt weak and inept. Moreover, he was cowed by the explicit and singular anger of his father — who probably was the "monster" he feared — and could not compete with him directly. Indirectly, he probably played one parent off against the other. Obversely, he was the vehicle through which disagreements between the parents were expressed.

All of these statements were, of course, hypotheses to be checked against other data both from the assessment and later in the treatment of the child.

Such thematic analysis is based on inductive reasoning. Admittedly, it consists of seeing what can be made out of the data, post hoc. It depends a great deal on the scientific knowledge of fact and theory and on the clinical experience and acumen of the assessor. At the same time, there is always the danger of stretching the data to fit some theoretical bias or of failing to take account of the data because of theoretical prejudice. For example, the psychoanalytically oriented assessor may gladly accept any thread of evidence which might support his preconceptions, while those skeptical of Freud's concepts might ignore repeated evidence of psycho-sexual conflict. Ideally, an assessor should have a variety of concepts and fit them against the data, accepting those which yield the best fit for the evidence. It should be emphasized that all behavior is multidetermined and that several explanatory concepts might justifiably be entertained. Moreover, it is to be hoped that an assessor would be free to invent new concepts if necessary for the particular child at hand. He most certainly should not merely repeat old shibboleths, but should use his concepts in such a way and with such variation as to emphasize the uniqueness of this child. If the interpretative concept gives meaning to the child's behavior, it is also true that this child and his behavior and history often add to and expand upon the meaning of the theoretical concept.

Even when a case history has been so analyzed, the chief inferences are yet to be drawn. The assessor must then ask himself, given these patterns of behavior as shown in these data, how do they relate to the development difficulties currently presented by the child? *The purpose of reviewing the past development is to understand the present.* However, in making such inferences, an assessor should be just as cautious and parsimonious as he would be in making inferences from any other kinds of data. He should be particularly careful to keep a "null hypothesis" in mind, that is, the possibility that past experiences and stresses have *not* necessarily led to the present developmental difficulties. All too often it appears easy to explain much or all of the child's current behavior in terms of history, as if current stresses were relatively unimportant. Such a tendency to argue in terms of the past is particularly tempting when analogies are used. An assessor should ask himself: Given the child's current stresses, how do the child's past experiences contribute to his present difficulties in a way that distinguishes him from other children under the same current stresses but with different histories? How might the child react to the current stress had he had a different background or experiences? These questions assume considerable importance when the assessor begins to make recommendations for changes in the child's behavior. Then it becomes necessary to know to what degree the behavioral changes should emphasize reorganization of his current environment and relief of current stresses and to what extent it is also necessary to assist the child in healing old wounds and unlearning old habits and attitudes.

C. STRUCTURED TECHNIQUES BASED ON SUBJECTIVE REPORTS

Since the time of Galton, a wide variety of structured samplings of subjective self-opinion, such as true-false or multiple-choice tests, self-rating scales, Q-sorts, etc., have been employed by psychologists to study attitudes and feelings. Many were called "personality" tests or tests of "temperament." Most of these techniques were built for adult and adolescent literate populations, and only a few of these ever enjoyed any prolonged clinical adoption. In this section, two children's questionnaires, currently used in many clinics, will be discussed: The Rogers Adjustment Scale (1931), and the Bene-Anthony Family Attitudes Technique (1957). Also to be considered are two subjective scales used for measuring ego functioning patterns among adolescents and adults: The MMPI (McKinley and Hathaway, 1943) and the Edwards Personal Preference Schedule (EPPS) (Edwards, 1959). The final technique to be considered will be the Vineland Social Maturity Scale.

1. The Rationale

The rationale behind these subjective scales is often neither clearly stated nor obvious to the user. Most of them propose to measure several different variables, and no two inventories assess the same set of variables. Inspection of these scales suggests that except for the MMPI, they appear to have been constructed on an a priori basis, that is, sets of items were selected that seemed to reflect those variables the author wished to measure; scores were then standardized on various samples and the interrelationships between the scores were studied. Rarely, however, were there studies made of the interrelationships between these scores and other kinds of behavior. Rather, the items, and thus the sets of items or scales, were assumed to have a face validity. The simplest rationale behind such personality scales is that the subject's score on any one of the categorized sets of items represents his subjective opinion of himself with regard to the variable in question, in comparison with the self-assessments of other members of the sample. If the items do form a reasonable and statistically unified category, and if the subject does try sincerely to express his feelings about himself in objective fashion,

then this type of scale may very welll yield a fair measure of such subjective behavior. Except in those rare instances where there is research regarding the relationship between subjective and objective behavior, it cannot be assumed that these subjective opinion scores necessarily reflect anything other than self-appraisal.

Although the instructions vary somewhat from technique to technique, in essence the operations are about the same. Except for the Vineland (and the Bene-Anthony when it is read to the child), these scales are usually self-administered; the child or adult is given the questionnaire and a pencil and, after the assessor assures himself that the subject understand the directions, the subject proceeds to give his responses silently without the intervention or assistance of the assessor. This operation in which the subject and assessor are not in immediate contact creates several other special conditions. For some subjects the fact that he does not have to say these things aloud with someone making note of his remarks frees him a bit more to express himself. Many adults will accept MMPI items as "true" which they do not mention in the initial interview or later deny. When given a range of choices to describe their behavior on the Rogers, children also may tend to be more frank than when asked similar questions in interviews. On the other hand, there are probably just as many children who are willing to discuss things about themselves in interviews where they can defend or explain themselves but are quite cautious or compulsive about committing themselves on paper with a "yes" or "no" answer. Sometimes the items will suggest to the subject things which neither he nor the assessor has thought to discuss in the interview, thus adding to the subject's opportunity to evaluate and express himself. Just as often, however, the subject may feel that many of the items have little to do with him or are out of the range of his experience or knowledge. Some items may only serve to intensify his defensiveness.

However, these or other "test-taking" attitudes are not accounted for in the test scores per se. Even the MMPI "validity scores" are more concerned with other variables, such as social conformity, self-denunciation, and suppression. These variables are related to "test taking" but are at best only indirect measures of the operational conditions mentioned above. Sometimes by inspecting the subject's responses, it is possible to make a reasonable guess as to how the subject regarded and used these operations. One can see if a disproportionate number of his responses were self-derogatory (thus usually resulting in high scores on all subscales), or if he consistently gave socially acceptable, self-approving responses, denying any discomfort or dysfunction (usually lowering all scores). However, this information alone does not indicate whether the subject is actually expressing a bias or whether this represents how the subject actually regards himself. If the child tends to give mostly "yes" responses, or to mark only on one side of the answer sheet, or to show signs of responding randomly, the whole test may be held "invalid" but there is no way of discovering what made the subject decide to avoid the test, other than to ask him. Following up such questionnaires with a brief interview or using them as one basis of the main interview during the assessment is therefore recommended procedure. Such a follow-up interview gives the assessor the chance to explore with the subject both his feelings about taking the test and some of the pertinent test items. One can also compare the defensiveness and kind of defenses used in the interview with that demonstrated or suspected on the tests.

One other limitation to these scales is the fact that they depend on the ability to verbalize feelings and attitudes, or at least to comprehend such verbalizations. Occasionally even very bright children cannot reveal how they feel even when the task is merely to check "true" or "false." All of these scales require that the child be able to read — at the fourth grade level or better — and that his intellectual development is average or better.

2. Methods of Analysis

The standardized metric scores provided by these scales lend themselves easily to pattern analysis. On the MMPI in particular, such pattern analysis of the subscales has been so intensively studied that profile analysis, as it is called, has become a complex "cook-book" art. Pattern analysis for the other scales to be discussed here has not been so finely developed and is still a matter of rough inspection and estimate. However, any assessor attempting such profile analysis, even on the MMPI, should take into account the nature and size of the sample, the variability of scores in the original standardization (the raw scores upon which standard scores, if computed, are based), and the intercorrelations between the scales. For no matter how exact a science one may make of profiles of scales, if the scales were constructed on small samples from limited populations, then profile analysis is similarly limited; if the raw scores of the original sample were highly skewed, no amount of standardizing of this variability will change the profile's ultimate skewness. If the intercorrelations between the scales are not established, then it is impossible to know to what degree high and low spots on a profile are significant variations and to what degree they merely represent overlaps between scales. Thus, when analyzing a profile of scores, the assessor should be sure that the high and low points are not merely the results of artifacts in the test standardization.

Another approach to analysis of these techniques that is commonly used by clinicians is the qualitative inspection of the items themselves. When there are not very many items involved, it is possible to look through the subjects' answers booklet and note patterns of responses, perhaps not measured directly by the test. A test constructor seldom ferrets out all the possible factors from his items, even if the test is constructed on a factor analysis basis (and those in clinical use are rarely so constructed). Often the subject has expressed, through his responses to these structured items, attitudes of his own, not represented in the scales. The perceptive assessor may even be able to spot repetitive themes across scales by examining the individual items making up the various scaled scores. For example, on the MMPI, it is quite possible for two or more subjects to obtain fairly high scores on any particular scale and yet be responding to quite different items, for each of these scales covers several different facets of a general category. Moreover, when one is examining a profile of two or more high scores, the characteristic attitudes of the individual under consideration may be hidden in the overlapping items. However, in any such qualitative analysis of items, one must be very cautious about attributing meaning to any one item, for there is no indication of what interpretation the subject placed on an item when he made his self-rating of "yes" or "no."

3. Rogers Adjustment Inventory

Turning now to some of the specific techniques, the adjustment inventory for children which Carl Rogers* published in 1931 probably is not used as much as it should be, for many clinicians today may be unfamiliar with it. This inventory consists of six sets of items: Part 1 consists of "vocations" of which the child is asked to choose the three he "would most like to be." Part 2 similarly asks the child to select three wishes from a list, for example, "To have my parents love me more," "To be stronger than I am," etc. Part 3 asks the child to write the names of three companions he would like to have on a desert island. Part 4 asks him to compare himself with an imaginary child, for example, "Fred is the best ball player in the school," by checking a square on a nine-point scale from "Just like him" to "Not at all like him"; simultaneously the child is also asked, using the same type of scale, "Do you want to be like him?" and this part ends with the questions: "Which of these children would your mother like best?" and "Which would your father like best?" Part 5 consists of a variety of multiple choice items of the form, "How many friends do you have?" (a) hundreds, (b) quite a few, (c) several good friends, (d) no friends at all." In Part 6, the child is asked to list the members of his family, including himself, and his "best boy friend" and "best girl friend" and then to rank this list according to whom he likes best. Separate forms were designed for boys and girls. From these items, Rogers derived four variables: Family Adjustment, Social Adjustment, Personal Adjustment, and Daydreaming. Each scale draws on items from several of six parts of the test. The manual lists norms for separate age groups for each sex for ages eight to 13. However, Rogers was most concerned with the qualitative clinical use of his technique, and he cites case material illustrating this approach. The items are usually quite comprehensible to literate children in this age group who are of average intelligence or higher. Moreover, the items are attractive to children, despite the fact that they are quite direct in approaching children's anxieties. Admittedly, its standardization is now quite dated and there has been very little research using this test subsequently. It badly needs some kind of "test-taking" attitude scale. In

the original study, Rogers was able to distinguish "well adjusted" from "poorly adjusted" children on the basis of the test scores but this finding was not cross-validated nor replicated. Clinicians used to dealing with more modern "dynamic" concepts and terminology may look askance at the old fashioned adjustment concept of these scales. Yet, using these simple measures, plus a qualitative analysis, one can gain considerable information about the child's subjective picture of himself, which can be translated into whatever set of theoretical concepts with which the assessor may be familiar.

4. The Family Relations Test

This test, constructed by Bene and Anthony (1957), is an excellent example of a well thought out and imaginative subjective technique. The intent, to quote from their manual, is to "indicate objectively, reliably, and rapidly the direction and intensity of the child's feelings toward the various members of his family, and, of no less importance, his estimate of their reciprocal regard for him." That these authors consider their technique a subjective approach is revealed in their statement regarding interpretation of the test results (*Manual*, page 15): "For clinical purposes, however, it is his 'psychic reality,' his own idiosyncratic concept of his emotional environment, that has operational value, and is likely to be more relevant to the etiology of his symptoms than the 'objective' reality assessed through careful social enquiry." (Evidently, when these authors speak of their test as "objective," they mean "structured.")

This technique consists of a set of statements (47 in the version for younger children, 86 for older children). In the version for younger children (ages eight or younger) the statements are subdivided into "positive feelings coming from the child; negative feelings coming from the child; positive feelings going toward the child; negative feelings going toward the child; and dependence." For older children, the items are further broken down into "mild positive, strong positive (sexualized), mild negative, strong negative (hostile), maternal overprotection, paternal overindulgence, and maternal overindulgence." The novel feature of this technique is that as the child reads each statement, (or, for younger children, as it is read to him), he is asked to consider it as a "message" to a member of

* Many psychologists of this generation may be surprised that Rogers ever published a test, since he is much more widely known for his non-directive and experiential approach to counselling and psychotherapy in which testing was seldom used.

his family and to deposit it in a little box attached to a cardboard figure which the child has previously indicated as a family member. The statements are in the form, "This person in the family is kind to me," or "This person in the family does not love me enough," or "This is the person in the family whom father spoils too much." Or for younger children: "N (names of the child) wants you to come when he (she) has hurt himself (herself). Who is it N . . . wants when he (she) has hurt himself (herself)?" If the child feels a statement does not apply to any of the members of his family, he can deposit it in the box attached to a figure labeled "Nobody." The child also selects a figure representing himself.

In discussing these operations, the authors quite carefully consider some of the problems mentioned above regarding subjective techniques with children. For example, they note that children may well have considerable guilt and anxiety when asked to apply these statements to parents, especially those involving considerable negative feelings, and they discuss at length the necessity for establishing a supportive rapport with the child, advising that wherever possible the child should be encouraged to read the statement silently and make his choices independently without interaction with the assessor. Moreover, although no validity score or other direct measure of defensiveness is included in the analysis of the results, a great deal of consideration is given to the kinds of defenses indicated by the distribution of the various kinds of items among the family members. For example, an overall defensiveness would be indicated if most of the very negative statements were given to "Nobody." Other defensive attitudes discussed in the manual are "Idealization, Displacement, Wishfulfillment/Regression, Projection, and Reaction Formation."

To analyze the child's responses, the kinds of messages that he sees as sending or receiving from various members of the family are to be carefully recorded and counted. Actually the number of items in each subcategory is so small, usually eight to ten (and their variability is not stated), that statistical differences in the distribution of any one type of response among the various family members or between the types of statements attributed to any one family member probably would be significant only when in such extreme ratios as 8:2 or greater. In fact, in all of the many

examples cited in the manual, only such extremes are mentioned. Although no one score is considered in itself, and analysis is almost entirely in terms of patterns of scores, once again one might question to what degree the variability of the individual scores affects this pattern analysis. For example, if out of the 86 items, 20 are attributed to the mother by the child, of which 16 are positive and four negative, and another 15 are attributed to the father, of which 12 are negative and three positive, the authors would probably conclude that the child sees the mother in a far more positive light than the father. Yet, without any knowledge of the normal distributions of positive and negative statements toward mothers and fathers, such conclusions cannot be made with any degree of security. It might well be that negative feelings about mothers are made by children much less frequently than about fathers, especially at certain ages. Despite the authors' psychoanalytic, developmental approach, no age norms are given! Nor is the possibility of sex differences even discussed. Thus, despite the fascinating clinical potential of the data of this technique, the analysis of score patterns is seriously weakened by the absence of normative standards.

The inferential interpretation of this pattern analysis (as suggested by Bene and Anthony) is chiefly inductive (although deductive inferences also could be as easily drawn) in terms of psychoanalytic developmental theory. From the various patterns of attitudes expressed by the child toward each of the parents and toward various siblings and other family members, the assessor can infer various internal psychodynamics. The authors discuss two "syndromes": "egocentric states — auto-aggressive variety" and "egocentric states — auto-erotic variety." Certainly from such data it would be quite possible to inductively infer many other kinds of syndromes of subjective attitudes and their meaning for the ego functioning of the child. Although the authors mention independent "blind" analysis and interpretation as part of their validation studies, it is evident in their discussion of case examples that in clinical use the technique is intended to be used in conjunction with other clinical materials.

The problems of validating such a technique are discussed very cogently by the authors in their manual. They cite several well thought out "comparisons between test results and case history material," studying four major questions regarding the validity of their interpretations; although the results of these studies are given in metric form in several tables, unfortunately the *n* of their samples is quite small and in only one instance was it possible for them to make a statistical statement. In another study, it was statistically determined that the sex of the assessor did not affect any of their variables (when testing boys). A split-half (odd-even items) reliability study, on samples of fairly respectable size, yielded intercorrelations ranging from .68 to .90 (corrected for attenuation), which for this kind of material are certainly above reproach. All in all, this Family Relation Test has much to commend it for both clinical and research use.

5. The MMPI

Of all the structured questionnaires invented for the study of personality dysfunction, the MMPI is by far the most widely used and thoroughly studied. The normative "atlases" for analysis and interpretation of profiles both for adults (Hathaway and Meehl, 1951) and for adolescents (Hathaway and Monachesi, 1961) are standard equipment in many clinicians' offices. Several studies have been made of the types of profiles given by parents of children brought to clinics (Marks, 1961), thus providing a basis for its use as a technique in assessing the relationship between the emotional attitudes of parents with the developmental difficulties presented by the child. Over the past decade the considerable study which has been made of adolescent profiles has extended the clinical use of this instrument to any literate person over the age of 12. Because this technique is widely known and so much information is available in the literature, discussion will be limited to a brief review of the rationale, some cautions concerning standardization (especially regarding adolescents), and some remarks concerning its use with parents.

The construction of the MMPI was so strictly empirical that the term "rationale" may not at first glance seem to apply; indeed few, if any, of its promulgators ever gave the rationale more than passing consideration and then only to reemphasize this empirical approach. It is repeatedly pointed out that none of the items contained in so-called clinical scales was selected on the basis of any theoretical premise but, instead, that these scales were constructed purely by comparing the differences between samples of patients with established psychiatric diagnoses and "normals." Only on the "Masculine-feminine" and the "Lie" scales were items arbitrarily assigned (and the rationale for the M-F scale has never been clearly stated). Thus, if the MMPI can be said to have a rationale, it is the simple statement that it is the *number* of responses that a subject makes rather than the content of these responses which determines whether he is responding similarly to the criterion groups. Thus, the theory behind the MMPI is that any kind of item or behavior might have been used, as long as it discriminated between persons diagnosed as emotionally disturbed and those not showing such disturbance. If one holds strictly to such a rationale, interpretation of the results would be limited to the dichotomous discrimination between "mentally ill" and "normal." In fact, a great deal of the application of the MMPI has been concerned with this dichotomy, of working out profile formulas for distinguishing "psychotic" from "nonpsychotic," etc.

However, both MMPI literature and the handbooks leave no doubt that the promoters of this instrument are concerned with many more subtle personality discriminations. Consequently, the rationale of the MMPI has been undergoing considerable implicit change. With the advent of complex profile analysis, from which inferences are drawn not only about diagnostic differentiations, but also about personality traits and defenses, it can no longer be maintained that the content of the scales is purely empirical and meaningless. Although the items in the scales were originally empirically selected, the traits and defenses, which it is often implicitly hypothesized these scales and scale combinations measure, *are* often based on generalizations about the item contents of the scales. Quite a few of these hypotheses have been checked out and cross-validated. Moreover, some of them concerning the content of the scales have been drawn from empirical observations, from noting and cross-checking the behavior of individuals with specified profiles.

Profile analysis of this sort has greatly enriched the usefulness of the MMPI beyond the sterile differential diagnosis rationale of its origin. Profile analysis permits the expansion of the MMPI rationale, which may be stated as follows: The subjective impressions that a person expresses in judging him-self on their 566 items may be analyzed into traits and defenses by comparing the relative identification of these responses with each of the eight clinical standardization groups. The subtle but definite change in this rationale lies in the degree to which the test is regarded as subjective. When one merely counts responses, disregarding content, in order to make dichotomous discriminations, there is no implication that the subject necessarily is judging himself in any particular fashion. In this instance, how the subject interprets the item is not only unknown but is considered to be of no importance! However, once traits and defenses are attributed to the profile, the assumption that the meaning of the item to the subject makes no difference can no longer be maintained. In fact, this assumption probably was invalid even for such dichotomies as psychotic versus nonpsychotic, for even these simple distinctions carried many implied trait assumptions.

The fact that the interpretation of an MMPI profile depends in so large a part on the comparison and contrast with the traits of the criterion groups makes critical the constitution and definition of these criterion groups. In his original description of the development of the MMPI scales, Hathaway (1940) emphasized that the criterion groups consisted of persons who clearly represented the diagnostic syndromes in question, and about whom there was no disagreement as to the diagnosis. Nevertheless, despite the many other studies in which it has been shown that psychiatric diagnosis is often very unreliable, there has never been any study of the reliability or homogeneity of these criterion groups. Even more serious is the absence of any discussion of the criteria upon which these diagnoses were based; since the MMPI was devised before national diagnostic criteria were established (as in the APA Diagnostic Manual), there is no indication of the kinds of behavior, symptoms, and traits that were used to make these diagnoses. This absence of any clear-cut and detailed description of the criterion groups, other than by diagnostic label, has continued to be a major flaw in the MMPI. Even in the many subsequent studies, cross-validating and expanding on profile analysis, rarely are the characteristics of the criterion groups discussed, although many post hoc assumptions are made. When profiles based on these original criterion groups are further compared and cross-checked on new criterion groups, also undefined, the error is compounded. Fortunately, in the more recent studies of the traits and defenses associated with certain profiles, the question has more frequently been asked: Are the traits and defenses which are assumed to be present in the diagnostic patterns actually reflected in the behavior of the groups being studied, regardless of diagnosis? It is where such trait patterns can be established that the MMPI gains strength and validity.

Although in the 30 years since its inception, the MMPI has been administered to thousands upon thousands of subjects, the number of subjects in the original criterion groups was surprisingly small. For example, the Hypochondriasis Scale was based on an n of 30, and few of the other criterion groups exceeded 100. One wonders about the stability of the enormous superstructure of profile analysis constructed on the basis of such small n's. Of course, in subsequent studies, many further cases have been considered, thus adding to the knowledge of the types of persons included in the criterion groups. Nevertheless, at no time has there been any revision of the original scales (apart from the addition of the K correction). Moreover, it has been implicitly assumed that the same thing is meant by the diagnostic classifications currently as was meant in 1937, although the standard nomenclature has twice been changed; at least two of the 1937 classifications (Hysteria and Psychaesthenia) no longer even exist as diagnostic categories! Admittedly the MMPI has in great measure helped to strengthen and clarify this diagnostic system by developing as part of the research better definitions in terms of behavior and symptoms. In effect, these diagnostic headings on the scales have new meanings and are personality syndromes rather than merely measures of degree of pathology. This change is emphasized by the fact that in MMPI literature the scales are referred to by number in the order in which they appear on the profile sheet rather than by name.

Although the MMPI was originally designed for use with adults, the application of this technique to the assessment of adolescents has received considerable study over the past decade or more, climaxing in Hathaway and Monachesi's *Adolescent Personality and Behavior: MMPI Patterns* (1963) and their *Atlas of Juvenile MMPI Profiles* (1961). Although the items and scales remain unchanged, their studies of over 10,000 adolescents in effect yield new norms (the authors advise correcting the usual profile sheet for the juvenile means and standard deviations). Moreover, they recognize well that emotional disturbance in this turbulent period of development does not have the same meaning as in later life. Although they do not discuss the topic of diagnostic nosology, they make no use of it and proceed directly to their "predictions" about delinquency and emotional disturbance. Both of these terms are operationally defined by their rating scales. The authors report that despite the adult psychopathological content of some of the items, the normal adolescents they tested seemed to understand the items quite well and to be unperturbed by them. This writer's experience with the MMPI in the assessment of adolescents continually has convinced him that it is a most valuable screening device, especially for outlining the systems of defenses used by the adolescent ego.

Since the MMPI has shifted from a diagnostic technique to a set of fairly well-defined personality scales, it is possible to translate the profile patterns into terms of ego functioning. Such a dynamic approach to the interpretation of the MMPI requires a knowledge of the empirical findings regarding the characteristics of individuals who are known to produce various commonly obtained profiles. The psychologist can then combine this information with his theory of ego-functioning, that is, he can recognize the dynamics within the MMPI profile of symptoms. Only a few examples can be included here. The most frequent profile among both normal and emotionally disturbed adolescents is '49 (*Pd* and *Ma* highpoints, between T–60 and T–70). In fact, '49 profiles are much more common today in both the adolescent and adult profiles than when the MMPI was standardized in the 1930's. This change reflects the change in personal and social value systems in the mid-twentieth century American culture. People are becoming increasingly open about their aggressive and sexual impulses; adolescents, in particular, are less inhibited affectively and are more assertive of their independence than were the good Lutherans of St. Paul and Minneapolis upon whom these scales were standardized. Currently, these scales measure, among other things, the degree to which the adolescent is participating in his social revolution. Commonly the '49 profile (without a tertiary peak) from an adolescent who is referred by his parents for psychological assessment is facing a generation gap. Often the parental MMPI profiles are marked by peaks on 7 (*Pt*), indicating obsessive concerns, by high *L* scores, with excessive social conformity, or by other high score profiles, indicating personal anxieties and the inability to accept normal adolescent rebellion. A 49' profile (T scores between 70 and 80) might suggest that the adolescent in question was at a peak of a rebellion normal for the current generation, while scores above 80 usually are obtained only when an adolescent is struggling with serious family and social disruptions. In this latter instance, this disruption usually also is represented in other high scores, such as 8 (*Sc*) or 2 (*D*). A tertiary peak on 8 would indicate that this social struggle is accompanied by poor contact with reality, possibly by ideational and behavioral confusion. Thus, a 49"8' profile, for example, would suggest that the adolescent faces this normal stress of his time without either internal or external guides, and is floating helplessly in the current of these stresses. In the histories of this very common adolescent profile, it is often found that the parents have been preoccupied with their own problems, and have ignored and denied the stresses on the child. A 492' profile (with 8 below 70), on the other hand, would suggest that the adolescent might be temporarily depressed by his conflicts with adult authority. A tertiary peak on 7 (*Pt*) would suggest brooding guilt over the rebellion, especially with a rise in the *F* scale. Such youngsters are tempted to rebel but face the conflict of the continuing ties with parents. All such hypotheses must, of course, be checked out against other assessment data.

The MMPI is also a very practical and helpful technique for assessing the personality functioning of the parents who bring children for assessment. Extensive assessment of parents is often prohibited both by the lack of time on the part of the clinician and by the resistance of the parents who see the child as "ill" but are only half willing to admit to their role in the child's disturbance. However, most parents are willing to "fill out a routine questionnaire" about "their attitudes and feelings." Quite often the parent's responses to MMPI are among the first indications of marked emotional disturbance within the parents which, when compared with the child's symptoms, may give clues as to the sources of the child's difficulties. Often these MMPI results suggest a need for further assessment of the parents. Most frequently parental scores fall within the 50 to 70 T-score range. Even so, variations within this "normal" range often reveal personality patterns of defenses within the parent which suggests clues about the parent-child interaction.

6. The Personal Preference Schedule

The PPS (Edwards, 1959) is another subjective technique used in many clinics to assess adolescent and adult attitudes. It consists of nine scales, each of which purports to measure the strength of a need. Although the titles of these scales are drawn from the same list of needs used by Murray in his discussion of the TAT (1938), for example, N Achievement, N Aggression, N Order, etc., they are actually defined by the content of the items within the scale, as stated in Edward's Manual for the PPS (op.cit.). It should be noted that the content of the scales, while roughly comparable to the variables discussed by Murray, are not identical with Murray's definition of these needs. Nor has there been any study of the relationship of the PPS scales to the TAT. Even if both techniques do tap the same variables, it is theoretically doubtful that there would be well-defined relationships between them, since one would not expect individuals to express their needs consistently or in the same manner on both the subjective and associative levels.

Edwards was most interested in the construction of scales which control what he has called "social desirability." As he points out, all other similar subjective tests are biased by the fact that most subjects tend to answer in a direction which they consider socially acceptable or proper. For example, on the MMPI, such a tendency is measured in a gross fashion by the L scale, but exactly how a high score on the L affects other MMPI scores is unknown. In the construction of the PPS, sets of statements each of which describe personal values, attitudes, and motivations were selected from a pool of similar statements in which the "social desirability of every statement had been previously agreed upon by several judges." The statements used in the final form of the schedule were selected on the basis that their social desirability ratings were equivalent.

Thus, in responding to the PPS, a subject indicates preferences rather than affirming or denying that the statement is true or false about him. In fact, he may on one item prefer one statement over another, but on another item, prefer a third statement to the first, and so on. The significance of this test-taking operation is that it results in patterns of relatively preferred values rather than dichotomous acceptance or rejection of self-descriptions. However, these responses in themselves do not indicate whether the subject manifests such values in his overt behavior or in his fantasies. As with other subjective techniques, the PPS indicates only that the subject "prefers" to ascribe these values and attitudes to himself. "Social Desirability" has been controlled, leaving "Personal Desirability."

Prediction from these patterns of personally preferred subjective attitudes to other behavior depends on both an acquaintance with the increasing research on the PPS and the application of the principles of ego dynamics. Over 400 research studies had been published by 1966, either studying the PPS or using it as a research instrument. Many of these studies, although only indirectly bearing on the predictive validity of the PPS, do further delineate the relationships between these patterns of preferred attitudes and other kinds of behavior. Most pertinent for clinical use are Klett's study (1957) of high school children and Mainords' (1956) dissertation on parents' responses.

The thorough standardization of the PPS includes percentile scores for both sexes, for both adolescents and adults. A profile of percentile scores can be drawn on the score sheet. (Standard scores are also published in the manual.) Thus, the psychologist can easily spot the extreme scores, that is, where the subject differs from other members of his sex and age, and he can then analyze patterns of intraindividual attitudes.

It is from these patterns of PPS scores that hypotheses about ego functioning may be conceived. For example, an adolescent boy whose preferences result in high percentile scores on N Achievement and N Order but who shows little or no preference for N Sex or N Aggression would seem to be using achievement values and orderliness as a defense against expression of sexual and aggressive impulses, especially if *N* Blame-Avoidance were also high. Since open expression of sexual aggressiveness does possess considerable social desirability among adolescent males in American society, this adolescent might well be in conflict with his peers, and suffer some social isolation. Moreover, such a profile would suggest that the adolescent was avoiding the development of normal coping mechanisms for these needs, and relying on general coping methods more appropriate to latency. The obverse of such a profile would indicate that the adolescent had developed few or no controls over these drives.

7. The Vineland Social Maturity Scale

This scale is one of the most widely used techniques for assessing children's development. Based on interviews with parents, this test scales social behavior from age one year through adolescence. The items are grouped together in age levels much like the Binet mental age scales, and by comparing the average "social" age to the child's chronological age, a "social quotient" analogous to an IQ can be calculated. Furthermore, the items in the manual (Doll, 1947) are classified into various areas of social behavior: "Self-help, Eating and Dressing, Locomotion, Occupation, Communication, Self-direction, and Socialization." As a result, it is also possible to extract from the classification of these items the various kinds of social behavior in which the child seems to be advancing and those in which he has not yet developed.

The chief difficulty with the Vineland is the fact that its original standardization was very inadequate. It needs restandardization on the current generation and some of the old-fashioned items need updating. Since it is based on the parent's report, there also should be a better standard than that of clinical hunch for estimating the reliability, defensiveness, and social desirability of the parent's responses. Little is known about the reliability or validity of this widely used technique. Although these objective items would seem to have face validity, parents of emotionally disturbed or handicapped children — and even parents of relatively normal children — often unwittingly report in a defensive manner or are poor observers of their children. Thus, this face validity should be seriously questioned.

Nevertheless, the Vineland is most convenient as an introductory device for interviewing the parents. However, an extensive inquiry is necessary into the nature of the parent's observations and the parent's attitudes toward the social behavior in question. Only by such interviews can the validity and reliability of this technique be estimated for the case at hand.

TECHNIQUES BASED
ON ASSOCIATIVE BEHAVIOR

A. THE NATURE OF FREE ASSOCIATION

The term "associative" really has two distinct meanings in psychology. In traditional experiments on memory or judgment, two stimuli are presented and the subject is asked to "form an association." It is discovered later that even if the subject is not so instructed, the hypothesis that he does this is confirmed in some fashion. It is presumed, usually correctly, that the subject finds some communality between the two stimuli, and makes a generalization or mnemonic so that he can remember the arbitrarily paired stimuli of the experiment, for example, between nonsense syllables, etc. Such experiments explore the subject's ability to abstract and thus remember. "Free association," although probably quite comparable as regards the thought processes involved, differs in that the associative link is between some presented stimuli (not always of great import to the matter at hand) and the individual's personal memories, experiences, attitudes, imagination, and feelings which those stimuli arouse. To identify this type of associative behavior, the term "projection" is often used. In a projective technique, the stimuli are often pur-posely vague or unstructured and not considered to be of great import to the real inquiry except to facilitate the flow of associations. The rationale is that the subject projects or reflects his personal associations as stimulated by the materials of the technique. As will be discussed later in detail, the nature of the presented stimuli often *does* affect the associative processes which the psychologist seeks to elicit, sometimes considerably more than is commonly supposed. Moreover, there is always the question of how the subject forms his associations (the associative linkages): is he following whatever instructions are used to promote free association, or is he attempting to make associations of the first type mentioned above, that is, is he "stimulus bound" and analyzing rather than free associating?

Before discussing some of these problems in using and analyzing associative techniques, it may be helpful to review briefly this concept of free association. When Freud introduced what he himself labeled the "free association *experiment*," the novelty lay not only in a new form of treatment for hysteria, but rather in the concept that every conscious thought, manifest or subjective, also included like the tail of a comet a trail of personal associations of which both the individual and others interacting with him might often be unaware but which were an integral part of the behavior. Experimenting almost exclusively with emotionally disturbed adults, Freud was impressed with the extent to which his patients repressed these associations "into the unconscious," that is, how these patients avoided focusing on their associations which were threatening, frightening, or guilt-ridden. Moreover, because the anxiety-producing nature of some of these associations became generalized to other associations, Freud and his colleagues discovered that in these emotionally disturbed adults, the associative process per se became blocked. Such patients, although quite aware of their manifest and even subjective behavior, often could not actually account for many of their experiences, acts, or feelings because they had not taken into account the associative aspects of their interactions with various stimuli and situations. This phenomenon was most dramatically illustrated by the cases of "grande hysterie" with the fugue states, functional paralyses, etc. Only after several decades did Freud realize that this was part of what he called the "psychopathology of everyday life." Because fairly well-adjusted persons made "slips" and appeared altogether unaware of this aspect of their acts and thoughts, he assumed that they also were repressing some possibly anxiety-ridden associations.

While this may often be the case, for everyone makes such associations, there are at least two other explanations for such behavior in the normal individual: (1) The individual may be quite conscious of the associative aspects of his behavior and thoughts but not speak publicly of them because of social prohibitions against verbalizing one's private thoughts or because to verbalize them would reveal his intentions, which for various reasons the individual would prefer to keep hidden. This Freud called "suppression" but because it played only a minor part in the types of emotional disturbance with which he was then concerned, he tended to dismiss it. (2) Associative aspects of behavior may be unconscious not because of repression but merely because no one can possibly pay attention to all aspects of his behavior at any one moment. In this respect, a person is also often unconscious of his manifest and subjective behavior as well. People do many things automatically because they have learned

to do them without thinking, find their learned habits successful, and therefore do not need to focus awareness on them. Only when learned habits fail to bring about the desired results does a person have to stop and examine the various aspects of this action, including his presumptions and associations.

Thus, it should be noted, the behavior revealed by free association, even of a sexual or anxiety-provoking nature, is not necessarily repressed or unconscious. The individual responding to the Sentence Completion, the T.A.T., or the Rorschach may be well aware of the associative facets of his behavior and their relationship to other aspects of his deeds and thoughts. Only when there is positive evidence that the subject denies any such attitudes as may appear in his free associations may one speak of repression. For example, if a subject outwardly idealizes his mother and behaves toward her in a submissive fashion, but on the T.A.T. tells disparaging stories about maternal figures or plots rebellion against overprotective mothers, one could posit with some reason that his anger toward his mother is repressed. But, if the subject says: "I love my mother very much and have never raised my voice against her, but sometimes I wish that she wouldn't always wait on me and try to tell me what to do. Once I even had a dream that she died and I wasn't sorry. It sure startled me," one might speak of suppression of conscious ambivalence, but the associations are not unconscious.

The nature of free association during the childhood years has been more assumed than specifically formulated, even in the psychoanalytic literature. Certainly the use of play materials in psychotherapy with children and the application of the associative techniques used originally on adults to the assessment of children attest to the assumption that children can and do free associate. In fact, it is sometimes assumed that because the ego of the child and its defensive systems are still in the formative stages, children free associate better than adults. They tend to work things out in play or appear to voice their associations openly and naively at times. However, it should be noted that the child's use of free association in everyday life (and on formal associative techniques) varies considerably depending on the stage of his development. During the accumulative stage of infancy (see Chapter 2), children usually engage in what to the adult appears to be uncontrolled associations. Such free-floating associative thinking is often an attempt to explore and accumulate the emotional as well as the intellectual aspects of their experiences. However, as they enter into the integrative stage in latency, this public display of associative behavior decreases sharply. The child becomes engaged in distinguishing fantasy from reality. Although he may enjoy fantasy, he is quick to identify it as such. Loosli-Usteri (1931), in her study of the response of eight year olds to the Rorschach, speaks of *"la notion du hasard,"* the awareness of taking a chance, that is, in committing oneself to identifying the inkblot as being anything but an inkblot. During this period of childhood, children appear to practice "defenses" and are relatively unaware of associative aspects of their responses.

Adolescents, in another upswing of accumulative development, appear to combine their previous experiences of infancy and latency. Associative behavior reappears (often repeating some of the feelings and attitudes of early childhood), usually followed by quick defensive covering. Adolescents make nonsense remarks, sing meaningless ditties, invent languages of their own, but are embarrassed and defensive when anyone notices. Every assessor has heard teenagers begin a T.A.T. story with "I could tell a wild one to that picture," then make a descriptive statement, followed by several free associations, and conclude with defensive facetious remarks. Rarely does a teenager have the courage to free associate in uninhibited fashion, nor does one often meet an adolescent who has enough control to exclude completely all free association.

Free association often seems a mystery to those untrained in this technique. Since uninhibited expression of one's associations is at least partially tabooed in Western culture (other cultures freely recite their dreams as part of normal communication), getting a subject to free associate without any stimuli is often difficult. Even children learn this taboo quite early in life when they embarrass their elders. Freud found that he had to train his patients to free associate. For this reason, the instructions given the subject on projective techniques and the kinds of stimuli used to elicit free association become very important. While procedures, including the setting and instructions, will be covered in the next sec-

tions, it should be noted that there is considerable research, reviewed by Murstein and his colleagues (1965 — see particularly Chapters 4, 5, and 11), which clearly indicated that responses to these projective techniques can be quite definitely altered by the immediate situation and stresses on the subject, by the nature of the instructions, and by the attitude, character, and even appearance of the assessor. The same is true for the objective and subjective techniques, also; but assessors are usually more precise in administering intelligence tests, and subjects are more used to such techniques and are not as much at sea as on associative techniques.

When projective techniques were first introduced and became widely used, the idea was advanced that the nature of the stimulus was of little importance, that subjects if properly instructed would associate to most any inkblot or tell stories to any picture. However, Rorschach, in his original monograph, says that he produced hundreds of blots before he selected the ten he thought most suitable — but he did not reveal the criteria of selection. Similarly, Murray chose his pictures out of a large collection, probably on the basis of clinical intuition. Studies on the stimulus value of the Rorschach blots have been reviewed by Baughman (1965). There are indications that certain T.A.T. pictures "draw" certain kinds of stories most frequently (Eron, 1950). There are "popular" or near popular responses to each of the Rorschach inkblots, and certain blots are more likely to produce movement responses or to be rejected, etc. There are also studies of the relationship between the degree of structure in the stimulus and the freedom of the association (Lazarus, 1965). In general, these studies indicate that this relationship is not exactly linear, that completely unstructured stimuli (such as the blank card, 16, on the TAT) may not give the subject quite enough to get him going and responses are often brief and superficial, while very structured stimuli do tend to evoke stereotyped responses. Evidently, the stimuli should have enough structure to start the subject associating but not enough to restrict him entirely. Most of these studies of the nature of the stimuli have been concerned with the responses of adult subjects, and there is very little research on the question of whether these originally adult techniques are actually appropriate stimuli for children. As far as can be ascertained, it has always been assumed that Rorschach's ten inkblots are just as appropriate for children as for adults, but it is quite possible that another set of blots could be constructed which would draw more free association from children. Murray maintains that the Harvard set of pictures is appropriate for children ages four and older. However, the difficulty many young children seem to experience in telling stories to these relatively complex adult stimuli caused Bellak (1949) to invent the Childrens' Apperception Test (CAT) consisting of ten much simpler stimuli depicting animals in various human actions and situations and concerned with such childhood stresses as sibling rivalry, separation anxiety, Oedipal conflicts, and toilet training. However, numerous studies (see Murstein, 1965, pp. 525 ff.) have been conducted which indicate that pictures using humans instead of animals (in the same situations) draw somewhat longer and more meaningful stories, even from kindergarten children.

B. VERBAL ASSOCIATIVE TECHNIQUES

For heuristic purposes, associative techniques may be divided into those in which both the stimuli and responses are primarily verbal, those with visual stimuli and verbal responses, and those with either verbal or visual stimuli but which call primarily for a nonverbal or motor response. Although in part such a classification is artificial and purely for purposes of discussion, it does focus on the type of function that is being elicited from the child. With children it is necessary to consider the fact that their associations are not as well verbalized as adults and that they often express their fantasies in nonverbalized play.

1. Word Association and Sentence Completion Tests

The purely verbal associative techniques, such as the Word Association and Sentence Completion, are seldom used with preadolescents. In part, this is because of the level of literacy these tests require. Very possibly, the Word Association could be adapted to younger children if adequate norms were available, but this grandsire of all associative techniques does not appear to be in popular use any

longer, even for adults. However, there are several well-standardized versions of the Sentence Completion for adolescents (Rotter, 1965; Rohde, 1957). The rationale of the SCT is generally the same as other associative techniques, but there has been considerable discussion in the literature over the level of associative material elicited by this method, largely in terms of the amount of structure offered by the sentence "stems" that are presented as stimuli. There is the question of person reference, that is, whether the stem begins the question with "I," or "My," or whether the sentence is started relatively impersonally, for example, "When a boy . . . " or "Most mothers . . . ." Goldberg (1965) summarizes research on this topic by stating, "What empirical evidence there is favors the first person construction. . . . " Again, the studies that Goldberg cites were limited to adult subjects.

By far the most important aspect of the SCT stimulus stem is the nature of the content of these stems and the rationale behind this content. Goldberg (op.cit., p. 813) concludes, "Most researchers using the Sentence Completion have seemed little bothered by the absence of a theoretical rationale underlying the use of the Sentence Completion method." But, he adds, "there have been sentence completion forms that have been developed more systematically. . . . " The selection of stems has sometimes been systematized on the basis of "areas of conflict" (for example, Forer, 1950), such as important interpersonal figures, dominant needs, environmental pressures, and aggressive tendencies. Other SCT collections seemed to have been derived, as was admitted by Holsopple and Miale (1954), because "they seemed a good idea at the time." Rohde (1957) lists six general criteria for her selection of 65 items.

"1. The range of stimuli must be broad enough to elicit information from all areas and phases of behavior reaction.

2. Areas likely to be foci of conflict must be stimulated.

3. The responses must be controlled as little as possible by the stimulus phrases.

4. The items must be arranged to lead the subject from everyday life to the more inaccessible areas of personality, in order to avoid engendering resistance.

5. The stimuli must be comprehensible to persons of mental age ten and up.

6. The total time required for the method must not exceed a period convenient for the schedules of schools and other institutions."

Summing up these criteria, it appears that the aim is to stimulate associations (sometimes in specific areas) and to avoid resistance but not to control the association. Evidently the nature of the stem depends a great deal on the variable that the test constructor intended to assess. Forer, with his fairly structured set of stems, was evidently hoping to get associations to well-defined areas of adjustment. Rotter was interested in the single variable of "degree of conflict." Rohde describes a much broader aim, that of getting at the same interacting need-press system of variable as originated by Murray. She is thus less concerned with the structure of her stems per se as with the variability of the responses they draw, which she illustrates at length in the description of the construction of her particular set of stems.

Both Rohde (1957) and Rotter (1965) have constructed well-standardized forms for adolescent groups. Rotter differentiates his Adolescent and Adult forms, chiefly by content. Rohde's test was standardized on ninth grade children, but she uses it for adults also. Both authors present data showing respectable repeat reliability and scorer reliability. Both present data that support their claims that their tests differentiate between adjusted and maladjusted children. Rohde's correlations between test scores and teachers' evaluations are among the highest this author has ever seen for studies using this criterion, but her questionnaire presented to the teachers was ingeniously extensive and elaborate.

A metric method of analyzing responses to the SCT is provided both by Rotter and by Rohde. Rotter's single variable measure is far simpler than Rohde's very complex scoring of needs and press. The latter requires considerable familiarity by the assessor with the Murray system and considerable practice and training to attain the level of reliability Rohde cites in her text. Rotter's test does have the advantage of a single neat score indicating the degree of conflict, but Rohde's system yields a much richer set of personality variables. Although neither author restricts his analysis to this metric approach, Rohde's system does lend itself to much more extensive pattern and thematic analysis. Thus, once the need-press system is scored, it is possible to group the scores into patterns and to analyze sequentially the responses into themes.

Although almost all of those who have used and studied the SCT agree that it is often quite successful in eliciting associative responses that give many clues to the functioning of the adolescent, all agree that this technique is also very susceptible to being neutralized by the defensive individual who realizes from the nature of the stems that his personality is being probed. Rotter and Willerman (1947), in testing a group of psychologists, found that this group in effect was saying "It's none of your business" while a college group was saying "Although it is undoubtedly your business, I will tell you only nice things about myself." Even where people come to a clinic or hospital for the purpose of studying themselves and their behavior, they often give stereotyped neutral, seemingly meaningless and ambiguous responses to the SCT. Adolescents in particular often respond with flippant, impudent sentences which seem to say "I dare you to make anything out of this." While such responses indicate the degree of defiance of authority and general resistance against anxiety, they thwart the assessor who hopes to find out anything else about the adolescent's functioning.

This resistance is, of course, heightened by the way the test is usually administered; the subject writes out his responses on an answer sheet without intervention from the assessor. Although these flip responses might be less frequent if the operations were altered to have the subject dictate the responses to the assessor, thus also forcing a response from the subject and avoiding omissions, this change of operations would not only be tedious but also would alter the standardizations when the metric analyses were used. However, this writer once used such a procedure with blind adolescents and there appeared to be no untoward restriction of their associations; admittedly blind adolescents often are more verbal than are the sighted. All in all, the SCT may be thought of as a step between the subjective report and the associative process. The subject usually realizes that the stems dealing with family life, personal attitudes, etc. are asking him to subjectively report how he feels, but they do not give him the structure of the subjective questionnaire and thus do encourage his associations.

However, a major shift in emphasis occurs

if the assessor does regard the subject's responses not only as subjective reports but also as associations. For example, if to the stem "My main trouble is . . . " an adolescent responds "my mother," the psychologist would certainly want to note that the adolescent subjectively sees his mother as his chief source of trouble, but the psychologist should also note several other facts about this associative report: Rotter would score the response as conflictual; Rohde might further note that the association suggests that there are probably internalized conflicts within the subject between feelings of resentment and dependency; moreover, the subject is very possibly defending himself against such a conflict by externalizing the blame for this trouble and protecting his ego. Whether such interpretative hypotheses are tenable would depend on the appearance of similar evidence in the responses to other stems. If there were no such general themata over the whole series of responses, it would be difficult to analyze this single response without further inquiry with the child. Thus, such a "conflictual" response given in isolation warrants a discussion with the child.

2. The Picture-Frustration Study

The Rosenzweig Picture Frustration Study for Children (Rosenzweig, Fleming, and Rosenzweig, 1948) differs from most other associative techniques in that it is aimed at measuring one general variable and is derived from a fairly well-defined theoretical schema. Concerned with children's reactions to frustration, Rosenzweig conceived of these reactions as having two dimensions: a "direction" (extrapunitive, intrapunitive, or impunitive) and a "type" (object-dominated, ego-dominated, and need-persistent), thus providing nine possible categories to classify the responses to his cartoon situations. There is no presumption that the manner in which the child responds reflects his behavior in social situations. There are, however, several studies, [for example, Levitt and Lyle (1955)], which suggest that extrapunitive, ego-dominated children are more aggressive than children showing other predominate patterns on the P-F. The chief rationale of the P-F seems to be that the child's responses represent his view of how frustration is to be met, either in what he sees as the socially approved fashion or possibly in some idiosyncratic fashion, ex-

pressing his own values and attitudes toward frustration. Rosenzweig was obviously more concerned with the latter and sought to account for the tendency for children to respond in a socially stereotyped fashion by scoring the most frequently given responses as "popular." Evidently he hoped that by assessing the patterns of attitudes toward frustration, it might be possible to uncover relationships between such patterns and other personality variables.

The P-F stimuli consist of 24 line drawings (like cartoons) in which one figure, adult or child, addresses a child with a statement which most children interpret as socially or personally frustrating. The sex of the frustrator and that of the child is clearly indicated in most of the drawings. The subject is then asked to write in (or in the case of very young children, to dictate) "what the other person in the picture (whose "balloon" has been left empty) might say." The structured nature of the stimulus and these instructions raise several questions for the user of this technique. Because more stimulus cues are provided the child than in most of the other projective techniques, some critics have questioned whether the P-F can be classified as projective. Moreover, although the child is instructed to say "what the child in the picture" might respond, children often ask if they should say what they themselves might say or give some indication that they are trying to figure out the "right" or socially approved response. Rosenzweig (1950) discusses this question in his classic paper on levels of response to projective technique. Thus, the child may be attempting to be objective (looking for the right answer), subjective (saying how he might respond), or projective (responding with an association stimulated by the cartoon and reflecting his own internal attitudes rather than either socially popular response or his own behavior).

However, this question is answered in part by the use of the standardized scores which Rosenzweig provides for ages four to 13. By using this metric method, one may distinguish the child who is attempting to be socially conforming by the fact that he has a high conformity or popular score. Such a child avoids direct expression of ego-defensive extrapunitive responses in favor of more impunitive defensive responses or polite submissions to adult authority (slightly higher than the mean on M', I, or M). In contrast, the child who is attempting to be subjective or is associating would be expected to come up with patterns of reactions somewhat more deviant from the norm. Of course, there is the possibility that a child who is socially conforming in other everyday situations will respond in a similar manner on the test, but it is just as possible that such a child might well take the opportunity of expressing his extrapunitive feelings on the test which he dare not in the face of live authority or peer figures!

Thus, one child may perceive that the way to handle frustration is to be conforming, whether or not he himself can conform; another may view frustration as calling for intrapunitive, guilt-ridden responses or for defending himself against blame by denying — but as an ideal rather than a representation of his own behavior Whether the child perceives himself as behaving in the same manner as he reports for the child in the cartoon cannot be answered by the test score alone. Frequently a child comes to the clinic with a long history of socially nonconforming, aggressive, extrapunitive behavior and not only gives largely "good boy" conforming responses to the P-F, but stoutly maintains that this is the way he would behave! Such a child does not necessarily see any discrepancy between his test responses and his actual behavior under frustration.

Despite this problem of levels of interpreting the responses, the Rosenzweig P-F can be a clinically useful tool to assess the child's social functioning and social perceptions, especially when used with other materials. Because it is concerned with a rather circumscribed area of the child's ego rather than the broader and more general dynamics of the T.A.T. or even the Rorschach, it has not received the wide usage of their other techniques. Very likely the difficulty lies in the fact that there is not enough known about the relationship between such perceived patterns of reaction to frustration and other kinds of ego functioning. The theorists with whom Rosenzweig was associated at the time he began his studies (Dollard, Doob, et al, 1939) posited that reaction to frustration or, more broadly, stress was a central variable in personality functioning, a theory to which many psychologists still subscribe. Unfortunately, the exact role of reactions to frustration, especially to the social frustrations depicted in the P-F, in the ego dynamics of the child is still being explored. Most research on the P-F has been concerned either with attempts to get consensual validation or with diagnostic differentiations and only a handful are concerned with the constructs underlying the technique.

Of all the structured associative techniques, the Blacky Pictures (Blum, 1950) is unique in that it was constructed to investigate variables derived from a specific theory of psychoanalytic development (Blum 1949). The ten pictures of this test represent various aspects of the psychosexual stages: "oral eroticism, oral sadism, anal sadism, oedipal intensity, maturbation or penis envy," plus five other psychoanalytic concepts, "sibling rivalry, guilt feeling, ego ideals, and love-object." In each cartoon, a dog hero, Blacky, is depicted reacting to some other family member or combination of family members (or his "ideal"). The scene is defined by the examiner, for example, Cartoon V, "Here Blacky is discovering sex . . ." and the child is instructed to "make up a story about each picture," which is very similar to the TAT. After each spontaneous story, the child is asked several standardized questions, for example, Cartoon V, "How does Blacky feel here? (a) happy, without a care in the world; (b) enjoying himself, but a little worried, or (c) mixed up and guilty."

The analysis of responses to the Blacky is not as structured as the theory behind it or the stimuli. There is no scoring system, and the psychologist is expected to thoroughly understand, and accept, the theory. This has subsequently been made more explicit by Blum (1953), and users of the Blacky should familiarize themselves with this separate volume. The spontaneous stories and responses to the inquiry are thus analyzed thematically according to the theory. The reliability of this technique is respectable (Blum, 1949) and a noteworthy study of its validity is reported by Blum and Hunt (1952).

As to some of the advantages of this technique, its primary value does appear to be, as Blum (1950) states: "its clinical orientation toward therapy." Admittedly this orientation is restricted to one therapuetic method, but it is used by many clinicians. Those clinicians who use psychoanalytic theory, even very broadly, in eclectic fashion will find that the Blacky does assess variables relevant to their work. Moreover, it is easy to administer; it could be given by a psychometrician or trained clerk. Like the CAT, the animal figures are attractive to children and they are usually quite responsive.

However, the main value of the Blacky is also its chief disadvantage. Many clinicians are unwilling to accept without modification the rather simple, orthodox psychoanalytic theory as outlined by Blum. Psychoanalytic theory is no longer widely rejected, as it was prior to 1940, but it is not so blithely accepted as at the time the Blacky first appeared. More and more the inclination of clinicians is to merge these constructs with social learning theory. The psychoanalytic "stage" is usually not considered separately from the ways the child is learning to cope with other stress, in addition to these primarily internal conflicts. Thus, in current use of the Blacky, one might want to add into the analysis other considerations and variables, such as the nature of the family constellation, the stresses from this constellation, the past experiences of the child, and the stresses from both the immediate environment and the cultural milieu. As with other specifically oriented techniques, the Blacky is most valuable when used as one of a number of assessment tools. For example, a combined use of the Blacky and the Bene-Anthony Family Relations Test might yield valuable data on the child's view of his family and the effects thereof on his psychosexual development.

It should be noted that the Blacky was originally standardized for use with adults. Blum (1950) does present a modified version for children. Here again a theoretical question arises. Psychoanalytic theory as applied to adults assumes that difficulties in emotional and social functioning are caused by reaction formations or regression of the ego to one or more of these developmental stages. It is assumed that the adult either has never passed through the psycho-sexual stage or has reverted to this stage under the pressure of some life stress. However, these concepts do not apply to children in the same fashion. Their reaction formations and regressions are far more fluid and temporary. As was previously noted in the introductory chapters of this book, the child who, in the Oedipal stage, is attempting initially to resolve these fantasies, is not necessarily abnormal or maladjusted. Moreover, none of these psycho-sexual stages are resolved all at once in a precise sequence, with one stage resolved before another begins, as some readers of Freud seem to presume. Similar to the development of other psychological functions, psychosexual

growth is a gradual and overlapping process. For example, a five year old may be in the throes of an Oedipal conflict, while at the same time still attaining controls over his oral and anal impulses. Moreover, as the child advances to a new stage, he may at the same time, under this new stress, regress slightly and temporarily in his adjustment to previously mastered stresses. For example, a five-year-old boy who may have achieved bladder control many months previously may suffer a relapse of a brief period of enuresis as he attempts to free himself from his initial Oedipal attachment to his mother. As has been discussed previously at several points, these psycho-sexual stresses of infancy are not completely resolved when the child enters latency. Rather, the latency period consists of the development and practice of self-controls. Finally, these self-controls are tested at puberty when the psychosexual stages are revived and reenacted. Thus, in interpreting the Blacky, it is most important to take into account the overall developmental progress of the child.

3. The Thematic Apperception Test

Among all the associative techniques, Murray's Thematic Apperception Test is undoubtedly the most widely used, both clinically and in research. Its rationale and method of analysis is a model for other associative and even subjective techniques (see the discussion of Sentence Completion and the Edwards Personal Preference Inventory above). Although Murray advances this technique and his set of instructions and pictures as appropriate for both children and adults, there is little in the research literature to support this specific claim. Lacking such research, it may be worthwhile to raise this question of the applicability of this primarily adult technique to children (or at least its advantages and limitations when used with children). As with the other techniques, this question may be raised separately for the rationale, the operations, the methods of analysis and inference, and the reliability and validity. The rationale is succinctly stated by Murray (1965, p. 430):

"1. In characterizing the hero of a story and in portraying his actions and reactions, the storyteller will commonly utilize some of the components, conscious or unconscious, of his own past or present personality, for example, an assumption, an expectation, an idea, a feeling, an evaluation, a need, a plan or a fantasy that he has experienced or entertained.

2. In characterizing the other major figures of a dramatic narrative and in portraying their actions and reactions, the storyteller will commonly utilize some of the personality components (as he had apperceived them) of persons — such as parents, siblings, rivals, loved objects — with whom he has had, or is having significant interactions.

3. In constructing the plot, describing the endeavors of the hero, his transactions with the other major figures, and the outcome and final consequences of these efforts and interactions, the storyteller will commonly utilize memory traces, conscious or unconscious, of some of the actual or fantasied events that have exerted a significant influence on his development."

Other authorities, for example, Stein (1948), have emphasized that each story simultaneously reflects three levels of experience in the subject's life: (1) the manifest content of the subject's interactions with his environment; (2) the feelings and attitudes of the subject himself about such manifest experiences; and (3) the interaction of needs and stresses within the individual.

However, most authorities agree that any manifest or life history material present in TAT stories is usually masked and distorted by the associations which the subject introjects and then projects onto the characters and the plot. The subject is not asked to tell stories about his family or his own life and, when he does so, it is considered a special instance of the inability to get away from the self. The emphasis and the intent in the interpretation of TAT stories are on the interpersonal and intrapersonal dynamics of feelings and attitudes. Thus, the TAT is aimed almost entirely at the assessment of the *internalized* associations and perceptions with which the subject views the world about him and with which he views himself. Such associations presumably are part of the forces that guide his manifest behavior.

When the TAT is used to assess children, two related questions about this rationale need to be considered: (1) What is meant by assessment of *internalized* attitudes and feelings during that period of a person's life when such inner perspectives are still in the process of being internalized? (2) What are the roles and purposes that fantasy plays in ego functioning during childhood, as contrasted with the uses that adults make of fantasy?

Unfortunately, the answers to both of these questions are at best speculative. Turning to the first question, from the hypotheses advanced in the previous chapters, very little internalization takes place during infancy when the child is still busy exploring his environment and mastering it and himself in a rapid accumulation of learned skills. As a result, it is a rare child under the age of seven who can do much more with the TAT pictures than describe them, make one or two identifications of central figures, and give more than one or two associations. More involved stories from kindergarten age children are a sign of intellectual and emotional precocity, and frequently indicate a "forced growth," that is, the "little adult" phenomenon. However, during latency, when the child begins to integrate and practice what he has learned during infancy, he becomes more able to organize some semblance of a plot to his associations to the TAT and to add voluntarily the feelings of the characters. Even the stories of most adolescents are still much less complete and involved than those told by most adults. Some children are able to weave very lengthy and wordy stories, with multiple plots and many characters, but usually such stories consist of a relatively tangential series of associations, with phantasmagorical characters who shift in feelings and attitudes in chameleon fashion, much to the puzzlement of the assessor. Thus, it would seem unreasonable to assume that the feelings and attitudes reflected in children's TAT stories represent permanent, established internalizations. A more tenable hypothesis would state that these associations represent the child's *attempts* to internalize his experiences and the conflicts he encounters in this process. With children, then, the TAT may most reasonably be used as an assessment of the *extent* and the *process* of internalization.

This hypothesis leads to a second set of speculations concerning the role of fantasy in the functioning of the ego. For adults, fantasy often appears to serve the purpose of the sublimation of unattainable or unacceptable wishes, feelings, and attitudes in which the adult experiences vicariously what he cannot satisfy in overt behavior. Seldom, however, are adults able to indulge themselves freely and completely and express all wishes in fantasy; their publicly expressed fantasies are often stopped short by defensive guards, repressions, and compensations. Children seem to learn this use of fantasy relatively early (even before the end of infancy) but, for several reasons, it appears neither to play such an important part nor to be quite as central a purpose in children's fantasies. Children are still learning what is attainable and what is socially acceptable; they are still attempting to test out interpersonal relationships in everyday life. They may retreat temporarily to fantasy but return to active interaction with their environment rather rapidly. Moreover, a great deal of the child's fantasy is of a nonverbal type and is enacted in playing games and make-believe with peers and adults. When a child retreats to solitary play and fantasy, even the layman is aware that there is something wrong. The adult use of fantasy as sublimation is relatively rare among children, for sublimation is developed much later — usually in adolescence. Before that time, the child sees no great need to sublimate for he still hopes in dependent fashion that his needs will be satisfied and his stresses relieved by his adult protectors.

Adults may also use fantasy in a creative and imaginative fashion in contemplation and reflection, in the introspective analysis of their experiences, in a review of their hopes and plans for the future expansion of their lives. Even more extensively, children appear to use fantasy in an analogous, albeit simpler, fashion, that is, to review and examine what they are currently experiencing. Play and fantasy, as students of child behavior have long recognized, are among the chief methods by which children practice and integrate what they are learning. In this sense the TAT may be thought of, perhaps somewhat surprisingly, as a technique for assessing learning, that is, learning of concepts about interpersonal and intrapersonal experiences. It is not, however, a learning test in the same sense of achieved skills or accumulated knowledge as intelligence tests. The affective and social functions of the ego which presumably are being tapped by the TAT do not appear to be accumulated in quite the same direct and stable fashion as are cognitive skills, but are more tenuously and erratically learned. The TAT often does

appear, however, to yield very valuable clues about *how* the child is learning to evaluate his social interactions and himself. In the child's TAT stories, it is possible to see evidence of the types of coping mechanisms which the child is developing to handle both external and internal stress. The TAT thus does not reveal essentially what the child has learned but what he is trying out; it shows how he is handling his environment and how he is defending himself against both internal anxiety and external stress.

Thus, the rationale of the TAT should be modified when used with children. Rather than reflecting established, internalized patterns of attitudes or feelings as with adults, it mirrors the process of internalization. For adults, fantasy usually serves as sublimation and escape; for children it is more often primarily a mode of learning. The TAT assesses this process of learning affective and social skills and controls.

Operationally, the TAT is described as an unstructured technique but there are some structural limitations set by both the instructions and the stimuli, which are especially important to note when using this technique with children. The instructions as given by Murray (1943) require more than simple free association; the subject is asked to "tell a story" and to conform to a definite story outline: "What is going on in the picture; what brought it about (the past); what is going to happen (the conclusion); and what the characters are thinking and feeling." Moreover, the technique is defined for the subject as "a test of your imagination" and he is encouraged to be imaginative; this instruction is repeated with renewed emphasis halfway through the test. Subsequently, Murray (1965) also recommended that the subject be requested to examine the picture for about 20 seconds before beginning his story, then to put the picture aside. "Also, in order to facilitate the establishment in the patient of a single individual point of orientation through identification with a preferred figure, we ask him or her to choose a proper name for the chief character before proceeding with the story" (ibid., p. 427). As Murray says further, ". . . the TAT is rarely administered as . . . it should be. . . ." Too many clinicians seem careless when administering this and other projective techniques, perhaps in the delusion that because they are dealing with an associative technique the instructions do not matter. Nevertheless, if the types of analysis recommended by Murray are to be applied, even in a gross scanning of thema, strict adherence to these instructions is necessary, as it is if one is to obtain stories of sufficient length to give a reasonable sample of the subject's fantasy. In his opinion, much of what is obtained is chaff or at least is not readily meaningful to the assessor, and stories of 200 words or more are what Murray believes necessary to get at the grain. The need for a story of reasonable length is furthered in the instructions by telling the subject to devote about five minutes to each response.

Since, as was discussed above, children's fantasies are often fleeting and lacking in structure, the use of Murray's instructions are doubly necessary to assist the child in constructing a story. Murray recommends repeating the instructions once, and only once, if the subject does not seem to understand immediately. It is often necessary, however, to encourage children several times, repeating the parts of the instructions which the child is not following. (See Chapter 11 for further suggestions on how to encourage the child.) Even so, the average length of stories told by children is usually less than Murray's requirement.

Most users of the TAT would probably agree that Murray's pictures have proven to be a most ingenious and inspired selection, providing just enough stimulation to fire the imagination yet being vague enough to permit a wide range of idiosyncratic responses. Even though most of them depict adult scenes, children are attracted and challenged by them. Of the series specified for children (marked B or G), none seem to be too stimulating or anxiety provoking; picture 15 (not marked either for children or adults and presumably to be used for both) does seem a bit too grim. To maintain a standardized approach, Murray urges that the entire set of 20 pictures be administered in two sessions, but he himself notes that the complete set is seldom used. Even with very compliant children or those who enjoy exhibiting their fantasies, ten to 12 pictures seem to be the limit of their endurance. Beyond that, one is very apt to meet with considerable resistance or, at best, with hasty and empty responses. Although there is no rationale offered for the ordering of the Harvard series of pictures, it would seem reasonable to administer them in numerical order if only to establish and maintain a standard approach. As several critics have noted, the pictures often pull dysphoric responses because of their content and shading. Further, as Murray admits, the Harvard series does not contain "certain often critical conditions such as sibling rivalry, separation from a supporting person, and so forth." Nevertheless, when the child is concerned with these conditions, they usually appear in his themes, sometimes with little or no relation to the stimulus.

It has been shown that there are marked differences from picture to picture on the TAT on such variables as story length, variety of thema, plot construction, and "pull" for Murray's needs and press (Eron, 1950). Despite this knowledge, the stimuli have never been revised nor have norms for the various pictures ever been compiled. (Picture series designed for special age or social groups have been advanced and will be discussed below.) It would be helpful to know, for example, which pictures draw what kinds of themes or need-press, so that if the assessor wished to investigate certain variables that might be mentioned in the referral, he would have some basis for a selection of pictures. The popular responses and their variants should be determined. When a child gives a socially popular response, one may say that his associations represent the needs and press which he shares with a population of children. This sharing of social norms indicates the degree to which the child is internalizing these social values and stresses.

An extensive metric method of analyzing TAT stories was introduced with the technique. Knowledge and use of the details of Murray's need-press system are required to score each story or sentence within the story. (The unit of response has never been precisely specified.) This scoring system, however, has never been widely used, perhaps because it does require much detail. Moreover, this aspect of Murray's theories has not been widely accepted, even though it is quite possible to relate Murray's schema to other approaches to personality analysis, either psychoanalysis or social learning theory. Thus, this detailed scoring appears only as a specialized research technique, such as in McClelland's N Achievement studies (McClelland, et al, 1953). It is also quite probable that Murray's schema would have to be modified somewhat if applied to children, who are still in the process of internalizing needs and reacting to press. McClelland notes, for example, that N Achievement may be developed only late in adolescence, after controls have been somewhat established. A kind of N Achievement does appear quite frequently in children's TAT's, but is very probably quite different from that with which McClelland is concerned among adults.

By its title the TAT invites thematic analysis, as is described by Murray (1965) and by Stein (1948). A theme is a boiled-down restatement of the story which describes the interactions of the characters and their feelings and moods. Let us take a fairly common response to Card 1 (boy with a violin) as an example.

"This boy . . . I'll call him Alex . . . is looking at the violin. He's thinking if he wants to practice. Maybe he's thinking he might become a famous violin player." (The child starts to put the card away and the assessor asks, "How does he come to be looking at the violin and thinking these things?") "Oh, his mother told him he'd better practice or else!" ("How does he feel about *that?*") "He doesn't really want to practice but he knows he won't get any supper 'till he does!" ("Well, what happens?") "I guess he practices all right," the child sighed, "but then he can go play 'till suppertime." ("How come he thought he might become a great violinist someday?") "Maybe his father was a good violinist. But I guess he'll never make it. He's too little and besides he hates to practice."

The central theme of this story is one of uncontestable compliance with maternal demands for control and learning in order to obtain immediate rewards. Along with this central theme, the storyteller, a bright six-year-old boy, entertains the possibility of being motivated to accept emotional control, symbolized by the violin, on the basis of modeling or identification with a paternal figure, but at least in this stage of his development it seems a remote possibility to the child.

This story may be contrasted with a similar interpretation by a 13-year-old boy.

"This kid is just sitting and looking at this violin. He's 'sposed to practice but he's tired of it. He'd rather be outside playing". ("How did this come about?") "Well, maybe he really wanted a violin in the first place and told his parents to get him one for his birthday. Then he found out about practicing and he hated it, but his father told him that since they bought it he's got to learn to play it". ("What happens?") "I guess he has to prac-

tice, but maybe he makes so much screechy noises that his parents give up and let him trade it in on a guitar."

Here the theme is of self-initiated attempts to learn control, of internalized ambition reinforced by adult authority, which leads to a passive-aggressive rebellion and a search for adolescent peer identification, symbolized by the guitar.

As each story is analyzed, it is possible to note repetitive themes or variants around a central theme. One may also observe the sequence of themes from story to story. Consider, for example, the following comments of the same 13-year-old boy to three other TAT cards. To Card 2, a girl and a farm scene, he told a story about "a girl who doesn't want to live the same kind of life as her parents . . . and leaves home as soon as she is through school." When presented with Card 3BM, a figure crouched against a bench with a gun on the floor, he described the figure in the following way, "He's run away from home; now he's in jail and his mother is coming to get him." About Card 4, young adults, a man faced away from a young woman, he commented, "She's always nagging at him and he's tired of it and he's going to leave and she'll be sorry." Gradually from these and subsequent stories, it became evident that this youngster in his fantasy was concerned with loosening ties with maternal authority, but with feelings of guilt and with insecurity concerning what the next step may be. These feelings were brought out in his story to Card 13B, a boy sitting in a rustic doorway:

"He's just sitting there doing nothing. Maybe his family has gone to town and left him behind. Or maybe he said for them to go and he didn't want to; he'd rather do something by himself for the day. But now he doesn't know what to do. Maybe he wishes he'd gone with them after all." (What happens?) "I don't know. I guess he tries to have fun. He goes for a long walk or something. But it's no fun by yourself."

This story focuses on the child's conflicts between a nascent need for independence and his continued need for familial affiliation, and between his need for a self-recognition as a separate identity and his inability to define that identity.

The associative material from the TAT is so impressively rich with the feelings and attitudes of the storyteller that most clinicians and even many researchers do not question its reliability or validity, but assume that each story is an adequate representation of the child's fantasy. Even in most experiments using the TAT, a kind of face validity is assumed. In most studies, the reliability of the judges is not questioned and, in general, it appears that given a well-defined scoring system or thematic schemata, two or more judges can easily be trained to come to the same conclusions about categorizing the stories. Whether several judges would agree as easily on the meaning or interpretation of the stories is another matter which is seldom investigated. It is probable, however, that a similar consistency could be maintained given the same theoretical constructs.

Whether the TAT provides a reliable sample of child's fantasy is a complex question, for many different factors enter into such an overall reliability. The fact that card pull for either need-press scores or for themas has not yet been established makes it difficult to begin such a reliability study. Therefore, it is impossible to study the consistency of the Harvard pictures either by using an alternate set or by splitting the test into an odd-even series. Using the full series of 20 pictures does seem a rather exhaustive sample of a child's fantasies; yet, it is not known whether one might obtain a whole new set of themas or need-press scores on a second "equivalent" set of pictures a week later. Moreover, fantasies which are mostly idiosyncratic inventions of the child are sometimes difficult to distinguish from those which the child has selected from what he has seen on television or has read and is presenting as a screen over his own feelings and attitudes. Perhaps in some instances it would be most reasonable to be quite conservative and limit interpretation to the assumption suggested above for the P-F studies: that the story represents what the child thinks is socially acceptable in the way of fantasy! As with dreams told during psychotherapy, the import of the story may not always be so much in the content of the story as in the setting or situation in which and to whom it is told. Therefore, probably any set of TAT responses is strongly influenced by the fact that the child has been brought in by the parent or some other authority, and no matter how much anxiety he may be enduring, he faces a representative of parental authority who asks him to reveal his fantasies. In this writer's experience, the TAT more than any other technique draws from the child the request, "You're not going to tell my parents what I've said, are you?" TAT stories, like any other kind of response, can be masked intentionally or at least at a "preconscious" level. Thus, the defiant but guilt-ridden child can, as he approaches some revealing material, quickly change his story, skip over parts of a plot, renege on his "slips," or be so blocked as to be unable to respond. For these reasons it is recommended that the TAT be administered in the latter part of assessment, after rapport has been well established.

Given these limitations about the representativeness of the sample of fantasies obtained from TAT pictures, how valid are the psychologist's interpretations? Again, most of the research on this question is based on data from adults, and very little is known about the validity of children's TAT's. The correlations between the feelings and attitudes expressed in TAT's and those assumed from observed or reported manifest behavior seldom reach any more than bare significance above zero (Samuels, 1965). Of course, one of the difficulties in such studies is that the criterion, the behavior observed or reported, is usually not as explicit or as well categorized as is the TAT response. Still, it is very likely that, as is assumed in the rationale of the TAT, the attitudes and motivations expressed are relatively distinct from the behavior manifest in overt social relationships. The TAT is intended as a device to assess what cannot be directly observed or reported. It might correlate better with dreams or, as Murray suggests, with associations in a psychoanatytic therapy. Perhaps, as psychologists come to know more about the kinds of fantasy themas associated with various patterns of overt behavior, it may be possible to make predictive statements. For example, it would be helpful to know what kinds of themas are associated with enuersis, school phobia, delinquencies of various types, and suicide in children. Until such research is available, the best one can do is to lean heavily on theoretical hypotheses and assumptions about such patterns of symptoms. Thus, what one can depend on is the research on these and other kinds of behavior in children, hoping that when the feelings and attitudes expressed in TAT stories appear similar to those found in research studies on a specific kind of child or childhood symptom, one can reasonably suppose a similar relation between behavior and fantasy in the child being assessed.

4. *The Children's Apperception Test*

Because the TAT pictures did not seem appropriate for young children, Bellak and Bellak (1949) constructed a series of ten plates for children ages three to ten, known as the Childrens' Apperceptive Test, or CAT. These plates use animal figures, many performing human acts, on the theory that children would be more attracted by animals, and that many childhood fantasies in literature and in the children's own productions contain such figures. Moreover, it is argued, children who are engaged in testing and conceptualizing reality have more difficulty than adults in separating fantasy from reality and need the animal figures as an aid in "distancing" themselves. Bellak invented an interesting and helpful outline for analyzing CAT responses, but presents no normative data. Indeed, as Haworth (1966) reports (p. 62), "Bellak cautions that while norms may be useful as a frame of reference and as an indication of developmental trends with age, the statistical treatment of separate responses destroys their meaning as integral parts of a total universe. He maintains that norms are not essential for projective techniques and that actually, each person and each record constitutes a sample population of needs and behavioral variables."

The CAT pictures, unlike those used in the TAT, were purposefully aimed at tapping a general aspect of childhood development and conflict. Bellak intended, for example, that the first picture, which shows three little chickens around a dining table with bowls in front of them and a vague image of an adult chicken in the background, brings out childrens' feelings about eating and orality, especially in relationship to a parent figure and to siblings. Similar hypotheses about each of the pictures were also advanced. Further, Bellak conceived the series as interrelated, so that the stimuli presented to the child first would influence his response to the next picture and so on through the series, somewhat according to the psychoanalytical theory of psycho-sexual development. Thus, a set of hypotheses are present to be checked out in a study of card pull and normative data.

During the next decade, a body of research on the CAT gradually accumulated, including normative data (despite Bellak's contentions). Normative card-pull studies for various age groups, for both sexes, and for both normal and disturbed children have been thoroughly reviewed by Haworth (1966). In general, most of Bellak's hypotheses about the nature of the stimuli have been supported with some age and sex variants. Summarizing the data on thematic norms by age and sex, Haworth reviews thoroughly the studies on reliability and validity. Intrascorer and interscorer reliability have been shown to be very respectable. Test-retest reliability, always a stumbling block for projective tests with children, remains an unanswered question; there seems to be a general tendency toward consistency of response by children to these pictures over time, but there remains considerable variation in stories told from one administration to another, in themes, in needs expressed, and in figures with whom the child appears to be identifying. Haworth points out some of the difficulties inherent in attempting to study reliability of the CAT, not the least of which is the rapid change and fluctuations in the functioning of children during this phase of development. She suggests longitudinal studies as the model for further evaluation of reliability. At the time she wrote her book, several longitudinal studies were in progress employing the CAT. Until further evidence is provided, however, the CAT will have to be used with caution as the variables in the normal child's responses may well change as much as 50% on a second administration even a few weeks later. Whether such fluctuation in response is also true of the emotionally disturbed child or children with other developmental difficulties is unknown. One might expect that a child who give markedly deviant responses suggesting considerable emotional difficulty on one administration of the test would likely show a great deal of the same gross signs of dysfunctioning on a second testing, if no major changes of his functioning were accomplished in between the two administrations.

Validation studies of the CAT, as reviewed by Haworth, show a similar difference between samples using normal and those using disturbed or handicapped children. Correlations between CAT scores and similar variables on other measures on normal samples are barely above zero in most studies. On other studies comparing normal and disturbed children, CAT scores usually differ markedly. Longitudinal case studies, one of which Haworth cites in detail, show "marked congruence" between CAT variables and case history materials. Thus, it appears that while the CAT may not distinguish with acceptable reliability or validity the nuances of development in the normal child, it does demonstrate and discriminate gross difficulties in development.

One factor in considering both the normative and the reliability and validity studies is the very short length of the stories (sometimes only two or three phrases) that are given by children, especially by those under age six. Thus, the data from any one story are often so brief and so sparse that norms are difficult to accumulate and reliability and validity depend upon an extremely narrow range of scores. In this writer's judgment, ten such brief samples of the child's fantasies are often insufficient for clinical assessment purposes also. More recently, Bellak has constructed an additional series of ten pictures, the CAT Supplement (CAT-S), for which there is some initial normative data (Haworth, op. cit.). Thus, it is possible to double the sample of the child's fantasy by combining the two sets. To avoid fatigue and resistance, the sets probably should be administered at separate sessions.

Analysis of CAT or TAT stories told by young children is also curtailed by the fact that their stories often consist of very brief series of disconnected associative phrases rather than therelatively more integrated and sequential plots constructed by older children and adolescents. Thus, there are less clear-cut themes in the responses of children ages four to seven. More often children of this age group describe what they see, attributing little action to the characters, and only single word characterizations of the "heroes." Thus, it is often difficult to determine which character the child is identifying with if, indeed, the child seems to make any definite identification. Of course, at this age the individual's thought processes in every other respect are often described as "concrete"; for example, on the Stanford-Binet, it is not until age seven that one may expect a child to recognize "what's foolish about this picture," which is a "recognition" and not an "inventive" response. Neither should one expect these younger children to attribute much action to their characters, for at this stage of development they have only begun to control, internalize, and project action sequences; their own behavior either in play or work usually consists of very simple, single, and relatively disconnected acts. To cite the Binet again, the item "Memory for a Story" (The Wet Fall) is not successfully passed by 50% of children until age eight.

In young children identification processes are just beginning to develop. Preschool children commonly use some play object, such as a favorite stuffed animal, as a means to express many of their feelings and as a substitute for practicing interpersonal relationships. While the child may seem to project onto such transitional objects, as the psychoanalysts have labeled them (Winnicott, 1953), the nature of such projection is quite different than that shown by older children in verbal responses to the TAT. The infant's play with his Teddy bear, although it may be accompanied by verbalization, is chiefly of nonverbal motoric responses, for example, cuddling, stroking, pounding, clinging, tossing, kissing, and biting. For the most part such transitional objects are "security blankets," not so much objects to be projected upon as to be incorporated into the child's feelings. The infant uses the stuffed animal as part of himself, pulling it into his feelings. Only at the end of infancy does he begin to distinguish objects as different from himself, as capable of having feelings different from his own, which is the essence of projection as applied to the developing child. Projection is thus a process, beginning at the end of infancy, in which the child attempts to separate other people from his egomaniacal, narcissistic self and to perceive others as having feelings independent from his own. In the process of projection, he often attributes his own feelings to others, but the fact of projection presumes that there are others onto whom the child is projecting.

Analysis of the CAT thus requires a different approach than the traditional theme analysis of the TAT. For example, while purely descriptive responses to the TAT by an older child might be considered as indicative of emotional construction, defensiveness, or "immaturity" (sic!), for the four to seven year old, accurate and detailed card description can be considered not only a fair indication of adequate intellectual development but also of the child's ability to separate objects from himself and identify them.

During this latter half of infancy, the number of confabulated, automatic, and perseverative responses to the CAT should decrease and the number of accurate, concrete, reality-oriented responses should increase. The four year old may hit the picture or gesture with it, or he may act out his stories, but such motoric expression would be much less common by age seven. Who is who is often not clear in the stories of the four year old; more definite character identification may be expected by age seven, with less shifting of sex identification or mixing up of identities. In psychoanalytic terms, "primary process" associations, suggesting relatively uncontrolled and generalized impulse release, might well pervade the CAT responses of the four year old but there is a gradual shift during the immediately subsequent years so that these impulses appear in the responses of the seven year old in much more controlled and differentiated form. In summary, the CAT used with this four to seven year old group provides much more of a sampling of the development of ego controls than of definite and differentiated internalized need systems or thematic leitmotifs.

5. Other story-telling techniques

A full review of all storeytelling and similar techniques and methods of analysis is beyond the intent and purview of this book. At least passing mention should be made, however, of two tests, which although not in widespread use, have been fairly thoroughly developed: The Symonds Picture Study Technique (PST) (Symonds, 1949) for adolescents, and the Michigan Picture Test (Andrew, et al, 1953). Both have extensive normative data as an aid in analysis. The PST scenes have been criticized as even more depressing than those of the TAT and do not, in this writer's opinion, depict or elicit adolescent conflicts with any greater specificity than does the TAT. Moreover, whereas the animals of the CAT do seem to attract little children, the specific depiction of adolescents in the stimuli does at times have the effect of making the adolescent even more embarrassed because his problems are being investigated, and thus his defenses rise. The Michigan Pictures are directed more specifically at interpersonal relationships, consisting of photographs of families and other groups in interaction (including school situations). In these respects they leave less to the imaginative processes than the more vague TAT pictures, which permit the child to introduce characters not present in the stimuli.

Another variation of the TAT, which is particularly attractive to children, is the Make-A-Picture Story Test, or MAPS (Shneidman, 1952). In this technique, the child is presented with 67 cardboard cut-out figures and 22 background scenes and is instructed: "You will have figures like this one and your job is simply to take one or more of any of these figures and put them on the background picture as they might be in real life. You might start by putting the figures out on the table so that you see each one." After the child has selected the figures he wants and placed them on the background, he is asked to ". . . tell a story about the situation you have made. In telling your story, tell we who the characters are, what they are doing and thinking and feeling, and how the whole thing turns out. . . ."

Shneidman maintains that the rationale behind the MAPS is essentially the same as that of the TAT. Furthermore, he recommends that the MAPS be used with the TAT as anextensionof it. He lists five general approaches to the analysis of thematic test interpretation: the *normative* approach, using normative tabular data; the *hero-oriented* approach, the classic identification with the hero hypothesis of Murray; the *intuitive* approach of psychoanalysis; the *interpersonal* approach, in which the interaction between characters is emphasized; and the *formal* approach, in which formal (noncontent) aspects of the story such as length, plot construction, etc. are taken into account. This writer is in agreement with Shneidman that all of these approaches need to be used.

Shneidman does, however, emphasize the interpretation of the particular formal aspects offered by the MAPS. He notes the process that the child goes through in selecting the figures and placing them on the background card, and raises questions in his interpretations about why the child selected the kind and number of figures, how these are related by the child to the background, and how they are moved about on the background. (More movements of the figures is possible when the theater form of the test is used, where the background can be placed in a special box at right angles to the table and the figures can be mounted on small metal spools.)

Shneidman presents no particular signs or rules for analysis of these formal aspects of the MAPS test but calls upon the clinician's general background in personality theory and in behavioral observation and logical speculation.

6. *The Rorschach as an Associative Technique*

Although as discussed above, the Rorschach Technique is basically a sampling of modes of perception, the associative content of the responses may be quite revealing of the ideation of the child. Some Rorschach authorities have put primary emphasis on interpretation of content, most notably Schafer (1954), almost to the neglect of the perceptual approach originally proposed by Herman Rorschach. In adult records, content may often play a larger part in Rorschach interpretation than in children's responses. The fact is that the ten cards, which draw some 20 to 30 responses from adults, are actually a very small sampling of ideational content, since many of the responses are often "popular" or relatively banal and stereotyped. Less than one half, and often fewer, adult responses seem to be definitely idiosyncratic or significant in content. Children's records are even briefer on the average; with young children one response per card is quite common, and cards are more often rejected. Children's responses tend to be much less detailed and specific, replete with vague "bugs, butterflies, doggies, trees, etc."

Despite the limited sampling of ideational content which children's responses to the Rorschach provide, in most records, especially among children with developmental disturbances, several such idiosyncratic responses or a definite set of responses usually appear which, although not unique, do carry a marked emotional edge. For example, a child may see only very passive animals, flowers, etc., or predominately "scary" monsters, animals, and people. Clues about the psycho-sexual development of the child may be suggested by examining whether he pays attention to oral details such as animals eating, mouths, etc., or is compulsive about detail, picking out phallic details, or concentrates on feminine genital areas of the cards. In forming hypotheses about psycho-sexual development from such minute clues, however, one should keep in mind not only the limited sample but the developmental level expected of the child and the relevancy of this set of hypotheses to the overall development of the child's ego.

The assessor who attempts to utilize the associative content of Rorschach responses needs also to be aware that these associations are determined to no little degree by the nature of the stimuli and of the task. The nature of Rorschach associations may be realized by contrasting them with the TAT. In contrast to the TAT, the Rorschach presents no content in its stimuli. In administering the TAT, the child is instructed to be imaginative and to utilize the pictures to stimulate his fantasy; he does not expect him to describe the picture. On the Rorschach, the child's task is to structure the stimuli himself, to "make something out of the inkblot." Thus, the task is primarily one of structuring with association following. The psychological meaning peculiar to Rorschach associations arises from the fact that the response is determined by perceptual factors, not by content. The Rorschach is not a projective technique in the strict sense of this term; it is not designed to produce fantasy projections, for these imply an *un*reality or *non*reality process. Instead, Rorschach's instructions require a fitting of nonsense into sense, a making of reality out of a nothing, a process which is the reverse of that of projection. In contrast to the TAT, in which the child projects his feelings, the Rorschach taps the *selective* process of the ego; the determinants are designed to show *how* the child determines perceptually the unknown realities of his world; the content of the responses yields at times a sample of what he *selects* as associations and thus represents what the child *takes in* as regards ideas, feelings, attitudes, symbols, etc.

As Rorschach cautioned consistently, what the child takes in or how he selects is not necessarily directly related to what he gives out, that is, how or with what he responds. In Rorschach's terms, these responses represent *Erleben*, experiencing or perceiving, but not necessarily *Erlieben*, living or manifest behavior. For example, the child who sees one aggressive animal or explosion or destructive association after another would appear to be experiencing his world (here including his inner world) as quite hostile and destructive. He is responding to and selecting the hostile aspects of unstructured situations. He may or may not, however, project these experiences outward onto the environment or permit them to appear in his verbalized fantasies on the TAT. How he handles these depends, of course, on the structure of his ego and its defensive mechanism. For example, he may try to counteract these experiences by dreams of affection and wishes for love in his TAT stories.

For example, a nine-year-old girl who had been deserted by her father and lived with her psychotic mother responded to the Rorschach with associations marked by violent upheaval, clashing forces, and threats of destruction; her TAT stories were wound about "Santa Claus" (in mid-July!). This child appeared to have been too terrified by her experiences to project them into fantasy, let alone into actual interpersonal relationships. Moreover, many of her experiences came from within herself, from her own drives and impulses—as indicated by the many movement responses in her record. Thus, these feelings were not reflected in her manifest behavior *or* in her fantasies of interpersonal relationships. Conversely, the child who fantasies violence in interpersonal relationships, who is projecting, may be quite obtuse to actual indications of violence and hostility either in his environment or on the inkblot shapes. Of course, in many instances the child whose N aggression and feelings of hostility are so strong that they break through his defenses, may be sensitive to clues of aggressive hostility on the Rorschach and express these feelings also both on the TAT and in social interactions as well.

How then may the assessor begin to judge the import of such contentual associations that seem significant on a child's Rorschach? First, one should examine the modes through which the child is perceiving and experiencing such associations. Are they stemming from within him as a part of his instinctual life, his personal attitudes and ideation, or are they chiefly stimulated by environmental contacts and interactions? Or, might they be an intellectualization, a defense against something else? In the case of the child threatened by hostility, is the feeling of hostility derived from his internalized preconceptions, from his aggressive impulses, from his awareness of environmental threats, or from his interactions with the environment? Might he be expressing phobic or counterphobic defenses against some other conflict or anxiety?

According to the Rorschach hypotheses, the source of the child's experiencing may be suggested by the perceptual determinants, by the inferences based on whether the child's response is dictated by color, movement, or shape as discussed in Chapter 7. Quite often, of course, the child may experience the same kind of association from several sources.

Some of the ways in which the Rorschach determinants and the associative content of the child's responses, including those on the CAT or TAT, may be used in combination, will be discussed in greater detail in Chapters 13–15. It is through such combinations of perceptual mode and associative content that a start can be made toward an understanding of the emotional dynamics of the child. The nonverbal activity and productions of a child are essential to assessment of his ego functioning because they contain clues for which the child may have no verbalization. Nevertheless, they are efforts of the child to communicate to others or to work through his emotional interactions with his environment and within himself. There are many gestures, actions, and productive expressions for which there are no adequate words in English. An assessment of children depends a great deal on observation of nonverbal behavior because of the fact that the developing child is, of necessity, engaged in continuous exercise of motoric activity as part of his growth. Even if there were no prohibitions on verbal expression and children were taught the appropriate terms, they would probably still express many of their feelings through physical activity.

C. NONVERBAL ASSOCIATIVE TECHNIQUES

Under the heading of direct observation, some types of children's nonverbal activity which the assessor should note during the examination have already been mentioned; his gait and posture, gestures and facial expressions, and the amount and kind of overall bodily movement. Such physical activity is also very important to note as the child is responding to associative techniques. The way the child scuffles his feet, slams the card on the table, or even tilts his head may often give more clues about his affect than the words he uses.

In addition to observing such spontaneous motoric activity, the psychologist should be prepared to use techniques specifically intended to sample such behavior. Some of these techniques, for instance, Draw-A-Person (Machover, 1949) or House-Tree-Person (Buck, 1948), are widely employed but there are some that are less well known such as the Make-A-Picture Story* (Shneidman, 1952), the Structured Doll Play (Lynn, 1959), and The World Test (Buhler, et al, 1951) with which the assessor should also be familiar.

1. Drawings

Drawings of the human figure are one of the oldest, most clinically fascinating, and at the same time, one of the least scientifically established of all associative techniques used with either children or adults. Because children need to engage in motor activity and in spontaneous creative activity, they are often attracted to this task. Thus, this is often where the child invests the most devotion and energy and, in so doing, appears to spontaneously express many of his unspoken feelings. The operations involved in the drawing of a person actually create several interlinked tasks for the child. This writer and his colleagues employ the following instructions: "Draw a picture of a person, any kind of person you want, just for fun. But make a whole person, not just a stick figure." These instructions require first that the child envision a human body, probably foremost from his own body, although some children may be observed to try covertly to draw the assessor. Second, these instructions require that he transfer this image via motor activity into a reproduction. The added instruction to make a whole person is intended to prevent the child's drawing only a head and shoulders. This part of the instructions does approach the distinctly different instructions for the Goodenough IQ scale ("Make the best drawing you can"), but the slight push toward an achievement motive is purposefully counteracted by the phrase "just for fun." The combined task is quite similar to that demanded by the Rorschach which also asks that a mental image or "engram," as Rorschach

called it, be conceived before the actual response is given. The phrase "not just a stick figure" encourages the child to go beyond any stereotyped set of symbols and to express himself as freely as he chooses.

Therefore the rationale of the D-A-P is that this sample of behavior may divulge the extent to which the child has developed some image of his own body and the physical beings of others. It also yields cues about the manner in which this image is transmitted into more or less controlled motor activity. It is often proposed that one may generalize from this behavior to the image which the child may have of himself as a social person as well as his ability to control or express himself socially. This rationale and its second level of generalization, although not stated in these words, appears to be the basis for the use of this technique by most leading proponents of the D-A-P such as Machover (1949), Hammer (1958), and Buck (1948).

After the drawing is completed, the subsequent instructions to associate verbally to the drawing vary widely. Machover employs an extensive verbal inquiry and bases a great deal of her interpretation on this verbal association. Hammer discusses the D-A-P as though no inquiry were demanded of his subjects, but in discussing the House-Tree-Person Test, he gives an example of a case of a child with an extensive inquiry which he notes is routine. In another case (in Rabin and Haworth, 1960) he does not mention such inquiry at all! In this writer's experience, inquiry seldom yields more than sparse replies from children of any age, and often meets with considerable resistance. Machover (pp. 238 ff., in Rabin and Haworth, 1960) gives samples of the responses by a nine-year-old boy to two sets of 33 questions about his male and female drawings. Twenty to 25 of these responses are insignificant stereotypes or blanks, such as "regular" (how healthy is she?), or "yes" (will she get married?), or "nothing" or "no" (to 13 questions); 21 of the 33 questions about the male drawings were similarly answered. Perhaps other children yield richer protocols to Machover's questions, but responses such as those quoted above are quite typical of most children, including adolescents. Most children present their drawings as a finished product and seem resentful when extensive inquiry is conducted, as if the assessor should be able to comprehend their unspoken graphic message

---

* The MAPS, discussed above as a verbal technique, does not necessarily involve much verbalization. It is especially recommended for exploration of fantasy in cases when the child is relatively nonverbal.

without additional verbiage. At most, children seem willing to answer one or two associations, such as age (and sex if indefinite), and "What is this person like? What kind of personality does he or she have?" Strangely enough, it is not very difficult to get a child to make up a story to his own picture, particularly if the drawing is administered after a relatively successful TAT. It would seem that such a spontaneous association to a creative work is most acceptable to the child than a formal inquiry.

Despite the fact that Goodenough long ago devised a standardized method of scoring the child's drawing of a man as a measurement of intelligence, no such actuarial measurement exists for analyzing the many other ego functions which these drawings are purported to sample. [An exception is Buck's (1948) very complicated system for obtaining an estimate of intelligence from his House-Tree-Person Test.] Most of the experts argue that a metric approach is not applicable, and even antithetical, to the understanding of the overall psycho-dynamic operation of the ego. As was discussed previously regarding other associative techniques, it is this writer's contention that greater psychometric precision, far from violating the assessment of psychodynamics, could well be introduced as a first step in analyzing these samples of behavior. Moreover, such precision might well help to sharpen and specify the second and third level generalizations, which as presently made, often appear to be so vague that they are meaningless stereotypes. In practice, the advocates of these drawing techniques do make use of very specific signs, interpreting them quite concretely. Indeed, some of these interpretations seem to smack of the "Dream-book" analysis of symbols used in the early days of psychoanalysis, but which have long been discarded in current psychoanalytic practice. For example, Levy (in Hammer, 1958) makes such statements as " . . . stroking toward the body is suggestive of introversive tendencies whereas stroking away from the body is often associated with extroversive tendencies" (p. 110), and "the size relationship between the drawing and the available space may parallel the dynamic relationship between the subject and parent figures. Size is suggestive of the way the subject is responding to the environmental press" (p. 101). Hammer, on the other hand (in the same volume), says, "The size of the drawn concept contains clues

about the subject's realistic self-esteem, characteristic self-expansiveness and fantasy self-inflation" (p. 64). Although these statements are not necessarily contradictory, it is difficult to tie them together. Hammer does cite research findings in support of some of his interpretive suggestions; however, Arbit, et al (1959) found that taken one at a time these signs are quite unreliable and have little predictive or even descriptive value. In defense of these experts, it should be pointed out that all consistently warn that no one sign can ever be taken as predictive in and of itself, but must be viewed in the light of the entire configuration of the child's production. Thus, for example, although dark and heavy lines may suggest a depressive mood, one might be more inclined to predict that a child had a depressive outlook if the drawing were also shaded, the eyes downcast, the figure inert or listless, and the drawing as a whole carelessly constructed, etc.

At least on dimensions such as depression, anxiety, overt and even covert hostility, there is a possibility of constructing concrete scales, for which behavioral criteria might be established. Such scales could be validated by the usual statistical processes and then cross-validated. Such scales would be of considerable aid to the clinical intuition demanded by any projective test and might relieve the present chaotic seat-of-the-pants approach. Given such scales as a beginning, it would then be possible to proceed with a profile analysis, that is, with broader generalizations about the patterns of signs. Such psychometric scales would not prevent the clinician from noting and utilizing even broader generalizations based on his analysis of the overall appearance of the drawing and its theme. In the present state of development of these drawing techniques, such overall impressions relp entirely upon the best clinical fit. As presently used, the children's drawings often provide dramatic illustrations to the case history, but the generalizations made on the basis of the drawings are among the most tenuous and least specific of all clinical predictions.

2. Free Play as an assessment technique

The main advantage of drawing is that it is part of the child's normal play activities. That the child expresses many of his conflicts, practices many of his ego functions, and reacts many of his social and personal life situations in his play has been well established both in research and in the clinic. Observing the child in a play setting is a classic assessment procedure. Quite frequently clinicians take the child to a playroom, permit him to explore the room and its materials, and play with whatever he chooses, talking to him about what he is doing and engaging him in an unstructured interview about his play in general. Such observations and conversation are intended to obtain a sample of the child's freedom to play, his ability to use play materials to express himself, and his interactions with an adult in a permissive play situation. In an hour in the playroom, the assessor should observe the following.

1 The child's reactions when given a variety of play situations from which to choose. Does he explore? Does he settle down immediately to play? Is he overwhelmed? How does he make his choices and with what emotions? How restless is he? How compulsive? His responses give possible clues as to how he may make similar decisions in other situations.

2. The use he makes of the play materials he selects. Does he attempt some organized play? Does he use the materials in an appropriate fashion, recognizing them as defined objects or games? Or is his use of them primarily to express some of his own feelings, for example, flinging them about in an angry destructive fashion or pressing them to his body or face as if incorporating them? Such use of play materials may give clues concerning how the child uses reality: whether as something outside of himself or as an extension of himself. The choice of toys or games may also give clues about the feelings that the child needs to play out. He may select objects to work out objectively his angry and hostile feelings, such as military toys, or a ball that can be slammed against the wall, or a punching bag doll. He may want something that he can use to show his achievement and prowess, something to cuddle, or something to express his sexual excitement.

3. The manner in which the child relates to the adult examiner and his presence in the child's play world. In the first place, can he accept the examiner's offer to play freely and yet permit the examiner to be present? Does he allow the adult to observe his play expression or is he uneasy about his play being observed and his feelings revealed? To what extent does he involve the adult in his play? Does he need the adult to play with him? How dependent on others is he in his play? What kinds of things does he seek from the adult: Assistance in decision making? Information about the play materials? Engagement in competitive play? An obedient servant? Observation of such behavior may be very helpful in direct assessment of how the child uses significant adults (or how he would like to use them) in his everyday life.

Two major aspects of the operations involved in the observation of free play need to be considered: the nature of the stimulus (the playroom and its materials) and the activities, chiefly the structure or control, offered by the examiner. First, if free play is to be observed, then the playroom should be set up to permit it. Such a room should invite play and be as free from restrictions as possible. For example, if water play is permitted, the walls and floor should be of a material that will not be harmed by water and water paints; there should be a drain in the floor and a mop handy in case the child becomes anxious and wishes to clean up his mess. If a rubber ball is available, it should be possible to bounce it against the wall without disturbing the assessor's colleagues in the next room or against the ceiling without danger of smashing a light fixture. All in all, the room and its materials should not require the assessor to say, "I'm sorry, we cannot do that here." The rule should be the same as in play therapy: "We can do and say most anything we want here, except that no one should get hurt by anything we do. I won't hurt you and I won't let you hurt me or yourself."

More positively, the playroom should invite play. First, it should be pleasantly decorated without being so elaborate that it is stilted; it should be free of outside distractions but should not seem altogether enclosed. For example, one very inviting playroom has long windows, letting in light from about the ceiling level, screened on the inside to avoid breakage from overactive play, but giving a sense that the room was not completely closed in. Another very ideal play space consisted of a roofless garden court, surrounded by a high fence, which led into the examiner's office through sliding screen doors. This could be protected against inclement weather by pulling down a canvas. The floor area should be large enough to permit some physical activity, at least 100 square feet, but should not be so large as to make the child feel lost in space. For example, it is difficult for a child to feel comfortable playing by himself in a room designed to hold a whole nursery school class.

Second, the number and kind of play materials to be made available to the child should be carefully considered. Murphy and Krall (in Rabin and Haworth op. cit.) list six types of play materials that "one will want to include": the miniature life toys: housekeeping objects and family dolls, tiny soldiers, animals, cars, planes, etc.; "materials which will permit regressive play in conjunction with the miniature life toys: sand, water, clay"; "larger toys for more realistic play"; regular size dolls and trucks; "materials which permit aggressive play: guns, rubber knives, punching bag, "Bobo the Clown"; junk toys, containing fragments such as pegs, light switches, string, tops, balls"; and "materials which permit communication and expression: a toy telephone, crayons, pencils and paper, chalk, paints, finger paints." For older children or even for young ones who need to express their feelings of competition and achievement, it is a good idea to have a few simple competitive games, such as checkers or Parchesi, or a deck of playing cards. These latter materials give the child a chance to involve the assessor in his play and challenge him should he choose to do so, as well as the opportunity to express his feelings about rules and restrictions. If all these materials are immediately available, especially if they are scattered about the room in a jumble, the child may be overwhelmed and spend the major part of an hour sorting them over. Or he may feel that there is no need to play with anything definite since disorganization is presented to him. To avoid this, the materials should be segregated in cupboards which can be opened one at a time. If the assessor has reason to believe the child might be overwhelmed by or distracted by the number of toys, he can say, "All these cupboards have different kinds of toys. We won't have time to play with all of them today but let's look in these (selecting those containing materials the assessor wishes to present) and we can look in the others the next time we get together." If the child is dissatisfied or overly curious, it is still possible to open all cup-

boards. In some instances, the assessor may want to present a limited set of materials. Some thought should be given beforehand to the appropriateness of the play materials to the child being assessed and to the kinds of play materials that might best aid the assessment. For example, one might want to see how a compulsive child might behave if given the chance to be messy with fingerpaints; or a child who is experiencing considerable familial dissension which he cannot voice may be able to express his feelings in play with the doll house or with puppets.

If free play is to be elicited, the assessor must reverse or alter the role he normally plays in structured assessment situations, and stand back giving little or no instructions or limits other than the general limitation mentioned above. As indicated, it if often possible to carry on a conversation with the child as he plays; in fact, many children invite such conversations and even seem more at ease if the adult behaves in a natural and interested way than if he sits silently, taking surreptious notes. The adult need not participate in the child's play, and should not do so unless invited. In some instances, when it is obvious that the child is anxious lest the adult feel hurt that he is not included or if the assessor wants to test the child's ability to play independently, the assessor may want to reassure the child that he need not be included. The conversation should not take the form of an inquiry as on the Rorschach, or of confronting interpretative statements, for these approaches tend to inhibit the child's play. Such commentary is appropriate only after the child is definitely engaged in a play therapy, not in the assessment period per se. The playroom observation may constitute a prelude to play therapy, giving the child a chance to get used to the clinician and the play situation and forming a baseline for the clinician in his subsequent efforts to alter the child's behavior.

Since a playroom as described above is not always available, it is a good idea for an assessor to keep on hand some simple play materials which can be used in an office situation, for example, a doll house, a set of miniature toys (similar to those of the World Test), and a set of hand puppets. A child might thus be invited to play with the materials on a table or the floor for a half hour or so after the formal testing is completed. (If these materials are presented to the child earlier in the assessment, it is often difficult to persuade him to return to more structured tasks.)

Although several methods of scoring free play observations with rating scales, etc., have been devised for specific research purposes, none of them appears to have been adopted clinically and most have been too specific for the more diverse multipurpose needs of clinical assessment. As Murphy and Krall say:

"Since the child's use of play may express the most personal, idiosyncratic experience reflected in any medium, no standardized set of criteria, signs or scores can offer an adequate approach to the evaluation of play. Just as the analyst is constantly on the outlook for new experiences not previously discussed in the literature, the psychologist who evaluates the play of a child needs to be sensitive to the unforeseen events which may carry him closer to the experience of the child than scores on standard lists could do. Anyone undertaking to use play for general diagnostic purposes should be thoroughly familiar with the discussion by Erikson, Peller, Despert, Murphy, and Loomis at a minimum. . ." (Haworth and Rubin, 1960, p. 290).

The fact that there is no comprehensive scoring system for evaluating play observations does not, however, excuse the assessor from a careful recording of his observations nor from a thoughtful and systematic analysis of his data. Although some children are made uneasy when the assessor takes notes during the observation period, usually the child is unconcerned since his responses to other techniques have been written down in prior contacts. It is then possible to go over such process recordings of the child's behavior, noting (1) the sequence of events and then (2) as on the TAT, the general themes. Viewing these in light of the rationale discussed above, one may obtain many clues about various aspects of the child's ego functioning.

There are really no established norms of clinic playroom behavior; one can only guess by what has been reported from nursery school and other free play observations. Even these have largely been of children playing in groups. Such norms can only be gathered through experience by the individual assessor. He learns, for example, not to be very impressed by the fact that an eight-year-old boy takes a couple of swings at the "Bobo" punching bag as he enters the room and a couple more before he leaves, and to be quite aware of the possible sexual implications of the behavior of an eleven-year-old girl who spends most of her time wrestling "Bobo" to the floor and squirming around over him.

The reliability of such data obtained from one or two play sessions has never been established, to the best of this writer's knowledge. The assessor should keep in mind that this sample of the child's play is probably biased by several factors, such as the relative artificiality of the setting, the fact that the child is being observed, and that children's play probably varies extremely from time to time in both the amount of expressiveness it contains and the intensity with which feelings are expressed. In addition to these unknown reliabilities of the data, there are even larger questions about the reliability and validity of the inferences drawn from these data by the assessor. The reliability of his judgments depends essentially upon his experience. Unfortunately the emphasis in the training of psychologists on exact measurement is not always balanced by training in careful observation and recording of behavior. When no rating scale is provided for the novitiate, he tends either to become lost or to overestimate and overgeneralize from the scraps of behavior he is trying to analyze. Only by careful practice in systematic observation can an assessor become consistent.

The validity of generalizations drawn from free play presents essentially the same dilemmas as do the projective techniques: against what criteria does one compare the expression of unconscious feelings and emotions? Although no validation method has univocal acceptance, at least an internal validation may be obtained by noting the consistency of the child's behavior through the comparison of these play observations with other data obtained from projective materials and from the case history. However, there are two possible fallacies in such an internal validation process: (1) The assessor must be careful that he does not contaminate his conclusions by selecting only those data from each set of observations which support his overall hypotheses. His hypotheses must fit a majority of the data. (2) Conversely, the assessor should not expect that data obtained from one level of ego functioning will necessarily be consistent with that obtained from another level. In fact, it is quite reasonable to suppose that these data may actually seem at odds, especially in the ego functioning of emotionally disturbed children. For example, it would not invalidate one's hypotheses to find that a neatly dressed and well-behaved child who has a history of enuresis gives largely compulsive and stereotyped responses to most of the projective tests, with only minor signs of repressed hostility, but in the playroom becomes so involved in messy water play that he accidently wets the assessor, albeit with considerable signs of guilt!

3. The World Test and The Structured Doll Play Technique

Although most clinicians are aware of the values and hazards of free play observations, many do not seem as familiar with the possibilities of more structured play techniques, involving the use of more or less standardized materials, more well-defined methods of analysis, and more limited rationales. Two such techniques which have received at least occasional use in clinical settings are the World Test (Buhler, et al, 1951) and the Structured Doll Play Test (Lynn, 1959). The World Test consists of a set of miniature buildings and other objects which can be used to form a village, human figures to people it, military personnel and equipment, and a set of domestic and wild animals.* The child is invited to sit on the floor and open the case. Buhler used the following directions to the child: "See all these things. You may play with them and build something with them here on the floor. You may use as many as you like. Here are houses, trees, people, soldiers, cars . . . " and the assessor points out each item, naming it. "Now you may play." She recommends that the child have an area six feet square in which to construct his world and that the child be allowed to play 20–30 minutes. She suggests that the examiner ask the child what he is making after about five minutes and make further inquiry after 20 minutes. Thus the element of the child's world are identified for him,

but the arrangement of these elements is left up to him.

In this set of test operations, the assessor withdraws after having acquainted the child with the stimuli and the child is free to utilize the stimuli as he sees fit (or not utilize them, as is frequently the case). Although Buhler and her cowriters do not remark on interactions between the child and the assessor, it has been this writer's experience that many children try to involve the assessor in the construction of the world. They frequently ask for further identification of the items, ask advice about using them, or permission to use their own ideas, or even invite the assessor to join in the play, giving directions, sharing items, etc. One child went so far as to divide out the entire box of toys between himself and the examiner, one at a time. "This is for you, and this is for me." He directed the psychologist to play with his half on the opposite side of the room and kept coming across to see how the psychologist was proceeding! Each time he would "borrow" one of the "doctor's toys" to add to his world, so that in effect the toys he left for the psychologist were those he was omitting from his world. Although such extreme interactions are rare, the kinds of interchange which the child voluntarily creates between himself and the assessor should be noted. In this interchange, the child may be demonstrating the amount and kinds of support and help he needs in organizing his world. Through observing this interchange, the assessor may gain clues about how dependent, demanding, manipulating, seductive, or rejecting the child may be in relation to adults when he has to organize the elements in his environment.

When this technique was constructed, the criterion for a clinical instrument was that it could statistically distinguish normal children from emotionally disturbed or retarded children. Thus, most of the original studies were concerned with the discriminative value of various signs, such as use of aggressive elements, the absence of human figures, the number of items used (50 or less), the number of types of items, closed versus open worlds, schematic versus disorganized worlds, and so on. Unfortunately, in these studies of signs and symptoms, the basic standard data were almost forgotten and only the barest age norms are given.

As is indicated by the cases cited in these

---

* Unfortunately this original set does not seem to be commercially available at present, but most of the materials may be purchased in many toy stores using the list in Buhler's *Manual* as a guide. This author recently replaced most of the plastic buildings by having more sturdy wooden ones built in the hospital's Occupational Therapy Shop as a patient project. Although the test's standardization is undoubtedly weakened, the *Manual* suggests that the number and types of materials used do vary.

original articles,* the World Test provides much more data than a mere discrimination between normal and disturbed children. Although there does not appear to be any further research on this technique, and no systematic validation, this writer is continually impressed with the fit between the child's use of these materials and other clinical data. More than on any other projective technique, the child displays on this well-named World Test how he organizes the elements of the world about him, what kinds of emotional stimuli he accepts and rejects, the interactions of these elements, his attitudes toward them and his methods of coping with them. Most of all, the World Test shows the child in action, with a minimum of required verbalization.

As to methods of analyzing responses to the World Test, the rough classificatory signs or "symptoms" which Buhler lists are scarcely metric scores, but they do provide beginning steps. Thus, the gross number of objects used does seem an indication of how many stimuli the child can admit and handle; this measure also reveals how empty or overcrowded the world seems to the child. The number of different types of elements may be taken as one measure of the complexity of his world. Buhler also stresses observation of the way the materials are organized by the child. As she notes, some children systematically organize the play materials into a village with an outlying farm area for the animals and a nearby military post and a zoo, etc. Others, particularly younger or retarded children, may line up the materials in neat rows but with little or no systematic arrangement. Still others present some partially organized sections but with disparate elements intruding in bizarre fashion, as if the child were trying to use and absorb something into his world which he does not understand or is out of place. The content of such intrusions often gives clues to some of the child's conflicts. For example, Bobby, age six, had built a relatively well-organized village and peopled it with several human figures, but had not used any of the animals or soldiers. Then he proceeded to place a wild animal behind each of the buildings. "They all got loose from the zoo and are hiding," he explained. Then he brought in several soldiers to hunt down the animals. None of the human figures were

disturbed. Questioned about this, he looked puzzled, then he decided, "They don't see it—they don't see all the lions, 'cause they're invisible. Only these guys (the soldiers) can see 'em." It was noted that Bobby's parents had been unable to see his aggressive behavior at school, and openly expressed their feelings that the school authorities were unjustly critical of him.

Another variable in the child's organization of his world which Buhler observed was the closure or openness of the overall gestalt. Some children built very tight little worlds, with everything crowded together in a small circle. Others scatter their buildings and people loosely across the floor, freely utilizing all the available space. Some use the fences and other materials to enclose many elements. Many children make sure that the animals, domestic or wild, are corralled. Marlene, age seven, built two squares of four buildings facing in toward one another. Inside one square she put the boys and in another the girls. The assessor also noted that on the DAP, Marlene, after drawing a girl, specifically asked for a separate piece of paper on which to draw a male figure and continued to remark on and emphasize the sex differences in her drawings. In the initial interview, the assessor discovered that Marlene had four brothers, but no sisters, and that there were no girls Marlene's age in her immediate neighborhood. However, neither Marlene nor her parents had seemed particularly concerned with the fact that Marlene's world was chiefly male. These data suggested that Marlene might be struggling to separate out and establish her feminine identity.

Another major variable—not specifically noted by Buhler—is the sequence in which the child selects the objects and inserts them in their world. Most commonly children of all ages begin by selecting buildings and other inanimate objects and then adding animals and people. Most children put in houses before they use other buildings, usually putting in the school, hospital, or jail last—if these buildings are used. Domesticated animals and human figures are usually inserted before the wild animals. However, it would not be unusual, for example, if a normally aggressive five-year-old boy played first with the soldiers or aircraft, and then set them to one side to become occupied with building a village, finally constructing a military airport on the outskirts. The sequence

---

* All were published together, see Buhler, *op. cit.*

of choices is most important to note when the child's world is chaotic, for the sequence of associations often reveals the defenses and conflicts which disturb his world. For example:

CASE 13

Lonnie, age nine, was both threatened and fascinated by the wild animals. Initially he brushed them aside, making a sound that suggested both fear and disgust. He sorted over some of the buildings but used none. He then selected the policeman and the jail and placed them in the center of the floor, without comment. Then he added several soldiers, the "Stop" sign, and a dog. Two houses were placed far from the first objects. He returned to examine the wild animals and asked the assessor to name each and to tell him if they were dangerous. When he was asked to name them, he became upset and stopped playing for a second but began to identify them to himself, *sotto voce*, with his back to the assessor. His attention returned to other objects and he played momentarily with cars and planes. Then he gave the monkey a ride in the car, adding in a bear and a lion. He concluded by crashing the cars and wild animals into the policeman and jail.

In the initial interviews with Lonnie's mother, it was discovered that Lonnie's personal world was also chaotic. From ages three to seven, he had been a "football" between his parents in the divorce court, each claiming custody over him. This battle was not resolved when Lonnie's mother remarried, for his father continued to give him treats and did not discipline him. In his mother's home, Lonnie responded to this discipline with temper tantrums and angry rejections of his stepfather and his mother. His reactions caused so much dissension between his mother and stepfather that their marriage was about to be dissolved. However, when Lonnie's parents quarreled, he became extremely upset. During one such parental quarrel, he ran screaming into the street, declaring he was going to be killed and would have been hit by a car had not the driver quickly swerved and crashed into a neighbor's house.

In the Structured Doll Play Test (SDP), Lynn (1959) presents a technique which uses cardboard doll figures and simple settings to sample the child's perceptions of and reactions to a variety of parent-child situations. These situations include: separation from parents and choice of parents, feeding, sleeping, toileting, discipline, aggression toward peers, and affection. In the administration of the SDP, the assessor first introduces a family trio of father, mother, and a child (of the same sex as the client); subsequently a child of the opposite sex is also used to obtain intersex peer attitudes by both parents and child. Lynn notes that he specifically limited the family to three in order to standardize the situations. However, it does seem that a younger sib and older sib situation might well have been added. The assessor illustrates how figures can be made to talk and walk and encourages the child to use them in the settings provided. For example, the child is shown a "pottie" and an adult toilet and asked which the child doll is to use and which parent is to help.

Although some free association is called for in the operational procedures of the SDP, it is, as the title states, quite structured. The assessor sets up situations and asks the child to make choices. Only in a few situations is the child offered the opportunity to express his own ideas. However, as Lynn notes, most children verbalize many feelings during this doll play or act them out with the dolls. As with the World Test, the manner in which the child relates to the assessor should be carefully noted. In this procedure, the assessor is inviting the child to join him in play; not all children accept this invitation in the same way. Some do wait for instructions, recognizing that it is the assessor's game. But many children regard play as their perogative and resent the intrusion of adult instructions. Even children who accept a test situation, such as the Binet, or stories to the CAT, may decide to play with the dolls as they please and make up their own situations. Many children communicate through play, as some adults use dreams to voice their feelings. The child who disregards the SDP instructions often seems to have something special to communicate to the assessor. Thus, it may be wiser to permit the child to act out his own play with the dolls if he wishes and note such play carefully as a special communication. Usually the child will subsequently accept the assessor's directions.

Lynn advises that the SDP may be used with children from ages two to 11, but provides normative data only for ages two to six. These normative data are in the form of percentages of children who make various kinds of responses in each setting, using Lynn's classifications. It should be noted that these percentages are based on samples of only 30 children. Moreover, most of these children were from upper-middle class families, and were attending a private school. No reliability or validity data are supplied in the manual. It is to be hoped, as Lynn mentions, that more complete normative data are to be provided. More than most associative techniques designed for children, the SDP does take into account developmental changes and is designed to assess the maturity and immaturity (to use Lynn's terms) of the child in his relationship with his parents.

In analysis of the child's responses to the SDP, there are no scores or scales. However, using the preliminary norms in the manual, it is possible to outline patterns of reaction. Thus, a child may show a relatively rare response to some situations and standard responses to others. For example, he may make mature choices concerning objects, but have difficulty separating from his mother. Another child may give unusual responses only to the situations involving aggression and toileting. Although it is usually difficult to state definite themes in the brief associative responses to the SDP, this sample of the child's play often does appear to reveal a leitmotif or overall pattern. For illustration of the use of the SDP, see Case 50 in Chapter 17.

Part III

PROCEDURES IN ASSESSMENT

Chapter 10

THE ASSESSMENT
MILIEU AND THE REFERRAL

A. THE ASSESSMENT MILIEU — A COMPLEX OF INTERPERSONAL RELATIONSHIPS

In clinical assessment, as in any scientific study, the procedures of data collection are dependent upon and secondary to the goals and purposes of the investigation. Children are interviewed and tested, not merely to see "what the tests show" (a phrase too often found in student reports!), but rather to determine, quantitatively and qualitatively, the level and variation of the development of ego functions. As in any scientific study, assessment of these functions requires a systematic, precise, and careful collection of data.

In Part II the methods and techniques for collecting data were reviewed. However, the setting in which these techniques are used and the procedures in administering these techniques also constitute important facets. These procedures include: the environmental setting in which the clinician works, the nature of the referral, the planning and preparations for the assessment, the setting of appointments and fees, the initial contact with the child, the introduction of the child to the assessment, procedures in interviewing children, procedures in testing, handling resistances during the assessment, procedures in interviewing parents and others concerned with the welfare of the child, and procedures in reporting findings and follow-up.

As the ramifications of these steps in carrying out an assessment are explored in detail, it will become obvious that the procedure as a whole involves many different variables which affect the assessor and his procedure of gathering data about the child and, ultimately, his analysis of these data and his reporting of that analysis. As the assessment proceeds, these variables become even more complex and interwoven in interaction with one another. These variables are considered separately in the initial discussion of the environmental background in which the assessment is carried out. Thereafter, however, these assessment procedures are examined sequentially in order to emphasize the manner in which this complex of variables does develop. A recognition of this procedural process may help the assessor to keep track of these variables, to manage them, and even to take advantage of this sequence per se as further data in his evaluation of the child's behavior.

As will soon be obvious, the variables which most significantly affect assessment are most commonly called "interpersonal relationships." Before examining the procedures of assessment, it may be helpful to define this term operationally. First, there are the interactions between the child and the assessor, that is, how the child views the assessment and the psychologist conducting it; how the psychologist regards this particular assessment and child; how the behavior of the psychologist affects the child and his motivation and achievement; how the child and his problems, personality, behavior, and even his performance and achievement affect the psychologist; and how they interact from the moment they meet. All of these interactions taken together constitute a major variable in the assessment process. Yet, this interaction between child and assessor is seldom an isolated experience for either of them, but is nearly always affected by and embedded in a complex of other interpersonal relationships, directly and indirectly bearing on the assessment. Often one of the most important of these sets of interpersonal relationships is the one involving the child's parent (usually the mother), the child, and the psychologist. How the mother's attitudes, expectations, and behavior affect those of the child—and of the psychologist— and the relationship between child and psychologist, and how these in turn condition the mother's reactions, constitute a second major issue in the assessment process, as will be discussed in detail in this chapter. Third, it is necessary to consider how the relationships between these central figures are affected by and have effects upon many other persons concerned with the assessment and the welfare of the child. These include the person who refers the child for assessment, other parental authorities, staff colleagues of the psychologist who may or even may not be directly involved with the assessment, school, medical, and community authorities, and even at times siblings and peers of the child—as, for example, when the child is being assessed at school or in other institutional settings.

B. THE ENVIRONMENTAL SETTING

1. *The Community*

In the broadest dimension, both the relationship between child and psychologist, and the purposes and import of the assessment, are delimited by the nature of the community in which the psychologist works and the community in which the child lives (which, as will be seen, are not necessarily the same). Attitudes toward psychology as a profession and as a science vary from community to community and in different segments of any one community. Most commonly, psychological assessment is a middle class phenomenon, sponsored chiefly by the upper-middle class, utilized by a broad span of the middle class, and conducted by middle class professionals. Although in such communities there may be a minority which has negative views about anything associated with mental health, for the most part, psychologists and their clients will usually be in agreement that such services are worthwhile and necessary. However, some communities, even those which are predominantly middle class, barely tolerate anything associated with psychology, especially where the clinic is sponsored by some agency not directly under the aegis of the community, such as a university or a state government. In such settings, the child and parent who seek psychological assessment run the risk of at least silent if not vocal disapproval from their respective peers. Although driven by dire necessity to seek these services, the clients may themselves regard the psychologist with grave reserve and feel considerable shame and guilt. At the other extreme is the community which hires the professional expert as a kind of shaman to solve a hidden agenda of problems, such as is described in *Crestwood Heights* (1956).

In other institutional settings, such as in the juvenile hall or welfare agency of public hospitals and clinics serving largely lower socioeconomic clients, the services are nevertheless largely paid for by the middle and upper class taxpayers, who sit on the governing boards of these institutions, and who expect the institution and its employees to foster middle class standards and behavior in their work with their clients. Even where the professional attempts to bridge the gap between the section of the community which governs the institution and the clientele it serves, the lower class client usually recognizes, albeit covertly or unconsciously, that the institution was set up with the idea of reforming and rehabilitating them away from their mores. Thus, they may come overtly hat in hand, cooperative, and obsequious, but also with unspoken suspicion and resentment. The psychologist should be quite aware of the relationships between his institution and the community and between the power structure of the community which sponsors him and the clientele he serves.

Sometimes, such as in the isolated state hospital or institution for delinquents, the child may not even be a member of the communuity surrounding the institution. For example, this writer once was employed in an institution which was the major employer in a small rural community, so that community consisted chiefly of the employees of the hospital. Yet the power structure of the community was most hostile toward the hospital and its patients and carried on legal and social war to attempt to drive the institution out!

2. *The Nature of the Institution*

The second factor in this general environment is the nature of the institution and the psychologist's position in it. In settings where the institution is generally run on democratic principles, with little or no competition between staff members and with a general problem-solving orientation, the assessment would be treated as another and important step in service to the child. In other settings where there are intrastaff power struggles or battle lines drawn along theoretical differences or personalities, the psychologist's work may be severely hampered. He may feel that he must watch his step in conducting and reporting his assessment. If the child under consideration presents problems which might sharpen staff differences, the psychologist may have to take care that he does not unconsciously treat this particular child in a defensive way which might bias the observation. Insofar as possible he should try to prevent such intrastaff difficulties from entering his relationship with the child, and attempt to seek solutions for these problems in a more appropriate arena. One of the most difficult positions for a psychologist is when he feels that his work will not be appreciated or will be disregarded by other staff, so that he begins to go about his assessments in a listless manner. On the other side of the same coin is the tyro who feels that his observations constitute the only answers. In fact, the novitiate sometimes actually has both opinions of himself. However, the psychologist who is oriented toward problem-solution rather than his own status wins the respect of his colleagues in the long run.

The nature of the institution may also directly affect the attitudes and expectations of the child and his parents. If the agency is part of a line of bureaus through which the client must make application before his is able to get service, he is often very frustrated and may thus arrive on the psychologist's doorstep feeling both negativistic and hopeless. Where the client has direct access to the agency, especially where that access includes a friendly and perceptive receptionist who is not made defensive by angry or distraught parents, the child and his family's expectations are more likely to be positive.

Many other aspects of the institution's public image may also affect the client's perception of it: its professional reputation, its location, its title, etc. The assessor should be aware of these factors and in his initial interview, when he inquires how it was that the client sought help from this particular institution, he should be alert for indications in the client's response as to whether these factors are playing a part. For example, the middle class parent whose financial straits prevent his seeking private care and who finds himself in a dingy hallway at the back of the public welfare building in front of a door labeled "Psychiatry Clinic" may feel very let down—and defensive. Or, on the other hand, the family from the lower socioeconomic strata who makes a long trip across town to the seemingly palatial new buildings of a university, located in an upper-middle class suburb, may, after paying a parking fee and lining his own car among newer ones and entering the marble halls, wonder in embarrassment what he is doing there! Such a client may even question whether his child's needs will be considered in such a setting. Very often it is necessary for the psychologist to be aware enough of these attitudes and frustrations for him to allow the parent and child at least a few minutes to rest up after their efforts to get to his office and to ventilate briefly some of their difficulties in finding and adjusting to its surroundings. A pleasant waiting room, a helpful and cheerful receptionist, and the greeting given by the psychologist usually serve to ameliorate such negative first impressions.

3. *The Assessment Room*

The environmental aspect of the assessment which bears most immediately on the psychologist-child relationship is the room in which they work. The setting for an assessment should be one in which both the child and assessor can work comfortably, at ease and without distraction. The room where the assessor works should be located close enough to the clinic waiting room so that the fearful child can be reassured that his parent is near at hand, but far enough way so that he knows the parent is not listening. Ideally, there should also be a supervised waiting room for children, where the child can stay during parent interviews. Child-size lavatories and low-level drinking fountains should be included in plans for any clinic serving children. All of these environmental details make a child feel that the assessment situation has taken account of his physical needs and implies to the child that his psychological needs may also be met.

In building a new clinic, a room should be set aside for assessment purposes, separate from either the office or playroom. It should not be much larger than eight feet by ten feet, so as not to give the child too much opportunity to move about, but spacious enough to contain a work table for the assessor's materials, his chair, a table adustable in height for the child to work on, and a chair appropriate to the child's size. This ideal room should be free of all other distracting materials. Assessment of children in the usual office setting has the disadvantage that the child may be attracted by many other objects that he may want to explore or ask about and to which the clinician may want to deny the child access or about which he may not want to have to explain. The assessor should not have to answer the telephone or protect his papers and books from the hyperactive and possibly destructive child. The child should not have to feel that he is in the adult's domain, for example, the formality of desks, file cabinets, bookcases, typewriters, and dictaphone equipment. A playroom is often at least equally distracting, unless entirely cleared of all play materials. Doll houses, dart boards, and Bobo punching bags are far more fascinating than most test materials and offer a fine target for the child who seeks to avoid the job of assessment. This ideal room should be brightly lit, but preferably not with any source of flickering light (which can induce seizures in brain-damaged children). A window in any room does give a sense of openness and freedom,

but is not necessary. It should be draped or shaded both to avoid distractions from the outside and the possibility of glare. Such a room, while as devoid as possible of things other than the work materials and furniture, need not be absolutely bleak; the walls may be painted in warm colors preferably with washable paint and decorated with simple prints—or even children's drawings. If the room abuts on other rooms where the sound of a child's voice or of kicking feet or scraping furniture might be undesirable, sound-proofing may be needed. Floors need not be carpeted but definitely should not be waxed or slippery for, no matter how children are warned, they tend to lean back in chairs, to push on the table, or otherwise slip and slide across waxed floors. An assessment session can come to an abrupt end when a child's chair slides from under him as he moves to the front edge of it to handle test materials on the table, only to crack his chin on the table edge as he goes down! The temperature of a room where one is working with children should be a few degrees lower than might be comfortable for an adult without a sweater or coat, for children's body temperatures tend to run a few degrees warmer than adults' and they are too warm when the adult is just warm enough. The room should have a hook on which the child's coat can be hung, so he can work free of the encumbrances of jacket sleeves. If the room is in a hospital or school or an institution other than a purely psychological clinic, then it should be isolated as much as possible from the sight, sound, and smells of the institution. It should be evident to the child that he is in an assessment room, not a schoolroom, and not a medical examining room.

All these may seem rather petty and evident details. However, too often assessments are deterred unnecessarily when the assessor attempts to work in quarters where both he and the child are continuously distracted and where the setting so intrudes on the child's consciousness that it affects his responses. For example, in the usual office setting, the child has only to look around him to name 28 works in one minute as required on item of Year X of the Stanford-Binet. IQ or Rorschach responses or interview material may be deflected or deterred when a child sits in an adult chair, half sliding off, his feet dangling, and facing a window with the sun streaming into his face, with a ballgame going on in the playground outside. Small wonder that he jumps to his feet and peers out the window when the assessor's office phone rings. Nor should one be surprised that his next response is contaminated by the distraction.

Of course, such an ideal situation is seldom attained. If one does have to assess in an office, care should be taken to keep distractions to a minimum. Admittedly, there is some advantage to working in a room where the assessor feels at home; if his office is his castle which children can invade without causing him undue anxiety, he may feel enough at ease and accustomed to the exigencies of his office that he can account for the distractions. The writer admits that he prefers to operate ensconced in his own "cubby hole," even though hyperactive children occasionally knock over his personal possessions, stare at his books, or stand on the chair to gaze out the window. But to assess a small child, the typewriter and calculator are moved out and a child's table and chair are brought in; the drapes are drawn and the secretary takes the phone calls. Each time the writer assures himself that next year he will ask the clinic for a separate room.

Sometimes it is necessary for the assessor to leave his setting and assess the child elsewhere, for example, at a school, in a hospital room, at juvenile hall, or in the child's home. Even in these situations, it is sometimes possible to approximate the general conditions mentioned above. For example, on a pediatric service, it may be necessary to assess a child who cannot leave his bed. Even so, one can establish the atmosphere of an assessment situation by drawing the curtains around the bed, asking the nurse—in front of the child—that there be no disturbance and making sure that the usual nursing operations for the comfort of the child have already been performed. In such instances, the child may feel more at ease and even be pleased by the assessor's visit if, during the orientation (see below), the assessor mentions in passing that since the child could not come to see him, the assessor has made this special trip to see the child.

C. THE ASSESSOR AS AN ENVIRONMENTAL VARIABLE

Last, but certainly not least, the assessor himself should be considered as part of the environmental setting. The impression given by his appearance, demeanor, and behavior often affects the attitudes of the child and parent toward the assessment. Although any particular initial impression may change as the assessment proceeds, the assessor should be aware of the impressions he makes on his clients in general. He should also be alert for clues from any particular client about the way the client is reacting to him as a person and how this may be affecting and shaping the assessment. This alertness to the sensitivities of the client, so basic in every step in assessment, thus requires that the psychologist be able to see and hear himself as he appears to others.

1. *The Assessor's Appearance*

Some aspects of the assessor's appearance, such as dress and grooming, may on first thought seem too superficial or picayune to warrant much consideration. In many agencies and institutions, it almost goes without saying that the professional staff should conform to relatively conservative middle class standards in their dress and behavior, even though their clients may not themselves come from the same background, or, as is often the case with adolescents, be attempting to revolt against it. On the other hand, psychologists themselves, as members of the intelligentsia, may well argue that a person's dress and appearance are matters of personal choice and *should* make no difference—forgetting that they themselves often make inferences about their clients from just such clues! If there is any general rule about the psychologist's manner of dress, it is largely in terms of broad limitations; insofar as possible, the psychologist should avoid offending or startling his clients with his dress and grooming or, on the other extreme, setting them too much at a distance by an overly formal or stiff manner of dress or uniform. Actually the psychologist working with children can and should be a bit more informal in dress than perhaps may be required when working with adult clients. Shirt sleeves and slacks for the men or a housedress or smock for the women are not only excusable, but appropriate and acceptable. It is difficult sometimes for either child or psychologist to relax when he is dressed for the adult office. The psychologist who adopts the white uniform of his medical colleagues is apt to be mistaken for the fearsome laboratory technician who stabs the child with a needle. It is inevitable that some client is going to take offense at the way a psychologist wears his hair or other details of grooming. If a psychologist enjoys wearing a beard, he must at least recognize that children will regard him as "different" and probably expect him to be different in his behavior and attitudes as well, which may have both advantages and disadvantages. Such deviations in the appearance of the psychologist may help to make some clients feel that his own deviations in behavior and attitude will be tolerated but, on the other hand, the compulsive parent or phobic child may recoil.

Although the psychologist may make some adjustments in his dress and appearance, the best he or she can do about physical build is to be aware of the client's reactions—and of their own feelings about their body image. Such self-awareness about one's own physique and attitudes toward it has special import when dealing with children who are just forming their own images of themselves, are quite sensitive to such impressions, and what is more, are sometimes quite frank in mentioning them. Since psychologists come in all sizes, shapes, and colors, there is no way of avoiding this factor. Even "good-looking" psychologists may be at a slight disadvantage at times when the child who is disfigured or feels ugly fears he will not be understood or is jealous. The young and shapely woman psychologist often finds herself regarded as seductive by boys or a potential object of envy by the girls. On the other hand, the psychologist who suffers some physical deformity or handicap may not be at such a disadvantage as might be thought. Strangely enough, clinics who preach "hire the handicapped" too often express doubts about hiring a psychologist in a wheel chair or one who has a sensory defect, only to find that most children including those with emotional or social handicaps themselves usually accept such obvious defects in the assessor.

2. The Assessor's Speech

The child also judges the assessor on how he sounds, the tone, pitch, and volume of his voice, the speed with which he speaks, his enunciation, pronunciation, and accent, and other peculiarities of language. While a psychologist can look in the mirror to assess dress and appearance, it is sometimes more difficult for him to be aware of how he sounds; if for no other reason, it is therefore a good idea for the student to tape and listen to his own interviews. At times it may be necessary to learn to modulate one's speech, both to be more comprehensible to children, or even to avoid distracting them by speech mannerisms. Too often, the adult who is not used to working with or being around children unconsciously adopts an artificial manner of speech, for example, a slightly saccharine tone of voice, increased volume (with the mistaken idea that a loud voice is needed to command the child's attention), an affected enunciation, and an attempt at what is thought of as a child's language. One should, of course, modify his college vocabulary and use words that are comprehensible to the child, but this does not require "baby-talk"; the child expects the assessor to speak in normal adult fashion, albeit with words he understands.

The psychologist may be even less aware of the possible cultural and subcultural differences in language between himself and the child. Where such differences are very marked, as when either speaks with a foreign accent, the difference may be forgiven by both, just as in the case of the obvious physical handicap. However, for example, the Bronx born and educated psychologist may be only partly aware of his communication difficulties in dealing with a child from an Ozark family, even though both have emigrated to California! Again, it may not be possible or even necessary for the psychologist to alter his language habits completely and, in fact, if he attempted to imitate the child, it might seem quite artificial. It is necessary that the psychologist be aware of his cultural language habits, so that when he finds that he is not communicating to a child from another subcultural background, he can be flexible enough to express himself in other words and phrases. It is equally important that he be able to translate the child's phraseology and pronunciation. Above all, the psychologist should be aware of the subtle but definite ethnocentric and sociocentric prejudices which surround speech and language differences. Not only should he avoid being caught up in his own provincialism of the academic forum, but he should be able to appreciate the possible richness of expression of the child "from the streets" or the "hill country."

3. *The Assessor's Demeanor and Physical Contacts with the Child*

As to the psychologist's general demeanor, he should interact with the child in a relatively relaxed and informal, but adult, manner so that both psychologist and child feel comfortable. One of the most commonly discussed aspects of this interaction concerns physical contact with the child. Since physical contact between adult and child is more common, at least in our culture, than between adults, it does leave the door open for the adult to take the child's hand, to put an arm around the child, to pick the child up in his arms and comfort him when necessary, or even to take a playful poke at him. Children often use physical contact or motor behavior as one means of communication. Whether the assessor should initiate such contact, or even engage in it if initiated by the child, has to be carefully weighed in each instance. One good clue as to how the child accepts or uses such contact may be gained from the initial handshake. Some children refuse to shake hands and want no part of physical contact with a strange adult, at least to begin with; from others one may obtain every sort of handshake, from a limp wet paw which barely touches to a vigorous yank which practically invites a wrestling match.

Some children may seem to invite such contact but then shy away from it, suddenly embarrassed, seeming to play a game of seduction and rejection. Others may use such contact as a method of detracting from and avoiding verbal communications. As a rule, the child does not necessarily expect the adult to respond to physical contact with much more than a casual recognition, that is, in adult fashion, unless the child is in dire need of physical comfort at the moment. For example, a four year old was brought to the psychologist's office from the pediatrics ward and left for a few minutes by himself in the cold hall, dressed in his pajamas and sitting in the wheel chair. Suddenly he burst into uncontrollable tears. When he was picked up and cuddled for a moment, the storm quickly stopped. This physical contact created an appropriate and warm beginning to the assessment session. In contrast, when the five-year-old girl stood on the chair and with a sly

smile jumped onto the psychologist, grabbing him with both arms around his neck and both legs around his waist, the admittedly surprised psychologist gently set her down and asked, "Hey! What's going on here?" Although the child did not directly answer him, she showed no signs of requiring further physical contact, but accepted his friendly but businesslike approach to the assessment and became involved in the tasks set down before her.

On the part of the psychologist, some introspection is necessary concerning his needs and feelings about physical contact with the child. Undoubtedly and quite appropriately, many psychologists work with children because they enjoy the emotional rewards children often offer, including physical contact. Normally, an adult enjoys having a child take his hand, give him a hug, engage in a momentary physical tussle, or finding the child receptive to his overtures. Thus, it is tempting to initiate such contact, and it is understandable that an adult may feel a momentary hurt if rejected. Of course, the psychologist cannot depend exclusively on his professional contacts for such satisfactions but instead must limit himself to the needs of the child. The corollary to this rule is that the psychologist should again look at his own feelings if he finds that he cannot relax his adult behavior and accept physical contact from the child when it is appropriate.

In summary, then, the assessor behaves most appropriately as a relaxed and comfortable adult. He need not speak nor take on the demeanor of a child. He should be prepared to offer comfort to the child, like any adult, if it is required, or to repel, in adult fashion, an attack on his person. He should be accepting of the child's natural contacts, but should not depend on them.

D. THE REFERRAL AND THE SPECIFIC PURPOSES OF THE ASSESSMENT

The opening key to any assessment is the nature of the referral, that is, the questions which the person who requests the assessment* has concerning the child and which the psychologist is expected to investigate. Finding out what these questions are and what kind of answers are expected is the first step. When one has a collaborative working relationship with other professional colleagues who also have some understanding of the general principles of child development, these questions may be stated clearly and relevantly, with an awareness of the advantages and limitations of assessment procedures. However, referrals frequently come from someone who has only passing knowledge of what assessment can and cannot answer and who may not phrase the question in the professional terms which the psychologist might prefer. Much of the time, the main and only reason the child is referred is that the persons dealing with him are puzzled by his behavior and symptoms, and have at most some vague and ill-defined hypotheses concerning them.

Often the referrant has several questions in mind. He may want the psychologist to provide both some possible explanations of the child's behavior and some more clearly defined working hypotheses. Sometimes the question is even broader, for example, simply "how is this child progressing?" Usually the referrant also has some practical, decision-making questions: Should the child be placed in a special school? What kind of treatment, if any, does he need? What kind of care in what kind of setting? At least a brief discussion with the referrant is usually necessary to understand what he expects and, sometimes, to clarify with him what pertinent information an assessment may provide.

Not infrequently a referrant has questions that cannot be answered and, at the same time, does not realize that an assessment might help him with other aspects of the child's case which he has not thought to bring to the psychologist. Where the psychologist is a member of a staff which is working collaboratively on the child's problems, it is a good idea to discuss the referral in a staff conference in order to clarify the questions of all involved. In other situations, the psychologist may have to contact several persons independently, for example, if a teacher has advised a parent of school problems the child may be having and has suggested that the child be taken to the pediatrician who then requests the assessment from the psychologist, the psychologist may need to contact physician, parent, and teacher.

Two questions face the assessor at the time of referral: (1) How does the assessor obtain the information he needs in the referral?

* For want of a better term, this person will be called the "referrant."

(2) What information is usually necessary? Before going into the details of these two questions, one variable that is central to both should be considered: the relationships between the referrant and the assessor.

1. *The Relationships Between Referrant and Assessor*

The assessor's attitudes toward the referral are derived from his interactions with the referrant. These past experiences with the referrant may well affect the assessor's initial attitudes toward the child and the assessment. A referral from the hospital superintendent or the president of the Board of Education might well be given different attention with different emotional reactions by the assessor than if the referrant were a ward nurse or a substitute teacher. A referral from a friendly colleague, one who "appreciates the contributions" of the assessor, would certainly be more welcome than an "order" to "give tests" from some administrator who never lets the psychologist know how his ideas and recommendations are received. The assessor may well feel more free to inquire further about the needs of the referrant if he is a friendly colleague with whom the psychologist has collaborated for a number of years than some stranger with whom the psychologist has had only a single telephone contact and who initially gives him little information. The psychologist thus should consider whether such natural biases, present in almost any referral, are possibly preventing him from questioning the referral further, either because his relationship with the referrant is too distant, or perhaps too close. Most of all, he should take pains to distinguish his relationship with the referrant from his pending relationship with his clients.

This relationship between referrant and psychologist may be reflected by the methods used to obtain information about the child. Most agencies and institutions have some kind of formal referral sheet or card, such as shown in Figure 5. This form, in addition to asking for certain identifying data about the client, and other facts which might affect the assessment, leaves space for the referrant to state some of the general and specific reasons for the referral, his working "diagnosis" or impressions, and the hypotheses which he hopes the psychologist will be able to test or at least add information about. By and large, these formal written communications between referrant and psychologist are quite helpful, particularly if the psychologist has given some thought to making up the referral card so that the referrant can understand what the psychologist wants to know quite clearly and definitely and if the referrant knows how and bothers to state his answers on this sheet equally clearly. However, referral forms are too often given scant thought by either party. They frequently show signs of hasty construction, containing vague headings without any instructions. Understandably, the busy physician, teacher, or social worker, commonly disliking the flood of forms he has to fill out, may give this referral sheet only perfunctory attention.

Personal contact between psychologist and referrant is thus usually necessary, even where a generally acceptable written form has been devised. In such contacts, while using the referral card, the psychologist should make clear his interest in the specific problems which face the referrant. What information does the referrant need which is not provided from other data about the child? What decisions does the referrant have to face about the client? And, what is most often important and not always easy to discover: what are the referrant's attitudes toward and relationships with the client? Is he, for example, a teacher faced with a class trouble maker, a judge who must pass sentence, a pediatrician who specializes in bone-growth problems and is uncomfortable about emotional problems of children, or possibly a minister with a missionary zeal to save this child from his divorced parents? Has the referrant already made up his mind about what is "wrong" with the client and what he is going to do, and merely wants the psychologist to confirm his findings and opinion? Or might he only thinly veil his hope of passing the responsibility for all decisions and future care of the child to the psychologist, without really releasing his authority? Quite often a referral contains some such hidden agenda, not recorded on any referral card and at most mentioned casually in passing in conversation by the referrant. However, in a personal contact, the psychologist should politely but nevertheless directly, discuss such factors with the referrant. Even though the contact between them may be relatively brief, the psychologist using his interviewing techniques can usually establish how the referrant feels

about the child and about the assessment. In many instances, one or both parents are involved in the referral, and in some cases they are the main or even only referrants. Determining the nature of the referral in this instance will be discussed below in a separate section of this chapter.

2. *The Referral Data*

The basic information that the psychologist needs at the time of referral is listed in Figure 5. This "model" referral form is admittedly much longer than that used in most agencies or institutions and would be most appropriately filled out by the psychologist in discussion with the referrant. To begin with, if the child is referred by any agency or institution, the assessor needs to know the file number, if any, used by that institution, so that his report will be properly identified. (Large agencies and schools or hospitals often have several children with the same name.) The child's exact legal name should be obtained. Sometimes a child is known by several different names; for example, a child may legally bear the name of a divorced or deceased father, but also use the surname of a stepfather, even though never formally adopted. Such information is necessary if only because it may have a bearing on the child's psychological as well as legal identity. The name or nickname by which the child is usually addressed is needed so that the psychologist will know what to call the child when he meets him. An assessment can easily get off on the wrong foot if the child is inadvertently addressed by a formal name that he seldom uses or might even dislike. Even so, it is wisest to check this information with the child when first meeting him: "What do most people call you? What do you like to be called? Is it all right if I call you _____?"

The date of the child's birth should also be rechecked, at the time of the first appointment, with both parent and child. Sometimes records differ completely about birthdates, or parents' memories are vague, and such differences need to be resolved before assessment can proceed. It is, of course, often of interest why a birthdate is in error. For example, parents who are anxious to place the child in school at an early age have been known to add an extra year to the child's age when entering him in kindergarten, giving the school a false birthdate a few months to a

Your file # _____   Date referred: _____

Child's name: _____
       Last   First   Middle

By what name or nickname is the child usually addressed?

_____

Date of the child's birth _____

Name of person(s) or institution with whom the child is currently residing:

_____

       Address: _____

       Telephone: _____

       Relationship to the child:_____

Father's name:

_____

       Home address: _____

       Home phone: _____

       Business address: _____

       Business telephone: _____

Mother's name:

_____

       Home address: _____

       Home telephone: _____

       Business address: _____

       Business telephone: _____

Name of the person or institution who has legal guardianship of the child:_____

_____

       Address and telephone, if different

       than above: _____

_____

Name of the school the child is currently

attending: _____

       Address: _____

       Telephone: _____

       Principal: _____

       Teacher: _____

Name of the child's physician: _____

       Address: _____

       Telephone: _____

Name of any other persons concerned with the child's care and welfare who are concerned with

this referral: _____

       Address: _____

       Telephone: _____

Name of person who should be contacted for

appointment: _____

       Address: _____

       Telephone: _____

Who has been advised that this referral is being made:

_____

_____

What have they been advised regarding the purposes and the nature of the referral:

_____

_____

What has the child been told regarding the purposes and the nature of the referral:

_____

_____

Prior studies: Has the child been previously assessed psychologically? If so, where:

_____

Address of clinic, hospital, or psychologist

       When: _____

         Date(s) of prior assessment(s)

If copies of reports of prior assessments are available, please attach them to this referral.

Reasons for the Referral

Please summarize on the reverse of this sheet or on a separate sheet: (a) Under what circumstances and for what reasons did the child come to your attention? (b) What kinds of problems and/or symptoms does the child present? (c) What are your findings and impressions? (d) What questions are there concerning the child's care, training, treatment, and disposition? (e) What are the specific questions regarding the child's psychological functioning?

Conditions Affecting Assessment

What physical handicaps does the child have?

_____

_____

What medications is child receiving and how might they affect his responses?

_____

Figure 5. *Referral for psychological assessment of children.*

What speech or language handicaps does the child have? _____

Who will be responsible for payment of the fees?

_____

Are there financial limitations which should be considered regarding the fees?

_____

To whom should reports of findings be sent?

_____

Has permission been obtained for the release of the assessment report?

_____

Referrant's name_____

Position_____

Address and phone_____

FIGURE 5.—*Continued*

year earlier; several years later, when the child is having difficulty at school or home, the parent may give the correct date to the psychologist, forgetting that the school has another date. Even if such a parent continues to falsify the child's birthdate, the child of school age will likely know and give his correct age and birthday (if not year).

Since many children referred for assessment may not currently be living with their parents, it is necessary on any referral form to allow space for several different addresses and names. Item 7 on this model form asks with whom and where the child is currently living, and their relationship with the child. Additionally, one may need to know the name(s) and address(es) and telephone number(s) of the parents so that they may be contacted if necessary for further information about the child. (Where the child is residing with his parents, it would not be necessary to fill in Items 8 and 9). Since legal guardianship may not lie in the hands of either parent or even in the hands of the persons currently caring for the child (as in the case of foster homes under court order), it is a good idea to note who is legally responsible for the child; in any instance it is necessary to obtain permission from the legal guardian before beginning an assessment. If the legal guardian (or, in the case of a public agency or court, a representative of the agency) does not bring the child to the psychologist in person, thus giving verbal permission, the psychologist is legally bound (in most states and countries) to obtain written permission from the guardian before examining any minor.

Identifying data about the child's school is always valuable but becomes of primary importance when the child has originally been referred by the school or is presenting school difficulties. Similarly, it is often vital to know from the very beginning of the psychologist's contacts with the child who is responsible for his medical care, his pediatrician or family physician. Sometimes even before assessment begins it may be necessary to contact either the school or the child's physician. In such instances, it is usually necessary for the psychologist to obtain written permission from the parent or guardian for release of school or physician records. Figure 6 shows a model form for obtaining permission to procure such information which, when signed by the child's legal guardian, can be mailed to the school or physician with a cover letter stating the kinds of information needed.

Not infrequently, persons are also involved in the referral other than the parents, school, or physician, such as other close relatives, ministers, attorneys, or agencies other than the one making the referral. Their names, addresses, telephone numbers, and relationship to the child should also be recorded.

To: (name of physician, school, or social agency)

This is to give my permission for the release of any or all information from your records concerning _____
Name of child

to _____
Name of the clinic or the psychologist

_____
Parent or guardian

_____
Date

Figure 6. *Model for obtaining permission for the release of confidential material.*

Finally, among all these names, the one of most immediate importance is the name, address, and telephone number of the person whom the psychologist needs to contact in order to make an appointment for the child. Sometimes this person may not be any of the above! Along with this, the psychologist needs to know who has been advised by the referrant that the referral is being made, and what the referrant has advised these persons about the purpose and nature of the referral.

Equally important, of course, is what the child has been told. Some of our professional colleagues, those used to working in close collaboration with psychologists, are aware of the necessity of clarifying with the parent and child the reasons they are asking them to come for an assessment and, in general, what they may expect. In instructing medical students, this writer suggests that the student tell both the child and parent that he is making this referral and that it is to help him better understand the child's problems and symptoms. Further, the student is advised that he need not mention "tests" per se, partly because other techniques may also be used and partly because this word is so often misunderstood by both child and parent. Instead, it is suggested that he merely say that he is asking them to see the psychologist, "who is interested in how children understand and do things." If the child or parent seems anxious to know more about the examination, they should be referred to the psychologist for further information. If they ask specifically about tests, they should be told that tests may be part of the assessment but that he and the psychologist are most interested in how the child is developing or "getting along." Similarly, parents may be advised to tell the child directly that he is going to see a psychologist, that the psychologist is a person "interested in how children do things, understand things, and the things which make children happy or unhappy."

Furthermore, the parent should tell the child the reasons he, the parent, believes the assessment to be necessary. In this regard, this writer usually advises parents to be fairly direct but at the same time supporting and to say, for example, "You know all the trouble you've had with _____ (school, bedwetting, stealing, etc.), which we've not really understood. Your (doctor, teacher, parole officer) tells me that a psychologist may be able to help us both understand better what is the matter and how things may be helped." Although such direct information may create other resistances or raise further questions in the child's mind, the child who has at least this general orientation is usually better prepared and less resistant than the one who is told little or nothing or is told that he is going "to get a mental examination."

The next item on the referral sheet, *Prior studies,* tells the psychologist whether the child has had a previous assessment, thus indicating whether the child is familiar with the procedure. If there has been such a study, and the report is available to the referrant, the psychologist may want to inquire further as to why such a study needs to be repeated currently. What were the purposes of the prior assessment? Is it out of date? Have there been changes in the child's behavior since the prior assessment? How did the child react to the prior assessment? How might he feel about being reassessed? In many instances, the psychologist may want to obtain a report of any prior assessments and review them in planning the reassessment.

The central and most important part of the referral is contained under the heading, *Reasons for referral.* Here, the psychologist hopes to obtain a concise but definitive statement of the child's problems and the referrant's view of them, and the questions that the referrant poses for the assessment. How did the child come to the attention of the referrant and for what reasons? What kinds of problems and symptoms did the referrant discover and what were his findings and impressions regarding them? What decisions have to be made about the child concerning his care, training, treatment, or possible disposition? In these questions, the psychologist seeks to get a preliminary view of the child as seen by the referrant.

None of these questions necessarily asks the referrant to pose the problems in psychological terms. For example, a probation officer might state that the child came to his attention because of an infraction of the law, often one of a series of such infractions; that he had found out that the child was also failing at school, was truant at home and was in serious conflict with his parents, that the parents were about to get a divorce, etc. The parole officer may be requested to recommend to the court whether the child should be removed from the home, whether he needs to be placed in an institution for juvenile delinquents, whether he needs remedial education, etc. However, the final question under this heading gives the referrant an opportunity to phrase his question in psychological terms if he so chooses. Thus, the parole officer might ask, in response to this last question: "Does the child have sufficient stability to adjust in a proposed foster home? Does he have enough intellectual ability and motivation to succeed in public school if he were removed from the emotional stress at home? Does he show any guilt over his actions? Are his crimes a part of some overall emotional disorder?" Such questions do not necessarily limit the psychologist's investigations but at least will orient him to some of the questions that the referrant has considered, and pave the way for better and continued communication between them.

The final series of questions on this model referral form is concerned with possible practical limitations on the assessment of which the assessor must be aware before beginning his evaluation. He needs to know whether the child has any physical handicaps, especially in vision, hearing, or motor coordination which might have to be accounted for in selection of his techniques. Parents should be advised that a child with even a mild visual handicap should bring his glasses. With the widespread use of various psycho-pharmaceuticals today, the psychologist needs to know if any medications are being given to the child, and what kinds of effects these are having. Individual children vary so widely in their response to drugs that it is always necessary to know how the child in question is reacting.* Especially in a hospital situation, the psychologist should learn to check thoroughly on what medical, surgical, or other procedures the child has been experiencing during the hours prior to the assessment. Any child who has spent the morning undergoing exhaustive medical examinations, X-rays, EEG's, etc. is usually in no condition for an afternoon of psychological tests. The child who has had a barium examination, a spinal tap, or some other extensive examination which seriously affects his whole system may need at least 24 hours to recover before he is in condition for psychological assessment.

Although this referral form does not provide space for notes regarding other kinds

* This topic is discussed in more detail in Chapter 19.

of stress that the child may be experiencing, the psychologist should be alert for any indications of such stress also. For example, in any institutional setting, the psychologist as a member of the staff should be aware if the child were, for example, recently subjected to punishment, in a fight with other children, feeling very dejected because his parents failed to visit, etc. Under such circumstances it might be well to postpone the appointment with the child for a short while. If an appointment has already been arranged, the psychologist might mention that he is aware of these extenuating events, and offer the possibility of postponing the appointment, leaving the choice to the child. On the other hand, some children might actually see and use the assessment as a means of diverting their feelings and attention away from the immediate stress.

Information about the language the child speaks or is used to speaking in his home and how well he speaks or understands it is, of course, vital to planning the assessment. His assessment procedure will be quite different if he is going to evaluate a child who speaks only a language foreign to the assessor, or who cannot make himself understood clearly in any language. Many young children from bilingual homes may appear to speak the language of the community but in fact have considerable difficulty either in understanding it or communicating in it. If the assessor has any hint that a second language is used in the home, he should inquire further about it.

The next two questions have to do with the setting of fees. Although the fee probably will not be set on the basis of this preliminary information, the response to these items will serve to forewarn the psychologist of possible difficulties. Occasionally a client who is in financial straits or whose income is limited may fear that he cannot meet whatever fees he thinks may be charged. He may be too proud to discuss the matter and use some other excuse for avoiding an appointment. If the psychologist is aware of this difficulty, he may be able to bring up the matter with the parent when making the first appointment, and discuss the possibilities of an adustment or delay in fees.

The final questions in the referral deal with distribution of the psychologist's final report of the assessment. Sometimes only the referrant needs a report. In other instances, several other persons should or will want to be advised of the psychologist's findings. If persons other than the referrant are to be sent reports, the referral may have to be expanded to obtain further information about the questions and interests of these other persons. Moreover, if someone other than the referrant is to receive a report, the psychologist may need the permission of the child's guardian, as his report is legally confidential information. In many states, the psychologist's report, like medical data, is legally the property of the client (unless it is obtained by a governmental agency).

E. PLANNING THE ASSESSMENT

On the basis of this preliminary data from the referral, the assessor can construct some beginning hypotheses about the case which will, in part, determine his subsequent procedures and his choice of techniques. By studying the data he has collected so far, he can surmise what some of the important psychological variables may be. His working hypotheses may be based on the identifying information, the reasons for referral, or the circumstances surrounding the referral. The following cases illustrate how such working hypotheses are derived.

CASE 14

Dr. Smith, a staff psychiatrist, telephoned to request an assessment on Leslie, who was being considered for admission as a patient in the out-patient clinic. The date of the referral was January 15th, the parents having first contacted the clinic on January 5th. Leslie, more commonly called Lee, was born on December 25th, 14 years previously. He was residing with his mother and stepfather at an address in an upper-middle class section of a large city. Business phones were listed for both the mother and stepfather, and the psychologist was advised to contact the mother at her office. The parents' last name was not the same as that used by Lee. The mother was listed as legal guardian. Lee was beginning the ninth grade in a private boys' school. The names of his teacher and principal had not been ascertained, nor was the name of the child's pediatrician known. However, both the teacher and pediatrician were interested in this referral, according to the mother;

both had urged her to seek psychiatric help for Lee.

Both Lee and his mother had been told respectively by the psychiatrist and the social worker at the clinic that Lee would need to have an appointment with the psychologist, as a further step in assessing the nature of his problems. Customarily, this psychiatrist told children, "I can understand some of your problems by talking them over with you and our social worker can similarly see how your mother feels about them. However, it is also helpful to us to see how people do things and think about things. This is why I want you to meet our psychologist who will talk to you too, and give you some things to work with and think out." Lee had accepted the referral without comment or question. His mother also agreed and informed the social worker that Lee had been given some psychological tests at the local Children's Hospital about three years ago, when hospitalized after being knocked unconscious in a bicycle accident.

As to the reasons for referral: Dr. Smith reported that Lee had been brought to the clinic by his mother because the school had reported to her that Lee was made very anxious by any form of competition, and that he would easily become enraged or burst into tears during sport activities or when reciting in class. Shortly before the holidays, he had become so excited and upset over a football game in which he had been the star player that despite the fact that his team won the championship, he burst into tears, ran from the field, and hid for an hour. When found by the coach, he seemed quite confused; he thought the team had lost and that it was his fault. His stepfather, who had encouraged him in his athletics and was extremely proud of his prowess, was very worried; the mother wondered if sports had not been overemphasized by the stepfather and if Lee perhaps should withdraw a bit from sports for the spring semester. Moreover, Lee's grades had fallen markedly over the past two years, and he had barely passed on all his subjects the past semester, although he had been a slightly better student up to the sixth grade. His school grades were even more of a concern since his twin brother, Lester, known as "Les," had maintained a B average all along. Les, however, had not matched Lee's athletic record, although he, too, was quite active in sports. The parents had at first ignored the school's suggestion that Lee might have a serious emotional problem and decided that the whole incident arose from too much investment in sports and the "big game."

At home they had noticed no signs of emotional disturbance in Lee, whom they saw as a model boy, usually obedient, although showing some signs of adolescent arguing back, and mildly mischievous. "An all-around American boy," his stepfather remarked. They denied any evidence of sibling rivalry between the twins, who had always been "very close." Both were very proud of their two-year-old half-sister whom they seemed to adore. However, during the holidays, Lee continued to appear morose and irritable around the house, "flying off the handle" whenever his stepfather spoke to him and picking quarrels with Les. He was adamant that the family should not hold the traditional Christmas birthday party.

Finally, much to his mother's dismay, Lee secretly contacted his father, whom his mother had divorced six years previously and whom Lee had not seen for three years, and made arrangements to visit him on Christmas Day. After the holidays, Lee refused to return to school; he asked to be transferred to the local public school and hinted that if more consideration were not given to his desires, he might choose to go live with his father. Lee's mother took him first to their pediatrician who referred them to the clinic.

Dr. Smith had had two interviews with Lee and the staff social worker, Mrs. Morse, and had one interview with Lee's mother. Dr. Smith found Lee unwilling to discuss any of the problems his mother had mentioned; instead, he denied that there was anything really to be concerned about and complained that his mother was making too "big a deal" out of everything. He admitted that he did get a bit excited over football, but the football season was over now and there would be no more trouble; he now could return to his studies and catch up. He did not mention his visit to the father or the birthday party incident. When asked about them, he became a bit irritated and argued that it was just that he and Les both felt that they had outgrown "those babyish" birthday parties. As to his visit with his father, he shrugged and said he just had suddenly wanted to see his father, that he was sorry he'd upset his mother, that he had no intention of seeing

his father any more; "He's just a drunk and a bum, like mother always said." He averred that he really loved his mother and "dad" (stepfather), and had no intention of leaving them, "though I really could if I wanted; the judge said so." As to the school, he admitted he had seriously considered changing to the public school where many of his neighborhood friends attended, but Les had about talked him out of it now. He added with a smile that if the psychiatrist really wanted to help him he should talk his mother out of continuing the piano lessons which the twins hated.

Dr. Smith's initial impression was that Lee had really reached some kind of impasse both at school and home just before the holidays and thereafter, but had reconstituted enough so that when faced with the possibility of having his difficulties examined, he was able to maintain that they were unimportant. Dr. Smith particularly wondered if Lee might be struggling to form some identity separate from his twin, perhaps struggling extra hard to establish his own masculine role (which might account for the visit to his father), and perhaps be indirectly beginning a rebellion against the stepfather. Dr. Smith noted that neither twin had shown much adolescent interest in the opposite sex, but suspected that this might be the real reason that Lee wanted to go to the coeducational public school. He did wonder about Lee's intellectual functioning, since the school grades had been low, but was more interested in Lee's fantasy and in his "basic personality structure and emotional development." The application for treatment was to be considered two weeks hence, at which time it was hoped the psychologist would have completed the assessment. Dr. Smith planned to have at least one more interview session with Lee, and perhaps one with Les. Mrs. Morse planned to continue contacts with Mrs. R, Lee's mother, especially to obtain more information about the family's functioning and Lee's developmental history. Dr. Smith said the staff would try to decide whether (1) to let the application drop at present, in view of Lee's attitudes; (2) to conduct individual psychotherapy with Lee, with perhaps intermittent collaborative contacts with the mother; or (3) perhaps to consider family therapy sessions with both parents and the twins.

The psychologist's first response to the

referral was to ask if, in view of the last possibility, it might not be helpful to include Les and perhaps the parents in the psychological assessment, to which Dr. Smith readily agreed. Mrs. R had already expressed concern that Lee was singled out for psychiatric attention, and although she had no questions about Les, had asked if he might be seen at least once so that Lee would not feel he were "different." Dr. Smith also believed that the R's would be cooperative if asked to participate in the assessment.

Next, the psychologist reviewed the referral data, particularly the findings and impressions of Dr. Smith and the questions he had posed. Considering these data, Dr. Smith's formulations seemed to the psychologist to be reasonable as tentative hypotheses, but for the purpose of assessment, it might be necessary to rephrase them slightly to permit testing of them by his techniques. Considering the problem in terms of development, Lee, at 14, was at an age when adolescent "identity"—social, emotional, and biological —normally is being formed. The question could then be posed: Might there be any evidence to suggest that this normal identity formation was not proceeding smoothly for Lee? If so, what might be the nature of this possible identity crisis? What factors might be contributing to it? How severe a disruption might it be? Was it, as Lee and his family maintained, possibly a disruption related to immediate stresses for which he had now recovered? Might these stresses have caused a continued disruption? Or might the symptoms be a sign of some more long-standing developmental disturbance which came to the fore under these pressures? If no identity crisis seemed evident, what alternate hypotheses might be entertained about Lee's symptoms? The psychologist considered the possibility that Lee might have already formulated some unconscious image of himself, for example, as an Esau, the nonintellectual brother whose identity depended on physical accomplishment, and who was beginning to demand his "pottage." In terms of classic psychiatric diagnosis, might Lee have already developed a "character neurosis?"

Another possibility was that Lee might not yet be struggling with adolescent problems at all but, instead, still be psychologically in latency, perhaps even attempting to prolong the little-boy stage in order to avoid the problems of adolescence. Certainly some of Lee's reactions, his hyperexcitement and his tears, would not be considered quite so unusual on the part of a child of seven or eight. Last, but certainly not least, was the possibility that Lee's outburst represented a release from strained but covered family relationships which, though not affecting the normal development of an identity, might constitute a developmental problem per se, that is, a freeing of the self from the childhood parental and sibling bonds.

As the psychologist thought over these possibilities, he recognized that they were not necessarily alternatives, and that it was quite possible that the evidence might support more than one of them, or a combination of them. For example, it might be possible that Lee was trying to maintain a preadolescent adjustment in order to avoid the kind of identity he was already beginning to formulate in response to the family stresses.

Added to these broad developmental hypotheses were several more specific questions. Might Lee be having rather specific problems in relatively isolated or autonomous functioning, such as the handling of social stresses or in competitive situations, rather than some broad developmental progress? The question of Lee's intellectual functioning might or might not be related to his overall development or his identity but, at least in view of the practical question posed by Dr. Smith concerning Lee's academic progress, assessment of Lee's intellectual functioning did seem called for. Then, there was the hint that Lee had previously needed an assessment after a head injury; had there then been some behavioral evidence of a perceptual-motor dysfunction or other defect? If so, had it persisted and might it be playing a part in Lee's difficulties in emotional control and academic achievement?

A telephone call to the Children's Hospital revealed that Lee had been given several psychological tests shortly after his accident; he was found to be functioning intellectually at a low average level, but there were no indications of any gross intellectual or perceptual-motor dysfunction and it was concluded that at least behaviorally his accident had left no immediate sequalae. A permit for release of information was signed by the parents to obtain a complete written report of these findings.

With these data and hypotheses in mind, the psychologist turned to choosing his techniques and mapping out his procedures. If he had had time to gather as much pertinent data as was feasible, identical assessment techniques for all members of the family might have been worthwhile. However, limited by time, the psychologist decided to devise a similar procedure for the twins, a more limited assessment for the parents and, unless time permitted, to bypass assessment of the half-sister. For the twins, he decided to allot two two-hour sessions each. Since all family members (except the sister) were being interviewed by other staff, and their data were available to him, he decided to keep his interviews at a bare minimum, dealing chiefly with their feelings about the assessment. For the twins, he decided to begin with a structured test of intelligence, since Lee was reputed to function with a little less anxiety in structured situations. The Wechsler Intelligence Scale for Children seemed a good choice, since on the Binet a child ends in utter failure which might be too anxiety provoking to Lee; on the other hand, several samples of Lee's reaction to failure, followed by successes on subsequent subtests, might help to evaluate his reaction to failure a bit better than on the Binet. The WISC also lends itself more readily to analysis of perceptual motor functioning and details of thought processes than the Binet. Ending the WISC on the coding subtest (where failure is less obvious), the child has the pencil in his hand and it would be natural to go on to the Memory for Designs or the Bender-Gestalt, for a further check on perceptual motor functions, perhaps adding in the Porteus Mazes.

The second session might begin with the Rorschach, both to complete the assessment of perceptual functioning and to begin study of the boys' emotional functioning. For study of their fantasy, the psychologist considered Lee's reputation for preferring motor expression over verbalization and thus decided to use the MAPS, selecting in addition several pertinent pictures from the Michigan pictures and Symonds' pictures for adolescents should there be time or should Lee be more verbal than expected. He hoped to end this session with two self-administered techniques: the P-F Study, since there was specific question of Lee's attitudes toward frustration, and the Bene-Anthony Family Relations test, since

there was the question about the family structure. After completing these individual assessments of the twins, the psychologist planned to bring both parents and the boys together for further study of their relationships in a two-hour session. He thought it might be possible to have each family member (1) take the Edwards Personal Preference Schedule, (2) describe themselves and each other member of the family on the Leary Interpersonal Checklist, and (3) make drawings of a male, a female, and of a family. It was hoped from this latter battery of techniques to obtain data about the need patterns within the family, the perceptions each held of the other, their relative positions in Leary's "love-dominance" scheme, and the perceptions of each regarding sex role and identity both for themselves and for a family.

Another type of referral, with different complications is illustrated in the following case.

CASE 15

Tina, age about five, was referred for assessment by a Childrens' Care Center operated by a religious order to whom the psychologist served as an outside consultant. No referral form was used, but the case was reviewed with the Center's social worker. Tina had first come to their attention approximately five years previously when, as an infant, she was abandoned in a basket at the doorstep of the church. She appeared very malnourished and ill and was hospitalized for the next several months in the hospital operated by the church. The pediatrician estimated her age at that time to be approximately three to four months. Medical examination revealed that, in addition to the malnutrition, she was suffering from a severe amibiotic infection, disrupting her entire digestive and excretory functioning. She had not been kept clean, and her skin was covered with small sores. With special diet and medication, these conditions cleared up in about six weeks and she grew rapidly. Further medical studies indicated that she was otherwise a fairly healthy and normal infant. Her skin coloring was a light olive, her hair dark and curly, and her eyes blue, and she was small boned; her nose tended to be flat and her lips large: all suggesting a mixed racial background. Her condition attracted the sympathy and attention of the nursing staff, who spent extra time playing with her and being affectionate to her. She blossomed under this care and appeared to be a happy and relatively contented baby.

The Center sought to place her in a foster home but partly because of Tina's "race" and partly because the agency limited itself to homes practicing their religion, no immediate placement was found. Finally, one of the nurses volunteered to accept Tina in her home. This nurse had one infant of her own, was expecting a second, and planned to quit her job and devote herself entirely to caring for her children. She spoke of adopting Tina but the agency advised her to delay this decision and accept Tina on a foster-child basis. Legal papers in Tina's case folder showed that a local court had awarded guardianship to the agency, granting them the right to place her in a home of their choosing, had designated a name chosen by the agency, and had ordered a birth certificate made out and filed in that name and stating an approximate date of birth. As was customary, the agency remained responsible for the child's medical care and offered a small stipend to the foster parents designed to cover clothing needs.

Although the agency usually tried to make periodic contacts with the children placed in foster care under their guardianship, there were only two brief notes about such contacts during the subsequent two years. At that time, the foster parents regretfully informed the agency that they were no longer able to care for Tina as the foster mother now had four children of her own including a newly born pair of twins, and their housing and finances were limited. No record was made of Tina's condition at that time nor of her reactions at being removed from this home. The social worker recalled that Tina seemed in good health. For the next eight months she remained in the Center's residential institution while a second foster placement was sought. Records were kept only of her health, physical development, and "discipline"; her physical development and health were normal, and there was no indication that she was a discipline problem.

At approximately age four, she was placed in the home of a middle-aged couple who had two other preschool foster children; arrangements were made for this couple to receive monthly allotments from county funds for Tina's care. The social worker visited this home four times during the next year, and

the foster mother came to the agency regarding Tina twice, both times to complain that the allotment checks were not forthcoming. The worker noted that the home was very neat and clean but it was very crowded and there was little play space. As far as the worker could tell, Tina seemed happy playing with the other children. However, after about six months, the foster mother complained that Tina was becoming a "naughty" girl, would not mind, and fought with the other children. She frequently wet the bed and even soiled herself though previously she had been completely continent. These complaints increased and shortly after the end of the year, the foster mother called to report that Tina had run away and had been picked up by the police and was being held at the juvenile hall; the foster mother refused to take her back so the worker brought Tina again to the Center's Home. Tina seemed very unhappy and depressed, complained that the foster parents were "mean" but could not say how. Now, three weeks later, Tina had recovered her spirits and seemed her usual self.

Several questions faced the social worker: Had Tina shown a change in attitudes and behavior which disrupted the last placement? If so, might this change make further placement difficult? Did Tina need any special kind of psychological care? Or was she merely reacting to a situation containing more stress and possibly less emotional support than the first placement? Might Tina have been reacting to the loss of the first foster mother? Tina would be old enough to start school within the year; how well might she be expected to perform? One possible placement would involve attending a public school where there were many bright children and thus expectations of high achievement. In discussing these questions with the social worker, she admitted that although she was aware of some of the variables, she had not been trained in methods of assessing them. She had tried to interview the most recent foster mother but had not succeeded in getting past the mother's complaints.

The psychologist, in turn, suggested several other possibilities. Might it be that Tina, now almost five, had been reacting in fairly normal fashion l.b., active, testing things out? Or might she be regressing slightly? Even running away is not altogether unusual at this age, although admittedly a cause for concern. If so, why was the foster mother unwilling to accept and deal with a four year old's behavior? Another question concerned the sibling patterns in the two placements. How did Tina react to the birth of the children in the first home, and her eventual displacement? What was the sibling pattern in the second home? What kind of rivalries existed and on what basis? What kind of discipline and training was used in each of these homes? Most of all, the psychologist needed to know in much greater detail how Tina had actually developed if he were to make any predictions about her future placement and education.

To answer these questions, the psychologist needed data from several sources. He decided to observe Tina, first on the playground and at mealtime at the Center's Home, and to interview the Center's matron who had known Tina before, on her return from the first placement. From this matron, he hoped to find out how she reacted after the change of placements. Then he planned to observe Tina in a playroom by herself, talking with her first about what she was doing while she played in front of him and then about herself and her placements. During one of these sessions, he planned to remove the toys and give her the Binet and some projective tests, such as the CAT and the World Test.

The psychologist hoped to obtain the bulk of his data from interviews with the two foster mothers. The social worker assured him that the first mother would undoubtedly be most cooperative, and that she had inquired about Tina from time to time and still felt a little guilty that she had not been able to keep her. The second mother might be reluctant to discuss Tina further, had seemed defensive about discussing her all along, and probably now would like to forget the whole affair. However, the agency maintained a guardianship over one of the other children placed in that home and there was some question about continued placement of that child. Thus, there was a definite reason for further contact between the agency and the second foster mother. It was finally decided that the psychologist would join the worker in making visits to both homes and interviewing both foster mothers.

In these two instances, the psychologist was acting as part of a staff, and someone other than the parent made the referral. However, in private practice or in such agencies as University Psychology Department Clinics where all of an assessment is conducted by a psychologist, the client (parent) is often the source of referral per se. It is the mother, most usually, who calls the clinic or practitioner and asks for help with a problem concerning the child. In such instances, the questions may be about the same but the technique of handling the referral will differ somewhat. Some clinics do have an "intake" form, essentially like the referral form in Figure 5. However, it is even more usual to interview the parent briefly either in phone contact or in an intake interview. The main difference, of course, is that the referrant is also the client and that here the client-psychologist relationship starts with the referral. How this referral is taken thus may set the tone and framework of the ensuing assessment, as illustrated in the following cases.

CASE 16

Mrs. T telephoned the psychologist and, speaking hesitantly in an anxious voice, asked if he knew anything about teenagers and narcotics. Assured that he was interested in such problems, she went on to explain that she feared that her 15-year-old son, Dale, had been using marijuana. "He comes in after being with friends whom he knows I disapprove of and looks awfully funny." She had found cigarettes in his room which she believed were marijuana, "But I really don't know for sure." Dale avoided her questions neither denying outright nor affirming her suspicions. Instead, he counterattacked by accusing her of invading the privacy of his dresser drawers and calling her a "snoop." Against Dale's will, she had taken him to the family doctor for a physical examination and was told by the physician that he was in good health and that she should stop worrying because "marijuana is relatively harmless." Mrs. T appeared most worried lest Dale become involved in more harmful narcotics, get in with the "wrong" company, and be arrested. At the same time, she wondered if she were overconcerned, perhaps "making a mountain out of a molehill." She wished that her husband were home but he was away on overseas military duty. She hesitated to bother him with this problem, at least until she found out how serious the situation might be. The minister of their church suggested that she call the psychologist.

The psychologist asked if Dale were aware of her call. She replied that she had told

Dale and that he was willing to go along with her request for help, "if only to get me to shut up." The psychologist assured her that her concerns were worth looking into and proceeded to make an appointment to see both Dale and Mrs. T. In this instance, he made little other inquiry over the phone, hoping to investigate in his intake interview with Dale and his mother the facts as well as the nature of each of their concerns.

His referral contact led him to guess that there might be a great deal more conflict between the mother and son than this one statement indicated. However, he realized that his first task might be to win Dale's co-operation and confidence. He decided to interview Dale first, getting his view of the situation in general and of the referral specifically before talking to the mother further.

CASE 17

Mrs. V phoned the Psychology Clinic and asked the secretary "if they gave tests." The clinic secretary informed her politely that no staff member was immediately available to discuss this with her but that someone would return the call within the hour or at her convenience.* Mrs. V was a little annoyed, repeating her question. Assured that "testing is part of our service but that better information could be obtained from a staff member," Mrs. V left her telephone number and requested someone call before "3:00 when Bobby gets home from school." When her call was returned, Mrs. V seemed quite anxious, talking rapidly and loudly. She explained that Bobby, age ten, had not been doing at all well in school, making C's in most subjects and a D in arithmetic, that she was most concerned and had tried to help him with his homework and had conferred with the school. The school had seemed to her to be unconcerned: "They have so many kids they just don't care about one." Her husband too had been no help: "After all, he's just a house painter and he dropped out of high school to go in the Navy when he was seventeen. Now he says I'm nagging Bobby, that I should let the kid alone." Mrs. V added, "Bobby feels that his Dad is on his

side and doesn't bother with his homework. I know Bobby is smart enough to make B's and A's, but my husband just laughs and says 'he's as dumb as his old man.' I get so mad I could kill 'em both, I really could!" When the psychologist inquired whether she had told her husband that she was going to call the clinic, Mrs. V sighed and said, "He'd just laugh at me and tell me to forget it." The psychologist reflected that it sounded as if this concern caused considerable conflict between the parents and wondered if Mr. V might also like the problem cleared up. Mrs. V seemed hesitant but agreed, "They'd both like me out of their hair." The psychologist then suggested that she discuss with Mr. V the possibility of a joint conference and, if Mr. V agreed, to ask him to call and arrange an appointment at their mutual convenience. Mrs. V remained doubtful but agreed. The next day Mr. V did call to say that he too was concerned about Bobby's achievement at school but that he felt that his wife was a chronic worrier and "makes the kid's life unbearable." He accepted the psychologist's offer of a joint conference quite readily.

In this case the psychologist was forced to make a quick analysis of the referral and some decisions about his procedures during these initial contacts. He recognized that Bobby's problem might very well be only one sample of parental differences over his training and discipline, and that he would very likely need the cooperation of both parents from the very start. Although he would very likely comply with Mrs. V's request for "tests" at some time during the assessment, it was necessary first to set the stage by inquiring further into the parents' hopes and expectations and attitudes toward Bobby's achievement now and in the future. He also wanted to explore to see if there were further questions and differences between the parents about Bobby. He hoped to establish some common concerns between them, as Mr. V had already indicated, and to use these as a basis for the assessment.

Some referrals are unacceptable. If, despite all efforts, the psychologist is unable to discover from the referrant the reasons and purposes for the referral, he should inform the referrant that he does not understand and cannot carry out the referral. Thus, a request for "psychometric tests" with no indication of what the referrant needs to know or what decisions are going to be made on the basis

---

* In some clinics, the initial referral information is obtained by a secretary, but in general this has not proven satisfactory even when the secretary is an experienced and trained employee. More usually, a secretary merely obtains and records the caller's name, telephone number, and address and the introductory question.

of the assessment is unacceptable. Usually when this is explained to a referrant, the referral can be clarified. Occasionally the questions are posed to the psychologist in such a way as to be unanswerable.

A classic example is the "McNaughten Rule," which asks whether an adult knew the difference between right and wrong when he committed a crime. Similarly a parent or other referrant may want to know if a child has told a lie or has performed a specific act. For example, this writer has been asked to decide whether a child who has accused an adult of sexual molestation is (a) falsely accusing the adult; (b) has invited the molestation and/or (c) has been psychologically damaged by this specific incident. In such instances, it has been necessary to explain to the referrant that assessments give a general description of the child's development rather than specific information about particular events, but that the psychologist might contribute information about the child's behavior and development which might be pertinent to the specific behavior. For example, although the psychologist has no way of knowing if the child is lying (unless the child reports this and agrees to so inform authorities), he can ascertain whether the child "generally distorts reality" or "is so negativistic as to make things out of nothing." Similarly, the psychologist may not be able to discover whether a child has initiated an act, such as participation in pederasty, but he might estimate how much impulse control the child shows, how seductive he might become, or obtain other data about the child's sexual development and behavior in general. The psychologist cannot even say for sure whether a child has been disturbed by a specific incident, but can attest to the child's preoccupation with such incidents, and give reasonable opinions as to the possible relationship of such an incident to whatever behavioral and developmental difficulties the child may demonstrate.

Similarly, a referrant may ask the psychologist to make an impossible prediction, for example, "Will my four year old be able to go to college?" At times considerable persuasion is necessary to convince a parent that such predictions cannot be made. Once this writer was asked by an anxious parent if his very bright and seemingly effeminate six-year-old boy was in danger of becoming a homosexual. The parent finally accepted a restatement of the referral in terms of the child's current development and of questions which dealt with the care and training of an apparently precocious child.

The psychologist must also tread lightly when he has any reason to believe that the assessment might not be used to the best interests of the child or that there is some hidden agenda or unspoken reservation in the referral contract. He must make sure that the confidentiality of his data and report will be maintained. The psychologist should reserve the right to decide whether certain materials might be used adversely, either at present or in the future life of the child. The classic example here is the old-fashioned school system which rigidly classified its students on the basis of IQ scores. This led a generation of psychologists to refuse to report IQ scores at all! Some physicians, who would ordinarily lean over backwards to avoid making the patient anxious by revealing any details of their own findings, have been known to bolster their own ignorance of psychological factors by reading the psychologist's report verbatum to the parent! It is to be hoped that such incidents will become less frequent as students in education, medicine, law, and the ministry, now are being trained in the use of psychologists' reports. More difficult to ascertain sometimes are those occasions where the referrant, especially the parent, intends to use the assessment for purposes other than to help the child.

CASE 18

Mrs. Q brought Arlen, age ten, to the clinic to find out why he was not succeeding in school. In the initial intake contact, she stated that she was "absolutely certain" that Arlen was intellectually retarded and that she hoped to be able to convince the school that he should be placed in a special class. The clinic accepted the referral with some reservations, explaining to the mother that no such assumption could be made in advance of the assessment and that there might be other reasons for the child's school difficulties. Mrs. Q seemed to accept this restatement of the referral, but became quite resistant to the clinic's request to contact the school. The assessment work with the child himself was completed before the clinic discovered that the mother had filed a formal lawsuit against the School Board. Arlen reported that he had difficulties with his relationship with the teachers and principal because of his mother's constant interference with school activities. His test responses showed that he was actually above average intellectually. Mrs. Q was advised of the latter result and an attempt was made to discuss further her relationship with the school and the child. She became enraged at the slightest suggestion that her child might be anything but retarded and demanded that the clinic write a letter to the School Board confirming this. Later, she included the clinic in her ultimately unsuccessful lawsuit. On court order, the clinic was forced to release its findings to public record. Finally, when the mother refused to enter the child in any public school, and could not find a private school which seemed acceptable to her (or which would accept the child), the court ordered an investigation into the capability of the mother to care for the child.

Last, but not least, a psychologist is bound by his ethics not to accept a referral that is beyond his competency. Thus, a psychologist who has never dealt with the case of intellec-tual retardation or of childhood schizophrenia, or is unfamiliar with some other type of special problem, should, before he accepts such a referral, obtain consultation or supervision from some colleague who is knowledgeable about the specific problem. Similarly, the psychologist is ethically bound to use only those techniques which he has been trained to use, and only those which he has reason to believe will contribute to the referral questions. Sometimes as he proceeds he may discover hints of other kinds of disturbance than that originally suspected. For example, he may be asked specifically about intelligence, but find emotional disturbance also. Unless an extensive investigation was requested, it is at least professional courtesy to confer with the referrant, including the parent, before proceeding. Nor should the psychologist include techniques merely for his own curiosity even though it be his scientific curiosity or research, unless he has specifically asked permission of the referrant and parent.

CONDUCTING THE ASSESSMENT

A. ON MAKING APPOINTMENTS

It may seem that "giving" an appointment is a simple operation, which would warrant little or no discussion. In many settings, arrangements for the client or patient to meet the professional man is handled by a receptionist or appointment secretary. However, in psychological work the appointment is where the patient contact begins. In essence, this is the first implementation of the assessment "contract"; quite often it is a continuation of the making of that contract, whenever the client is referred by someone else. When the appointment is made, the psychologist begins negotiations with the client, at least the parent, toward fulfilling the obligations contracted for in the referral.

For these reasons, it is much wiser for the psychologist himself, rather than an appointment secretary (no matter how well trained), to arrange the appointment. The main element of this step in the assessment has to do with *time,* with the psychologist's time and with the child's time — as managed by the parent. In making this time arrangement, the psychologist begins his relationship with the parent and child (even if the child is not personally contacted). In clinic settings, this appointment continues and expands the client's

relationship with the attitudes toward the clinic. In addition, the appointment contact is often used by the client and possibly the psychologist to obtain and give additional information. In fact, the manner in which the client handles the making of the appointment may in itself yield further data about how the parent handles the child and social situations. The position of the psychologist in a private practice rather than in an agency or institution who makes the initial contact entirely on his own had already been discussed. Two other situations need to be considered: the out-patient clinic or agency and the hospital or institution situation.

In the out-patient situation, the psychologist has to contact the parent to bring the child to the office. He may arrange with one of his colleagues to introduce him to the parent when the parent comes to the clinic to see the other staff member. Such vis-à-vis introductions are ideal, since the client has some idea who will be seeing the child, can think through the matter of time arrangements, and can raise any other questions that come to mind. However, in the everyday workings of most clinics, such arrangement for a personal introduction of the psychologist and client is not always feasible. Quite commonly, the decision to make a full assessment may not be made until the initial contact has been reviewed by the staff. The usual practice is to review an "intake" and decide whether the clinic can possibly help the child before proceeding with further interviews and examinations. Thus, most frequently the appointment for psychological assessment is made over the telephone.

Whether the contact is vis-à-vis or via telephone, the psychologist should ascertain beforehand, during the referral, whether or not the client has been apprised that an appointment with the psychologist is to be made, and what the client has been told about the nature of the assessment. After introducing himself and identifying himself as a member of the clinic staff, the psychologist should remind the client about the referral, for example, "Mrs. S, this is Dr. T of the Child Guidance Clinic. Mrs. J asked me to call you to make an appointment for me to see Bernie. I understand that you have already discussed this with her?" Such an introductory question-statement allows the client to introject any further questions she may have. When it is clear that the parent does have a general idea of why an appointment is to be made, then the psychologist may inquire about the question of time; usually he begins by informing the client of approximately the amount of time that will be needed. Then he can inquire if there are time limitations for the child and parents. For example, "Are there any times when it would be impossible for either you or Bernie to come in?" Note that such a question includes the child.

Once the limits of the client's time are established, the psychologist will want to mention his own availability to see if a mutually agreeable time can be set. This presumes, of course, that the psychologist arranges his own time so that he can offer more than one possible opening to the client. Again, such flexibility is not nearly as possible when an appointment is made through a secretary. If the psychologist has no after-school time, and after-school hours are indeed precious when one is working with children, then there should be some discussion about both the parents' and the child's feelings about missing school. The psychologist is usually able to reassure the parent that only one or two such arrangements will be required and that the child will not regularly be missing school. If an after-school appointment is being arranged, the psychologist should in-

quire what the child usually does on that day, with at least the suggestion that he is interested in how the child feels about giving up his time.

If the parent does not ask about or mention what the child has been told about the appointment, the psychologist should bring this up directly. If the parent has any doubts, the best and most honest approach that one can suggest is that the parent tell the child that the appointment will be one which is intended to help the doctors better understand some things about his "problem" for which they have started going to the clinic. Suppose that Mrs. S has discussed Bernie's enuresis and night terrors with the social worker, but Bernie has not as yet come to the clinic. The psychologist discovers that Mrs. S has not told Bernie about her visit, but that Bernie has been taken to the pediatrician about these problems and he advised contacting the clinic. The psychologist should then advise Mrs. S to remind Bernie that their doctor did tell her to contact the clinic, that she has talked to one of our staff members, and that she wants him to come to the clinic next Tuesday. Since Bernie's prior experiences concerning this problem have been medical, the psychologist should advise Mrs. S further to tell Bernie that there will be no physical examination but, rather, that the psychologist is a different kind of doctor who is interested in what children do and think about and that he will talk to Bernie and ask him to do some different kinds of interesting things, all of which will help the doctors at the clinic understand Bernie's problem a little better. Not infrequently, parents raise further questions, such as, "What shall I tell him if he wants to know more about what he will be doing with you?" or "You mean you will be giving him some tests?" Quite often when parents raise such questions, they are voicing their own curiosity and anxieties about what the psychologist is going to do with or find out about *their* children and thus about them. Rather than enter into any extended explanation at this point, it is usually wiser to gently repeat the instructions and add that if the child does have further questions that the parent tell the child that the psychologist will be willing to talk this over with him when he comes to the clinic.

When the child is a resident in some institution, or is being seen at a school, the psychologist should begin by checking the child's schedule of activities with the institutional authority who is responsible. He should talk first with the nurse, matron, or teacher, finding out when the child is most free and what activities he may miss if the appointment is made at one of the times the psychologist has available. He should also inquire as to how the child might feel about missing whatever activity might be scheduled at that time. It is also wise to find out how the person who would be supervising the child during that time will feel about the child being taken out of the activity. For example, if the athletic director at the hospital has just about succeeded in getting a frightened and withdrawn child involved in a ballgame, then it might behoove the psychologist to take this into consideration, even though one might feel that a patient could miss his recreation "just this one time." Next, the psychologist should meet the child and discuss the appointment briefly with him, much in the same way he would advise the parent in the out-patient situation, for example, "Dr. V, your doctor, has asked me to get together with you soon. I guess he talked to you a little about seeing me. I want to talk a little with you too and ask you to work on some things with me so that I can understand better how you think about things and work at things. This will help Dr. V, too, to understand your problems. Nurse R has told me that she thought you wouldn't mind too much missing OT tomorrow morning for a couple of hours. Would that be all right with you?" Again, such an introduction helps to tie in the assessment procedure with the other attention the child is receiving and recognizes that the child's time is considered important. Of course, the psychologist should be prepared to offer the child an alternative time — but not too many alternatives as this may confuse an emotionally disturbed child or give him too much chance to manipulate the adult. If the child raises further questions, suggesting some anxiety about the assessment, the psychologist should indicate, as in the out-patient situation, that these questions can better be discussed when they meet. "Do I have to?" is the common resistant question, to which the answer is "Dr. V and I think it will help." If the child completely rejects the appointment, then it may be necessary to contact the staff colleague who made the referral and inquire if

further steps need to be taken to help the child accept the assessment or if possibly the assessment should be delayed until the child is able to accept it.

B. THE INITIAL CONTACT WITH THE CHILD

The relationship between the child and the assessor usually begins when they meet in the waiting hall or at the assessor's door. In this meeting there are often many subtle clues about the parent-child relationship and their attitudes about the assessment. Most commonly, when the assessor introduces himself to the parent, the parent introduces the child; if not, the psychologist should ask directly, "Are you (child's name)?" Most children appreciate being offered an adult handshake when introduced. Frequently, anxious parents act as if the child were deaf and start giving additional information about the child or instructions on how to handle him. The assessor should note how the child reacts to being talked about in front of him to a stranger. As one might expect, even very young children who commonly experience such adult behavior are usually somewhat embarrassed and may react by hiding further behind mother's skirts or by creating some diversion so as to interrupt the parent or turn the parent's attention away from the assessor. Older children often directly show their embarrassment, reddening and remarking, "Oh, mother!"

If this writer has planned to see the parent first, as I commonly do in the case of younger children, I may remark, "I guess your mother has some things she wants to talk to me about. Would it be okey if we talked first — if you don't mind waiting here?" Children may be a bit relieved to find that the assessment is to be delayed a few more minutes, but also apprehensive about what mother may tell the assessor about them. With adolescents to whom independence and privacy are so often very important, I most commonly meet with the child first, telling the parent, "We will have an opportunity to discuss that later, after your son and I have had a chance to talk things over." Of course, there is no strict rule about whether one meets first with parent or child; this decision depends on factors such as whether or not the assessor has had a chance to gain enough information to know some of the purposes of the assessment, and other vital information from the referral, the relative anxieties of the parent and child, the child's ability to separate from the parent, and the exigencies of the waiting room. If the assessor has previously had a chance to interview the parent briefly over the telephone, it may be quite feasible to see the child first. In other instances, the child may show signs of being too anxious to wait.

Most important to observe, especially with younger children, is how the child and parent separate. Often there is a slight delay with the preschool child, while he makes his separation. He may hide his head in mother's lap for an extra second (even though he may have been exploring up and down the hall a few minutes previously), give her an extra hug or kiss, or go through some diversionary actions before accepting the examiner's hand. The intensity of the child's anxiety in this separation and the mother's reaction to it provide one clue about their relationships. Sometimes this is a prolonged and elaborate ceremony, or a "game" as Eric Berne (1964) would label it; or at the other extreme, the child may desert the parent without a glance behind him. Parents have their separation anxieties too. The mother who has a lot to talk about with the assessor in the hallway may be delaying separation from the child. Parents have been known to urge the child verbally to "go with the doctor" while at the same time holding tight to his hand. At the other extreme is the mother who pushed the child out of the car in the parking lot, scarcely stopping before she wheeled around and sped off. In most instances, it is usually best for the assessor to patiently step aside and let the child and parent work out the separation on their own.

Only occasionally is it necessary for the assessor to intervene by firmly requesting the parent to leave and wait "down the hall" and reassuring the child in a matter-of-fact voice that "you and I will be talking and doing some things while mother waits." In those instances where the mother abandons the child in the waiting room, the situation should be at least mentioned by the assessor to the child, with an eye to the child's reaction. Such children may be used to such maternal desertion and be able to maintain a stiff upper lip. Even the five year old who stumbled out of the moving car into the parking lot picked himself up, and when the psychologist rushed

out to inquire what had happened, he was able to muster a noncommital "hello" as if ignoring the whole incident. When the psychologist remarked, "Your mother seemed in an awful hurry!" the child replied somewhat bitterly, "Yeah, she's always in a hurry!" However, he seemed rather listless and preoccupied, gazing away from the psychologist toward the door; the psychologist inquired again, "Are you still thinking about how your mother was in a hurry?" whereupon the child burst into tears and permitted the psychologist to pick him up in her lap and comfort him. The assessment was discontinued that day, and the mother was asked to stay for an interview with the social worker during the next appointment. This time the child rushed in to greet the psychologist, sat as close to her as possible, was eager to please and even motivated to achieve.

Some children, especially very young children, cannot make this separation from the parent easily. They may continue to cry, to demand to return to mother, or at least need to go periodically and check to see if mother is still there. Usually some verbal recognition of the child's anxiety suffices, for example, "You seemed scared — are you afraid mother won't be out there? Shall we go see?" Of course, fear may not be the only emotion the child is experiencing over the separation; he may also be angry, and both feelings may have to be recognized before the child can settle down. With exceedingly anxious or shy children who do not seem to be able to make the separation at all, it may be necessary to bring mother into the room for a little while, and to condition the child gradually to mother's leaving. Occasionally, a child may make several visits to the assessor's office in which nothing more is accomplished than that he permits mother to leave for increasing periods of time. The manner in which the child and mother achieve the separation under such extreme circumstances is often as revealing as any tests one might administer.

Another source of anxiety for the child is the stranger, the assessor. According to Spock (1946), a mild shyness in front of strangers is normal for the three year old. Emotionally disturbed children of all ages usually show some indication of anxiety in relating to the strange doctor. They may be initially very stiff, reserved, and guarded, or obversely defend themselves by intrusively detracting, asking a million questions, looking out the window, playing with something, etc. If the referrant or parent has helped to define the situation for the child, some of his anxiety may be deterred. However, no matter what he may have been told, the fact that he expects to be observed and examined in some as yet undefined manner often creates considerable initial anxiety.

Thus, once some sort of separation from the parent has been achieved, the psychologist's first job is to relieve this anxiety. One should begin by helping the child define the situation more clearly. First it is a good idea to orient him briefly to the room: "Why don't you sit over there. Is that chair comfortable for you? We probably will be doing some work at this table, and I'm going to sit here." Once the child is seated, one should proceed to introduce oneself a little further, repeating one's name and letting the child know how it is he has come to know of the child: "I'm Dr. P, and Dr. C called me the other day and told me he's been talking to you a bit and that he wanted me to meet you and do some things with you. Did he talk to you too about seeing me?" Even if the child does indicate that he remembers the referrant orienting him to the assessment, a brief discussion of what the child expects and about the nature and purpose of the assessment is usually necessary. The question, "What did you think we were going to do here today?" may meet with a noncommittal shrug, but even so the child usually gives some indication that this was exactly what was on his mind. If the child was referred by a physician who has physically examined and treated him, then it would be appropriate to ask: "Did you think I was going to do the same kind of things with you that Dr. C. does?" "What does he do?" Then the psychologist should differentiate his role for the child: "Yes, I see, Dr. C. helps you when you're sick, or gives you shots" (or whatever the child mentions). Or, if Dr. C. were a psychiatrist, "Of course, Dr. C. is a psychiatrist, he talks with children to see how he can help them. Well, I'm a different kind of doctor, I'm a psychologist. Do you know what that is? A psychologist is interested in understanding how boys and girls think and feel about things, how they go about things, the things they like and don't like, and what makes them happy or unhappy."

As may be noted, in such a discussion the psychologist is not only introducing himself and differentiating himself from other people dealing with the child's problems, he is also beginning to relate the assessment to what the child has already experienced in the way of help. This association should be continued to assist the child in recognizing that the assessment is part of an overall effort to understand his problems. How such an association is made for the child depends, of course, on the nature of the referral. If referred by the pediatrician, one might say, for example, "Dr. C. told me that he had been giving you some shots for some kind of allergy, but that the shots didn't seem to help you much. Is that right?" "Why do you think Dr. C wanted to have you come see a psychologist like me?" "Perhaps if we understood more about some of the things I mentioned, it might help to solve some of the mystery of your allergy." Such questions then might lead to a brief discussion of the child's medical complaints and of his current behavioral difficulties associated with being allergic, and on into his current adjustment in general. Where the child is being seen by some colleague in a clinic setting, this discussion might run this way. "I know Dr. C and you have been talking about your problems but, of course, what you talk about with him is just between you and him so he didn't tell me much about what you said. That's the rule here, you know. However, because he knew you and I were going to work together, it was necessary for me to know about the problem that brought you to the clinic. So I do know that one of the main reasons you came to see Dr. C. was because of your problem in . . . ."

Depending on the child's response, one might continue, "Since you and Dr. C are already talking together about that and other things, we don't have to go into that, unless there is something more about it or some other problem you think I should know about. Talking about one's problems and the things that go with them is very helpful — after one gets used to doing it. But that's only one way we have of understanding about children and their lives. Often it helps us, too, to see how children do things, think about things, and look at things. That's what you and I are going to do today, so as to help you and Dr. C as you talk more together." Such an introduction would presume that the assessor was leaving the interviewing of the child to Dr. C and going to proceed with other techniques. On the other hand, if the interview is to be part of the assessment, then the psychologist may want to establish a bit further the relationship between the referral and the assessment, especially when the parent is the referrant: "When your mother phoned me, *she* told me that you'd been having a lot of trouble getting along at school — and with her and your father too. However, I didn't get a chance to talk with her very much about it and, besides, I really wanted to meet you first and understand how *you* saw it and what you thought about it. This gives you and me a chance to talk together in private. You see, what children and psychologists talk about together is just between them, and no one else gets to know." If necessary, the fact of the confidentiality of the assessment can be discussed further: "Of course, if psychologists told other people what they talked about with their patients, no one could trust them and tell them how they actually felt or about what was going on in their lives, 'cause sometimes it's very personal. That's why we have this rule."

For older children, the initial resistance may result not so much from separation anxiety, but from both the interruption of their normal activities and the prospect of facing uncomfortable, anxiety-producing topics they fear will be brought to light by the psychologist. If the psychologist has any inkling that the child is coming under protest, this resistance may have to be explored even before the introductory discussion outlined above — or at least as part of it. To the glum and glowering adolescent who does not respond to a greeting or even rise from his seat in the waiting room until his exasperated mother says, "Well, aren't you going with the doctor?" and who shuffles along behind you down the hall and stands staring out the window at the warm afternoon sun, one might as well begin by directly recognizing, "It sure seems evident to me that you may not have wanted to come here at all this afternoon. What's the trouble?" One may then proceed directly to a discussion of the resistance in a sympathetic fashion. Such a recognition can usually lead into the type of introduction as outlined above. Where the resistance is less marked than in the above illustration, where the child seems apathetic or bored, one might ask, "On a day like this, I'd guess most boys might want to do most anything rather than come to see a doctor. What might you have been doing if you didn't have to come to see me?"

To summarize: In the initial contact with the child, the psychologist should: (1) allow for, observe, and, where necessary, recognize and deal with the child's separation from his parent; (2) introduce himself and his role among those adults interested in the child's problems; (3) investigate the child's concerns and attitudes toward the assessment, being alert to the child's fears, hopes, and resistances.

This introduction serves yet another purpose: the psychologist also meets the child. Like the child, the psychologist undoubtedly also has some preconceived notions about the type of person he is going to meet and deal with. He has heard the "complaints" (a term which has an unfortunate association with courts of law) and symptoms, knows some of the ideas that others have about the child, and has some ideas of his own about how children of this age should function. Moreover, by then he has had at least a phone contact with the child's parent, and has formed some impressions about how a child might react to "that kind of mother." He may be prepared to be sympathetic or he may be girded to meet a hostile or resistant child. Having studied the referral and made the appointment, he has made plans about the kinds of techniques he wants to use, and hopes that he is correct in his choices and that the child will be cooperative. During this brief introduction period, the psychologist should silently check out these preconceptions about the child. What kind of behavior does the child initially show? How is the child accepting him and the proposed assessment contract? What are the possibilities that he may run into resistances or that the child may be cooperative? How verbal is the child? How restless? How much does the child volunteer? How guarded is he? Observing the child's behavior during these first few minutes of the assessment will help the psychologist to decide whether his plans for the assessment can proceed or whether he needs to revise them.

C. TIMING AND SEQUENCE

This initial contact will also help the psychologist double-check two other aspects of his plans: the possible division or utilization of the time which he and the child may have together, and the sequence of activities in which the psychologist may wish to engage the child. As to the timing, under ideal situations, a thorough assessment would not be time-bound, and the psychologist could take as much time as he needs. However, in practice, the amount of time available is limited by the psychologist's schedule, the clinic or referrant's schedule (when the assessment data are needed for the referrant's decision), and certainly by the parent and child's schedule (when they can come in). Early in the referral stage, the psychologist should make some rough estimate of how long it may take him to gather the kind of data demanded by the referral. Such an estimate may not be easy to make, especially for the novitiate, but as one gathers experience, it becomes more possible to guess how long it might take to interview and administer a proposed set of techniques to a certain age child with certain characteristics and handicaps. The psychologist can also usually make a guess as to whether all that he plans to do can be done in one session or in several. In negotiating the referral, he should inform the referrant of this time estimate. If there is a decision pending for a certain date, will it be possible for the psychologist to complete his study by the time the referrant has to make the decision? If not, should the psychologist limit his assessment to certain essential facets of the referral, possibly continuing the rest of the assessment thereafter? Or might the decision be delayed until the psychologist has had a chance to make a complete study? If these timing elements are not worked out between the psychologist and the referrant, the psychologist may feel rushed, then rush the child and, as a consequence, end up with inadequate and insufficient data; or, obversely, he may make an excellent and thorough study of the child and write a scholarly treatise, only to find that the referrant, weary of waiting, has had to go ahead and make a decision without benefit of the psychologist's findings.

Similarly, the time budget of the assessment needs to be discussed with the parent. In part, this is usually begun between the parent and referrant, who says, in effect, "Next, I want you to take the child to the psychologist; after that we can begin to make some decisions." Some parents react with anxiety,

often typical of the anxiety they experience in other similar situations, and jump the gun, making contact with the psychologist and seeking an appointment almost before the psychologist is aware of what is going on. Others, who may be seeking to delay the opening up of their Pandora's box, delay and seek more time before allowing an appointment.

It is during the making of the appointment that these attitudes of the parent come to light. The psychologist needs to explore with the parents their pressures as to how soon they want to make a decision and to help clarify with them the clinic's time limits and flexibilities. For example, to the parent who appears to be wondering if she should put aside other obligations to meet a proffered appointment, the psychologist might explain, "If you can bring your child in this week, then our staff might be able to discuss all our findings the following week and Dr. C could advise you of our suggestions soon thereafter. However, if it is necessary for you to delay, we would understand and you could call us when you are ready to have your child seen." At the same time, the psychologist should acquaint the parent with his prospective time budget for the assessment, the possibility that he may need around so many hours and so many visits — a budget which may have to be tempered to meet the resistances and anxieties of the parent.

This time budget may again be altered once the psychologist meets with the child. His hopes that he can interview the child and administer such and such tests in a two-hour period may be dashed by the anxious child who defends himself either by passive resistance and silence, or by hyperactivity and a running interference with the best laid plans of the psychologist. Dealing with these resistances is the subject of the next section of this chapter. Suffice it to say, it is usually useless to barge ahead and try to obtain a history or give an IQ test in the face of a child who is either "taking the Fifth Amendment" or conducting a guerrilla war. In such instances, the time is much better spent by dealing with these resistances. Often, by so doing, much more assessment data can be accumulated directly about the behavior of the child.

Assuming that the child's anxieties are successfully alleviated in the initial five to ten minutes of the introductory discussion, how long might a psychologist expect to spend in contact with the child for the average overall thorough assessment? Although to this writer's knowledge, no time-motion study has been reported for assessment of children, in an unpublished survey conducted by the writer (1957) as part of the planning for staffing the state hospitals in California, staff psychologists reported that the patient contact of their assessments of adult in-patients ranged from two and a half to four hours. The longer assessments were broken into two appointments. In the experience of this writer and his colleagues, the time needed for assessment of children is more variable, depending as it does on the age of the child — as well as the nature of the referral. With younger children, (under age eight), it might be possible if they are very cooperative and involved with the procedures to maintain their interest and cooperation for a full two hours; however, most preschool and younger school-age children begin to be restless even before an hour has passed, and fatigue sets in. If the assessment has to be continued, then a run down the hall and a trip to the bathroom or drinking fountain is called for. It is usually wise to have a second session arranged in reserve for children in this age group.

However, the total time needed for the assessment of the younger child is usually a little shorter than that required for older children and adolescents. The overall responsiveness of the younger child is on the average more limited. They may be quite verbal but on the whole they find less to talk about than their older sibs (although some have learned at an early age how to entertain adults by being garrulous). Unless one is dealing with a very bright or unusual child, it is usually possible to administer a Binet to a five year old (encompassing about 25–30 items) in about a half to three quarters of an hour. In contrast, giving a WISC to an average ten year old (50–75 items) takes from an hour to 90 minutes. Similarly, the preschooler's responses to the Rorschach, his CAT fantasies, and drawings and other productions are more brief than those of older children. With this three to eight year old group, two one-hour sessions are often quite sufficient (not including parental contacts). "Tests" to infants under three may require even less time but often extra time is needed for general observation, and more than one session is usually required because of the variability and unre-

liability in the reactions of infants. Extended assessments of older children and adolescents may require almost as much time as the assessment of adults, up to two, two-hour sessions.

The above mentioned time estimate presumes that the assessor has made at least preliminary plans as to which techniques he will be using before he meets with the child. It presumes that the assessor has laid out the test materials he plans to use and has checked to see that they are complete and in order so that he does not have to hunt around among them or rearrange them before presenting them to the child. It presumes he is skilled in the use of these materials, that he does not have to flip pages of a book to read directions or questions, or even to score items, and most of all that he knows the tests so well that he can listen to and follow the child's responses and pick up clues from them without having to think about what comes next on the test.

Another skill that an assessor needs to develop is the ability to plan out the sequence in which he is going to use the techniques, which incidentally also can conserve his time. Ideally, one task should lead into the next, so that the child does not have to shift his set too extensively or rapidly. At the same time, the tasks should be varied enough so that the child does not become bored. As one shifts from technique to technique, the sequence of events should lead naturally one to the next. For example, the introductory discussion leads easily into the interview; at most, one might remark, "Perhaps I could better understand about your problem if you could tell me a little more how it began . . ." and then, after obtaining some history of the complaint and its circumstances, lead the child into discussion of his family, etc., by saying, for example, "You mentioned something about your mother and father. Could you tell me a little more about your family? Who else is there?" and so lead into a gradually expanding investigation of the child's current world and its history.

After 50 or 60 minutes and a short break, the assessor might remark, "We've been talking together quite a bit, and talking helps me understand about you and your problem, but as I told you before, it also helps to see how people do things and think about things. So now I'm going to ask you to work with some materials and puzzle out some questions." In the normal course of events, a child's expectations when he hears about tests are on the order of the kinds of tasks included in intelligence scales. Thus, he may not be surprised when the assessor says next, "Let's begin by seeing what words you know." In most instances, such relatively emotionally neutral problem-solving tasks are less threatening to the child than the more unstructured associative techniques. The short and varied items of the Binet are particularly designed to hold the attention of the young child, while the older child is able to stick to one type of task a little longer on the WISC. Although the vocabulary subtest of the WISC is numbered 5, beginning with the Vocabulary, switching to Information (a comparable task), on to Comprehension, and then to the more complex judgments required in Similarities and Arithmetic makes a natural sequence. If one ends the verbal tasks with arithmetic or digit span, the shift to the nonverbal tasks is not too great, for example, to digit symbol. There is less of a smooth sequence among the performance subtests, and occasionally the assessor may need to call the child's attention to the fact that a shift of set is required, for example, if picture arrangement is presented after picture completion, the assessor might explain, "Now I'm going to show you some more pictures but this time I want you to do a different kind of thing."

If the Bender-Gestalt or Memory-For-Designs are to be used, this type of visual motor task fits in nicely with the IQ scale tasks; however, one would want to consider whether a visual motor task should be introduced after an hour of problem-solving intellectual work, or whether one should wait till the child is more fresh, especially if one were dealing with a child whom one suspected might be neurologically handicapped and quickly fatigued. In any case, at the end of an hour and a half or two hours, one should remark, "You've worked awfully hard today, and some of the things you tried were quite difficult. Perhaps we should stop now. I do want to see you again next _____ at _____ o'clock. When we get together again, we can do some more, slightly different things, which I'm sure you'll find interesting." Such a conclusion to the first session rewards the child for his efforts and lets the child know of the continuing interest of the assessor in his work, including other possible ways the child might have of showing the assessor about himself. If, to carry on this example,

the assessor decides to open the second session with a visual motor drawing task, he might say, "This time let's begin by having you use the pencil. Here are some designs." Subsequently, "While you have the pencil, here's another sheet of paper and now I'd like to have you draw me a picture of a man . . . (and proceed to the Goodenough or to the Draw-A-Person, or House-Tree-Person). Such a shift makes it easier to proceed with other associative tasks. For example, "When children draw me pictures, I understand a little how they look at things. Now I want you to try a little different way to show me how you look at things. Here I have some cards with inkblots on them and I'm going to ask you to . . . (giving the Rorschach instructions)." Although the Rorschach instructions do not mention "imagination," one can turn from the Rorschach to the TAT or CAT by saying, "Making things out of those inkblots did require some imagination, didn't it? Now I'm going to ask you to do even more imagining, as I think imagining is pretty important for children. Here I have some other pictures, not just inkblots, and instead of just describing them to me I want you to think up a story for me, to use all your imagination . . . (and continue with the TAT instructions)." Often, if the Draw-A-Person has not yet been administered, this writer says, "I've shown you a lot of pictures, now I'm going to end by asking you to draw me a picture." Or, one might conclude a session with some questionnaire, such as the Bene-Anthony, saying, "This time I'm going to let you read the questions and make your answers to yourself without having to say anything or me having to write anything down. Here we have . . ."

Many other sequences are quite feasible and it depends a great deal on the kinds of techniques being used and the reactions of the child. One might not need to give an intelligence test and want to start directly with associative techniques. For small children, drawing is usually an attractive task and one which they often are used to doing at the request of an adult. As was noted above, the shift then can be made to the Rorschach, then CAT. Play techniques, such as the Lynn Structured Doll Play or the World Test, are best left to the end of the assessment as it is usually difficult for the child to shift away from play back to a work task, even to other associative tasks. It is just as possible to start off with the Rorschach, remarking "What I'm most interested in is how *you* look at things, *your* ideas and feelings."

D. ON HANDLING RESIST-ANCE—"THE GAMES CHILDREN PLAY"

Assessment carries with it some element of anxiety for nearly every child. There is the stress of having to perform. Most of all, there is the anxiety, albeit often unconscious, over revealing hidden feelings or inadequacies. Even the very conforming and competitive child who is challenged by his own achievement motivations holds back as these anxieties arise. Those children who are less driven to please or to achieve may become even more defensive as they become threatened by certain kinds of demands made upon them or as their secret fantasies are pried from them. Such defensiveness may be lowered, of course, by the methods mentioned above, that is, by the introductory discussion of the purposes of the assessment. During the assessment, as the child becomes blocked, restless, or lags and drags his feet, it is often necessary to give him a chance to recover from such moments of anxiety, and even to recognize with him that there is a threat present. When the child blocks after having expressed some anxiety, it may be helpful to remark, "This is a difficult thing to talk about." Or, "That picture (or that inkblot) does make one think of some depressing things." Or, "That was a pretty scary thought," etc. Usually such recognition of the child's anxiety is sufficient to allow him to recover and tackle a new stimulus. Of course, the way in which the child handles the anxiety engendered by the stress of the assessment is often characteristic of how he handles other, similar stress. Thus, the kinds of defenses he uses and his ability to recover from anxiety during the assessment is part of the data available for estimation of his ego strength.

For some children, the stress of the assessment is so overwhelming that they offer massive resistance. For various reasons, they do not accept the assessment contract set up for them by the adult authorities. Again, their rejection of adult pressures to conform and perform is often a basic part of their life problems. Usually such a child has been referred for assessment just because he or she is engaged in a battle of resistances with adults. These battles often take the form of what Eric Berne (1964) has labeled "games," games in which, in the transaction between child and adult, the child seeks to impose his own restrictions upon the adult instead of accepting the adult's terms. Children bring their transactional games of their everyday life to the assessment, and try to renegotiate the assessment contract according to the game. In order to understand and handle such challenges to the assessment transaction, it may be helpful first to examine and define some of the common games children play in assessment, that is, the nature and manifestations of such resistances.

1. *The game of "No!" or "Make me!"* This game, played most commonly by younger children, consists of very open and direct negativistic verbal expressions, often with the response "No," no matter what the question. Usually this "No" is given with a smile or giggle, in a seductive fashion, as if to say "Go ahead: make me!" The child expects the adult to play the game by responding, "Come now!" and wheedling or cajoling. The child then repeats his "No" with even more relish, and so the game goes on in rounds of "No" and "Come now" with the child offering just enough tidbits of cooperation to entrap the adult into the game, or until the adult becomes exhausted and gives up.

2. *The game of "I can't"* also played more by younger children, but also commonly by immature or passive adolescents, the aim of this game is to seek reassurance from the adult authority by claiming inadequacy. Here, the child says in effect, "I just can't" expecting the adult to respond, with encouragement and reassurance, "Oh, yes you can." Often this game is played by children who really do have some doubts of their abilities and some feelings of inadequacy. Thus, they seek to avoid any assessment of their functioning. If they can get the adult to reassure "Oh, yes you can" then there is really no need to prove whether they can or not. Thus, the assessment has been turned into a reassurance transaction. Although the intent is to gain reassurance against feelings of inadequacy, the player is never really reassured and has to keep demanding, because the reassurance per se is no proof.

3. *The game of "Fifth Amendment"* * is another version of the game of "No!" but is played for different reasons. Where "No!"

is essentially a seductive game, the "Fifth Amendment" is an attack. In this defensive tactic, the child maintains silence in order not to "incriminate" himself. The child fears that "anything he says may be used against him." It is the response of the guilty and angry child who fears that the assessor may discover how he feels. Just as when the Fifth Amendment is used in Congressional hearings, the refusal to respond usually incites anger in the inquirer, and the other "player" is expected to cite the child for contempt. The child argues (to himself) that he has a right to privacy, while the adult seeks to "get at the truth." It is a common game between children and parents and is frequently brought into the assessment situation.

4. *"My game first"* or *"Promise me"* is a game of blackmail. In this game, the child proposes alternate activity which he demands that the assessor promise to permit before the child will accede to the assessor's demands. If the adult agrees to play this game, he finds the price constantly raised at each step. Often the child claims the prize before cooperating, then makes new demands. If the adult refuses, then the child can claim to be cheated. Again, the child who plays this game is not accepting the assessment contract of cooperation in return for psychological understanding; rather he seeks some concrete prize for "being good." Such a child doubts the sincerity of others, cannot accept a promise on faith, but needs immediate evidence, and even when so rewarded recognizes that he had to be bribed and is not really loved.

5. *The game of "silly-billy"* by younger children or *"Flip"* by adolescents is like "No!" often seductive, but like "Fifth Amendment," also hostile. In this game, the child gives a nonsense answer, or the adolescent a flip or impudent response. The expected response is "Gee, you're cute!" or "Don't be silly!" — but with a smile. It is a teasing game, intended both to delight and irritate, but mainly to divert.

6. Closely allied to this latter game is a tactic known as *backward talk*. Not really a game in the transactional sense, backward talk is really a version of simple denial in which the child gives a response entirely opposite to what he might say if he were agreeing to the assessment contract. He is particularly likely to deny his true feelings, during the interview, and in extreme instances may give antonyms for synonyms on a vocabulary test or make reversals on the Bender-Gestalt or the Block Design (which have nothing to do with "organicity"). Backward talk does become a game when the assessor silently assents, saying in effect, "I believe you." Rorschach discovered backward talk when, annoyed by individuals who used the white space between the blots he had so carefully selected, he recognized that the responder was being "oppositional." In essence, backward talk reverses the figure-ground of the assessment, in that the child puts the assessor on the spot to see if the assessor can come up with the answer.

7. *"Uproar"* has been well defined by Berne (1964). In the assessment version it may start with "silly-billy" but proceeds to an increasing number and intensity of diversions which are no longer "cute." Like the adult game, this diversionary tactic becomes a game if the assessor roars back, in the form of increasing demands on the child to "Stop it" and conform. Again, as in backward talk, the child is reversing the assessment procedure and testing the adult. As in "No!" he says in effect "make me" but this game is a more grim one. Here, the child defends against feelings of inadequacy by proving the adult incompetent to control the situation and thus proving the child to be superior. If the child succeeds in getting the adult to lose his temper, the child righteously feels he has won, even though it be a pyrrhic victory.

8. The success of the child in any of these games depends on whether the assessor is also playing a game — which might be labeled *"Score!"* In this game, the assessor is concerned with obtaining a "scorable" response. Rather than accepting and utilizing the response given by the child, the assessor wants the right (or wrong) answer. Usually he is concentrating concretely on the child's verbalizations or test performance, rather than on what is going on between him and the child. In playing the game of "Score," the assessor is in a sense also violating the assessment contract, for he puts his interest in the technique over and above his interest in the child. He can very easily become a victim of any of the child's games mentioned above, for

* This title is taken from the Fifth Amendment to the United States Constitution, which protects a person from testifying against himself. It has become popularized in recent years in Congressional investigations where witnesses have refused to "incriminate" themselves.

all that he knows is that he is not getting any cooperation with his game.

As Berne points out, a game may be disrupted by pointing out that there is a game going on. The assessor sets his pencil down, and says with a knowing smile, "I know the game you're playing. It's called "No!" The three year old usually screams with delight, says "No" several times loudly, and the assessor says, "Of course, I can't *make* you do anything. So I can't play the game of "No!" But, if you'd like to play, I'll show you what I can do. Then I'd be glad to play." Most of the time the child gives up the game, perhaps with one or more feeble attempts. If he persists, the assessor says sadly, "I guess you don't feel like playing anything but 'No!' Let's stop now and we can get together again when you feel like doing something else." Since the motivation for "No!" is seductive, the child probably will feel rejected at that point but is likely to completely avoid the game at the next session. "I just can't," "silly-billy," and even backward talk are likely to be denied with more backward talk and are thus more persistent. "Promise me" has to be dealt with quite promptly. The assessor cannot give bribes without being caught in quicksand. The first time the child even hints that "I'll do what you say if you let me . . . " the assessor must quickly say, "I can't play 'promise me.' The only thing I can promise you is that I'll try to understand what you have to say and how you do things."

"Fifth Amendment" needs to be handled with more sympathy, though no less directly. Here, the assessor must let the child know that he realizes that the child may be afraid, but he may feel that his privacy is being invaded; in fact, that this is true. The rationale of the assessment contract must then be rediscussed and the child's fears be investigated in a kindly sympathetic manner: "When children won't say anything to me, I often wonder if they aren't scared to trust me. Maybe they think we'll tell their mother everything they say." "I don't care, tell her anything you want," snarls the child. "If I did that, I wouldn't have any right to ask you to do anything. The only reason I have any right to ask you anything is if I respect your rights too. And I don't even have the right to expect you to answer my questions or do any of these things unless you want me to. I think I can understand you better

by asking these questions and seeing how you do things, but I need your permission if I'm to help you." The child who plays this game often needs time to think this over; and a second session may be necessary before he is willing to accept the assessment transaction. Where the child persists, formal assessment may have to be abandoned — with an explanation again of the reasons. Attempts may have to be made to establish some other kind of relationship with the child, that is, in therapy.

"Uproar" also calls for immediate action: "It sure seems like you want to create an uproar and get me angry. But I don't know what you're angry about." If the child can't explain, the assessor may make some guesses. "Did I interrupt something you were going to do today?" or "Are you scared what I may do?" or "Were you angry about something when you came today?" Again, if the child persists, the assessor says, "We can't do much when you're feeling so angry. I'd really like to get to know you better and have a good time talking with you and doing things. Perhaps we can get together next . . . and you would be feeling better."

This list of games does not begin to exhaust the defenses that children can put up against the anxieties engendered by the assessment situation. Nor are the suggested ways of handling these defenses more than illustrations. Most of all, the assessor must learn to distinguish between such defensive games and actual depression or schizophrenic confusion. The depressed child is not playing a game; rather, his feelings so overwhelm him that even though he eagerly accepts the assessment contract, he is actually unable to perform. However, once the assessor recognizes his mood, the depressed child is usually able to discuss the things he is depressed about, or at least openly acknowledge his depression. The confused child who has only a tenuous hold on reality may also defend himself by withdrawing and being noncommittal, but is also often feeling so uncomfortable that he will at least accept some offer of support and make some attempt to explain how he feels.

E. THE ASSESSMENT OF PARENTS—THE PARENT CONTRACT

As indicated in the previous sections, the involvement of the parents in the assessment of children is inevitable if only to obtain their cooperation in bringing the child in and orienting him to the assessment. Moreover, in most cases, wherever the child is being reared and cared for by parents or parent substitutes (other than institutional employees), it is necessary at least to interview the parents to obtain information about the child, his current behavior, and his history. Even when the contact with the parents is focused entirely on the child, their attitudes, behavior, and personality enter at least indirectly into the assessment, if only from the way they discuss the child. Recognizing that the development of the child's personality takes place in this parent-child interrelationship, the clinician usually finds that he must attempt to study the personality of the parents and often of other immediate family members, in a family assessment rather than focus entirely on the child and his symptoms. In fact, as will be discussed further in detail, it is often the case that the child's symptoms and behavior actually derive from and represent a family maladjustment, so that the child constitutes a scapegoat for the neurotic interaction of the whole family. Thus, instead of making assumptions about the behavior of other family members from the child's reports and views, or from the parents' behavior as they discuss the child, it is often necessary to obtain data directly about the parents' attitudes and behavior, and their history. These data are obtained by asking the parents to become involved in further interviews and to take tests, and to allow observation, directly in the playroom or in the family home, of the interaction between the parents and child.

The parents' acceptance of this aspect of the assessment depends a great deal on the manner in which the assessor handles his initial contacts with them. Many of the predominantly middle class parents who accept referral of their child to a psychologist or to psychological service centers often realize that they also will be subjected to assessment. Even those who may know little of assessment procedures seem aware that in some way their actions and attitudes may be related to the child's symptoms, and expect to be questioned about it. However, whether sophisticated or naive, the parents usually feel that they will be blamed or that they are at fault. In order to assuage their guilty feelings, parents may defend themselves in a variety of ways, ranging from a stiff-necked avoidance of discussion of any of their own feelings or background to an open confession (hoping thereby to gain reassurance from the assessor). Thus, one of the first steps in involving the parents in the assessment is to neutralize as much as possible this blame-avoidance behavior.

Much of the parents' initial guilt can be assuaged by the general attitude of the assessor, who seeks to understand and assist with the solution of a problem rather than to determine blame. In the initial interview with the parent, while the child's behavior and symptoms are being considered, the assessor lets the parent know that his purpose is *problem-solving* rather than judgment. This is indicated by the way he phrases his questions, his line of inquiry, and his tone of voice. The assessor may imagine or have good evidence that the parents may have seriously mismanaged the care of the child for their own neurotic needs and feel sympathetic with the child and critical of their failures. Nevertheless, in order to help the child in his contact with the parents, he must shift his sympathies and seek to understand the parents and their problems. Unless he can approach the parents with a "how can I help you" attitude and regard them as much his clients as is the child, it is quite possible that he will meet with such resistance, overt or covert, that he will be unable to help the child. Because this shift in sympathy from child to parent or parent to child is not easily accomplished, and no one is ever entirely neutral, assessment of the parent is often carried out by a different assessor in collaboration with the assessor who is working with the child. Where it is necessary for one assessor to work with both parent and child, the assessor must carefully examine his own feelings and attempt to view his assessment task not as a purely child-centered, but as a family-centered problem to be defined and resolved.

If the assessor can approach the parent with such a problem-solving attitude, he is then in a position to help the parents view their problems in the same manner. Often it is necessary to say directly to the parent who is demonstrably guilty — or defensive — "It really isn't a question of who's to blame. Establishing blame doesn't help anybody. Rather, we need to examine in detail what the problems are and have been, and then we can think about ways of handling them more effectively . . . . Therefore, I do need to understand more of what you are up against and even some of the pressures you've been under in the past." Usually even the most guarded parent inadvertently mentions some of his own stresses, present or past, while discussing the child, if only to explain and excuse what has happened. Thus, it is often possible during the initial interview with the parent, while focusing on the child's behavior, to guide the parent into a discussion of some of his own feelings. However, merely luring the parent into discussing his role with the child without openly recognizing with him that this is part of the process often results in continued resistance. Although the parent may go along with such a discussion for a while, it usually occurs to him that he is being trapped into revealing things about himself that he may not have intended to discuss. Rather, it is much wiser to let the parent know that such a discussion is proposed as part of the assessment contract. Thus, the assessor might remark at the close of the initial interview, "Some of the things that you have mentioned about your feelings and about your past do seem to help us understand your problem with your child. I wonder how might you feel about discussing these further in more detail next time?" Such a question may mobilize the parents' anxieties for the moment but, as it is discussed further, it is often possible to alleviate the parents' fears of exposing himself to blame. Similarly, the assessor can say at the opportune moment, "I can understand many of your feelings and attitudes as we talk together, but another way we have of getting your viewpoint is to ask you to fill out some questionnaires and work with some other materials the psychologist has. How might you feel about doing that?"

Once the parent realizes that the assessor is concerned with him and his problems and stresses and anxieties, he is usually more than willing to cooperate. Some may persist in maintaining, "My child is sick, not me, but if you insist . . . . " Others may in effect respond, "Yes, I'm part of the problem," and still others may plead, "I am most disturbed and it is really me and not so much the child who needs help." The assessor's response should not be to agree or disagree with any other of these statements, but to continue to maintain that who is to be helped and how the help is to be given requires a careful and thorough assessment.

After the initial appointment and introduction, the sequence of procedures in the assessment of the parents usually begins with an interview about the child, his symptoms and their onset, the conditions surrounding them and their history, and then about his environment and his history. As was noted above, by recognition of the importance of the parents' stresses and their feelings, it is thus usually fairly easy to proceed to explore the parents' own stresses. Once it is established that they also are the focus of the psychologist's attention and sympathy, it is possible to introduce other techniques and ask them to take tests or to observe them in the playroom with their child or to request permission to visit the home. Preparation for either of these latter two techniques may require further exploration of the parent's feelings — and of the child's. For example, the assessor may say, "It does seem important for us to understand clearly how you and your child interact. As you know, I have been observing him at play in our playroom. I think I would understand even more clearly if next time you and he come to the clinic, you and he played together for a little while and I sit back and observe. Would that embarrass you to have me watch the two of you together?" And, to the child, "You and I have been having a good time in the playroom here and doing some interesting things. I wonder how you would feel if we invited your mother to join us next time, at least just once, and you could play with her. Of course, what you and I do together and talk about together is just between us, so you don't have to let her know about that unless you want to. But I'd like to see how she plays too." A home visit should be similarly discussed with the parent and then the child, using again the grounds that this would enable the assessor better to understand the family and its interactions and settings.

F. PROCEDURES AND TECHNIQUES

The details of how to observe and interview children and of administering specific techniques have been discussed in Chapters 7–9. However, it may be helpful at this point to consider some of the general procedural problems common to most of these techniques. The five problems to be discussed below might be subsumed under a single question: How can the assessor maintain rapport with the child, motivate him to respond and achieve, and at the same time, conduct a precise and systematic scientific inquiry?

1. *How Formal Should the Assessment be?*

Should the assessor and child "just talk" or should the assessor conduct a formal structured interview? Should the assessor and child engage in play, or should the assessor stay in his corner and observe? Should the child be told that he is taking tests or should he be invited in to "play games?" The answer to all these questions is that both are possible and necessary. It is quite possible to carry out an interview which is planned to at least touch upon many facets of the child's life but in such a fashion as to continually make the child feel that his interests are foremost. Such an interview is possible if (a) the assessor does not have to stick to a rigid plan or sequence of topics, but can follow the discussion of the child and then introduce new material when the child has completed discussion on one topic, and (b) the assessor makes clear his reasons for asking about topics which the child has not introduced. For example, in interviewing a ten-year-old enuretic boy, one might want to obtain data about the occurence and circumstances of the bedwetting, the interaction between the child and his parents regarding it (the details of training efforts and of possible feelings of shame and of the punitive actions of the parents), and about possible sexual overtones associated with the enuresis — all of which are delicate and embarrassing topics. If one begins with a restatement of the purposes of the assessment, as suggested above in the initial contact, it might be well to remark at the very beginning, "Wetting the bed! That's an embarrassing thing to talk about! At least most of the boys and girls I talk to find it embarrassing, even when they're talking to a doctor. Do you feel that way too?" If the child admits to some embarrassment: "Yes, I thought you might feel that way," or if he tries to be nonchalant and deny it: "I guess you've gotten a little used to talking about it by now . . . " and then, in either instance: "I guess if you and I are going to understand this problem of yours, it will be necessary to think about many different things connected with it, and I may have to encourage you to talk about some more embarrassing things. But, you know, I've found that after one gets into talking about it, a lot of the embarrassment goes away and it becomes interesting. It becomes interesting just because it's about us. However, if it gets very embarrassing, we can stop and talk about some other things till you feel easier. Okay?" Then initially one might discuss with the child the general history of the complaint, the frequency of its occurence, perhaps in a relatively detached fashion. If the child becomes too anxious, topics such as training and punishment might be delayed until parent-child relations are being discussed or when sleep habits are the topic. In fact, reintroducing the complaint at various points does help the child to maintain and recognize the purpose of the assessment. The sexual aspects of such a complaint might be investigated at several different points; for example, when discussing sleeping habits, one might ask about times the child enjoyed joining his parents in their bed, or about the circumstances when he is tucked in bed or awakened to go to the toilet. Or in talking about going to the toilet, one might gently inquire if the child had seen others in his family go to the toilet, his parents, for example — again, mentioning that "this *is* a personal topic, isn't it!" Again, in talking about health and growth, one might ask a ten year old, in contemplative tones, if he had noticed any differences in his sexual growth, now that he "is almost a teenager" — "as this is a time most boys do become more aware of changes in their organ and how it works." Recognition with the child that his natural bodily functions are an acceptable topic for the purpose at hand, just as other topics have been, will often help him to get by the immediate anxiety. Indeed, he may be delighted to find that an adult is willing to discuss what he and his peers have been whispering about.

Similarly, in play observation the assessor may engage in the play, if invited by the child, or even suggest things to play if he wishes to see how the child engages in play with an adult — and at the same time be quite open about the fact that he is studying the child's play, even to the point of taking notes! If the assessor wishes to take notes on the spot (and such immediate notes are more reliable than one's memory after the hour), he should enter the playroom with the notebook and pencil openly displayed, and tell the child at the time he first makes a note: "I just want to make a note about what we're doing so that I can remember it better." If he and the child engage in a common activity, the notebook can be set aside for the moment and taken up again when the child turns to something else.

Testing, too, is both a serious challenge and a game. The general directions of "I can understand from how you do things as well as talking about them" indicates the serious purpose of the assessment but there is no need to make an inquisition out of an IQ test or to play "Score" when administering the Rorschach. Actually, it is not difficult to make the challenge a game for most assessors themselves enjoy intellectual games and fantasy — which is probably one of their own motivations for engaging in this work. If one enjoys testing, the assessor's mood will be conveyed to the child. If the child does seem to be enjoying himself, a direct recognition of it will help to reinforce this mood. If the child is having difficulty and is obviously not having any fun, then as the assessor turns to another task, he may remark, "That doesn't seem to be something you enjoyed working with. Let's try something else now." Or, to the child who appears to be struggling in perfectionist style with a drawing, one might remark, "I think you're making it like work. Why don't you just show me how you make a drawing for fun?" Similar remarks often help the fearful or cautious child on the Rorschach or TAT.

2. *Instructions*

Allied to this problem of "formality versus informality" is the problem of instructions. Certainly standardized instructions are a necessary part of a scientific assessment. For the most part, these instructions appear to have been worked out with a definite rationale by the test constructor, who attempts to design them so as to orient the subject to the task without giving him exact clues as to the solution of the task. The difficulty arises when the subject does not seem to understand the directions or appears to be misconstruing them. The question then arises, may one repeat the directions or even possibly add to or reword them without so varying the task as to change its nature and thus the analysis of the response? Some techniques do specifically allow for repetition of the instructions, for example, the Cattell Infant Scale, where several illustrations and trials are standard procedures for many tasks, or the Rorschach, where the instructions may be repeated at least once, and the TAT where the instructions are repeated and enlarged upon as part of the standard procedure after Card 10. However, if after one repetition of instructions on the Rorschach, the subject remains under the impression that he must interpret the whole card and find one best response to fit the whole inkblot, no further instructions are allowed, and his response set is interpreted as a personality variable. While such interpretation may at times be quite valid, Klopfer (1956) does advise that after the inquiry, in the "testing of limits," one should encourage the subject to associate to smaller pieces of the blot, and notes that some subjects then realize that the instructions did not limit him as he may have supposed. The problem increases on techniques that do not specify what to do when the subject does not follow directions, the major intelligence tests being the most prominent examples. For example, despite the instructions on the vocabulary tests, subjects frequently associate to the words rather than define them. Small children frequently confuse differences and similarities, particularly on the Binet, where one follows the other from year VI to year VIII. Except where there are definite prohibitions against giving further help, a repetition of the instructions would seem very much in order, even with a correction of the subject's misperception and a reemphasis of the correct orientation: "No, please tell me what the word *means,* not what it makes you think of." Or, "I'm not sure you have the idea here. It isn't necessary to try to find the 'right' answer to the inkblot. Merely tell me the *different* things that it looks like to you, or makes you think of or even just *suggests* or brings to mind." In the examination of deaf children or those who do not speak English, directions are usually given by hand signals and illustrations, which usually can be repeated several times until the subject appears to comprehend or until it is obvious that no amount of illustration will suffice to communicate the instructions. If instructions are to be translated into another language or into hand signals to the deaf, the assessor should carefully check with the translator regarding any changes in meaning that might be present in the translation.

3. *The Child's Perception of the Task*

Since whether or not the child has understood the instructions can only be determined from his first responses, the next question is: How can one tell whether the child has understood and is giving the best response he can or whether he is still trying to comprehend the task? For example, if after studying Card I of the Rorschach for 20 seconds or more, a child solemnly announces that it "looks like someone has splattered ink on this card," is this an association or has he misinterpreted the instructions? Or similarly, if he describes the TAT picture but does not tell a story, is he "blocking" and unimaginative, or has he failed to understand the directions? Or on the Stanford-Binet vocabulary, he defines "roar" as "a lion roars," is he defining or merely repeating? Or, if he just sits and stares and bites his lip, is this a response? Of course, the assessor may repeat the instructions with gentle encouragement. Or he should, if puzzled, inquire further: "Tell me a little more what you mean?" Or, "Yes, it is an inkblot — what does it look like?" Or, "Yes, but what is roar like a lion roars?"

Some techniques have an inquiry as a specific part of the test; on the Rorschach, the inquiry is an essential part of operations. The TAT is less specific in its instructions, although it is common practice, particularly with children, to inquire about the essential parts of the plot if the subject has ommitted them, at least on the first several cards until the child begins to realize that the instructions call for more than description or a present tense. "How did that happen?" "Well, what happens next?" "How did he (the person in the story) feel about that?" are almost standard TAT inquiries. "Tell me a bit more what you mean?" can be used on many items of the Wechsler tests. Such inquiry should, of course, be voiced in a nonchallenging manner, perhaps prefaced by "I think I understand, but . . . . " Or, "I guess I'm a bit puzzled . . . . " The assessor should accept the child's wording and phrasing as long as it is comprehensible, but can plead ignorance when he does not understand clearly. Once the child has made an attempt to clarify his meaning, even if his response is not adequate,

the assessor should praise him for his effort in order to reinforce such efforts on further tasks.

How far one may carry such inquiry is a matter of clinical judgment. Obviously, if one expands on the instructions or asks additional questions beyond those specified in the standardization, the task is changed. Yet, since the purpose is not merely to obtain a score, it is often necessary to pose additional questions. One may need to inquire further to the WISC Comprehension Test or to Similarities to follow the child's logic or to see whether or not with one more clue or one more thought he might be able to make a more effective solution. Commonly the child is asked to "tell the story" to the Picture Arrangement Test, even though Wechsler does not include such an inquiry in his instructions — and it is quite possible that in so doing the child is helped in his further PA items by giving him the practice in verbalizing his logic. A similar situation arises when the child is permitted to finish the Block Design or Object Assembly puzzle after the time limit.

The answer to this dilemma is that such necessary and informative inquiry can be considered as an addendum to the test per se. Though not included in the score, it becomes part of the data, enriching the score and enabling the psychologist to understand the thought processes and ideation that accompany the response. When one allows the child to finish a Block Design or add a response to a previously rejected inkblot, it is possible to estimate what the child may be able to do over and beyond the time limits of everyday life. Thus, the score indicates what the child can do under the pressures of time or on his own and the inquiry shows what he might do if given more time than usual or if encouraged.

4. *Silence and "Don't Know"*

These are special responses which pose a slightly different problem. When a child quickly responds "don't know" or sits silent, should the assessor accept this as the response or should he give encouragement? Should the assessor let the child off the hook, so to speak, or should he sweat it out patiently and, in effect, through his silence pressure the child into some kind of response (if possible). The answer lies in the assessor's clinical judgment of what the child is trying to do and his mood and motivation. Usually, after the initial contact period and a few trial test tasks, it is possible to make some estimate of what is going on. If one has the advantage of having conducted an interview with the child before attempting tests, it is much easier to guess at what the child's silences or "don't knows" are about. The hasty shrugged "don't know" may be a version of the game of "No!" which is easily spotted beforehand in an interview. The shy, fearful, or depressed child may need support, a friendly repetition of the question or a few more seconds of the assessor's patience. The contemplative child may need more time to respond. To the compulsively perfectionistic child who would rather say "don't know" than be wrong, one might remark gently, "I think you're making all this too hard. Just tell me in your own words what your idea is." On the other hand, the child who sits in embarrassed silence when he does not know what to respond may have to be reassured that "there may be some problems you won't know the answers to, but unless you tell me that you give up, I can't tell whether you're still thinking or are ready for the next one."

G. SPECIAL PROCEDURES WITH HANDICAPPED CHILDREN

The motorically disabled, sensorily handicapped, or severely retarded child does present special problems in assessment, but in general, as far as procedures are concerned, many of these problems can be handled by an extension of the procedures used for the nonhandicapped. Thus, with the handicapped, one may need a little longer initial contact, more careful observation of nonverbal cues (even with the blind who are frequently very verbal), and a more generous allowance of time and patient waiting for responses. However, the main problem presented by the handicapped child is not so much strictly procedural as it is in the way that the child views and uses his handicap — and in the way that the assessor, too, approaches and interrelates with the handicapped child. A handicapped person (child or adult) may, at one extreme, thrust their handicap into the center of any interpersonal contact, using it as a guilt-creating weapon, either defiantly and

aggressively or in passive dependent fashion. Others may act as if there were nothing special about them, in fact try to pretend that the handicap does not exist — although it is never for a moment truly forgotten. Most handicapped children, when not under any special stress, are able to carry on the everyday routine of life without either overemphasizing or denying their disability, but taking it into account somewhat realistically, resorting to these defensive moves only when they feel threatened. However, since the handicapped child is usually referred for psychological assessment because he may be experiencing some generalized anxiety, the assessor is more likely to be met with defensive behavior. Added to this is the extra threat the handicapped child feels when his abilities are challenged.

The average nonhandicapped person reacts to the handicapped child with twinges of guilt and disgust. Basically, the common underlying reaction is, "There but for the grace of God go I!" Usually he covers these feelings in much the same fashion as the handicapped person himself, by overreacting to the handicap, going out of his way to make sure the handicapped person is helped, and making doubly sure he is understood (people often raise their voices to the blind, as if they were also deaf!) but, at the same time, politely avoiding any reference to the handicap — as if it did not exist. Even though the child may be demanding special treatment, he is likely to be angered by the "Oh, you poor thing" approach of the nonhandicapped. In turn, the nonhandicapped person finds himself grimly having to hide his anger at being pressured and made guilty.

The assessor who recognizes some of these possible emotional interactions between the handicapped child and the nonhandicapped adult will be at an advantage. He does not have to feel pressured or threatened by the child's handicap, nor accept the child's defensiveness and play "blind man's bluff." Rather, he can begin with a realistic and frank recognition that a handicap exists and approach it as part of the child's life problems. Thus, in the initial contact the assessor should ask about the handicap, how it occurred and to what degree it interferes with the child's life. How much does he need to be helped to deal with it? How much has he learned to do on his own? Moreover, there should be open recognition that the assessment is being carried out both despite of and because of the handicap. Thus, initially the assessor should remark, "I've found that children with handicaps like yours often feel a little bit anxious when somebody asks to see how they can do things because it draws attention to their handicap. Do you feel that way too?" And, "Perhaps one way these tests and our talking will help is that we, you and I both, will understand a little better just what your handicap *does* mean for you." Such an introductory recognition of the handicap and brief exploration of the child's feelings about it usually does help to dispel some of the anxiety for both parties. Thereafter it is much more possible for both the child and assessor to proceed, taking into account the child's actual physical limitations but at the same time examining them. Naturally the assessor will not expect the child to perform tasks completely beyond the range of his limitations. However, when the child is not completely handicapped, when his vision is limited but not blinded or when he can make some movements but not freely, then some materials might be presented just to assess what the limitations and possibilities are. Thus, the question may arise of how the child with severe visual limitations visually conceives his world, and his Rorschach and TAT may yield considerable data when so utilized. Or of how the spastic child behaves when he attempts to draw or to manipulate blocks? Can he see the pattern even though he can't reproduce it?

The mentally retarded child may seem to present a special problem. In the first place, he lives with a handicap which often has little outward manifestation except in his behavior. Whatever outward stigmata may be present is not usually recognized as definitely part of the child's main handicap but rather is experienced by the child — and the observer — as an additional handicap, a repulsive detraction. Second, there is even more social taboo on open recognition of mental retardation than with other handicaps, as witness such euphemisms as "exceptional child." As a consequence, there is even more of a tendency for both the retarded child and the nonretarded adult to overact to the handicap; the retarded child becomes overly dependent and overly demanding as the adult becomes overly guilty and overly solicitous. Third, and more seriously, the child's handicap often does make it difficult for him to communicate

his feelings verbally or to understand what others are trying to communicate to him. Nevertheless, it is possible and necessary for the psychologist to be a notable exception to the usual social mores in his approach to the mentally retarded child. By couching his words in a socially acceptable manner and by simplifying his phrasing, it is quite possible for the assessor to recognize with the child the fact of his intellectual restriction. Thus, just as one would do with other children, the psychologist also asks the retarded child what it is that he needs help with and inquires about the nature of his need for help. The usual response is in terms of school achievement or social adjustment with other children, etc., but as these are explored, the retarded child usually gradually reveals that he is at least not able to understand at school or is teased or not accepted because others consider him "stupid." Thus, it becomes possible for the psychologist to sum up for the child by saying, "You have a lot of difficulty understanding the work at school and other children don't understand you. Is that it?" And then, "Not being able to understand things is very difficult at times, especially when other people don't understand us either." And then, "As I ask you to do things and figure things out, it may help us both to find out where and how you have difficulty in understanding. I won't expect to understand about everything, but I do want to know about the things you can and can't do."

The difficulties in communication of the deaf or mute child also require special consideration. If the deaf child has some speech and can read, the assessment is merely slowed down while the examiner writes (or more usually prints) out instructions. Many deaf children, even preschoolers, have learned some lip reading. Although the international hand signal language is no longer as commonly taught to deaf children as it used to be, most deaf children have learned to be attentive to and interpret the gestures and signs used by the hearing person in his attempts to signal to him. With preschool deaf children, communication through drawing pictures can be helpful. For example, in beginning the assessment of a deaf five year old, the psychologist drew a stick figure with ears and then crossed off the ears and smiled and pointed to the child. The child acknowledged the drawing with a vigorous nod and smiled back. Then three more stick figures were drawn, of a baby, a toddler, and a slightly larger child, each with crossed off ears and a large "?". The child understood that the psychologist was inquiring as to when he was deafened and pointed to the baby and then with a smile to one side of the baby, suggesting that the disability occurred before birth. The psychologist pointed to his own lips and asked in a normal tone, without emphasis, "Can you read my lips?" The child shook his head. Then the child looked all around the room and spoke, "You gonna give me a shot!" The psychologist laughed as he shook his head, and continuing with pictures and gestures, indicated his interest in how the child was getting along and what he could do. From then on in the child responded verbally to the assessor's nonverbal communication with great delight. With mute but nondeaf children, the situation is reversed. The psychologist vocalizes but encourages the child to gesture, point at pictures, draw pictures, and, if possible, to write.

H. CULTURAL DIFFERENCES

The child who speaks a different language from the assessor may be approached somewhat similarly to the deaf child, through gestures and pictures or via a translator. If the parent is bilingual, he or she can act in the latter capacity, but it has been this writer's experience that parents make poor translators in the assessment situation as they become too emotionally involved. Thus, if at all possible, a professional translator or at least a person generally familiar with the child's language is to be preferred. As was noted above, the differences in meaning presented by translation, especially with a child, need to be taken into account and discussed with the translator. Unless he is himself a native of the same country as the child, he may not be familiar with the childhood idioms of the language and, in turn, his accent may puzzle or confuse the child. American tests should be used with considerable caution; not only is the content culturally determined but even the types of tasks are peculiar to American achievement drive and American thinking. For example, a Puerto Rican child who spoke only Spanish was asked to name "the four seasons of the year." The translator, also a Puerto Rican, thought a moment and repeated the question somewhat hesitantly. "Caliente y frio," replied the child ("hot and cold"). The question was repeated and the same answer given. Then there was an exchange in Spanish between translator and child. The translator explained, "In Puerto Rico there are only two seasons, hot and cold!" The story, probably apocryphal, is told of the psychologist sent to test an Indian tribe to determine if they were "educable." He found the children most cooperative and tractable, but seemingly unable to solve the puzzles and block designs he presented. Yet, he observed that the Indians were most ingenious in their business dealings and their art and could not really believe they were as unintelligent as his tests suggested. Finally, he discussed this with one of the English speaking chiefs. "Why can't the children solve my puzzles?" he asked. "Solve them!" the chief replied. "Is that what you want them to do?" It was only then that the psychologist realized that this tribe not only did not recognize the intellectual achievement drive of the white culture but even had prohibitions against children demonstrating to adults their ability to think. A similar conflict commonly appears in the Negro child facing a white examiner as Negro children learn early in life that one should not appear "smart" to white people, that it is safer to "keep one's place" and say as little as possible. Fortunately, with desegregation and the civil rights revolution now in progress in America, Negro children are somewhat less timid and even encouraged to "speak up." This social handicap does not have to be verbally recognized in the same manner as the physical handicap. A Negro child usually soon responds with openness when greeted with the same friendly interest that an assessor uses with any other child.

I. CONCLUDING THE ASSESSMENT

Although the total assessment involves only a brief contact between assessor and child, it usually is a more intense emotional interaction than the child commonly experiences in contacts with strange adults. No matter how resistant he is, he usually is aware that attention has been focused on his feelings and his needs, and many of the children brought to assessment have been seriously deprived of concern and understanding. Often they are hungry for such attention, openly or secretly, but at the same time they may greet it with distrust and anxiety. Unconsciously, at least, they realize that it is a temporary relationship, that it will not last, and that they should steel themselves against a false hope. The more infantile child will make obvious moves to win over the assessor, to charm him or to begin to make demands on him which go beyond the assessment contract. Such children frequently try to stretch out the assessment hours and so delay the inevitable separation.

For these reasons, some time is needed to allow the child to make a gradual separation rather than have it occur as a sudden impact. As was mentioned above, in making the appointment, one should inform the parent of the approximate time the appointments will involve and ask her to tell the child. This should be repeated to the child on initial contact: "We'll spend about an hour and a half together today. I don't know whether that will give us enough time to do all the things we want to, but we can always set up another appointment if necessary." If the child is anxious and wants to negotiate the time right then, one may reply, "Let's wait and see what we need." Shortly before the end of the first contact, one should warn the child, "We have about ten minutes left," or "We've just got time for one more thing; then we can meet with your mother and see when you can return." Then, at the beginning of the second — or final — contact, one can tell the child and mother, "We'll probably need another hour and a half today to finish up." The child who protests that he wants more time may be reassured that this does not mean he will not receive more attention at the clinic but rather that this particular kind of contact or this beginning step will not need much more time.

On the other hand, the resistant child, particularly the glum teenager who drags his heels and protests that there is "nothing wrong with me" and thus does not need so much time, may be countered with raised eyebrows: "I thought you needed someone to understand, so I was giving you as much time as I could." Again, shortly before the end of the assessment, the assessor should warn, "There's just one more thing I want to ask you to do before we stop." The assessor should plan to make this task one which may not be so vital to the assessment that a serious lack of data will occur if the child rushes through it or dawdles over it to the point that it is not possible to complete it. Usually there will be little problem if it is some interesting and relatively nonthreatening task such as drawings or the World Test. Of course, if the child has been rushing through things all along, the assessor should have taken note of the child's attitudes long before and raised a question with him about it: "You seem to be rushing and not giving yourself enough time. I wondered whether you were anxious to get through or thought you didn't have enough time?" Obversely, if a child is dawdling, interrupting, or otherwise obviously taking up more time than necessary, it is necessary to raise some question about it: "It seems as if we have a hard time getting going on things this afternoon. I wonder if you need more time or possibly even really don't like what we're doing here today?" If the child agrees that he is rushing or needs extra time, one might inquire further about how he approaches other tasks at home or school to see if this is habitually his approach to task-oriented situations or if it is related specifically to the assessment and his anxiety about it.

During the final task, the assessor should observe particularly how the child is reacting to the announced separation. Besides observing the alacrity with which the child proceeds, one may look for such signs of anxiety as extreme carelessness or extra precision, apathy or restlessness, increase or decrease in verbalization or other extra activity, changes in facial expression and bodily movement, watching or studiously avoiding the clock, etc. Once the final formal task is over, the assessor should specify that the session is ended and spend a few moments inquiring about the child's feelings and questions about it: "Well, those are all the questions I have and all the things I planned to ask you to do. But I wonder if you have any questions you wanted to ask or anything you wanted to tell me about that I may have forgotten to ask you about?" Even if the child denies that he has anything more to say, the assessor should reinforce whatever efforts the child has made to reveal his feelings and to cooperate: "You've really worked awfully hard, even though I've asked some very personal questions of you and asked you to do some things which were not so easy. I know it's not always easy to show other people how we do things or let them know what we think about, especially when we're afraid other people will criticize us or won't understand. But I think I do understand a little bit more now. How you you feel about it?"

This question and whatever discussion ensues will allow the assessor to introduce the fact that although the assessment per se is over and, perhaps, this particular relationship as well (unless the assessor is going to proceed with whatever treatment or disposition may be in order), the child's needs will receive further attention and the assessment will contribute toward the planning of this attention. Thus, the assessor should check with the child about his next appointment at the clinic or with the referrant: "When will you be seeing Dr. X again?" And then, "By that time I will have a chance to think over what we've done together and will be able to talk with him. That way he can understand a bit better also. If you have more questions then about what we did here, you can ask him about it." Quite often children will show some anxiety about what the assessor will communicate to the referrant and will want to discuss it, particularly if the referrant is an authority figure for the child. "What are you going to tell him?" The assessor may point out that he is still thinking about it but should inquire what the child is worried might be said. Often the child's reply will reveal his concern about his performance or some revelation of his feelings. "Would it help if Dr. X or the teacher or the probation officer did understand that you have difficulty doing arithmetic or that you have angry feelings sometimes toward your mother?"

Sometimes a child will admit to being puzzled or concerned about some of his responses. In such instances, he may be encouraged to contemplate, at least momentarily, what he has said or done and what it might mean to him. In general, the assessor should avoid explaining or interpreting the overall results of the assessment (particularly since he has not had an opportunity to digest them himself). However, if the child is trying to recognize further some of his feelings, and is close to some insight, the assessor should assist him, if only to reinforce the message that further help and understanding is in the offing. For example, a shy and retiring ten-year-old boy remarked that he was surprised how many "murder" stories he had told to the TAT. "I guess you didn't know how much

murder there was in your imagination," remarked the assessor. The boy shook his head. "From what you told me about yourself you don't actually murder anybody or even hit anybody very often. But apparently these kinds of feelings are inside your thoughts even though you don't do anything about it. Can you think of any times you feel like murdering somebody but just keep it to yourself?" The boy reminded the assessor that he had said this about his younger brother in the interview and on the Bene-Anthony Family Relations questionnaire. The assessor suggested that maybe the boy might want to think more about this and other things that had come up during the assessment and discuss them with his therapist.

More frequently, the child and especially the parent pressure the assessor for some immediate advice or report of findings. In such a situation, one may tell the parent that it is not possible to answer this question before the data are analyzed. In any event, the assessor should not attempt to intervene until he has conferred with the referrant or before he has some idea how the client may use his opinion. This is not to say that the results of the assessment should never be conveyed to the client; on the contrary, it is to be hoped that the assessment is not performed purely for the information of the referrant, but that eventually the assessment data can be used, sometimes fairly directly in further counseling or therapy. However, at this point, interpretation of the assessment findings is not appropriate. However, rather than refusing the client's request, even with a polite explanation, the fact that the client does want to know about himself or his child should be reinforced. Moreover, by exploring the client's question further, the assessor may both obtain additional data and assist the client in making a transition from the assessor back to the referrant. Thus, the assessor might respond, "I am not sure I know what to recommend right at the moment, but I will be conferring with Dr. X very soon, and I know you will be in touch with him. But I wonder what ideas have occurred to you while you were talking to me and doing these things here? Has this given you a chance to consider your problem further?" Whatever response the client may give, he should be directed back to the referrant for further discussion. Even if the assessor himself is going to carry the case, he should defer further discussion until he has had a chance to study the data.

After the assessor has assured the client — and himself — regarding the client's next appointment with the referrant, the contact with the client can be concluded. The next major steps in the assessment are the analysis of the data and the formulation of a report, tasks which often take as much of the psychologist's time as the actual contact with the child and parents. As was mentioned above, the assessor should take this time factor into consideration in planning his assessment, setting time aside for it in his schedule, so as to be able to inform the referrant and client when his results might be ready for their use. Moreover, the assessor should plan his own schedule so that he can work on the analysis of data and his report as soon as possible, not only because of the client's needs, but because it is likely that he can do a better job while the experience is still fresh in his mind, before the data get "cold." Last week's data, at the bottom of the "to be done" basket, too often become a chore and the inspirations and scientific curiosity present at the end of the patient contact may fade.

Unfortunately, there are those instances when, despite the efforts of the psychologist to establish an effective liaison with the referrant, the psychologist cannot in good faith promise the child that the assessment will definitely be used. Referrants do not always follow the psychologist's recommendations; they may not comprehend or even read the report. In such instances, the psychologist should be more cautious and remark only that he will talk to the doctor, probation officer, or parent. Sometimes the child himself senses that there is difficulty in communicating with the referrant: "I don't think he'll listen to you!" The psychologist should reassure the child that he will do his best to communicate clearly — as is his obligation.

One method to resolve such doubts, which this writer has found satisfactory, is to arrange for further appointments to discuss the results with the child, and subsequently with the referrant — and possibly with the two together. Such an arrangement should, of course, be explained to and be agreeable with the referrant. This method is particularly reassuring to the child if the results are subsequently to be discussed with parents or some other authority. It is also helpful to a prospective therapist.

Since a child is often aware of some of his failures and successes on IQ or other achievement tests, and of the fact that he reveals his feelings on subjective or associative techniques, such a discussion of results should center about those items which the child recognizes as meaningful. Where appropriate, the psychologist might remind the child of those tasks which the child had previously remarked that he found difficult; or a seemingly "significant" TAT story might be read back to him to see if the child might contribute further associations. However, such discussion should be limited to those behaviors which appear to be near the level of the child's consciousness; so-called "deep" interpretations should be avoided. For example, the child might remark that he found the arithmetic subtest (on the WISC) difficult, or at least that he did not like it. If appropriate, the psychologist might remark that this was understandable since the child had told him of his difficulties with arithmetic at school, but at the same time note with the child that such difficulty might be hard to understand since his reasoning on other tests was above average. Even when a child has many areas of poor functioning or is performing at a retarded level, it may be quite possible to use the IQ or other test to help him recognize and understand his difficulties. It is quite inappropriate to tell him that he "did good" when he actually failed. On the contrary, he should be told that the psychologist also is aware that the child "has difficulty learning things and figuring things out" and might help the child speculate why this may be true. Since such an interpretation may be quite anxiety provoking to the child, the psychologist may help the child face the truth and remind him that he probably has been aware of this all along since, for example, he has received poor grades at school and is in special classes. Although the assessing psychologist may not be the person who subsequently aids the child in the resolution of the anxieties engendered by his handicaps, he can help the child face them and recognize them more realistically. Of course, if there is no definite plan for the child to receive further resolution of these anxieties, then the psychologist should be most circumspect in his interpretations and avoid arousing more anxiety in the child than is already present. Sometimes, however, such discussions can serve to motivate the child and parent to seek further psychological counseling.

Similarly, the psychologist might ask the child which Rorschach responses or TAT stories he remembers and what they meant to him. Or, the psychologist might remark, "You remember the several stories you told in which the hero got rid of his enemy. You also told me a lot about what a pest your brother can be. Could he be one of the enemies you daydream of getting even with?" Often when the psychologist connects such consciously reported feelings to the fantasies, the child will respond by making other associations on his own.

At the conclusion of such discussions with the child, I usually ask him what he thinks I should communicate to the referrant. I usually agree not to reveal anything which the child wishes kept private, but I also point out that the parent already seems aware of such and such aspect of the child's problems and that further discussion with the parent may clarify issues. If feasible, the child can be invited to share the discussions with the parents, which should follow the same approach, that is, beginning with those facets of the child's behavior and functioning which the parents already recognize and understand, at least partially, and expanding into those areas which the parents may be able to use or consider further. Similarly, I may ask the adolescent what he thinks will be helpful to him to be revealed to his probation officer or his therapist. "Should he know," I might ask, "that you panic easily, that you cannot think at school or on IQ tests when you are tensed up, or even that your mother confuses you? Do you think he would understand? Might this help the two of you to work out a solution of your problems?"

Part IV

ANALYSIS OF THE ASSESSMENT

SPECIFICATIONS OF THE EGO FUNCTIONS

Although scoring and analysis organize data according to the theories of each of the assessment techniques, the focus of the analysis is not on the technique per se, but on the overall functioning of the child's ego. Thus, it is necessary to examine all of the data from all techniques for the evidence pertaining to the development of each function. Perhaps the most difficult lesson for the beginning clinician is this task of recognizing and interpreting the evidence. The purpose of this section is to demonstrate one system by which the data of an assessment may be used as evidence of the child's ego development. In order to conduct this analysis, it may be helpful to add yet another step in this classification of ego functioning, specifying further the different aspects of each function. The categories which follow are purely heuristic and are intended only as an aid in organizing the data:

1. The *modality* of the function, that is, the bodily—or social—organs through which the function operates.
2. The *input* and *output* or receptive-expressive aspects.
3. The development of the ability to *focus* on and to *differentiate* stimuli.
4. *Interferences* with the functioning.
5. *Coping mechanisms.*
6. The *content* or subtypes of each function.

These categories may be most clearly defined by the manner in which they are applied operationally to each function.

THE ANALYSIS OF PERCEPTUAL-MOTOR AND COGNITIVE DEVELOPMENT

A. PERCEPTUAL-MOTOR MODALITIES

The most common modality of perceptual-motor behavior as sampled by the techniques commonly used in assessment is *visual*. The child is asked to draw what he *sees* on the Bender, tells us what he *sees* on the Rorschach, sort out what he sees on Picture Completion or Picture Arrangement, or identify what he *sees* on Picture Vocabulary tests (Binet or Ammons). Some of these tasks depend on hearing also, at least in the instructions, but this auditory aspect is usually a minimal part and if a hearing deficit is suspected, the test may be given with gestures as if administered to the deaf. The Knox Blocks subtest of the Grace Arthur is a good example of a technique that involves vision alone. On the other hand, other tests of attention, such as the Digit Span subtest of the Wechsler or Binet, involve only audition. Differences in the modality of perceptual functioning may thus be evidenced in the differences in scores on tasks involving mainly one modality as opposed to another. However, the evidence may often be more qualitative than quantitative.

For example, an auditory perceptual dysfunction may show up chiefly in constant misperception of verbal instructions, for example, when the child asks repeatedly to have instructions repeated or repeats verbal problems to himself before proceeding. This type of dysfunction is illustrated in Case 19.

The lack of any direct assessment of tactile perception in the usual clinical battery may be excused on the grounds that tactile perception plays such a relatively small part in the overall intake of stimuli in contrast to vision and audition, except among infants. Moreover, tactile dysfunctions are extremely rare and are usually compensated for by vision or hearing. On the other hand, tactile dysfunction may be one sign of brain damage, and neurologists commonly do make gross tests of the child's tactile discriminations. Inversely, the overuse of tactile perception, that is, where the child seems to have to touch everything before he can react to it, may be one tell-tale sign of a visual or auditory dysfunction. Such a child may be attempting to cope with a defect in the other senses or with an overall perceptual imbalance. Even the neurotic child who has to touch

209

things compulsively is, in a sense, touching to reassure himself that what he sees or hears is real and permanent. Such touching behavior is fairly common among preschool children as a normal way of integrating perceptions.

The other perceptual modes are also not commonly assessed by psychologists, much for the same reason. Again, disturbances of kinesthesis is also common in some types of brain damage or are symptomatic of gross developmental lag. Differentiation between poor 'balance" sense and inadequate motor coordination is sometimes difficult, and requires close observation of the way the child moves and sits as opposed to his ability to perform motor tasks when his whole body is not reacting to gravity. The possibility of an akinesthesis should be entertained if the child can pass most of the psychologist's motor tasks, but has trouble standing erect, hopping on one foot, skipping, leaning, etc. Dysfunction in pain perception is a rare childhood complaint. Some children do seem overly sensitive to pain; it is very rare that a child fails to experience pain with trauma. Since pain is difficult to localize and identify even for an adult and can easily be generalized, careful interviewing of the child is often necessary to determine exactly how and where the child does experience pain. Although such interviewing about complaints of physical pain lie chiefly within the province and skill of the pediatrician, the data from psychological interviews may be of assistance to the physician, especially where the child has difficulty distinguishing physical pain from affective experiences or where complaints of pain are heightened by emotional states. Pediatricians may also request psychological assessments of cases of childhood analgesia. Sometimes such imperviousness to pain may be part of an overall lag in perceptual development such as in the severely retarded child, or possibly (but among children very rarely) a hysterical symptom.

B. PERCEPTUAL-MOTOR INPUT-OUTPUT

Distinguishing between input and output difficulties in perceptual-motor behavior is a crucial question in determining the type of retraining required. Since most assessment tasks involve both perceptual and motor be-havior, the evidence regarding input versus output does not come from any one set of scores or responses, but from qualitative observation of the way the child performs the task. For example, if the child struggles in drawing the Bender figures, holding extra tight to his pencil, erasing and correcting, evidently dissatisfied with his production, Koppitz (1963) suggests such behavior is indicative of an *expressive* difficulty. The child perceives the figures but has difficulty in motorically reproducing them. On the other hand, if the child draws a figure quickly and easily but erroneously and without recognition of his error, Koppitz takes this as a sign of a perceptual or *receptive* difficulty rather than purely motor. Similar behavioral evidence of input versus output difficulties may be drawn from many other techniques such as Block Design, Object Assembly, or even on the Rorschach. For example, any child over age five who sees the whole of Rorschach Card II as a face, with eyes at the bottom (D-3),* a nose in D-4, a mouth (D-5), and D-1 as ears, is evidently experiencing some kind of perceptual disorganization. However, another child may give the same response, but during inquiry says "it just looks like it . . . here . . . here . . . ." This child may have an anomia or other difficulty in expression. It is possible that he may be able to identify the parts of the face with adequate perceptual organization when specifically asked about them.

Discrimination between receptive and expressive dysfunctions is not always easy. For example, one way children have of coping with motor difficulty is to deny it by hastily scrawling something and pushing the product aside as if content with it. Only through specific inquiry can it be determined whether or not the child actually has misperceived or if he has tried to avoid the motor task. In such instances, the assessor can ask, "How might your drawing be changed to look more like this?" Inversely, the child who labors in dissatisfaction over his Bender drawings may be hesitating not so much because of his motor difficulties, but because he has not been able to focus or discriminate perceptually.

One test designed specifically to explore this differentiation is the Goldstein-Sheerer

---

* For those familiar with this system, the numbers in parens refer to Beck's numbering of the Rorschach Inkblot parts.

version of the Kohs Blocks (1945). On this test, if the child fails the original design, he is given one with the block boundaries drawn on the design, then a larger design, and finally one with both perceptual clues. Presumably, if the child can do the task with these extra clues, the difficulty is perceptual. On the other hand, if the child is given some motor training, for example, if he can then copy the design by seeing how the examiner does it, a motor difficulty would seem more likely. Tests like the Porteus Maze or the Arthur Scales or any of the trail-making tests (as in Part V of the Frostig, 1961) also allow for observation of input versus output difficulties. If the child accidently gets off the path in going around the maze but corrects himself, he most likely is having a motor difficulty in guiding the pencil; but if he keeps going into blind alleys and becoming blocked, his difficulty would seem more perceptual. Similarly, using any of the various aphasia test materials, if the child can name an object when it is presented to him separately but cannot select the object from a group of objects when asked for it by name, this would seem evidence of a receptive aphasia or agnosia (based on inability to recognize the auditory stimulus), but if he can select the object when given the name of it but cannot name it himself, expressive aphasia or anomia is presumed. It should be noted that input and output do not always develop uniformly in infancy; thus, the Binet in years II and III contains both kinds of items.

C. PERCEPTUAL-MOTOR FOCUS AND DISCRIMINATION

The ability to screen out stimuli and focus on an object or situation is measured by quite a number of psychological tests. Focus and discrimination of the stimulus is the central task on the Rorschach. At the simplest level, focus is merely the ability to concentrate perceptually and pay attention; at the more complicated level, focusing requires sorting out and bringing together a total Gestalt. The "DW" or confabulation type of response to the Rorschach, in which the child is reminded of something by a relatively small detail of the blot but then is unable to restrict his response to the single detail and expands it out of proportion to the whole blot, is a classic example of a difficulty in focusing.

Discriminating between several objects or situations is tested by such tasks as the Three-Figure Form Board or Aesthetic Comparison or Form Differences (on the Binet) or the Wechsler Picture Arrangement. It is central to the Raven Matrices and the Columbia Mental Maturity Scale. On the Rorschach, difficulty in discrimination is manifest when the child cannot separate two different engrams, but contaminates two disparate associations into one, without being able to see the inconsistency of the total response. For example, the child may see Card I as a butterfly and also as a face and call it a "butterfly face." Learning to make perceptual differentiation is, of course, one of the tasks of the preschool child, as witness the number of differentiation tasks on the Binet between years II and IV-6. Such contaminations must be distinguished from the sometimes bizarre combinations often given by preschool children to the Rorschach, which are evidence of creative imagination and the beginning of the ability to make complex associations. For example, the following response to Rorschach Card II (inverted) was given by a very bright and imaginative four year old: "It's an 'O' (D-5) walking. Here's its legs (D-3). And here's its wee-wee (D-4)!" Even though the combination of parts is fanciful, there is no contamination present in such a response.

Most techniques require both focus and discrimination. All the tests cited above as measurements of focus also require some discrimination and the tasks cited as measuring discrimination merely emphasize that aspect of the overall focus-discrimination process. Block Design on the Wechsler, for example, requires that the child make discriminatory choices between sections of the design and then focus on the section and the position of the block. On the Bender or the Graham-Kendall, the child must focus on the overall Gestalt but also discriminate between parts. For example, on Card A of the Bender, the child may see the figure as consisting of two parts but he may not discriminate between the parts, drawing both as circles, or he may see the two parts but not be able to bring them into focus as a unity.

Motor behavior also involves both focus and discrimination. Every child has to learn how to focus on one movement while controlling or excluding others. Specificity of motor control is a task of primary import during infancy but continues to be practiced throughout childhood. For example, before age four months, the infant may be attracted by an object held over his head and flail out with both arms and legs in an effort to grasp at it, but the average infant of this age is able at least to move both arms in coordinated fashion at the object, while holding the rest of his body still enough to make the grasping move. By the time a child is able to draw the Bender figures, he must not only focus on holding the pencil but avoid other motor movements which might make it difficult for him to draw. Very often, the hyperactive child may make gross errors on the Bender just because he cannot focus on the single movements of his arm but, wriggling and contorting his whole body, can only make a slap-dash drawing. His pencil runs off the edge of the page or past the point where he wants to stop or begin. Similar focusing of motor movements is required on other tasks, such as the Seguin Form Board, where the child must not only perceptually match the block to the hole, but must so control or focus his movements as to insert the block correctly. Typically, the child who has motor focusing problems makes a correct match between block and hole but, unable to insert the block, attempts to pound it in with both hands. The child must also learn to discriminate between movements, to choose the appropriate movement or pattern of motor behavior. He learns first to use his hands for some things, his feet for others. He learns to make circular motions as opposed to a straight line. He learns how to make his arm and pencil go to the right as distinct from the left. These discriminations are qualitatively demonstrated in such tasks as drawing a square (Binet age months), on the Seguin or the Knox Blocks (of the Arthur). Sometimes even an older child has difficulty in making such motor discrimination, for example, on the Porteous Mazes, and even though he has figured out the pattern of the maze perceptually, he still has obvious difficulty in guiding his pencil along the pathway in directions he desires.

D. INTERFERENCES WITH PERCEPTUAL-MOTOR FUNCTIONING

The sources of interference with perceptual and motor functioning are so multiple as

almost to defy description or even classification. Some may be so obvious as to seem fortuitous to mention. The perceptual motor limitations of the blind child, for example, may seem so gross that it is possible to forget the many little ways in which it interferes with his overall functions or the implications of it for his other ego functions. At the other extreme, there are often interferences to the child's functioning which may be so subtle as to defy direct observation. For example, the psychologist may know that the child has been upset by something that happened just before he came to the assessment which has unnerved him, so that he cannot pay attention to tasks presented to him. But the psychologist cannot always know what is going on within the child or even that anything is preoccupying him or pressing on him. For example, a five-year-old-girl seemed to be getting increasingly uneasy as the assessment proceeded; her attention wandered, she wriggled about in her chair, fumbled with the test materials, and after about three Rorschach cards, seemed almost in tears. Setting the cards aside, the assessor remarked on her obvious discomfort and asked her about it; whereupon the child burst into tears and admitted she needed to go to the toilet but was too inhibited to have voluntarily admitted it. On return from the bathroom, she was much more at ease and asked to look at the Rorschach cards "all over again." Thereafter she was able to give much more adequate responses.

Although temporarily inhibiting factors can be spotted by the astute assessor, it is often necessary to infer the presence of more long range and constant interferences with perceptual-motor behavior from the data. Sometimes the nature of these interferences appear in the perceptual-motor responses or in the behavior accompanying them. For example, if a child with a misshapen head and spastic extremities, who is cooperative, friendly, and smiling, takes the pencil in his fist and attempts to copy the Bender figures with glee, but makes only very simplified inadequate reproductions which he offers with satisfaction, the impression that his perceptual difficulty is related to a central nervous system* dysfunction would certainly seem quite reasonable. However, if the child were not so disabled but was very tense and glum and uneasy, openly voicing morbid and phobic ideas and elaborating his Bender reproductions to illustrate these fears, it would seem reasonable to assume that his reproductions were interrupted by his severe emotional disturbances.

In most cases, however, the nature of the interference is not so blatant. All that is seen is the struggle of the child to perform the perceptual motor task and the resultant distortions in his reproductions. To assess the nature of the interfering factors, it is necessary to examine other data from other sources, that is, to specify further the nature of other ego functions and their interactions with the perceptual-motor behavior. Even when the interference seems to be as obvious as in the above example, the data from the perceptual-motor tasks should be crossed-checked against data from other techniques. If, for example, the placid and seemingly brain-damaged child showed signs of emotional disturbance on other kinds of tasks, or succeeded on more complex tasks involving perceptual functioning — or if the phobias of the second child were demonstrated only on the Bender, then our initial hypotheses about these children would have to be revised considerably.

Although the variety of factors that interfere with perceptual-motor functioning are too extensive to be listed here and probably cannot be completely covered by any classification, most seem to fall within the following groups: (a) physiological limitations, such as brain damage, sensory deprivation, or muscular weaknesses; (b) physiological disruptions, such as injuries, illnesses, fatigue, etc.; (c) immediate, temporary environmental stress; (d) poor motivation; (e) affective disruptions; (f) intellectual retardation; (g) social or cultural deprivations or differences from the norms used by the test.

Perceptual-motor tasks have been so exclusively designed and used for the assessment of brain damage that they are commonly called "tests for brain damage" as if there were no other interferences with perceptual-motor functioning. When attention is so focused on this one type of interference, it is often difficult to even remember that perceptual functioning is affected by other factors. Moreover, there is thus a tendency to attribute all perceptual distortion to some kind of CNS dysfunction. However, the acceptance of the hypothesis that it is brain damage which is interfering with perceptual-motor dysfunction (even in a child with a history of presumed brain damage) requires very specific evidence.

Moreover, the type of evidence for brain damage from childrens' protocols is quite different than from the responses of adults, especially from children under the age of ten who are still developing perceptual-motor skills. Koppitz (1963) has derived a list of 29 signs of brain damage for the Bender but warns that "a tentative diagnosis of brain injury should only be made if *several* of these areas show positive findings" (page 106). She distinguishes very clearly between what she calls "developmental lag" and "brain damage," and between the child with developmental lag and the child with emotional disruptions. These signs of brain damage on the Bender consist of very gross distortions and rotations of the figures. However, it will be noted that Koppitz found that some gross distortions did not distinguish the brain-damaged child from other types of children with perceptual dysfunctions. Graham and Kendall in their Memory-for-Designs Scale also specify the kinds of gross alterations of the Gestalt which are significant, and they provide cutting points on their total score above which the hypothesis of brain damage may be entertained. They also correct this total score to take into account both age and intelligence. However, whether a corrected high score on the Graham-Kendall indicates that the perceptual-motor functioning of the child is deterred by brain damage or by schizophrenia or some other intense anxiety or by poor motivation can only be decided by examining data other than the reproductions per se.

Moreover, even when the data from the responses to the perceptual-motor tasks strongly suggest a neurophysiological dysfunction, this evidence alone does not tell us whether there may be additional factors interfering with the child's functioning. In fact, in most cases, even where there is a high probability of brain damage, there are usually other quite severe interferences with perceptual-motor functioning. Such a child is likely to be poorly motivated, feel very inadequate, and be quite anxious. In such instances the question arises, suppose these other factors could be alleviated, how significant would the interference of the brain damage be?

Evidence of the presence of types of interference other than CNS damage may be present in the perceptual-motor responses themselves, or inferred from them. Thus,

---

Often abbreviated CNS.

many investigators have agreed that drawings which are oversized or very tiny, which are heavily shaded or very lightly drawn, which are either extremely neatly aligned or organized, or which are drawn with no regard for organization on the page are all signs of possible emotional interferences with perceptual-motor functioning. However, these signs may also appear in the anxious brain-damaged child as part of his way of coping with the task.

Sometimes the child who produces grossly distorted Bender or Graham-Kendall drawings is suffering from an as yet undetected opthalamic condition. If disruptions are noted only on visual tasks, this possibility should be seriously entertained, even though there may be evidence of alternative or additional interferences. Similarly, difficulties in motor focus and control on these tests have been known to be the first prodramata of muscular disorders such as muscular dystrophy or multiple sclerosis. When such a muscular focus problem stands out, the possibility of the onset of such disease process must be ruled out before accepting some other hypothesis about the nature of the interference.

Poor motivation may result in a slap-dash performance, in careless errors, even in occasional rotations (which may be an indication of negativism as well as of brain damage). The child who is preoccupied with his own emotional problems may "forget" more than one drawing on the Graham-Kendall. The intensely angry child may mess up the drawings just to spite the adult authority personified by the assessor. In the past decade, psychologists have come to recognize that severe cultural deprivation can also result in a developmental lag in perceptual motor functioning. Unfortunately, the signs of this kind of interference in the child's perceptual-motor responses per se are not well established. By and large, perceptual-motor responses do not in themselves supply sufficient evidence about the nature of these other interferences. The kinds of data bearing on these interferences from other sources will be discussed later in this and subsequent chapters.

E. COPING MECHANISMS AND PERCEPTUAL-MOTOR FUNCTIONING

The presence of interferences in perceptual-motor functioning is often not grossly evident in distortion of reproductions themselves, but may be inferred from the coping mechanism the child may use to overcome the interferences. Koppitz points out that the mildly brain-damaged child may seek to cover his perceptual disability by drawing excessively slowly and in a compulsive manner, thereby concentrating his total effort so that his errors are minimal and only occasional.

CASE 19

Rick, age 16 years, who was being treated psychotherapeutically for his asocial acting out of his conflicts with his parents and other authority figures, suffered a massive head injury in an auto accident during a "joy-ride" while running away from home. After he recovered from the immediate injuries, his psychiatrist thought she noted some aphasia and possibly other perceptual-motor sequalae, although Rick averred he was completely recovered. During the therapy, Rick associated the injury with his angry and rebellious behavior and fantasied that the injury represented the punishment of fate for his wrong-doings. Nevertheless, the therapist requested psychological assessment of the possible effects of this injury both on perceptual-motor functioning and on his outlook on life in general. Rick continued to deny that he had any memory problem or speech difficulty. During the Graham-Kendall, he studied each card carefully, complained that he was not given enough time to see them, and then verbalized the shape of each design; thus he succeeded in drawing most of them without scoreable errors. When he began to have increasing difficulty in remembering them correctly, he remarked disgustedly, "I never was any good at this sort of stuff anyways!" Similarly, on the Digit Symbol subtest of the Wechsler, he verbalized each symbol as he drew it, so that he made no errors but his score was lowered because he lost time in being so meticulous. He passed the Digit Span, including the digits backwards, by whispering the numbers to himself as they were pronounced to him, but was unable to cope with the memory passages on the Wechsler Memory Scale in the same manner. When he could not justify his responses to the Rorschach, even some very simple "popular" responses, he denied the response, often remarking, "Well, I don't see it that way now. Instead, it looks like . . . " and gave a new response which he often could not justify either.

Another common way children have of coping with a perceptual-motor difficulty is by avoiding such tasks, by diverting attention, by making demands on others for help, or by rebellious angry behavior. The avoiding of perceptual-motor tasks may take the form of refusing to go to school or neglecting school work which the child cannot successfully perform. His feelings of frustration and inadequacy may be demonstrated in his disruptive behavior in the schoolroom which has the secondary benefit of getting him excused from the tasks he cannot do. Such a child may use the "game of uproar" (see Chapter 11) during the assessment, refusing the task and attempting to divert attention away from the demands of the assessor. One child, who it was suspected suffered a mild cerebral defect, succeeded in avoiding the Bender altogether by the following maneuvers over a half-hour period: he broke the pencil lead four times, dropped the paper on the floor three times, erased a hole in the paper or tore it up in disgust several times, went to the bathroom twice, twice sat and "studied" the initial figure for several minutes complaining it was too hard, asked several times to do some other task, left his chair to look out the window, knocked over a pile of books and insisted that he pick them up and sort them out, finally noted that time was running out for the session, and when more time was granted, claimed he was "bored" and refused to do his test altogether. His difficulties on other perceptual tasks were obvious. He guessed wildly on the Picture Completion, all the while looking at the assessor for clues and attempting to read the assessor's notes on the scoring sheet. His behavior on Object Assembly was quite similar. On Digit Span, he began to be more openly frustrated, tearful, and complaining. He also made a game of the Rorschach, avoided looking at the cards, saying, "It looks like that chair over there, doesn't it? Isn't that what you made a picture of here? Isn't it? . . . You tell me what you think it is and I'll see if you are right!" He refused to allow any inquiry into his responses saying, "I told you about that already. You ask too many questions. I don't want to play this game anymore. Let's play something else."

F. THE CONTENT OF PERCEPTUAL-MOTOR FUNCTIONS

The nature of interfering factors in perceptual-motor functioning may also be indicated by the kind of task the child is trying to perform, that is, the *content* of the stimuli. Some children with severe perceptual dysfunctioning may have difficulties across the board, on all kinds of perceptual-motor tasks. However, many children can perform some of them quite successfully or at least with only mild difficulty, but be quite helpless and fail at others. As was noted above, some children can perform relatively simple tasks which chiefly require focusing but have much more difficulty when the task involves discrimination. However, whether or not the stimulus has some kind of meaningful content may also affect the child's perceptions of it. Some tasks, such as the Bender or Graham-Kendall, are in effect "nonsense" tasks. Picture Completion, Object Assembly, or even Bead Stringing (Stanford-Binet) involves a meaningful context. For some children, the perceptual task is made easier when this context is provided; they can deduce what is to be done even though they may have perceptual difficulties. Without a context from which to operate, they may have no clues and, therefore, their perceptual difficulty may be more obvious. Such children may try to make up an association or create a content for the nonsense task so as to keep it in mind. Other children may be hindered perceptually by complex stimuli with associative content. They are able to focus on and make discrimination among abstract forms, such as the Bender or Block Design, but when meaning is added to the task, they are lost or confused.

Use of the content of the stimuli as an aid to perception is most common among older children whose perceptual-motor function has been damaged by some disease or injury to the central nervous system after infancy. They are able to call on old associations to assist them in new perceptual tasks. Children who can copy the Bender Designs or the Kohs Blocks but fail tests with a content would seem to have an associative rather than a strictly perceptual difficulty. Such a difficulty may occur among children who suffer a CNS injury or disease during the period where associative learning is occurring and after perceptual-motor learning is established, that is, after age eight. As will be discussed below, such disturbances of associative learning, as a part of cognitive functioning, are also characteristic of several different kinds of emotional disturbances in children. Where only certain kinds of content seem to deter perception, for example, only stimuli involving humans or only those with aggressive implications, an associative dysfunction involving affect or social functioning would seem present.

G. COGNITIVE MODALITIES

The modalities through which development of cognitive functioning takes place are commonly divided into *verbal* and *nonverbal*. The child learns to make associations, comprehend meaning, delineate, generalize, and analyze both through verbally communicating and through visualizing and manipulating objects. Most children need and use both modalities, but some think primarily with words or verbalized ideas, while others think by doing and are relatively less prone to utilize verbally expressed ideas or to put their own thoughts into words. This division of the modalities of cognition was recognized by inventors of intelligence long before Wechsler divided his scales into verbal and nonverbal. Arthur constructed her "Performance" scale in order to sample nonverbal thought processes. Terman and Merrill purposefully included both verbal and nonverbal terms in each of their mental age scales, and users of the Binet have long been accustomed to examine items across the age groups according to these two modalities. (The tasks on the Binet for older children are chiefly and sometimes exclusively verbal, however). What Wechsler provided specifically was a method of measuring and comparing these two modalities within one set of scales.

Scores from the Wechsler verbal subtests, from the Shipley-Hartford (both vocabulary and abstractions), from the upper age levels of the Stanford-Binet, and from other similar scales yield the best *quantified* data about verbal intelligence. *Qualitative* evidence of cognitive process involving verbalization may come from such tests as the Rorschach, Sentence Completion, or even the TAT. In addition to scores from such formal nonverbal tests as the Wechsler Performance Scales, the Goodenough Draw-A-Man Scale, the Arthur Performance Scales, the Leiter International, the Raven Matrices, or the Columbia, the assessor should examine cognitive aspects of other drawings and manipulation of objects such as during the child's play with the World Test materials or doll play on the Lynn Structured Doll Play test or on the Make-A-Picture Story (MAPS) test. The arrangements of the materials on the World Test or of the figures in the MAPS often give clues about the child's logic and comprehension as well as information about his affective, motivational, and social functioning. The Merrill-Palmer Preschool Scales offer a particular advantage in that the items are about equally divided into verbal and nonverbal; items may be omitted or rejected according to the needs of the child or exigencies of the situation, and an overall estimate of intellectual development still may be obtained.

Although a preference for one cognitive modality over another during infancy may be only a temporary developmental phenomenon, a persistence of such a preference may have considerably more widespread significance as the child grows older. In the current American educational system which leans so heavily on verbal skills, a child who remains verbally retarded undoubtedly will have educational problems, even though nonverbal intellectual faculties do develop at a normal rate. However, his verbal retardation may also reflect an educational deprivation or some other block connected with schooling. The inability to verbalize one's ideas or to comprehend verbally expressed ideas is also characteristic of several kinds of childhood emotional conflicts, as will be discussed below in greater detail. The child who develops only verbally without being able to solve intellectual problems by manipulating objects may be suffering from some perceptual-motor dysfunction, as was discussed above. Being able to talk about things but not to touch and do things may also represent a motor inhibition, arising from any number of emotional conflicts or social taboos. Where there is no marked disability of either cognitive modality but merely a greater skill and preference for one modality over the other, such a difference may be part of the child's character or style of life. The nonverbal roots of the future engineer or the verbal abilities of the lawyer-to-be are often seen in the cognitive style of the child long before adolescence.

H. COGNITIVE INPUT-OUTPUT

The receptive aspect of cognition is usually labeled comprehension or understanding. Comprehension tasks sample whether the child correctly receives not merely a perception, but the associative connections and meaning within the perception. This is the intent of not only the "Comprehensions" test on the Wechsler or similar items on the Binet, but also of Vocabulary and Similarities items and the Mincus Completion (Binet), and Picture Completion (WISC). These tasks all require essentially a verbal comprehension or at least some verbal expression. Picture Arrangement and Object Assembly on the WISC and "Ball in Field" on the Binet are examples of nonverbal search for the meaning provided by the stimuli. Among the best nonverbal tests of receptive cognition are the Columbia Mental Maturity and the Leiter International which depend solely on identifying the meaning of or communality among a group of items. All of these tasks also depend to some extent on memory, that is, on how well the input was established and retained. Although there are scales for "immediate memory," that is, for attention and concentration, such as Digit Span, about the only WISC subtest which essentially taps memory is Information. (Note that the child does not have to understand the Information questions; he merely has to remember the answer.)

Although the concept of receiving the meaning from a stimulus has been central to the study of cognitive development, the act of putting-out meaning (of formulating meaning where no meaning was inherent in the stimulus) has not been commonly conceived as part of cognitive functioning per se. Rather, such an act has been called associative or projective thinking and been seen as something somehow separate from cognition. Psychologists have occasionally tried to understand this process of inventive thought; over the past decade, there has been considerable research on creative thinking. On the other hand, philosophers have long maintained that most meaning constitutes an attribution of the mind to the object. There is not even a commonly used term to categorize this kind of thinking. This ability to formulate meaning, to pull together disparate meaningless parts into something and give them one

identity, or to analyze out parts not previously identified and to speculate, is, however, one of the most fascinating and unique aspects of the human mind. Psychologists are now beginning to realize that this mental faculty begins with the child's associative and imaginative thought. Since this aspect of cognition was not well recognized when intelligence tests were constructed, they do not sample it. The intelligence tests were constructed to measure educational achievement or aptitude in an educational system which promoted chiefly receptive, not inventive thinking. This social emphasis on having the child learn what he is taught rather than create ideas on his own continues to this day. Moreover, inventive, creative, imaginative fantasy was — and still often is — considered child's play, something which, if it persists, may be the seeds of insanity. Thus, the first tests of associative and projective thinking, Jung's Word Association Test and Rorschach's Inkblot Technique, were designed primarily to assess the *dis*associative aspects of associative thinking, or projective *dys*functioning.

However, Jung quickly began to see that associative thinking had positive normal attributes. Rorschach, too, spoke of sampling creative thought by means of his test. The task of the Rorschach Technique is to making something out of nothing, to create and impose meaning on a situation and to structure reality. Like the task of comprehension, the task of projection calls upon previous learning and memory (Rorschach speaks of "engrams"). Projection does not so much require the finding of meaning out of the stimulus but rather the integration of the stimulus into conceptualizations already present in the mind. For the child, this is a demanding task since his experience is as yet brief and his range of concepts with which to explain phenomena is thus limited. Moreover, his prior perceptions and comprehensions are still being validated through further experience. Thus, he may not be very effective nor accurate when he tries to fit an unstructured situation to a limited range of not fully established engrams.

Thus, the child's Rorschach responses may reveal the extent to which he can use the ideation and the organizational thinking process which he has developed to test out and formulate reality independently, rather than merely recite back what he has been taught. His responses and his explanations of them during the inquiry may be analyzed to determine: (1) the range of concepts he has used, (2) the ways he has selected out parts of the inkblot, organized these parts together, and utilized the whole blot in order to fit some concept, and (3) the congruence between this organization and the engram which he has selected. Projective intelligence requires that (1) the child can select out of his range of engrams the concept "doggy" to fit a selected part of the blot, for example, D2 Card VII; (2) he can show how he has arranged the part of the detail to fit his concept; (3) these parts have been organized to fit his engram. When the child projects onto the blot his prior motoric experiences, it is evidence that he has yet another dimension by which to judge the potentialities of an unknown situation, that is, the possibility that it may move just as he moves. Similarly, if he can integrate the more stimulating, space-filling aspects of the blot, the color, and the shading into his concepts, he may be credited with an ability to integrate and use external affective stimuli in other unstructured situations.

Perhaps in the mythical "average" child, comprehension and projective cognition develop at about the same rate. Theoretically, they are complementary; the expansion of each in the child's development permits the growth of the other. The more he comprehends, the better he is able to project; the more he can imagine, the better he will be able to comprehend. The fact that, on the average, these two sides of cognition are so related is shown in the significant correlations reported by several studies (Tucker, 1950; Altus and Thompson, 1949) between various facets of Rorschach responses and various intelligence tests; the fact that these two functions seldom match one for one in a child's development is attested to by their usually low correlations. Analysis of a child's cognitive development should include a comparison of the relative development of each of these sides of his intelligence.

I. COGNITIVE FOCUS AND DIFFERENTIATION

The ability to select out concepts, and to name, identify, and differentiate objects, is one of the chief initial cognitive tasks of the preschool child. Among adults such concrete thinking might be viewed as an inadequate, but for the younger child this ability to be concrete is essential. He must learn how to focus on one set of impressions and see them as a unit, grasp one idea and not get it confused with other concepts. He must learn that not all women are "mama's," that five is different than ten, etc. Only after he has become secure with this exclusion type of thinking can he progress to being inclusive, to making generalizations, seeing similarities, comprehending laws, etc. Thus, on the Binet, the child is asked to "tell the difference between" (age VI) before he is required to make similarities (age VII), followed by a combined test at age VIII (Differences and Similarities). "Vocabulary" is also a focusing and differentiating task. The Binet vocabulary contains many generalizations or class concepts words, even at a relatively early age (for example, "brunette") while the Wechsler contains mostly concrete items, even among the most difficult items. The Binet contains a variety of items at the upper age levels requiring generalization, for example, at Year X, Abstract Words and Finding Reasons; at Year XIV, Induction and Ingenuity 1, and Reconciliation of Opposites; and at Average Adult, Proverbs. Most comprehension items on both the Binet and Wechsler call for generalizations. On the Rorschach, gross, undifferentiated whole responses are the common approach among younger children; during latency, the child grows much more cautious about including every part of the blot in his response, and begins to limit himself to specific details. He is apt to exclude or even reject parts of the inkblot which do not fit and finds it difficult to fit everything in, which sometimes leads him to reject the whole idea. Gradually, he becomes able to put details together to make a whole, to both analyze and reconstruct. Such a dual process of analyzing out parts and reassembling them into a whole is the central task of the Block Design and Picture Arrangement subtests of the WISC. The Object Assembly test obversely calls for grasping an overall pattern and then pulling together parts.

In analyzing the data, the assessor should note how the child goes about these tasks. For example, does he put the Object Assembly pieces together in trial-and-error fashion, only recognizing the whole figure when he is nearly finished? Or does he stop to figure out what he is putting together before he proceeds? The older and more sophisticated child is able to begin the more complicated Block Designs by placing the corner blocks in first. The ability to combine ideas, especially in an independent expressive fashion, is nowhere better sampled than on the TAT. The younger child tends to give only card descriptions, with little plot. He finds it extremely difficult to conceive of causes (the past) or consequences (the future), and if pressed, his plot is usually incomplete and disconnected. As he becomes older, he is more able to string sequences of events together in a more integrated plot, with fewer non sequitors. Similarly, the young child's drawing of a man may have the parts complete but poorly arranged, and disproportionate in size. Gradually he begins to conceive of the human figure as a whole with parts in place. Many of the points on the Goodenough Scales are awarded on the basis of the placement and proportion of the details.

Although specification is the primary concern of the younger child, and generalizing is learned and developed at a larger age, these two functions do overlap considerably in developmental sequence and, to a certain extent, the age differences are determined by the complexity of the task rather than by the nature of the cognitive behavior. Thus, preschool children are making simple types of generalizations at the same time that they are learning a wide variety of concrete facts and discriminations. The older child, busy with constructing concepts, is still accumulating more refined distinctions and elaborations of his facts. For example, the ten year old in his drawing of a man is not only putting the arms and legs in the right place and drawing them both in proportion to the body, he is adding brows to the eyes and heels to the shoes.

The extent and nature of the development of these two aspects of cognitive functioning often provide major clues about the overall development of the child's ego. For example, the child whose thinking remains very concrete and detailed and who is unable to make generalizations may be developing compulsive traits, that is, isolating affect and drives by intellectualization. Such concrete thinking might also be characteristic of a culturally deprived child. Severe CNS trauma often interfere with development of the ability to generalize. Overgeneralization and intellectualization may also be symptoms of emotional conflict in children. The bright adolescent delinquent may argue with impeccable logic but on the basis of specious premises. The younger phobic child picks out the threatening aspect of every situation.

J. INTERFERENCES WITH COGNITIVE DEVELOPMENT

The general factors that deter cognitive development have been discussed at length in Chapter 4 and have been partially delineated above in relation to some of the specific aspects of intellectual behavior. The chief point to be emphasized is that, insofar as possible, both the kind(s) of interference(s) and the kind(s) of intellectual functioning and the interrelationships between them should be made specific. Such statements as "the child's intelligence is lower than it might be because of his anxieties" or "brain damage lowers his IQ" are of little direct help to those who may try to treat or retrain him. Instead, the assessor should search for clues in his data which would allow greater specification, such as: "At times he demonstrates an above average ability to objectively analyze a situation, or to generalize from situation to situation, but most of the time the potentially threatening aspects of the situation so preoccupy him that he can do no more than cautiously identify it." Or again: "Johnny loves to talk about things, using an extensive vocabulary and demonstrating a fairly extensive fund of information for his nine years, but even the casual observer will discover that he often does not really know the meaning of the words he uses nor does he make sense when he spouts out information. These verbal fireworks apparently are designed to hide his sense of inadequacy over his inability to really comprehend, which has as its base a marked perceptual motor dysfunctioning." Or: "Diane's need to repress any action which even smacks of being aggressive or assertive is so extensive as even to limit her intellectual functioning at times. Specifically, she falters when an intellectual problem contains any kind of aggressive content (such as the Verbal Absurdities items on the Binet). Moreover, she dare not argue her point, cannot explain herself when challenged, and prefers to give the simplest response possible, hoping it will not be challenged." And again: "Mark jumps from one idea to the next, often with little connection or logic. So many things enter his mind at once that he cannot seem to sort them out. His intellectual functioning is very similar to his social and affective behavior, all of which point to a serious difficulty in self-control."

K. COGNITIVE COPING MECHANISMS

These mechanisms for handling interferences with intellectual functioning and development are extremely variable. One very common way children deal with and mask intellectual deficiencies, arising from either a physiological or a social handicap, is by compensation. They avoid those types of cognitive tasks which they cannot perform, and they over-develop others. The classic example is the so-called "idiot savant" who cannot understand the meaning of things but tries to compensate by developing a hypertrophied memory for some trivia. Milton, age 11, could give the name of any car and the year of its make as it approached along the street, and he had picked up such miscellaneous facts as "Shakespeare wrote Romeo and Juliet," which so pleased his parents that they overlooked the fact that he could not differentiate words in a sentence on a printed page. Thus, they blamed the school for his poor academic achievement. Milton could recite back what he had seen on TV but then was at a loss to understand a game on the playground or a conversation between two peers; his mother considered the other children "cruel" because they rejected him.

Like the child with a perceptual-motor deficit, the child who cannot intellectually comprehend may distract from his disability by "acting up" or by some other behavioral reaction formation. In the classroom, he will keep the teacher busy with his misdemeanors in the secret hope she will not realize that he does not understand the classwork. During the assessment, this can be noticed when the child starts getting restless each time the limit of his abilities is reached on each of the WISC subtests, or from his diversionary tactics during the Rorschach inquiry. Because the child's behavior is so annoying, there is often a tendency by school authorities to blame his poor record of achievement on his behavior. An analysis of the assessment data may help to determine the extent to which the child is failing because he is not paying attention and where he is trying to hide an inability to comprehend.

The opposite type of reaction formation is also very common: the masking of intellectual inadequacies by very socially conforming behavior. Teachers and parents often tend to forgive the very "sweet" child who "tries." Because he gives the teacher no trouble, he may be allowed to sit hidden and neglected in the back of the class. At the end of the year, the teacher compensates for his (and her inadequacy) by giving him credit for "trying," and the child is promoted into the next grade where he faces even greater problems. Motherly psychologists (of either sex) are also occasionally seduced by such well-behaved children. For example, Lillie, age nine, was a very pretty child, with long blonde hair in pigtails, soulful brown eyes, and a sweet smile, who was very polite to adults. She was thought to be very bashful by her mother and teachers, and they decided not to pressure her to recite in class, hoping she would "outgrow it." When called on to go to the blackboard, she would stand there helpless with the chalk in her hand, and even when the teacher would encourage her or attempt to help her, the tears would well up and she would seem so petrified that she would be excused back to her seat. Her workbook was neatly filled with incorrect answers. During the assessment, she was so demure and so helpless that the student psychologist later discovered he had not pressured her for explanation of several of her vague Rorschach responses, and he kept looking through the data, emphasizing any adequate response he could find!

L. IDEATION

The content of the child's cognitive functioning (his ideation) is also a very important dimension. Sometimes a child has difficulty with a certain type of intellectual problem, such as arithmetic, or in judgments involving social interactions, even though his thought processes and cognitive modalities are in other respects quite adequate. Such a failure on a specific subject is often difficult to explain if one only examines the cognitive functions, as in the case below.

Case 20

Elizabeth, age 12, was failing most of her school subjects, including arithmetic, during her first year at junior high school — although she had made above average grades in elementary school. The initial intake history revealed no other complaints or difficulties. On the WISC, all subtest scores except arithmetic were above average, but she failed all but the first four arithmetic problems (Problems 4–8). Looking at other data from the assessment, the psychologist noted that while Elizabeth showed no signs of gross emotional disturbance, there was a consistent theme throughout her TAT stories of rivalry between the sexes, in which men were depicted as mentally or physically superior and very arrogant, but were nonetheless bested in the long run by the women who won emotional approval from others who felt sorry for them. Her father's responses to the Edwards Personal Preference Schedule indicated that he placed a high value on achievement and aggression, while her mother's preferences suggested that she was more feminine, and preferred to handle situations by being mildly exhibitionistic and seductive or by deferring to others. Noting that she had a brother, age 14, who was reported to be succeeding at school, the psychologist speculated that there might be more rivalry between the siblings than was originally mentioned. Further interviews with the parents revealed that they were quite proud of their son, who was graduating from the same school with honors and who was a top athlete. The parents, however, were quick to deny that there was any unusual rivalry between the children and vouchsafed that they "played no favorites." To prove their point, the father said he had praised Elizabeth for her cooking and her choice of clothes. The mother wondered if Elizabeth might possibly be a "little boy crazy," as she had overheard Elizabeth and her friends talking avidly about the boys, but denied that she could see that this new interest really interfered with her schoolwork. Several more interviews with Elizabeth were necessary before she began to talk about her "snotty" brother and how he "lorded it over everyone" and how he gained his father's approval by his achievements. "But," she said, "I don't have to be smart like that. I know what men like!" When asked what she meant, Elizabeth suddenly blushed and then retorted, "Well, they don't like girls that are smart." Subsequent interviews revealed that Elizabeth's interest in boys was far more intense than even her mother imagined, and that she was so involved in the social whirl at school and the rivalry at home that she had a real aversion for school achievement. In the background was her strong identification with her mother whose femininity included a denial of intellectual achievement.

The special intellectual preoccupations or aversions of other children may not always be so obvious. As was noted above, a child's cognitive functioning may at times be deterred by the intrusion of special fears or obsessions, as is shown in the following case.

Case 21

The first hint of Phillip's fulminating schizophrenia came during his responses to the WISC. He was a highly verbal youngster (age ten) who was considered to be potentially very brilliant by his teachers but was labeled as "underachiever" because of his unsatisfactory school performance. He talked incessantly about his interest in science, and it was difficult to get him to respond to anything else. He went into great length to explain why there were four seasons in the year, but he was not clear in his explanation, forgot the question, and actually forgot to name one of the four seasons. "What the stomach does?" and "Why oil floats on water?" similarly set him off on a frantic flight of ideas. On other items of this and other subtests, he tended to give only perfunctory responses. All of his subtest scores were in the low average range. Qualitatively, his failures seemed to result either from a disinterest in the topic or a highly catheted but very confused concern with how things work and why. Associations from other techniques suggested that Phillip might be very curious and very confused about sexual functioning. His responses also indicated that he was very attached to and dominated by his widowed mother. She, however, rejected the clinic's recommendation that parent-child guidance was in order; believing that Phillip had an educational problem, she sought private tutoring for him. Two years later, information about Phillip was requested by the Juvenile Court who was investigating an accusation that Phillip had sexually molested several younger children of both sexes. At the court's request, Phillip was again assessed by the clinic. At this time, evidence of intellectual confusion and emotional distress of psychotic proportion was rampant in his responses.

Chapter 13

ANALYSIS OF
AFFECTIVE DEVELOPMENT

A. MODALITIES

Usually when the term affect is mentioned, there is a tendency to think of the outward expression of feelings, of tears or laughter, of rage or affection, openly displayed in the child's behavior. Moreover, affect is usually thought of as a reaction to something in the environment; the child cries over frustration, he laughs at something funny; he gets angry at someone or shows affection toward someone. Since the control over affective expression is still developing during childhood, the experiencing of affect is predominately through *external* interactions. However, *internal* modalities of experiencing affect begin to develop very early in childhood. In fact, the initial affective states of infancy are chiefly internally experienced; the baby cries because of internal physical discomforts, or coos and even smiles because of satiation of his physiological needs, independently of whether anyone is cooing or smiling to him. Only gradually does he relate his discomforts and satiation to the outside world. *Expression* of the child's affect may appear chiefly external, but such signs of internalization as somatization also begin early in childhood, for example, through colic or in asthma.

However, it is not until the child builds up a bank of memories, of internal attitudes, and of contained impulses and tensions that his affective behavior can be said to be a response to internal sources rather than whatever is immediately going on around him. Usually it is some clue in his environment which sets off these inner affective states, even though the trigger is often hard to spot. Similarly, as the child learns to control and suppress affective expression outwardly, he develops means of internal expression of his feelings. In addition to somatic expression, he develops a fantasy life, playing out feelings which he has learned are socially taboo or would bring undesirable responses from others.

This theoretical classification of affective experience into *external* and *internal* modalities serves to clarify some quite practical questions. For example, is the child who angers so quickly in the classroom responding chiefly to some immediate social situation which may not be immediately observable to the adult observer, or does he carry a chip on his shoulder, fantasying enemies everywhere or seeing all other children as rivals for his unsatisfied dependency needs? Why is it that another child seems so bland and oblivious to the same group of teasing classmates and authoritarian teachers? The treatment or the retraining of affectively disturbed children requires knowledge of how the child experiences affect.

How children experience affect is not easy to observe directly. The child who seems oblivious to what is going on about him may actually be quite aware of his environment but reacting to it on a purely internal level. Another child may be crying his heart out for no obvious reason, although this apparently inappropriate affective behavior may have very good reasons in the child's fantasies and fears. Much of the difficulty psychologists have encountered in understanding affective functioning, especially in children, has arisen from the attempts to assume these reasons without any idea of how the child experiences affect, except by direct observation. Some adults seem not to realize that considerable additional data may be obtained simply by asking the child for his subjective opinion. Many children are able to verbalize the sources of their fears, excitements, depression, joys, or anxieties—particularly if they are external. However, when the child feels sad or happy "inside," he may be less able to verbalize further about it. Moreover, almost as soon as the child has learned to verbalize at all about his feelings, he learns to cover up his private world.

Clues about the modalities through which the child experiences affect may be gained from projective techniques such as Word Association and Sentence Completion. In his original work on Word Association, Jung posited that behavior such as long response time or idiosyncratic responses suggested the interference of internal affect, while indicators of a dependence on external clues for affective experience might be seen in "popular" responses, in rhymes and repetitious or "clang" associations. On the Sentence Completion test, the responses to stems with personal reference, that is, containing "I" or "Me," may be contrasted with relatively impersonal stems, with respect to affectivity. The child who gives predominately more affectively loaded responses to the personal stems would seem to be experiencing more affect more internally than the child who attaches his affect to the more impersonal stimuli.

For example, 12-year-old Mary gave the following responses: "I often *feel sad*," "Mother—*I hate her*," "School—*is out tomor-*

row," "Boys—*are alright*," "I get embarrassed when—*I think of some things*," "I get angry when—*EVERYTHING*." In contrast, her 10-year-old brother responded: "I often—*play ball*," "Mother—*is a klutz*," "School—*is a pain in the neck*," "Boys—*are better than girls*," "I get embarrassed when—*my father talks loud*," "I get angry when—*someone hits me*." This is only a brief sample of the many responses Mary gave indicating that her affect was chiefly internal. Her brother, however, experienced affect in response to something or somebody. The two children fought incessantly. Usually Mary began the quarrels, either by teasing her brother or by complaining about him when he fiercely claimed he was "doing nothing." He was more likely to respond by hitting her, invading her privacy, or destroying her property. When they were separated, she would continue to grouse, but he would quickly forget even the most vicious exchanges after a few moments. On the other hand, Mary was most likely to apologize, while "I'm sorry" never escaped his lips.

The one technique specifically constructed to sample modes of experiencing affect is, of course, the Rorschach Technique. Moreover, the genius of Rorschach lay not so much in his invention of the inkblot technique per se, for inkblots had been used previously as a test of form perception, but rather in his insight in connecting theory with technique. Drawing on the Jungian theory of his day he differentiated his "intratension" and "extratension" from the social introversion-extroversion concept, focusing not on how a person behaves or lives (Erleben), but on how he perceives or experiences (Erlieben). The ideas he used are common parlance. People speak of "being moved" by something, or "moved to speak" in Quaker style, thus describing an affective state or mode in terms of motion or tension within ourselves. On the other hand, when concepts and judgments are labeled "colored" by events and people around us, it means that affect is experienced passively and receptively, through contacts with the environment. Affect may be experienced through either or both of these modes, at various times or situations. Rorschach noted that many people appeared to use one mode much more than another, or even exclusively. This preference of affect modality is summarized in the *Experience Balance*, the ratio between *M* (responses containing human movement) and *C* (responses based on color).* Rorschach also recognized variations on these basic modes. Sometimes the movements are experienced in the form of raw impulses or, to use the vernacular, "animal spirits," or even pure tension without being precisely personalized. In contrast, there are shades of color, shades of affecting meaning, which are the "texture" of life. Some people are stirred up by instinctual forces within them, but are impervious and insensitive to environmental clues or nuances. Others are so sensitive, so aware of the sensuous stimuli about them that they dare not permit their own impulses to be loosened. A good deal of experience is emotionally neutral; people do not experience affect in every situation, but often attempt to consider situations purely intellectually. Approximately 30 percent of adult Rorschach responses are based only on the form of the blot. However, an inability to utilize and handle affect leads not only to a cold, impersonal approach to life, but to a dangerous ignorance of the affective aspects of reality.

The development of the modes of experiencing affect, and their representation in the determinants of Rorschach responses at different ages during childhood, is so extensively delineated by Ames, et al (1952) that only a brief mention of the highlights need be mentioned here. The preschool child is still accumulating affective experience, and his mode of experiencing affect is largely external. He is gradually learning to control and internalize his own motoric experiences but he is not "moved" by much until he enters latency. His own animal instincts, however, may play a prominent part in his affective life. It is during latency that the dual developmental processes of affective control and internalization are learned, practiced and reinforced. Dependence upon the environment for affective experience is characteristic of the preschooler and is represented on the Rorschach by the predominately color-determined records. During latency, the child attempts a neutralization of affect, in order to integrate his affective experiences. His Rorschach record is likely to contain less color than in infancy and the first movement

responses appear. Expansion of these modes of experience is the hallmark of adolescence. (Hertz, 1943a, 1943b). The adolescent varies from being the victim of his environment and its stresses at one moment, to imposing his will and his feelings onto it in arbitrary fashion in the next. Like Hamlet, he does not know whether the reality of what he feels is within him or without him. Ambiequal Rorschach records are characteristic of the normal adolescent.

B. INPUT-OUTPUT

In discussing affective functioning, the distinction between mode and input-output is often blurred. When one speaks of experiencing affect internally, there is a natural tendency to assume that the stimulus is necessarily an internal one, and that the expression is also internal. Similarly, extratensive experiencing of affect might be assumed to entail an environmental stimulus and an overt expression of affect. However, on reflection it is easy to see that the manner in which the affect is experienced does not necessarily depend on the stimulus nor does it determine the nature of expression of affect. Rather, the relationships between modality and input-output may be conceptualized as two dimensional, as shown in Figure 7.

Thus, the input may consist of such internal stimuli as spontaneous memories, dreams, values and attitudes, or the stress and tension of physiological drives. If such stimuli are received in an intratensive mode, the individual correctly identifies them as internal stimuli. His affective expression, however, is not necessarily limited to internal reactions. He may react with further memories, more dreams, changes or expansions of his value systems, feelings of tension and anxiety or guilt, or somatic reactions. But he can and often does also express his reaction to these inner stimuli by outward behavior which is manifest to others. The affect from his dreams may be expressed in his artistic productions, for example, or the values he has internalized regarding achievement may play a large part in the way he interacts with his teachers or peers.

These same internal stimuli may, however, also be experienced in an extratensive fashion. If so, they are disassociated from the self, and experienced as something external and

---

* For further definition of these modalities of the Experience Balance, a method of quantitatively distinguishing them, and some research validating these hypotheses, see Palmer (1955, 1956, 1962).

MODES

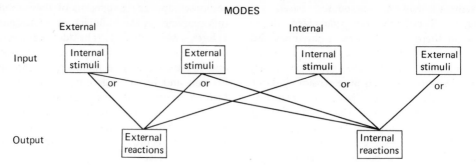

FIGURE 7. Interrelations between modes and input-output of affect.

separate. Such a disassociation is very common in the child who is still forming an integrated self — or in the neurotic or psychotic adult. Thus, children commonly experience dreams in the same way they experience environmental stimuli; they do not recognize themselves dreaming but rather as having a dream happen to them, much as anything else happens to them. They say, "I was scared by a bad dream" rather than "I dreamed a bad dream." They first experience values as external, as imposed by parents and other authorities, and thus the affect connected with such externally imposed values is also experienced as external. The child may get anxious about being "naughty" but he is uneasy lest he be punished, not because he is conscious-stricken. "Naughty" is an external concept. (For further discussion of this point, see Chapter 14 on conative functioning.) Even fears may be seen as external; a three year old runs from a dog and climbs in her grandfather's lap saying, "The doggie is afraid of me." Even if the internal stimuli are experienced extratensively, the output (the expression of the affect) may be internal. The younger child's super-ego is the external pointing finger of his mother, but his affect may be shown only in his fantasies about being naughty. Or he may awaken from a nightmare, screaming in terror, in the same fashion as he might from some external threat.

Obversely, the extratensively perceiving child will correctly identify an external stimuli as something separate from himself. He participates in the ballgame and is excited and challenged by it; but *he* does not win or lose, the *game* is won or lost. He may shout and scream or cheer or weep in chorus with others as part of the game. Yet, his affect may continue and be expressed also in restless sleep or a case of the hives. The intratensive child projects himself into the external event and identifies with it. When he plays ball, he is concerned with what *he* does, not how the game turns out. The excitement, challenge, glory, or depression is his own, not something he shares with a group. If he is challenged, he too may cheer with the group, and his external behavior would be indistinguishable from that of the extratensive child. But if he is disinterested, he does not have the need to cheer as might the disinterested extratensive, who shares the excitement of the crowd whether or not he likes to play ball. The intratensive child also may dream of ballgames, but his dreams are likely to be of his own glory or shame, while the extratensive child hears the shouts of the crowd in his dreams.

The assessment of the sources of affect is one of the most important questions in the overall study of the child with behavioral problems and, at the same time, is often one of the most difficult. Since the child's mode of experiencing affect may not be readily observable, identifying the source of a child's affect may not be easy. A potentially stimulating stress may be spotted in the situation by the adult, but the child may not see this stress as stimulating affectively and his outward behavior may be in response to some inner stimulus of which he is unaware. The ten-year-old stoic, wearing his "What, me worry" mask nevertheless experiences pride, disgust, shame or joy, just as much as his five-year-old brother who is shouting or crying or bubbling outwardly. But the ten year old is practicing containment of his feelings.

The assessment of the sources of the child's affect cannot be made on the basis of any one technique but instead is derived from a combination of variety of data, for example, the determinants of his Rorschach responses, the content of his TAT stories, his responses to Incomplete Sentences, and his World Test constructions and the subjective reports given by the child and his parents in the interview. Once his affective modality is established, it is possible to begin to spot the sources of affect. Looking across the board, the assessor notes the stimuli to which he responds with anxiety, depression, exhilaration, or satisfaction. For example, the assessor may note first that the child shows poor form level on the Rorschach or gives "tension" responses (Fm) whenever he attempts to deal with separate details of the inkblots; Cards III and X give him particular trouble and he likes Card V best. His TAT stories are replete with themes of people who leave never to return, of persons who don't communicate, or of lost objects. His "World" consists of a tightly packed village, fenced in. During the interview, he goes into great detail about the comings and goings of the family, who leaves the house and who comes back again. His mother reports that he had to be accompanied to school throughout kindergarten and first grade, and notes that he always checks up to see who is at home when he arrives. As further data are accumulated, it becomes more and more obvious that separation is one source of anxiety for this child. The meaning of this separation anxiety is then established by taking into account the modality. If the child is functioning chiefly on an extraversive level, then it is likely that he is responding (or overresponding) to separation stresses in his environment, to threats to his dependency on environmental clues. If he is more intraversive, then this separation may be concerned with some inner struggle. He may need people around him not for their own stimulation per se but, for example, as a protection against his own inner impulses, his own anger, his own sexual impulses, or his fantasied fears. In this latter instance, the separation would be secondary to other affective arousals, requiring further analysis of sources of affect. Since the developing child continues to be dependent on his environment for emotional support and, at the same time, is increasingly internalizing his experiences, this analysis of the sources of his affect is often quite complicated. If separations make him anxious, he may be responding to real separations in his environment, while simultaneously working out some inner conflicts.

The reason for this complicated analysis of affective *input* is, of course, to understand the child's affective *output*. The aim is to understand why he gets so anxious when he has to go to school, why he screams at his mother, why he seems to be hyperexcitable, or what depresses him. In studying the input, it may be discovered, for example, that his affective reaction in the school situation has little to do with school per se but, for example, may be aroused by his fears of his own hostility toward his parents, and that he has to stay at home to see that the awful things he has imagined and wished would happen to them does not occur. His screaming battles with his mother may be directed both at her overprotective controls and at his need to drown out his own erotic attachment to her. Sometimes the relationships between the internal sources of the child's affect and his outwardly expressed affect may seem quite obvious but often they are complicated and indirect. For example, much of the data may give evidence that the child feels emotionally deprived in relationships with his parents and family, and thus depressed, angry, and guilty; perhaps the child may voice such feelings as subjectively and consciously experienced, and even the parents may be aware of this possibility. However, all may report that aside from an occasional sullen reaction in the face of discipline, the child shows little outward manifestation of such feelings at home, rather that he is obedient, compliant, even outwardly cheerful in interaction with his family most of the time. In such an instance, it might be quite difficult for anyone, child, parent, or psychologist, to explain his affective outbursts, his disruptive, angry, and excitable behavior in the school situation, as arising from this depression over his family interrelationships. Very often, the key to understanding how the affective input and the expressed affect are related lies in analysis of yet another aspect of the child's affective functioning, namely, the kinds of interferences with affective functioning which the child experiences and the mechanisms with which he attempts to cope with these interferences.

However, before turning to a discussion of these interferences and coping mechanisms, some further thought needs to be given to the kinds of data commonly obtained regarding affective output. Usually, any direct observation of affective reactions is very brief, and under the very special and limited circumstances of the assessment situation itself. It is usually difficult for the psychologist to observe the child in prolonged interaction with his parents, peers, or other situations. Projective techniques may yield many clues about input, but they are notoriously poor predictors of output. Therefore the chief source of data is the subjective reports from the child and his parents. However, it is in the area of affective functioning that such subjective reports are likely to be most unreliable. Children have enough difficulty admitting that they are impudent to teachers who restrict their activities or get furious at playmates who disregard them; they usually find it even less admissible at first to mention that they glower at their parents (if they even realize that they do!), or that they are panic-stricken by an erotic dream (even if they remember it). At most, one can observe their affect during the interview when parental discipline is discussed or when erotic feelings are hinted at.

CASE 22

Mary, age five, who was so excitable that she had trouble sleeping, responded to the assessor's question about sleeping arrangements in her home by changing the topic and avidly reciting a rambling, disconnected spy story she had seen on TV; her drawing of a house contained a large keyhole in the door, which she called an "eye-hole." Her parents initially said nothing about the possibility that she might have considerable sexual curiosity, even when asked directly about it. Only later did it occur to Mary's mother that Mary always seemed to have to go to the bathroom when her father was there or asked to have her father take her to the toilet or bathe her (all of which was permitted). No one noticed at first that Mary seemed to manage to be present when her mother changed the diapers of her four-month-old baby brother or that she made frequent excuses to get into the parental bed. The possibility that the parents might well be unaware of and guilt-ridden by the recognition of Mary's excitement in such situations was, however, foreseen from their responses to the Edwards PPS. Her father's responses indicated very strong N Exhibitionism and

N Heterosexuality, suggesting that he might well be quite seductive. Mary's mother proved to be a very modest and compulsively orderly person who repressed sexual needs as something "dirty." For the father to report Mary's behavior would have meant admission of, or at least arousal of, guilt feelings over his own behavior. Mary's mother tried to blind herself to any indication of erotic ideation. Thus, although Mary's behavior during the assessment, as well as many of her responses to the tests, suggested that she was at least responding to erotic stimulation and curiosity, support of the hypothesis that her excitement was actually enhanced by erotic experiences was not obtained until long after the assessment, during subsequent counseling interviews with the parents.

In order to assess affective output, the psychologist must be most alert to small cues dropped by the child and the parents, and must follow through on these side remarks or hints regarding affect. In a supportive and non-threatening fashion, the psychologist needs to inquire further about the affective behavior of the child. Even though the informants may at first deny any affect or be unaware of it, they may reveal whatever affective reactions the child may be demonstrating in their description of the child's behavior. Often the assessor may be able to use clues gained from the child's responses to the projective techniques as a guide in conducting the interview, as was done in Mary's case.

The Bene-Anthony Family Relations Test (see Chapter 8) is especially designed to sample affective input-output. The items of this questionnaire are worded to distinguish between those feelings expressed by the child (labeled "outgoing"), and those expressed to the child by someone else in the family ("incoming"). The way in which the child distributes these two sets of items in the boxes behind the family figures is often very revealing of his affective patterns. Most children tend to attribute most outgoing feelings to the parents and most incoming feelings to the children. A reverse pattern would be very unusual, and would suggest that the child sees his parents as depending on him and his sibs for emotional stimulation. Of special interest is the child's use of the figure "Mr. Nobody" (where he deposits items he does not want to attribute to members of the family), and of the figure representing himself. Some children may attribute many incoming feelings (especially negative feelings) to "Nobody," thus denying that anyone is the receptor of negative affect. The child who lives in a family who represses positive affect may designate "Nobody" as receiving comfort or affection. The child who feels rejected puts the incoming negative items in the "Self" box. The guilt-ridden child may attribute the outgoing negative items to himself. The very repressed child who feels alienated may not put any items in the "Self" box.

The Rosenzweig P-F Study for Children (see Chapter 9) was constructed specifically to measure the patterns of affective modality and input-output. Rosenzweig's schema is very close to that presented in Figure 7. Although the distribution of the responses of the child among the various categories of the P-F may have little relationship to their manifest behavior, they may be taken as evidence of the child's values regarding affect. Thus, some children believe that frustration should be responded to by outwardly expressed complaints, aggressive actions, or demands for assistance. Others depict internal reactions to frustration as their model. The child who believes that all frustration has to be denied probably has considerable difficulty in maintaining these values in his external behavior. The child who thinks that he is primarily responsible for a solution of frustrations may react outwardly with depression or compulsive behavior. Aggressive and demanding children are likely to make similar responses to these techniques, but not all children who so respond do demonstrate these feelings internally. These "false positive" cases may be using the P-F as fantasy. As noted in Chapter 9, the level of response can only be determined by reference to other data.

C. FOCUS AND DISCRIMINATION OF AFFECTS

Very frequently the critical aspect of a child's emotional adjustment is his ability to differentiate affects. The child under stress may experience a variety of affective stimuli from his environment which are disparate and confusing. His sensitivity to such incoming affective stimuli may be compared to a radar screen, and he has the task of sorting out and identifying the various "blips," recognizing the friendly objects from the hostile. If the air is full of affect, it may be difficult to make these discriminations. Moreover, the child is also experiencing internal affects, both from his struggles for need-gratifications and in reaction to the external stresses.

The development of this ability to discriminate affective stimuli follows the general pattern discussed in Chapter 4, Section E. Very likely, this discrimination develops at least parallel to perceptual discrimination. Early in life, the child is unable to make much more than simple pain-pleasure discriminations, but during tne preschool years he begins to experience a variety of affects and to attempt to discriminate between them. For the most part, the preschooler experiences affect as something external to himself but, as he enters latency, he has already begun to sort out which are his feelings and which are the feelings of others. Although the latency age child often appears oblivious to feelings, he is actually making efforts to control and discriminate affects. He attempts to keep feelings to himself and to appear to be obtuse to the feelings of others, but his blocking of affect allows him to practice this task of affective discrimination without becoming flooded with affect. As an adolescent, he is often forced to make increasingly refined affective discriminations in a variety of interpersonal relationships. He becomes more sensitive to the feelings of others and also more introspective.

The methods by which the child copes with these affects will be discussed below. At this point, consideration needs to be given to the manifestations of affective discrimination in assessment data. The child's ability to discriminate affect is often revealed in the discussion of his feelings during an interview. "How do you feel about that?" and "How do you think other people feel about that?" are questions which should be interjected at every appropriate part of the interview — if the child does not voluntarily state his feelings. Some times it seems that a child is so overwhelmed by his own anger, depression, or excitement that he is unable to discriminate any other feelings. Even so, the assessor should inquire and determine the extent to which the child's affective perception is out of focus. Other children appear to have an affective tunnel-vision. They cannot say how they feel nor how others feel. Others experience affective double-binds; they receive two (or more) affective messages. Internally they experience a conflict of feelings, for example, love and hate, shame and pride, etc. (see Section F below).

Since the child is still learning the difficult and imprecise language of affects, it is often not easy for him to differentiate his feelings in words. Moreover, a great deal of the child's affective expression is motoric. Thus the child's subjective reports of his feelings normally have to be supplemented by reports from his parents and by other methods, particularly associative techniques. Some parents are acute observers of their children's affects and can report the child's efforts to differentiate them. Others, less cognizant of their child's feelings, nevertheless naively reveal the child's affective discriminations as they describe the child's behavior. For example, one mother remarked of her ten year old, "Why he knows I love him!" "Yes," replied her husband "and he knows when you're out of sorts — even if you don't say anything." Or another mother speaking of her adolescent daughter, "She's so moody; it's hard to say how she feels. You can say this for her — if she's in a bad mood she keeps it to herself and stays clear of the family up in her room. If she's in a good mood, she's all over the place." However, many parents of emotionally disturbed children are poor observers of the child's feelings — which is usually one of the child's problems. They are often wrapped up in their own affective states and ignore the child. They are unaware of the emotional messages they send the child and react defensively to his confused or angry responses. Sometimes they may not even recognize the child's overt anger or depression and are only able to complain about his acts, much as though they were complaining about a machine.

The ability to discriminate affect is evidenced in children's Rorschach responses by the form level of his affectively determined responses. If the form level of the child's movement, texture, or color responses is markedly less adequate than in the purely form-determined responses, this may be one sign that he has difficulty in discriminating those situations which are affectively loaded. If CF is much greater than FC, the child is making less well-formed perceptions of external affective stimuli. If his movement responses are largely vague whirlings or tensions rather than well-defined M or FM, it may be his internal affects which are unclear to him. When the child gives few or no affectively determined responses, it is impossible to tell whether the child is unable to make such discriminations or whether he is blocking out all affect — or both. One indication in such records is the differences in form level between the child's responses to the colored and achromatic cards. If his form level drops on the colored cards, it would seem that he has more perceptual difficulty in responding to external stimuli. (Lower form level on the achromatic cards, which is rare, is more likely to occur as a reaction to the ideation suggested by the card, but it is also possible for the child to be confused by the shading or the achromatic coloring.) The best way to determine the child's affective discrimination when he gives chiefly affectively neutral responses is in the "testing of limits," that is, requesting him to respond specifically to the color and shading or to find movement responses or to detail a movement response pointed out by the assessor. Not infrequently the tightly defended child who has made only cautious responses will, when encouraged in the testing of limits, respond with well-defined color and movement responses. However, the very threatened child may not be able to handle either external or internal stimuli — even when they are pointed out to him.

Evidence of the child's affective discriminations on the TAT or similar techniques is often more subtle but nonetheless revealing. As was previously noted, children's TAT's are more likely to be action stories, with little or no mention of the affects of the characters. Usually the feelings are revealed in the actions — much as the child expresses his feelings. However, it may be possible in the TAT situation to get the child to verbalize the feelings behind the character's action. One may ask directly, "How does (the character) feel?" but the child is more likely to respond to the simpler question, "How come he did that?" "He was mad," or "He was bad," the child may reply. "How can people tell?" the assessor should persist.

Sentence Completion techniques often offer a particular opportunity to test children's affective discriminations, as most SC forms contain many items which require explanation of affect: "I feel most angry when . . ." or "The things that make me uneasy are . . . ."

The child who has difficulty making affective discriminations may respond, "Nothing" or "Everything" to such stems. Last but not least, the child's drawings of human figures often illustrate very dramatically his affective discriminations. Even sketchy or poorly formed drawings often contain expressions in the curve of the mouth, the glance of the eyes, the turn of the head, the gesture of the arm, the position of hands or the overall posture of the body. In contrast, some children may produce very elaborate but lifeless mannequin figures. The overall amount of expression in the drawing may be one measure of the child's awareness of feelings — his ability to make affective discriminations. The kinds of affects illustrated in such drawings should also be noted. Affectively disturbed children often illustrate their confusion by drawing one kind of emotional expression in one part of the body and another somewhere else. One such child who was trying to mask his anger at his parents who were in the middle of a divorce battle drew a little boy with a big smile, waving goodbye. Yet the eyes of the drawing strongly suggested anger and the left hand of the drawing was clenched in a fist at the side of the body. Another child, struggling with the problem of controlling his hyperactivity, drew a figure which portrayed excitement, but loaded the figure down with a huge hat.

D. INTERFERENCES WITH AFFECTIVE FUNCTIONING

So many different kinds of factors can limit the child's reception of affective stimuli or block his affective expression that any listing would be incomplete. Many of these factors have already been discussed in some detail throughout this volume, especially in Chapter 4, and in the immediately proceeding sections of the present chapter. This section is concerned with the ways in which such blocking of input or expression is manifested in the responses children give to our most commonly utilized techniques. For example, a child may be completely unresponsive to the color or the shading of the Rorschach inkblots; he may attribute all negative feelings on the Bene-Anthony Family Relations Test to "Mr. Nobody"; the feelings of his TAT characters are not mentioned or even suggested. During

the interview, he may spend 15 minutes describing the pesty behavior of his younger sib but when asked if he is annoyed, he looks surprised and says it really doesn't bother him, that he just shrugs it off or doesn't pay any attention to the sib. To describe such behavior, psychologists commonly use such terms as "denial of affect," or "blocking," or under special circumstances, "bland affect."

Such terms may describe the response, but they do not indicate whether the interference lies in the reception of affect or in the expression. Does showing no affect under circumstances where most children would indicate that a child is obtuse or insensitive to the normally affect-creating stimuli, or is it his expression that is blocked? Often it is assumed that the child does recognize and feel a stress but for some reason or other cannot respond outwardly. However, it is also possible that for this child the stimuli may not be affect-producing. Or, he may actually have so steeled himself against such stimuli that he actually does not recognize them when faced with them. In dealing here with the absence of a response, there is no easy way of knowing whether the child is unaware or just unresponsive.

Distinguishing between receptive and expressive blocking entails other aspects of the response. If the child says "ooh" and "ahh" only to the colored cards of the Rorschach, if he mentions that they are colored but does not use the color, if he hesitates for many seconds before responding and then carefully notes that he is not including the colored parts of the blot, it may be assumed that he at least recognizes the presence of affect-arousing stimuli from his environment even though he cannot respond to them. Similarly, if on his TAT he describes how the antagonist does things to get the hero angry or to make him sad, etc., but fails to mention how the hero responds, an expressive blocking can be assumed. If on the Bene-Anthony he describes various members of the family as having incoming feelings but denies that he has outgoing feelings in return, it would seem likely that he is suppressing his expression of feelings. In contrast, if his affective life is chiefly intratensive, if he is unaware of incoming feelings from his family, or if only the heroes of his TAT stories have feelings, then his blocking of feelings would seem to be more receptive. Quite frequently, such a repression of affect is widely generalized, covering all sorts of feelings and blocking both the reception of feelings and their expression. As was noted above, such a "coarctate" (to use the Rorschach term) emotional neutrality is a fairly common characteristic of the latency age child. Certainly, if the child's responses to the color cards of the Rorschach are given without hesitation or other signs of tension, it does not seem meaningful to speak of "color shock" even though color is not used. If the child's stories to the TAT are not only lacking in affective content but are told without affect, there is little sign of awareness of affect. If he mentions neither his own feelings nor those of others in describing his everyday life, then it would appear that he is quite obtuse to feelings. In essence, then, it is the nature of the coping mechanism which tells us whether the reception or the expression is being blocked.

Interferences with affective functioning may also result in what is known as "inappropriate affect" or in overreactivity. The child cries endlessly over what appears to be a slight hurt, is terrified by what seems an innocuous stimulus, laughs uproariously at something no one else thinks is funny, or goes into tantrums over "nothing."* In these examples, the word "seems" is important because the affect may be inappropriate in the eyes of the observer but not necessarily in the eyes of the child. It may well be that to him the loss, the terror, the joke, or the insult may be very real. Thus, it may not really be the affect that is inappropriate but rather his perception of the situation. Such hyperaffective reactions may also be displacements or counterphobic phenomena. Classic is the "laugh clown laugh" reaction to cover depression, or the whistling through the cemetery to cover fear. One teenage boy wept copiously throughout the initial interviews, without being able to say what he was weeping about. There were some signs of depressive affect in his responses to the projective techniques but the predominate affective content of his responses was anger. Only much later, in subsequent psychotherapy hours, did he volunteer that he himself realized his tears

covered his anger. Quite commonly such inappropriate affective outbursts may be the overflow of bottled-up feelings. The previously meek and compliant child, who has never responded with even a sign of annoyance, suddenly becomes murderously enraged at the last straw, or the joking "life of the party" bursts into tears when he can no longer contain his depressions. Very often the affect that is being displaced, reacted against, or bottled up is revealed in the child's responses to the projective techniques, thus exposing the reaction formation.

Sometimes the source of the affective disturbance is very obvious. For example, a bright ten-year-old girl who had been failing at school told the rather unusual story on Card 7GF that the mother and little girl were crying because the dog had died; on the Rorschach, Card IV, she saw a "dead giant," and then on the same card, D1, "a weeping cow"; finally, in drawing her family, she made a circle of her mother, brothers, and herself around a coffin and said with tears in her eyes that her father had just died. The fact that the father had died about two years before was not mentioned in the intake interview with the mother because it was later revealed that the mother felt guilty for having divorced him the year before his death. She had told the child of the father's death at the time, but had avoided showing any grief "so as not to upset the child," and the child had not seemed moved at the time by this announcement. The child's underlying grief was manifested chiefly in her apathy toward her schoolwork and in her social isolation.

Quite often the source of affective inhibitions may be much less obvious. They may lie in unconsciously assumed taboos, possess guilt-ridden associations, or be part of a role played within the family by the child.

CASE 23

For the past month, Amy Lou E., age 13, had frequently awakened in the night, tearful and shaken by nightmares which she could not recall. She had always been subject to mild attacks of uticaria or "summer hives," and was thought to be allergic to certain foods or to summer pollens, but this year her skin rash persisted into the fall and she was continually scratching — "all through the night," her mother reported. The dermatologist could find no source for her skin outbreak and had diagnosed it as a "neurodermatitis."

---

*The term "lack of *affective control*" is much more specific than the term "lack of *emotional* control," which, as it is usually applied, includes conative and social functioning as well as affective.

The possibility that Amy Lou could be emotionally disturbed seemed unimaginable to her parents or her teachers or those who knew her. They regarded her as essentially a "happy" child, who "seldom complained," was "obedient," "helpful around the house," "has many little friends," "adores her little brother," and "loves animals." Her school-work was generally superior; "very neat in her work," "well behaved," read the teacher's notes. In appearance, Amy Lou was a pretty, fair-haired child, neatly and attractively dressed, who smiled sweetly and sat demurely and expectantly in her chair awaiting the psychologist's questions.

Her "problem," she decided solemnly, was that her "kitty had been put away." "Daddy put him to sleep with a little ether in a box and we buried him in the backyard. Mother thought his fur made my skin itch — but he was getting old anyway. He didn't do much but sleep most of the time." Amy Lou's eyes teared as she spoke and as she wiped them, she continued "One shouldn't cry over ani-mals. They're not humans, you know. We didn't have a funeral or anything. That wouldn't have been appropriate. After all, there isn't any kitty heaven, really." And she smiled. She contrasted this incident with another, when "the neighbor's dog died . . . they all cried something awful, for days, and held a big funeral. Isn't that silly though! They're kind of awful people, but maybe I shouldn't say so." She stopped, embarrassed. Encouraged to go on, she described how these neighbors shouted at one another, "the father swears sometimes . . . the mother has the funniest laugh, you can hear it a block away" and "they're always kissing one another, right out where you can see it. My mother says they're the kissiest family she ever saw." She described her own family as always speaking in modulated tones. "Even when angry?" asked the psychologist. Surprised, Amy Lou denied they ever got angry. "My little brother sometimes yells and stamps his foot, but then he's only six. He'll learn though. Daddy never puts up with that!" The punishment for such a display of anger in the E. family was to be isolated in another room. When asked about kissing in her family, "Mommy kisses me on the cheek when she says good-night, and Daddy gives me a little peck right here" — pointing to her forehead. Asked if her parents kiss, "One another?" she said in amazement, and then burst out laughing so hard that the tears ran down her face. " 'Scuse me," she apologized in embarrass-ment.

That Amy Lou inwardly experienced con-siderable exuberance was evident from the dancing, jumping, whirling figures she saw on the Rorschach cards. However, the same figures were sometimes also described as fighting, "clawing one another until the blood drips down." Aside from this response (to Card II), she made no reference to the color of the blots, and was unusually hesitant in response to the last three colored cards. On the other hand, she was quite aware of the texture of the blots, mentioning "fur" (Card VI), and "icy water" (Card VII), and "sherbet" (Card VIII) "because it looks so creamy and drippy" — but did not mention the color and could not say what flavor it made her think of. Stories about people who were stiffly polite to one another prevailed on the first half of her TAT, but before she was through, she was reciting one fantasy after another about bloody murders in which the criminal killed in anger. The murderer was always caught, tried, electrocuted, and "went straight to you know where." Her drawing of a person was a svelte feminine figure dressed in an off-the-shoulder evening dress with feminine curves (although no breasts were indicated) and long flowing hair and long lashes and heavily emphasized lips, iden-tified as a "party girl, about 20." She made a grimace when asked to draw a male figure, and produced a smaller cartoon-like boy in an aggressive stance, with prominent teeth, identified as "a little monster, about ten — all boys are really monsters, like my brother, sometimes," and she laughed merrily.

The affective rigidity of Amy Lou's self-righteous parents was obvious during the initial interviews with them and became even more manifest when Amy's concern with and conflict over affective expression were used as a clue to discuss with them affective ex-pression within the family. An almost puri-tanical ethic concerning affect was revealed. In subsequent interviews with both the parents and with Amy Lou, it was discovered that her itching and uticaria occurred most severely following incidents in which affect of various kinds was almost consciously suppressed. Then she began to recall her nightmares, which contained obvious angry feelings toward authority figures, and then with considerable guilt Amy began to admit feelings of hostility, first toward her little brother, then toward her parents.

Both reactivity to and expression of affect may be interfered with by trauma to the central nervous system. Again, such affective dysfunction is often subsumed under the more generalized term "lack of emotional control." Inappropriate laughter or tears, inexplicable irritability, or even periods of seeming imperturbability are frequent symptoms among brain-damaged children. While the term "happy moron" is a misnomer, it is true that severely intellectually retarded children do seem slow to react affectively with either happiness or sadness. They are seldom if ever entirely without feelings, but they are more likely to react only to the immediate situation and are less likely than the normal child to accumulate regrets and fears and expectations for happiness, since their memories are short lived and their range of experience very narrow. It is this shallow, brief nature of their affect that distinguishes them from the neurotic or even psychotic child, who may appear on the surface to be affectless but who shows signs of considerable tension accompanying the repression of affect, a tension not often present in the child with a neurological deficit.

E. COPING MECHANISMS

Usually when one thinks of coping with affect, it is in terms of "emotional control," that is, the suppression of affect demanded by the social group surrounding the child. In this sense, psychologists also speak of the uninhibited affect or spontaniety of the child in contrast to the seemingly more inhibited adult. However, certain amounts and certain kinds of affect may be a threat to the child's ego functioning. Children who are as yet still internalizing the adult inhibitions are easily overstimulated and "flooded" with affect. When something strikes them as funny, they may laugh till they choke or, when disappointed, they may cry without surcease. Affect can be infectious among children, as any school teacher knows too well; one joker can "break up" a whole classroom; one crying infant can set off a whole nursery. Such floods of affect may temporarily incapacitate the child, so that he cannot study or even play. Gradually he learns to suppress and

internalize affect, not just because society demands it, but because it disrupts his ego. One particular kind of affect problem not infrequently encountered in the clinic is the overstimulated child, for example, the child who is teased or seduced or overly excited. The unconsciously sadistic teasing adult, the bullying older sib, or the pesty younger sib can keep a child in a constant state of tears. The parent who constantly fondles the child or unconsciously teasingly seduces the child can keep him or her in a state of erotic excitement. Families who play a constant game of "uproar" can wear a child into a state of affective fatigue.

CASE 24

Jay, age 11, often became so flushed with excitement on the playground or even when called on in the classroom that he could not function at all. He would fumble the ball, run into the fence, or become mute. At other times, he would be so listless as to seem depressed or be fatigued and fall asleep in class. In moments of excitement, his facial muscles jerked in an uncontrollable tic. Almost constantly he seemed to be furtively touching the area of his penis or his rectum. Although intelligence tests administered by the school psychometrist showed him to be a very bright boy, his schoolwork frequently was at the near failure level.

During the assessment, Jay was very tense and his face frequently flushed bright red. His hands often dropped suddenly toward his crotch, and several times he rose suddenly from his seat as if jabbed from behind. During the Rorschach, his facial tic was most marked as he struggled for many seconds to get out some response. His Rorschach psychogram was most remarkable for an 11 year old in that there was not a single response based exclusively on form; all of his responses contained some kind of affect, either internal or external. Often this affect had no boundary at all; it was pure sensuousness, labile reactivity, explosive tension, or free-floating anxiety. His TAT was most dramatic; he played all parts, voicing the affect of each character. These characters screamed and shouted, spoke in seductive whispers, threatened and cajoled, wept and laughed without end. By the time the assessment was over, both Jay and the psychologist were exhausted.

Jay's mother was an obese, large-breasted young woman, who, except for her weight, could have been fairly pretty. Her unkempt hair fell about her shoulders and she often sat sprawled in her chair, or with one leg across her knee, idly rubbing her calf. Her cheap housedress was rumpled as if she had slept in it. At one point, when giving an example of her poverty, she mentioned that she owned no brassieres or panties, but "I hate'em anyhow." During the interviews, she also displayed considerable volatile affect. As she told of how her husband had abandoned her in poverty, leaving her to care for Jay and his younger brother, she filled the air with four-letter invectives in bitter denunciation of him. Nevertheless, she revealed that even after two years of separation, her husband, who now lived with another woman, would return to visit almost weekly, supposedly to spend time with the boys. However, these visits usually consisted largely of recriminations and quarrels between the parents and concluded either in physical violence or in sexual relationships. At these times, the boys either ran to the neighbors or retreated into the bedroom. In another context, she mentioned that the apartment was tiny—one bedroom, bath, livingroom, and kitchenette, and that the walls were so thin "you could hear a whisper in the next room." It seemed quite evident that the boys were witness to the parents' quarrels and love-making. Moreover, it was discovered she and the boys shared the one bed—"because we only have one coverlet." When this situation and its possible relationship to Jay's affective overstimulation were questioned further, she protested, "But I always wear something to bed; I never sleep naked!" Unemployed, she was entirely dependent on welfare, and the severe limitations of her income also depressed her. Sometimes she would spend whole days in bed, or sit around the house depressed and in tears. Jay would try to cheer her up and comfort her, waiting on her and bringing her little things. On the other hand, when the boys disobeyed her, or particularly when they did not stay around the house when she wanted them, she would become outraged, screaming at them and striking them. However, her rage would be short lived, for the boys had learned that if they quickly apologized, kissed her, and climbed in her lap, she would melt and forgive them. All in all, it was apparent that Jay's environment was intensely affectively overcharged.

With considerable reluctance and ambiva-lence, she yielded to the social worker's recommendation that the boys be placed temporarily in a residential childrens' care center. She visited them twice weekly and received continued counseling from the social worker there. Subsequently, she decided to break off all relationships with her former husband, and sued for divorce and child support. Through the State Vocational Rehabilitation Service, she received training as a nurse's aide, and after six months was fully employed. Jay's symptoms abated almost immediately after being placed in the Center. When he and his brother returned to live with his mother, Jay was making above-average grades at school and presented no behavior problems. Two years later, she and the boys dropped by the Center to introduce her new husband to the social worker. All seemed prospering and happy.

Coping with such external overstimulation is often very difficult for a child. Jay's tics and compulsive gestures were indicative of the tension which he felt from his highly charged environment. Another common response of the overstimulated child is some type of psychophysiological response, such as Amy Lou's uticaria or the "fainting spells" of the Victorian teenager. Every mother knows that when a child is overly excited, he may vomit or have a bloody nose. The asthmatic or epileptic child will be subject to an attack when under emotional stress. In assessment interviews, the assessor should particularly investigate the events and surroundings leading up to recent attacks or to physiological upsets. Sometimes the child's TAT stories or other fantasies will give leads to the possible affective antecedents to such psychophysiological reactions. Somewhat less commonly, children are able to escape the stimulating situation—as Jay tried to do at times by staying away from the apartment until forced by hunger or bedtime to return. Other children escape by busy work or even by overachievement at school.

Coping with internally experienced affect is also frequently a distressing problem for a child. In fact, what is most disturbing about external stimulations is that they arouse and exacerbate internal affective states which the child is attempting to control. Jay's tics did not serve as a method of coping with the external stimulation, but rather with the tension aroused within him. His own anger, his own anxiety, and his own sexual excitement had to be controlled. However, most children who are attempting to cope with affective stimulation are not so externally stimulated. Their affects lie within them. They may be enraged or disappointed over external events, but these events in themselves may contain little affect. The most commonly internally experienced affect is, of course, anxiety. This generalized sense of insecurity may have very definite sources in the environment. The child is anxious about something, but the anxiety itself lies within him, even if he is reflecting the anxiety of someone else. Coping with such internally experienced anxiety is the most common trial for the latency child or the adolescent.

Methods for coping with anxiety are almost as varied among children as among adults, but children's defenses are usually not as well perfected nor as much a consistent and integral part of the ego as among adults. Gross, generalized defenses such as outright intellectual and perceptual distortions are more common among children. They are less able to adopt the more subtle denials and evasions of the adult. Their evasions seem outright fantasies or "lies." The adult tries to appear "reasonable," to ignore the anxiety or to evade it by compulsively turning his attention elsewhere. Only rarely is the child able to deflect anxiety through sublimation. Intellectualization of affect does occur among children, even among retarded children, but it is more commonly an adult defense. Children's reaction formations to anxiety, too, are likely to be more gross and more simplified than those used by adults. Among children, the most common reaction formation is some kind of physical or social activity. Children cannot long endure anxiety. They have to *do something,* anything, almost as if they hope by being active they can expend the anxiety itself in the energy used up in the activity. Such motoric release of anxiety results in such symptoms as hyperactivity or, in adolescent restlessness, in fisticuffs between sibs and in increased masturbation (without necessarily any heightened sexuality). Often such hyperactivity occurs when the child reports subjective feelings of boredom, for it is in such periods when the child is not otherwise occupied that his internal fears come close to consciousness. One very emotionally constricted 14 year old reported that every morning he ran steadily around the block between the hours of 6:30 and 8:00 A.M., ostentatiously to prepare for a track meet. However, he was frequently so exhausted that he fell asleep in class, and by afternoon had little energy left to make practice trials around the school track. He also had many fears of and considerable anger toward his rigid and distant father. Later, it was discovered that by practicing for track, he avoided having breakfast with his father.

Restless activity is also the major coping mechanism used by children to counteract depression. Although adults may also react with "manic" activity to mask their depressions, this defense is even more common among children. Often such hyperactivity has a compulsive quality to it. The activity is intended not only to distract from or counteract the depressive affect, but often also seems to contain elements of undoing the experience of loss which underlies the depression. The child who is depressed because he feels neglected or rejected engages in an activity which denies these feelings. For example, Billy, age 12, was taken to a new community by his mother after she divorced his father. While she worked, she left him in the care of her maiden aunt, who disapproved of her divorce and was annoyed by boyish noises and activities. Billy tried to make friends at school but failed to get into the main clique. He was temporarily accepted by an outcast group and, as an initiation rite, was required to steal something. He elected to steal food from the market. His mother could not understand; "He gets plenty of food at home," she cried.

F. AFFECTIVE CONTENT

Recognizing and specifying the feelings and moods of a child should not be, but too often seem to be, a difficult task. Children do not and cannot mask their feelings as successfully as adults, and any attentive adult and most other children can, by observing the child carefully, make a fairly reliable and valid description of the child's feelings. These emotional states of a child are such a commonplace occurrence and so much of the child's everyday behavior that it does not really take a psychologist to recognize them. The difficulty is that many adults, especially those who have to deal with the emotionally disturbed child who does mask his feelings or who annoys the adult, blind themselves to the child's affects. Indeed, the central affective problem for the child quite often lies in the fact that he happens to live in an environment that is blind to his affect, that is, among particularly insensitive adults or in a cruel peer group.

Another factor which makes this simple observation seem difficult to adults, including psychologists, is that they are used to verbalized statements of the adult, although most people know that verbalized statements of affect are often masked and evasive. Moreover, because affects have not been subjected to psychometric measurement nor the subject of much experimental research, psychologists often approach them as if they were something ephemeral, an ascientific phenomenon. It was the work of Carl Rogers and his students that brought the feelings of the client into focus and made them a central aspect of clinical psychology. The beginning student should familiarize himself with Rogers' approach (as represented in his earlier books, 1942 and 1951). Special attention should be paid to the way that Rogers, in his published interviews with clients, recognizes the feelings of the client as the client describes his own behavior, even when the client does not himself specify his affect in direct terms. Of course, the Rogerian therapist, and therapists of almost any school, often ask the client to specify his feelings, since clarification of affect is one of the beginning aims of therapy. However, neither Rogers nor any other therapist considers the client's statement alone to be evidence of how the client "really feels." The therapist is interested in getting the client to explore and uncover repressed or hidden affects. Of course, the assessor does not have the time nor is he in a position to so explore affect. He must be able to recognize unspoken feelings, but since he is not in a therapeutic relationship with the child, he cannot demand that the child recognize feelings.

A complete catalogue of children's affective behavior and its manifestations is beyond the scope of this book. However, it may be helpful at least to review the main affective categories, especially those of clinical concern, with some explanation of how such affective behavior may be recognized and specified in the responses of children to the most commonly used techniques. Again, in dealing with children, it is necessary that these affects be considered developmentally.

For this purpose, five categories of affect may be considered: (1) security-anxiety, (2) happiness-depression, (3) affection-anger, (4) pride-shame, and (5) innocence-guilt. Personalogists would probably differ as to whether these particular categories were independent and as to whether they are actually continua. However, the purpose here is merely to provide some organization and distinctions for discussion.

Security and anxiety. Certainly, from infancy on, the child's needs for a feeling of security are obvious. As an infant, he particularly needs to feel physiologically secure, to rest assured that his physical needs will be supplied. Gradually this need for security becomes expanded to include his social needs. It should be noted that this need for security is affective, not conative. It is a feeling of security, not a drive per se—although getting rid of anxiety does form a motivation. (See further discussion, Chapter 14.) Thus, a child may have all his needs answered but if he is not sure they are to be fulfilled, if satisfactions are erratic and inconsistent, or if there is some threat, real or imagined, to their fulfillment, he may be overanxious. On the other hand, children may not feel insecure even if they receive only minimal satisfaction of their needs as long as they feel certain that these needs will be met consistently and without threat of deprivation. As the child grows older, these possible anxieties become more extended and complicated. As an infant, he experiences anxiety largely on the basis of external events, on the basis of here-and-now conditioning. As he begins to internalize experiences, to build up "sign-gestalts," and to foresee the possibilities of deprivation, the source of his anxieties also becomes internal.

The anxieties of the older child have two main antecedents. First, he learns that he must comply with adult wishes and demands if his own demands are to be met; if he does not obey, he may be deprived. He must increasingly learn to satisfy at least some of his own needs. Thus, security does not depend wholly on the environment but on the child himself. Second, there is the social demand that he delay some of his needs, particularly his sexual drives, and that his needs be satisfied at particular times and in particular forms. Indirectly and gradually, the responsibility for satisfaction of his needs are placed upon him and his anxieties concern himself and his ability to conform to social demands. Often these anxieties are accompanied by other affects, that is, frustration and rage, depression, shame, and guilt. However, anxiety without feelings of anger, of depression, or of blame is also frequently observable. This pure anxiety is often associated with the inability to "tolerate ambiquity" as Frenkel-Brunswick (1948) has described it.

Three kinds of anxiety are commonly differentiated. The term "free-floating" anxiety is used to describe those overt and generalized manifestations of insecurity which are readily observable by most of the people around the child and often by the child himself. He expresses apprehension in many situations; he cries easily; he trembles; his sleep and appetite are disturbed; his palms perspire constantly; he looks and acts "afraid"; his voice breaks. When such manifestations of anxiety are not so generalized but occur only under specified conditions or in response to certain people, the child's anxiety is often labeled as "fixed." It should be noted that the object of such fixed anxiety may be a displacement. In the famous case of Little Hans (Freud, 1909), the child was "afraid" of horses, and became anxious only when in the streets of Vienna, then filled with horse-drawn vehicles. Subsequently, the child's associations revealed that his real anxiety concerned his father. Such anxieties may be expressed in the form of childhood fears or phobias but in this writer's opinion, this term is often overused and misused. Specific phobias are actually rare among children. For example, the term "school phobia" is a misnomer. In most such instances, the child is not anxious about anything at school; indeed, he seldom manifests a fear of school; more often than not, he is afraid of what is going on at home, or of what he fantasies might happen if he were not there to prevent it.

The third form in which anxiety appears in children's behavior is when it is repressed and is manifest only in otherwise inexplicable behavior, such as the hyperactivity or "acting out" (as described above). In this form, the child himself may not overtly experience any anxiety, and may deny it completely; nor will others think of him as a "nervous" child. His anxiety shows itself in his inability to do his work at school, in his somatic symptoms, or in the "immaturity" of his social behavior. However, the presence of such repressed anxiety may be noted both directly and in-

directly in the nature and content of his responses to techniques such as the Rorschach or TAT. On the Rorschach, such anxiety is manifest in the vagueness of responses, or in the selection only of details which are obvious and clearcut, in the hesitancy of responsiveness, in the overuse of shading, especially chiaroscuro, or of the white space, or most severely in the record devoid of any determinant except form. Although a "monster" or two appears among most latency age children's Rorschach responses, since all such children experience some threat from within, intense feelings of anxiety are demonstrated when the child's Rorschach responses are replete with threatening content. Underlying anxiety may be demonstrated in TAT stories by themes of insecurity or themes in which everything is altogether secure, with all threat denied. Often these themes reveal the source of the anxiety, even when threat is omitted or specifically denied.

The ambiguity in the structure of the stories may also be a sign of anxiety. Some children cannot specify anything, but give only a series of descriptive sentences; they cannot commit themselves to any one story or make up their minds about the character of any of their heroes. The hazard of speculation is too threatening to them. Other children manifest anxiety obversely by becoming overly detailed, having to account for everything. The interference of anxiety with formal problem-solving behavior on intelligence tests has previously been noted. Thus, the inability to concentrate as represented by low scores on the Digit Span subtests of the Wechsler or Binet is traditionally considered as a possible sign of tension. The anxious child, unsure of himself, may be slightly more at ease on structured materials, such as offered on IQ tests, but nevertheless require more support, express more self-doubts, be less willing to "guess" when he reaches the upper limits of his ability. On the DAP, Machover (1949) and other authorities (Hammer, 1958) argue that extra shading in of figures, comparable to the Rorschach shading, is an indicator of free-floating anxiety, as are very sketchy or lightly drawn drawings. Similar interpretations are made of Bender Gestalt reproductions (Clausen, 1962).

Blocking and refusal to enter into unstructured tasks often indicate a panic in the face of the unknown. For example, one very anxious seven year old spent a half hour with the World Test merely opening and peeking in the test case; when the psychologist opened the case wide and took out some materials for him, he became rigid with fright and quickly returned the materials, slamming the case lid shut. Although such anxiety often seems quite generalized and unattached to any specific stimulus, careful examination of the overall protocol, across techniques, often gives clues as to the specific types of situations and persons who most threaten the child. The number of signs of anxiety on any one technique may actually be insignificant, for example, perhaps one or two shading responses or only one white space response, one prolonged response time or card refusal on the Rorschach, one or two "phobic" responses, a horror story or two on the TAT, and an anxious moment or so on the WISC. Yet, if one looks across the board at all the responses of the child, it is possible that one might find that these indices of anxiety follow some pattern, for example, that they always follow upon or substitute for associations about female or maternal figures, or about sexual symbols, or about threats of injury or of loss.

CASE 25

Jimmie F., age ten, came to the clinic because of his obstinate attitudes toward adult authority both at school and at home. He also seemed to have alienated many of his playmates by being demanding and "bossy." The initial interview with his father revealed that Jimmie's parents had divorced about five years previously and that he had been placed with his father since his mother was hospitalized for alcoholism. Two years thereafter, the mother was killed in an auto accident. A year prior to his coming to the clinic, Jimmie's father had remarried to a much younger woman, who tried to win Jimmie over by being at least mildly seductive toward him.

That a great deal of anxiety underlay his behavior and that this anxiety was specifically associated with the shift in maternal figures was indicated by the following set of responses:

To the Rorschach: Card I, "A witch . . . no two witches, flying away with somebody. And he's lost his head"; same card, inverted, "It's an iceberg, cold grey ice, dripping"; Card II (to D5 + D3) "a rocket ship, a jet taking off, with the exhaust flame below." Card III, "Two women, I think, pulling something apart. It looks like a

skull." Card IV, "I can't see nothing, except maybe some big old boots." Card V, "Looks like a bat, doesn't it?" Card V, "A totem pole, stuck in the ground.' Card VII (after a long pause, and much turning of the card), "Could be two rabbits, no . . . two women, Indian women, saying 'goodbye' "; same card inverted, "Like a cloud, a kind of unhappy cloud, all full of rain, just about to rain." Card VIII, "Two lions walking up the mountain." Card IX, after considerable pause, "Jezz, that's a 'mother' " (obviously using the word "mother" as a vulgar expression indicating that he was puzzled), but could give no further response. Card X, "A crab (D1); two beavers eating at a tree and its going to drop into the water (D8)."

In reviewing these responses, the assessor noted that Jimmie's first response, the two derogated female figures who have captured a male figure, seen as "headless" or without power, was in itself a rather unusual and anxiety-provoking concept; moreover, this response was followed by a depressing thought, stimulated by the shading of the card; the response to the space in Card II indicated a rejection of the blot itself, an escape form situation, although Jimmie was not able to completely reject the blot, being attracted by the extra stimulation of the color. Analogously, one might suppose that when Jimmie experiences anxiety, especially concerning female figures, he tries negativistically to escape the situation, but at the same time becomes involved in it in labile fashion. His response to Card III is the popular one, but he adds in the detail that the female figures are splitting a skull apart; both female figures and a skull are commonly seen here but this interaction which Jimmie projects onto these concepts is idiosyncratic. Again, after such a response, similar to Card I, he has some difficulty on the succeeding card. Thus, on Card IV, he notes the popularly seen "boots" but feels he is not doing justice to the possibilities of the blot. On Cards V and VI he recovers, expressing no direct anxiety and giving fairly popular responses. On Card VII, he is again struck with the feminine figures, being unable to stick with his concept of "rabbits"; again, his response is not markedly unusual, but they are depicted as Indian (suggesting again the possibility of females as aggressive), and most notably he specifies that they are "saying goodbye"; this response is again followed by a dysphoric reaction to the shading. He is subsequently able to pick out the popular response to Card VIII, but as on IV and V, he is unable to do anything further with this card. His choice of vulgarity to express his bafflement at the complexity of form and stimulation of the color to Card IX now seems most significant. Under pressure of environmental stimulus, he blocks and his anxiety is expressed with overtones of erotic hostility. Again, on Card X Jimmie is able to give a popular, everyday response, ignoring now the extra stimulation of the color. But he ends where he began with a response in which two figures are destroying or eating away at something which will fall into space.

On the TAT, also, Jimmie's anxiety seemed focused on relationships with mothers, on their loss and on their possible threat to his manhood. In Picture 1 he depicted the boy as having broken the violin and "now his mother will be broken-hearted" because it was she who liked to hear him play. "Maybe his father will get him a new one," Jimmie concluded. To Picture 3BM, the boy is crying because his dog has died. His father (not his mother) comes in to comfort him and will buy him a new one, but he really wants the old one back. To Picture 5, a maid is looking in to call the family to dinner. When the assessor asked about the woman being a "maid," Jimmie explained that maybe they had a maid so that the mother wouldn't have to work too hard: "Maybe she is sick or something." To Card 6BM, Jimmie blocked for over two minutes, finally asking, "That's the grandmother, not his mother, isn't it?" He couldn't think of a story right away, finally decided that the young man had come to live with his grandmother "because his parents had died." He couldn't expand on this story. To Card 7BM, the young man is listening to his father, who is giving him some advice, "like about business or getting married; maybe the young man wants to get married. Or maybe he is telling him something sad . . ." but Jimmie could not continue either of these themes. To Card 8BM, Jimmie perceived the prone figure as a woman (it is almost always seen as a male), and told a story of a boy who wanted to grow up to be a doctor and operate on people and save lives, like the doctors who are operating "on this woman." To the assessor's question, Jimmie decided that maybe the woman was having a baby or perhaps "she had been hurt in an accident." The hero in his story would grow up and be a better doctor than

those shown in the picture; "He'd be able to save people's lives." On Picture 11, Jimmie described how the hero had "looked into the cave of doom" and was being chased by the dragon but would make it to safety. Then the hero would be able to "fight back." To Card 12 BM, Jimmie told a version of the Snow White fairy tale; the figure bending over the reclining figure was seen as the Prince about to kiss and awaken the sleeping beauty (ignoring the fact that the reclining figure is wearing a necktie!). He remembered that Snow White had been poisoned by the evil witch, but he completely forgot about the seven dwarfs and other details of this fairy tale. The hero in Jimmie's version was not Snow White, but the prince, who had "searched all over for the woman he loved." On Card 13B, the little boy is waiting for his mother to come back from the store with groceries, but she is late and he worries that something may have happened to her. Finally, she appears and they all get to eat. On Card 17BM, Jimmie portrayed the figure on the rope as "escaping something" or "rescuing somebody"; maybe, Jimmie speculated, "he is a fireman going up the rope to rescue some woman. He saves her and everybody is happy—except the fireman's wife." And Jimmie laughed. In his final story, to Card 18BM, Jimmie decided that the hero was being helped away from the scene of an accident. "He didn't get killed but somebody else did; maybe his wife." As to how the story might end, Jimmie concluded, "Maybe he'll get married again someday—but he'll never forget her." These stories appear to contain many references to the loss of maternal figures, or their feared loss, and the need for rescue or reviving them. He is so concerned with this loss that he actually misperceives the depicted sex of some of the persons and changes the pictures to fit his concerns. Jimmie's responses strongly suggest that he was still grieving over the loss of his mother and perhaps was not too sure of the stability of the new mother, and not too willing to accept her. Yet, his heroes do look for some resolution, some rescue, and are able to "fight back."

Happiness-depression. Jimmie's responses not only indicate a sense of insecurity and anxiety, but perhaps even more reflect his grief and depression. In fact, these two affects, anxiety and depression, so commonly appear together that neither the observer nor the subject himself can quite distinguish them. Perhaps the child who continuously feels insecure over a long period will also experience some depression, for the insecurity itself will be experienced as a loss. Children who experience a loss may also feel insecure and feel a threat of further loss. Obversely, happy children do not usually feel insecure. However, even children can and do distinguish between these two varieties of affect, both subjectively within themselves and in their behavior. Children's facial expression may appear strained and tense but not necessarily clouded with depression. The apathy of children's depression is in contradistinction from the hyperactivity of their anxieties—although at times this hyperactivity may be a mask for and a reaction to the anxieties created by depression.

Depression as a reaction to a loss is not the only type of depression, but it is the most common source in children. Such depression can be noted even in infancy, as witness the severely depressive reactions of infants who are deprived of mothering (Spitz, 1946). The loss may be of a loved one, but children like adults also suffer depression when the loss is part of their own bodies, as in an operation or amputation. This loss may only be temporary in reality, for example, when a parent goes to the hospital or has to leave the home for awhile, the child may not be able to comprehend or be assured of the parent's return. Or the child may experience loss and depression when the parent is unable to care for him, so that the child feels a loss of love even though the parent be physically present. Even such a normal loss as the loss of "baby" teeth traditionally is compensated for by the parent in the ceremony of hiding the lost tooth under the child's pillow and replacing it with a coin while the child sleeps. Sometimes a child's depression derives from a single, intense loss (a single incident learning), such as the loss of a parent through death. More often, however, such a single loss results only in a temporary grief episode, from which the child recovers, as he becomes again involved in and driven by the push of his development.

Pervasive, extensive depressions are more likely to occur when the child experiences a series of losses, or prolonged deprivation. Because these may be small and almost forgotten individually, careful interviewing may

be necessary to elicit what does underlie the child's depressive affect.

CASE 26

Connie R., age seven, often seemed listless and unhappy, not joining other children in play, not even watching TV which once fascinated her. She spent long periods of time just sitting and moaning slightly to herself. She frequently complained of stomach aches but refused medicine and seemed to recover rapidly; the pediatrician could find no physical reasons for these complaints and advised psychological help. Sometimes she seemed abnormally hungry and kept asking for food and at other times refused to eat altogether for a whole day. Most of all, she was completely disinterested and apathetic at school, making no effort to become involved in the work, although tests showed her to be intellectually above average. Often she tried to get out of going to school because of her stomach pains or other excuses. Although Connie's mother used the term "depressed" in describing Connie's behavior, she could think of nothing which might be depressing her. Inquiring further, the psychologist discovered that Connie's parents had been divorced about three years, partly because the father's work had kept him away from the family for many days at a time. After the divorce, Connie and her little sister were supposed to be visited by their father every other weekend, but in the last year Mr. R had not been able to visit even once a month. Mrs. R admitted that Connie "used to be" very attached to her father, but did not seem to miss him much at present. Mrs. R and her two children were living with her mother, who cared for the children while Mrs. R worked. Her father had died about a year ago. At this point in the interview, Mrs. R wept for a moment. When she recovered, she remarked, "It's been too much!"

Connie clung behind her mother's skirt and left reluctantly for the playroom only when assured that her mother would remain nearby. She stood, silent and glum, staring at the play materials until she saw a stuffed toy dog which she picked up and cuddled. On inquiry from the psychologist about doggies, she told of having to give up her dog when she moved to Grandma's because Grandma disliked dogs. Subsequently, she had a kitty, but it got run over. She spotted another doll and noted it looked like one her father had given her. At this point, she fell silent, sitting on the floor, her face buried in the stuffed doggie. When asked further about her father, she stared straight ahead for a moment, then complained of a stomach ache and demanded to return to her mother. On the next appointment, Connie was given the Binet; she responded very slowly and with little drive, but nevertheless achieved an IQ of 114. On the Rorschach and TAT, she gave brief responses that were gloomy and dysphoric.

Connie's case also illustrates another common cause of depression in children, that is, a reaction to depression in the parent, especially in the mother. Further interviews were held with Mrs. R and she took the MMPI, the Sentence Completion, and Draw-A-Person. Despite her attempts to deny and repress, it was evident that she was experiencing considerable depression. She was angry, bitter, and had intense feelings of rebellion, but was able to hide them by keeping busy at work, yet she suffered intense headaches in the evening. Her anger and grief over her divorce had never been resolved, and had been exacerbated by the death of her father, with whom she had retained strong infantile ties. Nor could she break away from her mother, who passively dominated her by being dependent on her and making her feel guilty. Interestingly, Connie and her mother drew almost exactly the same female figure (discounting Connie's more primitive form-level): a sad-looking, heavily shaded little girl!

How Mrs. R's depression was transmitted to Connie was not clear until much later in the therapy, when Connie dramatized it in dollplay: the mommy doll was crying 'cause the daddy doll died and then the girl doll cried too. At the same time, Mrs. R, who had questioned whether she spent too little time with Connie or whether she might be neglecting her, began to realize that she was most likely to cuddle with Connie and pay attention to her when she herself felt sad and lonely, or to be rejecting of Connie when she felt angry and rejected. Thus, she began to see how she had treated Connie as an extension of herself and of her own depression, and to relate how Connie had responded with depression. This insight temporarily increased her guilt feelings, but she was able to look at her relationship with Connie more

realistically and then to seek new and more appropriate outlets for her needs in more adult fashion, that is, with her boyfriend. Connie saw her mother's depression as a rejection, and thus as a loss.

The pattern of anger, guilt, and then depression, as demonstrated in the case of Mrs. R, is most common. As children begin to internalize their feelings and to experience guilt rather than loss of fear, they also can become depressed like the adult. If Connie had been slightly older, it would not be surprising to find evidence that she vaguely blamed herself for her losses. On the TAT, one might find themes in which the girl was to blame for the father's leaving, or had to be punished for murderous feelings toward the mother, or for robbery of the mother. Adolescents who have a history of losses similar to those experienced by Connie, frequently relive these depressions as they struggle with the adolescent drives toward independence and sexual maturity. Symptomatically, adolescent depression is often acted out, for example, in truancy, school failure, or mild delinquencies. Thus, the sullen, seemingly rebellious adolescent may give responses that spell out considerable underlying guilt and depression. Since adolescence is a time of life in which mild, temporary disappointments are normally quickly sloughed off, even slight indications of continuous depressive affect are to be considered significant. For example, on adolescent norms for the depression score of the MMPI, as given by Hathaway and Monachesi (1961), T-scores are much higher than for adult norms. Since adolescents tend to cover depression by hypermanic behavior, extremely high "Ma" T-scores on adolescent MMPI Profiles may also indicate depression. On the Rorschach, the depressed adolescent may respond with use of achromatic color or shading, but more often depression at this age is marked on the Rorschach by apathy, by an absence of color, shading, or movement responses. The presence of color responses in an adolescent Rorschach is not contraindicative of depression but, in combination with other signs, may indicate a continuation of infantile dependency on the environment, an effort to reestablish and regain infantile relationships, and to compensate for the earlier losses. On the TAT, the guilt-ridden depressed adolescent is likely to respond with themes of hostility, guilt, and punishment, accompanied by depressive affect.

Affection-anger. From the discussion about security-anxiety and happiness-depression, it is obvious that these two affectional dimensions become intertwined with various degrees of affection and anger. Although these affects may be highly intercorrelated, and in the younger child experienced without much differentiation, they are quite distinguishable affects both theoretically and in the behavior of the child, even in infancy. For example, receiving affection may or may not lead to security and happiness; where such affection is eroticized, as is often the case, by either the parent or child, the child may experience anxiety rather than security, and consequently feel guilty and depressed. Obversely, the anxious or depressed child may appear very affectionate, searching for love. Anger may lead to feelings of anxiety, guilt, and depression, but the child who is able to express anger—or to receive it—appropriate to the situation may feel more secure in the long run, and feelings of depression may actually be relieved.

It is easier to differentiate love from the other affects than to define it. Definitions of love have defied poets and philosophers through the ages, and most psychologists avoid the term (if not the whole concept) by using euphemisms such as "positive" feelings, etc. In using the term affection rather than love, one may be able to distinguish between the more erotic implications of adult love, and the positive interactional affect between children and others. However, it is to be admitted that in so doing this author, too, may be euphemistic and not allow for the erotic overtones present in much of the child's affectional experiences. Love is love, and cannot be diminished by other terms.

Anger, too, is a definite and directly experienced affect, so common a part of our experience that it may not seem to warrant description or behavioral definition. Manifestations of covert anger have been illustrated many times in the cases throughout this volume. Anger is not the opposite of love; the term "hate" describes the far end of this dimension more accurately, but hate is a rather rare affect in childhood (Redl and Wineman, 1951). At least for purposes of discussion, anger may be thought of as a relatively temporary negative affective reaction to some definite person concerning some definite situation; when such anger is prolonged or becomes generalized, the term "hostility" is used. Intensified, continuous, and generalized, such hostility is commonly called hate. While anger is on the opposite side of this dimension, children from infancy on experience the conflict of both love and anger toward the same person, almost at the same moment. A full blown hatred seems to blanket out love, although the two commonly alternate. Affection-anger thus may be considered a "dimension," but not a continuum.

Another reason for using these terms is to distinguish the affect from the drive. Such distinction needs to be made in the case of all affect, for each can become a motivation, but the need to obtain love or to express hatred is such a strong motivation that it is sometimes difficult to conceive of these drives as primarily affective, or at least experienced by the individual as affect.

Since a major concern in assessment of children is the development of interpersonal relationships, expression of affection and anger is often a focal point. However, too often the novitiate reports only the fact that the child has such feelings: "This is a very angry or hostile child," or "Johnny lacks affection." Such statements often have a taint of value judgment to them, as if there were something wrong with having angry feelings or even being hostile per se, or that it is unusual to "lack affection" in itself. The main question is, of course, how the child copes with these affects. Continuous or frequent states of anger, or generalized feelings of hostility, may, of course, be draining in themselves. Even being in love is, as every teenager knows, both delightful and enervating at times. In most instances, the child—or adult—who feels injured or insulted and can express righteous anger feels relieved. His communication of his anger is in a sense a normal human interchange, a statement to others that they are injuring him and that he will defend himself. Similarly, his expressions of affection tell others that he will exchange emotional support with them that he seeks such support and will defend and support them.

Anger or affection becomes a "problem" when such expression is blocked. A conflict is created when the child perceives anger as threatening a loss of love. He avoids expression of his own feeling of anger if it is directed toward someone upon whom he is dependent or from whom he needs emotional support. Similarly, he avoids making these persons angry. During his preschool years, he learns to "control his temper" for fear of rejection; later in childhood, when he begins to internalize, he stifles his anger because of his feelings of guilt. The two or three year old tells anyone "No" if he feels like it; he also is quite free with his affections. However, before he reaches latency he has become considerably more discriminating. He has learned by then who will permit "No" and who will respond to his offers of love. Thus, it is rare to find a preschool child who so represses his anger that it becomes a generalized state of hostility. Likewise, the latency child who is indiscriminate in his affections would be considered "immature."

Anger also becomes a "problem" for the child because it is so commonly associated and confused with aggressive impulses and behavior. The untrammeled, yet normal aggressive drives of childhood create social problems and make others angry. The child often interprets the efforts of others to control his aggressive behavior as anger, even if these efforts are not accompanied with anger. Thus, being aggressive creates anger and may be interpreted as such both by child and by others. Children do learn to discriminate between aggression and anger but often it is a fine line of distinction. Thus, children push and pull on one another or even hit one another "just for fun"; getting ahead in line or in a game can also be a nonangry competition. But feelings of hurt and anger begin to enter in. Making these discriminations is almost a preoccupation of social relationships during latency. Children continuously test how far they can go with one another —or even with parents and teachers—until the line is crossed between aggression and anger.

As has been repeatedly illustrated in the cases cited here, when the child has intense conflicts about expression of anger, he often throttles his aggressive drives. Thus, a child who has intense and generalized feelings of hostility is often quite passive. The so-called "passive - aggressive" personality probably should be labeled "passive-hostile," at least in childhood. The child's efforts to remain passive and contain his hostility are seldom if ever quite successful. His hostile feelings are likely to burst forth, in aggressive form occasionally, like an erupting volcano. Even his passivity may be an indirect expression of his hostility if he is unable and unwilling to take the independent steps expected of him by others. This passive expression of hostility often underlies such symptoms as enuresis or underachievement at school. The child who is full of his own repressed hostility is also likely to be very sensitive to anger in others, to easily feel hurt, rejected, and to interpret the actions of others as anger, projecting onto them his own hostility. A mild form of paranoia or at least feelings of persecution is common in early adolescence. Not as yet prepared to handle the normal surges of aggressive and sexual impulses, the 13 year old projects them onto others. He or she (girls almost more frequently than boys) complain that adults are "picking on" them; "get them off my back" is the cry. Similarly, at this age girls are "crushed" by rejections, especially of their affections.

Feelings of affection may also become loaded with anxiety or guilt for the child. Even before love has sexual overtones (in the usual sense of sexual), the child begins to experience moments when those he loves cannot reciprocate. Mother is not always right there at the moment the two year old needs love or wants to tell her he loves her. Moreover, just as anger and aggression become intertwined, so do love and aggression, especially in infancy. The infant wants to hug the mother, to devour her. In fact, mothers, too, express their love for the baby in similar terms: "I love you so much I could eat you!" Such "oral aggressive" love, as Freud called it, is often difficult for parents to endure; if it expressed by the mother it may cause panic in the child. Of course, if expressed by the mother in response to the child's "oral aggressive" behavior, such a statement as quoted above may also act as a reassurance to the child in that the mother in effect accepts and recognizes the child's wishes.

As sexual and aggressive impulses become stronger and even more interlaced later in infancy, the child becomes more cautious and discriminatory in his expressions of affection. At four and five, he tells his mother "I love you" but watches her reaction, and then does something naughty to test her. Or, he asks repeatedly, "Do you love me?" and then tests her. Similarly, with his peers, he may bring a gift or kiss a friend one moment and hit and pull on him the next. Such open expressions of affection are much more dampened during latency and early adolescence, while feelings of affection are being internalized. Once the child learns that his affection is acceptable to others and that others will respond, he does not have to test it as extremely as he once did. He begins to accept affection as part of himself, without being rewarded constantly.

In early adolescence, affectionate feelings again are tinged with sexual drive. The adolescent tries to make sure that no one recognizes this and that these drives do not enter into parental or other relationships. Only after he begins to enter the stage of normal heterosexual relationships, can be once again permit overt expression of affection. One mother noted that her son scarcely had said "hello" to her between ages 13 and 15. Now, at age 16, "He has a steady girl-friend and they smooch for hours—but I get a goodnight kiss too, for the first time since he was 10!"

Manifestations of these various patterns of affection and anger can often be gathered directly from the reports of the child or his parents. However, where these feelings are strongly repressed, the child may be entirely unable to bring them up in interviews and blocks or denies their importance when questioned. Since the difficulties in exchange of these feelings often are present in both the child and in his parents, the nature of the conflict may only be hinted at in the parental interviews, in subtle clues or in the tone of voice or phrasing of the subject. Thus, quite commonly the referrant will remark to the psychologist, "This child seems very sweet and denies any anger but I sense an underlying well of hostility. His mother acts this way too. Please see what you can find."

Sometimes the evidence of bottled up rage is quite clear in the associations of the child to the projective techniques. Angry, mean, threatening faces or attacking vicious animals appear in the child's responses to the Rorschach or in his drawings. Here the psychologist must be careful to distinguish between expressions of anger and signs of aggressive impulses. Not every explosion means anger, not every powerful aggressive

animal necessarily indicates hostility. For example, one ten year old drew a man with boxing gloves; "Who's he going to hit?" asked the psychologist. "Why, nobody," replied the child in surprise. "He isn't going to hit someone. He's just working out." "But, isn't he going to hit someone some time?" persisted the psychologist. "Well, he might get into a boxing fight," admitted the child. "Who would he like to box with?" inquired the psychologist. "Oh, someone else who likes to box for fun," replied the child. The conflicts surrounding feelings of anger are often most dramatically revealed on such techniques as the CAT, TAT, or MAPS. Some sample responses (from different children) follow:

3BM. She just shot somebody. There's the gun on the floor . . . (?) . . . Maybe she's sorry and is going to kill herself . . . (?) It coulda been her boyfriend. He coulda told her he didn't love her anymore . . .

6BM. They're just standing there . . . I don't see no story . . . (long pause) . . . They look kinda angry but they don't seem to be saying anything . . . (angry about?) . . . Well, maybe he wants to leave home, or get married, something like that and doesn't want to tell his mother 'cause it'll hurt her, but she already knows and is angry anyhow. (He is angry?) Yeah . . . he wishes she'd understand and is mad 'cause she doesn't. She isn't going to say anything either, just looks out the window, mad like . . . That's all I can see. I don't know how it ends.

MAPS Living Room Scene: This little boy is waiting for his father to come home. He's seen a Cadillac stop outside and goes to greet his father. But it isn't his father, it's this gangster, who is going to shoot everybody. His mother screams and his sister cries. He runs out the door and gets a policeman who comes and arrests the gangster. (How does the boy feel?) He's angry 'cause his father didn't come home.

MAPS Street Scene: Here's this man and here's his wife, and they don't see this car coming and they get runned over and get smashed to death (patient laughs nervously). (How come they didn't see the car?) They were having a big fight as usual. (What about?) . . . I don't know. Maybe she wanted something and he didn't think they had the money for it. (What did she want?) How should I know! (angrily).

CAT 1. The baby chickens have to eat their mush and they hate much. The mother says, "Eat your mush or I'll eat you up." But they don't want to . . . (what happens?) They eat the mother up instead . . . Eat'er all up . . . They eat everybody up (child screams with laughter).

To the Rorschach:

Card II. These two dogs . . . no, bears . . . having a big fight . . . blood all over them . . . they bit off each other's legs . . . blood shooting up in the air . . .

Card III. These two cannibals . . . cannibal ladies . . . fighting over the guy they're eating . . . they're fighting over his brains . . . that's 'sposed to be the best part, isn't it?

Card IX. It looks like a volcano exploding. Here's some people down here trying to run away but they're going to fall in and get burned up.

Affectionate feelings and the need for affection also are often dramatized in children's fantasies and associations, sometimes in the same set of fantasies expressing considerable anger. For example:

11BM. His father comes in and sees him sleeping on the couch. He thinks maybe he's sick or something 'cause he is sleeping on this couch instead of his bed. But he isn't, he's just tired. So the father is worried over him and goes to feel his forehead. He doesn't want to wake him up, just wants to see how he is. The boy wakes up and he's scared for a minute but the father tells him it's okay and he's glad he isn't sick, and the boy isn't scared anymore. (What was he scared about?) He didn't know what his father was going to do. He thought maybe his father was mad 'cause he was sleeping on the couch, but he was glad his father wanted to see how he was.

7GF. This mother is trying to read the girl a story, and the little girl isn't listening very much . . . (How come?) . . . Maybe she didn't have anything to do. She was through playing with her doll and hadn't anything to do. Now she wants to go out and play 'cause she hears the other kids outdoors. (What happened?) Her mother knows she wants to go out and play and gives her a big kiss and tells her, "Okay, run out and play."

To the Rorschach:

Card I. Two ghosts, right here in the middle . . . They're right up against one another, like they're kissing (laughs). I guess ghosts kiss! And here's two more big ghosts, with wings, on the side. And they look like they're patting the other ghosts on the head. (In the inquiry, the child noted that "you can see right thru 'em . . . They're ghosty-like." This use of the shading suggested considerable anxiety intermixed with the affectionate feelings).

Card III. Two people picking something up. Like each is reaching for it. Like they were saying, "Let me pick it up for you . . ." "No, permit me!"

Pride and shame, like anger and affection, are also in essence social or interpersonal affects. Pride is a little more than a feeling of confidence or of self-worth. It implies that the child is expecting or receiving rewards for achievement or for some kind of socially approved behavior. A child does not know to be proud unless he has experienced praise, or is seeking praise. Similarly, he is ashamed only in respect to what others think of him or might think of him. These affects appear relatively early in childhood, becoming first most noticeable somewhere between ages three to six, when the child becomes deeply involved in self-mastery and in being rewarded for such abilities. The psychoanalytic school relates these feelings to what they call the "phallic" stage of development. This is an age when little boys flaunt their masculinity, both directly and indirectly. They exhibit themselves sexually with pride and are not very secretive in their masturbation. More evident is the four year old's boasting of what he can do, with exaggerated claims of his powers and prowess, and his constant requests for adult attention to his abilities and for their praises. At this age, children are testing not only their abilities, but what others think of them.

When they cannot control themselves, they become dreadfully embarrassed. "Aren't you ashamed!" the three year old says to his Teddy bear, echoing his parents. The five year old bites his lip and tries not to cry when hurt, because as a boy he would be embarrassed to be seen crying. Kindergarten and first-grade children taunt one another with cries of "Shame! Shame!" That the term "phallic" applies to the girls as well is difficult to maintain. However, little girls at this age are also unconsciously very vain little creatures. They pose and cavort in seductive fashion, enjoy dressing up and grooming (much like their teenage sisters, but in striking contrast to the latency "tomboy"). At other moments, both they and their little brothers in this age group are suddenly very embarrassed by their bodies, and become quite modest. As with other stages of early childhood development, these affects of pride and shame are repeated during early adolescence. The latency child can be shamed and does exhibit pride over his accomplishments, but embarrassment, particularly as a response to social failures, is most marked in adolescence.

Although in the long run shame is not usually as disturbing to the ego structure as anxiety, depression, or guilt,* it is usually acutely painful at the moment and children as well as adults make immediate moves to cope with it. To "face up" to errors is difficult for the child. Such admission, with the possibility of learning from the error and correcting, has to be rewarded if the child is to learn. "Hanging one's head in shame" typifies the tendency to try to escape the pain of social embarrassment. The child quickly learns to avoid situations where he might be embarrassed or people who shame him. Since he does not experience his social inadequacy as his fault (see the discussion on guilt below), he is more likely to be angry at the persons who embarrass him than to become depressed. Thus, the child who is frequently shamed is also quick to feel falsely accused. He becomes sensitive to the weaknesses of others and quick to embarrass them in return. He is apt to seek out other acts of skill or positions of social status of which he can be proud and to be boastful of these.

Shame, rather than guilt, is most likely to be experienced when the child does not possess the ability to perform the acts expected of him or the status which permits him entry to his peer cliques. Feelings of shame are thus experienced more frequently by the novitiate, the socially and economically deprived, and by the physically handicapped or scarred. In fact, shame is the affect associated with inadequacy whereas guilt derives from blame.

Case 27

Vera L., age 15, was born with one leg shorter than the other, and a small but noticeable red birthmark on her face. Her mother, who had delayed having any children until age 40, was most disappointed. Her father, who really had not wanted any children in the first place, maintained a sneering attitude about Vera's disfigurement, an attitude which he commonly took toward disappointments and which characterized his

lifelong and barely concealed depression. Mrs. L counteracted her disappointment by an anxious, hovering overconcern in her care of Vera. She was easily convinced that every time Vera coughed she was catching some dreadful disease, so she constantly protected her and ran to the pediatrician at every occasion. By the time she was five, Vera was also very anxious — and very spoiled. She had already learned how to panic her mother and to control both parents by causing them to disagree about her care.

Vera's start at school was a tremendously anxiety-laden event, both for her and for her mother. Mrs. L warned Vera "not to mind" if other children made fun of her, which made Vera even more anxious. Vera did not want to separate from her mother, and Mrs. L stayed around the school until asked to leave by the teacher. At first Vera was very shy, hanging around the edge of the schoolyard and refusing to play with the other children, sitting in the back of the room, covering her face. The teacher made special efforts to introduce Vera into peer activities, and gave her a "special" seat near her desk. It was easy to praise Vera for her accomplishments, since she was bright. Vera's physical development was also slightly precocious, and despite her slight limp, she became quite adept in gross motor coordination and at playing active games on the playground. Thus, after only a year, she changed from being shy and retreating to being a dominating leader—at times almost a bully. She tended to boast excessively and to make fun of others. Yet, she still had moments of intense embarrassment, almost without provocation, during which she would giggle without being able to stop, embarrassing her further. When her mother was advised of Vera's uncontrollable giggling, she again assumed that Vera was defective in some way and carted her off to a series of neurological examinations until she found a neurologist who conceded that Vera's behavior "might" be an "epileptic equivalent." Thereafter, Vera's parents treated her as an epileptic, filling the medicine chest with anticonvulsants; anytime that Vera became angry, anxious, or excited, her mother changed medicines. Mr. L, who had ulcers, decided that Mrs. L was mistaken in "drugging" Vera, and insisted that the whole problem was Vera's diet.

Vera's pediatrician, now very aware of the family situation, tried desperately to stop the

---

*Shame or "loss of face" is a more severely disturbing emotion in such cultures as the Chinese where the child's errors are seen principally as reflecting on the parents.

medication and the dieting but without effect. He pointed out that these ill-advised medications had unknown but possibly deleterious effects on Vera, both physiologically and psychologically, and that her father's diet was making her anemic. The parents responded by demanding a new diet and new medications. In recalling this, Vera was quite embarrassed and tried at first to deny that her parents' concern was of any importance, but admitting that she was always fearful that other children would find out about the medications or that her mother's fears might be realized and that she would have some epileptic accident which would shame her in front of her peers.

The culmination of Vera's difficulties began with the onset of her menses, which, since her growth was generally precocious, occurred at age 11. Even at age ten she showed marked breast and hip development which embarrassed her as other girls and boys remarked on it with giggles. Her mother tried to dress her to hide this development, but Vera quickly outgrew the loose blouses and sweaters. By age 12, Vera was already acting like an adolescent. She was in full rebellion against her parents, rejecting their attempts to control her, coming and going as she pleased, entirely neglecting her schoolwork. Painting herself with cosmetics, she joined a mildly delinquent group of older adolescents. As Vera admitted, almost defiantly, her behavior embarrassed her parents acutely.

Mrs. L continued to conceive of Vera's behavior as a defect. This time she concentrated on Vera's physical blemishes, and after more doctor-shopping, found a surgeon who agreed to try to correct Vera's leg. He warned the L's that surgical correction of this defect was risky, especially since her bone growth was almost completed, but, he admitted subsequently, he felt pressured into attempting reconstruction of her leg by the mother. For the next two years, Vera was in and out of hospitals. Several operations were required. Long periods of recuperation in bed followed each operation. Mrs. L hovered over her, granting her every request, and Vera was very demanding. Her only friends were disabled children whom she met in the hospital. At home in bed, she was very lonesome, restless, irritable, and depressed. She kept up with her studies via a home teacher and special tutors hired by her parents. She sat like a queen in her traction bed at home, telephoning her friends on her private line and writing endless letters to various boys she had met previously. The seductive tone of these letters and phone calls worried Vera's parents, who further embarrassed her by shouting at her while she was on the telephone and by reading her letters and diaries. Vera retaliated by being most demanding and outrageously impudent whenever her parents' friends were in the house. When her parents reprimanded her, Vera screamed with anger, heaping curses on them and striking them with her crutches. Mr. L stated that he felt "ashamed" to enter his own home.

When, at age 15, Vera was able to return to public school (with her leg in a cast), the separation anxiety of starting school in the first grade was reenacted. Mrs. L demanded extra assurances from the school authorities about Vera's "safety" at school, raising questions in their mind about Vera's ability to attend. Vera's preparation for return to school consisted of dying her hair and buying the shortest skirt possible (which didn't fit over her cast). Within three days Vera had (1) lost her temper at a teacher, (2) vomited up her breakfast in the classroom, (3) been brought into the dean of women's office on charges of "lewd" dress and behavior. Mrs. L quoted the dean of girls as saying, "Vera says the most shameful things!"

Prior to entering public school, Vera had been attending special classes for the handicapped. Most of the children in this class were permanently handicapped in contrast to Vera's temporary disability. Many had intellectual handicaps. Vera was insulted and embarrassed at being placed with this group. Asked what irked her most, she replied, "Their boasting!" During her stay with this group, she constantly derided the other children, making fun of their handicaps and punching holes in their claims to adequacy. It was obvious what Vera resented most was that very behavior of which she herself was most guilty.

Although pride and shame are everyday affective phenomena in human behavior, especially in children, there has been almost no systematic study of these affects nor even recognition of them and their manifestations in clinical assessment. In reviewing 100 randomly selected reports of assessment on children, this writer found none mentioning the words shame or pride; only two referred to "embarrassment" and then only in describing the behavior of the child during the examination. Although it was not possible to check further into the data per se, it did appear that in many instances the assessor may have confused feelings of shame with more adult guilt reactions, and pride with the need for achievement or ambition. It seems inconceivable that psychologists cannot recognize these emotions in children. More likely the reason that they are not mentioned is that they are considered unimportant or only temporary affects, relatively unrelated to long-range affective development. In any event, there is no rating scale in common use to define "shame" nor any projective technique which includes this concept in its sampling of associations.

Thus, the clinician is dependent chiefly on the subjective reports of the child or parent or on his observations for assessment of the child's feelings of shame or pride. However, shame is often too painful for children to report directly, and they have learned that they must soft-pedal admissions of pride, in order to avoid appearing boastful. Adults, especially those who turn for assistance in understanding their children, are often poor observers of their children, and part of the problem may well be that they are obtuse to the child's feelings of embarrassment or of their pride in their achievements. Such parents may view the child's feelings of shame only as resistance to doing what they want to the child to do, especially to achieve. In fact, if the parents admit that the child is ashamed of a failure or inadequacy, they might have to admit that they, too, are ashamed of the child. The same parents are also unlikely to recognize and praise the child for other accomplishments, or to recognize what the child may take pride in; too often they see these accomplishments as unimportant or as "childish."

Thus, it is usually necessary during assessment interviews for the psychologist to inquire with the child and the parents about possible situations in which the child may experience shame or pride. The clinician should be particularly observant of the child's face and his voice when topics such as physical disabilities, school failure, or social failures are discussed. The adolescent or prepubescent child may be able to shrug off feelings of shame in discussing such failure, but the presence of this affect often shows through in his tone of voice, gestures, and posture. Blushing, of course, is the classic manifestation of embarrassment. The experienced interviewer will also make efforts to introduce topics wherein the child may have an opportunity to talk about things he is proud of. Even before discussing painful topics like school failure or physical inadequacies, the assessor should inquire about what the child likes to do "for fun," what he is good at, etc. Some very depressed children or those who feel very inadequate may be threatened by such questions, but such an approach is welcomed by most. After talking about those things they enjoy and are proud of, they are often more able to mention, even voluntarily, the situations that embarrass them.

CASE 28

Kenny, age ten, was referred for assessment by the school primarily because he had been apprehended peeking into the girls' restrooms and gave other indications of sexual curiosity. His parents were also concerned with his continued, intermittent enuresis. Kenny was pushed into the psychologist's office by his mother, who was obviously embarrassed by his reluctance. He sat scrunched up in the chair, looking furtively about the room and out the window. The assessor remarked on his reluctance to come to see him, noting that many children were embarrassed by having to see a psychologist. "They are?" responded Kenny tentatively. "Especially when embarrassing things have happened to them," responded the psychologist. Kenny reddened and drew himself tighter up into the chair.

Asked if he knew why children came to see psychologists, he nodded, " 'Cause they have problems." He only shrugged when asked if he had any problems, or if his parents thought he had some problems. "Didn't you talk with them?" he asked suspiciously. Informed that the psychologist had heard the parents' "story" but wanted to know how he felt, Kenny fell silent. "What did you expect we might do here?" asked the psychologist. Kenny said he had been told he was to take some tests, and thought they might be like the "Iowa" test he took at school. This opened up a discussion about tests and school. Kenny said he "hated" that achievement test but said, proudly, he had been told he made a high score on it. He was embarrassed to admit that he had not made grades to match this test score; quickly he mentioned that he had gotten an "A" on a special project and in several tests where he enjoyed the subject matter. He admitted he was often bored at school (subsequent testing revealed he had an IQ of 144!) and liked to make up games to amuse himself or to tell jokes to amuse others.

"Would you like to hear some of my jokes?" Kenny asked, and proceeded to tell several little jokes in a self-assured manner almost like an adult raconteur. Responding to the assessor's laughter, he became more expansive, obviously proud of his story-telling ability, ending with one story with obvious sexual overtones. Realizing suddenly that he had told an "off-color" story, he blushed markedly. When the assessor noted he seemed embarrassed, Kenny said cautiously, "I'm sorry. I thought maybe you wouldn't like that one." Asked more about his joke telling, he admitted he liked to "show off" among his classmates, and often disrupted the class by whispering stories to his buddies, "especially like that last one." "That's why I get sent to the principal's office." After further discussion, Kenny agreed that he did have a problem "in keeping my lip zipped up," and "not paying attention to the teacher" and "that's why my grades are no good." As he came to these conclusions, he was much less embarrassed, but actually seemed somewhat self-satisfied that he had found a reason for seeking psychological consultation.

Children, especially adolescents, also commonly mention feelings of shame and pride in their TAT stories. However, since these feelings may not be mentioned spontaneously, the assessor should inquire about the feelings of the "hero" whenever the situation in the story implies shame or pride. The experiential basis of these feelings may also appear in the Rorschach determinants. Since shame and pride are affects in reaction to and in association with environmental stimuli, one would expect these affects to be experienced by those sensitive to environmental stress. Thus, Rorschach responses which contain both shading and color, while not evidence of these affects directly, do indicate that the subject is more likely to experience shame and pride when he does fail. One type of response which, in this writer's opinion, suggests the experiential basis for these social

affects is when the child sees color as indicated by the shading, for example, the top of Card VI is said to "look like a bright colored flower," or "the sun rising, all orange." This projection of "coloring" into sensation is what happens when shame or pride is experienced.

These affects may also be illustrated in the stance and expression of the child's drawings. One five year old, for example, drew a figure with the head off to the right, almost on the chest; when asked about this head, the child remarked, "He's hanging his head. He's ashamed," but could not decide what the figure might be ashamed of. The figure did seem to have an erect penis, but when asked about that part of the drawing, the child remarked, in embarrassment, that he had made a mistake and erased it. On the adolescent forms of the Sentence Completion, the stems, "The things that embarrass me most are . . . " and "I was most proud when . . . " are commonly used. Embarrassment over "goofs" and pride over achievement on IQ scales are another common indicator of the child's experiencing these affects.

Innocence and guilt are so much associated with legality in our culture that even when these terms are used by psychologists to describe subjective feelings, the fact that they are subjectively experienced affects may be forgotten. Thus, it may be surprising to discover that a person may feel very guilty even when "he has done nothing wrong." Obversely, people often are outraged when it appears the person feels very innocent even though he may have committed what, in the eyes of society, is a heinous crime. These reactions occur because the person's affective state is presumed to be synonomous with the value system of his society. Even psychologists may fail to understand that affects and value systems may not or need not be equated.

As was noted in the discussion above on pride and shame, shame and guilt are often confused in the mind of the beholder, and even at times in the report of the subject. Shame is an affective response to external, environmental stimuli, that is, to social situations. Guilt and innocence relate to internal, self-actuated phenonema. A person feels ashamed in response to the opinions of others. He experiences guilt in response to his own opinion of his own behavior. The subjective experience of shame is quite different than guilt. Thus, the child may feel shame, particularly when accused by someone else, but at the same time feel self-righteously innocent and thus quite angry. For example, he may be embarrassed over a social *faux pas* or a disability but not blame himself at all. The confusion arises when such terms as "ashamed of one's self" are used which in a sense describe guilty feelings. When the child is told, "Aren't you ashamed?" he is really expected to feel guilt rather than merely embarrassment.

Perhaps the main reason that shame and guilt are so often confused, especially in regard to children's feelings, is that they are related developmentally. Shame, in a sense, is the developmental predecessor of guilt. Both do relate to blame, and thus to the child's superego. Shame is the affect associated with an external control system. It occurs when the child depends on others to exercise control over him, or at least to assist in his learning control. Shame is thus most closely tied in with the learning and establishment of physiological controls and becomes generalized to other social behaviors. However, during infancy the child is learning the mechanism of controls, but he does not as yet accept responsibility for independent self-control. Even during the early years of latency, the child is still testing the external authorities who demand these controls.

It is during latency that the internalization of control takes place. During these years the adult sense of guilt begins to appear but, even at this time, shame is still the more prevalent affect. Guilt and shame are both experienced by the adolescent, often at the same time. Since an adolescent is subjected to new lessons in social behavior, he has new things to be ashamed of. Since he has already learned to take some responsibility for himself, he also often feels guilty over his "goofs," as if he should be able to manage the things he is just learning about. Here again, it may be noted that guilt and shame are not the same affect. The teenager may secretly be quite proud of his sexual development, but feel quite guilty that he cannot always control these urges. The affects associated with adolescent masturbation may thus be both pride and guilt.

Both guilt and shame are related to the child's feelings about himself. The child may feel ashamed when he cannot live up to what is expected of him—by others. He feels shame over his disability or ignorance. He thus may feel inadequate and helpless. However, when he begins to blame himself for such disability or ignorance, when he feels "worthless" rather than merely inadequate, he is experiencing guilt. Both shame and guilt are related to depression, but the depression felt by the ashamed child is the infantile depression of the loss of external social approval. The depression experienced by the guilty person is the more adult type of depression, the feeling of worthlessness and of self-blame.

Manifestations of guilt in children's behavior, particularly in adolescent behavior, has been discussed at length at many points in this book and does not need repetition at this point. Suffice it to remind the reader that the child, like the adult, is often prone to gloss over feelings of guilt or to deny them altogether. The presence of this affect among adolescents is most often manifested in their behavior, in the actions they take to deny and avoid guilt and depression.

Evidence of feelings of guilt is also found in response to various kinds of associative techniques. As an internal affect, the experiential basis for feelings of guilt are evidenced on the Rorschach by movement responses. It is when the child is capable of withholding and internalizing kinesthetic motor responses that he is able to experience guilt. Again, such movement responses do not in themselves represent or predict the subjective feeling of guilt. The tension represented in the inanimate movement response (*Fm*) is more likely to denote feelings of guilt, especially when the content of the response has to do with falling or being destroyed. On the TAT, guilt may be specifically mentioned as the feeling of the hero but is more often represented in the behavior of the hero who "acts" guilty, and in the punishment meted out by the story teller to offending criminal "heroes." Children rarely punish heroes who are ashamed; the shame itself is enough punishment.

The presence of guilt may also be deduced from adolescent MMPI patterns. Feelings of guilt are particularly present in the "472" profile (*Pd, Pt,* and *D,* above 70). At first glance, "psychopathic personality" traits may seem the opposite of guilt but it must be remembered that adolescents respond to guilt by "acting out"; at this age, guilt and rebellion are closely associated. The obsessive mulling over of feelings and behavior included under the "psychaesthenia" scale is more obviously part and parcel of the experience of guilt. High depression scores are relatively rare among adolescents, who cannot endure depression. Thus, even scores between 55 and 70 are more significant for the adolescent than for the adult. The "479" profile is similar, except in this instance the adolescent is masking his depression by manic behavior and ideation. Quite frequently, K is also elevated in the profiles of guilt-ridden adolescents, representing their efforts to suppress guilt. K also has the implication of internalization. However, as guilt mounts and becomes unbearable to the adolescent, F and Sc also tend to rise. The adolescent then begins to exaggerate his complaints, often in a plea for relief, and experiences increasing confusion. The hallucinatory and delusional experiences of the schizophrenic adolescent often reveal very open feelings of guilt.

The interpretation of manifestations of guilt in children requires some different considerations than for adults. In the treatment of adult neuroses, the relief of neurotic guilt has been such a common problem that psychologists frequently forget the role of guilt feelings in the development of the normal child's ego, particularly the superego. Guilt is the affective component which heightens the child's motivation to internalize and adopt social behavior as his own. It is the leaven in the child's rising sense of an identity. Just as anxiety is a warning signal against possible insecurity, shame is a warning signal against social injuries and guilt against loss of independence.

Thus, while the child is forming a conscience and a sense of self-regard, he may show extra amounts of guilt feelings. The latency child, as has been illustrated elsewhere in this book, is involved in rules and regulations, in right and wrong, and in who is to blame. Thus his TAT stories are often full of crime and punishment. At least two such stories may be expected in the protocol of the average nine year old. Unfortunately, there are no norms for estimating exactly whether these themes or other signs of guilt are merely part of normal superego development or whether they represent a conflictual, hypertrophic development. Although normative data certainly would be helpful, an analysis of the details of the stories and of the sequence of stories is informative. The question is not so much the extent of the child's guilt feelings, but rather what he feels guilty about and how he is handling these feelings.

For example, a nine-year-old boy who tells a series of stories about burglary, especially about women who get robbed—some ending with the apprehension and execution of the criminal hero and some with his escape— would seem particularly concerned with control over his needs for succor and narcissistic supplies, especially in relation to his mother. Another latency child might still be attempting to work through intense rivalries with his father or sibs, fantasying "accidents" and "murders" in which who is to blame is controversial. Robberies and murder stories by latency girls, although not as common, also often contain hints to the effect that they are working through and internalizing controls over their needs to possess love. Little girls also often struggle with their burgeoning femininity at this age, and their fantasies become concerned with giving up masculinity. Guilt over aggressiveness is thus quite a common theme in latency girls' fantasies.

Chapter 14

ASSESSMENT OF CONATIVE DEVELOPMENT

The chief question in the assessment of childrens' motives is not so much the identification of the drives per se, as it is the comprehension of the methods which the child is developing for channelizing, controlling, delaying, and redirecting his impulses. As was described in Chapter 5, this development of need-gratification skills constitutes one of the principal aspects of ego-development. In order to spell out the kinds of evidence relative to this aspect of ego-development, and the interpretation of such data, some further details of this concept of conative development need to be considered. As was considered with the other ego functions, discussed in Chapters 12 and 13, the motivations of the child need to be specified as to: (1) modality, (2) input-output, (3) focus and differentiation, (4) interferences, (5) methods of coping, and (6) the different kinds of skills associated with specific motivational patterns.

A. CONATIVE MODALITIES

As was indicated in the discussion of modalities in the other ego functions, the primary consideration is not so much the physiological or social source of the function as it is the manner in which the child experiences the function. Since the overall aim in describing the ego functions of the child is a description of the development of his sense of identity or self-concept, the first aspect to be considered about his needs and drives is how the child experiences these drives in relation to himself. The chief question then is: Does the child experience these needs and drives as chiefly *external* or ego-alien or as chiefly *internal* or ego-integrative?

Most adults, except those who are severely emotionally disturbed, generally accept without question that most of their physiological drives are a part of themselves. However, under times of stress even "normal" adults may speak of their drives in an ego-alien sense, for example, hunger or sex may be referred to as some kind of homunculus or "devil" within. This external experiencing of even physiological needs is, however, much more common during early childhood. Since food and other need-gratifications have to be supplied to the child externally during his infancy, he often acts as if his needs for these supplies are also external. It is only when the normal child begins to be deprived temporarily of food at weaning that he experiences internal hunger to the point that it can be identified as part of himself. Similarly, as his other physiological needs, for elimination, comforting, or sex, are delayed by social regulation and by social demands for self-control, he begins to see himself as having and experiencing needs. However, since the regulation of the child's food intake and defecation of wastes and of his needs for sleep and for activity begins very early in infancy, the child usually recognizes these needs as part of himself soon after he has words to express them.

The exception to this development of internalization of the experience of physiological needs is, of course, his sexual needs. Since direct gratification of his need is strictly tabooed in most cultures, one might imagine that such regulation would rapidly cause the child to experience his sexual needs as part of himself. However, even casual observation indicates that for several reasons the average preadolescent child does not experience his sexual impulses as part of himself. If sex is talked about, most children speak and act as if sex were something people other than himself experience and do. When an infant's genitalia are stimulated, either in masturbatory activity or by his clothes, etc., he can be observed to have a puzzled look on his face, as if he were experiencing some strange force. Frequently adolescents, or adults remembering their adolescence (for example, during psychotherapy), speak of their masturbation as if they were driven to it by some external force.

The reasons that sex remains experienced chiefly as external are several fold. First, although sexual sensations occur from birth on, the maturation of this drive does not occur until puberty, when it becomes a primary need. Not only can sex be delayed, but such delay is needed until sexual maturity. The child is not able to satisfy this drive, and society protects him from undue stimulation until puberty. For these and other reasons, the child often does not clearly differentiate his sexual needs from other drives (see differentiation and focus of drives below). Frequently, if other needs are gratified, the child may feel sexually gratified also. Obversely, his lack of sexual gratification may result in the heightening of other needs, but when these needs are gratified, his sexual drives may be lessened also, in sublimated fashion. Most of all he learns to gratify these sexual needs on an ideational level (see discussion below on input and output). In fact, as has been described in previous chapters, conceptualization of sexual need-gratification has as its epitome the Oedipal fantasy. Once a fantasied solution of sexual urges has become possible, the child drops most overt sexual behavior on a motoric level, even refusing such normal sexual contact as kissing and caressing.

At puberty, when the child begins to experience increased sexual urges, he begins to recognize these urges as part of himself. Often the 12 year old, for example, shows many signs of experiencing sexual urges but as something ego-alien. Stories of being robbed or raped, that is, of being sexually attacked by an external force, are very frequent in the TAT responses at this age. In girl's stories to 6GF, the man in the picture is commonly seen as a robber, or even blackmailer, or as making some untoward and unmentionable advance or suggestion. Girls of this age seldom see the man in 13MF as the sexual object, but rather depict him as a lover or husband who finds the girl has been murdered or robbed, with the implication of rape. Boys of about 14 respond in similar fashion to Pictures 4 and 13MF.

Most informative in this respect are the child's responses to the TAT primeval dragon-in-the-cave, Picture 11. Although no "card pull" norms are available, in this writer's experience children before pubescence are likely to tell stories to Card 11 in which two monsters are battling for existence. During the early years of pubescence, the typical story runs as follows: The dragon suddenly appears and threatens to destroy a hapless and innocent traveler who is trying to get through a strange passage in the rocks. Only after ages 15 to 16 is the following type story common: The hero is exploring the cave, a scientist looking for the dragon, which the hero captures and preserves for humanity and is honored for his prowess. Another common story to this picture at about ages 12 to 14 is that the dragon comes out of the cave and is accidentally destroyed while searching for food, suggesting that the search for gratification of the fiery impulse may lead to destruction.

Recognition of the secondary physical sexual growth as part of the self is often manifested in the adolescent's drawing of a human figure, especially in the drawing of the female figure (although such recognition may also be indicated in the clothing put on the male figure, or in his stance). Again, the presence of breasts or well-defined hips, etc. on the drawing of the female figure would suggest a precocity in a 12-year-old girl or boy. At this age, they are much more likely to draw slightly younger children, or parental figures. It is only after they have become comfortable with their own pubescence and accepted it as part of themselves that they project it as part of their body image in their drawings.

The fact that children have engaged in sexual relationships with each other or adults does not indicate that they necessarily experience sex as a part of themselves. Strange as it may seem on initial consideration, the 13- or 14-year-old girl who has been quite promiscuous and who even talks about it in adult nonchalant fashion usually does not see her behavior or her impulse as part of herself. Her seeming sexual precocity makes more sense when, as is commonly the case, it is discovered that her behavior is based on motivations such as a rebellion against her parents, a bid for their attention, or even a counterphobic reaction to her sexual impulses themselves.

CASE 29

Sandy, age 13, was described by the Juvenile Hall physician as "a well-nourished, well-developed female without signs of physical illness or distress." She had been examined to determine if she had been sexually violated after she was apprehended in a motel room in the company of three older "juvenile males." She had been reported as a missing person by her parents after she had not returned the previous Friday night. She was picked up by the sheriff the following Sunday on a report by the motel owner. The physician's report regarding possible sexual molestation was "indeterminate." Sandy refused to discuss the question. She was released to her parents on Monday morning. They immediately called the psychologist, requesting an emergency appointment that day.

Sandy's appearance suggested that she might be quite sexually provocative. She was dressed in the current urban teenage style, her brightly colored loose dress was so short her thighs were exposed. She was barefoot and her long, streaked blonde hair fell loosely to her shoulders; she wore eye-makeup but no other cosmetics and her skin was quite tan but free of adolescent acne. In the waiting room, she sat across the room from her mother, looking away at the wall, her face in a pout. Her mother, Mrs. Y, was, in contrast, plainly attired, an almost dowdy woman who showed no special attention to dress or grooming. Although only 38, her hair was beginning to gray and the lines in her face were accentuated by her harried and depressed expression. She rose to greet the psychologist and called hesitantly to Sandy who did not respond. When the psychologist went over and introduced himself to Sandy, she rose silently, made a spiteful face at her mother, and accompanied the psychologist to the office.

Soon after the interview began, Sandy's sullen hostility ignited into open expression of anger against her parents, her two younger brothers, her teachers, and even her girlfriends. She accused her mother of being too critical and always treating her like "I'm a child." "Daddy's even worse; he just agrees with everything she says! He comes home and doesn't know what it's all about and then opens his big mouth." Her chief complaints were that her parents did not accept her clothes, her friends, her use of the telephone, etc. They did not understand the problems she was having at school with teachers whom Sandy considered prejudiced against her. Instead, her parents kept nagging her for better grades, and about homework. She claimed she got "mostly B's and C's, with a D in gym." She "hated" gym because she did not want to have to change clothes, and get "all sweaty and have to shower." She had forged her parents' names to notes excusing her from classes, and had been caught in her forgery by her father, who told the school authorities to take whatever measures they saw fit. However, her mother had intervened when she was threatened with expulsion. She felt her parents let her brothers (ages nine and 11) "get away with everything."

At the end of the interview, Sandy was asked about the incident that landed her in juvenile hall, which, the psychologist noted, they had neglected to discuss. Sandy made a sour face, "Oh, that!" She suddenly looked quite depressed but began to talk. She had gone to a show with a girlfriend that Friday night and had met several boys there. After the show, they all drove around for a while with one of the boys who was older and had a car. She realized that the hour was growing late and that she would be scolded for returning home after hours. She was also angry at her girlfriend who was flirting with the driver who was an acquaintance of Sandy's. "He wasn't my boyfriend or anything, but I'd introduced her to him and she had no right to crowd in like that." She asked the boy to drive her over to her aunt's home, in a nearby small town. After he drove away she found there was no one home. She wandered down the street, met some other boys whom she did not know but who offered her a ride home. Instead, they took her still farther away to a resort town. She escaped from them, met some other adolescents and slept most of the day on the river bank. Saturday night she joined these adolescents for a "party." "There was a lot of sex there, but I didn't do anything, honest I didn't." Later, one of the boys offered to drive her home, but instead took her to the motel with two other boys. When she resisted their sexual advances, they let her alone. Very tired, she lay down to sleep, "but I got a big knife out of the kitchen and had it beside me" for protection against a possible attack.

Whether Sandy's story was fact or fantasy, her responses to the projective techniques did indicate that she was very immature for 13. Of her 14 responses to the Rorschach, 11 were based entirely on the form of the blot and three were rather generalized reactions to color. She saw no human figures. Card III was "a monster's face"; Card IV also "a big hairy monster" (she was using the term "hairy" in the current teenage slang meaning "horrible"); Card VII was "clouds" and "rabbits." Cards VIII—X were, respectively, "ice cream flavors," "some kind of flowers, all the colors," and "paint spilled over." Most remarkable in this 13 year old's responses was the lack of FM; none of her responses showed any indication that her perceptions included her "animal instincts." On the other hand, she was overly respondent to and dependent upon emotional stimulation from the environment. This pattern of responses did support the possibility that Sandy would be easily influenced by others, that she could be led astray, but that her sexual and other instinctual drives were not only part of the picture, but probably strongly repressed, as in latency.

Similarly, in Sandy's very brief TAT stories, the heroines had very few, if any, motivations of their own; rather, things happened to them that made them unhappy. The boy with the violin was forced to practice by his mother, but Sandy could not imagine what he might be doing if he were free. On Card 2, the girl "had to go to school" and is "looking back to watch her father working"; on Card 4, "Her boy friend has to go in the Army and she's scared she'll be left all alone." 6GF: "He's criticizing the way she's playing the piano and she's mad." Card 11: "It just looks like there's a lot of rock and stuff, all bare. Like the end of winter and pretty soon it's going to be all spring, but there's nothing there right now." Asked about the dragon: "Oh, that! I don't know where that goes in." Card 12F: "Looks like that old fairy story about the witch that fed the girl the poisoned apple." Asked how it turns out, "I don't remember; I guess she spits it up . . . right in the old witch's face," answered Sandy and laughed. 13MF: "Looks like she's very sick and her father, I mean her husband, thinks she's going to die and he's very worried and crying and everything. It turns out she really isn't sick at all. Maybe she just got drunk and is sleeping it off!" These fantasies indicated that Sandy conceptualized the factors affecting her life as chiefly external, with little recognition of the play of motivations of her own. Symbolically, Sandy remained frozen in the winter of latency, and though her spring was not far away, she ignored and was unable to include the phallic symbol of the snake-dragon. Nor could she visualize or even remember that Snow White would be rescued from the witch-mother by a Prince Charming. Finally, it is the father-cum-husband who is to be made concerned when her impulses overcome her.

Mrs. Y's first remark during the interview with her was a seemingly guilt-ridden, "I guess we've just done everything wrong with Sandy!" but immediately thereafter she began to describe the pressures that she was experiencing in a self-pitying martyrish fashion. Her children took up all of her time and energy, cooking what each wanted, picking up after them, driving them everywhere, etc. Sandy particularly seemed very demanding to her, ready at a moment's notice to throw a tantrum when she thought she might be refused what she wanted, never contributing anything to the care of the house, always squabbling with her brothers, and never saying "thank you." "Instead, for all your efforts you get a sneer or a snarl." Like Sandy, she felt unsupported by her husband; indeed, she felt her husband protected and spoiled Sandy. "Of course, he's very embarrassed by what has happened." Mr. Y was a city official who had risen in the ranks because of his political and community activities—which often occupied his evenings and weekends. Mrs. Y expressed the fear that Sandy's escapade might reflect on Mr. Y's reputation and damage his career. "He just got appointed on this new Youth Commission and now *this* had to happen," she moaned.

It was noted that Mrs. Y, like Sandy, also felt that things happened to her, rather than that she caused things to happen. It was not her motivations but those of others that concerned her. Regarding Sandy's escapade, Mrs. Y remarked, "I don't know what caused her to do something like that. She never seemed interested in sex. She just seemed like a little girl to us. I guess we didn't realize she's almost a teenager." The lack of communication between Mrs. Y and her daughter, especially regarding Sandy's development, was even more evident in a subsequent interview. When Sandy's menses had begun the previous year, she had not informed her mother and had secretly helped herself to sanitary napkins from her mother's supply. "If I get cramps, the family just thinks I'm sick. My father's so funny! He tried to make me take an Alka-Seltzer. I pretended I did and then spit it up in the toilet."

The degree to which sociocultural values are being internalized by the child and the manner in which this internalization is taking place are often of central concern in an assessment. Although the child's physical needs become part of his identity at a relatively early age (with a recurrence of this process at puberty), the acceptance of these social values as part of the self is a continuous process throughout childhood. There seems to be no point in the child's development where the infusion of these values into personal motivations is not of active concern both for those responsible for the child's care and for the child himself. The ways that these social values become personal motives have been discussed in previous chapters, and will be considered further in Chapter 15 as part of the discussion of social development and its interpretation. Suffice it to say that this internalization of social values and mores is the hallmark of social development. As regards conative development, the important aspect is that these external social pressures do become motives.

At this point, the question is simply whether or not the child experiences such social stress primarily as external to himself or as coming from within himself. Does he strive at school in order to satisfy his parents' ambitions for him, or because he himself feels some need for achievement? Does he join the crowd because one is supposed to be sociable and a member of the group, or because he likes people and has seen himself as wanting affiliation? Does he do things on his own because his mother rewards him, or because he takes some personal pride in being autonomous? Where such social values concern prohibitions of behavior, control can also become a personal motivation. Thus, the child learns that certain kinds of aggressive behavior (or even aggression, in general) are prohibited. At first the child controls his aggressive actions, whether positive or negative, because he fears punishment or desires praise. Even his aggressive exploration of his environment may be curtailed. Later, in latency, this control becomes the basis of an internalized guilt.

Data about this process of the internalization of social motivations can be garnered from many of the techniques of assessment. In the interviews, the question, "How did that happen?" is better than the question, "Why did you . . . ?" for it allows the child a bit more freedom to choose between mentioning external pressure and personal desire. A neutral question permits an analysis of the wording used by the child to explain his behavior or the situation in which he finds himself. Often such attitudes are expressed in the very first remarks in an assessment interview, when the psychologist inquires, "How was it that you came to see a psychologist?" After a few shrugs of the shoulder, most children start describing the complaints either their mother or the school has made, that is, the external stress. Fewer mention their own internal unrest, needs, or guilt feelings. Further questioning is usually necessary to determine whether such statements reflect internal or external motivation for accepting the psychologist's implicit offer to help. If the child states the parents' complaints, the assessor should determine whether the child accepts these as part of his behavior or whether he merely wants his parents to "get off my back." Inversely, his complaints against the environment may be voiced as frustrations of his motivations, for example, of his needs for narcissistic supplies or for independence. Or, they may constitute a protest against the impositions placed on him to do things which he does not regard in any way as need-gratifying.

Since children and even their parents may be unable to discuss the reasons for their behavior, either because they are unaware of them or ashamed of them, it is often necessary to gather additional data from projective techniques such as the TAT and Sentence Completion. However, even in TAT fantasies, the child may fail to include the motivations of the hero and it is necessary in such instances to make an on-the-spot inquiry of: "How come?" "What would make him do that?" If the child indicates that the hero was reacting in an affective state, for example, "Cause he's mad, that's why!" the assessor should continue to inquire, "What's he so mad about?" As in the analysis of interview data, it is the phrasing of the child's explanation of motives in the fantasy which is important. Compare the following stories to Picture 1 (which often draws stories about achievement), all of which were told by ten-year-old boys:

ART'S STORY: "He's just sitting there looking at this violin or something . . . (?) [in a resigned voice] He has to practice it, I guess. (He feels?) He hates it . . . (How come?) How should I know? He just hates it. (What does he hate about it?) I guess just having to do it. (How come he has to do it?) I guess his parents or somebody . . . (What happens?) He practices all right! Else he gets a whipping. [Art laughs in a hollow tone.] (How does it turn out in the long run?) Huh? (Does he just keep on practicing everyday?) I don't know . . . Maybe it wears out. . . ."

BOB'S STORY: "Should he have a name? I'll call him Jake . . . That's a good name, isn't it? I don't know any boy named Jake, but I read it. Like 'everything's Jake!' [Bob laughs at his own pun.] Jake has to practice this violin here . . . He's stopped cause he sees some other kids out the window playing and they want him to come out. He'd like to run out and play too but his mother has told him to play the violin, or else. He'll make some more racket on it and then his mother will let him out. (How does it turn out in the long run?) You mean in the future? Well, let's see . . . We'll say his mother gets tired of making him do it and listening to him play so awful and stops making him practice."

CHUCK'S STORY: "This kid has been practicing his violin and he's tired of it and wishes he were through so he could go out and play. (How does

he come to be practicing?) Well, maybe his father gave him this violin and wants him to learn to become a great violinist. (How does he feel about that?) Well, he's too young now to appreciate it. He just wants to finish his practice and go out. Maybe when he learns to play it better, he'll like it more."

DAN'S STORY: "This guy's studying the violin. He's sitting there and thinking how to play it better. (How come?) He wants to become a great violinist. (?) Maybe his father or grandfather were great musicians or he's heard some famous violinist and liked it. (What happens?) He asks his teacher to show him how to play it better. (And then?) He practices a lot more and becomes very good at it."

Art feels that controls are imposed on him for no purpose. Unlike Bob, he does not even express needs of his own. Bob has needs to gratify, but they are the needs of his environment, that is, his peers want him to play. Chuck has both sets of needs and both are his. Note he says "his" violin. Dan's need to control and achieve are almost entirely his own; although modeled after his father, he drives himself.

If the gratifications of a child's needs have been inconstant and unsure, he will feel threatened when he has to compete with others or is required to gratify his own needs. He will continue to seek infantile gratification from others, and his social behavior will be immature also. Such immaturity is a common cause of behavioral and educational disturbance in the elementary school child and is often evidenced in the complaint per se. For example, such a child may be described by the teacher as "demanding of her attention"; he does not learn anything unless she hovers over him. It may often be noted, in further interviewing about his schoolwork, that he perceives the teacher as the source of motivation of achieving. His attitude is that he goes to school because the teacher wants him to, not because he has any interest or curiosity of his own. Such an attitude is often blatantly displayed by the adolescent school dropout; in such cases one often need only scratch the surface to discover a chronic immaturity of motivational experiencing, which usually begins in latency.

B. CONATIVE INPUT AND OUTPUT

Whether the child considers his needs as part of himself, or internal, or as something alien to his ego, or external, depends to a considerable extent on the *input* and *output* of the motivation. The term input is used here to describe the form in which the motivation is experienced by the child. Output refers to the manner of expressing the need. (The source of the motivation is the topic of a subsequent section of this chapter, under the heading of "Content.") There are basically two ways in which the child both receives and expresses his needs and drives. The first may be called "motoric" and the other "ideational."

Perhaps physiological might be a better term than motoric, but the latter draws attention to the fact that many needs, particularly physiological drives, are experienced by the child in terms of visceral and skeletal sensations. Hunger comes to one's attention through a contraction of the stomach walls, and sex through a tumescence of the genital organs. Lack of oxygen results in severe muscular contractions. A drop in bodily temperature makes the child shiver and realize that he is cold.* Such motoric input is not limited to physiological drives. The secondary or social motivations are also frequently motorically instilled in the child. He may learn about property values by having his hands slapped when he reaches for something he should not touch. He may learn to curb his aggressive impulses by having his nose punched by a peer when he invades the other child's activities. Such motorically induced pain may thus teach him to avoid certain activities and to conform to social norms. At the same time, it is to be hoped his social motives will also be reinforced through more pleasurable motoric experiences. Although he may conform partly through fear of pain, his motivations are more strongly instilled if he receives caresses or is fed or played with. Such motoric instillation of motivation does not prevent the child from perceiving the need as external. How he *perceives* the need and how it is actually instilled may be quite distinct.

In contrast, many motivations, especially for an adult, have little or no motoric component, but are largely ideational. Adults behave in the way they do, not because of any special physiological tension or sensation, but because some concept or memory in their mind drives them. Many adult social needs consist of such ideational values. Sometimes even physiological needs are on an ideational level. For example, adults sometimes eat because it is dinnertime when one should eat, whether he is hungry or not. Or, an adult may exercise because he thinks exercise is good for him, even though he is fatigued. However, as parents often discover with considerable vexation, children do not readily grasp the idea of eating at a definite time, whether or not they are hungry, and they have to be taught to defecate in the proper place and to withhold defecation until a time can be allowed for it. How these essentially motoric needs become ideational, or at least attain an ideational component, is an important aspect of child-rearing and is often a focal point in assessment.

As has been discussed at several points previously, the training of the child in the control and management of these physiological drives is often the prototype of his learning of the control of his other, more social drives, which, is essence, are largely ideational. Thus, if the child does not learn "going to the bathroom" or "eating dinner" as an idea as well as a motoric act, it may be difficult for him to learn such concepts as "going to school," "staying out of fights," "obeying the teacher," "respecting property," or "being polite" as other than motoric acts. One very common reason behind the referral of a child for assessment is that he has learned as an infant to perform these social behaviors as automatic motoric acts without any idea of why or when they are appropriate but only because he is conditioned by the punishment or praise he receives from them. His social behavior in relatively unstructured situations outside the home may then be naive and even inappropriate. He may become anxious and fearful when no immediate conditioning agent is present. Moreover, in such situations he may express some of the pent-up resentment and frustration over the meaningless conditioning of his behavior.

On the other hand, the input of the child's motivations may have little or no motoric base but be almost exclusively an abstract idea. Such is the case with most of his social motivations. The child has to learn what "being good" or "well behaved" means, or what it is to "want to get ahead." A great

---

*Admittedly, the child does not directly experience the contraction of his sweat glands when he is hot nor of his salivary or other muscuous glands when he is thirsty but, instead, experiences dampness or dryness, respectively.

deal of how to be nice or not to be naughty and what these terms mean in concrete acts is learned prior to entering school. The child must first learn the specific motor acts which are covered by the ideational term. This requires at least a modicum of intelligence and is part of the cognitive development of the child. The child whose intellectual development is slow will also be slow to grasp the meaning of these social motivations. A retarded child may want to be nice but not be able to comprehend exactly what being nice is. Sometimes even bright but socially isolated children have difficulty in grasping the meaning of some social concepts; for example, such a child may want desperately to affiliate with his peers but through lack of experience be unable to specify the kinds of behavior which would mark him as being "in" with them.

Motivational output may also be classified as motoric or ideational. Children of all ages, but especially the preschool child, express their wants by primarily physical movements. They touch, reach, and grab for what they want, and even their verbalizations are often accompanied by a great deal of motor activity. Although this may be intended to fulfill the need, there is often a great deal of excess or nonfunctional motor activity accompanying the demands. The child almost seems to experience the need through the motor arousal and release. As the child learns to delay need-gratifications, this excess motor activity may increase temporarily, but subsides as the child learns ideational expression.

As has been discussed in the earlier chapters of this book and will be mentioned in more detail in Chapters 14 and 15, *the development of the ability to withhold gratification of needs and to control motoric release, taken together, is a keystone to all ego development*. It is the basis of abstract thinking, of affective internalization, of the comprehension of social behavior and the ability to meet social norms in nearly all major cultures. Most of all, it is the basis for the formation of both the social and personal sense of identity. Only when a child begins to conceive of need-gratification as an idea rather than simply as a motor reaction is he able to begin to form other concepts and abstractions. Only when he can begin to contain and delay the need can he begin to contain and channel his affects. Both of these developments are necessary

for effective social functioning, and both are necessary for the child to experience himself as an independently functioning person.

Since the ability to delay and conceptualize need-gratification is so important to all of ego development, attention to the data bearing on this question is usually a focal point in any assessment. As is the case with other aspects of ego development, no special technique has been designed specifically to sample this ability. Rather, evidence concerning the input and output of need-gratification is present in nearly all clinical procedures and tests. Indeed, it would be difficult to construct a technique just for this purpose, since conative functioning so pervades the child's behavior. It is thus necessary to focus on the need-gratification aspects of all the data collected about the child's functioning.

These techniques also do not distinguish between input and output. This distinction can only be made by looking very carefully at the child's behavior and responses. As has been mentioned several times throughout this book, the distinction between perception and response is often very difficult. This distinction is somewhat easier to make once the child is able to conceptualize at least some of his needs—and can verbally express such concepts. Direct observation of the preschool child yields data primarily about the expression of output of needs. During these preschool years, the input of motivation is so much a part of the parent-child relationship that assessment necessarily turns to techniques which sample parental attitudes and behavior as well as the child's development per se.

Data concerning the manner in which the child experiences and expresses his needs may be gathered by examining concretely the kinds of skills the child is developing for need-gratification. The level of development of these skills is in itself one indicator of conative development. However, in assessing input and output of motivations, the main aspect with which the assessor needs to be concerned is not the skill itself, but the ways the child is experiencing and expressing these motivations. By beginning with the concrete aspect of skill development, it is often possible to expand the interview with the parent or even with the child and discuss how the skill is being taught and learned.

Doll's Vineland Social Maturity Scale (1947) was one of the earliest and most notable attempts to assess the "self-help" skills during infancy and latency. It focuses attention on the need to investigate how well the infant is learning to do things for himself. It can form the basis for a more extensive interview with the mother about these behaviors and for more detailed observation of the child. This self-help development is, of course, dependent upon and intercorrelated with his development of motor skills. His motivation for the learning of these motor skills is, in turn, the desire for independent need-gratification. In the interview with the mother, the psychologist should investigate the degree to which this motivation is fostered. How much does the mother encourage or even tolerate the child's efforts to help himself? To what degree does the mother wait on him and to what degree does she push him to do things for himself? Is she made anxious by his failures? Is she easily pressured by his demands that she satisfy his every need? Does she attempt to teach him how to answer his own needs or does she find it easier just to go ahead and do things for him since he seems so helpless and takes so long to feed himself, or dawdles over dressing himself?

For example, many mothers take what seems the easy way out in toilet training by conditioning the child through "establishing regular habits," that is, putting him on the potty at regular intervals. Such a routine is admittedly very helpful in the beginning of toilet training, but in the long run the child has to learn to go to the toilet on his own when he needs to. Despite any conditioning, a child is liable to have little "accidents" in between the potty sessions. The average mother then quite appropriately loses patience, scolds the child, insisting that he make efforts on his own to control his body eliminations. Her anger becomes the reinforcing agent for the child's independent action. It is possible, of course, with the utmost patience and suppression of anger to toilet train the child entirely on routine conditioning. It is not uncommon to hear mothers of emotionally disturbed children boast that the child "gave me absolutely no trouble" when he was toilet trained, describing such a pure conditioning. However, such children frequently have difficulty in learning to satisfy their needs independently. Moreover, they also learn that anger has to be suppressed as much as possible.

Again, toilet training is only a prototype of the mother-child relationship in the training of self-help. The assessor should explore other types of training and the mother's methods and attitudes. Does she insist the two year old attempt to feed himself, using a spoon, and reward him for his attempts, even if he is sloppy? Does she foster his curiosity by providing the opportunity for him to explore or attempting to answer his questions, rather than put everything out of his reach and shushing him when he interrupts her activities? Does she button his buttons and tie his shoes for him rather than attempt to teach him these skills, even though it takes more trouble and even involves some fuss?

As might be expected, most mothers would maintain that they do make efforts to teach the child these skills. Thus, direct questioning of the mother often results in denial of any failure or restrictions on her part and an insistence that there is something wrong with the child since he is not learning. More information is gained if the interviewer inquires in a neutral tone about the efforts the mother has made and the conditions under which self-help was learned or not learned. Very often, when the kindergarten child is retarded in the development of self-help skills, when he passively waits for others to take care of his needs and seems helpless, the mother appears physically or emotionally unable to make the efforts to teach the child to care for himself. Another common situation is the working mother who has to leave the training of the child to a baby-sitter or to a grandmother who "spoils" the child by waiting on him, and does not tolerate his motoric activities. When there are no such extenuating circumstances, the psychologist should explore further to see if the mother has needs of her own to overprotect the child or is herself a passive, helpless person, relatively incapable of making the effort to train the child. The handicapped child, in particular, needs extended and intensive training toward self-help, and there is much more temptation to wait on the blind or crippled or intellectually retarded child, thus inadvertently reinforcing his helplessness.

Such self-help training extends, of course, beyond the simple motor skills needed for eating, dressing, keeping clean, and avoiding physical hazards. Even before the infant starts kindergarten, he develops needs for social affiliation. By the time he has learned to walk and talk, his mother is also weaning him from her side, so that she is not his constant companion. If he hangs at her skirts, she begins to brush him away and return to other duties. He has to learn to occupy himself, with only an occasional glance and word from her. If he has older sibs, he may seek companionship from them and join in their achievements and play. Mother may seek out other toddlers for companions for him. Nursery schools were invented for this purpose (not only in our culture, but also in primitive cultures). It is the credo of the nursery school and kindergarten that they are not just to baby-sit and entertain the infant, but rather are to provide a "head-start," an opportunity for activity, for socialization, and for achievement. They are aimed at creating independent goal-achievement, even though they do not always obtain this ideal. In contrast, one of the untoward side effects of television is that it is too often used as a passive baby-sitter, discouraging activity, curiosity, and socialization.

In assessing the development of the preschool child, the psychologist should collect data about the child's opportunities for independent acquisition of his affiliative and achievement needs. Again, subtle interviewing of the mother is necessary. If the child has not had these opportunities, she may blame the neighborhood or kindergarten. However, one must listen carefully to her complaints to understand the extent to which her own attitudes may enter into the restriction of the child's opportunities in this regard. Is she reluctant to separate from the child to permit him to go to nursery school? Does she have undue fears of his health and welfare? Is she too passive to make the effort? Would it threaten her ego for someone else to care for and be close to her "baby?"

The separation of the infant from the family in the quest of these social drives is important not only because these needs must be gratified, but also because in satisfying these social needs the child begins to develop ideational modes of gratification. Although these secondary needs probably have their basis in physical needs, they become autonomous and do not require physical, motoric gratifications. Thus, the need itself becomes in the long run ideational. Being affiliative for example, is a concept, not a physical hunger. Therefore, attempts to gratify such social needs force the child to begin to conceptualize. He begins to discover that he cannot answer all of his needs purely by motoric responses. Instead, he has to develop concepts of human interaction and affect. The emergence of conceptualization as a mode or aspect of need-gratification is evidenced in many aspects of the preschool child's behavior. His play, for example, although still primarily motor activity, begins to include acting out fantasies, practicing social interactions, and imitating adult need-gratification modes. He still spends many hours just riding his tricycle up and down, or swinging, manipulating, and hitting things. But more and more he engages in games of "pretend," usually with slightly older children. The five year old begins to play house, school, store, or war, practicing concepts of human interrelationships. Through this play, he begins to imagine how his social needs may be gratified.

As was noted in the introductory chapters, the development of ideational modes of need-gratification has as its prototype the child's development of the ability to delay and conceptualize his sexual drives, in what Freud labeled the Oedipal conflict. Whether one accepts the hypotheses of this psychoanalytic concept, most observers do agree that the overall bond with the mother does have to be relaxed enough by the time the child leaves the home to enter school to permit the child to seek gratification of his needs for affiliation outside the family circle. Whatever erotic component there is in the gratification of social needs has to be repressed at this time, as society forbids him to attempt to satisfy these needs with other children— even if it were possible. The child has to learn how to get along with others outside of his family before he can enter into the more complicated social world of sexuality. Thus, in assessment it is important to gather data about the child's affective interrelationships with his parents as evidence of his development of the ability to find social gratifications on his own. Has he learned to conceive of his parents as individuals rather than merely as extensions of himself? Is he still altogether mama's boy at seven—or is she exclusively "daddy's little girl?" Has the child broken away from this bond sufficiently to allow him to seek gratifications elsewhere? Although no little evidence concerning this development of internalized, conceptualized gratification can be obtained from indirect clues supplied by the mother or father in parent interviews, it is at about age six that the process of internalization and ideational need-gratification is revealed in the child's associative responses. On the Rorschach, for example, prior to age six, children tend to respond primarily if not exclusively with vague form or nearly pure color reactions. The first M responses appear at about age six or even slightly later. This ability to delay kinesthetic action and to project associatively heralds the appearance of the development of ideational need-gratification. As Ames, et al (1952) point out, this step in ideational modes is presaged at age five by the appearance in five year olds' Rorschach responses of the nonhuman, m response.

This development is dramatically evidenced in the change in childrens' TAT stories. Prior to age six, children generally merely describe the card, with occasional mention of affects but little or nothing regarding the motives of the hero, and very little plot. At about age seven, the child is a little better able to answer the examiner's questions as to "why?" the hero did this or felt that way. The nine to ten year old voluntarily attributes motives to his hero in about half of his stories. Although the seven year old may have an outcome for his TAT fantasy, it is likely to be farfetched and unrelated to the plot. He cannot tell how the hero finally achieves. The 10 to 11 year old can tell you that the boy in Card 1 becomes a "great violinist" because he practices hard, etc.

Preoccupation with concepts of need-gratification is the hallmark of adolescence. The daydreaming Hamlet is perhaps an overdrawn stereotype, but even the most philistine "surfer" does not entirely escape the idealism of youth. Even in their seeming antithetical attitude toward values and ideals, such adolescents reveal their concern. More than at any point in childhood, indeed in their whole lives, they are concerned with how and when needs are gratified. They outdo their six-year-old sibs in finicky food habits. They can only dress in the fad of the moment, speak certain words, and answer their need for excitement with certain thrills. The approaching possibility of gratifying long repressed sexual drives now haunts their every thought and deed, intermixed with aggressively charged achievement needs. Yet, the

morals and values surrounding need-gratification becomes almost obsessive concerns.

Estimation of the normal development of such ideational need-gratification during adolescence is often difficult. At moments when an adolescent is struggling with some specific problem, his ideational confusion and his erratic behavior may be almost indistinguishable from what would be unhesitatingly labeled "schizophrenia" in an adult. It was not purely by accident that Kraepelin originally called schizophrenia "dementia praecox," the dementia of the young. At other moments, however, the adolescent may evince a blasé disregard for ethics or, like a small child, demand gratification immediately. Behavioral reports from angry, disappointed, or astonished parents are likely to be quite unreliable. The adolescent may report only his "crazy" thoughts or erratic behavior and try to argue that they are normal and sane. His Rorschach is apt to contain some mildly contaminated responses, reflecting these obsessions, and some of his TAT stories may be "way out."

What needs to be determined is the extent to which such adolescent extremes of ideationalization actually deter the development of other functioning. Thus, in interviewing the adolescent and his parents, the assessor should divert them from merely reciting "crazy" ideas and behavior and to inquire about his other functioning. For example, is he so obsessed with this particular need-gratification problem that he cannot eat or sleep? Is he suffering from some somatic disturbances? Even if he is neglecting his schoolwork, is he actually not absorbing what the teacher says? Does he have moments when he does behave "sanely?" In connection with this line of inquiry, the psychologist should take a look at the adolescent's responses to relatively neutral problem-solving tasks, such as on the Wechsler. Only if this ideational concern has spread across several areas of the adolescent's functioning can one begin to think in terms of schizophrenia.

Second, one should inquire about the history of such behavior. Again, unless there is a history of "prodromal" signs of a prepubescent thought process disturbance, one should be extremely cautious about applying such socially pejorative labels as schizophrenia. Although psychiatry is now beginning to distinguish more definitively between the long-term ego deterioration called schizophrenia and what are now labeled "adolescent behavior disorders," in this writer's opinion too many adolescents are still labeled schizophrenic purely on the basis of temporary need-gratification confusions. In fact, it is quite possible that this distinction is the basis for the differentiation of the "process versus reactive" schizophrenia. Many of these adolescents who seem to have a sudden onset of schizophrenia may actually be experiencing a need-gratification crisis.

The following case may serve to illustrate some of the problems that arise in the development of need-gratification input and output and how they are assessed.

CASE 30

Milton G., age ten, was referred to the clinic by the school for assessment of his educational needs. For the past three years he had been placed in special classes for the "educationally handicapped," but the teacher and the school psychologist questioned this placement and requested further clinical evaluation. His mother also was dissatisfied with his educational progress, but rather than questioning his need for special classes, was insistent that he needed even more individual instruction. Further inquiry regarding the referral revealed that although Milton had not progressed satisfactorily in the first two years in regular classes, the school authorities would not have placed him in this special class but for the insistence of his mother. She took the initiative and informed the school that Milton was a "premature" baby who had been diagnosed as "cerebral palsy" at age three. The school records showed further that at the usual age five years, eight months, on finishing kindergarten Milton did not seem ready to enter the first grade. His score on a "reading readiness" test was below the level which predicts success in reading at the first-grade level. His kindergarten teacher noted that Milton "was very demanding of my time and attention," was "possessive of playthings," "did not socialize well," "had crying tantrums when disciplined or when other children frustrated his activities." Nevertheless, Mrs. G insisted that Milton be placed in the first grade and hinted that she regarded the kindergarten teacher as prejudiced against Milton. The first and second grade teachers recorded very similar notes about Milton. He "insisted on pursuing his own interests, disregarding what the class

was engaged in and disrupting others"; "he brought toys to class and was preoccupied with his own play." His word recognition was satisfactory, but his reading comprehension was inadequate. He seemed to be learning to add and subtract by rote memory; he memorized the sum of 5 and 6, but if these numbers were reversed, he considered it a new problem and had to learn it all over again. Similarly, he could successfully memorize a list of words for spelling but could not even guess at the spelling of a new word even though he could spell another with the same phonetic base.

Mrs. G boasted of how smart Milton appeared to be to her, citing as an example that during Sunday afternoon excursions, she and her husband would make a game of drilling Milton on his arithmetic and spelling, helping him to memorize problems and words. However, at school Milton was a resistant pupil, constantly complaining that the work was too hard and that the teacher demanded too much. When the school psychologist attempted to administer the Wechsler Scale for Children to Milton, Milton was similarly resistant and querulous. He needed continuous encouragement and kept expecting to be prompted. "I haven't had that yet," he would complain. "Milton refuses to try to think on his own," remarked the school psychologist. Despite this resistance, Milton achieved an overall score within the "normal" range: IQ 94. Both his verbal and performance IQ scores were within a few points of this total. He made above average scores on subtests involving chiefly recognition of and memory for concrete details (Information, Digit Span, Digit Symbol, and Picture Completion), and his vocabulary was average for his age. However, he had considerable difficulty on any test involving abstract reasoning and conceptualization.

On initial contact at the clinic, Milton was very tense and apprehensive. Before he entered the psychologist's office, he was reassuring the psychologist of his success at school. Talking more about school, he first boasted that he was a "lot smarter than those dummies" in this special class and that he would like to be put in regular classes. At the same time, he complained of how hard the work was and how tough his teacher made things and how the children in his neighborhood who were in regular classes teased him and called him a "dummy" and a "spaz." He reluctantly agreed to show the psychologist how he did think things out, but when the WISC materials were brought out, he cried, "Oh no! Not *that!*" His behavior during this administration of the WISC was similar to that previously reported by the school psychologist, and his responses and scores were practically identical. He copied the Bender figures very slowly and meticulously, but quite accurately. After much complaint and resistance, he finally dashed off a scribbly drawing of a man who, he remarked, looked "scared and mad." Each Rorschach card looked harder than the last one to him, but he consented to "make a guess" and then demanded that the examiner affirm his response or tell him what it really was. His responses were relatively accurate as to form but did tend to be very simple, without much detail. Of his 13 responses, ten were simple form, two were primarily determined by the bright color, and one by achromatic color. There were no movement responses of any kind.

Yet, Milton did not lack a fantasy life, and his fantasy on the CAT, in contrast to the Rorschach, was full of "movement." He told fairly long and elaborate stories in which the characters did such and such and then they did something else. The actions of these characters did not follow one upon the other in any logical fashion, and it was difficult to understand why they were doing these things. Milton ignored the examiner's questions about the characters' motivation. For example, to Picture 1: "The babies are eating their dinner. The mother gave them their dinner. She brings them more dinner. Then they go out and play. Some other kids come over and play. He [pointing to one of the babies] is crying. Then they go out to play. (Why is he crying?) When they get through playing they have some more dinner. Then they go to sleep. Their father comes home and brings them a present. That's all. (What do they play?) They're asleep now." To Picture 6: "He's asleep and he wakes up. There's nobody there. He eats breakfast and then he runs away from home. (How come?) He finds a million dollars and he's very rich now. He buys two bicycles [Milton describes the bicycles at length]. Then he goes out to play. (What does his parents think?) They go in a big fight and they're dead now. (How come?) A big gorilla came along and killed them dead." All in all, Milton's fantasies

suggested that although he experienced considerable infantile hunger for love, he had little or no idea how to gratify this need. Similarly, his need for aggressive activity was plain but he had no concept of how to achieve this need. He often felt frustrated and very angry, but these feelings seemed disconnected, random, and generalized. As Milton saw it, things just happened without rhyme or reason.

Although Milton's perceptual-motor functioning seemed intact, there was the possibility that his inability to conceptualize (a fundamental part of his cognitive as well as of his conative functioning) might be due to some general central nervous system defect. Strangely, Mrs. G was somewhat resistant to the clinic's recommendation for neurological assessment. In her mind, the cause of Milton's retarded development was already established as brain damage, and she was reluctant to question it. Yet, she yielded to the psychiatrist's insistence. When the neurologist reported, after extensive examination, that he could find no indications of CNS disturbance, or even of cerebral palsy symptoms, Mrs. G remained unconvinced. However, the point was not argued with her. While she remained fixed in her opinion, she did continue to bring Milton in for psychotherapy and to discuss with the social worker her behavior and attitudes toward Milton and the interactions within the family.

Using the results of the assessment, the treatment was aimed at (1) helping Mrs. G to see how she infantilized Milton, and why, and urging her to adopt tactics designed to promote his independent need-gratification and (2) exploring with Milton the possibilities of conceiving ways for such independent gratification. Both in his play and conversation, Milton soon began expressing considerable dissatisfaction and anger over his lack of gratifications and with his interpersonal relationships both with his peers and at home. He became angry with the therapist's questions regarding his role in gaining these satisfactions, derisively labeling him "Dr. Why." As Mrs. G began refusing to wait on Milton and to insist that he do things for himself, Milton was at first even more resistant and angry but admitted he was secretly glad to find he could and wanted to do things on his own. Without parental help, his schoolwork improved markedly within a year and the following year he was placed in a regular class, only a half year behind his age level where he continued to perform successfully. He remained somewhat isolated socially from his peers until he entered junior high school two years later. The psychotherapy was discontinued when he was graduated from elementary school, but a follow-up interview was conducted two years later when Milton was 13 and in the eighth grade. At that time, he was making average grades at school, seemed to have several close friends, and to be accepted by his peers. A reassessment showed that his IQ had jumped 16 points to an IQ of 110. His responses to the Rorschach and TAT at this time revealed much more ideational conceptualization of need-gratification. Mrs. G, a very bright woman who had quit college after two years to get married, had now returned to college to get her teacher's credential. She remarked, "I used to really hate Milton and all the problems and care he required. None of my needs seemed satisfied, but I thought I had to do my duty and I felt so guilty hating him. Now I see I did have some real needs, and that caring for children can be fun, if you see how they can grow up. I'm proud of him now, and proud of myself."

C. FOCUS AND DIFFERENTIATION

The ability to differentiate one need from another and to focus on the satisfaction of one need at a time develops slowly over the years of childhood. The neonate appears to experience all needs as a generalized tension, and it is difficult initially to discover the sources of this tension. However, it does not take most mothers very long to distinguish from the baby's cries and other behavior whether he is hungry, restless, in pain, or in need of comforting. Even before the child himself can speak, he usually is able to make simple distinctions between his physiological wants. He can respond to questions such as, "You want something to eat?" or "You want to go potty?" By age three, he should be able to verbalize the form of need-gratifications to these wants, as witness the Stanford-Binet item at this age level, "What do you do when you are thirsty?" Even so, when these needs arise, it is sometimes difficult for even the average child to think of anything else. The need becomes generalized, affecting much of his behavior. For example, Sanford (1936) found in one of his early studies on the TAT that schoolchildren gave many more responses and themes concerning eating and food if the test were administered just prior to lunch. Such a generalization of a need may occur even more persistently if the child continuously or even periodically experiences deprivations. For example, a three year old who had been placed on a very restricted diet because of her diabetes was always preoccupied with food. She named her stuffed animal "Candy" and was forever biting on it. She startled both the children and the teacher at nursery school when she greeted them by licking their hands, and later became quite a problem when she began biting others.

CASE 31

Norman, age three, in the same nursery class, had just completed a prolonged battle with his mother over bowel control. However, he had learned his lesson well and was very concerned about cleanliness. As far as Norman was concerned, getting dirty was a capital crime, to the point that he was almost immobilized. Keeping immaculate made it difficult for Norman to eat and, even though he was sorely tempted, he could not bring himself to participate in the admittedly sloppy afternoon snack. In the play yard, he finally latched onto one tricycle and kept riding back and forth carefully avoiding touching anything or anybody. He screamed with fear when the teacher invited him to join the others in the sandbox. Norman's impasse was finally broken when the teacher prevailed upon his mother to spend an afternoon at the school and suggested to her that she specifically give Norman permission to get dirty. Although Norman's mother at first was unconvinced, and not even quite in agreement of the necessity to do this, she agreed to attempt it. At first, Norman did not believe his mother when she encouraged him to abandon his tricycle and join the other children in the sandbox. What did convince him was when his teacher involved his mother in finger painting. When he saw his mother getting dirty, and even enjoying it, he began to believe her. Although his mother had feared that he might revert to his previously "messy" habits and even break his recently obtained bowel training, she was relieved to find that this did not occur. Moreover, Norman rapidly learned to distinguish getting "dirty" in play from defecating.

It is in these needs which entail avoiding or in the more abstract social needs that the child has the most difficulty in differentiating motives. Freud labeled the child's initial sexual drive, which is also experienced in terms of suppression, with the rather clumsy term "polymorphous perverse," by which he meant nonspecific and nonfocal. His detailed study and classification of the stages of the child's differentiation of the need for erotic stimulation and gratification is a classic model for the study of need-differentiation patterns. If there were similar studies of the child's differentiation of other needs, it might be much easier to investigate Freud's hypothesis that the differentiation of the sexual drive sets the pattern for other needs. The child's need for affiliation, for example, although probably closely allied to his sexual drive as Freud maintained, may not follow exactly the same pattern of development. It does seem true that the neonate will accept any mother for a brief period, thus making adoption quite feasible at an early age. However, it is not long before he distinguishes the affiliative bond with mother from other interpersonal relationships. Although this affiliative bond is reinforced by feeding and comforting, most observers of infant behavior agree that the child seems to need to have these wants satisfied by one person consistently. A series of mothers rather than one affiliation often appears to result in difficulties in forming meaningful relationships later in life.

Weaning away from this bond and learning that affiliative needs can be met by someone other than the mother occur in very much the same way as Freud describes the weaning from oral satisfaction of erotic needs. The child has to learn to delay satisfaction of affiliative associations, to wait till mother is available or till father comes home, or a peer or sib is available. Learning to endure even brief moments of loneliness is one of the most painful lessons of childhood. As with his sexual drive, satisfaction on the ideational or fantasy level soon plays a major role. Indeed, it is during moments of social isolation and loneliness that the child experiences fantasy most vividly. He creates imaginary playmates with whom he plays imaginary games. The Oedipus complex of his affiliative drive involves not so much the parent of the opposite sex as his sibs, who are his rivals for the affiliative bond with the parents. This process might be better labeled the "Cain complex." By murdering the hated sibling rival in fantasy, and experiencing the guilt, the child is better able to be his "brother's keeper." For example, Mike, age five, carried about an empty gunny sack which he explained was to "pick up the pieces" just in case his three-year-old sister Nellie was "run over." However, he never attacked her and was even quite protective of her when other children pushed her around. He was even disturbed when she was punished by his parents. An only child appears to develop more slowly in this respect and to have more difficulty in making affiliative discriminations than children who have sibs.

As may be gathered from the above discussion, the ability to discriminate need-gratification requires not only differentiation of needs per se, but also of potential gratifications. The child learns what is edible, who will give love, who reciprocates in his affiliative needs, whom he can compete with in his drives for achievement, etc. Early in infancy, the child is surprisingly flexible about the exact form of need-gratifications. Most infants will eat almost anything, go to sleep anywhere and even under conditions which would preclude sleep for older children or adults; it makes little difference to them where they go "potty"; and they can be comforted by any adult. However, this stage evaporates very soon, and at least by the beginning of the third year of life, the child requests specific foods and rejects others, is comfortable only in his own crib, has to have his own potty and his own mother to comfort him. Such rigid limitation is, in this writer's opinion, associated with the fact that need-gratification during infancy is chiefly motoric, and the association between need and gratification is learned principally through simple conditioning. Although this conditioning can be and usually is generalized, it is when the child is able to conceptualize need-gratifications that he also becomes able to make discriminative choices. For example, the infant soon learns that specific foods not only satisfy but are particularly enjoyable and are associated with pleasurable eating. Other foods that may not be as tasty to the child are rejected as not satisfying the hunger—very often because they are also associated with unpleasant eating circumstances.

For example, one mother presented her rather pear-shaped, flaccid ten-month-old baby to the pediatrician in a Well-Baby-Clinic, complaining that the baby had troubles sitting up and made little effort to crawl or pull herself erect. Noting the baby's obesity, the pediatrician began inquiring about the baby's diet and was horrified to learn that she was fed largely carbohydrates. The doctor began advising the mother to add strained vegetables and meats to the baby's diet, but noticed the look of disgust on the mother's face. Further questioning revealed that when the mother had tried feeding "those things" to the baby, the child had regurgitated. Moreover, it was evident that the mother "could not stand the sight" of these strained baby foods and disliked vegetables in any form. Her husband too was a "meat-and-potatoes" man. When the mother first came into the examining room, it appeared as if she were pregnant. Later, it was discovered she was merely obese, like the baby, and equally listless.

In the assessment of this ability to discriminate needs and their gratification, data may be obtained from a variety of sources and techniques. For example, in the interviews with the child and also with the mother, the assessor should inquire about likes and dislikes in need-gratifications. One such like or dislike might be explored in some detail: how did it develop? What are the respondent's own associations concerning this particular need discrimination? What does the mother recall about Johnny's food finickiness and his distaste for vegetables, for example? How does the child recall it and what associations does he bring up? Sometimes such questions may seem very far removed from the immediate complaint, but nevertheless be quite revealing about motivational differentiation. For example, one mother had been very concerned about the company her 13-year-old girl was keeping and a battle ensued which reached a climax when the girl ran away from home for the weekend. The interviews with the mother revealed that she had never trusted the child to make decisions about need-gratifications in choice of food, clothes, or recreation, that she had long worried about the health and welfare of the child in an overprotective fashion. Consequently, the child did not know how to make discriminations on her own. The girl was very resentful that her mother tried to intervene in her choice of friends, but oddly enough did not seem even aware of the degree to which her mother had made decisions for her about

need-gratification choices. She reported in a puzzled childlike tone that she had not eaten for the two days she had been away; although she had money to buy food, she had been unable to select from a menu at a restaurant and had left in embarrassment.

Although the inability to make discriminative independent choices about gratifications is in itself a sign of immaturity, a child who confuses one need with another usually is demonstrating an extensive ego disturbance. Most often such a confusion of needs begins with the acceptance of the gratification of one need for the lack of satisfaction of another. For example, an obese child may be found to be substituting food for affection or for sex. Or, as was illustrated in Case 29, Sandy tried to substitute sexual behavior for parental affection. However, what may begin as a temporary or causal substitution often becomes such an autonomous habit pattern that, in the child's mind, one need is no longer merely substituted for the other, but they are actually equated. One depressed and overweight nine-year-old girl denied that she was substituting food for affection. "Chicken soup *is* love!" she declared solemnly.

D. INTERFERENCES IN CONATIVE DEVELOPMENT

Many of the factors that often impede the normal developmental process of the attainment of independent skills for need-gratification and of the internalization and channeling of drives and impulses, have already been discussed in Chapter 5, and in the previous sections of this chapter. The anxiety and other affective factors accompanying conflicts over need-gratification were also discussed in Chapter 13. In the following section of this chapter and in Chapter 15, the role played by social taboos and compunctions and their internalization into personal guilt will be given further consideration as a major factor in conative development, both as a normal developmental process of the attain-principal deterrent to need-gratification skills. At this point, what is most important to consider are the manifestations of these interferences in the child's everyday behavior and in the samples of his behavior which may be gained from administration of psychological techniques. In general, these manifestations may be thought of as taking three major forms: (a) *hypotrophic,* (b) *hypertrophic,* and (c) *compensatory.*

a. Hypotrophic Conative Development

Some aspects of a child's conative development may lag while others progress normally or even quickly. One of the most common patterns of behavior, which indicates an interference in conative development, is what might be called "hypotrophic," that is, an overall retardation of either impulse control and need-gratification skills, or both. Sometimes the outward manifestation of such hypotrophic conative development takes the form of purely "impulsive" behavior, that is, the child seems to have no control over his impulses, makes continuous demands, and grabs what he wants. Since such children have fair skills in maneuvering the environment into answering their needs, they may seem to have developed need-gratification skills. However, such a skill in maneuvering or forcing others to meet one's needs is not the same as development of skills for *independent* need-gratification. Very often such a combination of a lack of impulse control along with the development of skills at demanding and exorting need-satisfactions from others is associated with a history of severe neglect of the child by his parents, both in need-gratification and in the teaching of impulse controls. Such children "grow like Topsy" as described in Stowe's *Uncle Tom's Cabin.* No one tells them what to do, but neither is anyone particularly concerned with their needs, especially with those needs involving interpersonal care. The child is thus forced by circumstances to scrounge for his own satisfactions. Although these children are quite often very aggressive in seeking their own need-satisfactions, molesting and annoying those about them, they are often also quite depressed. As their efforts to supply their own gratifications become more futile, and as they meet with increasing repressive reactions from social authorities, they may have periods of massive and overwhelming depression. Although such a hypotrophic growth often appears in children of very socially deprived families, where very few physical or personal gratifications are available, it also can be present in any home where only perfunctory physical care is given the child and little or no attention is paid to his needs for affection or no attention paid to his impulse controls.

An equally frequent manifestation of such hypotrophic development appears in the seemingly passive and even well-behaved child who, in fact, is quite dependent upon the environment for control and channelization of his impulses. Not knowing what to do when there is no one there to guide him, his behavior becomes suddenly bizarre and out of place. Very often this lack of conative development appears when such a passive, compliant, and seemingly good child enters into one of the crisis points of childhood, such as separation from the parents upon entering kindergarten, the onset of puberty, or graduation from high school. Such children, when they leave the guidance of the overprotective and everfeeding mother, become terrors in the kindergarten and first-grade classrooms, much to the amazement of their parents. Teachers and other observers may call such a child "spoiled." The child makes immediate and constant demands for narcissistic supplies from the teacher and his peers. Similarly, the well-behaved but very dependent latency child, who has always made good grades and practiced his piano faithfully, may panic when he shifts from junior high to high school. He may become either so depressed as to be unable to attend school or plunge suddenly into teenage social and sexual activities in haphazard form, seeking the same emotional support and guidance from his peers which he has learned to obtain in previous years from his teachers and parents. Quite commonly such children experience considerable overt depression when they are left on their own to manage their need-gratifications. Such depression may be manifested outwardly in apathy, a sudden fall in grades, or adolescent restlessness. Disappointment, hurt, and anger may be themes on the TAT, and increased use of shading or achromatic color may appear in such a child's Rorschach responses. Strangely, such children may appear to be both severely repressed and impulse ridden. As long as their needs are gratified by others, they accept the repressive forces of an external super-ego and their impulse life is not outwardly manifested. However, such seemingly very well-behaved children may give Rorschach responses dominated by the animal movement category. They relate fantasies to the TAT which are replete with scenes of uncontrolled and immediate need-gratification or of guilt-less anger toward those who might attempt to frustrate such impulses. Such "spoiled" children do not develop independent need-gratification because their needs are constantly gratified by others. Nor do they independently control impulses because they are constantly bribed.

A most serious form of retardation of conative development occurs when the child shows repression of impulse life at all levels. As has been noted in previous chapters, such overall repression in a mild form is the hall-mark of the latency child. However, even in latency most normal children show some signs of the stirrings and waxing and wanings of impulse life in their play, intellectual curiosity, and in fantasies. When a child demonstrates little or no such evidence of even a latent impulse life, he is not pro-gressively developing means of handling and controlling his impulses but, instead, is quite stultified in his growth. Such a massive overall repression in the child immediately before and during the onset of puberty may well be the prodromal signs of a later ex-plosive emotional disturbance in adolescence. If such an overall repression continues for that length of time, there is the possibility that at least a very passive-aggressive char-acter structure if not a schizoid pattern may develop.

A history of such repression is often seen in the person with a "schizophrenic break" in the latter years of adolescence or of early adulthood. The manifestations of such over-all repression often seem benign in the his-tory; such children are often quite compulsive "grinds" at school, sometimes overachieving, worried about their schoolwork, and using it as an excuse for social isolation. Their parents and even teachers, far from being disturbed by the child's lack of socialization, often support his repression and in fact de-mand it. Unless these children become so depressed as to be physically ill, they may not be seen in psychological clinics, but their hypochondriasis is often treated by pedi-atricians. When they are referred for psy-chological assessment, their responses to projective techniques are often quite sterile, lacking in imagination, and void of signs of emotional life. Such a child frequently will compulsively strive for achievement on an intelligence test, but become quite stultified when faced with the Rorschach or TAT, and

be unable to do much more than describe a TAT card, apologizing profusely for his lack of imagination. The MMPI profiles of such adolescents are marked by the height of the K or repression scale, a general flatness of most of the other scales, with perhaps a slight rise in hypochondriasis or depression (both of which are usually lower among normal adolescents than among adults). A T-score of 65 or above on schizophrenia for such a child is not unusual. In contrast to the profile of the spoiled child, the PD and MA scales of such repressed children are usually low. Much like the impulse-ridden child, the repressed child suffers from de-privation of need-gratifications; it is because he has been given the hope that if he con-forms and achieves, he will win parental support and affection and he will be allowed full need-gratification. Children—and adults —who have severely and chronically repressed their impulses often have grandiose dreams of gluttonous revels or sexual orgies. When the parents remain cold and distant and the dreams of need-gratification fade, the re-pressed adolescent slumps into depression or schizophrenia.

b. Hypertrophic Conative Development

The opposite side of the coin is the child who shows hypertrophic development of need-gratification skills and impulse controls. Such a child may also show considerable academic success but, if so, he is also likely to be socially successful. He may also be quite adept in manipulating his environment, con-centrating his efforts on pleasing adults and wheedling things out of them or commandeer-ing his peers, while neglecting any actual achievement in the classroom or on the playground. For example, he organizes the ballgame but avoids going to bat. He charms the teacher and makes many promises, but acts surprised when demands for productivity are made upon him. He may be able to charm his way through elementary school, but finds his techniques of manipulating teachers are ineffective when he is in junior high school with many different teachers to please. Often such a child is quite able to get what he wants even on his own. Mothers of such children will report that the child learned to feed and care for himself at an early age. The usual complaint against such a child is that he is exceedingly "willfull." However, such hypertrophic development of need-gratification skills often proves to be a defensive measure of the child. Such rapid growth is fostered when the child feels his needs will not be met unless he makes immediate efforts to gratify them himself, or to maneuver other people into meeting his needs. This maneuvering of the hypertrophic child is much more subtle than the screaming, demanding negativism of the impulse-ridden child.

Among the children who manifest such precocious development are those who face inadequate or ill parents or the absence of parents. For example, such behavior may be manifested by children of psychotic parents who are unable to provide for the child's needs and who force the child to handle a great deal of reality on his own, including the reality of the parents' confusion. Although some children are made psychotic by their psychotic parents, this reaction of becoming precociously able to manage their own need-gratifications is also a common phenomenon. Similarly, although children in orphanages or other institutions may remain quite infantile and even retarded, it is not unusual to find an orphan who develops very rapidly and becomes quite independently skilled in the gratification of his own needs, albeit in a "psychopathic" fashion. Such children, however, often manifest signs of being quite untrusting of others. Although they may learn painfully not to go afoul of the law, they may remain cynically aloof from society. In the long run, such children run into trouble because their dependency needs are never really affectively met. Despite their ultra-independence, they inadvertently and circuitously set up situations wherein they may test out whether they can depend on others. Basically they feel very cheated and often plot a very generalized revenge against the world which they feel has deprived them. The Rorschach protocols of such children often are characterized by a predominance of human movement responses, but they are very cautious and restricted when stimulated by the color of the inkblots. Their confusion and blocking increase when stimulated by the texture of the blot. This latter inability to handle texture is one manifestation of their ambivalence over need-gratification and dependency. In TAT stories, such children emphasize the hero's ability to meet his own needs, but scenes of revenge against cheaters or robbers are also prevalent.

Although this syndrome is more commonly seen in the clinic among adolescents or latency children, such precocity is also occasionally a defensive measure in the late infancy period.

CASE 32

Andy's paranoid mother had the delusion that he was not her child. He was a very bright five year old who showed every sign of rapidly developing methods to defend himself and answer his own needs. In responding to Schniedman's MAPS tests, this little boy utilized the Superman figure in every one of his little plays. Superman became superego, controlling the evil characters, including naked, seductive, and confusing mother figures. Superman aided a giving and rewarding paternal figure, but this father was often removed from the stage and Superman had to protect the child. However, Andy's need for further emotional support in his confused world was also manifest by his use of another figure who assisted Superman whom he called the "doctor" who seemed to understand where the child had pain. Andy was quite aware that his mother was delusional. He was no little depressed, since his sense of identity was affected by her delusion, but he appeared to be maintaining his own hold on reality by this precocious development of controls over his own impulses, and of need-gratification skills.

c. Compensatory Conative Development

A third general pattern of disturbance in conative development may be labeled compensatory. Rather than a simple hypotrophic absence or repression of need-gratification skills and impulses, the child may seem to neglect the gratification of some needs and hypertrophically develop skills and interests in the satisfaction of others. Such compensatory behavior may be seen in physically disabled children who become superior in their intellectual achievement. In a sense, the child who concentrates on the "good boy" or "good girl" role and represses impulses to obtain social rewards may also be thought of as compensating. However, such children often do not receive much reward for their good behavior and are constantly pressured for an increasing amount of achievement and made to feel guilty about any manifestation of their impulses. More subtle forms of compensation may be commonly observed in what might be labeled the "cuteness" and the "naughtiness" syndromes.

Children who have the good fortune to be physically attractive and who are rewarded for being socially "cute" may develop and foster these socially rewarding attributes which do gain them, at least temporarily, the need-gratifications they seek. The beautiful little girl or handsome boy may unconsciously depend on good looks, expecting others to reward them for being attractive. They learn that parents, teachers, and even peers may not demand as much of them in the way of impulse control or deny them need-gratification. Such children may avoid intellectual or physical competition with other children and compete only in the area of "looks." They are often referred to the clinic at about junior high school age when their scholastic achievement is not up to par and when they begin to make extra efforts to be ostentatious in their dress and grooming. Although actually physically attractive, in their emphasis on their body image, such children begin to develop doubts of this image if only because they place so much emphasis on it.

In what might be called the "naughtiness" syndrome, the child misbehaves just enough to get attention without actually getting himself into trouble. He plays the clown in the classroom, often getting others into trouble as well. His parents, although sometimes disturbed and angry at his mischievousness, may privately describe his naughtiness as "cute." It often turns out that they tolerate or even encourage such behavior, vicariously enjoying the child's antics and even boasting that he does things which they would not have dared to do. Such parents may complain bitterly about how much more "freedom" children of this generation are allowed in contrast to their own childhood, but often they do little to control the child. By being "naughty," the child attracts the attention of the parents, inveigles them into rewarding him in order to avoid further naughtiness, and then reneges on his promise, in a continuous cycle of defrauding his parents. This constant maneuvering through "naughtiness" eventually becomes a need-gratification skill itself and, in the long run, compensates for the lack of development of other need-gratification skills.

Moreover, neither the "cute" nor the "naughty" child actually expresses his own impulses, but instead represses some of his basic needs. For example, the very pretty adolescent girl who has always depended upon being pretty may, in fact, repress her sexual needs and be quite uncomfortable when she finds that boys are sexually attracted to her. Similarly, the naughty child, although seemingly aggressive, may actually be quite dependent and passive and never develop ways of handling his needs to be aggressive and independent.

Such disproportionate or compensatory conative development is evidenced on techniques such as the Edwards Personal Preference Schedule or the TAT (both of which use Murray's Need-Press System). For example, a 15-year-old boy who obtains a high N Achievement and N Endurance may be compensating if, at the same time, his needs for Succorance or Heterosexuality and Aggression are abnormally low or absent. A similar though obverse pattern is also quite common in adolescence. For example, many teenage girls overemphasize romanticism and utilize their newfound sexuality in quite a compensatory fashion to avoid independent achievement while disclaiming adult values on Order or Endurance. For example, one 15-year-old girl, although of above average intelligence, was repeating the ninth grade and it appeared that she might fail again; she told the following story to Card 2 of the TAT:

"The mother is the boss. She is making the boy work hard and has told the girl that she must go to school. The girl hates her mother for making her brother work and is thinking of running off with her boyfriend to get married. She fakes out her mother by carrying the books but she meets her boyfriend and they go off to the city. (Examiner asks if there is no father in the story. The storyteller laughs.) I guess I just forgot him."

And to Card 8 GF: "She's supposed to be studying but she's daydreaming about her boyfriend. [Pause] I can't think of much more. (What might she be daydreaming about?) I don't really know; I guess maybe he's a pretty groovy guy; she's all hot for him. (How does the heroine feel about her studies?) Maybe she thinks they're pretty feeble. She doesn't look very smart, maybe she's kind of dumb."

E. COPING MECHANISMS IN CONATIVE FUNCTIONING

As has been amply demonstrated throughout this chapter, it is almost impossible to discuss any aspect of conative development without at the same time discussing the ways in which a child copes with his impulses and becomes skilled at meeting his needs. In fact, what has been discussed as modes, input and output, and differentiation all may be viewed as various ways of coping conatively. Nor is it possible to discuss interferences in conative development without mentioning coping; the three types of interference patterns mentioned are in effect coping patterns, albeit neurotic and, in the long run, ineffective. The purpose of this section is to look at the underlying attitudinal "set" with which the child approaches coping with his drives. In so doing, it is hoped the interrelationships between the various patterns of coping already discussed above may be more clearly defined and delimited.

Although a theoretical formulation of the interrelationships between various coping mechanisms is beyond the scope of this book, a rough schematic model may be helpful, purely for heuristic purposes. Clinical experience suggests that coping involves at least two major attitudinal dimensions, which in the diagram of this schema (see Figure 8) form the axes of a circle. The horizontal axis describes the amount of energy or activity which the child deems necessary to attain need-gratification. This dimension may best be understood by applying the commonly used terms "passive" and "aggressive" to the extremes. The extremely passive child waits for others to satisfy his needs and even to stimulate his drives. The extremely "aggressive"* child seeks out his own need-gratifications without waiting for others, and imposes his impulses and drives on the world about him whether or not he is stimulated by his environment.

The vertical axis of this diagram is intended to describe the interpersonal attitude or stance of the child in coping with his drives, that is, his dependency on others. Because passivity and dependency are so often found together, it may seem at first glance that they are synonomous. The very passive, dependently "receptive" child appears quite frequently in the clinic. However, it is also quite possible for the child to be passive and conforming and at the same time to try to independently seek need-gratifications. This coping pattern is illustrated in what was labeled above as

---

*The term aggressive is used in so many ways and has so many affective associates that were it not popularly used to describe coping attitudes it might almost be preferable to use some other less common term, such as active. In particular, the psychologist should distinguish between aggressive coping and aggressivity as a need, as will be described in the following section of this chapter.

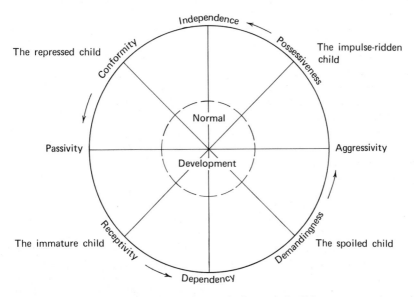

FIGURE 8. A schematic representation of the interrelationships among coping

"the repressed child," who does what he is told, who is expected to achieve independently, but not aggressively. Similarly, being aggressive is often associated with being independent. The extremely aggressively independent child is typified by what was described in the previous section as the "impulse-ridden" child, who in nonconformist fashion rejects any controls and seeks, often because of his circumstances, to gratify his own needs. Yet, there is also the child who is both aggressive and dependent, who depends on others in demanding fashion. This was illustrated in what was labeled the "spoiled" child. These terms on the outer edge of the circle describe extremes of behavior. In the normal development of any child, all of these attitudes may be involved in the child's attempts to cope with his drives. The inner dotted circle denotes these "normal" limits. As those readers familiar with Leary's (1957) Interpersonal Adjective Check-List will immediately note, this schema is analogous to the one Leary constructed to describe interpersonal relationships. Obviously it is also quite comparable to the schema presented by Erickson (1950) in his psychoanalytic constructs concerning need-gratification.

Although it would be interesting to explore this theoretical scheme further qua theory, it may be more meaningful for assessment purposes to review briefly what has been described in more detail in prior chapters concerning the development of these coping mechanisms. Observers of neonates (Call, 1964) have noted differences in their approach to need-gratification while feeding at the breast. Some newborns have to be propped up and have the nipple pushed into their mouths. Others grab at their mother's breasts, making sucking noises and motions. Such observations have led some to posit that such passive receptivity or "aggressive" possessiveness is possibly genetically or congenitally determined. However, it is also observed that the newborn's behavior is often fostered or at least abetted by the mother. She can condition receptivity in the baby by making the breast available immediately and holding the suckling against it—or she can let him struggle slightly for a second. In turn, such behavior on the part of the mother may reflect her own need-gratification attitudes. Those mothers who take an aggressive stance toward satisfaction of their own needs may "possess" the child, pushing him into her breast, to satisfy her

maternal needs.* A more "receptive" mother might await the child's demands to be fed. Where very strong receptive or possessive attitudes are a part of the mother's neurotic character structure, the reactive attitudes of the infant are likely to be equally intense. Thus, coping attitudes may be formed at a very early age.

In most instances, however, the way the infant perceives and expresses his need-gratifications is not dependent so entirely on this relationship with his mother but, in the normal course of events, is part of his further maturation. Unless his mother forces him to grab at the breast continuously, he is most likely to begin life expecting to have his needs gratified. As the mother begins to regulate his need-gratification, she fosters independence. As the child becomes more able to satisfy his needs, the infant accepts the mother's urging of independent need-gratification and he begins to attempt to possess things for himself. During the preschool years, this predominately receptive attitude continues. A four year old who attempts in most situations to make the first move toward need-gratification in a majority of situations would be quite precocious and "hypertrophic." By the time the child starts to school, he is expected not only to be able to answer many of his own needs, at least within the limits that such need-gratification is available, but he also should have developed a sufficiently aggressive attitude that he generally desires to take the first step toward need-gratification. He should be capable of —if not responsible for—feeding himself, keeping himself warm, avoiding hazards, obtaining affiliative contacts with his family and with peers. Moreover, it is expected that he take steps toward exercising these skills independently rather than waiting to be urged or merely receiving satisfactions.

This development of an aggressive attitude is necessary before the child can achieve in the school situation. He can sit back and absorb some knowledge at school, but in the long run, if he is to achieve he must aggressively seek knowledge. If education entailed

---

*Psychotherapuetic interviews with mothers of emotionally disturbed infants often reveal that breast feeding and comforting, etc., of the infant may serve to gratify many different needs for the mother. For example, many women are sexually stimulated during breast feeding, and their attitudes toward breast feeding reflect their attitudes toward sexuality.

only repetitive memorization of information, as it once did, then a passive receptive absorption of "facts" would be all that was necessary. However, even in more authoritarian-oriented educational systems, some independent cognitive processes are required, some "possession" of an idea. Present-day American education, of course, strongly emphasizes such active possession of learning from kindergarten on. In fact, this aggressive, independent attitude has so been fostered by this educational system in the current generation that many college and even high school students rebel against teachers who expect them to memorize facts or to learn what the teacher thinks is best! Teachers also resent students who expect them to "spoon-feed" them with learning.

During the adolescent years, being receptive versus being independent frequently becomes a conflict both within the adolescent himself and between the adolescent and adult authorities. The teenager wants to see himself as being able to satisfy his own needs, is impatient with those who try to wait on him, and is embarrassed and depressed momentarily when he is unable to independently gratify his needs or control his impulses. At the same time, he often behaves as if he expected the whole world to provide for him exactly as he wishes. Being passive is so closely associated with being dependent that because he takes advantage of the last chance to gratify this dependency need, he may often assume that it is also necessary to be passive. For example, an adolescent may make extra efforts to earn the money to buy something which his parents could supply him, and might even be willing to buy for him; then he will turn around and make some seemingly outrageous demand on them, fully expecting them to meet it, and even argue that he deserves it because he has gratified his own need on the prior occasion!

Turning now to the task of assessing coping mechanisms, referrals about the child seldom directly indicate that such attitudes are a central and definite complaint, but the assessor should read between the lines. For example, referrals which read "poorly motivated, makes no effort at school" or "very selfish and rivalrous with sibs" would suggest that the assessor keep his eye out for possible further data concerning need-gratification mechanisms. Even such varied symptoms as "petty theft," "obesity," or "sexual promis-

cuity" might lead one to entertain the hypothesis that coping with need-gratification may be disturbed and inadequate.

Data for the assessment of these attitudes toward need-gratification can be collected on a variety of techniques. Clues that there might be problems in the development of these attitudes often appear in the side remarks and descriptions of the child's behavior in interviews with the parents or with the child. Thus, the parents may describe the child as quite capable of caring for himself, but note that he waits for others to do things for him, or that he "expects too much" or "is demanding"; such clues should be followed up by the interviewer with further questions about the circumstances, descriptions of how the child "expects" or "demands" and how the parents regard and treat such behavior. Clues regarding precocious independence often are phrased in terms describing "aggressive" behavior: "just helps himself to what he wants," "has little regard for rights of others," "acts as if he owns the world," "hates to be waited on," "hates to be told what to do," etc. Either overly passive or hyperaggressive attitudes may be masked in the parents' reports if they unconsciously encourage the child's attitude. Thus, the parent may describe with pride how compliant the child is, how he accepts without complaint whatever they say or is always ready to take whatever is offered; or, inversely, how independent he is, how he goes ahead and does things on his own: "Eddie (age 5) is so sweet," reported his mother, "he gets up in the morning and helps himself to breakfast, and is out playing before I get up." "Yes," added his father, "and he can take his own bath and puts himself to bed." Only later in the interview did the parents admit that Eddie seldom obeyed them, and they failed to understand how Eddie could be so very disturbing in the kindergarten class, where he ignored the teacher, played what he wanted, and entirely disregarded the rights of others. The interviewer in this case noted also that these parents were "cooperative" but they seemed to expect the clinic to "straighten Eddie out" for them, and did not seem to understand their role in the proposed treatment plan for family therapy.

The child's behavior as well as his responses often offer opportunities to assess his need-gratification attitudes. Some children sit back and wait for the assessor to approach them, volunteering little, but compliantly receptive. However, as was noted above, dependently oriented children may also be quite aggressive and demanding. Such children may reject the psychologist's requests to talk or to take tests, but instead seek to be entertained or to be released from the situation altogether. They may perceive the assessment situation as making a demand on them and offering little for satisfaction of their needs. The more independent child may also be quite cooperative but is likely to decide for himself how he goes about the task. If something interests or challenges him, he may put forth quite a bit of effort but slack off when his motivation wanes. Moreover, he is more likely to lead the interview where he wants it to go. Eddie, for example, helped himself to a box of crayons and some paper off the examiner's desk and sat down and started to draw before the psychologist had a chance to do or say anything. He scarcely waited for the psychologist's introduction before volunteering a little story about one of his playmates and a fight he had had. Later, when the psychologist stopped to answer the telephone, Eddie took off for the bathroom without saying a word and returned on his own without so much as an "excuse me." At the end of the hour, when a second session was to be arranged, Eddie considered his free time much as if the psychologist were to make an appointment with him!

Among various techniques that offer special opportunity to observe need-gratification attitudes are the CAT or TAT and the Rosenzweig P-F Study. In CAT or TAT stories, these attitudes may be observed in the manner in which the hero achieves his needs. For example, to Card 1, how does the hero get out of practicing the violin—or become a great violinist (whichever common plot is given?) Does he sneak out when parents are not listening or does he wait till given permission? Does he become a great violinist overnight as if by magic, or does the story teller explain that the hero "earned the money to buy the violin by working every night after school, then finds himself a good teacher, and practices every day. . . . " Is the young man in 6BM or 7BM asking permission or hoping that his mother or his father will do something for him? Or is he telling them something or "plotting a robbery?" Another indication on the CAT or TAT of these attitudes is the degree to which the child depends on the stimulus in order to invent a story. The more receptive child adds relatively little to the stimulus; although he may construct a whole plot, he sticks pretty much to the clues given him. The more independent child makes the card his own, weaving into it some of his own fantasies, adding characters and objects, not present in the card, for his own ends.

Since the P-F for children deals with the frustrations experienced in social situations and the verbalized attitudes toward such frustration, it offers specific data regarding need-gratification attitudes. Among younger children, the most frequent responses to the P-F Study are the "Object-Dominance" and "Ego-Defensive" categories in contrast to what Rosenzweig calls the "Need-Persistent." This suggests that children are more likely to focus on the frustration and on defense of their ego (blaming others) than on resolutions of the frustration.

Further data about the case of Eddie may serve to illustrate how these attitudes toward need-gratification can pervade and affect the overall development and behavior of the child.

CASE 33

Eddie B.'s behavior at school and in the assessment situation have already been described above. At age five, he evidently had the attitude that he possessed the world and that it was his to manage for the satisfaction of his own needs. This attitude also appeared blatantly throughout his test responses. In his drawings for the House, Tree and Person, he drew the tree on the same page as the house; it was an enormous tree which overshadowed the small sketchy house. It was quite elaborate for a five year old. Buck, in his interpretative manual for the H-T-P (1948), suggests that the drawing of the tree represents the self as contrasted with the house which is more associated with the home and environment. In his drawing of a person, which was superior for a five year old (yielding a mental age of 7–6 on the Goodenough Scale), he added the unusual detail of muscles (indicated by round bumps on the arms and legs), and announced that this was the man who planted the tree and built the house! In responding to the Rorschach, he was quite critical of the blots, announcing that he could make better blots himself. Some of his responses seemed most original and unusual for a five year old, but it was difficult to assess his form level, since he disdained explaining himself in the inquiry. For example, he responded immediately to Card I, "The guy in the middle is swinging these two other guys around and around," but when asked for more details, he inverted the card and said only that it was necessary to cover the spaces in order to see what he had mentioned. Card II looked like "the same things . . . that's what I'd call it" and, after some pressure by the examiner, he decided that the space (D5) was the man in the middle and the rest of the blot (inverted) were the other two men, but he could not specify any details. He was able to perseverate with the same response on Card III, using the popular human figures, and becoming more precise by deciding that D8 was the head of the person in the middle, around which the other two figures were "having to dance." Card IV he associated with a "puppet doll" he had seen at school, identifying D1 as the "hand" inside the puppet and the rest as "a big monster puppet . . . with big feet." Card V was a big bird, or "no, an airplane" and he ran around the room imitating jet noises and flying the card as if it were the plane. Reluctantly giving up his play with Card V, he made a sour face at Card VI, and immediately rejected it. Urged to take a second look, he peeked at it inverted and announced it was a "hammer" pointing out D3 as the handle. Card VII, also given only a cursory glance, was "something smashed by the hammer." On VIII, he saw the popular "bears" (D1), "walking over the world." He completely rejected Cards IX and X: "It's silly," he announced, but could not say why they looked silly. Although Ames, et al (1952) found that crude *M* and *m* responses are not uncommon among five year olds, Eddie's perceptual attitudes were most extreme; he excluded any recognition of emotional impact from the environment, (the color of the blots), and emphasized entirely his own images, tensions, and impulses (3 M, 3 Fm, and 1 FM and 1 F).

His dominating possessiveness of the world was equally dramatized in his responses to the CAT. The little chickens on Card 1 were "getting their dinner . . . while the mother chicken watched." On Card 2, which is usually interpreted as a game of tug-of-war between one parent bear and another, with the baby bear on one side, Eddie decidedly depicted one big brave bear rescuing two other bears. Eddie admired the lion on Card 3, remarking that he was the king, and making roaring noises. "He makes everybody do what he wants," remarked Eddie. He did not notice the mouse in the background until it was brought to his attention. "The mouse is looking at the lion — how big he is!" Eddie decided. Eddie also identified with the tiger (Card 7) who "is going to get his dinner." On Card 8, the little monkey "is telling the big monkey something so the big monkey will know all about it."

Eddie had all sorts of solutions to the P-F situations. Twelve of his 24 responses were "need-persistent." In contrast, only one could be classified as "obstacle-dominated." Most unusual were his ten "intrapunitive" responses, most of which indicated that he assumed the responsibility for the solution of the situation, scored *i*.

Although Eddie's drawings, Rorschach, and CAT all suggested that he was intellectually superior, he actually did very poorly on the Stanford-Binet. He often disregarded instructions, recast the problem, and went ahead and used the materials as he saw fit. Some of his responses were difficult to score by the strict rules of the test. For example, to the "Aesthetic Choices," where the instructions are to point to the prettier one (Year V), he gave the wrong answer to both of the first two; then with an impish glance, he asked to see the third card and taunted the examiner, "I can show you the dumb one on that one too!"

Eddie's mother had suffered two miscarriages within the first five years of her marriage; she was 34 the following year, when at her husband's urging she agreed to adopt Eddie. The adoption was arranged through an attorney friend of Mr. B. All the B's knew of Eddie's background was that he was born out of wedlock to a 16-year-old girl who had made good grades in high school until forced to leave because of her pregnancy. Eddie was five days old when they picked him up at the hospital nursery. Mrs. B admitted that she was a bit nervous, since she had had no experience whatever with babies. She had been told that infants set their own schedules and that she needed only to feed and change him when he cried or seemed uncomfortable. She found him an easy baby to care for and found herself enjoying cuddling him and playing with him. However, from the first he did not seem to respond to her cuddling and after a few moments would struggle from her arms.

He grew rapidly and his psychological development seemed advanced to Mrs. B, although she could not remember exactly when he began to crawl, walk, or talk. (The fact that Mrs. B did not note these hallmarks for her only child, nor could not remember them only a few years later, did seem unusual). To Mrs. B it seemed as though Eddie was up on his feet and out of his crib and playpen before she quite had got used to having a child at all. However, she continued her laissez-faire approach, and did little to restrict him; she removed possible dangers and continued to enjoy watching him grow and answering his demands. "He seemed so cute and so spunky then (at age two). We just adored him and couldn't refuse him anything." To the best of her memory, he was talking fairly fluently by 24 months, without use of "baby-talk." She also remembered that he loved to sit at the table and eat what the adults were eating and delighted his father by teaching himself to use a spoon by imitation. "He's a great mimic," Mr. B added proudly.

Eddie was about three when Mrs. B's mother visited the family and she was scandalized to find him still in diapers. Mrs. B described her mother as a dominating person who took charge of any situation in which she was involved. Mr. B nodded in agreement, making a sour face. "She took charge of Eddie, all right!" he remarked. "It was summertime and everytime he soiled himself, she stripped him and took him out in the yard and turned the hose on him, and then put him on the toilet and stood over him. He screamed like mad but he learned quick enough," Mr. B chuckled and added, "When she came back the next summer, he turned the hose on her!" Eddie continued to wet the bed for another six months, but gradually ceased and had been completely toilet trained for the past year.

Until Eddie started kindergarten, the B's had considered him a well-adjusted, healthy child. They had centered their lives about him. They had led relatively socially restricted lives prior to his adoption, and for the past five years Mrs. B had not ventured far from the house except for necessary errands. Eddie usually accompanied her wherever she went. Mrs. B had thought he might have a difficult time separating from her the first day at school, and she had stayed around the school for several days, but he had quickly rushed off to explore the kindergarten and did not seem to notice that his mother was in the background. "It was harder on me (to separate) than on him," she remarked ruefully. It was only when the school authorities reported to her how disrupting Eddie's behavior proved to be that she became aware of the difficulties he was causing. Even so, she did not really seem to appreciate the school's problem. "I guess he's a little monster," she remarked at the conclusion of the first interview — but she laughed. Mr. B seemed more serious. "He should have some discipline," he said thoughtfully, "but I'm not sure how to begin."

Mrs. B had a slight build and was neatly but conservatively dressed; although not yet 40, she was graying noticeably and might be taken for several years older than her stated age. She spoke very softly, almost inaudibly at moments, with considerable hesitancy. However, as the interview proceeded, she began to volunteer information about Eddie, evidently enjoying talking about him. She was more reluctant to discuss her own life or feelings, tending to brush aside the interviewer's questions about herself as if they were unimportant. An only child, she admitted that she had always been dominated by her mother, and although she was conscious of considerable resentment over her mother's domination during her adolescent years, she had not openly rebelled partly because of her fear of her mother's anger and partly because she did not want to hurt her father, whom she adored. She had little social life during high school; "My mother never told me that I could not go on dates, but I knew she disapproved and she kept me busy with church work." Although she made only passing marks at school, she did attend the local college for one year because she thought it would please her father. Thereafter, she went to work for her father in his real estate firm. Mr. B joined the firm three years later. "It was love at first sight," she noted. "But it took you four years to make up your mind," he responded with a smile. However, it did appear that their courtship was cut short by the death of Mrs. B's father, when she was 25. She quit work, remained at home with her mother in what seemed like a prolonged grief reaction. She did not consent to marry Mr. B until three years later.

Mr. B, who was 12 years her senior, was the third of four sons of a "hard rock"

Missouri farmer, who believed and practiced hard work, stern discipline, and "fire-and-brimstone" religion. His mother was tubercular and died when he was 12 years of age. His two older brothers ran away during the following year. He and his younger brother kept house and helped their father on the farm for the next five years. "It was a hard and lonesome life," Mr. B said sadly. "My father seldom spoke unless necessary and never smiled after my mother's death." He completed high school and left home the next week to join the Navy. He remained in the service for the next 20 years, retiring just after World War II, at age 38. He tried going to college but quit after two years when he joined his father-in-law's firm. Despite this relatively harsh and unrewarding existence during his younger years, Mr. B did seem to be a warm-hearted man who evidently was quite supportive to his rather passive and dependent wife and, in turn, seemed to receive considerable affection from her. He also seemed to have a genuine affection for his son, and expressed a concern for Eddie and his problems at school, openly asking for help from the clinic. "I guess I need some advice about being a father. I didn't like the way my father was, so glum and so unloving, and I thought If I just loved Eddie that would be all that was needed. . . . But maybe it isn't!" However, it soon became clear in the subsequent interviews that Mr. B, never having experienced love from his own father, did not really know how to give love to Eddie. In fact, it was Mr. B's underlying hope that he would receive the love from his son that he had so sorely missed during his own childhood. Thus, the passive dependent attitudes of the parents drove Eddie to gratify his own needs aggressively and independently, without regard for impulse controls.

F. THE CONTENT OF CONATIVE FUNCTIONING

Earlier in this century, personologists were preoccupied with the classification and measurement of different drives. At least implicit in their thinking was the assumption that differences in behavior could be explained, rather simply it may seem now, by differences in drive strength. Thus, it was assumed that some people had less sexual drive than others, or more intense appetites. Even the more socially learned and developed needs were considered as separate "traits" rather than forces within an ego-structure. It was to measure these drive strengths that Murray (1938) originally constructed the TAT. But Murray envisioned even then that these needs were not entirely independent "habit strengths," but rather were enmeshed in a relatively fluid, functioning ego. The fact that when the TAT became a popular clinical instrument few clinicians bothered to utilize Murray's need-press system was not so much because the system was very cumbersome or that clinicians disdain measurement but, instead, that clinicians were more interested in how these drives were handled by the ego than the name or strength of the drive. However, in an "ego-psychology," such as espoused in this book, there is a tendency to overlook drive strengths and to confuse drive nomenclatures.

One other reason that the amount of the drive is no longer the focus of assessment is that psychologists have learned that drives are so easily and frequently repressed or compensated for by other satisfactions that it is often difficult to distinguish what is actually motivating the child, let alone to measure the strength of the drive. The basic physiological drives of sex, hunger, and waste elimination are difficult to measure with psychological instruments, perhaps just because they are primarily physiological. Moreover, although there may be individual differences in the strengths of these drives, for the most part their psychologic import lies in how people learn to cope with them. As was discussed in Chapter 5, even such social drives as N aggression, N achievement, or N Affiliation very possibly have some physiological basis, also unmeasurable by psychological techniques. These latter "secondary" drives are even more easily masked by repression and compensatorily interchanged, making precise and independent measurement extremely difficult.

Murray's contribution to psychology was not merely the ingenuous selection of a set of pictures, but rather the construction of a method, the projective method. This method was based on the psychoanalytic concept of unconscious motives, but it provided a means of assessing the presence and import of these underlying motives without the extended process of therapeutic free association. Nearly all projective techniques, except for the

Rorschach and the Word Association Test, followed upon Murray's invention. In these verbal associations and fantasies and in graphic free expression, it is often quite possible to see the underlying motives reflected, motives which are usually masked by repression in everyday life. Subsequently, Edwards (1957) has provided a means of measuring many of the same variables from subjective data by eliminating the element of "social desirability" through paired comparison of items. Any comprehensive discussion of the measurement and nature of these separate drives is far beyond the purview of this book. Many of them have already been considered in some detail both in this chapter and in Chapter 5. Suffice it at this point, for purposes of illustration, to discuss briefly the assessment of several principal drives.

Physiological drives are present in every child, and in assessment the concern is not with the presence of the drive, but with how the child learns to channel and handle it. That such a physiological drive is of particular concern to the child may be evident in the content of various associative techniques. For example, the budding sexuality of the pubescent child, while seldom demonstrated in direct sexual content, is often quite manifest in symbols and slips of the tongue. Between ages 11 to 13, the child begins to draw the human figure in profile, and although he may not indicate actual secondary sexual body features such as breasts or hips, the overall attitude of the figure often begins to take on slightly more adult stance. By ages 12 to 13, the presence of a definite hip and chest area or of a rump are not unusual. Lips and eyes may also indicate some sensual interest. As Machover (1949) and others have noted, the child of this age often shows particular concern with the point at which the legs are attached to the body, either having difficulty drawing the crotch or giving it special emphasis. Boys whose sexual urges and curiosity are rising may draw a male figure and take extra care to pencil in the fly to such an extent that it may look as if they had drawn a penis underneath the pants. In drawing a figure of a girl, boys of this age often start to draw the girl's legs up through and underneath the skirt. Girls' sexual interests are more likely to be shown in fancy clothes, breast lines, a seductive pose of the figure, or extra emphasis on hair and decorations.

The need for affection [which may actually be a physical drive as suggested by Harlow and Zimmerman (1959)], may be assessed from TAT stories, doll play, or the MAPS. For example, one five year old who had spent most of her life in the middle of a marital battle, and who had been recently abandoned by both parents to her resentful, bitter, and depressed maternal grandmother, poignantly spelled out her concern on the MAPS, arranging the adult figures so that they were being affectionate to each other and at the same time centering affection upon child figures. Intermixed with these affectionate scenes were battles between the Superman figure and the ghost in which Superman prevented the ghost from breaking the affectionate bonds between the parents and between the parents and the child. In the concluding scene, the child picked out the backdrop of the desert, and depicted a child figure wandering back and forth across the desert, weeping and afraid to be rescued by an old witch figure. The child imitated what must have been her grandmother's voice harshly ordering the child to come with her to get food.

Whether aggressivity is a psychological drive as Freud and others have maintained, the manner in which this drive appears and the way that the child handles it is often a crucial variable. As was discussed previously in this chapter, aggression becomes a need as the child is forced to learn to seek his own need-gratifications actively and independently. Such aggressivity should not be confused with the affect anger, nor the accumulative effects of anger which are called hostility. Rather, such aggressivity consists of the child's drive to explore and test out his environment, his imposition of his needs, impulses, and feelings onto the world, and his assertion of his own identity as a separate and unique force in his environment. It is the accumulation of all these aspects of his behavior into a need or drive that particularly characterizes the shift from infancy to latency. However, as this assertion of the self takes on such an active form and becomes in effect a drive, the child also finds himself increasingly in conflict both with adult authority and other children who are also asserting themselves. Thus, "being aggressive" is often a complaint lodged against the latency child. The assessor must be particularly careful in understanding this complaint. He must distinguish the degree to which the complaint reflects the inability of the adult authority to accept what may be a natural developmental phenomenon.

At the same time, the possibility should be entertained that whether the parents do accept this change, the child himself may be having difficulty with it. The child may interpret even mild criticisms of his aggressivity by the parents as a threat of loss of love. He may find that his aggressivity runs him into more competition with other children than he is immediately prepared to endure. He may wish for the protection of his mother and try to retreat to a state where she entertains him, feeds him, and keeps him safe from harm. He may find his mother willing to resume this role, but as his need aggression increases, his conflict with his mother may also intensify. Moreover, the child who withdraws from aggressive interaction with his peers is likely to be the object of their attack. He will likely find himself alternately teased and isolated. Instead of entering into the normal games of push and pull, he attacks with anger and receives anger in return. Evidence of such difficulty in handling aggression may come first from teachers' reports or parents' complaints about the way other children treat their child. The themes of such children on the TAT, Sentence Completion, or the World Test usually consist of mixed aggressivity, fear, and anger.

CASE 34

Sherry Y, age eight, in playing with the World Test, built a very neat and orderly world at first, omitting all such aggressive symbols as the military figures or the wild animals and even carefully corralling all of the tame animals. Suddenly she spotted the bull and, almost without warning, started to break down the entire world, remarking that the bull was getting even with all the bad people who were in its way. Her drawing of a person was not easy to identify by sex, but carried a spear. When asked about the sex of the person whom she drew, Sherry added a skirt and identified the drawing as Jane from the TV series "Tarzan."

Mrs. Y had brought Sherry to the clinic because she refused to go to school where all the children teased her. In further discussions, the mother agreed that Sherry was often demanding with other children who came to the house. Although Mrs. Y had given it little thought at first, she now realized that Sherry may well have isolated herself in the neighborhood because she was quick to anger, very possessive with her belongings, and unwilling to be competitive. When Sherry had complained to her mother about other children, Mrs. Y had been quick to comfort her and divert her attention from the situation with other pleasures.

In the initial interviews, it seemed that Sherry's difficulties in handling aggression might well have arisen from her jealousy over the birth of her little brother two years before. She had been particularly curious about her mother's pregnancy, and Mrs. Y had given Sherry considerable explanation about this event, including the fact that the father had "planted the seed which grew into a baby." Although these explanations did help to satisfy Sherry's curiosity, she had presumed that the baby would be a girl. When she discovered the baby was male, she was very angry and demanded that her mother take her brother back to the hospital and "exchange" him, as she had seen her mother exchange purchases at stores. When it was explained to her that this was impossible, she asked if the doctor could operate on him so he would be a girl. For weeks after the sib was born, she was sullen and irritable, and would not go near the baby.

However, Sherry's open rivalry with her male sibling did not seem to explain Sherry's particular modes of handling aggression. Mrs. Y, once she had described this sibling rivalry, was insistent that this was the source of Sherry's difficulties. She denied that Sherry had shown any tendencies to be demanding or explosive prior to the sib's birth. She argued almost defensively that Sherry had been an easy child to care for. "Perhaps we did spoil her a little since she was so sweet, but we also disciplined her when necessary." The discipline which Mrs. Y described consisted chiefly of isolating Sherry briefly in another room, whereupon Sherry usually became contrite. At first Mrs. Y could not identify the kinds of behavior for which she punished Sherry: "Just different little things. We seldom had to punish her," but on second thought, she did remark that Sherry often was "greedy" and "grabbed at things." "I tried to teach her what was hers and what belonged to someone else." She explained that it had been difficult to keep Sherry out Mr. Y's study, where Sherry might destroy books and papers. Sherry also loved to explore cupboards and drawers. "She always made such a mess."

In response to the social worker's questions, Mrs. Y provided the bare facts about her own background, but it was difficult from this initial interview to obtain much information about her own attitudes and behavior. Like Sherry, she had a brother approximately five years her junior. She denied any memory of rivalry with him or jealousy toward him. "We each had our own interests and went our own ways," she explained. She remembered her own childhood as generally happy and uneventful. In contrast to Sherry, she recalled that she had many playmates and seldom quarreled with any of them. As evidence, she named two with whom she continued to correspond. Until she married Mr. Y she had always "lived in the same town in the same house." Her school achievement had been above average and she had attended two years of college when she met and married Mr. Y. For the first two years of their marriage, she had worked as a secretary while Mr. Y completed his training as an accountant. She denied that she had had any particular vocational ambitions of her own, but had attended college chiefly because "it did seem better to have some college education." Shortly after Mr. Y finished his training, the couple moves from Mrs. Y's home town to a distant large city where he found employment. That year she became pregnant with Sherry. She averred that her marriage was generally happy, that "Mr. Y provides a good living," and that "we seldom quarrel."

On the Edwards PPS, none of Mrs. Y's scores was excessively high. However, percentile scores around 70 on "Order," "Aggression," and "Autonomy" did suggest that Mrs. Y's own values might entail a mildly compulsive ordering of her environment in order to maintain her identity. Such a pattern was further emphasized by percentile scores below 25 on "Intraception, Abasement and Sex." Mrs. Y thus evinced little interest in the feelings of others, was not inclined to blame herself, and placed little value on sexual drives. This pattern of scores thus suggested that Mrs. Y tended to be somewhat impersonal, unresponsive to stimuli, and concerned with her own security.

As it was the clinic's policy to involve fathers in the assessment and treatment of the child, Mr. Y was invited to make an appointment with the social worker. He cancelled the first two appointments on the excuse that unexpected business had intervened. He appeared 15 minutes late to the third appointment, claiming again that his work day was rushed. He did seem out of breath and very tense, and sat quietly for a moment before asking, "What did my wife tell you?" The worker explained that Mrs. Y had given her view of Sherry's difficulties, but that the clinic thought it might be helpful to understand how he perceived the situation. Again, Mr. Y was silent for a moment, before asking, "I mean about us?" Mr. Y flushed and remained silent for several minutes. "I guess you thought I didn't want to come to see you, that I wasn't interested in Sherry," he said. "Well, I really was reluctant to come. Not because of Sherry. I'm very worried about Sherry. It's because of my wife—and me." He hesitated again and seemed depressed. "We've never gotten along well. She's a difficult woman to live with—perhaps I'm difficult too; I don't know." He went on to explain that he regarded his wife as "selfish," "demanding her own way," "sulking when she is slighted." "Sherry is just like her. She hasn't any friends either." He felt she was very jealous, complaining about and downgrading all of his friends and demanding that he spend "every spare minute at home." Now that he was working independently as a public accountant, he often needed to work evenings, which was the reason Mrs. Y had arranged a study for him at home. From his description, it appeared Mrs. Y was jealous of his attentions to Sherry, often sending her off to bed early in the evening when he was playing with Sherry or scolding her when she tried to get his attention or acted seductively toward him. Their marital dissension had become so intense about three years ago that they had contemplated a separation. However, soon afterwards Mrs. Y became pregnant and there was no further discussion of their separation. Since the birth of their son, Mrs. Y had completely rejected his sexual advances. Mr. Y admitted he was very depressed at times and that he regarded this marital dissension as the chief source of Sherry's difficulties.

However, he was very reluctant to discuss this matter with his wife. He seemed resolved to try to maintain his marriage on its present basis, and was afraid that further consideration in connection with Sherry's problems might again threaten it with dissolution. He begged the worker not to mention to his wife what he had said. He agreed that if his analysis of the situation were valid, it might be difficult to help Sherry without some further exploration of the marriage, but adamantly refused to become involved further. Rather, he begged the clinic to try to help Sherry as much as possible — "without going into any of this!"

Mrs. Y failed to appear for her next appointment, but did call later to make another, without explaining why she had not come in as scheduled. When she did appear, she seemed even more reserved than previously. She too wanted to know "what my husband told you," and seemed unsatisfied by the social worker's statement that they had discussed Sherry's problems. She agreed to the clinic's recommendation that both she and Sherry come weekly to the clinic, but remarked, "I don't know what more I have to tell you!" A week later, Mrs. Y called to cancel further appointments, explaining that Sherry's pediatrician had prescribed a mild tranquilizer which "seems to quiet Sherry down." There was no further mention of Sherry's social and school problems. This case illustrates how a child's aggressive social behavior may actually reflect the hostilities within the family, especially marital discord.

One of the most common human motivations is the urge for revenge. Strangely, this is seldom mentioned by psychologists, even though it is often emphasized in literature and history. Retaliation as a motive is part of psychoanalytic theory, that is, the fear of retaliation for the forbidden wish to possess the mother. Perhaps revenge is ignored in psychological literature because it seems only another form of anger, but it is a very specific anger which is unique to human relationships. It is as real and common a motivation as achievement or affiliation. Although there are no research studies on revenge and no scales to measure it, everyday experience does suggest that it is probably quite a common motive in childhood as well as among adults. "I'll get even with you!" is a cry which periodically comes from every child. Plotting revenge is a frequent theme of daydreams, and the ways in which revenge is attempted probably vary as greatly as any other comparable form of behavior. Often such plotting occupies much of the injured or insulted person's waking hours and his dreams as well. Revenge can become an obsession with children as with adults. Because destruction of the offender is usually not possible, and even more because even the thought of annihilating the enemy is often quite guilt creating, the child usually fantasies some substitute gratification such as humiliating the offender or making him feel guilty and apologetic for his act. One of the main aims of this obsessive plotting is to avoid having the tables turned on the plotter, that is, the act of revenge should not be committed in such a way as to make the revenger look as if he were an offender, guilty of an act of aggression. Moreover, the revenger has to avoid feeling guilty; revenge is only satisfied when the revenger feels justified. Thus, the dreamed of act of revenge often has to be very devious. Sometimes in order to avoid having any finger of guilt pointed at the revenger, the whole idea of the revenge itself has to be repressed, and thus becomes quite out of the consciousness of the child. In such instances, all that then remains is the act itself. Moreover, in seeking to avoid any blame, the child often chooses some other need-gratification, consciously or unconsciously, through which to express his revenge.

A few examples of how revenge becomes confused with and hidden in other need-gratifications may serve to illustrate how needs can be confused by the child. One of the most common needs confused with revenge is N achievement, either as underachievement or overachievement. A classic example is the underachiever who seeks revenge against parents whom he feels offer insufficient affection and succor, but place a high value on achievement. By playing the helpless, inadequate infant, the child wreaks revenge on the disappointed parents and, at the same time, subtly gains some of the attention for which he has longed. Most of all, achievement becomes the battlefield and the child's anger over his feelings of rejection remain hidden. Overachievement may be a child's means of revenging against the intrusion of a sibling rival. By overachieving, he seeks to show up the beloved baby. If he does everything correctly and properly, the sins of the younger sib will stand out. This wearing of the halo is a very common behavior pattern in which older sisters obtain revenge against a favored younger brother. The obstreperous and less successful brother then becomes the object of the parents' concern and in the referral to the clinic becomes what Satir (1964) calls the "identified patient." The behavior of the revengeful sister is revealed in his screams of pain. Again, *N* Achievement becomes the battlefield in which the family affections are the spoils of war. However, the sister's revenge is usually only briefly satisfied for although she may win approval for her superior achievement, the offending sib actually obtains the parents' concerns. However, substituting achievement for revenge easily becomes a pattern, and the sister may go on to higher levels of achievement seeking revenge against all offending males but always losing in the long run, for this behavior pattern seldom brings the affection and succor she seeks.

Revenge may involve physiological needs as well as other social drives. The use of sex as revenge either in the form of frigidity or promiscuity is very common among adults, both women and men. Sexual "acting out" by adolescents also can be a form of revenge against parents, as is illustrated in the case of Sandy (Case 29). Another syndrome in which a physiological need becomes substituted for revenge is the neurotic self-starvation called *"anorexia nervosa."* Because of the obvious concern of everyone involved with eating and because children who suffer from anorexia are usually quite passive and "sweet," the underlying obsessive, seething revenge may easily go unnoticed.

CASE 35

Janet B., age 14, was transferred from the pediatric to the psychiatric ward with a diagnosis of *"anorexia nervosa."* During the first month on the pediatric ward, her weight continued to diminish so that she weighed only 68 pounds when the transfer to psychiatric care was decided upon. At that time, she vomited up all solid foods and had been placed on intravenous feeding as an emergency measure. Upon her admission to the psychiatric ward, she was extremely emaciated and weak. She looked depressed, spoke very little, and seemed slightly in a daze. Janet expressed a distaste for the intravenous feeding, but became agitated when the psychiatrist assured her that this was unnecessary and that she would be maintained on a special dietetic fluid. She was not allowed to remain in bed but instead was required to join the activities of the other children on the ward including attendance at the hospital's school.

In the initial interview, Janet was unable to give much information about the onset of weight loss and vomiting except that as far as she could remember it began about the end of the prior semester and had continued throughout the summer. She was anxious to leave the hospital as soon as possible both because she missed her family very much and because she was eager to start high school the following week with her friends. There was no history of any prior major illnesses or accidents, and a thorough medical workup had not revealed the presence of a disease. Nor was there any history of prior weight loss. In fact, Janet's mother reported that her daughter had been quite "chubby" as an infant and slightly overweight throughout her childhood, until the previous year. At that time, Janet had become somewhat concerned about her weight and decided to diet along with her mother who was considerably overweight. Her loss of weight until that spring had been quite modest; she had lost approximately ten pounds over a six month period and had gained approximately two and one half inches in her height to her present height of five feet six inches.

Janet was the third of three daughters of a fairly well-to-do owner of a chain of bakeries. She laughed as she mentioned her father's occupation since the family name was Baker and, moreover, she had been known from infancy by the nickname "Cookie." The children at school had teased her at times about the fact that her name was "Cookie" Baker, but she claimed that she did not mind this. Her sisters were ten and 14 years older than herself and both had been out of home since she was eight years old, so that for many years she had been the only child in the house. As far as Janet's mother could recall, Janet's growth and development had been entirely normal. Mrs. B and her husband had not necessarily planned to have a third child but were quite happy over Janet's arrival. Mrs. B denied that she had any particular hopes concerning the sex of the baby when Janet was expected, and that she was quite content to have a third girl. She claimed that Janet was a very pretty baby and that they were delighted with her. She had been in good health throughout her pregnancy and her labor was brief and the delivery quite easy.

Janet was breast fed for almost six months, "perhaps a little longer than my other children." She was given a bottle in addition to baby foods until after she was two years old. Mrs. B could not remember exactly when Janet learned to walk and talk, but thought Janet's development had been quite comparable to that of her other daughters. She did remember that Janet seemed to be "less trouble" and more "quiet" during infancy than her first two children, but attributed this to the fact that she was a more experienced mother and less upset by babies.

She remembered being much more concerned with the care of her first child; as she recollected this, she smiled and added that when her two other daughters were infants, she had had the help of her mother who was living with the family. She recalled that she had resented the efforts of her mother to be helpful and had found her to be an interference. Her mother had died three years before Janet's birth and thus she had had Janet's care as an infant entirely to herself. Janet seemed to enjoy being cared for and played with, so that Mrs. B had found her a more enjoyable child than her older daughters. Even Mr. Baker, whom Mrs. B described as a somewhat distant man and not easily given to expressions of affections, was less reserved with his youngest daughter. He permitted her to climb into his lap and would even swoop her into his arms when he arrived home from work, which was something he had never done with the other two children. Even as an infant, Janet was quite sensitive to her father's moods and would cry if she thought that he disapproved of her. If he were cross over other things or preoccupied, Mrs. B would have to reassure Janet that he was not angry with her.

Mrs. Baker did not find it "necessary" to put Janet in a nursery school since she had "nothing else to do but take care of her." Janet was a bit tearful when she started kindergarten, and it took her several weeks to become accustomed to being separated from her mother. Thereafter, however, she was a model of good behavior both at school and at home and seemed very happy. Throughout elementary school she made all A's and B's. School records did show that Janet was considered a "timid" child by her teachers and that her main difficulty had been in reciting aloud. Her written work was considered exceedingly neat and always correct. Janet's grades dropped slightly as she entered junior high school but her record of A's and B's continued on through the eighth grade.

During the previous year, however, Janet did seem to have much more difficulty at school. She was placed in a slightly advanced class and seemed to have a considerable amount of homework. She pored over books in the evening and struggled to write compositions and reports. She complained about her assignments a great deal to her mother, who worried over them with her. She just could not seem to write a satisfactory essay and dreaded making verbal reports. Mrs. Baker tried to reassure her that it would be all right to get a C in her English and social science courses but Janet just "couldn't stand the idea of having a C," perhaps because her father had been so proud of her top grades. In fact, Janet worked so hard and was so very concerned with these particular courses that she slightly neglected her work in other areas and her overall academic achievement fell during the year. Mrs. Baker had considered obtaining some psychological counselling for Janet at that point, but Mr. Baker had disapproved.

Janet was also active socially both at church and with a girls' club, and there seemed to be a party or other social event nearly every weekend. However, Janet was often too tired to go out or, if she went, did not really enjoy herself. Mr. Baker had expressed some disapproval at the extent of Janet's social activities. He believed she might too easily become involved in what he considered the delinquent activities of adolescence, in "drinking, carousing around, and so on." Mrs. Baker tried to assure him that Janet's group of "little girls" were all very nice, that no alcohol was served at their parties, and that although there were boys and dancing, none of the girls did any individual dating. As the year progressed, Janet became worried lest her father disapprove entirely of her social activities. She particularly feared that he might believe these activities caused her decline in school achievement, although Mr. Baker never openly made such an association.

Janet became especially concerned that her father might not permit her to attend the social events during graduation week if she did not improve her school grades. During the weeks just prior to graduation, Janet was most anxious and tense and sleepless. She concentrated for hours on her schoolwork. Mrs. Baker prevailed on her husband to praise Janet for her efforts and to buy her the special clothes that she wanted for the parties. On the night of the graduation party, Janet was at a pitch of excitement and tension. At the last minute, she almost did not go because her menses had occurred a week early. Nevertheless, with her mother's support she went to the party. She was particularly excited because her escort was a boy upon whom she had a particular crush. However, Janet was most disappointed at the party because this young man had not paid any particular attention to her, but had chased after some other girl. Moreover, there was alcohol in the punch and Janet became slightly inebriated and then ill. She was terrified that her father would discover this. It was that night when she arrived home that she first began to vomit. During the subsequent week, she seemed depressed and physically ill, had little appetite, and continued to vomit. The situation did not clear up the entire summer. Significantly, Janet did not remember this incident nor did Mrs. Baker herself associate it with the onset of Janet's symptom. Only later did Janet admit that she had expected this party to be "just everything."

That this very passive and sweet child could possibly be motivated by revenge seemed most unimaginable. Moreover, food was such a life-and-death struggle, in which Janet involved the nurses, doctors, and her parents, that at first it seemed that this rejection of food was in itself the need. In fact, the resident physician initially posited that the problem was "an oral aggressive fixation." Certainly the fixation was oral, and in the struggle to maintain Janet's life and in her obstinate resistance to food, there was no doubt that aggression was also involved. However, the nature of this aggression was not easily definable from immediate clinical observation nor from the history. Psychological assessment was requested "to determine some of the sources of her underlying anxiety and her defenses against it,

especially concerning being aggressive." In further discussion with the psychiatric resident who asked for the psychological consultation, he remarked that he guessed that Janet was probably a very angry girl but that anger made her very guilty.

When Janet was introduced to the assessment, she made a sour face and said that she had heard of "these 'psych' tests from the other kids on the ward," and that "I don't see what they have to do with my problem." However, she had consented to her doctor's request that she go through with the assessment, so she decided to accept the situation albeit with obvious distaste. Although there was no question about her intellectual functioning, she was given the Shipley-Hartford Intelligence Scale first as a "warm-up," that is, as an emotionally neutral task. Her scores on both parts of the Shipley indicated above average intelligence, with a WAIS equivalent IQ of 117. She expressed annoyance with the Abstraction Test, asking "Who thought these up anyway!" and then remarking "I must be pretty stupid!" She accepted the Rorschach with a noncommital shrug, but soon become quite involved in it so that by the time she was presented with the TAT she was relatively relaxed and was almost enjoying her own fantasies. When asked to draw a person, she wrinkled her nose in protest, but said nothing and immediately became engaged in drawing, carefully selecting her colors. Given the MMPI to complete on her own in the ward, her reaction was again negative: "Do I have to?" She worked very slowly, read and reread each item carefully, stopping periodically to rest in her room until urged by the nurse to return to the task.

Janet gave the following responses to the Rorschach:*

---

*Locations are indicated by reference to Beck's (1945) details, by number. Scoring, however, is according to Klopfer (1956).

Administration	Inquiry
Card I 3″	
1. Ew! How ugly! Like an ugly mask.	The whole thing. Like a robber wears. Black. With mean eyes and a mean mouth. *W Fc; Fm Mask*
Card II 17″	
1. Could be two lambs, black lambs, just their heads. And they're nursing out of a bottle.	This (D1) is their heads. Here's their noses, nuzzling at this bottle (D4). Ears here and you can see their eyes. *D FM, FC′ A P, O*

Administration

Inquiry

2. Or it could be a face, the whole thing. A real mean face.

His mouth (D5) is wide open, like he was yelling. Or it could be a she, I can't tell. Her eyes (D2) are red! Like she'd been crying or was angry. Angry, I guess. She's sticking her tongue (D3) out.
Like a nasty person.

W, S M, FC Hd

Card III 20″

1. I don't know. Looks like it might be some kind of X-ray or somebody's insides.

(D1) Like the bones right here [points to own pelvis]. It's that shape. (X-ray?) Dark and shadowy. I don't know what that red could be. (?) All bloody. But that wouldn't show on an X-ray, would it?

D Fk At (D CF At)

2. Ick! This way (inverted) it looks like a big monster, coming right at you.

(D1) He's got his hands up (D5) like he was going to pounce right on you. Big black eyes (D8). And his mouth is open, with white teeth. (?) I don't know if it's human or animal. Like something from outer space.

D M, FC' (H)

Card IV 22″

1. Another big ol' monster. Are they all going to be monsters? With giant feet and arms like hooks.

The whole things. Like he was clumping out like this [makes a menacing gesture] humped over, going to grab somebody. You can't see his face, just mean eyes (D1?) I don't know. A big tail? (laughs)

W M (H)

Card V 4″

1. Here it is again. All monsters. This is a monster bat.

Swooping down. Big claws (D10) on the end of his wings. Ugly. (?) So black. Big horns and curved in feet. Ugh!

W FM, FC' A P

Card VI 25″

1. I don't know what this could be really. This (D1) like some kind of skin, but this (D3) . . . I know, that (D3) could be the tail, like a beaver skin.

It's just shaped like a skin .There's where the feet were before it got skinned. And beavers have big tails don't they? (skin-like?) I don't know. Just couldn't think of anything else that shape.

W F Aobj. (P)

Card VI 8″

1. Oh, this is kind of cute. Like two puppy dogs, with their ears up. Or kitties. More like cats and they are spitting at each other, with their fur sticking out.

(D2) Their mouths are open and their eyes big like when cats fight. All their fur's one end. (de). Their paws are out like this, ready to fight. Upon on a fence (D4).

W FM A

CARD VIII 13″

1. Two dogs, one on either side. . . . Like wild dogs. . . .

(D1). They're stretching out to this hand here. Like smelling it. They look awfully fierce. You can see it in their eyes. *D FM A P*

2. And here's a hand right at their noses, like reaching out to pet them or something. You'd think who ever's trying to pet something like that'd get bit.

Here's the hand with long fingers, and part of the arm. (?) Just arm and hand.

dr M Hd

3. This red . . . could be meat . . . but it's too red for meat. Like poisoned meat. Maybe somebody put it out for the dogs. (laughs) Maybe that's why they're going to bite!

(D6) It's all pink and whitish . . . like spoiled or poisoned.

D FC, Fc Food

Administration	*Inquiry*

Card IX 52″

1. Ugh! The top (D3) might be like two witches, and they're standing over a big pot, stirring up some evil of some kind. It's all streaming up in their faces. Here's the fire down below.

D3. They got pointed caps and long noses like horns and big fat tummies.
  D, W M (H)
Here's the pot (D1). (poison?) The greenish color. Isn't that poison color?
  D FC Obj
And the hot fire below, all this pink.
  D CF Fire

Card X 5″

1. Crabs snatching at
2. some seaweed.

D1. All these legs. *D FM A D* This green stuff

  D CF Pl

3. Here's two guys up here, lifting up a big pole or pillar, standing on his cliff, like they were going to drop it on
4. these two other guys who are climbing up the mountain.

(D8) Real weirdos. Like cave men. They're on top of the cliff (D9). They're trying to destroy these guys (D6) *D M (H)*
(D6) They got big fat bodies and big fat arms but little teeny hands. They'll get smashed.
  D M, Fm H

5. And this guy down here has fallen off. Maybe the other guys got him or maybe he was dragged off by
6. these two big snakes. They're bigger than he is! It sure looks like a big ol' war is going on.
7. Explosions all around.

D Here's his legs, and his mouth is open like he was screaming as he falls. *D M, Fm H*

D Long, green snakes all curling up. (green?) More poison, I guess.
  D FC, FM A P
Things bursting in different colors.
  D CF, Fm Explo.

SUMMARY, RORSCHACH SCORES, CASE 35

	Main	Add		Main	Add		Main	Add
W	6	*1*	M	8	*1*	H	2	
D	15	*1*	FM	5	*1*	(H)	4	
Dr	1		Fm		*4*	Hd	2	
S		*1*	F	1		A	6	
R	22		Fc		*1*	Mask	1	
P	5	*1*	FC′	2	*2*	At	1	*1*
O		*1*	FC	3	*1*	Aobj	1	
			CF	3	*1*	Food	1	
Experience Balance:						Obj	1	
8 : 4½ = I 116 [a]						Fire/Explo	2	
						Pl	1	

[a] For calculation of this Experience Balance ratio, See Palmer, 1955.

Of Janet's 12 TAT stories, four were particularly pertinent to the question of the form of her anger.

Card 2 (administered first): "This girl is going to school, but it looks like she's turning around like she was watching what was going on behind her. That must be her mother; she's watching something too . . . whatever's going on. They're watching this guy, whoever he is. He looks too young to be the father, maybe her brother or just some guy working there. They're watching to see if he's working right . . . (story?)

. . . I don't know . . . maybe they're making sure he doesn't cheat 'em . . . (come about?) . . . Who knows! They just hired this guy to work on their farm. Maybe they don't really have a father. They have to watch that this guy doesn't steal whatever they're growing there. That's their food for the winter. But they don't look like they know much about farming. (Happens?) He probably takes the stuff and sells it when they aren't looking. (And then?) They starve to death! [laughs] No, don't put that down. Let's see . . . The girl goes to town and tells the sheriff and they get a posse and chase the guy and catch him and hang him. (Girl feels then?) Oh, she'd be happy." [laughs]

3GF (second card): "She's all busted up over something. Crying over something. Probably something silly! [laughs] (What has happened?) Oh, she probably caught her boyfriend making out with some other girl. (Next?) She goes out and jumps in the lake! . . . No, she wouldn't do anything like *that*. I know: she doesn't really jump in the lake; she just throws her clothes in and they float down the river and they find them at the bottom of the waterfall and they think she's drowned. Then her boyfriend thinks it's all his fault and he shoots himself . . . No, change that. The other girl thinks it's *her* fault and *she* shoots herself. Later this girl comes back and they find out that she didn't drown after all and she marries this guy and they live happily ever after . . . How's that for a story!"

Card 5: She sure looks like she's sneaking up on someone. Maybe she's looking in here to see what's going on behind her back . . . (?) Oh, maybe her daughter's in there making out with her boyfriend . . . (happens?) She screams . . . (Who screams?) [laughs] . . . I'll make it the mother screams 'cause the daughter knew her mother'd come sneaking around so she put a bucket of water over the door and when the old lady stuck her head in she got all soaked [Janet laughs] (And then?) I don't know . . . Oh, I got a really funny ending. Let's say she really wasn't sneaking up on them at all. She was going to call them to dinner. Now the joke's on them. She won't give them anything to eat."

18GF (final story): "Oh, oh. Caught in the act. She was sneaking downstairs to get something out the refrigerator and her mother caught her. Looks like the mother's trying to choke her, make her cough it up! [Janet laughs] That's all . . . (Come about?) . . . More story? Well, let's see . . . Let's say this really isn't her mother. It's her stepmother. Her father died and her stepmother is trying to starve her to death so that the stepmother can get all the money her father left her. The stepmother has her locked up so she can't get away. If she goes down the stairs, there's a squeaky board and the stepmother'll hear her and lock her up again. So she makes a rope out of her sheets and tries to climb down out of her window. But she can't make it 'cause she's so weak and everything. She falls down but she doesn't get killed. Maybe she falls in some bushes or something. Anyway, the neighbors see her and they call the police and they see her condition and they arrest the stepmother and put her in jail. So the girl gets all the goodies from her father. The end!"

The profile of T-scores obtained from Janet's MMPI was quite unusual: 216' 734-5. Her "lie" score was 68, K was 55, and F was

47. The amount of depression indicated in her score on Scale 2 was considerably higher than might have been expected from most adolescents. Although Janet complained bitterly about being hospitalized and kept wishing she could return home, she masked whatever other depression she might be experiencing by a set smile. Evidently she could not maintain this mask when presented with statements concerning depression; note that Scale 3 ("Hysteria") at T-score 60 does show use of repression and denial as a secondary defense. However, repression alone could not contain Janet's depression. Her sense of loss was projected on the one hand into somatic complaints and suffering (Scale 1) and, on the other hand, any guilt was deflected by "paranoid ideation" (Scale 6). The combination of these reactions with the indication of obsessive-compulsive trends (Scale 7) is consonant with the clinically observed compulsive fasting and vomiting, but in addition suggested an obsessive rumination over revenge. Her *Pd* score (Scale 4) was not particularly high for an adolescent, but considering Janet's history, it does indicate far more feelings of rebellion and of family discord than was mentioned in any of the initial interviews.

Janet's first drawing of a person did not seem to show any anger. It was a rather stereotyped figure of what appeared to be a chubby latency girl, with a round face and long curls and a set smile, dressed in an old fashioned frock with bows and ribbons, colored in pastels, and wearing little girl's black dress shoes; the figure was standing full face, with her hands behind her rather demurely. Janet described her as a "teenager all dressed up to go to a party." However, for a male figure, Janet began by drawing a horse, on which she placed a knight in full armor with his lance pointed out in front of him. "He's all set to kill the dragon or something and rescue the princess . . . Maybe she (drawing I) is the princess."

These data provided considerable evidence about the nature of many aspects of Janet's ego development. Evidently she was an intellectually bright and emotionally sensitive girl, whose affective life was far more extensive and expansive than seemed indicated in the initial clinical observations. Concentrating on the question in the referral, there was considerable evidence to back up the psychiatric resident's initial impression of "fixation at an oral aggressive stage." Obsession with food and with anger was present throughout Janet's Rorschach and TAT responses, until they became almost equivalent, as epitomized in the "poison" associations to the Rorschach. However, these responses suggested that Janet's oral aggressiveness had become more specific, that revenge had become an autonomous motive. Witness such Rorschach responses as the masked robber, the face with the tongue sticking out, the menacing monsters, the spitting cats, the dogs who bite the hand of those who feed them poisoned meat, the poisoned meat, the poisoned witches' brew, and finally the exploding battle on Card X. Revenge intermingled with food permeates Janet's TAT stories. For example, to Card 2, the heroine seeks revenge for stolen food; on Card 3GF, depression over lost love is satisfied by an ingenuous revenge obtained by creating guilt in the offending parties. On Card 5, food becomes more important to the teenager than sex, and the mother obtains revenge for her insult by deprivation of food; finally on Card 18GF, Janet's fantasy equated food deprivation with being deprived by her mother of

her father's love, and she found revenge by inciting the community to retaliate against her mother for her, thus saving her any feelings of guilt.

Combining these findings with the clinical history, it did seem highly probable that Janet had long felt deprived of her father's affections and although her strenuous efforts to please him had seemed futile, she had swallowed any anger she felt toward him. However, Janet's fantasies suggested that she blamed her mother. It was hypothesized that since Janet felt unappreciated by her father, it was likely that any normal jealousy she may have had toward her mother may well have remained unresolved and even magnified. The succor which mother had always so generously provided her now seemed like poison to Janet. If Janet could not reek revenge on her depriving father, she could attack her mother by refusing the mother's succorance. Yet, even her revenge against her mother had to be indirect. She could, and did, make her mother feel guilty, without seeming willfully to be the cause of her mother's distress. The revenge thus became masked in the anorexia.

Chapter 15

THE ASSESSMENT
OF SOCIAL DEVELOPMENT

For many years, the assessment of the child was aimed almost exclusively at his internal, personal behavior, with scant attention paid to the social pressures bearing upon him. However, as was discussed in Chapter 5, clinical psychologists now recognize that the development of the child's ego takes place within a social ecology which gradually becomes part and parcel of the child's ego itself. Moreover, one of the central aims of development of the child is to function in an integrated manner as an individual in society. Thus, no assessment, no matter what the complaint, can be considered complete or meaningful without data bearing on the social forces and the milieu in which the child is developing. As was discussed in detail in Chapter 10, the analysis of such data about the child's particular social forces depends upon the clinical psychologist's knowledge of the social forces extant in the immediate community and the sociological makeup of the society at large. Nevertheless, in the assessment proper, the psychologist must aim at least part of his data gathering at sampling the particular social forces bearing on the child and his family, and the ways in which they are handling and integrating these forces. As will be discussed particularly in this and

the ensuing chapter, assessment is very often centered on the degree to which and on the manner in which the child is forming a social identity.

Although the interview often provides a great deal of data about the child's and the family's social situation, evidence concerning the child's social growth is also present in nearly every other technique available to the assessor. Rather than discuss the techniques separately, this discussion will center around the various aspects of social development, citing examples of data gathered from various techniques, using the same heuristic outline applied in the previous chapters to ego development: the modality, the input-output, focus and differentiation, interferences, coping mechanisms, and content.

A. MODALITIES

The socialization of the child takes place through his interaction with and membership in social groups of increasing size and variety. The "modality" of his social development consists of the size, variety, and constitution of these groups. His initial social interaction —or, more specifically, personal interaction—

is with his mother; more strictly one may speak of socialization as beginning as he becomes a member of a family group. His family grouping may change, increase or shrink, during his childhood, thus changing his perspective of himself as a group member and affecting his identity. One of the important pieces of data to be gathered at intake is a statement of the family constellation and a history of its changes. Such information includes the birth or death of siblings, the presence or absence of parental figures, and data concerning any other types of family figures either present in the home or those outside the home which exert any kind of meaningful effect upon the child's social development. Who these family members are now, what they mean now or have meant in the past to the child, how they have regarded and treated the child, all should be explored in interviews with the parents and the child himself.

Moreover, the child's feelings about this family group and the degree to which these various group members may have affected him and become part of his internal feelings will be reflected in his fantasies on techniques such as the TAT, CAT, MAPS, and the World Test. It must be emphasized, of course, that these associative techniques do not tell how the family *actually* behaves but rather how the child *perceives* them and the extent to which they are part of his social identity. (The relationships between socialization and identity formation will be explored in more detail in Chapter 16.)

As was noted in Chapter 5, the child's social grouping begins to expand as soon as he begins to leave the family structure. Initially he may experience extra family groupings in his neighborhood play. His social world is perforce enlarged as he enters any kind of school situation, be it nursery, kindergarten, or elementary school. Here he finds himself in an extrafamilial, peer group society which expands his original family group identity. His relationship with and membership in this peer group society exist alongside the original family group and, at least until adolescence, the peer group is largely secondary to the family. Few, if any, of our popularly used clinical techniques yield much data regarding the child's peer group membership and adjustment. For the most part, the psychologist learns about it

from the child and his parents, both of whom are biased by their family group membership.

Teachers' reports occasionally mention how the child gets along in the classroom and on the playground, but even these are likely to be child-centered rather than group-centered reports. Again, it may be necessary for the psychologist practicing either in a clinic or privately to become familiar with the social makeup of the schools in his area. He should be familiar with the kinds of families in a specific area, what kind of social outlook the school authorities have, and what opportunities for peer interaction are offered to the child in a school setting. In some schools the child might well be a minority group member intellectually and socially, if not in the usual sense of race or religion. Moreover, schools vary widely in the degree to which they tolerate variations in behavior. Conflicts between the school authorities and the students are occasionally obvious in high school or even junior high school settings. Such conflicts may well be present on the elementary school level also but be less obvious to the casual observer.

As the child enters adolescence, his peer group begins to increase in importance to him, so that the kinds of children with whom he is associating and the settings in which these associations occur do become important variables in clinical assessment. Assessment interviews with the child of any age should include some discussion of his playmates and friends, and what they do together. In interviews with adolescents, an extended exploration of this aspect of his functioning may be necessary.

No few of the children who come for help in a psychologic clinic are social isolates without friends. In such instances, it is still necessary to ascertain from the child or his parents how he feels about his peers, what it is that he dislikes about them, or whether he may feel that he is disliked and rejected. For many children, the problem of isolation arises chiefly because they cannot or will not give up enough of the original family grouping to allow the establishment of this extrafamilial social membership. The parent who fears that his child may be influenced by other children in some untoward and undesirable direction and voices jaundiced and prejudices attitudes toward other children is often threatened by the separation of the child-parent bond. The child himself also may be threatened, although at the same time attracted by the opportunity for greater freedom and independence and so be greatly torn between peer and parent. He may have to find some excuse such as illness or devotion to studies to help him escape this conflict.

Again, in understanding the mode through which these peer relationships are established, the psychologist should be aware not only of the prevalent community attitudes and interaction, but of the very size of this grouping itself. To no small degree, the extreme concern and prejudice of the adult community today over adolescent behavior are derived from the increasing size of this minority within the society. It is estimated that well over one-fourth of the population is between the ages of 12 and 25, and there is every indication that this percentage will increase over the next several decades. In many urban areas, children attend junior high schools with populations of 2000 or 3000 and high schools with 3000 to 5000, and go on to a college along with 10,000 to 20,000 young adults. Social adjustment in such massive peer communities is quite a different matter from that in smaller communities or rural areas. Such massive educational "factories" do, in essence, prepare the child to live a mass society but the pressure for existence for both the child and the adult in these circumstances is often quite extreme. Psychologists are beginning to realize the severe difficulties created for the development of the child's individual identity by the enormity of educational institutions.

In general, the child may be thought of as deriving his socialization through two kinds of groups: an *ingroup* with which he identifies and feels a membership, and an *outgroup* or the "they" who set rules and controls over his behavior which he does not consider as part of himself and with whom he has no membership identity. Although in most instances the child is and feels himself to be a member of his family, there are often members of the actual family group whom the child does not include in his own perspective as family members and whom he considers as extragroup intruders. One of the best techniques for assessing the child's attitudes toward and inclusion of various familial members is the Bene-Anthony Family Relations Test (as described in Chapter 8). As is noted in the manual for this technique, the

assessor should ascertain independently the constellation of the family, for very often the child, in utilizing the Bene-Anthony, may leave out family members who actually reside in the home or add members who are not present. Thus, a child may fail to mention some sibling or parent or step-parent. He may add in parents who are not actually present in the home and with whom he has little contact. One child, for example, included in his Bene-Anthony family a baby who was not yet born, evidently because he wanted to express some feelings about this unborn sibling. Another child whose father had deserted the family several years previously and was almost unknown to the child put three fathers out on the table. Later, it was discovered that two boyfriends and an "uncle" of the mother were residing in the home and were considered as fathers by the child. Children from broken homes may not consider step-parents and step-siblings or half-siblings to be members of the family, but as part of the "they" outside of himself. In such multiple and often ill-defined family groups, the child often has to construct his own membership for what he considers to be his ingroup.

Sometimes such children are so confused about the family group to which they belong that they are unable to expand outwardly and begin to form peer group memberships. Other such children may abandon the problem of family group identification and desperately seek identification among their peers. Thus, one often finds that the child who seems easily led into delinquency actually seeks out delinquent children in order to find some kind of peer group that will accept him when he is confused or rejected by his family group.

One of the richest sources of data about the child's social behavior, particularly his interaction with his peers and with adult authorities, is direct observation of behavior in the classroom and activity on the playground through visits to the school. Unfortunately, not many clinics offer the opportunity for the assessor to leave his office and go out to the school; it is to be hoped that, as the clinic and other community agencies become more consolidated, classroom and playground observation may be a routine part of individual assessment. Even if the psychologist himself is unable to make such visits on a regular basis, many teachers are trained to observe the child as a member of a group and teachers' notes or conversations with teachers are a valuable substitute for direct observation.

Another way in which the child's membership within the family group may be assessed is to ask each member of the family to rate every other member on some brief scale as the Leary Interpersonal Check List (1957). This check list is particularly handy because the dimensions it allegedly measures are conceived in terms of interpersonal interactions and stress. In the assessment of one family constellation, the Leary ICL was given to all members of the family eight times. Each was asked to rate himself and all other members of the family, including the potential therapist, who was at that point assessing the family in a family group therapy setting. The results of these interactions, plotted on the love-dominance circle of the ICL chart, revealed that the "identified" patient, an anorexic 13-year-old boy, was in the middle of a triangular power struggle between the very dominating father, the passive-angry mother, and a manipulating nurturant grandmother. Other siblings in the family had evidently taken sides with one or another of these three adult authorities leaving the patient unable to dare accept succorance from any one of the three, lest the others reject him. Although there were other factors bearing on this child's anorexic condition, an analysis of and a working through of the family power struggle proved to be one of the major therapeutic moves.

B. INPUT-OUTPUT

Classical behaviorism holds that, in essence, the child is a *tabula rasa* to be imprinted by social forces. Very similarly, in classical psychoanalysis the child's libidinal instincts were thought to become incased in social taboos, thus creating neuroses. The fact that the child is conditioned by social forces and that these social forces become internalized into a personal sense of guilt are complementary truths, but that the child is merely a receptor of this input of social forces is only a half truth. As was described in Chapter 5, the child from birth on, if not actually when he is first thought of by his parents, is himself a social force and an *effector* in whatever social group he is a member. In fact, he is

actually an effector in groups in which he does not hold membership but with which he comes into contact, or conflict. The degree to which and the manner in which the child receives social stimuli and in turn affects his social groups, is a core part of his ego development. A great deal of the assessment is concentrated both on the child's sensitivity and awareness of his interpersonal environment and his ability to manipulate it, enter into it, and affect it. Assessment of the child's development as both receptor and effector of his social milieu can be made from a wide variety of techniques.

As was discussed in several of the preceding chapters, the Rorschach Technique, in particular, has as its central variable the "intratension" and "extratension" of his Experience-Balance which describes the degree to which the respondent allows environmental stimuli to impinge upon his judgments and the degree to which he impinges his own personal attitudes and constructs upon his environment. As was explained in this prior discussion of the Rorschach, what is reflected in the child's inkblot responses is not his sociability or social introversion-extraversion, but rather an attitudinal set toward this environment.

While the Rorschach gives a basic estimate of the child's interaction with the affective aspects of his society, other techniques may be helpful in estimating the child's cognitive recognition of social stimuli or, as it is commonly called, his "social intelligence." One commonly used estimate drawn from the Wechsler Intelligence Scale for Children consists of contrasting the child's score on the "Comprehension" subtest with his score on the "Picture Arrangement" subtest. The Comprehension scale yields an estimate of how well the child understands and recognizes social behavior and mores. It shows whether he knows why things occur socially and what they mean. In contrast, the Picture Arrangement samples primarily the child's understanding of how social events take place, that is, the sequence and arrangement of social situations. The instructions to this subtest require him to manipulate the cartoon scenes into a meaningful sequence. Comprehension thus may be considered as a measure of the child's intellectual receptivity of social events in contrast to Picture Arrangement which requires the child to manipulate environment. Thus, the verbally bright, achievement-oriented, but socially isolated child often achieves a high score on the Comprehension subtest but may have difficulty with Picture Arrangement. In contrast, there is the equally bright but much less achievement-oriented child who concentrates his efforts on social maneuvers and manipulation; such a child makes a much higher score on Picture Arrangement than on Comprehension. Of course, this single score difference cannot be used as an isolated index, but should be treated as only one indicator among the array of evidence.

Indications of the degree to which the child sees himself as a passive receptor of social stimuli or a controller of his social milieu may also be found in his TAT stories or in his use of the World Test materials. Thus, in analyzing the CAT or TAT stories or the MAPS, the psychologist should note to what extent the hero is the object or victim of his surroundings and to what extent he takes charge and manages or affects the plot. Of course, in drawing conclusions from such data, one must keep in mind that this is *fantasy* behavior. What one may conclude is that at least in fantasy the child can imagine himself as a powerful figure managing his environment or that in fantasy he sees himself as the victim. Thus, it must be remembered that some children who do suffer from being buffeted by their environment may take an opportunity in fantasy to see themselves in control through identifying with the hero of the story. Even so, such fantasied role of being an effector does suggest that whatever the actual position in which the child may find himself in his environment, he is at least able to conceptualize having some affect upon it. Obversely, the child who fantasies heroes as being passively the victims of social forces may be projecting his own feelings of guilt rather than an objective analysis of the social situations in which he finds himself. A guilt-ridden child may in effect manipulate his environment to a considerable degree but still feel the victim of some outside force.

On the World Test, one can see such receptor-effector behavior in the way the child selects and utilizes the materials rather than purely in the content of his production. Some children seem to search the materials for those that will fit into some kind of plan that they have in mind to build a world. Other children will pick out each piece of material and let it effect what they are doing so that the item in the child's hand determines what he will do next. For example, Grace, age five, had been ejected from kindergarten for being too "aggressive." Her father caustically remarked, "She's just like her mother; when they're a bitch at five, what hope is there?" Grace immediately dumped the entire World Test case upside down and, hunting through the materials, picked out those she wshed to have for a village, ignoring all materials that did not fit into her plan. Another five year old, Emma, about whom the school remarked that she did not seem quite mature enough to enter the first grade, dantily selected one piece at a time from the World Test chest, trying to find where it might fit and continually asking the advice and support of the examiner. For this second girl, what was in the world controlled her, and she was at a loss to deal with it.

Very commonly the child plays a role both as effector and receptor. Thus, even when he is helpless, he, in effect, draws support and guidance from others, or when he is most aggressive and attempting most to manage his environment, he may be subject to increased pressure from adult authorities or peers. This concept of a social interaction rather than that of a purely stimulus-response pattern is sometimes ignored in assessment particularly when there is an attempt to apply rigidly structured diagnostic categories. The primary example is childhood autism. In the controversy in the literature over the etiology of autistic behavior as summarized by Eisenberg and Kanner (1956), one school of thought maintains that autism occurs because the infant is emotionally and socially neglected by a narcissistic mother from the time of the child's birth. A great deal of clinical material has been collected to support this argument. On the other hand, there are those who maintain that autistic behavior is a symptom of a generalized congenital central nervous system dysfunctioning and that such disturbances as seen in the parents are the effects of attempting to deal with a child who does not respond. The error made by persons holding each viewpoint is that autistic behavior is necessarily a unitary syndrome with a single etiology. Autistic behavior (as opposed to "autism" as a diagnosis) may be observed both in children who have obvious central nervous system damage before birth and in children in whom such brain damage cannot be established. It is also true that in both cases there may be a narcissistic mother who rejects the child. Certainly not all brain-damaged children become autistic, nor do all mothers of brain damaged children react by rejecting the child completely. It also is possible that some brain-damaged children will show autistic behavior no matter what the reaction of the mother. Research about this behavioral syndrome could be greatly clarified if put in terms of the interaction between the child and mother rather than either the effects of the mother upon the child or the effects of the child socially upon the mother.

C. FOCUS AND DIFFERENTIATION

Both as receptor and effector in social situations, the child must learn to discriminate among the incoming social stimuli and to recognize differences and similarities among the people with whom he is dealing. He must also learn how to play distinct roles of his own in his interaction. For the infant, all people appear the same; they are all "mammas" or "daddies." Gradually he learns to discriminate the roles that people play with him, particularly if he has siblings or peers at his nursery school or in the neighborhood. However, even a five year old is not always able to discriminate other roles that people play with other people; for example, he may ask a grown woman about her "daddy," not distinguishing daddy from husband. This sorting out of roles played by people with him and with one another and of the roles that are assigned to him by others is an ever-expanding task for the child. Such a receptive differentiation is essential if the child is to be able to develop and differentiate roles for himself.

Take, for example, the physically handicapped child. His parents, in their depression and desperation, may assign him the role of the helpless cripple who needs constant care. The child may accept this role insofar as it gives him advantages as being the receptor of extra emotional support and other rewards and as being socially immune to the discipline and prohibitions applied to his siblings. Since in assigning this role to the child the mother inadvertently assigns herself the role of being an all-loving and all-protecting maternal figure, no matter what her needs and wants

may be, the child also is, is essence, assigned the role of depriver of mother's wants. Similarly, father's role as authoritarian may be limited and extra demands may be made upon him as the provider of financial and material goods. Siblings in such a family may find themselves in the role of second-class citizens. The child in question may wear this role comfortably at home for awhile, but as he enters school he may find that his peers will regard him as helpless and unwanted. His teachers, too, may not give him quite the special treatment that he is afforded at home. At school he may try to compensate for his rejection by his peers by playing an almost opposite role by denying his disability and attempting to force himself into the peer group. His fantasies at such a point may contain megalomanic dreams of war and glory. With such disparate roles, the child finds it difficult to take any realistic, objective view of his disability, or to develop a consistent image of himself.

Both the structured tests of intelligence and the associative techniques provide data for the assessment of the child's ability to make these social discriminations. Although certainly not purely intellectual discriminations, the ability to differentiate intellectually the roles that other people play is essential for the child. He has to learn what the different rules are in specific situations, and why people do the things they do, as is sampled on the Comprehension subtest of the WISC. However, a knowledge of these general rules may not always help in specific situations and thus he must also be able to spot what is going on in a specific situation and focus on it as is sampled in Picture Arrangement. Both the MAPS and the World Test provide an excellent opportunity for the child to demonstrate his social discrimination. The MAPS with its numerous figures of all ages, sexes, and even races, and of both real and fantasy figures, gives the child a chance both to find the type of person he needs for a specific fantasy situation and to assign roles to these characters. The younger child, below age eight, often does not make much discrimination among the stimuli provided by the test but assigns roles in general as his fantasy guides him. In contrast, the older latency child and the adolescent will look for figures to match whatever fantasies they are dreaming up. However, a younger child's consistent selection of a particular figure to play one role may be quite significant.

For example, one five-year-old boy, whose recently divorced mother often took the child to bed with her, consistently selected as mother figures the half-dressed and naked women of the MAPS. Halfway along in his fantasy, he began to confuse these figures with the witch figures. He became puzzled as to which figures he should include as daddies, picking one up and then another, and putting each back. At one point he even addressed the ghost figures as daddy, then apologized for his slip of the tongue.

The way that the child relates the figures to the selected scene may also give clues as to his ability to discriminate socially. Again, younger children make what seems to be almost random assignments of the MAPS figures to the scene, albeit with an idiosyncratic meaning. Considerably more discrimination would be expected of the older child, and thus his slips or fantasy intrusions are even more significant. For example, a 14-year-old voyeur decided to stage a gun battle between cops and robbers in front of the street scene of the MAPS. During his search for figures for this scene, he picked up the half-dressed female figure, fingered it and looked at it and dropped it on the stage. Ignoring it for the moment, he picked up other figures but then returned to it and as he noticed it on the stage, remarked, "Oh, I guess I goofed putting this one in!" Still holding it, he finally decided that he would make the whole scene very silly and put this woman in the middle of it. This intrusion of sexuality in an inappropriate form into a masculine battle scene was consistent with the child's actual social behavior, for he kept company with younger boys and had not started any normal heterosexual interests.

In playing with the World Test, preschool children use very few human figures and only slightly more animals; often they do not discriminate between the kinds of human figures or animals. Both adults and children are considered "people" and wild and tame animals are thrown together. Soldiers may be shown as going to the grocery store. The world of the latency child is somewhat more peopled and, as the child grows older, he will begin to pick out the policeman to direct the traffic, show the children going to school, and build a zoo for wild animals. One ten year old who decided finally to conduct a street battle through his village made sure

first that all of the children were tucked inside the schoolhouse outside of the way. The preschool child also tends to operate most of the equipment in the test himself. He flies the plane, runs the train, pushes the cars. The somewhat older child is more likely to get one of the figures to run the cars, tend the railroad station, or turn the signals in the street. The younger child dive bombs the airplane with his hands; the older child has the soldiers do the shooting while he makes the noises.

Most important, the child has to learn to play different roles himself. He has to know those settings where he can play the role of baby, those where he has to be tough guy, those where it pays to be smart, and those where it pays to act a little stupid. Being conforming and compliant he finds will pay off with the teacher but not with his peers on the playground. He may be able to play tough guy with his younger brothers but he has to be prepared for considerably more competition if he plays this role with peers of his size and intelligence. Children play such a variety of roles in their attempts to maneuver and test adults that their behavior might almost be classified as "psychopathic" in an adult. For example, it is not uncommon to find that a child, who is quite disorderly and impolite at home, who battles with his parents and resists their efforts to teach him to be "mannerly," may be quite the opposite when he enters the home of one of his friends. His mother thus will be quite surprised when the mother of the other child compliments her on how well behaved her child is. She may find also that although his clothes are scattered about his room and he gets angry when he is told to pick them up, his school-work may be quite neat. His teachers may vary in their reports of him. He discovers which teachers he can sass back and which ones to whom he must say "yes, mam" and "yes, sir." He may push his brothers and sisters around if permitted to do so but be considered a nice guy by his peers and rarely squabble with them. He may learn that dad will seldom sympathize with his hurts nor give him physical comfort but that he can always gain mother's support when he is feeling ill, hungry, or even out of sorts. On the other hand, he may learn that his mother does not understand or is out of sympathy with him when he is physically aggressive, gets into mischief, or demonstrates sexual curiosity, whereas his father may be the one who permits him to play the aggressive and sexual male role.

Even though the normal child, especially around puberty, may test many of these roles, he seldom finds it possible to present so many faces consistently but, instead, adopts those which are consonant with his image of himself. An inability to vary roles with different situations and people results in a social naïveté and in the extreme is characteristic of the schizoid child. At the other extreme, the child who constantly changes his face to fit the situation and seeks to maneuver others does seem to be failing to establish an identity of his own, and the formation of a psychopathic personality does become a possibility. Usually, this latter type of child faces a very inconsistent and frequently changing social situation. He may find marked differences between the expectations of each of his parents. Soon he discovers how to play one against the other. He may also experience considerable differences in expectations and mores between his home and his school or between the school and peers. If he is confused by marked differences in these social situations and is unable to play different roles, he may withdraw in schizoid isolation. Or, he may concentrate his efforts on adjusting separately to each situation, to "getting by" as best he can without adopting any one of these roles as an identity.

Such children often spend a great deal of the energy of their ego in playing such roles almost to the neglect of other kinds of ego functioning. Their N Achievement becomes concentrated on social role playing rather than on school work or anything else. As adults and other children find themselves maneuvered by such a child, they become more cautious with him and thus are less likely to accept the roles he purports to play. Such children are often hypersensitive to the feelings of others, and are quick to sense rejection. They rapidly change ground, renewing their efforts to manipulate people in some other direction with even more vigor. Such social role playing and hypersocial-sensitivity is frequently found among children who are labeled "delinquent." However, not all delinquents have this facility nor do all children who play multiple roles necessarily become delinquent. Because such children adjust themselves chameleonlike to any social situation, their difficulty may not immediately be obvious to the assessor, at least on the first contact. However, the assessor may come to realize, at least halfway through the hour, that he is being closely observed and that any clues he drops are being picked up. On the whole, the child is attempting to give the assessor what he wants while at the same time not giving himself away.

Case 36

Bob N., age 16, was brought to the clinic by his parents after having been expelled from school because of a locker room theft. His mother, who made the appointment, seemed grimly angry over the telephone and it was difficult to arrange an appointment since she seemed to have so many other things to do. She finally accepted the appointment time offered her, remarking that she should be present at the PTA meeting where she was an officer but that she was so embarrassed by Bob's behavior and expulsion that she doubted that she could face the other mothers. When informed that it was the clinic's policy that the fathers also be interviewed in the initial contacts, she retorted angrily that she could not account for her husband's time, and advised the clinic to call him. Finally, she agreed to inform him of this clinic rule and to ask him to call the clinic.

When Bob's father called, he seemed much less concerned, remarked that he didn't see why such a fuss was being made over what he evidently considered to be a childish prank, and said that he was getting in touch with the school to "settle everything out of court." However, he agreed to an appointment with the clinic's social worker at the same time arranged by his wife.

Bob's parents had not arrived at the time of the appointment, but Bob was in the waiting room by himself. He quickly put out his cigarette and limply shook hands with the psychologist. A tall, lean, pinched-faced youth with a bad case of acne, he followed the psychologist down the hallway, stopping several times to run a comb through his long hair and to get a drink of water. He slouched in his chair, looking around the room, fumbling with his cigarettes, but did not light one until given permission by the examiner.

Asked why he had come, he responded by asking if the psychologist were not aware of the reasons, since he knew that his mother had discussed it over the telephone. When invited to tell his own version of the problem, he replied in an offhand manner that the vice-principal, whom he referred to by his last name only, had made him stay out of school for a few days. Urged to explain further, he said "It was really nothing," that what had happened was that some friends of his had been playing a joke on another kid in the locker room and had hidden his wallet. Bob averred that he had been a witness, but not a participant, in this "joke," and that the vice principal knew this but had suspended him because he would not tell on the other boys. He made it clear that he considered the whole incident very unimportant and inconsequential. When it was suggested to him that he might not therefore regard the incident as a reason for being referred to the psychologist, he agreed but did not comment.

He suddenly asked the psychologist if he knew of several different youngsters who were being treated in the clinic. The psychologist asked him how he happened to bring up these names and Bob claimed he had talked to them and knew that they were coming to the clinic and that they had advised him that he was likely to meet the psychologist. Further questioning revealed that Bob had tried to ascertain as much information as he could about the clinic and about the psychologist beforehand. He had even taken the trouble of finding out what kind of psychological tests might be given and what kind of questions would be asked him. When asked why he was so interested in the clinic and in the procedures when he did not really see that he had any particular problem, Bob laughed and said that he had always been kind of curious about psychology and that he thought once that he might become a psychologist and so was interested in "that sort of thing." Asked further what he expected, he replied, "I guess you want to know all about me." The psychologist agreed that he was willing to listen to whatever Bob needed to talk about with someone if Bob saw some reason for it.

Bob then volunteered, "Well, I guess I do have a sexual problem." And then he paused, looking at the psychologist. "Don't you want to hear about it?" he asked. The psychologist agreed that he was willing to listen. "You won't tell my parents?" The psychologist agreed that the discussion was confidential. Bob paused again, eyed the psychologist and began, "Well you see, there is this little girl I've been making out with every once in awhile, nothing really very much you know,

never did really much, never went all the way, of course, but I just kind of wondered." He then paused, looking at the psychologist. When asked why he wanted to tell the psychologist about this, he replied, "I just thought you wanted to know about those things." He could not say why he thought such information might be important in his case, nor could he think of anything else important to talk about.

When the topic was brought back to the reasons for his referral to the clinic, Bob made a face, and commented "Oh, that!" In further discussion about his school situation, Bob agreed that he did not care much for school and that although he had made fair grades in elementary and junior school, his high school grades had been barely passing. He quickly said that he had full intentions, in this his senior year, of making up his grades so that he could go to college and that he had been studying extra hard this first month of the school year because he knew that he did have a great deal to make up.

He then began complaining about the assignment of classes, particularly in mathematics, giving a history of his difficulties in that subject which he claimed were not altogether his fault. He said he was particularly bored the previous year when he had had to repeat a basic mathematics course and had almost flunked it a second time. Further questioning revealed that he was bored in most of his other classes, and he agreed that he was tempted at times to skip them altogether. At first he denied any other previous clashes with the school authorities except for occasional truancies. At the end of the hour, Bob asked anxiously again about the psychological tests and was told that these would be given when necessary.

The social worker reported that Bob's parents also had been singularly uninformative. The parents seemed to feel that Bob had never done anything "terribly bad" but always seemed to be in hot water with the school authorities. The mother continued to be angry as she talked about the number of times that teachers and vice-principals had called her into the office. She complained that she received very little help or support from her husband about Bob's school behavior. Bob's father said that he did not see that Bob had done anything more than any other kid and that he was awaiting a conference with the vice-principal regarding the current incident. Nevertheless, both parents seemed to agree that they felt that Bob needed some kind of psychological help. His mother deplored his recent poor academic record and contrasted it with the excellent record of Bob's older sister who was now in college. The father, too, voiced the hope that the psychologist could find out "What's the matter with that kid," but could not specify what he thought was the matter. "It's hard to find out what's on his mind." The parents agreed that they might have "lost touch with Bob" and that they rarely could find out what he was doing in school or anywhere else, let alone what he thought or felt. Both felt uneasy about him but said that they had no cause for complaint about his behavior at home.

When they were asked about family schedules, it was revealed that the family actually spent little time together. Mrs. N was busy many afternoons a week with her community and entertainment activities and usually arrived home around six, the same time as Bob. She often gave Bob his dinner then, and waited until later to eat with her husband, who did not arrive from work until nearer 7:30. By that time Bob was usually out of the house—"studying" with some friends. On school nights he was usually back in the house around ten, and, they thought, usually asleep by eleven. On weekends, also, the family went separate ways. The previous summer Bob had been old enough to get a driver's license and was given a car and gas allowance. He had a generous cash allowance each week and always seemed to have plenty of money; neither parent could understand at all why he might be even interested in stealing anyone else's money. His father did remark that at times Bob did seem to have more money than could be readily accounted for, but Bob explained that he had been saving up his allowance and his lunch money.

After these interviews, the psychologist, with the permission of the parents, contacted the school vice-principal. The vice-principal confirmed that Bob had maintained that he was not involved in the theft but that the physical education teacher had found the missing wallet among Bob's possessions in his locker. Bob vehemently denied any knowledge of how the wallet came into his locker and tried to maintain that it was all a practical joke. The boy whose wallet was missing had claimed that Bob had stolen other things from him, and the two boys who were also implicated in this theft claimed that they had merely accepted money from Bob out of the wallet. The vice-principal did not believe Bob's story but said that Bob told stories so convincingly that it was often difficult to know what to believe.

It was not the first time that Bob had been implicated in a theft, but there had never been any proof before that he had really been involved. Nearly all of the teachers and school authorities were, however, very suspicious of Bob. He was known as a kid who always tried to get away with things. He always seemed to have some good excuse and to be very pleasant about it; a "charmer," said one teacher. If caught red-handed at some misdemeanor, he would apologize and try to make friends with the teacher or school authority. Several times it was suspected that he had forged notes to have himself excused from classes, but the school had found it difficult to contact his parents to ascertain whether they had signed the notes.

An hour prior to the next appointment, the mother phoned to inform the clinic that she would not be able to come in because of a previous engagement but assured the social worker that Bob would appear. No information was given concerning Mr. N's appointment, and he did not appear either. When Bob was asked about the fact that his parents did not come in, he shrugged his shoulders and remarked that he guessed that they were busy. When the psychologist asked if this might mean that they did not really consider Bob's problem very important, his face flushed and he bit his lip and replied in a manner as nonchalant as possible, "Well, you might think that." But he seemed to collect himself quickly and added, "It's really my problem, of course, and I am sure that they will be able to give you any information that you wish."

However, Bob disclaimed any knowledge of what his parents might have to say or even how they might feel about the incident at school. Pressed further, Bob said that he did not think that his father was very concerned about it, adding that "Dad always seems to find ways out of things." He could not explain this statement much farther but backtracked to emphasize that he had never really had any brush with his father and so was under the impression that this incident probably would not bother him much. As to his mother's feelings, Bob smiled wryly and remarked that he was sorry if it embarrassed her. He realized that she was most concerned about what other people might think because of these allegations. Asked if he thought she would be concerned if no one else heard of it, Bob said, "What do you think?"

The psychologist reminded Bob that he had remarked in the previous hour that perhaps the clinic should know "all about him" and asked Bob if there were things in his background that it might be helpful to discuss. Bob shrugged and said, "Ask me." However, it proved very difficult to get any kind of history out of Bob. He knew very little about his family except that his grandfather was reputed to have had quite a bit of money. The most he could remember about his early childhood years was that the family had moved around considerably to several different towns and that he had attended at least four different elementary schools by the time that he was ten years old.

At that time, his maternal grandfather died, leaving the family enough money to buy a home in a very nice district of town. His father had been a railroad engineer, but at his mother's insistence had quit his job so that their life would not be quite as irregular. Bob was not even quite sure what his father did for a living, but that it had something to do with his grandfather's business which he now operated, along with his mother's two brothers.

At age ten, Bob contracted rheumatic fever and was out of school for almost a year. He seemed to remember this year almost enoyably; he was waited on hand and foot by his mother and sister. "I never had it so good." When he did return to school, he was restricted from most physical education activities and it was only in this current year of school that he was permitted to be enrolled in a physical education class on a limited basis. He denied that this limitation on his physical activities bothered him at all, claiming that he never was interested in sports, and that he considered athletes to be "stupid." He denied also that he had lost interest in school while ill or that he had fallen behind in his studies.

The junior high school which he formerly attended highly emphasized sports. The psychologist knew that the vice-principal had been a football hero and that athletic competition had a high value among children at this school. Despite his denial of any interest in sports, Bob boasted that he had been invited several times to play basketball and that he had been one of the taller boys in the junior high school. He made further disparaging remarks about this school, and it was brought out that he really knew very few of the children there, most of whom had come from fairly stable families and had lived in the same neighborhood for many years. The student body was dominated by rather exclusive cliques. As a relative stranger, Bob had found it difficult to make friends.

Furthermore, the school district was divided rather strangely, so that when he started high school most of the children he did know at junior high school went to a different high school while his home lay within a district in which the high school was quite distant from his home. Thus, he again found himself in among strangers. This school contained many children from lower socioeconomic areas. Again the sports program dominated the social scene. However, academic achievement was not held in high value by his peers. Bob denied that he lacked friends but, when asked more specifically, he maintained that he preferred to go with one or two fellows. He claimed that the two boys allegedly involved in the theft were among his best friends and also named as friends two delinquent boys who were also patients at the clinic.

At this point, Bob suddenly asked the assessor what he thought of what Bob had told him the previous hour about his girl friend. The psychologist remarked that he thought that there was something there that concerned Bob but that he was not quite sure what it was. Bob smiled and remarked that what he had told the psychologist was not at all true and that he had made this all up because he had thought that psychologists were interested in "boys and girls and sex." The psychologist assured Bob that it was not necessary to make anything up just to interest him but rather that he was mainly interested in what concerned Bob. Bob suddenly admitted that he was unhappy that he did not have a girl friend, particularly since both of his friends were interested in girls and "make out all the time." The examiner agreed that this would be a definite concern and that it was only natural that one might at least pretend publicly that he had a girl friend so that he would not be embarrassed. He suggested that this might be something that Bob would like to talk over further at a later time.

Because the school was asking for some advice from the clinic about Bob, particularly regarding the possibility of readmitting him, the psychologist had been urged to complete his assessment at the earliest possible time. As part of the assessment, the psychologist had planned to use techniques other than the interview to explore Bob's social attitudes and his handling of affect and because of his recent poor school achievement, some measure of his current intellectual functioning. On the WAIS, Bob attained a full scale IQ of 119, a verbal scale of 110, but a performance scale of 128. Both his Vocabulary and Information subtest scores were quite superior and his verbal reasoning on the Similarities subtest was also above average. He made rather stumbling hasty errors on the Arithmetic subtest, but his real difficulty proved to be on Comprehension. For example, he said, "The smart thing to do (when a person saw a fire start at a movie) was to slip out the side exit and avoid the mob." People should avoid "bad company" because "they aren't any fun." (It seemed as though he interpreted the word "bad" as meaning uninteresting.) Criminals are locked up, Bob thought, "because that's what happens when they get caught." The proverb "Strike while the iron is hot" did not mean much to Bob, but he speculated that perhaps it would indicate that one should hit anyone who was angry and thus cool him down. He seemed to sense that he was not doing very well on these items and remarked after the last response, "I guess I'm not doing too hot. Is that what you wanted?" In contrasting his responses to the Comprehension test with those on the Picture Arrangement, it was noted that Bob succeeded in arranging all of the sequences correctly and with full time credit on all but the final one.

On the Rorschach, Bob studied each card for many seconds before responding and then usually gave some rather stereotyped and innocuous form response. None of his responses had any human movement; only two of his 15 responses contained animal movement, and the balance of his responses, except for one, was based purely on the form of his concept. The other response was the popular green worm on Card X. Out of these 15 responses, six were popular and none original. There were no human figures, even human

detail, anywhere in his responses. In a "testing of the limits," Bob readily agreed that the two figures on Card III did look human and perhaps in movement but remarked, "I didn't know you wanted that kind of thing."

He was most uneasy with the TAT, claiming that he had no imagination, and thus could not think of any stories. Again, he stared at the pictures for a long time before attempting any kind of response and then often merely described the cards. He denied that he could imagine at all why the boy in Picture 1 had stopped playing the violin, except that perhaps he just was not interested anymore. He could not imagine why he had been playing the violin in the first place or what he might be thinking at present. "You can't tell about a guy from the way he looks." Most of his other stories were in a similar vein. To Card 6BM, he remarked, "It looks like the old lady is giving him hell for something but I can't tell what. The boy in the picture is just taking it for right now, and knows that the old lady will forget it later. So he just goes and does what he want anyhow. She gets mad, but she gets over it. Guess that tell you all about me and my mom, doesn't it?"

Bob's drawing of a person, which he was also reluctant to attempt, was somewhat bizarre. The figure looked like a child with a big head and grin. Bob spent a considerable amount of time drawing the body of a rather muscular male figure, carefully shading in the shirt and trousers and finally putting two large guns in the figure's hands. He laughed at his drawing and remarked how silly it looked but could make no associations to it, just remarking that it was a ridiculous figure. He begged off drawing any female figure, and as the hour was growing late, the examiner excused him.

A further appointment was made with the parents, but neither of them appeared. When they were called, Mrs. N apologized and explained that Mr. N had been able to settle things with the school. Since it seemed quite evident that the N's were not motivated for any further help, the case was closed at this point. Three years later the clinic received a letter from the Dean of Men at a state college requesting a report of the clinic's findings on Bob, explaining that he was currently suspended for allegedly cheating on an examination.

Another syndrome which may be called "social retardation" is so widespread and is so commonly referred specifically to the psychologist for assessment that it warrants special consideration at this point. The model case is that of a child just entering pubescence who has always needed special help in his schooling and who has been slow to learn how to take care of himself. Often such a child is quite capable in his own home and even in many ways at school. He reads slowly, does some simple arithmetic even more slowly, but is basically literate at about the third or fourth grade level. He finds his way to and from school, and can even be trusted on brief and simple errands. However, his social naïveté is obvious to all. His peers reject him because he does not recognize the unspoken relationships and rules in his peer group. In fact, in many instances he ignores the open and declared rules. His parents are often embarrassed by his failure to learn how to "behave." He may have learned the words of politeness, even using them more compulsively and routinely than many other children. However, he remains very gauche, approaching strangers in such an open-faced manner that his parents fear that someone may take advantage of him. The family is tempted to hide him when guests come because he seems so socially childlike. Despite his relative successes at school, the parents begin to worry that he will "never grow up." They voice a fear that he will not be able to earn a living, not because he cannot work or do many simple jobs, but because others will reject him. More covertly, but with even greater intensity, they fear his naïveté because he is approaching puberty and they realize that his lack of social know-how may cause him problems with his social-sexual behavior, yet to be learned, as he enters adolescence. Case 9, Wayne, in Chapter 3, illustrates this.

This syndrome has many causes. Sometimes it is associated with a very mild central nervous system dysfunctioning, but in the majority of cases the neurological examination is essentially negative. Far more frequently the child has some mild physical handicap which may not even be noticeable but which makes him feel helpless and inadequate. In such cases, there is often evidence that the child unconsciously plays the role of social inadequacy because he feels helpless and fears that he really cannot get along socially. Most frequently such a social retardation is a reaction formation against parental demands and expectations that he act in a socially independent fashion. In his passive refusal to recognize social nuances, he often arouses hostility and rejection and thus his course of action is basically hostile. The essential hostility in the parent-child relationships which underlie this social naïveté syndrome is often demonstrated in the extremely phobic responses that the child makes to associative techniques. Even more dramatically, his anger becomes overt when some adult does not "play the game" with him. Various attempts to retrain such children are often met with storms of anger. Such children will scream repeatedly that they do not understand.

The compulsive, almost perseverative nature of such a child's social behavior is manifested not only in the simple and persistive response he makes to everyone, but in his fantasies as well. His TAT heroes will have few or no definite characteristics, and they behave in similar ways in story after story. It is often difficult for such children to differentiate one character from another in a TAT story. If someone is angry, the child may switch in the middle of the story and have another person be angry and then be unable to remember exactly who got angry about what. His drawings, which may score above the retarded level on the Goodenough Scale, will nevertheless look stiff and stereotyped. Sex differentiations on these drawings are usually vague. Nor are such children able to make any clearcut identifications or personality descriptions of their drawings.

At the other end of the continuum, the child who is hypersensitive to social stimuli may be either excessively shy or precociously socially adept or even both. A child who has been trained to be observant of others' feelings and to be aware of what others might do to him learns to be quite cautious. Some children who seem at first glance to be shy or withdrawn are merely standing to one side, carefully studying what is expected of them and what others are like. The training of the child to be socially perceptive is highly emphasized in oriental cultures, especially among the Chinese. Such acuity in the observation of social rules and behavior is taught to children, both consciously and unconsciously, by parents in any socially segregated group. Children of minority groups often have to learn several sets of spoken and unspoken rules and how to get along at several levels of society. They rapidly learn how to differentiate between life in the segregated ghetto and how to behave as they accompany their mother as a domestic in homes of the well-to-do or even when they cross town on a legally nonsegregated bus. In essence, social discrimination forces the Negro child to become more discriminative.

The responses of children with a hypersensitivity to social stimuli contrast sharply to those of their counterpart, the socially retarded child. Considering the indices mentioned above, the very socially aware child usually makes somewhat higher scores on both Comprehension and Picture Arrangement on the Wechsler, but not necessarily superior scores. He is likely to hedge his answers to the Comprehension subscale with many qualifications, sometimes to the extent that he may slightly contaminate his responses. For example, one such child considered seriously the question, "Why should one stay away from bad company?" and finally explained that he himself would not be so afraid that he would be influenced but that children who acted bad made other people angry and that he did not like to be in the middle of an angry situation. His sensitivity in interpersonal relationships also confused him when he came to the question of why women and children should be saved first in a shipwreck; his answer was that daddies might feel a lot worse if mothers and children were killed than mothers and children might feel if daddies were killed. He then thought this answer over and said that he was not sure of it because he thought that children would always feel bad if their daddies died instead of them. Thus, his sensitivity prevented him from taking an objective viewpoint, and illustrates how children who are quite socially sensitive can actually be somewhat stultified when it comes to making intellectual differentiations about social situations. Similarly, on the Picture Arrangement subtest, such children may get all the items correct but take an abnormally long time to sort out the cards, scrutinizing each detail and trying several arrangements before deciding on a final answer.

CASE 37

Margaret, age ten, made scale scores above 12 on all subtests of the WISC, except for the Picture Arrangement. There she went beyond the time limits on most of the items, and her score was only eight. Margaret had not been referred to the clinic but was seen in an extended clinical study as part of a research project. She had been selected for this individual study out of a sociometric study of the social interactions of very bright children. It was noted in the study that Margaret was a preferred partner in one-to-one relationships but was seldom chosen as a leader. Classroom and playground observations suggested that she seldom, if ever, intruded herself into any kind of activity although she was often invited by other children to participate. Her teachers rated her as a "shy but strange" girl. Her TAT stories were marked with a repetitive consideration of how people treated one another and what they thought of one another's treatment. Her characterizations of her heroes were very carefully and minutely drawn. These characters interacted with one another in consideration of how the other person would feel. Her plots were actually very simple, mostly in the present tense, and she often found it difficult to say what would happen next or how things would conclude. In fact, she felt very content with an elaborate statement of the interpersonal interactions without any conclusion.

Her Rorschach experience-balance was "ambiequal" with a high number of both movement and color responses, the latter being chiefly form-color. Her responses frequently contained additional use of texture such as shading in the highlighting of human faces or seeing the dual figures (as on III and VII) as having shadows. Such use of shading to denote shadows, which this child specified, is even rarer among children than among adults. One is reminded of the Jungian concept of the shadow as the social reflection of a person's personality.

Such children are not necessarily of superior intelligence; in fact, quite often they concentrate so much of the energy of their ego into this awareness of social stimuli that they may not achieve intellectually. However, they may have considerable interest in literature or other fine arts or, as they go on into high school, in the social sciences. One would imagine that if such a child learns to control and utilize this social sensitivity, he should eventually become an excellent psychologist.

On the other hand, some children are overwhelmed by the constant influx of such stimuli and do not develop either intellectual or other defensive measures to handle and assess it. (See Section E below on coping mechanisms.)

D. INTERFERENCES

Many of the factors that interfere with the social development of the child have been discussed above and in the introductory chapters and do not need to be explored further at this point. The important consideration here is the interaction between two main types of interferences: (1) those which arise from within the family grouping, and (2) extrafamilial or societal interferences. As has already been discussed, families have many ways of assigning roles to children which, in effect, keep them from developing into socially effective adults. Usually such family roles are relatively satisfactory within the family group. The difficulty arises when the child plays these same roles in the society at large outside of his family group.

For example, in a family that places an extremely high value on achievement, order, and self-control, a child may succeed in being a model of such behavior. However, he may find that he is "being good for nothing" at school. Particularly, he may not be appreciated by his peers who may see him as being overly competitive in classwork, a compulsive tyrant on the playground, and as being prissy and fussy. Even some of his teachers may be annoyed by such behavior.

In other families, with the same values, the child may be assigned a negative role in the family as a failure or scapegoat. If the parents project upon the child all their fears of failure and make him into the failure figure, he may well act out this failure syndrome at school as well as at home. Such a child may well become the socially retarded child described in the above paragraphs. The family history and parental responses to the Edwards Personal Preference Schedule in the following case give one example of this particular syndrome.

CASE 38

Saul H., age 12, was repeating the sixth grade and it looked as though he might fail once more. The pediatrician's referral stated that although "Solly" was rather obese, he was in generally good health and that a special neurological examination had been entirely within normal limits despite his mother's continued belief that Solly might have some neurological problem. Repeated intelligence tests at school had consistently shown Saul to be functioning at an average level, although his IQ had dropped from 113 in the first grade to 102 currently in the sixth grade. Such a drop in IQ over this period of childhood might be accounted for as a simple regression toward the mean. Saul's decreasing level of achievement had, however, been much sharper than could be accounted for by the drop in IQ. Teachers noted that Saul was "immature," "more concerned with neatness than the correctness of his answers," "quibbled often and becomes mixed up in details," and "a social isolate because of the ease with which he is frustrated."

When Saul was brought to the clinic, it was obvious that his parents had made an extra effort to have him neatly dressed and groomed. Although it was a warm day, he was wearing a jacket and tie, and his shoes were highly polished. Nevertheless, he had somehow succeeded in scuffing one shoe and in messing a chocolate bar across his starched white shirt. His mother was in despair because he had messed himself and was quite apologetic to the assessor about Solly's appearance. In addition, he had a slight cold, his nose was running, and his pockets were stuffed with used kleenex which he dropped in various parts of the lobby and in the office. Saul himself could not say what he thought was wrong but did show some vague self-concern, particularly surrounding his school failure.

Saul was more open about his negative self-concept on the Sentence Completion; for example: "I—am a slob," and "My father thinks—that I can't do anything right." To the item "Other children . . ." Saul wrote "Who cares?" His TAT characters were often helpless and ineffective and subject to considerable criticism. One such character, the male figure in 6BM, Saul labeled as a "nebish" (a Yiddish term roughly equivalent to "stumble-bum"). On the Rosenzweig's P-F Study for Children, Saul gave an unusually high number of ego-dominated, intrapunitive responses indicating that he was considerably concerned with self-blame. On the whole, intrapunitive responses dominated his P-F. His rather negative self-image was portrayed in his drawing which was of a rather tall and very thin man (in contrast to Saul's own obesity) but obviously a very awkward figure.

His difficulty in drawing, particularly in the placement of the facial features and details of the hands and feet, was so striking that the examiner thought that Saul might have some perceptual-motor handicap but Saul's performance on the Bender-Gestalt was well within normal limits. He had particular difficulty with the Rorschach because he continually criticized his own responses and thus found himself in a bind when he tried to justify inconsistent aspects of the blot. For example, he at first called detail 1 on Card VIII "a bear" but then said that it could not be a bear because it was pink. Then he could not decide whether one detail was a tail which would really make it a chipmunk or whether that was a leg and then "Where is the tail?" He frequently described things as "messy" or as "big, old, and hairy." (Using the word "hairy" to mean ugly.) Many of his responses had at least a mild phobic quality: "nutty people from out space" or a "big, hairy, old monster," but Saul chuckled and the tone of his voice suggested that the monster was not really frightening.

Mrs. H had brought along a written list of complaints about Saul, but before she could get very far in a discussion of them, she was already mentioning her own self-recriminations over her failure to raise Saul correctly. She accused her husband of being a failure as a parent, and he retorted that she was to blame. She was especially critical of Saul because of his sloppy eating habits, his failure to clean up his room, and his continual arguments with her and her husband in their attempts to discipline him: "He's a regular attorney, just like his father." Mr. H, stung by this remark, retaliated by describing his wife as a person who kept their home "hospital clean" and who constantly nagged when anything was out of place. Mrs. H retorted that she tried to do all of these things to keep a neat home for her husband, to have meals on time, and to do things correctly because she thought that this was what he demanded. When Mr. H shrugged off her attack, she was almost in tears, declaring that she had slaved all these years to make a "decent" home and that he did not really appreciate her. Furthermore, she remarked with acid bitterness that she thought

that a great deal of Saul's problems might be laid at her husband's doorstep because it was really he that constantly nagged at Saul and set high and perfectionistic standards for the child's behavior. It was Mr. H, she concluded who consistently corrected Saul's speech, his schoolwork, his manners at the table, and his appearance.

Mr. H, now nettled, retorted that if he had not done these things that Saul would be a perfect baby, that his wife spoiled Saul constantly by picking up after him, and by stuffing him with food and cooking special dishes for him until he was excessively overweight. He accused her of undermining his own attempts to discipline Saul through comforting him and giving him treats, especially when Mr. H had imposed some restriction on Saul or required some achievement from him.

As the staff reviewed this initial interview with the parents, it seemed obvious that each parent disliked his own role, yet feared that he would displease the other if he did not play it. In subsequent interviews, this possibility was explored with them. Mrs. H admitted that she might like to have some of the privileges of her sister-in-law who "sat in bed all morning and played bridge all afternoon." Mr. H laughed and remarked "Thank God no!" to which she said, "See see!" Mr. H, in turn, admitted that he really hated to discipline Saul and pointed out to his wife that despite his sister's seeming neglect of the household chores, she did pay attention to her children's behavior and that he envied his brother-in-law who did not have to fuss over the kids.

Both parents had been born and reared in Central Europe, had endured frightful hardships during the war, and had lost most of their relatives in concentration camps. Mr. H had just completed his training as an attorney when the war broke out and had fled to Switzerland where he remained working as an unskilled laborer until he was able to come to the United States. He was past 30 and spent the next three years training as an accountant, since his European legal background was not applicable in the United States. He did not marry until he was almost 40 and was 43 when Saul was born. He recounted his past with considerable depression; he was particularly bitter that he was never able to realize his career in law, and deprecated his own profession as an accountant. Although he was making a fair living, he put in many hours at his work, often arriving home after dinner, and bringing home work for the weekend. His wife was critical of his working habits, complaining that he took far more pains with his work than was appreciated by his clients, and that he troubled himself unnecessarily with many details. Moreover, she complained that he had difficulty in collecting his fees because he was not aggressive enough. She had tried many times to help him in his work, but there was so much disagreement between them that she no longer went to the office with him.

Mrs. H, who was ten years her husband's junior, had been hidden in an attic during the war in Holland much as was described in the report of *The Diary of Anne Frank*. This situation had required very strict compliance to routine as a life-saving measure. She had had little formal education, but her father, who was a religious scholar and teacher, had successfully carried on the education of his children during their long years of hiding. It was one of her regrets that she had never received any kind of formal certification for her education. She was very embarrassed by her European accent which persisted despite her several years in high school in classes in English for the foreign born. Consequently, there was considerable harping in this family over the correct way to speak. Mr. H took advantage of his wife's self-concerns to note that despite her avowed efforts to speak English correctly, she frequently lapsed into Yiddish or German when she was upset or when she wanted to discuss things with him which she did not want Saul to understand. Mrs. H complained that Saul was critical of both of them for their accents but that Solly had made particularly poor grades in English and grammar.

The profile of scores on the Edwards' Personal Preference Schedule for both Mr. and Mrs. H were remarkably similar. Both had scores above the 70th percentile on need-achievement and need-order and above the 90th percentile on need-abasement. This pattern of scores along with a relatively low score on need-aggression suggested that both set relatively high standards for themselves and were also quite self-critical and unable to really allow themselves to actively seek their goals. Both parents also made above average scores on Nutriance, suggesting that both (particularly the mother) placed a high value on waiting on others while, at the same time, both gave only few responses placing any valure on Succorance (particularly the father), suggesting that they did not allow themselves much satisfaction through receiving help from others. This latter set of scores seemed to be most important, as it indicated that both were denying themselves in almost martyrish fashion in an attempt to find satisfaction through Saul, yet were constantly failing to meet their need-achievement through him also. Saul, in turn, appeared to be acting out the needs of both parents to lower their need-achievement to a more realistic level and was reflecting their own self-deprecations and need-abasement. It thus seemed that Saul was a "failure" because the parents saw themselves as second class citizens who constantly failed to meet their own high ambitions.

Saul's case thus illustrates how an intrafamilial group pattern can be reflected out onto society, in this case in the classroom. However, the child also can disrupt the family group with pressures he may experience elsewhere. In a sense, this also happened in Saul's case, since the kinds of demands for achievement and for interpersonal relationships that he found at school were not satisfied by the kinds of responses he had learned at home.

The backwash of social problems into the home and the working through of these extrafamilial conflicts within the family setting are very common during adolescence. A seemingly peaceful family life may be disrupted when the child attempts to insert into it peer mores which may be quite inappropriate. Whether the family accepts the adolescent's attempt to adopt and internalize these peer standards will depend upon how rigidly the family had insisted upon its own internal regulatory measures. If the family is quite rigid, then the intrusion of these new mores may be disturbing. A child who comes from a family which might be described as "close-knit" may find his adolescence quite unacceptable by his previously approving parents, chiefly because adolescence breaks family ties. Many children from such families seem unconsciously to recognize that their peer standards will be unacceptable to the family and thus avoid becoming engaged in them. At least they are cautious about admitting to the family that they are interested in such peer activities. On the other hand, the same child may be most fascinated by those very peer activities which might be most disturbing to the family in his effort to free himself from the closeness of the family group.

CASE 39

The L family is a good example. All members of this family were very intelligent and energetic people. Mr. L, who made only a modest living, had nevertheless devoted all of his limited finances to his home and family, to the exclusion of any recreation for his wife or himself. Their large home with a swimming pool was obviously beyond their means. Mr. L took the bus and carried his lunch to work because they could only afford the single large station wagon which Mrs. L used to transport the children. All the L's time was spent in family activities. Although each child attended a school which started at a different time than Mr. L's own work hours, the entire family was aroused early in the morning so that they spent their early morning hours and breakfast together. Similarly, dinner was delayed until the entire family could be gathered. Even homework was a family-centered activity in which the parents participated by going from room to room where each child studied. All participated actively in church activities. Although Mr. L had a "bad back," he continually strained himself by participating in Little League with the boys and in family outings and camping, and teaching his girls to dance. Each member of the family played a different musical instrument and Mrs. L was very proud of their joint musical efforts which were displayed annually to all the L's friends in a huge Christmas party when they performed as a group. Seldom did the six L children go to other children's houses to play, but their playmates were constantly brought to their home.

When the oldest boy went away to college, he had never spent a night away from his family. The family came to the clinic when the second oldest of their two daughters, Stella, age 16, began spending many more hours with her peers than with her family. She began dressing in the most outlandish peer style, and she utterly refused to permit her parents to meet her boyfriends. Stella angrily declared that she would not permit her father to interrogate her boyfriends as she had seen him do with her older sister and with her older brother whom she declared "would not know what to do with a girl if he saw a live one." Her twin brothers, age 14, were also making many complaints against their father and then against their mother for supporting him. The twins also protested against their ten-year-old sister because she was playing the role of "little angel" in the family and their father held up her behavior to them as one who appreciated parental affection and family life.

The father's appeal for help from the clinic was heightened when his college son came home dressed in a very casual style, his hair uncut, and especially when he started an argument at the dinner table over the use of marijuana. Previously, intellectual discussions of the news of the world and of the daily comings and goings of the family members were commonly reported and commented upon during dinner. Much to the children's amazement, the father became outraged when this topic was brought up and forbade its discussion. Mr. L's behavior on this occasion was so unusual that even Mrs. L was quite concerned. After the initial interview with the parents, it was decided to initiate a brief series of family sessions. Only six sessions were required for the children to express more openly their need for extrafamilial identifications and for the parents to express their feeling of loss and yet to recognize that such activities and interests were to be expected.

Problems frequently arise in families, as is shown in the above example, because of the rigidity of the family structure in the face of extrafamilial pressures. Moreover, as described in Chapter 5, current social institutions frequently create almost overwhelming pressures on almost any family. The isolation of the nuclear family from any clan grouping, the constant mobility of the American family, the alienation of the individual in the mass culture, the new demands of technology for new skills and achievements, and the resultant alienation of the individual in the mass society all create problems for social development for every child. These problems are mentioned here for a second time to emphasize the necessity for the assessment of their effects in every case. It is necessary for the assessor to investigate how the child and his family are meeting these social stresses, what they mean to this particular family, and how the parents and child are coping with them. Although these stresses can disrupt development at any point in the child's life, it is more often that they become most marked at puberty. Thus, one should almost routinely ask how many times the family has had to move, what has happened to family possessions and ambitions through such moves, and how the family is meeting the problems of social and technological change.

The chief technique for assessing such stresses is, of course, the interview with the parents. However, it is often possible that the parents do not recognize the stresses that they themselves are under and hints from the child may give clues concerning what should be explored with the parents. The following case summary may suffice as an example.

CASE 40

Ricky M., age four, had been referred for psychological assessment by the pediatrician who had examined him when his mother had become worried over his listlessness, loss of appetite, interrupted sleep habits, and behavior at nursery school where he was reluctant to separate from her and seemed unable to join spontaneously in school activities. The pediatrician found Ricky to be in good health and felt that the boy might be depressed.

The possibility that there might be extraneous social pressures on this family was noticed immediately when it was discovered that both parents were working and it was difficult for them to find time for an appointment at the clinic. Mr. M was employed full time as an electronics technician, a trade he had learned in the Navy. He was also attempting to continue his education as an electronics engineer by attending university classes at night. This young couple had recently moved to Los Angeles from the midwest where Mrs. M had been living with her parents until her husband's discharge from the Navy approximately six months previously. Determined to establish a home for his wife and child, Mr. M had immediately purchased a tract house, which also demanded a considerable amount of his energy since it was not landscaped. The couple were also trying to pay for their new furnishings and to keep up the repairs on an old car. However, these facts were not immediately brought out in the interview, since both parents were preoccupied with Ricky's problems and did not perceive their pressures as related to Ricky.

In the initial playroom contact with Ricky, he preoccupied himself with the play house and dolls and enacted the parents' comings and goings and concerns. In this play Ricky had the baby left alone while the parents were preoccupied. Asked how the baby felt, Ricky stopped his play and sat very quiet, looking as if he were about to cry. Among his stories to the CAT, the following responses particularly suggested that his depression might be associated with the separation anxiety he experienced because of the busy routine of his parents.

Card 1: "The mommy is feeding the babies. Daddy isn't home yet. (How do the babies feel?) They save some for daddy." Card 2: "The baby is pulling on the rope. He wants to get them to come with him. (Who should come with him?) His mommy and daddy." Card 3: "The mouse comes out to see if the big tiger is still there. (Why?) 'Cause it's time for him to go to work." Card 9: "He's all alone. (How come?) Everybody's gone. All gone. (What does he do?) Cries."

Subsequently, the parents' situation was discussed with them; both admitted that they were somewhat depressed and felt under considerable pressure in their situation. Mrs. M began to talk about her feelings of loneliness in leaving her hometown and friends. Mr. M talked of his daydreams during his Navy years of having a home for his wife and baby and his disappointment since he currently was almost exhausted by the strain of trying to attain them. Mrs. M reported that her parents had offered to loan the couple money to ease their house payments, but Mr. M had felt that he had already asked too much of them as they had cared for his wife and baby during his stint in the Navy. He agreed that although it might hurt his pride slightly to accept this loan, it would make it possible for his wife to stop working.

After several interviews, this couple seemed to have some insight into the social pressures that they were under and were planning steps to change part of their arrangement. Mr. M decided to accept the loan from his in-laws and to register for summer session as he had previously planned. That fall, Mrs. M dropped by the clinic after a routine visit to the pediatrician to report that Ricky had blossomed during the summer while she was home and that she and her husband were attempting to lead slightly more relaxed lives although both were determined that he should continue to try to finish his college education. She did, however, plan to delay returning to full-time employment until after Ricky was well established in school. She also confided in the social worker that both of them were disappointed that they could not enlarge their family at this point. However, a year later Mrs. M again dropped by the clinic to show the social worker a new baby; she admitted that the family was again under considerable strain because Mr. M had finally decided to go to school full time on his GI Bill which really limited their finances since she was unable to work. However, both of them were now fairly cognizant of the strains that they were enduring and making efforts to make sure that these were not reflected in their relationships with their children. Ricky at this time was attending school and seemed "to be doing very nicely." Despite the increased social pressures, Mrs. M did not look nearly as depressed as she had when she first came to the clinic and she reported that her husband seemed to be enjoying a very busy and strenuous life.

E. COPING MECHANISMS

The myriad ways in which children cope with interferences in social development almost defy classification. Many of these have been described at various points throughout the previous and present chapter. A majority of these coping mechanisms reflect aspects of what has been already discussed as the process of internalization, in which the child copes with social stimuli by making them a part of himself. He adopts the family rules as his own, thus identifying with his parents. In a similar process during latency, he incorporates and internalizes the extra-familial, societal mores. However, seldom if ever is he able to internalize all the various stresses from his social environment and some of them perforce remain ego-alien. Thus, in general a child handles such social stresses by either internalization or alienation or a combination of these two. As a child's ability to focus upon and to discriminate various kinds of social stimuli becomes increasingly acute, it becomes more possible for him to accept and to internalize some parts of a social milieu and to reject others.

Sometimes a child can internalize two quite inconsistent or even conflicting viewpoints which may not, however, actually become conflicting for him unless he encounters situations in which he must make a decision between them. For example, it is commonly held by males in American society that the only marriageable women are virgins like one's mother. Many men holding this viewpoint also believe that any sexually approachable woman is at heart a prostitute. This virgin-prostitute attitude toward women is so widespread in Western culture, handed down as it is from father to son by looks, titters, and tone of voice, that it is well accepted by most 12-year-old boys—and many 12-year-old girls. For some teenagers such a mythology, if accepted, can create a serious block on adolescent heterosexuality. A young man who believes both of these myths might well feel that he should abstain from any normal heterosexual activity, such as dating, dancing, or petting, for fear that on the one hand he might be guilty of despoiling one of the virgins or, on the other, of being entrapped by one of the prostitutes. However, most young men succeed in refusing to accept one or the other side of this dilemma. Either they hysterically block out the prostitute side of the myth and thus presume that they are always pursuing only good girls, or they cynically decide there is no such thing as a virgin. Such a mythology is even more devastating to a young woman, who is often not sure which role she is expected to play and what kind of identity is being imposed upon her. If she acts in a sexually provocative manner (and finds this hard to control), then she may fear that she will be looked upon as one of the prostitutes. If she does not, then she may fear that she will be unattractive.

Another common set of conflicting viewpoints surrounds aggression. Boys are urged to be competitive, to be aggressive in sports or in business, or even to be intellectually aggressive. At the same time, any aggressiveness which adults may not necessarily associate with achievement is constantly dampened with do's and don't's throughout childhood. Many children do rapidly learn to discriminate where aggressivity is approved and where it is disapproved. Yet, gross inconsistencies regarding aggression are prevalent throughout our society and are often quite confusing to children. Many teenagers today are well aware of the Biblical commandment "Thou shalt not kill" and reject the government's encouragement of young men to join the military service and to kill the enemy.

Because of these and other similar inconsistencies in the American value system, the disillusionment of the current generation of adolescents is more extreme than that experienced by the other recent generations. Many brighter and more sensitive adolescents seriously question and consider alien many of the major social viewpoints held by their elders and the majority of society. However, when a child finds social dictums unacceptable, he also experiences a social rootlessness and an emptiness of identity.

As was discussed in previous chapters, children may use many other defenses when they are faced with conflicting ideologies or when they wish to hide the fact that an ideology is alien to themselves. Many adolescents may mask their feelings of alienation by simple suppression or repression. The surfer, for example, runs off to the beach and forgets about social problems; the "hippie" or "flower child" "drops out"; others project the conflict onto the parent, school, or other authority. These latter adolescents view the adult as having the conflicting viewpoint, not themselves. They tend to use such conflicts of ideology which they can pick out and enlarge upon from the adult world to mask and detract from some of their own personal conflicts. The brighter and more sensitive adolescent hopes idealistically to resolve the conflicts, but often admits to moments of confusion and feelings of helplessness.

Another common way children have of coping with ideological conflicts is to isolate or compartmentalize one set of values from another. The child adopts and uses an ideology when it is handy, appropriate, and approved of. But he may ignore it when the situation does not demand it or when it is inappropriate. Younger children often utilize this isolation of ideological conflicts far more readily than adults, since their internalization of ideology is still in process and is not nearly as rigidly fixed. For example, the author was interviewing children in the "authoritarian personality" study of Frenkel-Brunswick (1951). On the ethnocentric scale in the interviews, and on the special TAT, a ten-year-old white girl who had recently moved to California from the deep South showed every sign of race prejudice, ethnocentrism, and an authoritarian viewpoint. When dismissed from the interview and permitted to attend recess on the schoolground, she was observed to be playing merrily with a Negro and a Mexican girl. As she returned to the classroom, I invited her back in for a few extra minutes of interview and remarked on her behavior. She replied that I did not understand; what she had told me was quite true yet, she said, "It is like a stoplight at the street corner. If you are there with your mother and the light is red, you stop. If the light is red and traffic is coming, you stop. If there is nobody with you and there is no traffic coming, and the light is red, you may still go on."

The way in which children handle social inconsistency or discrepancy often is very comparable to, if not actually part of, the way they learn to handle any kind of perceptual inconsistency. Thus, the compulsive child who is thrown by changes in routine, imperfections, or other perceptual detractions very likely will be unable to handle socially conflicting stimuli. The child with a perceptual-motor handicap may have difficulty with social perceptions, and it is not infrequently difficult to decide which is primary —the social or the sensory perceptual difficulty. The child who shows a perceptual-motor blocking only after he enters school may actually be generalizing a difficulty in making social discriminations to making other kinds of perceptual discriminations. Such a regressive reaction to social conflicts is not uncommon in the latency child. For example, the child may be led to school, urged to achieve, and taught that he must honor his father and mother; at the same time, he may resent being pushed out of the nest, especially if it has been insecure, or if a rival younger sibling is going to enjoy much more of his parent's attention. Thus, the child may unconsciously mess this way through a Bender-Gestalt just as he behaves childishly in other situations to avoid resolution of his social and emotional problems. It is for such reasons that Koppitz (1963) carefully avoids designation of any particular etiology in her measures of perceptual-motor development.

Where such simple perceptual difficulty arises in the context of social conflicts, the assessor should take note of the possibility of *social*-perceptual rather than merely visual-perceptual regression. For example, if "minus" responses on a latency or teenage child's Rorschach are present, particularly where some human figure in interaction is commonly seen, one might well suspect that he may be having some difficulty in internalizing social perceptions. A good example here is where the child over age eight is unable to see the common M response on Card III and gives some distorted or vague response such as a "beetle" or "crab" to D1. Another common distortion occurs in responses to D1 of Card VIII, to which the popular response is an animal walking or climbing; most children ignore the fact that this "bear" happens to be pink. However, the child who is concerned with the color of the bear may be indicating some difficulty in the social integration of his impulse life with his emotional contacts with his environment. Of course, no one such response is predictive of such a difficulty, but such a clue puts the assessor on the alert to examine the data further for other possible indicators. Conflicts of ideology or of internalized social attitudes are also commonly portrayed in TAT stories and acted out on the MAPS.

F. THE CONTENT OF SOCIAL FUNCTIONING: ANIMISM, CONCRETIZING, AND DEPERSONALIZATION

Although there are many more kinds of childhood social behaviors than can be covered in this book, it is to be hoped that those already discussed and illustrated in this chapter (and in Chapter 5) will serve the purpose of orienting the student to the recognition and understanding of this aspect of the child's ego. Instead of attempting further to catalogue these social behaviors, it may be helpful to consider three common ways in which children commonly conceptualize social interactions: (1) animism, (2) concretizing, and (3) depersonalization. As will be seen, each of these forms occurs as a part of the normal development of most children. It is only when the child uses any one exclusive of reality testing or persists in using them that his social development is deterred. When such conceptualizations are used by an adult, they are symptoms of a severe psychological disturbance.

1. *Animism*

Animism is a term from anthropology originally used to denote the attribution of a human life to plants, stones, and other inanimate objects. As preschool children imitate adult behavior with dolls and Teddy bears, they also conceptualize the doll as alive. They may see objects as containing threats or promises, much as adults use charms or omens, but for the child these objects are very much alive. It is not at all unusual for the preschool child to have toys or even trees or other objects which he talks to and treats as friends. He needs a night-light to protect him from unfriendly objects who may come to life in the dark and harm him. Although adults may perceive that these are projections of his affections and fears, to the four year old they are very real. By the time he enters school, the child usually no longer needs these inanimate friends and enemies. Not only has he begun to repress fantasy in general and to explore and test reality, but he usually has plenty of friends and some real enemies among his peers.

Animistic conceptualizations are thus the first steps in the development of the child's formulations about his social experiences. Through such animisms the child reenacts his social experiences and affects. Psychologists utilize this tendency of the young child to humanize inanimate objects when they involve the child in doll play or present cards with animal subjects as stimuli, as on the CAT. On preschool IQ scales (Merrill-Palmer, Year II), the child is instructed to "make the block walk like I did." This animation of the inanimate was recognized by Rorschach as he studied the internalization of kinesthetic experience. According to Ames et al (1951), inanimate movement is a precursor of human movement and reaches a peak at age five. Typical is the previously mentioned response of a bright four year old to Card II (inverted): "It's an 'O' walking." She saw the space D5 as the "O" and D2 as the feet.

The socially isolated or lonely child may persist in using animisms for many years, substituting stuffed animals or other objects for friends. So do children who have met with rebuff and rejection. Animistic conceptualizations are often part of the phobic child's fantasy life, as is illustrated in the following case.

CASE 41

Maria, age eight, had an extensive and almost systematized set of objects that were either good or bad, safe or poisonous, which in effect constituted a delusional scheme.

Many objects in her house were evil to her and threatened to turn her into a witch. She could not touch them, sit on them, or go near them. Other objects were safe or even constituted refuges where she could hide from the evil objects. Objects as well as gestures could combat and destroy the evil if she become accidently contaminated. Her preoccupation with these phobias was so extensive that she could scarcely eat or sleep, let alone go to school. Often she lay awake at night in terror, lest she had accidentally contaminated herself and would become an evil person who might kill someone.

Her father, a poorly educated but highly successful businessman, considered her to be a contrary and obstinate child and punished her severely for her "silly habits" and thoughts. Her older sister made fun of her and used her fears to control Maria and to gain advantage in the father's eyes. Neither the father nor the teenage sister seemed at all aware that Maria's phobias had set in coincident with the death of her mother. Maria had really not known her mother who had been an invalid and who was isolated in a separate room for the first four years of Maria's life.

In the initial interview, Maria recalled with tears her memories of her mother's screams in the night as she lay dying of cancer. Maria readily admitted that she associated many objects in the house with her mother, either negatively or positively. The negative objects proved to be where Maria had happened to be sitting or things she was using when she felt angry at her mother or frightened by the recognition of her mother's dying. Other objects she had touched or used when she was dreaming of her mother's returning from death. Each object seemed to take on a different part of her associations and her relationship with her mother and thus became part of her own fears and hostilities. Maria's responses to the Rorschach and other associative stimuli were similarly both highly phobic in content and distorted in form.

2. Concretizing

At other times, children conceptualize human relationships and social stimuli in a very opposite and yet analogous form, that is, as if such social stimuli were actually inanimate. For want of a better term, this form of conceptualizing social experiences may be called "concretizing." Such concretizing, although fairly common among preschool children, does not seem as well-recognized as animistic thinking. More often concretizing appears to be merely a misunderstanding and, in fact, often originates in an inability to understand a concrete term. The child hears an adult use an abstraction or analogy to describe a person or a social experience, and then conceives of the abstraction in concrete terms. For example, one four-year-old child heard his mother exclaim to her professor-husband, "I can read you like a book!" Later the mother discovered the boy staring at his father and discovered that he was trying to "read" him. Even after she explained her analogy, the child persisted in concretizing his relationship with his father, noting that his father "always reads books." To this child, his erudite and literate father was a book. Years later he referred to his father as "bookish" and suddenly recalled his original concretism.

CASE 42

Mark, age six, who seemed to be having some difficulty conforming to and understanding the school rules, was asked about such rules. The child seemed at first to misunderstand the question and talked about "rulers." However, as the discussion ensued, it appeared as if Mark really perceived the school regulations in terms of the measuring stick, as if they were some kind of inanimate object. His confusion in part was explained by his association to regulations as being enforced by a slap on the wrist with the ruler. As the assessment proceeded, it was evident that he also conceived of other such social concepts in very concrete, inanimate terms. His drawing of a person had a distinct robot-like quality and on the World Test he used none of the human figures. When his attention was drawn to the fact that there were human figures available to people his village, he remarked that these were only tin people and that he wanted real people. His own speech and gestures were also quite stiff and mechanical.

That Mark probably lacked "real people" in his environment was suggested by the appearance and behavior of his father who reminded the assessor of a mannikin and who was obsequiously formal throughout the interview. Noticeably, this father referred to his child as "it." One of the complaints of the school was that Mark did not seem to realize that anyone had any feelings and was most surprised when other children complained when he hit them or interfered with their activities. Like Maria, Mark had lost his mother at an early age, and had been reared largely by a succession of part-time maids and tutors and spent most of his waking hours, outside of the classroom, wandering around a large and empty house where the servants moved like shadows.

3. *Depersonalization*

Here, as in concretizing, the child detaches the affective components of a social experience, but without turning the experience into an inanimate form. The child often denies social interactions and behaves as if there were no social interaction in a mechanical fashion. Much of Mark's behavior might also be described as depersonalization. Again, in mild form, depersonalization is one aspect of the normal development of the child's socialization. The latency age child in particular uses this coping mechanism to water down the myriad of social exchanges which he is experiencing so that they do not overwhelm him. Although he may consciously recognize that other children—and adults— have feelings, and that they arouse feelings in him, he often seeks to depersonalize his social relationships in order to keep his affect life under control. For the eight year old, anything can be excused with the phrase, "I didn't mean to!" The child is also implying, "It doesn't mean anything." In many instances, children depersonalize human relationships and social institutions in order to avoid conflicts.

Case 43

When Herb, age 14, was asked to draw a feminine figure, he drew a highly stylized sports car instead and handed over his production claiming that he could not draw any

kind of a woman and that he liked sports cars better than women anyway. As he made this statement and looked at his drawing further, he elaborately printed the word "Mother" across the car. Further investigation revealed that his life was highly programmed by his mother in almost computer style. She had arranged his time so that he was engaged in some activity at nearly every moment of his waking life. Every afternoon he was engaged in some kind of class or recreation which she had arranged for him. Dinner was served him in front of the television rather than with his parents and, during the evening hours before he went to bed, he was firmly isolated in his own room with his school books, apart from the family. His main moments of contact with his mother was in the family car when she drove him from one activity to another.

Further interviews with the mother suggested that her programming of the child's life was designed to keep him at a distance from her while she carried on her own activities. She was also very much afraid that if he did not have such a well mapped out life, he would become a "delinquent teenager," particularly that his sexual interests would come to the fore. In each of these activities arranged for him, the boy also found rather mechanical and impersonal relationships. He had few or no relationships with peers in these swimming lessons, guitar lessons, or religious classes. His only friend was the apartment house janitor whom he knew only by the name "Stovepipe," with whom his mother had forbidden him to associate. Thus, it was not entirely surprising that Herb had very little concept of others as real people with feelings or of social rules as having any humanistic meaning. The discovery of his inability to conceptualize either individuals or social groups as anything but inanimate helped in part to explain his lack of guilt after he was apprehended firing a rifle at passing cars on a highway.

ANALYSIS OF EGO FUNCTIONING
AND IDENTITY FORMATION

This chapter is concerned with relating assessment data to two conceptual constructs: the function of the ego as a whole and the formation of the sense of identity. As described in Chapter 5, these concepts are highly interrelated, both in theory and in their behavioral manifestations. They are also quite distinct aspects of the overall functioning of the child. Both are what might be called second-level abstractions, that is, concepts which link together and integrate the generalizations that have been labeled ego functions. Thus, the term ego refers to all the various functions: all modalities, all input-output mechanisms, all types of focus and differentiation, all coping mechanisms, and all the various contents of all functions. The concept "identity" is yet another across-the-board conceptualization of all ego functions. Since both of these second-level abstractions are derived from the primary classifications, they depend upon the same data from which the part functions were determined. However, merely summing the various ego functions does not result in a meaningful description of the overall functioning of the ego nor of the child's sense of identity. Rather, the assessor must integrate the data and abstract from them further. These second-

level generalizations, while not requiring additional data, do necessitate additional measurements or analysis of the data and other dimensions for interrelating them.

A. DIMENSIONS OF THE TOTAL FUNCTIONING OF THE EGO

Many different approaches to overall functioning of the ego have been suggested by various theorists. No brief review could possibly do justice to these theories, and such a review is beyond the purview of this book. However, there are at least three main dimensions which many theories of personality commonly utilize. The first of these might be labeled the overall "energy level" that the child seems to display and that is distributed in various amounts and various functions of the ego. The second may be referred to by the term used by Rorschach, "the experience balance," which covers many kinds of "introversion-extroversion" or "internal-externalization" concepts. The third, dilation-constriction, is also derived from the Rorschach theory and like the experience balance appears under different names in other theories such as "expansion and restriction" or "open-closed" systems.

1. *Energy level* refers to an overall behavior pattern which is very commonly observed and noted, but which is somewhat hard to define. Perhaps the psychological concept that comes to mind first is that of Freud's "libido," by which Freud meant the total instinctual forces of the person. Unfortunately, libido has become so confused and identified with purely sexual energies (even by many psychoanalytic writers) that it is no longer really a useful concept. Whatever term is applied, most theorists do seem to agree that children differ considerably in the amount of physiological and psychological energy they display. Physiologically, there is a fairly wide range in normal metabolism and other body functions that create physical energy. Individual differences in drive states have not been given much attention in experimental psychology, but everyday clinical observation suggests that there is considerable variation from child to child and at various times in the child's life. Then, of course, there is the diurnal variation of sleep and wakefulness for every individual. It has been observed that high drive states may result in either extreme tension and wakefulness or in apathy and sleep.

As regards individual differences among children, some children are quite obviously full of energy, always on the go, seem to require considerable amounts of energy-creating foods, and a minimum amount of sleep—although they might sleep quite soundly when they do sleep. Other children eat less, are more easy going and relaxed, and require more rest. These differences also occur among children who are under stress, or who are experiencing a considerable amount of tension or other disturbance. Thus, the high energy level child who is depressed may actually show his depression by increasing his normal activity to a point of exhaustion or his depression may be noticeable just by the fact that his normal activity level drops. The tension of a normally low energy level child may be easy to observe, since restlessness in such a child would be a marked change. However, a slowing down of the overall activity may also be a natural reaction under stress.

Because tension and depression often mask the basic energy level of the child seen in a psychological clinic, it is sometimes difficult to assess the underlying energy level from behavioral observation alone. One of the best indicators is the description given by the parent of the child's everyday activities, and of possible changes in activity level with the onset of the child's depression or of current stress. The mother may note, for example, that her son previously was always up early, ate a "good breakfast," and was out to play almost immediately and kept active the entire day. One mother, discussing her 11-year-old son, came to realize that there had been marked changes in his general activity level following the death of his father six months before. She had not, until the moment of discussion within the interview, realized that he was very probably depressed. Now he remained sleepy in the mornings, dawdled over his food, sat for hours in front of the TV, or hung about whining and making demands that she entertain him. His rest at night was now fitful. She contrasted him with her daughter, age eight, who had been a "sleepyhead" in the family and who was quite selective about what she ate and was a dainty eater, who preferred relatively sedentary activity, and who, although a good student, seemed to need more time for her studies. Following the father's death, she also complained more about little things, ate a great deal more—gaining 20 pounds. She fell asleep during the day, even at school, but was restless at night. Both had been examined physically, and there was no change in their metabolism.

Energy level differences within the family are often a point of conflict. Most people realize that it is difficult for an aging person to have full care of a high energy level toddler. Even the middle-aged parent can be exhausted by the pace of teenage children. What may not be discernible is that where there are differences between parents themselves in adult energy level, differences which might not cause excessive conflict within the marriage, the presence of one or more children in the family with the same energy level as one of the adults may cause the family dynamics to be thrown out of balance. Thus, a woman with a low energy level might marry a man with a much higher energy level, almost, it might seem, to counterbalance her pace. If, however, she is faced later with three sons whose energy level is like her husband's, she may find herself overwhelmed and her protests may seem to her husband and sons as nagging and complaining. In such circumstances, the boys may have biased views of women as extraordinarily weak, as needing protection, and as incapable of participating in male activity. An easy-going, sedentary, low energy man who selects for contrast a wife with a high pitched energy level and then finds himself with daughters whose energy levels are like his wife's may feel badgered and hasseled. His wife and daughters may see him as stodgy and unappreciative and lacking in affection. Such girls might grow up feeling that all men have to be pushed and pulled or tugged at.

When the assessor is faced with the complaint of the hyperactive child, he should be most careful to investigate the energy level of both parents. Not uncommonly, such a complaint arises from the low energy level parents who, hoping for a placid baby, find themselves with a child who to them appears extremely hyperactive but who, to other families, might seem quite normal or even below normal in activity. Obversely, in a family where the parents and most of the children possess a high level of energy, a more easy going steady paced child might actually appear slow and dull, and the child himself might come to feel somewhat inadequate and out of place. Thus, a review of family energy level patterns during both the parent interview and the interviews with the child is often essential in understanding family conflicts and the development of feelings of identity.

Although no one psychological test is aimed at the assessment of psychic energy level, it is possible to gain some estimate of the child's overall pace and push from his behavior in response to many different techniques. Classically, energy level has been considered to be tapped by the "timed" test. Thus, on the Digit Symbol Test of Wechsler, one child may attack it with vigor and consider speed the most important variable. Yet another child may view this task as one of precision and accuracy, rather than mere speed. Of course, in looking at these variables, one needs to take into consideration the amount of tension the child also shows and discount tension and depression in estimating basic energy level. No one such test would give us the entire picture, and it is necessary to note energy level throughout the assessment. Timing and pace appear as a variable in many subtests of the Wechsler, on the Bender, on the Rorschach, and even in the story-telling of the TAT. Although a high number of responses to the Rorschach or a quantity of detail in the TAT stories, for example, might indicate a high energy level, the child with a lower energy level may also be quite imaginative and productive, if one gives him enough time.

Extremes of activity and energy level may be signs of very severe disturbance in the child's development. Not only may they indicate considerable depression, as was noted above, but a child who demonstrates considerable alterations of energy level should be checked thoroughly by the pediatrician. These changes are frequently symptoms of endocrinological disorders or neurological dysfunctions. Even where there are psychological indications that a child may be severely depressed, if a child shows a marked drop in energy level or becomes extremely hyperactive, a thorough physiological examination should precede psychological assessment.

The distribution of energy within the ego among various ego functions is another major consideration. Most normal, low energy children appear to concentrate their energies when need be, for example, on their schoolwork—and then to let down and relax during playtimes. However, if a low energy child is a member of a high energy level family which sets an exhausting pace at home, he may not have the push to maintain himself at school. Nor can he compete if placed in a high energy level peer group. The high energy level child runs into the opposite kind of problem. If he controls and bottles up his energy and sits still in the classroom and adjusts to the overall pace of the average child, he will need to burst loose once he is freed from this social constraint. The author recently observed that a 12-year-old child in his neighborhood ran four square blocks every morning before breakfast and every evening before dinner. When the child was asked about this daily personal track meet, the child explained cheerfully that this exercise exhausted him sufficiently so that he could sit still in class during the day and fall asleep later in the evening. Further inquiry revealed that this boy was a top student, an excellent musician, and an outstanding athlete. Both of his parents were active physicians and community leaders, as well as quite successful in the rearing of five children. There is never a dull or quiet moment in their home.

The distribution of energy among the various ego functions may also be one sign of possible disturbance in the child's growth. Thus, the child whose need-gratifications are unsatisfied may pour a great deal of his energy in an effort to meet these needs and have insufficient energy to devote to other ego functioning. In a sense, such maldistribution of energy typifies, if not actually defines, depressive states in children. The child devotes a great deal of his psychological energy into compensating for whatever loss he has endured and controlling the resultant feelings of frustration and anger. The child who is depressed over a loss or a deprivation does not have the energy for normal spontaneous play or social interactions. The psychological tension he endures saps his energy level, so that he cannot achieve at school. He becomes too tired to think. An even more dramatic illustration of energy imbalance is seen in the obsessive child, who consumes so much energy in his compulsive acts and obsessive thoughts that, no matter how he may be driven to perfectionism, he may be very unsuccessful and unable to complete any task because of his exhaustion. Very often such compulsive behavior may also be viewed initially as merely hyperactive. Again, this term "hyperactivity" must be explored in detail in interviews with the parents to determine what is meant. Other children may bottle up considerable amounts of energy in order to conform to the demands of parents or other social authorities who consider such release of energy as "aggressive." In such instances, they may be quite inactive despite their high energy level. Such disparity between activity level and energy level may create considerable tension for the child. For examples, see the cases of Wayne, Case 9 in Chapter 3, and Ricky, Case 40 in Chapter 15, among others.

2. The term *experience balance* was originated by Herman Rorschach, but the concept itself is not really foreign to any theory of the overall functioning of the ego. Even in the traditional S-R learning theory of individual functioning, allowances are made for the possibility that the stimulus may come either externally to him from the environment or from within himself—if one takes into account the function of memory as a stimulus. The focus on this dimension of the overall functioning of the ego is, however, particular to Rorschach's theory. The balances between input and output for each of the ego functionings have been discussed in the previous chapters. Whether or not there is an across-the-board balance of experience, that is, a uniformity of input and output in all functions, may, however, be seriously questioned. At least theoretically, it would seem possible that an individual could be quite dependent upon the environment for the formation of intellectual judgments, but at the same time be relatively independent of the environment in his affective life. In fact, among adults, such a pattern of being quite sure of how one feels about something without actually being able to analyze it intellectually is a fairly common phenomenon. Equally numerous are adults who are quite capable of intellectually analyzing situations very independently, but whose value judgments are easily swayed by others. These two examples alone suggest that any rigid typology cannot do justice to the variety of the input-output patterns.

Although this concept of experience balance does appear in many theories (usually in other terms), it has not been the subject of much rigorous research. Because it is a second-level abstraction, it is difficult to establish criteria by which to measure it, outside of the Rorschach test, as this writer discovered in a series of exploratory studies (Palmer, 1955, 1956, 1957, 1962). Nevertheless, these studies do suggest a constancy of input-output in a variety of situations, such as intellectual functioning, subjective value systems, and fantasy production. Clinically, it does appear that most commonly a person whose input-output balance leans toward either the internal or external on one function seems to have similar balances in other functions. Individuals whose experience balance varies from ego function to ego function seem relatively rare. In Rorschach's day, it was popular to consider that such personality developments were very likely to be hereditary in origin. The developmental trends noted in the more recent studies (Ames et al, 1952; Hertz, 1943) do strongly suggest a maturational factor (see discussion in Chapter 5). However, there is some evidence that the experience balance can be altered under conditions of severe stress (Palmer, 1961), and it would thus seem reasonable to suppose that less severe but chronic stress might also affect this overall pattern of ego functioning.

Clinical observation also indicates that among children extremes of experience balance are rather rare. Young children are, of course, quite dependent upon the environment for nearly all stimulation and are unable to effectively form concepts of their own without cues from the environment. However, after the process of internalization—beginning at the close of infancy and during the early years of latency (as has been described in detail previously)—children are likely to attempt to use both internal and external clues for assessing the world about them. Moreover, as will be discussed further on in this chapter, they may use a variety of clues in formulating their own identity. The age at which one set of perceptual clues becomes preferred over another seems to vary so widely that no generalization can be firmly stated. One might at least hypothesize that a child who from the beginning firmly identifies with one parental image might well adopt that parent's experience balance at quite an early age and continue to view the world with the same perspective as that parent consistently throughout his childhood and as an adult. However, since it is much more common for a child to form some identity with each of his parents and more common for parents to vary at least slightly in their own experience balances, one might expect the majority of children to test a variety of patterns of experience balance until one or another becomes most effective or personally satisfying.

Although Rorschach hoped through further study to be able to identify pathological states, he made it clear in his original thesis that even the extremes of the experience balance were not in themselves pathognomic. Similarly, during childhood, neither the early onset of a particular experience balance trend nor the lack of any definite experience balance can in itself be considered a deterrent to development or a sign of psychopathology. Certainly there are personal and social values that may be well enhanced by a very stable and early determined pattern of ego functioning. There is also much to be said of a continuing flux and flow, and testing of patterns. However, an understanding of how the child's experience balance is developing may be very helpful in understanding if not predicting his method and ability to cope with either normal or unusual stress. For example, a child who early shows signs of a stable introversive experience balance and who maintains such a balance over most of the years of his childhood may present a stable front to others, so that they know how he will function and he himself will feel sure about himself in his patterns of behavior. However, should such an introversively oriented child face marked environmental stress and change, not consonant with his particular internal schema, he' might find it quite difficult to take such change into account, and to alter his internal perceptual framework. Commonly such children develop quite slowly during adolescence, requiring considerable time to absorb new stresses and strains.

In contrast, many children, although they make some internalizations, never quite trust their own internal experiences, and continue to demand empirical proof anew in each situation. Although much more flexible in the face of environmental change than their more introversive peers, such extroversive children do not feel quite sure about themselves and are more likely to be involved in an "identity crisis" during adolescence. The child who forms what Rorschach called an "ambiequal" pattern can utilize cues both from within himself and from his environment as he attempts to meet the external and internal stresses of adolescence. Such a child, however, does continue to face the problem of resolving inconsistencies between these two sets of clues. Least capable of facing adolescence and entering into adulthood is the child who attempts to judge situations purely on a bare-bones intellectual basis, without considering either the emotional and social clues of his environment or his own set of past experiences and personal attitudes. Such a "coarctate" individual is unable to judge the behavior of others or himself. Although a coarctate experience balance may be demonstrated from time to time, especially during latency in the normal child, a continuation of this pattern past puberty may be taken as a sign of serious ego dysfunctioning.

Although the Rorschach Technique is the only instrument specifically designed to assess experience balance, it is not the only technique which offers data in this area. In fact, in view of the limited number of responses that most children give to the ten inkblot cards, estimations of experience balance based solely on a child's Rorschach might be of questionable reliability. Taking the M: Sum C ratio from the Rorschach as only one item of data, the assessor should look at all of the various input-output patterns of each of the separate ego functions. Only if there appears to be a marked consistent trend across all functions can the assessor reasonably hypothesize that an overall experience balance type is being formed.

The import of this rather broad generalization about the function of the ego may not seem obvious, especially in the developing child. Admittedly, it was adopted from the philosophic writings of Carl Jung and may seem a far cry from the immediate and practical problems presented in a referral for an assessment of a child. In fact, such an authority on the Rorschach as Beck (1945) states in his introductory text that the experience balance is relatively unimportant. However, most writers on personality function do accord this variable or similar concepts a major role in personality function. In regard to functioning of the child, the experience balance may be considered as a long-range indicator of his final character structure. It is an overall indicator of the individual's relationship to his environment, and his perspective on the world. Occasionally, the manifest symptoms and behavior of the child may arise from an imbalance of input-output, but the main reason for considering the development of the experience balance is that it provides a glimpse of the future adult.

Even in considering extremes of input-output patterns, one should be careful about making value judgments. Becoming an introvert or extrovert is not in itself a sign of neuroticism. Rather, such trends constitute a way of life that is developed in childhood. The fact that a child at any one point shows a marked trend in either direction need not be of major concern, at least prior to adolescence. Usually during adolescence, such overall personality trends are tested and revised. The very extroversive child finds in adolescence that he must develop some strengths within himself and begin to depend somewhat on his own experience and memories and clarify some of his own attitudes as separate from those of others. He may remain essentially extroversive with just enough recognition of his own inner life to achieve an adult independence. Obversely, a child who is developing an introversive balance wil be challenged in adolescence to take some recognition of the emotional realities about him in his en-

vironment. Otherwise, as an adult he will be battered about the ears by others who feel ignored or intruded upon. Similarly one should not be too concerned about a latency child who gives minimum recognition to either emotional stimuli from his environment or from within himself. If, on the other hand, he is unable to expand his balance of experience and take into account such emotional stimuli, he runs into serious trouble during adolescence as he will be unable to evaluate either the world about him or his world within him.

To utilize these experience balance indicators prior to adolescence, the psychologist needs to note possible trends and their relation to the long-range development of the child. Thus, one might wish to use the experience balance as a basis for recommendations to a therapist or some other person planning out a program that requires estimates concerning long-range personality development. The assessor might, for example, indicate to the referrant a need to help the child utilize and recognize his inner impulses and fantasies. Or inversely, one might wish to recommend that an introversive child be placed in a milieu that might promote an exchange of emotional relationships.

3. The third dimension, *dilation-constriction,* is concerned with expanse or breadth of ego functioning. Again, this ego dimension is utilized by numerous personality theorists under a variety of blueprints. Lewin (1936), for example, speaks of the size and permeability of the "life space." Even laymen distinguish between a person who "spreads himself thin" and the person who "walks a straight and narrow path." This expansiveness dimension is interrelated both with energy levels and with experience balance, but may be distinguished from both. Thus, a person with a high energy level might be expected to live an expanded life, into everything with considerable emotional investment, but it is also quite possible for such a person to concentrate his energies on a narrow range of activities and interests. In fact, such a pattern of high energy level and restricted interests probably underlies a great deal of the productive work of scientists and artists who are able to pour all their energies into a single activity ignoring almost all other exigencies of life. Inversely, one might expect the person with a generally introverted or personally

determined outlook on life to tend to lead a relatively emotionally constricted life. However, it is quite possible that such an introverted person might have a very expansive life which, if combined with a high energy level, might lead to considerable creative productivity. Many other patterns and combinations of these ego dimensions are also possible. Prominent in the political life and the entertainment field are those persons with high energy levels who are quite extroversive and have an expanded horizon. In contrast, a low energy and introversive person may find adjustment much easier if he restricts his field of activities. Not all of these combinations are necessarily successful adjustments. For example, a person with a low energy level who is quite extroversive may try to be expansive but constantly exhausts himself, and thus easily turns to defenses such as obsessive hypchondrical concerns. Low energy people who are extremely introversive may float into an expansive fantasy which could become a near psychotic retreat from reality.

Such types are the extremes of what are probably normally distributed traits. Most children fall at neither extreme; they are neither altogether expansive nor altogether constricted. In considering the size of the life space of the child, it may be helpful to describe him as having some set point on a continuum, but it is necessary to keep in mind that this concept describes an overall dimension that is still developing. Far more than adults, children swing back and forth between being very expansive and spontaneous and retreating to a restricted and single-minded little world. The "mood swings" which are commonly experienced in children are manifestations of such an overall expansion and retreat. Such dilation and constriction is also observable in the child's intellectual behavior, as was discussed in Chapter 4. On occasion a child may be interested in a variety of intellectual stimuli and dabble in each one; later, he may devote himself almost exclusively to one activity, neglecting all others. Socially, he may have times of contacts with a variety of peers at different levels of society, and at other times exclude all others except a single beloved chum. As with the experience balance, a trend toward either dilation or constriction may not be obvious prior to puberty. A consistent trend during latency does not predict with any definite accuracy the kind of overall ego functioning the child will finally evolve during adolescence.

The assessment of the child's use of life space calls for a wide variety of data. As was suggested in the above paragraph, facts such as the spread of the child's intellectual interests and social interactions in his everyday life are one set of indicators. Remembering, however, that a child's life may be introversively expansive, one also needs to take into account the expanse and variety of his fantasy. Nearly every one of our multipurpose techniques provides at least one or more measures of expansiveness. The size of the child's drawings on either the Draw-A-Person or the Bender-Gestalt is one measure of this variable. The number and variety of objects used in the World Test is also considered by its author to be an expression of the child's dilation or constriction of his outlook on the world. On intelligence tests, items such as Digit Span on the WISC or Binet, or Response to Pictures, Level I (Stanford Binet Year III-6), or Word Naming (Stanford-Binet, Year X) are indications of the child's intellectual expansiveness. Other intellectual tasks require the child momentarily to focus his attention on a single task or a single aspect of a problem. On the Picture Completion subtest of the WISC, for example, a child must stay within the limits of a picture presented to him and the detail within those limits in order to succeed. He cannot look beyond the picture and reply that a man is missing from the coat, or that there is no nail on which to hang the thermometer.

Although like the experience balance, this dimension of dilation-constriction of the ego describes a long-range personality development, the immediate import of either an extreme dilation or an extreme constriction is of much more concern. Extremes at either end of this continuum may be one indication of a severe emotional disturbance in the child. A severe constriction of all ego functions in adolescence is strongly suggestive of depression or even of the onset of a psychosis. A manic dilation of the ego may be a defense against such a depression, a phrenetic warding off of a psychotic break. Although swings between dilation and constriction do appear to be more extreme in childhood than among adults, a child who is functioning at either extreme should be assessed very carefully for the presence of some kind of immediate stress. Not infrequently the stress may be nonspecific and general such as that experienced in a life crisis when the child shifts from infancy to becoming a school child or turns the corner from latency into puberty.

B. ASSESSMENT OF IDENTITY FORMATION

As defined in Chapter 5, the child's sense of identity lies at the core of his ego and involves all ego functions. It is both a part of the overall ego and distinct from it. While the ego is a set of interacting functions, the term identity refers to: (1) the child's perception of these interacting functions, (2) the roles assigned to him, and (3) his affective evaluation of these identities. Thus, identity may be considered as that part of the ego which looks at itself, which considers how the ego is looked at by others, and in which the sense of pride and guilt is centered. These three aspects of identity are, of course, highly related. How one perceives oneself is, in part, a result of how much self-regard one has which, in turn, especially for a child, depends upon the identity imposed upon him by his environment, the things expected of him, and the roles assigned to him. Inversely, the roles he plays and what the environment comes to expect of him depend upon his own attitude toward himself and his awareness of his functioning. Which of these three aspects should be discussed first is therefore an arbitrary choice. The main reason for so dividing the subject of identity into three aspects is that it serves to organize a variety of pertinent data.

1. Assessment of Self-Perception and Awareness

As was discussed in Chapter 5, most students of child development and personality agree that self-awareness is a developmental phenomenon which begins in infancy and expands over the span of childhood, reaching its critical point in late adolescence. Identity formation is both an unfolding and accumulative process and thus, at each stage of development, requires consideration of additional data and new criteria.

Imagine for a moment that there was a Stanford-Binet for ascertaining identity which yielded an "identity quotient." What kinds of items might each age level contain? During the earliest months of infancy, the child's identity formation consists of becoming aware of himself as a physical unity. The identity "age" in terms for this infant scale might consist of observations of the degree to which the child explores his own body parts, such as touching and manipulating his toes and fingers, or experiencing overall physical sensations in rocking, stretching, and then pulling himself erect. Similar items are present in the Cattell Infant Intelligence Scale and in the Vineland Scale of Social Maturity. Since identity also consists of recognizing differences between the self and others, the identity quotient scale would contain the Cattell items of recognizing and differentiating the presence of the mother. A few month's later on the Cattell also, the child recognizes himself in the mirror by patting it. Similarly, he turns himself over in the crib, manipulates other pieces of the environment, and sees them as separate from himself. Weaning is also an act in which the child separates himself from his mother and makes the first beginning toward the satisfaction of his own needs. Thus, the child says to himself in effect, "I am because I can do."

Thus, the child begins with recognition of himself as a behaving and even accomplishing person. This aspect of identity continues to play a prominent role in self-awareness in childhood, as will be discussed below. However, even during infancy several other elements of self-perception are present, at least in embryonic form. A second type of item of an identity development scale would consist of simple intellectual acts. The child begins to name and recognize objects and includes himself in this naming process by differentiating the objects from his own person. In fact, the use of his given name to identify himself precedes the use of proper pronouns; "Johnny want" appears in the child's speech before "I want." Actually, naming other people might be one of the earliest items in our identity scale, for example, beginning with the names "mommy" then "daddy," then sibs and himself. Later, the child distinguishes *mine* and *yours*, relating objects to the self. The names of objects and their possessors and the names of people are a preoccupation of the three- and four-year-old child.

At this age level also, the child begins to make sexual distinctions as part of identity. He identifies adults as "mommies" and "daddies" and himself and other children as boys and girls. The infant begins by identifying himself with a parent, first the mother and then the father. As psychoanalytic theorists have suggested, it is during weaning that the infant sees himself as separate from his mother. Perhaps it would be more precise to say that he sees mother and self as distinct once he is involved in actively feeding himself. However, such a separation of the child's awareness as being part of his mother is probably a very gradual process which still has remnants in adolescence. In any case, the child's social identity as part of the family and how he recognizes this would also be elements on an identity scale. By age three, the average child recognizes his father and siblings as family members distinct from nonfamily members. By age four, he begins to use his patronym as part of his own name and identity.

Last, but not least, some of the types of items that one might include in such an identity development scale would come out of the child's affective relationships. He is not only somebody because he belongs, but also has an identity because he is loved or hated. In turn, he experiences himself as someone who loves or hates. His identity is formed by his recognition of tender or angry feelings from others, and his experience of such feelings within himself. Again, this discrimination between feelings that belong to the self and feelings that come from others is gradually learned over the entire period of childhood, but has its definite beginnings during his preschool years.

Just as other kinds of development turn from an accumulation of experiences toward an integration and repetitive practice of learned experience in latency (see Chapter 2), so identity development proceeds in latency into a working-through of the basic facts of identification that the child has already learned. He has already discovered that he is separate from others, that he has a name, that he belongs socially to a family group, that he has a definite sex, and that he is both an object and an expressor of affect. However, by and large these facts about his identity are imposed externally upon him in the form of roles that he is expected to play or a lesson he is expected to learn. How well he learns these roles, and even more to what extent he accepts them, are the questions of identity formation during latency. Thus, in this imaginary "identity development" scale, the items for the latency years would be concerned with behavior manifestations of practicing these roles and with accepting or internalizing them. Although the child may begin practicing various imaginary roles during the preschool years, for example, playing cowboy or playing various family member roles in a game of house, etc., this playacting is even more intensified in latency. One of the items on an identity development scale might thus be the numbers and kinds of identities the child acts out, both in play and in various social situations. Does he play at being cowboy, fireman, doctor, etc. in a game with other children? Does he pretend that he is the various characters he sees on TV? Does he try out various roles with his family or with his peer group? Does he try being the baby in the family or the grown-up little man? Does he attempt to play the role of the "big man on campus" in the second grade?

During latency, it is traditional that boys and girls separately practice different roles. Although it is very probable that the psychoanalysts are correct in their hypothesis that children in latency have nothing to do with the opposite sex in order to resolve their Oedipal complex, it is also probably equally true that this separation of the sexes serves to give the child a chance to practice his own sexual role. Thus, a little boy may have nothing to do with little girls, chiefly to practice being a boy, to establish his masculine identity. It may be that little boys are driven to prove themselves to be different from little girls by a castration fear, and that little girls are not quite so involved in this establishment of their sexual identity so as not to expose their fantasy that they are castrated. However, the psychoanalysts point out that any child driven by this motivation alone may either overreact by attempting to be overly masculine or regress into a childhood state in which sexual identity is altogether avoided. More likely the driving force behind the practice of sexual identity roles in latency is the indication and identification with adult roles. Thus, the resolution of the Oedipal complex is not so much the avoidance of a castration fear, as it is the acceptance and identity with the parent of the same sex. An identity scale should contain items regarding the little boy's effort to imitate his father and to seek to join into activities with him. Since the little girl's identity development, particularly with regard to sex roles, is less definite during latency, little girls might be expected to be engaged in some doll play and in being mother's little helper, but one could not rule out that girls also seek to join in boy's games or spend some time with their fathers. One criterion for the sex-identity development of a little girl is her ability to handle the derogation she meets from her masculine peers or her feelings of rejection when she finds that her father spends more time with her brothers.

Identity development in latency is not, however, restricted entirely to the child's image of himself sexually. In fact, he continues to spend much of his time practicing his roles as an achiever both physically and intellectually. His sense of self as a moving and accomplishing person expands enormously between the age of 6 and 12. A boy's identity particularly derives from his activities on the playground, at home, and in his neighborhood in active physical games and play. Whether this play consists of organized sports or individual activity with his peers, it is often extremely competitive and the child searches constantly to see what he is good at and who he is better than. Similarly, he has an expanding intellectual achievement to depend upon as part of his identity. No longer is he merely naming things, or even merely getting their relationships established, but now he is thinking up ideas and making finer discriminations. Learning becomes a function which adds to his sense of identity. To a far greater extent than in his earlier years, he adopts the Cartesian philosophy "cognito ergo sum."

He begins to have a memory now, to see himself as an identity that exists over time. Even at age seven, he can tell you about things that happened when "I was a little boy." Although his chronology may be inexact, and his sense of time quite fluid, he definitely recognizes that he is the same person now that formerly existed as an infant. Yet, he differentiates his current identity from what he was like as a baby and can, on request at least, recite some of those differences. "How are you different now from what you were like when you were a baby?" might be an item on an identity scale which most eight year olds could easily answer.

The latency child's identity as a member of social groups also continues to expand. He sees himself as having membership in a school which has a name, as being part of a neighborhood, as belonging to a religious group, and as having a definite racial identification. Although the average nine year old may not know precisely what it means to be a Catholic, or a Mormon, a Democrat or a Republican, or all the implications of being white or Negro, he at least is well aware that such differentiations exist in the adult world. Thus, he flings these terms around and discusses them with his peers. He becomes acutely aware of his place within the hierarchy of his peer group. He knows how each of his playmates and schoolmates are regarded by the group as a whole. He may be less aware—or at least less willing to admit—how he himself stands with his peers. In this respect, an identity development scale might well adopt items from the Rogers Adjustment Scale (1931), which deals with the number of friends and the relationship to friends that a child is willing to talk about. In fact, a great deal of the Rogers Scale is concerned with various identity behaviors of latency.

Despite the fact that the term latency implies a repression of affective experience, the trying out and acceptance of various kinds of affective behavior is very much a part of identity formation during latency. Perhaps the reason that this may not be easily recognized is that the development of affective function to the ego is concerned largely with control of affect during this stage. As the child experiences affect as being part of the self, the self becomes responsible for the control and expression of affect. It is this internalization of affect which is the hallmark of latency. To an increasing degree, the child is expected to withstand disappointment without becoming enraged. Moreover, he is expected to find some solutions to his disappointments. If there is no one to play with, he is expected to entertain himself. If he is hungry, he is expected to wait until the family eats next. If he needs comforting, he is expected to come to his parents or other adult for surcease without excessive tears; the adult does not expect to have to see if he needs emotional support and affection. These affective self-sufficiencies become part of his advancing sense of identity.

His social and affective discriminations are also more refined. He may have some people whom he hates without reservation and some people whom he loves without reservation, but he is beginning to distinguish between the things he likes about one person and the things he dislikes about that same person. For the infant, "mommy" is all good at one time or all bad at another time. The latency child is able to tell you that there are things he likes about "Mom" and things that he does not like about her. He may mention some child about whom he makes generally derogatory remarks, but at the same time he may report that he spends time with this child occasionally in relatively peaceful play because this other child has some assets which he enjoys.

The acceleration of identity development with the onset of puberty is so remarkable that the concept is almost equated with adolescence. However, as is evident from the above discussion, the identity formation process in adolescence is actually the grooming period. As the adolescent rushes headlong from childhood into maturity, the fulfillment of his identity becomes a critical focal point. During these final years of childhood, the child attempts to integrate and finally establish the kind of identity that he has been developing. All along, his identity formation has been largely, although not exclusively, an unconscious process. During latency he can talk about himself if asked. During adolescence, self-awareness and self-contemplation become much more a manifest, conscious process, at times painfully obsessive.

Beginning in high school, if not in junior high school, he has to decide what kind of person he wants to be. He makes choices of electives in his schoolwork toward his eventual career. He enters into extracurricular activities at school, into certain kinds of peer groups, and makes other choices about himself which determine his identity. He choses between being an "egghead" scholar, an athlete or "surfer," or a "hippie" rebel. He may play all of these roles at various times but is almost consciously concerned with what he is doing and why. Peer heroes and peer causes are much more important to him now. He is even more conscious of his age and of age distinctions. He is extremely aware of his body and of his physical self: his dress, grooming, speech, language, posture, and the development of his body are all important items to him.

An identity formation scale would thus have many items concerned with the aware-ness of the teenager of the various facets of his identity development. A great deal of what is called adolescent rebellion is actually adolescent identity development. He has to says "no"; he has to set his own patterns; he has to determine his comings and goings; —all in preparation of seeing himself entirely separate from his parents and other adult authorities. He may not really expect these authorities to accept his declaration of independence, but it is necessary for him to assert it.

This action component of identity formation in adolescence is present not only in achievement in social behavior, but also in the sexual role. During latency, he practices being a man among men; during adolescence he has to practice being a man among women. For girls, the physical and sexual aspect of identity development in adolescence is even more marked. Although masculine virility is practiced and boasted about among latency boys, girls have little opportunity to be sexually feminine before puberty. With the onset of menses, a girl has proof positive that she is a woman. She no longer can play a tomboy role or avoid feminine activities with impunity. Her physique reflected in her own mirror tells her that she is becoming a woman. For a girl, feelings about body image are far more of an intense core of identity than for most boys. Although boys may take considerable pride in or have considerable concern with their muscular development, their height and weight or even their complexion, this masculine concern of body image is seldom as intense as is the feminine body image of most girls. Scarcely any girl escapes altogether from this physical feminine narcissism. Even the high school girl who appears to take only the minimum or practical concern with dress and grooming, who makes little or no effort to keep up with teenage girl fashions or fads, and who devotes herself to studies or athletics only barely hides her dreams and concerns about her body image. Any denial of this feminine narcissism is usually a reaction formation. Such girls frequently do not act like girls only because they fear that their physique is not feminine. Acting like a boy and acting like a girl—and *acting* is a very important part of adolescent identity formation—is not merely a pose but is a continuous interaction with the opposite sex. For latency girls, being feminine is being a little lady; after puberty, being feminine involves being flirtatious and seductive. Being a virile cowboy or baseball hero is part of masculine identification during latency whereas at least part of adolescent masculinity involves being able to attract girls and being a hero to them. On an identity formation scale, being somebody at age 13 for a boy would include being masculine enough to talk to girls, showing an interest in sex among his masculine peers, and taking a sudden and new interest in his grooming. An identity scale now definitely has to be subdivided according to sex, for the items will be quite different for girls. The items just cited for the 13-year-old boy might occur somewhere between 11 and 12 for girls. By age 13, feminine identification requires being entirely out of little girls' frocks and into teenage clothes, quite definite interest in grooming, and more than a casual interest in the opposite sex. Crushes on movie stars are part of being an adolescent girl, much more frequently than among boys. All of these items would measure the degree to which the child accepts the current adolescent roles as part of the self.

Although adolescent identity formation often appears to center about the adoption of the sexual role, such identity is certainly not the only aspect of this process. The sense of individual achievement and pride therein is a very essential part of adolescent identity formation, as are being a member of the clique or gang and of the school. One aspect of the adolescent's heterosexual relationship is also the feeling of belonging to someone. A girl feels more like she is "someone" because she has been pinned; and a boy is "somebody" because he has a girlfriend. Nor should an assessor ignore the emotional intensity of these girlfriend-boyfriend relationships, as do many adults when they refer to "mere puppy love." For the adolescent, these affective relationships are extremely intense and being in love is not merely a sexual attraction but is a very essential part of "being somebody who is in love" and is loved in return. The psychologist's identity test should take heed of what poets and philosophers have long known, namely, that the essential and complete feelings of an identity are derived through a love affair. Such affairs may be very brief and occur only once or twice before the end of adolescence, but nevertheless they are very important to the final stages of adolescent identity forma-

tion. They may not even include any actual sexual interaction. In fact, most adolescents become quite aware that there is a difference between being in love and having a sexual experience, even though the two are often combined. Currently, experiencing the full range of sexual activity before the age of 21 is often considered by the late adolescent as being essential to his or her achievement of being an adequate person. However, many late teenagers bitterly complain that they really do not know what it means to be in love. It seems almost the reverse of the previous generation who fell madly in love but could not allow themselves sexual interaction.

2. Identity Formation as an Interaction Between the Ego and the Environment

In the above section, identity has been analyzed as an accumulation of experiences leading to a sense of separate and total self. This discussion was concerned purely with the hallmarks of these accumulative experiences and perceptions, and only passive consideration was given to the forces that shape the identity. In contrast to intelligence tests which measure only the pace and accumulation of intellectual function, but not the forces shaping or actually deterring intellectual development, an identity formation scale should measure the interactions between the ego and the environment. An examination of some of the forces that shape identity is a necessary part of an assessment.

Since the motivational or shaping forces that form the child's identity also shift in nature and intensity over the childhood years, it would be quite possible in constructing this hypothetical identity formation scale to include items that would sample the nature and effect of these shaping forces.* During infancy, the forces that shape identity are largely external to the ego. The child is given a name, assigned roles in his family, and expectations of him are formed. He has a particular kind of body with a definite sex which develops at a certain rate. Whether he is adequate or inadequate, good or bad, acting like a boy or acting like a girl, or has other attributes that serve to delimit his

---

*In fact, had the constructors of our intelligence scales been aware of the motivational forces that shape intellectual development, these also might have been included at each mental age level.

identity, all depend largely upon what others say or how others behave toward him.

Although the young child is largely a passive receptor, the identity assigned him by others during infancy does not mean that he does not react to these roles nor that he receives them without affect. Certainly he may protest or react with depression to negative roles assigned or to disparagement of his identity. He may even at times assert and test roles of his own. However, such independent assertion is not the usual way identity is formed. In fact, when the parents say proudly, "He has a will of his own; he is a little character," they are, in effect, according him this role. For the most part, he adopts those roles which are positively reinforced and avoids those which are rejected or denied him by others. Even when he acts the little monster and is publicly denounced for it by his parents, it often turns out, on further investigation, that they passively permit this role or even secretly encourage it. Whether the child plays the role of passive invalid depends not nearly so much on how physically incapacitated he may be, but on whether this is the view taken by his parents.

Items on an identity formation scale during infancy should thus include a sampling of the parents' attitudes toward the child and the roles they assign him. In assessment, a great deal of this needs to be gathered from the interview with the parents. In such interviews the parents may not directly say how they regard the child or explicitly define the roles they assign him for, if they are aware of their behavior in this respect, they may feel very defensive. Rather, the assessor obtains his information by the description of their interactions with the child, the way they compare this child with other children in the family, what they deplore about the child, and what they hope from him. A very important item in the interview concerning identity is behavior for which the parents punish and reward the child—which reflects the parents' values. At this point of the child's life, the parents' values determine the limits of his identity.

The young child plays the roles assigned because he is as yet almost entirely dependent on the parent for satisfaction of his needs. However, as he enters latency and develops greater and greater skills at need-gratification, he is much less dependent on the parent and does not have quite as much pressure to conform to their identification of him. Moreover, he is practicing these skills for extended periods of the day away from his parents, in the company of his peers and under the direction of other adults. He may find that the roles assigned him by his parents are not appropriate away from home. He may continue to play some of these roles in order to pacify his parents or to manipulate them, but he does not necessarily see such roles as part of himself. Thus, what he accepts and internalizes out of these infant roles depends on other social pressures. His identity formation during latency depends more upon whether the roles that he plays gain him some need-gratification. Thus, he may continue to play some of the roles the family assigns him because they in turn allow him a greater freedom or self-assertion in return for compliance to their image of him. He may, however, play roles almost opposite those assigned him by his parents, if in so doing he can find the freedom to do other things which serve to enhance his identity. Thus, for example, if he is the fourth boy in the family and his mother has treated him like the little girl that she wished for throughout infancy, he may play that role until he reaches latency and then entirely reverse it when he finds it necessary to be a boy among boys. His reversal may also constitute an independent testing of identity in order to separate himself from his mother. As was noted above, latency is not merely a repression of affect, but rather an independence of affect in relation to others. The child's need for emotional independence drives him further into self-assertion and thus toward internalization of his identity. During latency, the child accepts roles as part of himself not merely to please others, but also to satisfy himself.

This internal motivation for identification becomes even more marked during adolescence. Now the child has to declare his independence openly and define his own identity if he is going to be successful in leaving childhood. During adolescence, he goes through the process of giving up parental pressure and parental example as external sources of identity formation. He does not necessarily give up all of these values, even though at times he may seem to reject them entirely, for many of these are internalized already as his own. What he does reject is the parental approval or disapproval of identity. Thus, he comes to feel that the things he wants and the things he does and the person he is are what he himself directs; they may or may not be what the parents also want for him. He may or may not imitate his parents. If he is like the parent, then it is because these values and this identity have become internalized.

If for various reasons the child has not actually internalized these values, if he does not see them as his own, then he will continue to be very dependent on parents and parent substitutes for direction. He will feel that he has little identity of his own and he will seek approval or test disapproval for every act, although he may resent having to do so. This failure at internalization of values and the subsequent search for identity are currently the most critical and widespread problems among adolescents. Such a failure in the development of an identity underlies a wide variety of behavior disorders in adolescence, ranging from depression to angry rebellion to open psychosis, often including elements of all three. The prevalence and severity of this developmental lag in identity formation thus warrant further examination.

In order for internalization of identity to take place, two general conditions must be present. First, during infancy the child should receive from the environment a generally positive picture of his identity. The parents may utilize both rewards and punishment for his behavior to condition a child to their sets of values and attitudes. However, if the child is to proceed to an internally induced self-image, then the rewards should be received more often than punishment. Particularly there should be rewards for avoiding tabooed behavior, as well as punishment for committing it. Moreover, the parent should distinguish between punishment of the behavior of the child and derogation of his identity. The child needs to learn that something is a "bad" thing to do, which he may be able to internalize as a value for himself, but he should not internalize the opinion that he is a "bad boy." Although a child may tend to believe that he is bad, he is not comfortable with such an identity and keeps testing it. The child who approaches latency with a feeling that the environment offers little love and mostly punishment or who has been told repeatedly that he is inadequate as a person will continue to seek external approval of his behavior and continue to attempt to revoke any externally created

negative identity. Such a child would then remain dependent on the environment for his identity.

The second condition necessary for internalization is that the child feel free to test what he has accepted as part of himself. In everyday terms this means that the parent must permit the child to guide his own behavior as much as possible. To internalize, the child has to feel trusted. Mother has to learn not to worry if Johnny, age eight, goes around the block to play because she knows that he will bring himself home. She knows that, given the opportunity and time, he will complete his own homework because he wants approval and pride for himself. She realizes that he will not do anything that will embarrass her because she knows it will embarrass him. Such trust does not, of course, develop overnight. But as the child enters latency, there needs to be an unspoken contract between child and parent that the child be given greater and greater permission and encouragement to utilize the values that have been externally conditioned during infancy. In many little ways, the parent conveys to the child that there are things that his own conscience will tell him to do. Certainly, this conscience or super-ego is not the same as a feeling of self adequacy or identity, but it is an important aspect of identity during this period of internalization.

Failures of internalization and identity formation thus may arise during early childhood from several situations, either separately or simultaneously. The child may receive inadequate affection and support and rewards, especially in relationship to punishment and derogation. Often, because of this he is not trusted by his parents, since he continues to test them, seeking their approval. He becomes unable to guide himself if they are not present. If both of these conditions for internalization are violated, it is likely that the child will present a major behavioral problem to all adults concerned—long before he reaches adolescence. Even if he does succeed in going through latency without any marked behavioral disturbance, it is very likely that the stresses of puberty will upset whatever uneasy balance he may have achieved. He will be unable to meet and handle for himself the stresses of burgeoning sexual impulses and pressures for independent behavior nor will he be able to participate in a peer society. Under such conditions, some children retreat in a regressive fashion, depressed and near psychotic. Others defend themselves by massive reaction formations, by rebelling excessively, explosively asserting their independence in an effort to hide their feelings of inadequacy, their continued dependence on their parents, and their negative self-image.

CASE 44

Larry G., age 15, was remanded by the juvenile court to the clinic for psychological assessment. In the past year he had twice been arrested for possession of marijuana; he had been put on probation both times and had violated this probation. Currently he had been convicted of selling marijuana and faced the possibility of one year in prison for his felony. It was only because his family was known as "community leaders" that the court agreed to the plea of the family's attorney and granted further probation on the condition that the parents seek psychological assessment and treatment. The court records showed further that Larry had had no other brushes with the law but that he had been expelled from two different high schools in the past year. The probation officer's report, which was rather brief, revealed further that Larry's father was a businessman with a gross income of around $30,000, that the family owned their own home, and lived in a respectable upper-midle class neighborhood. Mr. and Mrs. G were Larry's biological parents and neither had any previous marriages. In the home besides Larry and his parents was his sister Lisa, age 17. Larry also had an older sister, Elaine, age 20, who was married and lived away from the parental home. The probation officer noted that it was suspected that Lisa might also be using marijuana, since she associated with known users, but she had not been apprehended. He had not discussed this fact with her parents. He remarked that Larry showed no guilt over his actions. The parents appeared to him to be quite concerned about Larry's behavior and very angry at him, but the probation officer found no gross evidence of family dissention.

In appearance, Larry was a very handsome lad, slight in build, with very delicate, almost feminine features. He was dressed appropriately, casually and neatly, in expensive clothes. He appeared to be trying to assume an air of nonchalance as he came into the office, but his constant wetting of his lips, his perspiring palms, and his nails, which were bitten to

the core, all suggested considerable tension. He immediately lit a cigarette and started to put it out until the psychologist nodded permission. His face was drawn into a sullen sneer as he began the interview by defiantly defending an individual's right to use marijuana. The psychologist listened to his arguments which were very logically presented and which suggested that Larry was probably quite bright intellectually. Larry ended his diatribe with a challenging, "What do you think?"

The psychologist replied that he realized that Larry had very strong feelings on the topic and asked why he felt it was necessary to argue these feelings so vigorously. Larry retorted that he probably was wasting his breath, since he knew the psychologist did not agree with him. The psychologist agreed that this might be true but that he considered it important that Larry had opinions of his own and that he respected him for it. Larry replied rather despondently that he felt no one agreed with him or believed him. This statement lead to further discussion about his feelings that he was not trusted by his parents and that they did not understand him. With only slightly more encouragement from the psychologist, Larry plunged ahead into a description of a negative relationship with his parents and a history of his development as he viewed it.

He was particularly bitter and depressed as he discussed his father. He felt that his father had never understood or cared what he, Larry, felt or thought. Larry saw him as interested only in exacting immediate and complete obedience, no matter what the circumstances. He first blamed his father's behavior on the fact that he had been a military officer who had retired only recently. On further reflection, he became even more bitter, noting that he was acquainted with many other military families and that he had not seen other officers behave this way toward their sons. He even thought that his father acted in a more authoritative fashion toward him than toward the troops which his father had commanded. When he was younger he feared his father and stayed out of his way, which had been relatively easy since his father had usually been preoccupied with his work and social activities, or had been separated from the family by his military assignments. It was only after his father's retirement that there had been serious and continued clashes between the two. Larry laughed when he recounted that he had always called his father "sir" and found himself unable to break the habit, even adding "sir" when he swore at his father. He described how teenage interests and activities irritated his father who countered them with absolute prohibitions. He recounted with anger how his father had forbidden him to associate with certain friends because his initial impression was that these friends were "no good." He complained that his father had refused to sign his report card the previous year because he had two "C's" even though the balance of the grades were entirely "A's." The following semester Larry made no "A's" and there were two "D's" on the card and he forged a report card that looked more satisfactory in order to avoid his father's wrath. The forgery was subsequently discovered by the school and he was expelled.

The second expulsion occurred upon his first arrest for use of marijuana. However, Larry's biggest complaint was that his father had promised to get him a car when he was old enough to drive which would have been only two months away from the date of the interview, but that following his arrest the father had withdrawn his promise and told Larry he would not even be able to use the family car until he was past 18. Larry admitted that he also had a temper, that he could not contain his angry feelings, and had sworn at his father and had come close to hitting him at times. He had been punished with spankings and whippings when young, but more recently he had been restricted from all social activities. He had been forbidden the use of his record player allegedly in order to give him greater time to attend to his studies.

Larry was also very bitter because he felt his father favored Lisa, even though Lisa also had been openly defiant of him. He felt that the father did not punish Lisa and that she got away with "murder." He alleged that he had first learned about the use of marijuana from Lisa, but that she had never been "busted" (arrested). Larry was also angry at his mother but hedged his anger with many qualifications. His initial complaint was that he thought she should defend him more and that she tended to side with his father. "She has to, I guess," he added sadly. He also felt that she was full of complaints against him and that it was hard to

know what to do to please her. However, he was quick to add that he guessed he had done many things to make her sad and that he did feel most badly that he had disappointed her. He contrasted her behavior with that of his father, saying that he could never remember that she had punished him for anything but he still did not feel that she had much understanding of his needs or feelings. On further reflection, he admitted sadly that he could not remember her as showing much overt affection or attention to him.

He felt much closer to his older sister, Elaine, whom he felt had received the same treatment for the hands of his father. Three years previously, his father had driven Elaine from the house when it was discovered that she was illegitimately pregnant. Subsequently, Elaine had married the father of her baby only to divorce him a year later. Now Elaine had remarried and was pregnant with the second child. Larry enjoyed visiting his sister and brother-in-law and often retreated to their home when in conflict with his own parents. He felt he could confide in Elaine and receive comfort from her.

Larry was born in Germany where his father was then stationed, but moved soon afterwards back to the United States while his father was on duty in Korea. When he was approximately school age, he and his mother and sisters joined his father in Japan where they remained for most of his grade school years. During those years he was cared for largely by Japanese speaking servants who often fed him and saw that he was bathed and put to bed when his parents were otherwise occupied. In mentioning the servants, Larry made derogatory remarks about their habits and hinted that he often "put things over on them" or even teased them in order to annoy them. In a subsequent interview, Larry revealed that unbeknown to his parents he had had his first heterosexual experience with a Mexican servant girl who currently lived in the home. As Larry discussed this period of his life further, it was evident that a great deal of his behavior was unknown and unobserved by his parents. They knew very little of his friends, of his school, or of what happened at home while they were away. However, if their lives were disturbed he was punished severely.

Subsequently, Mr. and Mrs. G were interviewed. Although Mr. G's erect bearing and set jaw did attest to his military posture, he was surprisingly soft spoken and reflective as he discussed his problems concerning Larry. Mrs. G was a small, but strikingly beautiful woman, very tastefully dressed with a coiffure lacquered in the latest style. For the most part, she sat quietly by while her husband talked, her face set in a drawn smile. The interviewer was not surprised to learn subsequently that she had been a professional model until the birth of her children. It was also evident that Larry inherited most of his good looks from his mother. Mr. G opened his discussion with the interviewer by announcing his views regarding marijuana, initially blaming all their problems on the fact that marijuana was so commonly used by adolescents and that it was easily obtainable. Like Larry, he ended his pronouncements with the question, "What do you think?" Again, the interviewer reflected the fact that very strong views were being expressed and that Mr. G had a need to make his feelings clear.

This led to considerably more discussion of Mr. G's desperation over being unable to tell Larry how to behave and what was the proper thing to do. Mr. G readily admitted that he felt very ineffective and openly regretted that he had had so little contact with Larry during Larry's earlier childhood years. He did not openly blame his wife, but strongly hinted that he felt she had had little control over the children.

Mrs. G did not immediately comment, even though the interviewer asked her about her feelings and experiences with Larry during his childhood. However, as the discussion ensued, she became very defensive, stating that she had tried very desperately to teach Larry the right things, but had received very little support from her husband. Although he did not defend himself, she grew more and more direct in her accusations against him, to the effect that he had been unreasonably harsh in his discipline with Larry and that he had paid little attention to Larry's needs when Larry was younger. As she became more angry, she began to denounce her husband for his behavior toward Elaine, at which time she seemed near tears. Mr. G sat hunched over with his face in his hands. Finally he seemed unable to take her accusations any further and retorted that she could have handled things better if she had not been away from the home so often and if she had tempered her use of alcohol. Mrs. G, her face now flushed with anger and her voice shrill, retorted that he always accused her of being an alcoholic when he was trying to excuse himself and if she had ever drunk excessively it was because she was lonely and neglected by him. The interviewer pointed out that apparently some very strong feelings between them underlay Larry's problems and that further discussions might be helpful—to which both parents agreed.

These interviews suggested strongly that Larry had long felt that his behavior was more punished than rewarded, and that he had experienced little approval for any independent testing of his own ability to guide himself. Evidence from other techniques indicated that little in the way of self-substained controls over his behavior had ever been internalized and that Larry's sense of identity was primarily negative. For example, on the Sentence Completion Test he made responses such as: "A *mother* should show her son that she loves him," "My *father* can't be argued with," "*Who cares* if I live or die," "*I wish* I were never born." Although Larry gave 33 responses to the Rorschach inkblots, many of which were quite detailed and imaginative, only two could be scored as containing the human figures in action, one of which was the popular response to Card III. In contrast, nine of his responses were primarily based on the color of the cards and five of these were scored CF. This experience balance indicated that Larry remained chiefly dependent on cues from his environment and that little had been internalized. Moreover, such overdependency on the environment was accompanied by considerable feelings of tension and anxiety, as evidenced by responses such as to Card IX which he described as a volcanic explosion, the dark colors showing fire and lava, and the pastel shading indicating gas and clouds. Sensitivity was suggested in responses such as to Card VI which he saw not only as a soft and furry bear rug, but as a gasoline pump leaking a slick of oil. Other responses also suggested a considerable underlying depression and overt anxiety, such as to Card IV which he saw as the kind of stove used in military barracks (D1), bulging out a cloud of black smoke. In eight different responses he was fascinated by the white space; the most significant of these appeared on Card VII (often the card which is associated with feelings about maternal figures) which Larry saw as "a gaping canyon surrounding such high cliffs that no one can possibly descend into it." The psychologist interpreted Larry's attention to the empty space as indicating not only negativism and resistance, but also feelings of emptiness and depression.

On the TAT, Larry tended to describe his heroes as under the influence of other people or of circumstances beyond their control. For example, to the picture depicting the boy with the violin (1), Larry did describe the boy's anger and resentment as being forced to practice his instrument. Questioned further, he decided the boy would "put the violin down and split" when no one was watching. He decided that it had been the boy's father's decision that he play the violin and that he probably would "get hell" when the father discovered he had not practiced. Significantly, Larry made no mention what the boy himself would do. Similarly, to Card 3BM, Larry decided the boy in the picture was crying against his bed because he had been punished. In this story, the hero's parents had taken away his bicycle because "his teacher had given him a poor grade." To Card 6BM, Larry told the story of a woman weeping because her husband had been killed but then he changed to decide that she was really weeping and angry because the man in the picture, her son, had done something wrong. Asked what the son had done wrong, Larry hesitated and then decided that perhaps he had gotten into bad company. As to the conclusion, he thought that maybe the mother would forgive the son but it would take a long time. Presented with Card 7BM, Larry hesitated for quite a while remarking that he saw very little of a story in this picture and, when encouraged further, he decided that the young man in the picture had been accused of doing something wrong and was conferring with his attorney. Larry concluded that although the young man had done nothing wrong, he probably would be convicted anyhow and sentenced to 30 years in prison. In response to Card 8BM, Larry saw the man on the table as having been wounded in battle and now being operated on in primitive conditions by military surgeons. "Bad luck, they can't save him!" Larry concluded grimly. As to the figure in the foreground, Larry, when questioned, decided that he was "some character" who happened on the scene and "turned around because he couldn't stand the sight of blood." Card 11, Larry saw as depicting Dante's Inferno, which he had read in its entirety as a special project

in high school in his English class the prior semester. He could not tell a story about it but said that it probably depicted a scene where people were being punished in hell for their sins. As to the dragonlike figure in the central background of this picture, Larry perceived it as a monster which was specially designated to devour selfish people (the psychologist subsequently cited this response as evidence that Larry did have a sense of guilt, albeit a rather infantile fear of punishment). To Card 16, Larry tried to joke; "It's an invisible man who has just disappeared." When encouraged to expand this into a story, he decided that this man was able to disappear whenever he did not want people to know what he was doing, or when he wanted to escape from them. Asked what the man might want to do that he did not want other people to see, Larry could not decide but when pressured for a story, he decided that the man had been under attack from some bully and had been able to escape him by becoming invisible. He could not imagine what might happen further. Stories to the other TAT cards also suggested that people might have to escape from or bluff their way through hostile attacks from others. In no story was any hero actively seeking anything on his own, or deciding anything for himself.

Finally, Larry made a drawing of a small boy with face upturned and hands stretched up and out. "It looks like he's reaching for something he really can't get," Larry remarked. He could make no further associations to his drawing but remarked that the boy was probably about age seven.

Larry's lack of identity development thus was a result largely of a failure at internalization. Such inadequate development shows up even more strongly during the high school years because such children commonly see high school as an imposition upon them rather than as something that they are interested in or need. They resent authority not in the sense of adolescent rebellion, but rather in the sense of frustration of their needs which they themselves cannot control without an outside authority nor satisfy on their own. In contrast, the adolescent with a well-developed sense of self may rebel against authority not because he feels deprived of anything, but because he wants to do things on his own. Both the normal and the "emotionally immature" child, as children with poor identity development are commonly labeled, may use the same words in defying adults. However, their tone of voice is different and it is obvious that the normal child wants to be encouraged toward independence, whereas the emotionally immature child is making demands for someone else to supply his needs. Moreover, when the emotionally immature child is allowed to be on his own he remains restless and dissatisfied and does not know what to do with himself. Although he may want money badly to buy things, he characteristically does not seem to be able to find a job or keep one if someone else finds it for him. Although he may enjoy sports, such a child usually avoids athletic competition. In fact, he often is unable to entertain himself and goes looking for "kicks and thrills," associating with similar youngsters who passively seek "a way out." Although such children do not necessarily become engaged in gross social delinquencies, they are commonly on the fringes of delinquent groups or passively accept suggestions from more actively delinquent peers. Currently such adolescents may easily become involved in the use of marijuana or LSD and are found on the edge of the "hippy" movement. However, they are not the intellectual philosophers who lead such movements. Like Larry, they may initially voice an argument they have heard somewhere else for independent action, but soon they are reciting their complaints against an allegedly depriving set of parents.

Although this identity retardation, as it might be called, is far and wide the most common type of identity problem in adolescence, admittedly the term identity conflict or identity crisis refer to slightly different kinds of problems. Actually these terms are used to cover a wide variety of difficulties. Sometimes a child suffers because a variety of identities are externally imposed upon him, such as was illustrated in the case of Dana, Case 10, cited in Chapter 3. As was noted in that case, Dana's name was confusing to her from the first; she was alternately little princess and then scapegoat; she was mother's little girl and father's little girl but really neither; she attempted to identify with her sisters and was rejected by them. In her final psychotic state at pubescence, she rejected all of these identities and saw herself as a Cinderella.

The term identity conflict or identity crisis is most commonly associated specifically with the development of sexual identity. Like other aspects of identity, sexual identity has its roots in early childhood experiences, as detailed above. However, sexual identity crisis is particularly associated with adolescence, since it is during adolescence that the child not only accepts his sexual identity as a finality, but is forced to begin to practice it far more actively in interactions with others than at any previous time in his life. In the classic case of sexual identity crisis, the child finds it difficult to actively be male or female, often preferring to be sexually neutral and inactive, perhaps even denying any feelings of conflict or of inadequacy. However, such children often feel quite inadequate and display such feelings in other behavior or in their appearance. Thus, they may blame their heterosexual retirement on their size or looks, or lack of opportunity. Although such children frequently react in counterphobic fashion by suddenly becoming very sex conscious, displaying considerable sexual curiosity and alleged interest in the opposite sex, or dressing in almost bizarrely seductive fashion, they usually stop short of actually becoming socially and sexually involved with the opposite sex. Other children recognize and label such children as "phonies" and after one or two contacts have little to do with them. Such rejection leaves these children even more lonely, with increased feelings of inadequacy. As these experiences increase, the child becomes more and more worried and guilt-ridden over his sexual impulses, angry and depressed when he finds himself masturbating, and obsessed with the possibility that he might be homosexual. In the classic case, the parent of the same sex is either physically absent or psychologically distant or inadequate, thus leaving the child without a model for sexual identification.

Interestingly, in such cases of sexual identity conflict, responses to the psychological tests, especially in the early years of adolescence, are often similar to those illustrated above in the case of Larry. The sexual aspect of the difficulty in identity development is usually better represented in the problems the child has in everyday life, in his heterosexual contexts with his peers than it is in overtly sexual symbols or fantasies, in responses to such techniques as the Rorschach or TAT. Occasionally the older adolescent may, with some bravado, give a sexual response to the Rorschach or tell a sexy story to the TAT, or intellectualize about homosexuality during the interview. If such responses are associated with sexual identity conflict, they are usually given with considerably more anxiety and defensiveness than might be shown by relatively normal 16 years olds whose sexual impulses are spilling over into fantasies. Such overt sexual interests are almost par for the course for the normal, bright 18 year old. However, any child under 18 who obsessively verbalizes about sexual anatomy and sexual functioning during the initial context of assessment often proves to be expressing a breakdown in identity formation of near psychotic extent. The obsessive element often proves to be a more important factor than the sexual content of the adolescent's ideation. In most such cases, the history often reveals that the child has used obsessive and compulsive defenses throughout his childhood. Although the internal stress of burgeoning sexuality can be the precipitating cause of collapse of the child's ego functioning, the fact that the ego could be so precipitously overwhelmed does suggest that both ego development and identity formation are probably immature. Thus, such a preoccupation with sex in an adolescent would suggest that the control systems of the ego were never well formed in the first place, that they still remain largely dependent on external forces, and that they may have been successively weakened by each stress in childhood in accumulative fashion.

3. Self-Awareness

The formation of an identity includes a certain degree of self-awareness, of consciousness of ego functioning, the development of which is one of the most remarkable and most frequently noted facets of adolescent behavior. Adolescents are often uncomfortably aware of themselves and their functioning. At other moments they may seem to be most unconscious of themselves and behave in a completely free and straightforward manner. Yet, this awareness scarcely ever leaves them completely, and it takes most of their adolescent years for them to get used to it. A complete and continuous lack of self-awareness would suggest that the full blossoming of an identity is not yet attained. Such self-awareness may be noted at moments throughout childhood, even in the preschool

child, and becomes gradually more extensive throughout childhood, but it is not fully developed until after pubescence. It is this factor of self-awareness that makes it possible for the adolescent to assess and evaluate his own ego functioning.

For most teenagers, this self-awareness occurs with only minimum anxiety and guilt, but when considerable guilt has been instilled in the child and when his self-image is quite negative, this awareness is extremely painful and has to be closed off and repressed. Because this is often used as one of the keys in psychotherapy, at least a qualitative estimate of the nature and extent of the child's recognition of his own functioning is frequently an essential part of an assessment. Although there is no one well-defined instrument for measuring this variable, signs of introspectiveness and reflectiveness about the self may be seen on a variety of techniques. On the MMPI, for example, self-awareness would be indicated if the K and Hy Scales are relatively low. At least a moderately high Pt would suggest some concerns with the self. On the Rorschach, responses based on perspective or depth (FK using Klopfer's scoring or FV using Beck scoring) are commonly considered one index of reflectiveness. However, such "distancing" does not necessarily indicate introspectiveness. In order to interpret such vista responses as a tendency toward self-reflection, it is necessary to note the context in which they appear, for example, whether in company with internalized M responses or along with external, color responses. Not uncommonly in adolescence, responses containing perspective are associated with white space suggesting a more oppositional perspective rather than self-awareness. Self-awareness on the TAT may be indicated by fantasies in which the hero is reflecting upon himself. Probably one of the best indications of the development of self-awareness is the degree to which the feelings of the hero are voluntarily mentioned by the story teller. Not infrequently the story teller who becomes concerned with the ego functioning of his heroes will remark on his awareness of his own feelings and functioning. Even where this reaches the proportions of an obsessive excoriation, the very fact of this self-awareness, albeit extreme, is an indication that identity formation is reaching a climax.

Chapter 17

REPORTING THE ASSESSMENT

A. THE IMPORTANCE OF REPORT WRITING

The third and final step in assessment, after the data are collected and analyzed, is the communication of this analysis to the referrant and others concerned with the child. The importance of effective communication of these findings cannot be overemphasized. Obviously, if these findings are to be of any assistance to the referrant and are to carry any weight in the decisions which he needs to make in helping the child, they must be communicated as clearly and definitively as possible. Reports that are carelessly composed, that are replete with jargon, and that are a jumble of ideas without logic or organization often confuse rather than enlighten the reader. On the other hand, a report that states concisely and logically, in good English, the nature of the child's behavior and its causes provides a basis for the referrant in his organization of his work.

For many psychologists, especially those in training, the communication of their findings, especially in writing, is an arduous task. They enjoy the contacts with the child and are challenged by the analysis of the data, but shrink with distaste from writing a report. Undoubtedly, writing reports does become easier with experience. The chief difficulty

for the novitiate is in bringing together his miscellaneous observations and formulating his arguments. When a report seems particularly difficult to write, it is usually because the analysis of the data is incomplete or has not been thought through and logically organized. Thus, when one finds it difficult to compose a report—or when one finds himself writing endlessly—the best advice is to go back over the data and review one's analysis of it.

Report writing is also often difficult for psychologists—and, in fact, for many scientists—because they seldom receive any training in writing, beyond their Freshman English composition courses. Unfortunately, few universities provide special training in scientific writing. There are, however, several manuals on report writing (for example, Klopfer, 1960; Hammond and Allen, 1953) which provide guidelines for the student. Rather than reviewing these texts, this chapter is intended as a supplement in which the organization and logic of the report is emphasized.

Assessment results may, of course, be communicated either orally or in writing. Very often an assessor is called upon to deliver his reports in both forms. In many settings, the psychologist presents his report as part of a staff discussion and files a written report as part of the record. Oral reports are often easier and more satisfying because the psychologist has an opportunity in a discussion of his findings to clarify his ideas. He may even expand or revise his concepts as he compares notes with his colleagues who also observe the child and his environment. However, oral presentations also should be cogently organized and much of what is suggested in this chapter concerning written reports also applies to oral presentations. The written report is more exacting, since it does not allow for discussion and is part of a permanent record. Such records, although confidential and not to be used by any person other than the referrant or the hospital or clinic, can nevertheless be released to other persons by the permission or order of the child's parent or guardian, or a court. If a child should be seen by various agencies, these reports follow him. This writer has had the experience of having records of children that he has assessed requested by other clinics or by the military or the courts years later when the child has become an adult. Recently the United States Congress has been concerned with the possibility that "these invasions of privacy" might become public record and follow the person throughout his life. Thus, it behooves the assessor to be most circumspect and to have in mind throughout his report that he is writing for the welfare of the child. In clinical psychology, hasty analysis of the data and careless wording of the report are not only scientifically reprehensible, but are also professionally unethical.

B. THE REPORT AND THE REFERRANT

The first guideline for a good report is that it should be written for and to the referrant. It should reply clearly and succinctly to the referrant's questions. If these could not be answered, the reasons that they could not be investigated must be explained. However, the written report need not be this strictly confined. Very often the assessor uncovers data which may be quite important to the work of the referrant about which the referrant has not thought to inquire. However, such findings should be directly tied to the questions and the purposes of the referrant's work with the child. For example, suppose that the school is concerned with

the child's intellectual development and with his motivations toward learning. Suppose further that the data from the assessment indicate that the child is quite bright and is highly motivated to achieve, but that currently he is quite depressed over the death of his father and threatened by the fact that his mother is unconsciously turning to him for emotional support in a highly seductive fashion. This latter fact may well be of little concern to the school if, indeed, it is any of the school's business at all. However, it is quite proper and necessary to convey to the school authorities that the child's problem does not lie in poor intelligence or poor motivation, but rather in a depression related to his home experiences. One might suggest to the school that the child's school achievement is so severely deterred by depression that care and guidance of the child require the assistance of facilities outside the school system. On the other hand, should this question be asked by a psychiatric colleague in a clinic, a more detailed explanation of the possible causes of the child's depression may well be in order. Similarly, if the assessor were possibly the person to proceed with treatment and the referrant were the patient's mother, conveying these findings orally might in itself constitute an initial, if not an extensive, part of the mother's treatment. Both the content and format of the report thus depend on whom it is written for and for what purpose. The assessor should be most flexible in communicating his reports and no strict rules for report writing can be laid down that will cover every case. The discussions below are intended to be generalizations chiefly about written reports to other professional colleagues.

C. THE LANGUAGE OF THE REPORT

One aspect of report writing that has been given considerable attention in various books has been the language of the report. Sargent (1951), in particular, remarked on the use of psychological jargon. She noted, as have many commentators (Klopfer, 1960; Hammond and Allen, 1953), that there is a tendency for psychologists to speak in their own technical language which often confuses those who are not psychologically trained. She warns very properly that reports of assessment must be written in a language which is comprehensible to the referrant. Even when one is writing to other psychologists, psychiatrists, or mental health workers, there should be a minimum of the use of technical terms. However, Sargent argues that there are no few concepts about behavior that can be designated only by terms used mostly by psychologists. Many of these terms are at least vaguely known to most users of psychological findings, and so they are not truthfully jargon. This writer is slightly more conservative on this matter and feels that even when such terms are widely used, unless they are clearly understood by both the writer and the reader, they should be avoided.

In well functioning clinics and hospitals, part of the purpose of the staff conferences is to define clearly such terms in the communication between various staff members. Some opportunity for definition of terms is also possible in an ongoing relationship between a psychological consultant and an agency even when the agency is not primarily psychologically oriented, such as a school or an adoption service. As has been pointed out in previous chapters of this book, such common terms as "Oedipus complex" often are flung about with little recognition of their operational definition. In many instances it might be much more preferable to speak about "a prolonged and intense dependency on the parent of the opposite sex and an intense rivalry for affection of that parent with the parent of the same sex." Even widely used and well accepted concepts such as "perceptual ability" may at times be actually unclear to members of the profession as well as to laymen. Certainly perceptual development has a different meaning to the social psychologists, psychologists studying vision, and the Rorschach user. The author was once asked in court to define "perceptual functioning" and found it most difficult to explain to a jury of laymen.

Since such terms often have broad meaning and need to be specified for the case at hand, it is often helpful to accompany them with an illustration, a simile, or an analogy. Although idiomatic terms may not be formal scientific language, they often describe behavior vividly and concisely. For example, the phrase "mama's boy" conveys the meaning of Oedipal conflict, at least in part, to a great many people. A report should not be written in slang, but the vernacular need not be avoided and at times becomes the most meaningful and succinct way of communicating.

D. STEPS IN COMPOSING A REPORT

As was noted above, the composition of a report requires a careful and detailed analysis of the data. One of the best ways to begin is to go through the data response by response and make notes. Such notes need not be complete sentences, but merely words or phrases, itemizing the different aspects of the response. In order to comprehend the relationships between responses and to follow the train of the child's thought and feelings, it is a good idea to begin with the first responses, that is, in the referring contacts and in the introduction, and take each aspect of the contact in sequence, including the final handshake. These analytic notes may refer back and forth to other responses. Thus, although each technique should be analyzed separately, one should take note of the responses which are similar—or in contrast—to responses to other techniques. The patterns of scores and overall themes should be similarly noted. A summary of these notes from each technique helps to pull together the separate findings, bringing together the different themes and defenses and characteristics. A model for such outlining is presented in the chapter on the psychological examination in Menninger (1962).

Some psychologists proceed directly from these test-by-test notes to the composition of their report. In effect, these writers orient their report about the *techniques* rather than the child. In such reports, each test is analyzed separately and in detail. Sometimes each paragraph is labeled with the test name, such as "Wechsler Results" or "Rorschach Findings." More often these test-oriented reports have subheadings such as "Intelligence" or "Personality"; their hallmark is phrases such as "the Rorschach shows," the "TAT indicates," "an IQ of 110 was obtained," or "there were such and such signs of brain damage." A thorough-going test-oriented report usually contains considerable raw data in the separate paragraphs, cited in evidence of the analysis of findings. Because each test is handled separately, a subsequent section discussing and integrating the separate results is commonly necessary. The essence of all this analysis and discussion is then reiterated in a separate summary. These reports are thus often quite lengthy, running from four to six singlespaced typewritten pages. Such test-oriented reports may be advantageous when it is necessary to communicate much of the raw data upon which the analysis is based and the logic of that analysis. They are perhaps appropriate in the classroom setting where the student must demonstrate that each technique has been individually taken into account and thoroughly analyzed in detail and the method by which the student has drawn his final conclusions.

In most instances, however, the disadvantages of a test-oriented report far outweigh the advantages. In the first place, most referrants are not interested in "what the tests show," but in how the child behaves. In reading paragraph after paragraph of test findings, many of which may appear disparate and disconnected, it is often difficult to recognize how the child actually is functioning. Even though the separate findings may be subsequently integrated into a discussion, in the test-oriented report this discussion also is usually phrased in terms of test findings. Most of all, such reports reflect the testbound attitude of the writer. They suggest that the assessor has not been able to successfully look across and beyond his techniques to the essential overall functioning of the child.

In most situations, a report oriented in terms of the child's behavior rather than in test results is much more satisfactory as communication to the referrant. In such a child-oriented report, the functioning of the child's ego and his relationships between various ego functions may be reported in separate paragraphs but the analysis of each ego function may be drawn from a variety of techniques. Thus, in a paragraph discussing cognitive functioning, the analysis may be drawn not only from the Wechsler, but from the Rorschach or even the TAT. Perceptual motor functioning would include both the Bender-Gestalt, the Draw-A-Person, and parts of the Wechsler and the Rorschach. Such a report might contain quotes from the child's responses as illustrations of his behavior or report scores of subtests or from the Rorschach psychogram as supporting evidence of the kinds of behavior seen in the child. The phraseology in child-oriented reports disregards the test; thus, instead of saying "the Rorschach shows," the child-oriented reports states, "Johnny's perception of the emotional stresses. . . ." The child-oriented report is replete with such phrases as "Johnny understands," "Johnny feels," "Johnny fantasies," "Johnny avoids." The use of the child's name or the personal pronoun is thus the hallmark of the child-oriented report. Since there is no necessity to analyze each technique separately, a child-oriented report is usually briefer than the test-oriented approach. Even a very thorough assessment can be reported in less than three typewritten pages if the data have been thoroughly analyzed and integrated beforehand.

Such integration can be achieved if the psychologist goes over his initial notes in an effort to outline the development of the various ego functions. At this point in the analysis, one may write descriptive statements about the modes of each function, the input and output, the interferences, and the methods of coping. However, these miscellaneous statements do not in themselves constitute a report. It is necessary to organize them into a logical argument.

E. THE LOGIC OF REPORT WRITING

In reporting experiments, a scientist usually states his hypothesis and reports data bearing on this hypothesis which either supports or fails to support it. In some instances, assessments utilize this form of argument. For example, it may be hypothesized that the child's functioning is deterred by trauma to the central nervous system. Data may then be presented that give evidence for such a trauma or are contraindicative of it. Other similar hypotheses might be made concerning the effects of environmental stress or the presence of certain kinds of psychodynamics. Often, questions posed by the referrant can be phrased to state such testable hypotheses.

However, as is suggested in Chapter 1, assessments are far more often exploratory studies rather than purely experimental or actuarial in nature. The clinician is asked to look across the overall behavior of the child and discover "what is wrong" or indicate "why" the child behaves in such and such a manner. The clinician, in his exploration of the child's development, often runs across very important facts about his development, which, although unknown to the referrant, may nevertheless have considerable bearing on the questions at hand. Thus, the logic of reporting a clinical study usually differs from the experimental report. In clinical study, results are reported first and then conclusions are drawn. As was discussed in detail in the introductory chapters, these conclusions actually form hypotheses for further investigation in therapy.

Most commonly, then, a clinical report begins with a description of the child's current functioning and level of development, that is, with statements about the quantitative efficiency and qualitative nature of the various ego functions. The report should start with the "facts" of the child's perceptual-motor and intellectual functioning, the manner in which he expresses or fails to express his affect, how he copes with his impulses, and how he handles the stress from his environment. Such introductory paragraphs may only hint at the interrelationships between these functions and the forces that are affecting them. However, they should be written so as to lead logically into a more thorough analysis of coping mechanisms and defenses and a discussion of the motivating factors both from within and without the child. It is in this latter discussion that the assessor reports his hypotheses about the underlying dynamics and possible etiology of the child's behavior. However, such conclusions cannot be made meaningful until the reader is advised of the kind of behavior the child is actually showing. In logical terms, first-level generalization should precede second-level generalizations.

If the main body of the report of the assessment follows this inductive logic, the summary need not be a mere reiteration, but may be a recapitulation. Thus, the summary may state the conclusions succinctly with reference to the supporting data, in a more classical deductive fashion. For example, the main body of the report might begin with the description of the child's intellectual retardation and the quality of his thought processes. This may be accompanied by similar description of his difficulties in impulse control and in the lability of his affect. It might be concluded that the child's ego functioning seems retarded across the board. This introductory statement

might then be followed by a discussion of some of the stresses facing the child. The relationship between these functions and a history at birth might be considered, the nature of the child's relationships with his parents and other important persons in his environment might be discussed, and the possibilities of a relationship between environmental stresses and his retardation would be speculated upon. The summary, then, could begin with a restatement of these hypotheses. For example, "weakened at birth by his prematurity and deterred further by continuous illnesses during infancy, Johnny's development has probably been slowed even further by his resistance to the high level of expectations presented him by his parents. Since his parents also overprotected him, he was never really motivated to develop independent skills. Thus, he remains much more invalided than is warranted by his neurological weaknesses as he plays the role of the helpless and retarded child who sees no need to succeed at school nor to control his affect or impulses in any social situation."

F. REPORTING THE RELIABILITY AND VALIDITY OF THE ASSESSMENT

A report of a scientific study also includes some statement of the conditions under which the data were gathered and the methods of gathering those data. In research reports, the appropriateness of the techniques used in the research is usually discussed and related to the hypothesis. A similar brief statement of the conditions of the assessment and the techniques used should also be included in a report of an assessment — usually preceding the main body of the report. Since in the assessment the techniques used are fairly standard and well known to other assessors (if not always to the referrant), the mere listing of the techniques usually suffices. However, a statement of the conditions under which the data were obtained usually requires a brief paragraph, entitled, for example, "Behavior During Assessment." In this paragraph the assessor mentions the mood and motivation of the child, the child's understanding and acceptance of the assessment, and his behavioral reactions. Any conditions that might have biased or otherwise affected the assessment should also be reported. Cases

45 and 46 are examples of reports about the conditions of an assessment. Admittedly, both are related in greater detail than is necessary in most reports.

CASE 45

George, age 11, was brought to the clinic by his mother whom he had not seen for several weeks, as she and his stepfather had been out of town. The referral had been arranged by his father who was to pick him up later. The assessment had been demanded by the mother, however, as part of her continued battle with the father over George's custody. The father had arranged for the mother to pick him up and bring him to the clinic, but he was due to return to the father's home that evening. If George was upset by this situation, he did not show it overtly. Rather, he appeared nonchalant for an 11 year old, smiling and shaking my hand and did not even seem embarrassed when his mother requested that he kiss her goodbye publicly. That George was quite uneasy about the assessment was demonstrated initially when he pushed his chair up against the wall as far as possible from me. It was soon ascertained that George had not been informed at all that the assessment was to occur and had thought that he was spending the afternoon with his mother. He did admit that he had been advised by the referring psychiatrist that such an assessment would be in order. He denied that he had any idea why such an assessment would be required or even why he had even seen a psychiatrist in the first place. He averred that it was his mother's "big idea" and that she had alleged that he was not doing too well at school and that she worried about his seeming lack of friends. George completely denied that he found any problem at school at all and claimed that he was completely satisfied with his friends and had told his mother that she need not worry about him. Despite this, George did seem eager to talk about himself and his life. He readily chatted on about his play activities and his schoolwork and mentioned his family and their comings and goings voluntarily. He seemed actually to be taking an opportunity to review his life. However, any suggestion on my part that these might be of concern to him or be problems was quickly denied. Nor did he make any protest when the tests were introduced. Rather, he was most cooperative,

congenial, and seemed quite challenged to achieve. His demeanor was largely serious, though there were no gross signs of depression or anxiety, and he smiled on occasion quite appropriately. Given a break in the assessment, he took the opportunity to race down the hallway jumping into the air to touch some hanging signs. All in all, a fairly reliable sample of his behavior was obtained.

CASE 46

This assessment was obtained under very trying conditions which very likely affected the results. First, there was the fact that Carlos' parents were anxious to return to their home in Guatemala City after having spent an expensive and anxious two weeks while he was here in the hospital. Thus, there was an atmosphere of pressure for a decision. Second, there was every evidence that Carlos had been very unhappy in the hospital; his parents had visited him as frequently as possible but this was the first time that this seven year old had ever been separated from his mother. Moreover, since his English was extremely limited, he often found it very difficult to make his wants known. Last, but not least, the medical staff had planned to take one more barium enema that morning; thus, Carlos had not had breakfast and the plans were only changed when it was discovered that the appointment for the assessment had been made. When this was discovered, the assessment was delayed until Carlos was fed.

When the translator told him that the doctor would wait until he finished breakfast, Carlos seemed quite mollified and thanked the translator very politely. He was also very happy to find someone who spoke Spanish and queried the translator quite anxiously about what he might expect in the ensuing hour of the morning. He seemed a little puzzled when he was told that the doctor merely wanted to talk with him and play some games with him, but was relieved to find that there were no shots or other medical procedures to be endured. Carlos also seemed embarrassed when it was requested that he leave his bedroom in his pajamas and robe, and a further delay was caused when he insisted on dressing. When he finally arrived in my office, he was dressed in a suit, white shirt, and tie, and his hair was very neatly combed. Although most of the assessment was conducted through the translator, it did turn out that Carlos' understanding of English was far greater than had been expected. Often he replied immediately in Spanish to questions that were posed to the translator in English. However, occasionally the assessment was slowed further by the fact that he used childish expressions or local patois with which the translator was not entirely familiar and which required considerable explanation. He seemed to enjoy chatting about his school, family, and playmates, but since the setting of his life was not well known to the examiner nor translator, some of it was not too comprehensible. Initially, Carlos seemed rather unresponsive to the test materials until it was discovered that he was waiting for permission to reply.

None of the standard intelligence tests for Spanish-speaking people were available in our clinic, and the translation of the Binet was not entirely satisfactory, especially on those items in which the content is more familiar to North Americans than to Central Americans. Carlos was quite responsive to the CAT, although he remarked at times with amazement about animals dressed as humans and was particularly puzzled by the final card where the dog is displayed in the bathroom. Even the Rorschach, which is relatively culture free, seemed a little confusing to Carlos and it took him a while to realize that it was quite permissible for him to express his own ideas. The history obtained later from his parents did help to explain some of his responses and the perspective with which he viewed the techniques presented to him.

G. SAMPLE REPORTS

In the following reports, the raw data are presented first, followed by a detailed analysis, in order to demonstrate the steps leading to the report.

CASE 47

Danny DeV., age 12, was brought to the clinic by his mother upon the referral of the child's pediatrician. In the initial intake interview, Mrs. DeV. reported that since age nine, Danny had suffered from alternating periods of prolonged retention of feces, sometimes going without a bowel movement for up to

two weeks. Quite often after a period of bowel retention, Danny would have a subsequent period in which he would have difficulty in controlling his bowels and would soil himself. Mrs. DeV. was not sure as to the exact onset of these symptoms. Danny had kept hidden the fact of his constipation originally, and it was discovered only when he began to complain of "stomach aches." At first Mrs. DeV. reported that his soiling had started during a bout of the flu, but later remembered that several months previously she had noticed that his underclothes were stained and had scolded him about it. Following Danny's illness, he began to have an increasing number of "accidents," first at home and then at school. At the outset, Mrs. DeV. voiced her opinion that Danny's symptoms were "purely psychological" but could not specify at all what it was that gave her this impression. She remarked, with a smile, "that's why I brought him to you doctors here."

On further thought, Mrs. DeV. said that she felt Danny really had a "behavior problem" that should be "nipped in the bud." The school had reported to her that Danny always wanted to give all the answers in class that that he always seemed to be "on stage." "He needs to learn controls," the teacher had told Mrs. DeV. He refused to do routine schoolwork, which he saw as pointless. He felt picked on by some of the teachers, and had been suspended for two days recently because of a fight with another boy in the classroom over a piece of paper. Mrs. DeV. wondered if Danny's "accidents" might be associated with his boredom and frustrations at school, since quite often he had been sent home to clean himself up after such an incident. Over the past month he had missed an average of two half-days of school each week because of his bowel control problem. Mrs. DeV. went on to note that Danny is very easily frustrated over what seems to her quite small incidents. "He blows up over nothing. Only yesterday Danny went into a tizzy just because I had let his brother use his bedroom slippers." As Mrs. DeV. described Danny's "tizzies," it appeared that they were really temper tantrums in which Danny cried and screamed, pounded his fists on the floor, and sometimes destroyed things, most often his own possessions. However, he rarely attacked anyone. At other times, his "tizzies" seemed to contain little anger and consisted largely of frenzied excitement. When some special event was in the offing, Danny could scarcely "contain himself."

Danny was also interviewed briefly during his initial contact. He was a sturdily built youngster, who appeared slightly above average in height for his age. Towheaded and freckled faced with a winning smile, Danny was quite attractive. He was also very verbal, eager to talk about himself and his interests. He did not seem particularly embarrassed about discussing his symptoms, but tried to slough off the topic. He could not remember when the symptom began and tended to deny that it was of any great serious consequence or concern to him. It seemed to Danny that he always had "a little bowel trouble off and on" since he was a baby. He admitted rather nonchalantly that he had lost bowel control "once or twice" at school but denied that this had caused him any particular embarrassment. He explained that he would excuse himself from the classroom and report to the school nurse who would then send him home. By so treating this encopresis as an illness, Danny was thus able to avoid any major social embarrassment.

Danny was much more eager to discuss two of his current projects. He claimed that he was then engaged in "writing a novel" and had completed 80 pages in my "own handwriting." "It's a space murder story." Danny was even more excited about his invention of a rocket. He had carefully drawn the plans for this rocket and had painstakingly typed out a description of it, and without telling his parents had mailed it to the President of the United States. He was exceedingly proud because the day prior to this interview, he had received an acknowledgement of his letter to the White House.

Following this intake contact, appointments were made for Danny to return for further interviews with the psychiatrist and for a psychological assessment. The psychiatric social worker also made appointments with both parents to obtain further developmental history and data concerning the family. The psychiatrist planned to interview Danny further about his family relationships and his methods of coping with frustration. In making the referral for the psychological assessment, the psychiatrist hoped that Danny's fantasies might "uncover some of the under-lying dynamics." He said he was interested in what made Danny so explosive and yet at the same time so retentive. He also wondered if Danny was as creative and imaginative as was suggested in the brief intake interview. The psychologist suggested that in addition to the assessment of Danny, it might be helpful to have some brief assessment on both parents. Subsequently the social worker arranged for the parents to return and take the MMPI.

In planning the assessment, the psychologist noted that the chief questions posed in this referral concerned Danny's handling of affect but that the motivational factors which lay behind this apparent affect disturbance were probably the main points of the investigation. Further details were needed of Danny's methods of coping with frustration, but the larger question to be dealt with concerned the kinds of need-gratifications in which Danny experienced frustration. Thus, it appeared that the assessment should cover Danny's development of methods of coping with need-gratification as well as with affect. The initial history also suggested the disturbance of affect and conation might be affecting Danny's social development as well. The question of creativeness raised by the psychiatrist indicated a need to assess Danny's intellectual functioning. There seemed no question of his perceptual-motor development. To sample these functions, the psychologist planned to administer the Wechsler Intelligence Scale for Children in the initial contact and to follow this up in a second appointment for the administration of the Rorschach, the TAT and some drawings.

Danny had been prepared for the psychological assessment during the intake interview by the psychiatrist. He remarked that he thought "tests are fun" and hoped that they were "real hard." He enjoyed showing off his intellectual prowess, although he made no particular remarks about either his successes or failures on the WISC. When an item was presented to him which was beyond his ability, he merely shrugged it off. He was even more fascinated by the projective materials and was evidently eager to display his fantasies. Words seemed to tumble out of him as he dictated a TAT story, but he would check himself from time to time, "so that you can get everything down word for word." Even so, the TAT protocol was not completely verbatim.

WISC Results

Danny DeV.

Verbal Subtests	Weighted Scores	Performance Subtests	Weighted Scores
Information	17	Picture Completion	15
Comprehension	12	Picture Arrangement	11
Arithmetic	16	Block Design	17
Similarities	18	Object Assembly	13
Digit Span	12	Digit Symbol	13
Vocabulary	17	Mazes (Not given)	
Total	92		69
Prorated	77		
Verbal IQ	134	Performance IQ	127
Full Scale Score	146		
Full Scale IQ	133		

Danny DeV.   *Rorschach Technique**

(Response times were instantaneous and
thus not recorded)

I   ∧cv>

1. ∧ Looks like popular art.

Careless. Like thrown by some beatnik who
shot down balloons of ink.

W   F,m   Art

2. ∧ Keeps reminding me of a cat's face.

Just the eyes and nose.   (Sd 27+30).

S   F   Ad

3. ∧ Also looks like a map of Europe and
Asia. On each part here.

Here's Vietnam, Korea.   And Africa and
Spain.   (D8 + 9).

D   F   Geog.

4. ∧ Two big pincers holding out for something.

Like some crab.   (D1).

d   FM   Ad

II   ∧v

1. ∨ Two people that had walked all over

D2 are footmarks.

D   F/C   Hd

2. ∨ Australia and had red ink on their feet.

D1 + D1.   It's been split in half.   There's
red all through it.

D   F/C   Geog.

---

*Locations are indicated in ( ), using Beck's num bering. Scoring, however, is according to Klopfer.
Additional responses are scored in ( ).

3. ∨ Looks like blood splashed all over the place.

Like a big battle'd taken place. The red . . . the way it's spread out. . . .

D CF,m Blood

4. ∨ The bottom looks like a dragon.

(D4) is the eyes and mouth. You could attach the head to either part (D1). Looks like a gigantic something or other.

d W F (A)

5. ∨ A crab. A particular type. I can't remember what it is called.

(D3.) Two antennas. The general shape.

D F A

III

1. ∧ A dissected fly.

Two big eyes (D4) and claws (D5). This could be blood all over the place.

D F CF A

2. ∨ A gigantic monster, going after something.

Like a huge fly or giant ant from a horror movie, with a trail behind him. (D1)

D FM (A)

3. > Water splashed all over the place.

[Patient holds card at right angle to his face.] At an angle, it looks like a rainy street. You can see the shine off it.

W c,m Water

4. ∧ Two dogs dancing on their hind legs.

D1. The head, body and legs.

W M A (P)

IV

1. ∧ A palm tree with jungle growth all around it.

The fronds. (D4) and the base. (D1). All the circular motions could (points to the shading) be leaves closing in one on another.

W Fc,m Pl.

2. ∧ A king, with all the robes and everything.

(D1.) The crown and face. He's throwing off his robes (D2).

W M H O

V

1. ∧ A two-headed butterfly.

Antenna here and here. Big wings.

W F A P.

2. ∧ Two rockets that fell over. They didn't quite work.

(D10) are the rockets and all the rest is a big cloud of smoke after blowing up.

W Fm, K Explosion.

3. ∧ A raven's beak.

(D9) Sharp and well defined.

D F Ad.

4. ∧ A duck's beak.

Not so well defined. Thicker (D8).

d F Ad.

VI

1. ∧A rocket that *did* work.

(D1) All the flame and smoke. (D3) is the rocket.

    W   Fm,K   Explosion.

2. ∧Half the sun.
    .....V...

(D6) It's circular, cutting off the rays going up. Dark and light shows the corona.

    D   Fc   N

3. ∨Something in a book: It's called the two-headed, slimy-nosed bird. The Dirty Bird.

(D4) is the eyes. D6 the shoulder and beak. (dirty?) The uneven darkness.

    D   Fc   A   O

VII   ∧..V..∧

1. ∧Two girls looking at themselves in the mirror.

(D2) the hands, face and pony tail.

    D   M   H.

2. ∨A lion with a back like a camel. A hump.

(D2). The face, mane, and hump.

    D   F   Ad.

VIII

1. ∧The phoenix rising out of the fire.

No particular bird shape, just flame and the general rising motion.

    W   CF,   m   Fire

2. >Two bears

(D1) Four legs, general shape.

    D   F   A   (P)

IX

1. ∧Two gigantic dragons battling each other.

(D3) The head, eyes, mouth. Clawing away. The mist is rising from the battle. (D1.) Cloudy.

    W   FM,K   (A)

2. A^{c}frog.

Eyes like slits (D22).

    S   F   Ad.

X

1. ∧A big fireworks display in the sky. A pageant with a lot of color.

2. ∧People dancing, and a

3. ∧Guy at the bottom leading.

Splashes of color. All the darkness implies motion too. (D11) is the director with big arms, leading a choir. (D3) are two trumpets. The orange and part of the circle is the bell of the trumpet.
1. *W   CF,   m   Explosion.*
2. *D   M   H*
3. *D   M   H   C*

    Add: (*d   FC   Music   O*)

4. ∧A bird flying overhead.

(D10) Body and wings.

    D   FM   A.

5. ∧A lot of animals: an owl, and
6. ∧Ogres.

(D7) More movement. Eyes and body.

D   FM   A

(D8) Mouth, eyes. A monstrosity. Arguing, like brother and sister.

D   M   (H)

7. ∧Rabbits.

(D5) Long ears and smiling mouth.

D   FM   Ad   P.

8. ∧A flying squirrel.

(D7) All spread out.

D   FM   A

9. ∧The head of a cow.

The same as the owl, with horns.

D   F   Ad

SUMMARY OF SCORES [a]

Location		Determinants		Content	
W	$= 10 + 2$	M	$= 6$	H	$= 4$
D	$= 20$	FM	$= 7$	(H)	$= 1$
d	$= 5 + 1$	Fm,m	$= 2 + 6$	Hd	$= 1$
S	$= 2$	K	$= 0 + 3$	A	$= 8$
R	$= 37 + 1$	F	$= 13$	(A)	$= 4$
P	$= 2 + 2$	Fc	$= 3$	Ad	$= 8$
O	$= 3 + 1$	c	$= 1$	Art	$= 1$
		FC	$= 0 + 1$	Geog.	$= 2$
		F/C	$= 2$	Blood	$= 1$
		CF	$= 3 + 1$	Water	$= 1$
				Explo.	$= 3$

Ratios

Experience balance =

6:5; 103 Ambiequal [a]

$FM = m: Fc - c: 9:4$ [b]

$F\% = 38\%$. $A + (A) + Ad = 59\%$

N	$= 1$
Fire	$= 1$
Music	$= +1$

[a] For scoring of the experience balance, see Palmer (1953).
[b] Includes additionals.

DANNY DEV.   TAT

1: This guy has been trying to practice violin all afternoon. He has been playing all wrong notes and is about ready to give up. He sits and dreams, "This thing is hopeless; it's a wonder I ever got it." It had been given to him by an aunt or uncle who had money to throw around or didn't play it either. Hopeless. He thinks if he closes his eyes it'll go away. Eventually someone will wake him up and tell him to get practicing.

3BM: This guy's been out running around town and met up with a real good card player. He's just come from robbing the bank. He goes where a card sharp is and says "I can beat you again." He's also drunk. Finally, he gets wiped out; lost his $10,000. He goes around shooting in the air; everybody ducks. He grabs all the money. He runs to his house—no, to a train station. He is over the effects of alcohol.—He buys a ticket to Chicago and Ontario. He hides the strong box in a panel while the trainmen are out.—He gets away. Course, eventually he'll return to the scene of the crime; anyway they always do that—(?) He's blown all the money. Police sent out a bulletin to be on the lookout for a guy throwing around a lot of money. He wanders into the same gambling house. Bartender calls police who come just when he's winning back his $10,000.

6BM: The "army ant"—that grows in millions—Queen comes to Los Angeles in bananas and she lays eggs—and they've been brought into customs in larva. Queen taken out—ants marching out looking for food—second stage—thrown in dump—spread into 1000's, propagated fast—to 1,000,000's—marching thru Griffith Park—National news scene—planes flying over—firemen and police out—. This guy here's a scientist talking to his great aunt. He's been working on an insecticide—has produced some that have been shelved—. He decides to produce more. Ants are now on freeway—his home is overrun—. His great aunt evacuated—. He goes back to plant and gets packet that'll make 500,000 gallons; it is mixed in a pool in Valley—Ants march in to the Valley—now they're underground. He rushes the insecticide into the sewers—the ants dying out by 1000's—Queen is killed; found down gutter—. He mixed a second batch—he gets permission to release 1000 gallons into culverts—he kills all the ants—there's the smell of rotten meat which ants eat.

7BM: These two guys sitting in a bar telling dirty jokes to each other. [Laughs]—One had too much. The other has sour look. He says "all these guys stealing hub caps, etc. You think that's what America's youth is coming to?" The other hiccups. They could be any two guys in America with nothing better to do—If he was not drunk, he has a look that he'd really be ashamed if anyone else heard him.

8BM: Here's a private Army set-up. Fifteen guys go around to Vietnam; they're going round sabotaging, destroying things. They got a supply of arms on top of the hill—100 men are looking for them—so when they come after them up the hill, three guys get up there. All are killed but one. The commander, he gets hurt but doesn't tell the doctor. He gets hit again on other side—so now they take him to the doctor. This other

guy doesn't fit in the story—He just on guard watching the battle—the other 85 going up the hill—now they're reduced to 6—(turn out?) I don't know if all are wiped out or win—like just before—reinforcements come in like in old cavalry pictures—where the cavalry comes to the rescue.

11: A good one! [Patient almost drops the card] —Reminds me of the book I wrote, "Octa." Everything was prefaced with "8"—"Detail 1"—The characters were from various sciences and mechanics—here in Morocco—they're chasing a guy who's mugged the agent who carries secrets—who sells it to the Chinese Commies. They find the guy who throws his money around—They mug him in the men's room. [Patient laughs]—They rip his clothes off and find it in his heel. The Communists are determined to get it back. They chase them in the hills—they're blocked by a landslide—West hurls a homemade grenade and they climb over and get away with the secret—

12BM: This is an old man who's gone off his rocker in old age. His grandson's come over. They don't know how far off old man is but he's very rich and they bow to him like reeds in the wind. Unfortunate, since grandfather hates him—he's involved in big proxie battle, etc. The grandfather decides to kill him. He sees him sleeping on couch. The grandson is sleeping with clothes on just in case so he won't have to run out in street in pajamas. The grandfather knows karate and hits him on forehead and kills him. He drives him out and throws the body off cliff. Then he decides to destroy car by driving off pier, but fails to get out and is drowned in the tide—The stock goes to his enemies—the police never find out how grandson was killed.

13B: This is a boy who could read minds. He knows his mother didn't like him. She was a bit off. He has a dog named Bobbie—he knows Bobbie's food is poisoned by his mother who knows he can't live without dog. The dog can read boy's mind too. He throws food out after all. His mother runs to his father and yells, "He tried to kill me." The boy runs to his room. Father rushes up and pounds on door and demands he come out. They break in—Bobbie growls and rushes at his throat—the father and mother flee—Now the boy is waiting in the evening. Dog is missing—He also had a toy Panda—(How does it end?) Just leaves him there—I can't figure out an end as I can't see it happening in the first place.

17BM: This guy's breaking out of jail. He was innocent in the first place—So he found rope and decided to break out—they got a big light on him, and are about to recapture him. (How did it come about?) He was framed. Originally he was in politics but he had powerful enemies. A quirk of fate left him in office when enemies were elected—They trump up charges against him like running around with other men's wives—this guy had a queer way of doing things—like breaking out and then proving he was innocent—which he had to do to begin with—

16: It's a white cow eating marshmallows in snow storm—That's a private joke! This bridge has a car falling off—It's a bridge noted for suicide and accidents—has highest rate of anything. You name it—but it hasn't fallen—This guy is racing off to work—he was going too fast so he ran on the walk and crashed and went into the water below— That doesn't leave any room for development, does it?

18BM: This guy doesn't look real—Hands all over and pants 20 sizes too large—He's having a dream that his pants are 20 sizes too large. His tie is all messed; hands all over; his eyes are closed and he is stumbling around in a drunken trance. He sees the face of a friend who was killed in the war. Next morning he's sitting there. There's a knock on the door and sure enough there *he* is— sitting there—"Are you the parting breath?" —This guy doesn't know what to do, but then: "Smile, you're on Candid Camera"— but he had dreamed it. Later he was at horror movie about guy eaten up by ants and it was same face. He left movie and got sick and went to hospital. In hospital a guy next to him was brought in for surgery. It was the same face! The guy was shocked— He'd been bugged all day by it—On the way home he saw a body hanging from tree— So he threw the body in the bushes and took the rope and hung himself. That was the end.

Even as the psychologist attempted to record Danny's responses, he noted with amazement the high energy level displayed in Danny's mental activity and the expansive development of Danny's ego as represented in his productivity. After the psychologist had scored the tests and made some detailed notes concerning each test, he turned to the overall task of the analysis of Danny's ego development. Although the referral raised no question regarding Danny's perceptual-motor development and these data did indicate that his perceptual-motor acuity was on the whole probably superior to most children his age, there were some interesting aspects that seemed related to the questions at hand, par-

ticularly the child's symptoms. First, as regards Danny's motor functioning, it was noted that his drawings of a man and of a woman (see Plates I and II) were relatively static and even his volunteered drawing of a rocketship (Plate III) was not in orbit, but "landing on the moon." On the Rorschach a preponderance of Danny's movement responses were passive or, when active, the action had already taken place. For example, "the two big pincers" (see response 4 to Card I) are "merely holding out for something," the two girls on Card VII, response 1, are "looking at themselves in the mirror," and on Card VIII, response 1, "the Phoenix is rising out of fire," in a seemingly automatic "rising motion." Exceptions to this passivity, however, were present in the gigantic monster, response 2 to Card III, and in the first response to Card IX where the dragons are "battling each other." Note, however, that this latter aggressive movement is accompanied by an indication of anxiety. More frequently the movement of Danny's responses was half-hearted; the motion was completed or was included

PLATE I

PLATE II

accurate, being able rapidly and definitively to form percepts of incoming stimuli. By and large, his ability to perceptually differentiate was quite superior and, in general, his form level on the Rorschach was detailed and accurate. However, this made the presence of the few formless or inaccurate percepts even more remarkable. Note, for example, the relative loosness of Danny's very first response, response 1 to Card I, and his lack of precision throughout Card II. In contrast, on Card X Danny began with a gross overall percept which he then proceeded to define in precise detail. These variations in Danny's perceptual differentiation arose because of marked affective and conative interferences. Intense, aggressive impulses and intensely angry feelings seem to be the most obvious source of these interferences. Danny appeared to be attempting to deal with the stressful conative stimuli by becoming more and more expansive and by spewing out a wealth of detail in an effort to cover the underlying anxiety. Rather than freezing and blocking perceptually in the face of noxious stimuli, Danny actually appeared to be enlarging his perceptual field and extending his perceptual responsiveness. The psychologist wondered if by this mechanism Danny might be seeking to water down or even lose the disturbing affects and frustrations in this wealth of detail. However, handling this amount of perceptual stimuli appeared to be an arduous task even for such an intellectually bright 12 year old.

Danny's perceptual-motor functioning could be summarized as follows. Very sensitive to all incoming stimuli, Danny attempted to absorb and analyze as much of it as possible. Although his responses to these stimuli were primarily on an external motor level, the degree to which Danny attempted to handle stimuli on an internal visceral level was indeed phenomenal for a 12 year old. Despite the general superiority of his perceptual functioning, Danny was not successful in absorbing quite as much of the stimuli as he attempted to take in; nor was he able to contain this input and avoid external responses to it. This perceptual motor input-output probably was part of the general high energy level and expansiveness of Danny's ego, but it also seemed to be a coping mechanism for handling anxieties involved in the perception of affective and conative stimuli.

Cognitively, Danny functioned at a very

in something else. The inanimate movement in many of his responses was given to an act already committed such as response 3 to Card II, or response 3 to Card III. Even more remarkable are comments such as response 2 to Card V and response 1 to Card VI where, in the first instance, the movement was unsuccessful and, in the second instance, the fact of success had to be mentioned specifically and the act was already complete. Certainly Danny's motor activity on the subscales of the WISC was superior for his age, but his scores on tests such as the Object Assembly and Digit Symbol where he was working against time were slightly though probably not significantly lower than most of his verbal responses (the psychologist wished later that he had administered the Mazes). Danny's ability to fantasy a great deal of motor activity was demonstrated in every one of his TAT stories. These data, particularly the large number of inanimate responses on the Rorschach, suggested to the psychologist that, far more than most 12 year olds, a great deal of Danny's motor activity might well be expressed on a visceral level. Whether or not his motor functioning was also demonstrated outwardly in skeletal muscular modes could not be determined from these data alone.

In his perceptual functioning, he was very

PLATE III

superior level. He was highly verbal, but his nonverbal cognitive functions were also superior. His thought processes, though full of details, were nevertheless fairly well organized, especially for a 12 year old. His TAT plots, for example, were very elaborate, but for the most part he did not lose sight of the overall plot. However, his ideas spilled all over and, as with his perceptions, Danny seemed to have a compulsive need to include everything. There was evidence that his intense affective and conative impulses pushed his intellectual productivity rather than deterred it. It was hard for him to stop with one idea. It was easy to see how Danny would be bored with the routine of the average classroom, and that he would have a need to preoccupy himself with other activities. No intellectual problem, however, failed to interest or challenge Danny. He appeared curious about everything. Yet, his ideation did tend to be morbid; he was obsessed with destruction and death; insofar as there was a disruption to his intellectual functioning, it was this intrusive and obsessive preoccupation with his own hostility. However, the intrusion of such primitive processes did not really deter Danny from intellectual testing of reality; his fantasies were extensive and bizarre at times, but never reached the proportions of psychotic ideation.

If Danny's intellectual functioning was remarkable, his affective development was even more amazing. When one considers the affective obtuseness of the usual 12-year-old boy, Danny was certainly unusual in his sensitive awareness of the emotional components of his environment. Even more than most adults, Danny was immediately stimulated by the emotional aspects of his environment, and he appeared to respond to these stimuli in a highly diffuse and spontaneous fashion. Moreover, there were many signs that Danny was also beginning to be quite aware of affective stimuli coming from within him. His TAT stories depicted heroes who have inner feelings, as well as being stimulated from external sources. For the most part, Danny appeared to be still in latency and thus to be keeping a lid over sensuous feelings. Yet, there were many signs throughout his record that the stresses of puberty were beginning to impinge upon him, and that he reacted affectively, albeit probably quite unconsciously, to these new drives. As might be expected, these multiple affects and sensitivities are very difficult for any 12

year old to cope with. Thus, Danny found it much more difficult to form affective boundaries than he did perceptual or intellectual boundaries. One feeling floated into the next. Many feelings came up all at once, and Danny could not differentiate or separate these feelings very easily. He was happy and depressed, anxious and fearful all at once. Yet, when one looks at the input and output of Danny's affective functioning, a pattern does appear.

The pattern appears most clearly, for example, in his story to Card 3BM of the TAT: (1) An external affective stimuli incites (2) internal anxiety, which (3) expands into external reactivity, which (4) increases embarrassment and guilt and (5) leads to further depression and a need to cover depression by (6) exuberance, which then leads back in a vicious circle to number (1). Danny's coping mechanisms for dealing with affective stimuli were in general very ineffective. He tried to avoid them, but this was almost impossible because of his voracious appetite for stimuli in general. He tried to intellectualize, but his anger and depression particularly got away from him. He tried to joke about it, but his depression was close to the surface in his humor. Most of all, he tried to handle affect on an internal fantasy level, but he remained too dependent on his environment and too wrapped up in environmental interchange for his affect to be contained in fantasy. The chief affect with which he has the most difficulty is apparently anger, which, when internalized, leads to depression. His pattern of coping with affect thus parallels his pattern of coping with defecation. He attempts to contain his affect until he almost bursts, whereupon he no longer has any control over it.

It is Danny's conative function that appears to be at the source of his difficulties in development. In contrast to the hyperdevelopment of his intellectual and affective functions, Danny's development of dealing with methods of need-gratification are relatively immature. First, it is obvious that a great many of Danny's needs are external or ego-alien to himself. The referring psychiatrist noted that when Danny was describing his bowel "accidents," Danny said, "I guess I just get busy and then this thing *happens to me.*" Or, in describing a situation where he was hurrying to the toilet, "*It* caught up with me." Even such a basic physiological need as defecation was in Danny's view an external force beyond his control. A detailed examination of his TAT stories reveals clearly the extent of this ego-alienation of Danny's impulses. For example, on TAT 1, although he first had the hero "playing all wrong notes," the hero says, "This *thing* is hopeless." "If he closes his eyes *it* will go away." In the story to 3BM, the hero is excused from his impulsive behavior because of his use of alcohol. The overwhelming oral impulses symbolized in the marching army ants in story 6BM are also an external force. This story in particular illustrates Danny's struggle to destroy an impulse which is not part of himself. In 7BM, the hero would experience shame, but only if anyone external to himself knew of his purient interests. Story 8BM shows the private internal war which Danny is experiencing, but even here it is a war between two external, impersonal destructive forces. In story 11, Danny gets carried away with this theme and cannot contain himself. Note, particularly, that the "secrets" get taken from the hero "in the mens' room." In story 12, feelings of murderous rage and an impulse to possess the parents are projected outward onto the parental figure, the grandfather. On 13B, the hostility is externalized to what in an adult would be considered a paranoid degree. And in 17BM, the hero was "framed" and has to escape his powerful enemies but it is necessary first to break out and then to prove innocence. In Danny's story to Card 16, even suicide is externally caused by the bridge. And finally, in 18BM, Danny's extensive feelings of guilt over his murderous impulses are also external. Since Danny experiences most of his impulses in this way, it may not be surprising to find that his guilt feelings are also separate from his ego.

It was often very difficult for Danny to separate one motivation from another. He tried to specify on the TAT why his heroes were doing things, but as he expanded these stories, it became more and more difficult to define exactly why and who does what in these stories. Danny did strive to cope actively with need-gratification frustrations. Initially, in each TAT story the hero does struggle with the problem independently, but quite often the story is decided not by the hero but by some kind of fate. As with his rockets on the Rorschach, these efforts do not always quite work, but Danny continued to hope that he would find some way of independent need-gratification. The difficulty which Danny

faced was, of course, that these impulses were not part of himself over which he had some control but were external to him. He did not appear to recognize that the satisfaction of his basic infantile needs for succor, comfort, and solace depended in part on himself. These initial dependency needs were still extremely intense for Danny and continued to threaten him. The hunger for affection that he constantly felt became a destructive "oral impulse" which, in effect, poisoned a great deal of his interpersonal relationships. This unrestricted need for an infantile type of affection was apparently the unmentionable "secret" which Danny continually had to hide.

A detailed analysis of the needs and press in Danny's stories may be helpful in understanding both the sources of his need-gratification difficulties and how he coped with them. In story 1, there is the external press of a demand for achievement which the hero cannot accept; although he feels hopeless, the pressure is unending. In story 3BM, the hero, for an unstated reason, feels it is necessary to rob in order to obtain narcissistic supplies. Need-gratification was a gamble for Danny, a gamble which, when he lost, drove him to intense and destructive anger. The strength of his need for narcissistic supplies was so intense that he continued "to return to the scene of the crime." The pressure of his intense hunger, in the story to 6BM, affected all of society. This hunger was answered by poison, that is, it had to be met by a counterforce which, interestingly enough, considering Danny's symptoms, is poured down the sewer. In so doing, the externalized source of the hunger, the queen mother, is killed. In the story to 7BM, the "dirty jokes" of youth suggest that Danny was experiencing pubescent sexual drives which now were not differentiated for him from his preoccupation with oral and anal need-gratifications. The motivation behind the intense battle that went on within Danny gets completely lost in story 8BM. But the chase for the secret reenters on Card 11. This secret is revealed in 12BM where the hero, the grandson, seeks the old man's riches but loses in what is apparently an Oedipal battle, which was not a simple one for Danny. In the story to 13B, the hero feels poisoned by the food given to him by his mother which suggests that he might feel himself poisoned by mother's love. The Oedipal nature of

Danny's conflict is illustrated even further in story to Card 17BM. There are trumped up charges against him, like "running around with other men's wives." Evidently no little of Danny's expansive ego activity was to prove his innocence. However, in the story to Card 16, it is evident that Danny, at times, felt markedly depressed and foresaw that in his manic effort to work out all his problems, suicide might be a result. His murderous impulses constantly haunted him, as illustrated in Card 18BM. In every situation he was "bugged" by his own guilt.

Some of the external pressures that Danny experienced are shown in the responses of his parents to the MMPI.*

NAME: MR. DEV.

MMPI SCORES (CORRECTED FOR K): L56, F50, K54, Hs59, D65, Hy55, Pd41, Mf68, Pa52, Pt53, Sc49, Ma58, Si50, Es56.

TEST-TAKING ATTITUDE: He tended to be self-favorable in responding to the MMPI and was moderately minimizing of emotional problems. The profile appears valid.

SYMPTOMS AND PERSONALITY CHARACTERISTICS: The profile indicates a mild current depression. Tension, anxieties, worry, and self-criticism are suggested. He appears particularly vulnerable to feelings of guilt, and others could easily manipulate him in this way. Psychiatric patients with similar but more elevated profiles have complained of loss of appetite and insomnia, but such symptoms may be relatively mild in his case. Despite these depressed moods, his overall functioning and practical ego-strength appear fair to adequate in most areas.

The pattern suggests a few scattered physical symptoms lacking a sufficient organic basis. Symptoms such as gastrointestinal distress, headache, back pain, or fatigue are apt to be at least partly psychological in origin. The profile would indicate mildly more than average worry about bodily functioning. Psychiatric patients with similar but more elevated profiles were seen as mildly repressed and as tending "to look at the good side of things." Some complained of being sexually inhibited and "bottled up." His makeup tends mildly

toward the feminine, such as verbal or esthetic interests, rather than mechanical and outdoor activities. The pattern indicates strong and solid family loyalties, and his conscience would be strict but dependable. He would internalize family distress and be overly quick to blame himself for family struggles. He tests as practical and oriented toward tangible achievements and accomplishments. In similar cases, the needs for attention and affection repeatedly interfered with their capacity to act in positive and assertive ways toward loved ones, especially with problems such as misbehavior and delinquency by children and other impulsive and aggressive behaviors by loved ones.

DIAGNOSTIC IMPRESSION: The pattern suggests mild depressive tends. However, the profile is within the normal range, and it is not diagnostically definitive.

TREATMENT CONSIDERATIONS: The current level of disturbance would not indicate an urgent need for psychotherapy, unless clinical symptoms handicap functioning or there were any risk of suicide. Contacts with family members or other informants could help to clarify what the current stresses are, what secondary gains there may be from his symptoms, and how such gains could be minimized. Some psychiatric patients with related profiles showed a "flight into health," both as a positive response to reassurance as well as an avoidance of exploring psychological problems. The normality of his profile and the favorable ego-strength would predict a good prognosis and a positive response to treatment. He is apt to focus on his specific difficulties and distresses. Readjustment to the loss of a loved object, a recent rejection by a supporting family member, or a related loss of emotional support could be important in treatment interviews. A gradual ventilation and acceptance of aggressive feelings and sexual impulses could lead to more positive expressions of them. If a past role of hard work and self-sacrifice for his family had broken down, then he could benefit from new activities and a less dependent role without undue family demands and frustration.

NAME: MRS. DEV.

MMPI SCORES (CORRECTED FOR K): L42, F57, K53, Hs64, D64, Hy60, Pd64, Mf34, Pa38, Pt46, Sc59, Ma50, Si69, Es64.

---

* The following reports, derived from a computer analysis, were made available by Alex B. Caldwell, Ph.D., Medical Psychological Services, Los Angeles, California.

TEST TAKING ATTITUDE: She was straightforward in answering the MMPI without being unduly defensive or self-critical. The profile appears valid.

SYMPTOMS AND PERSONALITY CHARACTERISTICS: The profile shows mild personality disorder tendencies. At times she is apt to be seen as egocentric, immature, impulsive, and demanding. Recurrent family conflicts and guilt struggles are indicated. Occasionally self-defeating and self-punishing, she would then act against her own long-term interests with lapses in her judgment and forethought. Similar patients have used a variety of manipulations in order to evade difficult life situations. In some cases, the low tolerance for frustrations led to angry outbursts toward family members.

The profile indicates scattered physical symptoms and concerns on a psychological basis. Pain, weakness, and fatigue are apt to be partly psychological in origin. Such symptoms as G.I. pain or other G.I. complaints, headache, and undue menstrual distress have been associated with similar but more elevated profiles along with ulcers and histories of gastrectomies. Obesity, anorexia, nausea, or other symptoms involving eating were also typical in these cases.

The secondary depression tests as mild. Similar patients often have felt anxious, indecisive, unappreciated and misunderstood. They saw themselves as lacking in social skills with the opposite sex. Her balance of interests is rather feminine, including esthetic, cultural, or verbal interests and sensitivities. There is apt to be some rejection of aggressive masculine activities and a hypersensitivity to sexual roles.

Some similar patients were described as oral-dependent. Her father is apt to have been indifferent and lacking in affection. Family backgrounds consistently included indulgent and protective attitudes by their mothers. Difficult sibling relationships and other family conflicts were common, and the childhood homes had relatively often been disrupted by divorces and other upheavals. As a result, the lives of these patients became home oriented with an emphasis on food and nurturant care.

DIAGNOSTIC IMPRESSION: Although the diagnoses associated with this profile among psychotherapy patients are varied, they typically have reflected personality disorder tendencies; most often these were passive-aggressive in type. The pattern also suggests mild current depressive trends. Her profile is within the normal range, however, and it is not diagnostically definitive.

TREATMENT CONSIDERATIONS: Her ego-strength would predict good general effectiveness and self-sufficiency. However, the pattern predicts a future course of family struggles and of conflicts in her close relationships. It should be noted that males with this pattern are ulcer prone, and past workups on these patients have often been positive. Contacts with family members and other informants have been useful in similar cases in order to clarify what the secondary gains were and how such gains could be minimized. Such contacts could also help to evaluate possible paranoid trends. The anticipation of long-term psychotherapy is questionable, since her motivation may be mildly shallow and prompted by current pressures.

The pattern recommends the talking out of current distresses and the clarification of her immediate problems. She would seek to focus treatment onto her specific symptoms and situational difficulties so as to avoid facing the full extent of her contributions to them. The discovery and interpretations of her devices to keep others at a distance—especially as she uses them on the therapist—can be meaningful and important in treatment. She could benefit from learning to see how she aggravates these difficulties and what kinds of circumstances are personal "traps" into which she repeatedly falls.

After analyzing these data, the psychologist reviewed them in a staff conference with the psychiatrist and social worker. In this conference, his observations and conclusions were compared and integrated with the data gathered by the social worker and psychiatrist. The final written report without the preliminary paragraphs read as follows.

ANALYSIS OF RESULTS: Danny is evidently an intellectually very bright youngster, who has considerable potential for emotional spontaneity and sensitivity. Currently, however, his development appears to have reached a crisis as he enters adolescence. His normal spontaneity is accompanied by clouds of depression and his striving is accompanied by considerable tension. He faces adolescence with a great deal of ambivalent conflict. Outwardly, he piously mouths latency attitudes, like a little adult, denying interest in heterosexual peer activities and asserting independence from peer values—since they conflict with his "egghead" intellectual interests. He is secretly very curious about and excited by the prospects of adolescent activities, both sexual and rebellious. However, he perceives adolescence as a complete abandon of impulse controls, particularly as uninhibited aggression and as satiation of oral needs, but with only a hint of genital impulses. The prospect of puberty thus severely threatens his tight lid of repression and arouses considerable guilt.

Danny's difficulty is entering adolescence is much greater than normal because he is still fighting battles within himself over control of infant impulses. He has never adequately resolved the matter of control over aggression and hostility. Outwardly supermoralistic, he is preoccupied in fantasy with violence and destruction. At 12, he is still playing "cops and robbers," and "good guys versus the bad guys." Super-ego controls have been internalized, but Danny's super-ego is so rigid and so punitive that it is alien to the ego and thus not integrated into the personality structure.

Danny's fantasies provide a wealth of data about the dynamics of his conflicts. Problems in anal control are repeatedly evident, consonant with the presenting symptom. However, these fantasies suggest that underlying Danny's difficulty in accepting anal controls is a persisting oral aggression, a demanding, grasping hunger for maternal affection, which, still unsatisfied, leaves him frustrated, angry, and unwilling to accept social control. This unsatisfied and seemingly unsatiable hunger is the chief basis for his pervasive feelings of guilt. He fears that his frustration and anger would lead him to destroy the maternal bond and thus he would lose the source of succorance. To cope with his anxiety, he has mounted an accumulated reaction formation, through being overconforming and by striving to please, chiefly by intellectual achievement. He then relegates his anger to the fantasy and visceral level.

The roles of the parents and their interactions, both with Danny and between themselves, is outlined by their MMPI patterns. Although all of their scores fall within normal limits, both parents show signs of neurotic struggles within themselves, which are quite similar and also quite like Danny's conflicts. Both use somatization as a method of handling anxiety; both are easily made guilty and depressed. Mr. DeV. is a very passive, almost effeminate man, who is quite socially conforming and who would have little empathy for adolescent rebellion. Mrs. DeV. is relatively much more aggressive and striving; she controls and manipulates, chiefly in a passive, seductive manner, but sometimes without regard for reality and seldom with any insight into either her own behavior or the needs of those about her. Yet, both are conscientious parents who strive to provide for and train their children.

SUMMARY: The exciting prospect of adolescent impulse release reactivates Danny's childhood struggle over the control of both anal and oral impulses, exacerbating a well of hostility and ensuing guilt and depression. His psychodynamics reflect very similar patterns in his parents who also somaticize anxiety and are easily depressed. Danny "reads his mother's mind" and knows that behind her seductive manipulation lies considerable anger and rebellion. He is unable, except in fantasy, to separate from her and give up his infantile demands on her. Nor does he receive support from his passive and conforming father. In his most depressed moments, he sees no solution and suicidal ideas enter his fantasies.

CASE 48

Mrs. N first sought psychological consultation regarding her daughter Susan when Susan was age 11. The initial paragraphs of the first report read as follows:

Susan N., age 11 years, 5 months.

REFERRED BY: Mrs. N, patient's mother.

REASON FOR REFERRAL: Susan has always been unable to keep up with her schoolwork. She has been in special classes but is now placed in a regular fourth grade class, two years below normal age level. She is failing still and is the subject of teasing from other children because of her slowness and because she is older and larger than her classmates. The immediate referral question was whether Susan should change schools once more and return to a special class. There had been no prior psychological study, and Mrs. N accepted the suggestion that the assessment review Susan's overall psychological development for the purpose of further planning.

METHODS OF ASSESSMENT: Interviews with Mrs. N and Susan; Wechsler Intelligence Scale for Children; Graham-Kendall Memory for Designs; Goodenough Draw-A-Person Test; Rorschach Technique; Children's Apperception Test. A neurological consultation was obtained and a followup interview was held with Mrs. N.

APPEARANCE AND BEHAVIOR DURING EXAMINATION: Susan was an appealing child who, with a sweet smile, looked up as if expecting approval. She was a bit tense at first, but relaxed quickly. In the interview, she volunteered little; when she was encouraged, she was able to talk about things she enjoyed, but evaded questions about unhappy events. She accepted the tests with no question or resistance, in passive compliance to an adult request. She was outwardly unperturbed by her failures, but was reassured when successful. "That one's too hard," she would explain in matter-of-fact fashion. Her speech was clear and without noticeable defects, but her use of language was often more appropriate to a preschool child than an 11 year old.

Mrs. N evidently was attempting to take an objective view of Susan and of herself. Generally, she seemed a fairly reliable reporter. However, it was evident that she has many conflicting and guilty feelings about Susan's condition, which came to the fore during the interviews. It was particularly difficult for her to separate her feelings about Susan from her own anger and grief over her divorce. She came close to tears as she discussed these topics.

PRESENT SITUATION: Susan and her mother live together in an apartment which Mrs. N selected last year to be near a special school for Susan. Mrs. N supports herself and Susan by working full time as a saleswoman. Around the home, Susan is able to care for herself and help her mother, like a normal 11 year old. She comes home by herself after school, entertains herself, and often starts dinner before her mother returns. She has almost no close friends because of the present school situation and the changes of school but, with Mrs. N's encouragement, attends "Campfire" meetings. Mrs. N devotes most of her evenings and weekends to Susan, restricting her social life to a rare date.

During summer vacations and other holidays, Susan visits her father and returns to her mother for the school year. These partings, both from mother and father, are always stressful and tearful for Susan who openly says she wants to live with both parents and who urges her mother to move back to the hometown.

At school, Susan is well liked by her teachers. She is compliant, well behaved, and eager to please. Mrs. N fears that because Susan is no behavior problem, she may not receive the special attention she needs to improve her work.

PAST HISTORY: Shortly before Susan's birth, Mrs. N separated from her husband and filed for divorce. During her pregnancy, she was very emotionally upset and physically ill. Her labor was prolonged and difficult, but Susan was considered normal at birth. At this time, Mrs. N reconciled with her husband. Throughout the first year, Susan was a continual feeding problem; she "threw up constantly" and was "always crying." Mrs. N was hospitalized for surgery when Susan was eight months old, and Susan remained in the care of her maternal grandmother for several months. Susan's toilet training was started "immediately" when the child could sit upon the "potty." Although bowel training was established quite early, Susan was quite delayed in urinary control and continues to wet the bed periodically.

Much of Susan's life has been interrupted by prolonged physical illnesses or trauma, which probably have deterred her development. Beginning at about age three, she suffered from severe throat and ear infections which culminated in a tonsillectomy at age six. As a result, her first year at school was interrupted. At age seven, she had a severe bout of nephritis, was out of school almost a semester, and remained physically weak for some time thereafter. A year later she injured her knee, limped badly for several months, and was unable to be on the playground. Last October she had an appendectomy. For the past year she has been receiving orthodontic treatment. She suffers frequent severe colds, keeping her home from school.

The central trauma in Susan's life was the separation of her parents which culminated in divorce when she was about nine. To this date Susan cannot mention the divorce without tears. If Mrs. N's continued acrimony against her husband is any index, the dissension between the parents must have been very intense. At first, Mrs. N was given custody of both Susan and her brother (four years Susan's senior), but about two years ago, Mrs. N agreed to let the brother remain with her former husband, following his remarriage. Since the divorce, Mrs. N and Susan have moved several times, involving almost annual changes of school for Susan. The parents continue to disagree over Susan's care and each tries to get her to stay with them. Mrs. N declared in tears, "She's all I've got to live for!"

Before continuing this report, it is necessary to present Susan's response to the tests. Susan's scores on the Wechsler Intelligence Scale for Children were as follows:

Verbal Tests	Scale Scores	Performance Test	Scale Scores
Information	6	Picture Completion	12
Comprehension	6	Picture Arrangement	6
Arithmetic	5	Block Design	5
Similarities	10	Object Assembly	6
Vocabulary	8	Coding	7
Digit Span	5	Mazes (omitted)	
Verbal IQ	79	Performance IQ	80
	Full Scale IQ	77	

Susan's drawing of a man is shown in Plate IV. This drawing, when scored on the Goodenough Scale, yielded a mental age of 7 years and 3 months and an IQ of 66.

Susan's reproduction of the Graham-Kendall Designs are shown in Plate V. The scoring is shown only for those designs which were inadequate. The total raw score of 9, when corrected for age and IQ, yielded a corrected score of 5, which is in the "borderline" range between a normal performance and that considered by the authors of this test to be indicative of central nervous system dysfunctioning.

Susan gave the following Rorschach responses. She did not turn the cards.

PLATE IV

Free Associations	*Inquiry*

Card I—1″

1. A cat—no—

It's got big ears (D8), eyes, mouth [indicating the central spaces] (location?) [top half of card] If this [space above card] were filled in, it would be the hair.

DS F Ad

PLATE V

Free Associations	Inquiry
	This [indicating the bottom half] looks like a pumpkin. These two [spaces] are the teeth.
	(DS F Mask)
2. Sort of an upside-down spaceship—it doesn't look too good.	The wings and this tip and the windows. The capsule was up here and they threw it down and it blew up—(how does it seem to be now?) Oh, it's flying now.
	WS Fm Obj.
Card II 5″	
1. A skeleton of a butterfly or a moth.	The feelers, the wings, and the face. (detailed in D2) (including D3?) No. (What makes it look like a skeleton?) It's died or dissolved up or something tore the skin off [points to D5]. That looks like the skeleton.
	WS F- A O-
Card III 3″	
1. A beetle.	All around here D1. It's the skeleton of a beetle (?) The teeth or the bones and the skin. (Are D2 and D3 a part of it?) Maybe this is the heart and the flowers. (The heart?) It's the shape of a heart (and flowers?) They're hanging from the stem or it's a face hanging there, an ugly face tormenting the beetle. Are these really beetles?
	D F- A (D F At)
	(D F Pl) (D Fm Hd)

Free Associations	Inquiry

Card IV 7″

1. It's a monster with a sort of small face.

The whole things. It's got one eye and two arms and this and the tail (this?) Big feet.

W F A

(D3) looks like a skunk, it's the color, the shade —the white tone and the brown tone.

(D FC' A)

Card V 2″

1. *That's* a bat!

Wings, feelers and pinchers that suck up blood.

W F A P

Card VI 32″

1. Not much of anything.

Nothing.

Rejected

Card VII 10″

1. A girl with no body hardly.

(D2) The legs and arms, and hair. (?) So fat and flabby and big, but I don't know what this could be [indicating D6] Oh, it could be the inside of an apple.

D F H
(di F Food)

Card VIII 10″

1. Two bears on a mountain—well, not bears— birds or hawks or something.

Mice, they're mice! It looks like the legs and the face, like a mouse.

D F A (P)

The upper half looks like the skeleton of a coyote strung up there. (Coyote?) The feet and the body. It looks like it's yelling and this is the face.

(D FM A)

Card IX 30″

Not much of anything (encouraged) Well, it looks like they—in the middle—(40″)—

1. Looks like a bone.

1. [indicates the center D] It's shape in this little things (?) Just the shape.

D F At

Card X 15″

1. A big old monster—sorta—with big blue hand and all that.

(D1) are the hands and (D11) are the two cheeks. They're monster or bugs, or something— like outer space monsters, mad at each other.

DW M, F ⟷ C (A)

SUMMARY OF RORSCHACH SCORES, SUSAN N.—FIRST ASSESSMENT

Location		Determinants		Content	
W	= 4	M-	= 1	H	= 1
DW	= 1	FM	= - + 1	Hd	= - + 1
D	= 5 + 6	m	= 1 + 1	A	= 5 + 2
di	= - + 1	F	= 6 + 4	(A)	= 1
S	= - + 3	F-	= 2	Ad	= 1
R	= 10 + 7	FC'	= - + 1	At	= 1 + 1
P	= 1 + 1	F ⟷ C	= - + 1	Obj	= 1
				Pl	= - + 1
				Mask	= - + 1
				Food	= - + 1

Susan's responses to the Children's Appercep-tion Test were as follows:

1. The chickies are sitting down at the table and they're starting to eat dinner and the mother is coming to check on them to see if they're eating. So they say their prayers and start eating. (How do they feel?) They think the food is good, but it's chicken feed—(and then what happens?) They eat, they go to the bathroom, they brush their teeth, they wash their hands, and kiss their mother goodnight and go to bed.

2. The papa bear is tugging with the mother bear and the baby bear. All three fall off the mountain. (?) They go to the bottom and they hurt theyself. (How come?) They're pushing and tugging and then they have to go to the hospital. (How did it all start?)—[in a very sad voice] I don't know—(How did the baby bear feel?) He didn't like it, it was too much work and the mamma bear didn't like it, she just came out of the pet hospital.

3. The mouse comes out of the hole. The lion doesn't see the mouse. The lion has a cane and a chair and a pipe [continues to describe the card]—(What happens?) The mouse looks up at the lion and the mouse says to himself "Why shouldn't I go up and tell the lion he's a coward?" but he's afraid he'll get killed. The lion is thinking about the mouse. He's just getting ready to kill him. (How did it turn out?) The lion doesn't get to see the mouse and the mouse doesn't get to see the lion.

4. The baby deer is riding the mamma deer or kangaroo. The mamma kangaroo is carrying the milk home. The mamma kangaroo is carrying a baby in her pouch. There are two kids. They are going home to dinner—(?) He doesn't like it, it's too much trouble, it's tiring. He's tugging and pulling along. He's riding her on his bike. [Susan seemed to perceive the mother kangaroo as also on the tricycle.]

5. The two big bears are going to sleep. The mamma bear and the papa bear are asleep in their own beds—(What happens?) They wake up and find they have to eat breakfast. The papa has to go to work and the baby has to go to school.

6. Baby bear is going to sleep but not yet. The mamma and papa bear are already asleep—for the winter. But, the baby is just sitting thinking about the next day. Whether it's going to be raining, snowing, or sunshine. (What else might he be thinking?) He's thinking if he doesn't go to sleep mother and papa will wake up and spank him.

7. The lion is just about to jump for the monkey. The monkey is afraid. There are lots of rocks down there. The lion can't climb and the monkey is up the tree. The lion falls down but he isn't hurt.

8. The monkey's aunt is telling him something, and the mamma monkey is telling the father monkey something. There's a picture of grandmamma on the wall. (What is his aunt telling him?) "You'd better mind your mamma 'cause every little boy should do that." (How come?) He did something naughty. He threw her wristwatch on the floor, he was mad at his mamma 'cause his mommy wouldn't let him go to the show. (What is the mommy telling the father?)—I don't know what to make up about that.

9. —I don't know—A kangaroo—or a rabbit story: The baby rabbit is about to go to sleep but she's looking out the door to see what they're doing—(?) They're having a party—(What does she see?) A big man. No—a big fat woman. That's her teacher, she wonders what she's do-

ing there. She thought she might have did something wrong at school so she gets up and asks her mother and her mother says go back to bed. And she asks why the teacher is there. "She wants to know how you do at home and at school." (How does the baby rabbit feel then?) She doesn't like it, she thought the teacher would say she wasn't doing so good. It takes her two years to find out. The mother says, "You were very naughty that day." She says, "I wasn't either." They argue until something happens. The mother slaps the papa and the papa slaps the mamma, and the baby doesn't like it. They all settle down when the baby goes to school.

10. I don't know what he did wrong, but the mama is spanking the boy! (?) He thought he did something wrong but he didn't—I don't know what it could be.

These protocols were then reviewed with the prospective psychotherapist. The written report included the above reasons for referral and methods of assessment, the appearance and behavior during examination, the present situation and past history, and concluded with the following analysis of test results.

ANALYSIS OF RESULTS: Intellectually, Susan functions at a mildly retarded or "borderline" level: WISC Full Scale IQ 77, Verbal IQ 79, Performance IQ 80; Goodenough Draw-A-Man IQ 66. Her verbal skills, particularly information, arithmetic, and vocabulary, are undoubtedly depressed by her educational deficit. Even her social judgment is below average. In contrast, her ability to comprehend verbal abstractions is quite adequate and her performance on a test of attention to detail (Picture Completion) was above average. Low scores on tests involving visual-motor coordination and memory suggested the presence of a dysfunction of basic perception, of a type commonly associated with CNS damage.

Emotionally, Susan tries to play the role of the sweet and innocent child, but behind this mask she experiences considerable tension and confusion. Although socially compliant and friendly, she cannot really allow any emotional investment in her environment and sees no possibility of trusting anyone to answer her needs. She tries to repress her inner life, her daydreams and impulses, and handle all situations in a completely neutral fashion. However, fears of being overwhelmed and destroyed often break through her defenses, adding to her tension and depression. These phobic ideas suggest considerable underlying frustration and anger. She feels starved and deprived of love, angered and ready to devour others, then guilty and afraid of being devoured. Her defense is then to remain frozen and childlike in the hope that no one will know how angry she feels.

The main cause of Susan's fears of emotional deprivation, anger, and guilt appears to be her feelings about the divorce of her parents. Her fantasies support her mother's report that Susan has never acknowledged in her own heart the reality of this divorce, but keeps hoping for some restitution. Because she feels so insecure over the loss of her parents, she cannot allow herself even a normal expression of frustration, let alone her real anger at her parents. Moreover, her fantasies suggest that she has a vague feeling that she may in some way have been responsible for the divorce, that it was the result of some "bad" behavior on her part. On the other hand, she tries not to change anything, particularly not to grow up, not even to succeed at school, in order to retain the childhood state she was in when the divorce occurred. She seems to hope that by remaining static, restitution would be more possible.

SUMMARY IMPRESSION: Susan's school failure and even her low intellectual functioning are symptoms of her general emotional withdrawal and depression which is a reaction to the divorce of her parents and her underlying confused feelings of anger and guilt. Her school failure is further compounded by the fact that she changed and missed school so frequently.

NEUROLOGICAL CONSULTATION: Because of the history of frequent severe illnesses and Susan's poor performance on visual-motor tests, a neurological consultation was obtained. The neurologist reports that Susan shows no signs of any neurological disorder or dysfunction.

RECOMMENDATIONS: These results, including the neurologist's report, were discussed with Mrs. N. She was advised to (1) seek psychotherapy for Susan and (2) to apply for individual tutoring or to a school for remedial educational work.

A letter summarizing these results and recommendations was sent to Susan's father at his request.

Following this original consultation and assessment, Mrs. N accepted the recommendations of the psychologist. Susan was placed in a special remedial school and began twice-a-week psychotherapeutic sessions with another psychologist. Approximately 20 months thereafter, Susan's therapist requested a reassessment. The therapist was discouraged by what appeared to be very slow progress. Moreover, the therapist reported that Susan's mother and father independently had requested a summary of the progress of treatment.

SECOND ASSESSMENT, SUSAN N., CASE 48, AGE 13 YEARS 1 MONTH
WECHSLER INTELLIGENCE SCALE FOR CHILDREN

Verbal Tests	Scale Scores	Performance Tests	Scale Scores
Information	7	Picture Completion	10
Comprehension	9	Picture Arrangement	11
Arithmetic	4	Block Design	7
Similarities	9	Object Assembly	7
Vocabulary	6	Coding	8
Digit Span	(omitted)	Mazes	(omitted)
Verbal IQ	81	Performance IQ	90
	Full Scale IQ	84	

In the second assessment, Susan was asked to "Draw-A-Person" rather than to draw a man. Her first drawing, of a female figure, is shown in Plate VI. Although the exact instructions for the Goodenough Draw-A-Man test were not given, when Susan's drawing of a male figure (see Plate VII), were scored on the Goodenough Scale, a mental age of 8 years, 6 months and an IQ of 68 were obtained.

Susan's reproductions of the Graham-Kendall Designs were shown in Plate VIII. The raw score totals 7 which, when corrected for age and IQ, yielded a corrected score of 4.0 which again was in the borderline range.

RORSCHACH TECHNIQUE, SUSAN N., SECOND ASSESSMENT
Susan did not turn the cards.

Free Associations	*Inquiry*

Card I

I forgot what I said last time (encouraged)—50″
1. In my opinion, I think it's a cockeyed bear skin—(anything else?) Uh, uh.

There's no neck [indicating the tope space] and this [indicating the center space] is all burned out —(What makes it look like a skin?) The arms (D8) and it's kind of flat on a floor like (burned?) Well, there's no skin there. (skin?) It's all black.

W,S FC′ A obj

Card II 25″

1. A half of a butterfly.

(D2) and (D3) are the feet and head. The feelers are right here (D22)—(What kind of a butterfly?) It's a butterfly raccoon.

D F- A

PLATE VI

Free Associations	Inquiry
2. It's a half of a raccoon, that's what I'd say.	(D1) with a piece of (D5) taken out. The feet are (D22) (Is the butterfly and raccoon the same thing?) It's kinda—butterfly raccoon, just the feet.
	DW F- A O- (highly contaminated)
Card III 3″	
1. That's a frog!	(D7) are the feet and arms. (location?) (D7) (not a whole frog?) No.
	DW F- Ad

PLATE VII

Free Associations	*Inquiry*
Card IV 20″	
1. A lizard.	The whole thing, except for (D3). Well, maybe (D3), but not (D2). These are two monsters feet (what makes it look like a lizard?) The spine with this tail and his head (D1) plus (D5).
	D F A
Card V 3″	
1. A bat. I know, that's what it was last time.	The whole thing, the spinal cord, the head and ears, the pinchers and wings.
	W F A P
Card VI 23″	
1. A leopard.	A spinal cord and tail. The arms and the skin (skin?) It's all spotted.
	W F, FC′ A
Card VII 17″	
1. A bear.	Feet (D5), the arms (D21) and the fur on the head (D10). (The fur?) It's fluffy and spread out.
	D Fc A P

PLATE VIII

Free Associations	*Inquiry*

Card VIII 33″

1. Two mountain climbing rats.

Two of them. They're pink ones and they're by a mountain (pink?). The eye and the nose (?) Yes, I've read of white ones, the pink are uncommon. (Where's the mouth?) [points out the shape of (D1)]

$$D \ FM, \ F \longleftrightarrow C \ A \ P$$

Card IX 6″

1. A mouse.

The whole thing. This part, (D1) and (D3) and the spinal cord and where he's scratching his face (D21)—and his eyes and big pink ears. This fluffy part of the ink is his ears and these the feet (D3).

$$DW \ FM\text{-}, \ Fc \ A \ O\text{-}$$

Card X 15″

From the looks of it, I'd say it's a monster. I don't know what kind.

(D9) and (D1) (?) (D1) are big hands with the fingers spread out. The nose is (D8) and the feelers; a knife sticking in his mouth. (D9?) It's a pink ink splatter (?) Well, it's pink and spread out like fur.

DW FM, F   C (A)

Now it looks like crushed flowers (D's 15,7 and 13) (crushed flowers?) The green, brown and the yellow. (crushed?) That used to be a flower now it's crushed and the (D7) is the green leaf.

(D CF, m Pl)

SUMMARY OF RORSCACH SCORES—SUSAN N.: SECOND ASSESSMENT

Location		Determinants		Content	
W	= 3	FM	= 2	A $\longleftrightarrow$	= 8
DW	= 4	FM-	= 1	(A)	= 1
D	= 4 + 1	F	= 3	Ad	= 1
S	= - + 1	F-	= 3	Aobj	= 1
R	= 11 + 1	Fc	= 1 + 1	Pl	= - + 1
P	= 2	FC'	= 1 + 1		
O-	= 2	F $\longleftrightarrow$ C	= - + 2		
		CF	= - + 1		

On this second assessment, Susan was given the TAT rather than the CAT. She gave the following responses.

2: This is the daughter named Mary. She is wondering how she is going to earn some money to support her family and she is going to school right now. The mother is wondering how she is going to earn enough money to support the farm. (What happens?) Her son is trying to get the horse across the field to get the crop in to have enough food to eat and enough money to get things from the store. (How does it turn out?) She finds a job. She works at the store for $150 per week for enough to pay bills and stuff.

3GF: Like a show in a movie. The lady comes in drunk and doesn't know what to do. She comes home to her mother and wonders how she's going to earn enough money to pay her bills, about $300. She finds a job at a bakery. After that, she comes home and says to her mother, "I got a job at the bakery, cooking and serving. I get three million per week. I can pay the bills with that money." (She came home drunk?) She's an alcoholic.

4: This man came home and says to his wife, "I'm going out and find this man and fight him if he doesn't give me a job, I'm going to kill him." The wife doesn't approve and says he should stay home. (What happens?) They start fighting and she tries to hold him back and he's trying to get out the door which she won't let him do. So her kids come home and want to know what's going on and she accidently lets him go. She tells the kids all about what he's going to do. He comes home with his shirt torn and a black eye and the wife doesn't know what to do, so they call a lawyer. That's the end. (What all happened?) Nothing, the lawyer solved it. (But what happened when the man was out?) Well, he meets this guy in the restaurant and they go across the street and start fighting for about 15 minutes and came home. (What about the guy he was fighting?) He didn't get hurt; he was the one who started it.

5: This lady knocks on the door of a neighbor and she wants to know what's going on. She opens the door and sees nobody's in the house and she goes in and sees somebody lying on the floor. She finds her friend is dead. She calls the police and goes in their car and goes around, and as soon as she sees this man running, she knows that it's him. She says that's it. They ask his name. He says he's her husband and he killed his wife. (Why?) "She broke a vase." "I don't understand." "I had to kill her, but I didn't mean to but I did. She threatened me." He got put in jail and got out in ten years.

6GF: The guy comes in and knocks on the door and nobody answers. He comes in and sees a lady writing a letter. He sneaks up behind her and scares her. She sees it's her husband

and wants to know why he scared her. He said it's her anniversary and he brought her a present. "What is it?" She opens it and finds a diamond ring and in small letters it says that she's going to get killed that night at twelve o'clock. So it's only 11 o'clock and at 12 o'clock she's killed. That's the end of it. (How come?) Well, she asked him if she'd done something wrong. She said he killed his mark (?). That's all—(she gets killed?) The man's wife, the two of them were fighting and this lady pulled a knife and stabbed it into her (?). He was the guy what was going to kill her. He sneaked into her bedroom while she was asleep.

9GF: The lady sees this woman. She sneaks up behind a tree and she sees her husband and he doesn't like the way he's necking with her. She goes out on the beach and recognizes her. He calls her but she doesn't come because he's jealous of the lady. He calls and she goes away. She sneaks up behind the girl and kills her. Jealous, so she just kills her.

7GF: The lady's telling her to go into the other room. She'll tell her later what she's talking about. She calls the man and tells him and he goes out and goes home. She calls her daughter in and so—she says, "What happened?" The mother said, "What?" Oh, she's reading. She tells the daughter about it and tells her not to tell anyone. If she does, 'cause she gets $100 per week. 'Cause she does all the housework so—(What does her mother tell her?) This guy is coming to the house some Wednesday. It's Tuesday already. She's going to serve cocktails with a poisonous mix. Her daughter says, "Why?" " 'Cause I don't like the man." "Why?" " 'Cause my mother told me never to fool around with any man that's not nice." "How is he not nice?" "He goes around collecting money. He says for a good cause, but it really gives them counterfeit money." So she says to her mother that she wants to know what's going on and her mother tells her. Her mother tells her, "How come that man's so mean?"— "He says to women that he wants to go out with them but he gives them counterfeit and they get put in jail instead of him. Then they give it to the stores and liquor places. So she kills the man and comes home late—and that's about it.

12GF: The lady is wondering how she can kill this man. This lady is Catholic sister and she says, "Why don't you drop a poisonous stuff in his glass?" "That's a great idea"; so she did. The sister said, "A good job you did, you are a good agent." "You're a good agent too, sister." And she says, "We've work

to do and if you don't come along with me, you're going to get killed." "What for?" "Because you told me to put the poison in that drink." "But you said it was a good idea." "Never believe what you hear, sister." That might be the screams because she gotten killed (?) The sister got killed.

17GF: These people, the men on this ship, are loading the boat. The lady is on top of them, up above them. The sun is shining on the lady and the man says, "I'll be up in a minute." The lady says, "What for?" and the man says, "So I can marry you." "But I don't want to marry you." So they don't marry each other, so they go out with one another a couple of times and then they don't go out with one another anymore. (How come she doesn't want to get married?) " 'Cause he is mean."

18GF: The lady is looking at the other lady and says to the man who's married to this lady that she's going to die 'cause she has rabies. "Why don't you give her some shots?" They take her down but the doctor says it's too late. She's dead. (How come she has rabies?) This dog came up and bit her and he or it gave it to her.

APPEARANCE AND BEHAVIOR DURING EX-AMINATION: Attractively dressed and neatly groomed, Susan is developing into a very pretty youth, albeit a fragile appearing, pale beauty. She was much more poised and socially outgoing than before and accepted the assessment outwardly in almost adult fashion. However, she gradually lost her composure as the tests became more and more stressful, and she became visibly anxious. Although she tried to make up excuses to herself over her repeated and obvious difficulties, she was almost in tears by the time we were through. Otherwise, her affect seemed quite blunted, especially on the TAT. Although the content of her stories was highly emotionally charged, she told them in a flat, matter-of-fact tone.

ANALYSIS OF RESULTS: Intellectually, Susan continues to function in the dull normal range; the increase from a full scale IQ of 77 to an IQ of 84 is not in itself significant. Her overall Performance IQ increased by 10 points from 80 to 90 and Verbal IQ increased only by four points, from 77 to 81. However, there was an increase of two or more weighted score points on five of the scales and none showed any significant decreases.

Most marked was the five-point increase in Picture-Arrangement, suggesting considerable improvement in intellectual understanding of the sequence and meaning of social events. (Comprehension also jumped three points.) All told, Susan does seem to be developing intellectually at a slightly more accelerated pace.

Despite these gains in intellectual growth, Susan continues to show definite signs of a marked perceptual handicap. Her visual-motor coordination and perceptual grasp of even simple configurations is so poor that it is indeed remarkable that she has made any intellectual gains at all. Particularly in un-structured situations, as on the Rorschach, she becomes so perplexed and helpless that she is almost unable to respond. In despera-tion she grasps some detail and in vague fashion tries to fathom the situation, but is so confused that her responses are often close to complete confabulation.

Susan's perceptual handicap results in even more confusion when she attempts to under-stand and deal with emotional stimuli. Out-wardly, Susan has learned to mask her feel-ings with a socially acceptable smile and passive compliance. However, she remains very dependent on her environment for emo-tional support, absorbing in passive fashion any emotional stimulation and is thus easily influenced by others. Having formed little or no identity of her own, she remains in a symbiotic relationship with her mother. In mirror-distortion she reflects her mother's fears and frustrations. Thus, she echoes her mother's anxieties over their tight financial status, which fits into her own anxieties over being fed and of even being able to be inde-pendent and care for herself. Similarly, she reflects her mother's continued anger at the father which expands Susan's own conflictual anger at the father for his desertion of the family. Susan's fantasies of murderous hos-tility now include her mother, causing her even more confusion, guilt, and depression. She envisions most interpersonal relationships as a poisonous plot of jealousy threatening to destroy everyone concerned. Although emo-tionally still quite infantile, Susan nevertheless is beginning to experience the normal physio-logical stresses of puberty and thus there is an erotic overlay in her fantasies, again re-flecting her mother's sexual frustrations, all of which only serve to heighten Susan's anxiety and confuse her more.

SUMMARY IMPRESSION: Susan continues to show every sign of a moderately severe generalized perceptual handicap, which I am even more convinced probably stems from some overall neurological weakness or dys-function. She does show signs of a slight spurt of intellectual growth which makes her a bit more capable of conforming to well-structured situations, but she seems even more disabled emotionally by stress. She remains in a symbiotic tie with her mother, plus facing the stress of the early years of adolescence.

RECOMMENDATIONS

1. Susan should have another thorough neurological assessment. If, as I suspect, she does have some overall weakness, psychotherapy might have to be directed toward helping her accept and adjust to this handicap.

2. It would seem unlikely that Susan's sym-biotic relationship with her mother and her mother's anxieties can be resolved un-less Mrs. N can be helped to understand and deal more effectively with the situa-tion and some of her own stresses.

3. Susan's difficulties in dealing with un-structured situations and complex prob-lem solving suggest that her placement in regular classes in junior high school should be seriously reconsidered. In my opinion, the stresses involved may be far too great for this handicapped child. Admittedly, such a reconsideration could be quite anxiety-provoking for Susan who sees this placement as a promotion, that is, a re-ward for "good" behavior and a denial of her handicap.

These results and recommendations were discussed with the therapist and with Mrs. N. A second neurological consultation was ob-tained, but again there were no findings of any gross neurological difficulty. The neuro-logist, after looking over Susan's perceptual-motor responses on the psychological tech-niques, was of the opinion that this behavior was strong evidence of a generalized, but mild central nervous dysfunctioning and hazarded that this dysfunctioning might well be the sequali of possible damage which Susan probably endured during her mother's pregnancy and prolonged gestation. The fact of her many illnesses also suggested a generally weak physiological organism.

PLATE IX

PLATE X

Despite several consultations with Mrs. N, she remained quite resistant to any continued therapeutic consideration of her personal problems. In a matter-of-fact fashion, she admitted that she had been very depressed and volunteered that she at least had intellectual insight into the possibility that her depression had been a severe stress to Susan. She openly wept as she expressed considerable guilt about the possible damage she might have done. However, she averred that her life situation was now markedly changing, that she had been actively dating one man and was seriously considering marrying him. She recognized that this relationship with her boyfriend might be disturbing to Susan, but felt that with the therapist's help, Susan could come to accept the fact that she was not the only person in her mother's life. The therapist continued to be of the opinion that without at least collaborative treatment of Mrs. N, the prognosis for Susan was limited. However, in view of the findings in this second assessment which suggested that Susan was in a state where she was more cognizant of, but also more confused by, many of the realities in her life, it seemed it most urgent to continue Susan's therapy.

As to Susan's school placement, Susan adamantly refused to continue attending any sort of special classes for the handicapped. A conference was held with the assessor, the therapist, and the school counselor, and a program was worked out whereby Susan could attend regular classes for most of the day in largely nonacademic subjects, and remain in special classes for reading and arithmetic. The school reported that Susan's progress over the previous year had been very slow and that her continuation in the public schools was justified chiefly to assist her in her social adjustment and to prevent her from having a complete identity as a disabled person.

Mr. N was advised by letter of the progress of the treatment as seen from this assessment (without mention, of course, of the parts referring to his ex-wife). He agreed to continue to sponsor Susan's therapy.

Fourteen months later the therapist requested a third assessment of Susan's development. The therapist expressed the opinion that the intense anxiety which Susan demonstrated the year before had now largely abated, that Susan had shown no real changes in her attitudes or life situation over the past several months, that her mother's life situation continued to be a major source of stress, that there was no potential change in Mrs. N's behavior, and that generally there seemed to be little to be gained in continuing the psychotherapy. At this time Susan was 14 years and three months old.

Susan's responses to the Wechsler Intelligence Scale for Children on the third assessment yielded the following scores.

Verbal Tests	Scale Score	Performance Tests	Scale Score
Information	10	Picture Completion	9
Comprehension	10	Picture Arrangement	8
Arithmetic	9	Block Design	10
Similarities	12	Object Assembly	11
Vocabulary	8	Coding	8
Digit Span	11	Mazes (omitted)	
Verbal IQ	100	Performance IQ	93
	Full Scale IQ	96	

Susan's drawing of a man on this third assessment is shown in Plate IX. The Goodenough Mental Age for this drawing was 6 years nine months with an IQ of 51 (based on the Goodenough C.A. ceiling of 13-6).

Susan's reproduction of the Graham-Kendall Design at this time are shown in Plate X. The raw score of 5, when corrected for Mental Age and Chronological Age, yielded a corrected score of 3, still in the borderline range.

Susan's third set of Rorschach responses were as follows. (Again the cards were held up right.)

Free Associations	Inquiry

Card I 15″

1. A dress or coat.

The whole thing. It has a tail, arms, the back, the feet. It's a "mod" dress. These, (D5) snap together. (Mod?) The cut-outs. *WS F Clo O*

Card II 15″

1. How about a caterpillar?

(D3) are the feelers, (D2) are the feet, or the feet could be (D1) or that could be ears and these are arms [indicating the little dr center at the bottom of the blot] A long nose and eyes. *W F- A*

Card III 18″

1. A lizard.

(D3) are the sharp teeth, (D5) are the arms. Here's the leg [the outer edge], and (D8) are the cheeks. *W F- A*

Card IV

I remember this one, I liked this one. 20″
1. A space monster.

It has big feet (D2) and a long tail, (D1). Here are the little arms, (D4) and the face (D3). *W F (A)*

Card V 2″

1. A bat.

The whole thing, the feet, the long arm-wings, the eye-feelers. *W F A P*

Card VI 10″

1. I don't know what those green bugs look like. A green bug, I'll say.

(D10) are the teeth, (D9) the arms, (D23) the legs, (D3) the tail. Here's the spine down the center. *W F A*

Card VII 8″

1. A chipmunk.

(D4) are the big cheeks they store their food in. (D5) are the legs. Here are the arms, the little ones, and the fur. (The fur?) The puffy part [rubs the card]. *W Fc- A*

Card VIII 5″

1. Two bears climbing the mountain.

(D1) it's steep or it could be sorta like a tree. *D FM A P   W F N*

Card IX 12″

1. A giant mouse.

The whole things. (D11) is the sharp sting like the legs, (D4) the big ears. It looks kinda mad, the way the nose is. *W F-. FM A O-*

Card X [patient sighs] 12″

1. How about a spider, no . . . a bee!

The whole thing. (D1) are big muscles and (D3) a needle. Here are the feet, legs, and the inner part of the body. [Patient points randomly at various D's]. *W F- A*

SUMMARY OF RORSCHACH SCORE:, SUSAN N.—THIRD ASSESSMENT

Location		Determinants		Content	
W	$= 10$	FM	$= 1 + 1$	A	$= 8$
D	$= 1$	F	$= 5$	(A)	$= 1$
S	$= -1$	$F\text{-}$	$= 4$	Clo	$= 1$
R	$= 11$	$Fc\text{-}$	$= 1$	N	$= 1$
P	$= 2$	$O\text{-} = 1$			

Susan's responses to the TAT on this third assessment were as follows.

2: This is a man plowing the field and the girl is thinking of how it would be to be living in the big city. The lady is thinking of how it would be if it were more beautiful. (How did this all come about?) Well, she looks more like the city type. (What do the others think of the girl's idea?) They don't like it and want her to grow up and have farms of her own. (?) She goes up and tells her mother that she's going to go to the city. She marries a nice young rich baron and they live happily ever after.

3GF: Like in our modern times. They live in an apartment house. She opens the door to the apartment and she is crying. She tells her mother that she took LSD and was on a trip and she feels horrible, crazy. She puts on her pajamas and goes to bed, then she takes some more LSD and feels bad again. She keeps taking it. Her mothers says she should go to a doctor. So she wants to know why she keeps taking it. But the doctor has another patient and was terribly busy. She tells her mother and her mother says, "I'll go with you the next morning." So the doctor says, "Take pep pills." So she takes pep pills and is too busy to take LSD. Pretty soon she starts taking marijuana and the doctor says, "If you start you will never be able to stop."

4: The woman is going out with another man. She left her husband but she likes this other man too. The husband was a maniac on sex and the woman tells him not to go out and fight this other man. Se he goes out anyhow and picks a fight and the woman says, "He deserved it." (What does she mean?) The other man, he forced her, so they go out in the alley. The husband wins and kills the other guy. She wasn't too happy but she was glad it was all over.

5: The lady asks the daughter what time she was going out to dinner and the daughter says, "Oh, about 7 or 8." The mother asks her "What time is your date coming?" and the daughter replies "7:30." Well, it's 6:30 now, you've only got an hour." She is dressing and a man taps on the window. She screams. Her mother comes in, "What's the matter?" and she tells her mother "There's a man at the window who wants me to come with him."—"Maybe it's a dream." Her date comes and this man is out in the alley. "Who is that," asks the date. "I don't know, just ignore him." "How can I ignore him when he's in the back seat?" They go dancing and have a good time. They stay up to 4:A.M. They decide it would be nice to get married. The daughter gets married the next day. The mother wishes the daughter could have married someone else. Someone more pleasant. And the mother gets married and went to live with her daughter. Oh, brother! But the mother moved away after three years. Then the mother died and her husband died a few years later.

6GF: —I can't say too much about that one. —They're playing a play in dark shadows. A guy comes up and asks, "Is your father dead?" "In a way he is and a way he isn't. His name is Dr. Schneider." "What does Dr. Schneider do?" "He's a doctor in physical education." "What does he do in physical education?" "He has health." "Let's drop that subject." She pulls off her right white earring. He picks it up and a white sleeping pill comes out. He said, "What the hell?" The police came and she said, "That's the man who said my father was dead." So they pick him up and the lady got married to her father.

7GF: The title is, "The Mother who Died." This is the moral: while mother is reading a story, you should never listen to the story, but you should listen to the footsteps. The mother says, "Why don't you listen to the story?" "I hear footsteps." "It might be your father." The mother opens the door, and the daughter screams like she never screamed before. A high-pitched scream. The daughter picks up the mother and finds a knife in her back. "Was that daddy?" "I can't tell." "Fix me my dinner." "I can't, I'm a dying woman." But the girl doesn't know about death and things. She tries to fix the mother up. The moral is, never read a book to your daughter unless it's important.

11: What's that? It's a bee! These men are on a safari in the jungle. The picture shows a bee coming down the mountain. There's a falling stream of acid making the bee very hot. He wants to know why he's doing this and he jumps in the acid but it doesn't burn him up. He finally gets out and he's all burning. It flies around in a cave. It wants to know why it's doing that. It lands in a trail and goes back over in the cave where it belongs. The earth starts to shake and the bee is trapped 'cause a landslide closed the cave, so the world is saved.

12GF: This nun is the mother of the lady. The lady wants to know who the man is. The nun says, "Why not go see?" "You're kinda of a nut!" "You don't call me a nut!" So they pick a fight. They're in a museum. The man is her former husband. She wants to know if he is counterespionage spy. "No." "Well, why are you following me around?" "I'm not a child anymore and I can follow anyone around I like." (How does it turn out?) The man marries the lady and the mother goes in a nun's home. The nun is the tablesetter for the sisters. After years and years the old lady dies.

17GF: —I can't make up a story—The men on the boat, the lady is standing on a bridge. The sun is shining on the lady. The men come from Japan. They are hauling in lots of goods. (How about the lady?) She's just waiting for her husband.

18GF: Oh, the lady is supposed to be killing her, egads! The lady doesn't like this other lady. "What ever happened to Baby Jane?" That's not the real story, just the end of it. The lady doesn't like Baby Jane so she crippled her. "Why did you call the people from the insane society?" So she got her arm over her neck and she wouldn't talk, so she just killed her.

During this third assessment, a brief interview was held with Susan and she was asked how she herself looked at her therapy and what she felt about continuing it. Tears came to her eyes as she even considered the possibility of terminating her relationship with the therapist. She did agree, however, that such a termination would eventually have to come

about. Susan remarked, "I'll be a teenager then."

The following report was then made to the therapist: "Intellectually, Susan continues to make marked gains. She is now developing intellectually at a rate which might be expected for her age. Her intellectual development is the more remarkable since she continues to show signs of a perceptual-motor dysfunction. The perceptual-motor dysfunction is also not quite as marked as it appeared three years ago, but nevertheless is quite definite. In fact, Susan's responses in this third assessment even more strongly support the hypothesis that this perceptual-motor lag is very likely the sequali of some generalized central nervous system dysfunctioning suffered much earlier in her life.

"Although Susan now is able to handle relatively emotionally neutral problem-solving tasks much more effectively, she remains handicapped principally when she faces the task of perceptually comprehending and handling emotional stress. It is in unstructured emotional and social situations that Susan's perceptual handicap is most marked. Under the stress of emotional pressures, she becomes confused and severely distorts the situation. She finds it extremely difficult, if not impossible, to handle emotional stress from her environment or from her own impulses. Her fantasies, which read like psychotic poetry, reveal a conglomeration of raw feelings and impulses for which Susan has little resolution. However, it does appear that Susan no longer feels quite as intensely deprived and depressed as she did three years ago. Rather, she is now concerned with very definite Oedipal feelings. In her fantasies she expresses murderous anger toward her mother whom, it appears, she feels deprived her of her father. In fact, in one fantasy the heroine rediscovers the father and marries him, getting rid of the mother! Moreover, Susan appears now to question her mother's poisonous anger toward men. Nevertheless, Susan is also quite confused and threatened by her own sexual urges which now press on her as she advances into adolescence. She seems to fear that if a man came into her life it might be as destructive to her as she perceives it was to her mother. Yet, she seems to push on in these fantasies hoping that nevertheless there will be a Prince Charming for her.

SUMMARY IMPRESSION: Despite continued evidence that Susan is very probably mildly brain-damaged, she is evidently making marked strides in her intellectual development. Moreover, although the perception of social and emotional stress is particularly difficult for her, Susan is attempting to deal with the unresolved and prolonged relationships of her childhood which have been re-evoked during pubescence. In fact, Susan appears to be tackling these problems with somewhat less anxiety and depression, despite the confusion of her perceptions and the intrusion of primary processes into her ideation.

RECOMMENDATIONS: Although progress in treatment may seem very slow for this perceptually handicapped child, it certainly seems that Susan's development has been much more enhanced than could have been predicted three years earlier. Both consciously and in her fantasies, Susan pleads for continued assistance while she struggles with the adolescent stresses of sexuality. Thus, if at all possible, it would seem advisable to continue therapeutic support for the following year. It does remain questionable whether Susan can achieve a point where she can function emotionally and socially relatively independently. Nevertheless, it does seem possible that she might attain even more emotional stability and some sense of personal identity.

As might be expected, the therapist was most pleased and encouraged by these results. She remarked that she had been aware of them for some time, that Susan's Oedipal conflicts were coming to the fore, but she had felt that Susan might not be able to face these conflicts and thus had not encouraged discussion of them in the treatment. She agreed that as indicated in story 3GF, she had attempted to help Susan repress and avoid sexual excitement. However, she was now of the opinion that the problems of Susan's sexual maturation could no longer be avoided. Since Susan was determined to become a teenager, the therapist* agreed that Susan would need continued support. Mrs. N. was also greatly encouraged, not only by Susan's intellectual improvement, but

*Unfortunately, public credit cannot be given to this very skilled and persistent therapist, since to do so might identify the patient.

by the possibility that Susan could, in perhaps a limited fashion, mature to the point of a relatively normal social and emotional life. She reported that Susan was no longer a placid little girl, but at times was enraged at her in a rebellious fashion, "like any other teenager." Far from being upset by this change in Susan, Mrs. N was actually encouraged at Susan's development. She admitted that she had at times let herself daydream that Susan might enter into normal teenage social life. She bought Susan attractive adolescent clothes in the latest fashion. However, at that time Susan had no boyfriends and only one or two casual girlfriends. Mrs. N herself seemed to be breaking the symbiotic relationship she had maintained with Susan over the past year since her divorce. She was engaged to be married, although a date had not been set for the wedding. How Susan might take this additional stress was as yet unknown, although Susan seemed fond of her prospective stepfather.

CASE 49

Cindy K., age seven years, eight months, was referred by her pediatrician who had been treating her continued vaginal irritation and discharge. He had been concerned after Cindy's mother had reported to him that Cindy masturbated excessively and openly around the home and that she had been engaged in sexual play with other girls and boys of varying ages. The neighbors had become quite upset and had cautioned their children against playing with Cindy. The pediatrician was most shocked to learn that Cindy had been taught to engage in sexual play by Mrs. K's stepfather who, until about two years ago, had frequently been called upon as a babysitter for Cindy and her younger brother. Mrs. K had mentioned these facts to the pediatrician merely to explain the source of Cindy's vaginal irritation and seemed relatively undisturbed by any other aspects of them. However, when the pediatrician explained that he was concerned with the possible long-range emotional disturbances arising from the situation, Mrs. K agreed to accept his referral to the psychologist. When Mrs. K contacted the psychologist, an appointment was made for an interview with her. Subsequently Mrs. K was seen for two further interviews, and Cindy was seen in two two-hour assessment sessions.

During this second assessment with Cindy, Mrs. K filled out the MMPI. A follow-up interview then was held with Mrs. K to discuss the results of this assessment.

Mrs. K was a strikingly beautiful woman who was fashionably and expensively dressed. Although her constant smoking and such mannerisms as biting her lip suggested considerable tension, Mrs. K attempted to discuss Cindy and her own problems in an objective and intelligent fashion, as if she were telling a story about someone else. However, she was not able to completely contain her feelings and her voice became harsh and angry as she discussed her own relationship with her mother, and she was near tears as she recited some of her own difficulties. Although a great deal of the discussion centered around Mrs. K herself and her own background, she did seem genuinely concerned about Cindy, expressing the fear that "Cindy may turn out to be just like me."

Asked first about Cindy's symptom, Mrs. K explained that initially she had not been particularly concerned about Cindy's masturbation, as she had though that such self-stimulation was perfectly normal among preschool children. However, as this activity continued she had asked the advice of yet another pediatrician who had assured her that Cindy would grow out of it. When Cindy continued to masturbate every night as she went to sleep and began to rub her genitals frequently during the day in public, Mrs. K had tried to punish her by depriving her of things—but without effect. Mrs. K had wondered if punishing Cindy for masturbating might draw Cindy's attention even more to this activity and "besides I was not always around when she did it." Mrs. K was upset when she received vigorous complaints from nursery school teachers and from the kindergarten teacher. The kindergarten teacher had advised Mrs. K that "Cindy might not really be ready for school yet," largely because of this behavior. Thus, Cindy was excluded from school until she was six. Mrs. K was not disturbed at first when she learned of Cindy's sexual play with other children. "Isn't that normal too?" she asked. However, the complaints from the neighbors has grown to such a point that Mrs. K's landlord had refused to renew her lease and two months ago she had been forced to find another apartment. At first Mrs. K did not voluntarily mention what she had told the pediatrician about her stepfather. When asked about this, she sighed deeply and said that she had never really apprehended her stepfather sexually fondling Cindy; only recently, when Mrs. K was trying to discipline Cindy for masturbating, Cindy reported, "Grandpa used to rub me all the time and I used to rub him." Mrs. K then said in a very depressed tone that she believed Cindy's report, since both she and her sister had been similarly molested by her stepfather when they were children. After a pause, she remarked, "Maybe I had better begin at the beginning."

Throughout Mrs. K's childhood, she had lived in the home of her maternal grandfather with her mother and her sister who was two years her senior. The home was dominated by her grandfather whom she variously described as a "tyrant," "an ignorant old man who would still be a dirt farmer if oil had not been discovered on their ranch," and "a wicked old man who had nothing but sex on his mind." In regard to this last statement, she explained that her maternal grandmother had died shortly after her mother's birth and that her grandfather had had various mistresses in the home from time to time. Her grandfather and her mother often quarreled violently, but her mother had never left the home and continued to occupy the family mansion. Mrs. K's father separated from her mother shortly after Mrs. K's birth, and she had seen very little of him since. Mrs. K reflected that she thought it quite probable that her father could not live in the same house with her maternal grandfather, but that her mother had refused to leave home. She based this supposition on the fact that her mother's second marriage similarly disintegrated.

Mrs. K's mother married a third time when Mrs. K was approximately 11 years of age, and it was this second stepfather who had sexually molested her and her sister. Mrs. K boiled with anger when she recalled that when she complained to her mother about her stepfather's sexual advances, her mother had accused her of lying and refused to do anything about it. In giving this history, Mrs. K made no direct association between this sexual relationship with her stepfather and her own subsequent sexual behavior, but she did go on immediately to mention that she had developed physically very early and "started playing around" while she was still in junior high school.

When she was 17, she became pregnant in what she described as a casual sexual escapade. Her grandfather was outraged and forced her to marry Cindy's father, whose parents were socially and financially indebted to him. However, this young man refused to move into the grandfather's household and escaped from the situation by enlisting in the military service shortly before Cindy's birth. "I was really very wild after that," Mrs. K remarked, explaining that she became even more sexually promiscuous, became pregnant a second time two years later, but bore this second child, Cindy's brother, out of wedlock. At this time, her mother, with whom she constantly quarreled, demanded that she leave the house. In desperation, Mrs. K accepted a proposal from a man she had known only slightly and who had been pressuring her to marry him. At first, this second marriage seemed quite ideal; her husband was some ten years her senior, seemed genuinely fond of Cindy and the younger brother, and had moved them away from Mrs. K's hometown and had bought them a lovely home. However, Mrs. K soon discovered that her husband was impotent. Subsequently, he apprehended her in an affair with another man and divorced her. She returned to her mother's home quite depressed.

Her depression was increased by the death of her grandfather. She remembered that she had been very surprised to find herself weeping openly at his funeral. "I guess I really did love the bastard," she remarked. She resolved to attempt to become financially independent of her mother, particularly because their quarrels became even more violent. At one point, she actually fired a pistol at her mother and spent the night in jail, but was not prosecuted as her mother declined to sign the complaint. She trained as a model and soon thereafter found very remunerative employment in an adjacent metropolis. She was able to support herself and her children independently. She continued to have many boyfriends and many offers of marriage, but denied that she had any further sexual affairs. "I think I've been burned enough."

Because Mrs. K had not been altogether responsible for Cindy's care and training, she was rather vague about Cindy's development. During Cindy's first years of life, she had been cared for chiefly by Mrs. K's mother or by a hired nursemaid. She had not breastfed Cindy as she found herself unable to lactate. However, she could not remember that Cindy had been any particular feeding problem. It seemed to her that Cindy had always been hungry and always ate well. "When she was little, she always seemed to have a bottle in her mouth." Mrs. K recalled that Cindy was still requesting a bottle when she was three years of age and that she had decided to take the bottle away because she thought it might not look right to her second husband. Later in the interview, Mrs. K remarked that Cindy had always sucked her thumb and continues to do so especially when she is tired or ill. Mrs. K was not sure when Cindy was toilet trained, but believed it must have happened when Cindy was approximately two years of age. She could only recall that Cindy was completely toilet trained at the time that she remarried.

As far as she could recall, Cindy was relatively unaffected by the birth of her brother, David. She denied that there was any rivalry between the children, noting that Cindy actually seemed very fond of David and enjoyed trying to hold him or cuddle with him, calling him "my baby." Only recently had there been little fights between them, largely over favorite foods. Except for the vaginal irritation, which Mrs. K had first noted approximately two years ago, Cindy had been in relatively good health.

After she separated from her second husband, Mrs. K had found it difficult to obtain caretakers for her children while she worked or went on dates. Her stepfather, who had separated from her mother, lived nearby and she accepted his offer to watch over the children from time to time. About two years ago, he had returned to Mrs. K's hometown, and she was forced to try to hire other people to care for her children. Because she could not find babysitters, she frequently was unable to go to work and lost considerable income. Several times she was forced to borrow money from her mother which always resulted in another altercation. When it was suggested to Mrs. K that her situation seemed very depressing, she admitted that occasionally she was so overwhelmed with depression that she had actively considered suicide.

A slight-built blonde child who was neatly dressed and groomed, Cindy accepted the testing situation in a matter-of-fact fashion. However, it was apparent from the first that she was quite tense and apprehensive. In the initial session, the psychologist attempted to structure the situation for her, associating it as a follow-up of her medical treatment. This only caused her to be more tense and guarded. Regarding her physical symptom, Cindy said only that she "itched down there," but denied that this caused her any great concern or embarrassment. She also denied that she had ever known any other children who had a similar itch or had seen anyone else rub their genitals.

She relaxed noticeably when the discussion turned to her school and play activities. As her mother had reported, Cindy seemed to enjoy going to school and had been at least moderately successful in the first two years. Cindy described, with obvious enjoyment, some of her work at school, talked about some of her playmates, but froze perceptibly when asked what they did together. She talked excitedly about her hopes that she would receive a pet rabbit for Easter but then became sad as she remembered that her mother could not let her have a pet in the apartment. She described her brother David as "cute," but agreed that he could be "a little pest" when he got into her things. When asked about who took care of her when her mother worked, she replied that her grandpa used to, but "now we had other babysitters." She showed no particular affect when mentioning her grandfather. When asked about her father, Cindy remarked, still in her matter-of-fact tone, that he had gone away and that she did not expect him to come back. She denied that she missed him, and added that she thought maybe her mother would find them another daddy later. During the administration of the tests, Cindy was quite compliant and cooperative but she remained rather guarded and required considerable encouragement at times to respond.

Because the pediatrician had expressed the opinion that Cindy seemed retarded intellectually, the Stanford-Binet Form LM was administered. Cindy passed all items at the VI year level, four items at the VII and VIII year level, three at the IX year level, one at the X year level, which yielded a Mental Age of 8 years, 0 months and an IQ of 110. It was noted that Cindy failed "Similarities" at year VI but passed "Similarities and Differences" at year VIII. Her other failures at years VII and VIII were on "Comprehension IV." Her score of 7 on the Vocabulary was sufficient for age VI but not for age VIII. Cindy's verbalization, however, was adequate

enough for her to pass such items as "Rhymes: new forms" on year IX, and "Finding Reasons I" on year X. Her perceptual-motor functioning seemed effective as she quite easily drew a diamond for year VII and passed the "Memory For Designs I" at year IX, but not at year XI. However, she was not able to pass "Paper Cutting" item at year IX.

Cindy's drawing of a man yielded a Mental Age of 8 years 6 months, and an IQ of 107 when scored on the Goodenough Scale. This drawing and a subsequent drawing of a girl were quite stilted and the overcontrol of motor activity demonstrated in the drawings did suggest the possibility of a perceptual-motor difficulty. However, this motor behavior could also be explained in terms of the emotional restriction as was evident in Cindy's other responses.

Partly because of her age and partly because she seemed so very guarded, it was decided to inquire after her Rorschach responses as she gave them rather than subsequent to the free associations. Her responses were as follows:

Card I 40″
I can't make anything out of this one—(encouraged)—100." This looks like a dress, it's all I can make out of it (?) It's like this [pointing to the lower part of D4]. It's a shirt with a slip underneath it. *D Fc Clo*

Card II 4″
Rocks—and a bear—that's all. (Show me the rocks.) [Cindy points to a little d in D1]. They're kinda round. (Show me the bear). This shape, D1, the nose and the body (Anything else you can show me about it?) [no response] *Di F N D F A P*

Card III 4″
A butterfly (D3), that shape and a stick (D7) that shape. *D F A P   D F Pl*

Card IV 40″
Nothing out of this one—just nothing. It looks so ugly. (?)—90″ It really looks like a monster. [indicating the whole card with her finger] (?) Here's the feet, D2, and the body. (How about this, D4?) I don't know. (And D1?) His arm— (What makes it look so ugly?) The way the shape is, with his arm down here. *W F (H)*

Card V 5″
A cocoon web; a cocoon coming out of it. Here's the web [indicating the usual butterfly wings] and here's the cocoon coming out of it [indicating the center of the card] (What makes it look like a web?) 'Cause that's what cocoons got. *D FM A*

Card VI

Oh no!—30". Nothing out of it. The whole thing, nothing out of it [turns card over]. *Rejects.*

Card VII [sighs] 3"

A butterfly. That's all and two rabbits. The butterfly is here [points to D4 and 6] the shape and this thing here (D6). (D6?) I don't know (How about the rabbits?) [points to D2] The ear, the face, the nose, and the tail. *D F A   D F A*

Card VIII 5"

Two cats (D1) (How do they seem to be?) They look like bobcats, the face. (Anything else you can tell me about them?) No, and some mountains, this shape (D2) [outlines shape with her fingers]. *D F A (P) D F N*

Card IX 3"

Nothing—7". Just a blob full of paint—only one thing, a bear's head (D6) that's all (?) Here's his eyes. *W C Color   D F Ad*

Card X 5"

Two spiders (D1) and two flowers (D2). (What makes it look like flowers?) Just this shape. *D F A P   D F Pl*

Cindy told the following stories to the CAT.

1. Some animals are eating their dinner and a rooster is up here. (What happens?) The rooster is getting at them. (Why?) 'Cause they're eating without her, 'cause they were hungry. (What happens next?) She looks like she's going to give them a spanking after dinner. (How do the children feel?) They feel happy, they look happy without her.

2. The father is pulling away from the mother bear and the baby bear. (How come?) He's probably mad at them. (About what?) They're taking the rope away from him. (What happens?) The father bear looks disappointed. (And how does the baby bear feel?) Like he was mad, like he was going to bite his daddy. (How come?) He don't want his father to have it. He wants his mother to have the rope.

3. The lion is smoking a pipe and a mouse is peeking out at the lion and the lion is in a chair and he has a stick by him. (What happens?) The lion is mad. (What about?) 'Cause his wife isn't cooking dinner and he doesn't have anything to put in his pipe. (What happens next?) He's just sitting there waiting for his wife. (And the mouse?) He's just staring at the lion.

4. The kangaroo is trying to beat the other kangaroo on the tricycle and the baby kangaroo is holding onto the balloon. The kangaroo is holding a basket with milk and food in it. There is a house back here and it has smoke, and some of the trees are all burned up. (What has happened?) Maybe she's mad at him. (How is that?) 'Cause he did something wrong. He played out too long (?) He might get a spanking. (Why?)

He's sad because he didn't get a ride like him.

5. Two bears are sleeping in a crib and a father bear and a mother bear are sleeping in a bed next to them and they're asleep—(What happened?)—I can't—(encouraged). The other bear is sleeping in the crib next—(a brother or a sister?) A brother—(They're in the same room with their parents?) They're not afraid of the things that could happen to them in their own room.

6. The mother and the father and the baby bear are sleeping in the cave. The father is sleeping next to the door so no one can come in. (What happens?) The baby is awake—(what does he do?) He's just laying down; then he gets up, and he probably tries to get out and the mother and the father wake him and they say, "What are you doing?" "I'm trying to go outside." "Never do that again."

7. The tiger is trying to get the monkey and the monkey let go of the rope, and the monkey's afraid so he'll be real afraid and he tries to get away—all I can make up about that one. (What happens?) The tiger might get the monkey.

8. The baby monkey is in bed so the mother is being real mean to him and the other mother is talking and having coffee. (What did he do bad?) He did something wrong over at a friend's house. They're all telling him to go to bed. (How does he feel?) He's sorry he did it. (How does he feel about going to bed?) He don't want to. (What could they be talking about?) They're glad he has to go to bed; it's his next-door neighbor and he don't like it. He did it. (What did his neighbor do?) [no response]

9. The rabbit's sleeping in his bed and he thinks something's happening. So he looks out of his room and doesn't see his parents—(?) He thought they were in the next room but they were out taking a walk—(How does he feel?) He thinks somebody took 'em away. (How does he feel?) Bad, 'cause he has no one to take care of him.

10. The mother puppy is spanking the baby puppy 'cause he was a bad boy and he is saying ow, ow, ow. (What did he do that was bad?) He didn't come home when his mother called him.

When the World Test was opened, Cindy seemed relatively uninterested. She searched lackadaisically and apathetically through the test objects in random fashion. Once or twice she turned back to a house she had set out and peered under it as if she were looking to see what was inside. She fiddled with one which had windows and doors to open, and then placing her face down close to it, she stared into the windows. Then she shrugged as if she had expected it to be empty and returned to the case. Although she picked up several of the human figures and held them for a second, she returned these to the case but became preoccupied with the animals. She smiled as she found the horses and began to search for other animals which she placed in a little pile separate from her line of houses. She seemed a little puzzled by the wild animals, quickly rejected the snake and the dinosaur, but placed some of the others in the same pile with the domestic animals. Finally she seemed to be satisfied with what she had selected and, turning around, she stood the animals up but without any particular arrangement. She did find the barn and sat that next to the animals and then sat quietly looking at what she had done. When asked what she had made, she shrugged again and said, "Nothing." Asked what the buildings were, she replied "Some houses and stuff." Asked about the animals, she said "They're just eating." She picked up the horses again and stared at them, and then began to put things back into the case.

The following report was sent to the pediatrician:

To the casual observer, Cindy's psychological development might seem quite average for her age. Intellectually, she is functioning at a normal pace. As disturbing as her environment may be, it does not seem to affect Cindy's ability to solve intellectual problems, to learn at school, or to understand intellectually the meaning of rules of the society about her. Her choice of words is sometimes a bit immature, but she can generally say what she means even though she is not very verbal. Like most children her age, she feels that facts are facts and there is not too much need to explain them. However, she shows no special intellectual curiosity nor imagination. It is perhaps in this respect that she may, on first impression, seem slightly dull.

Although not intellectually dull, Cindy does lack the natural spontaneity one might expect of a happy and outgoing child. It seems difficult for Cindy to really become interested in or excited about anything. Although she does not openly express any sadness, for a child this age, this apathy in itself does strongly suggest an underlying depressiveness. Even more strongly than most latency children, Cindy is very emotionally guarded. She avoids the emotional aspects of a situation as much as possible. By and large, the emotional pressures and stimulations in her environment seem to have little meaning to her. Similarly she tries not to permit her own impulses to have any affect on her. Cindy's neutralizing of emotional stimuli is so extensive that it would appear probable that any kind of affective stimuli may be threatening to her. It appears as though Cindy could not become emotionally involved with others, nor permit her own impulses and feelings to be openly expressed.

Behind her mask, Cindy does have some very strong affects and impulses. There are many associations in Cindy's responses that strongly suggest that the sexual stimulation which she has experienced may be very threatening and confusing to her. Cindy's actual sexual development is symbolized by one of her Rorschach responses, "a cocoon web"; that is, still in latency, Cindy is like a larvae encased in a cocoon, but as further indicated in her Rorschach response, things are stirring in this cocoon. Cindy experiences sexuality as "an ugly monster"; when faced directly with even a symbol of sex, she rejects it completely.

Cindy's fantasies suggest that there are other aspects of her experiences that are even more disturbing to her. One of the reasons that this child is so very emotionally guarded is that she has experienced many emotional separations. Repeatedly in her fantasies, people are rejecting or separating from one another. Sometimes Cindy seems to feel that children would be almost better off without having to depend upon parents. Nevertheless, emotional succorance is very important to Cindy. In her view, the main reason people feel angry is that they are not fed, cared for, and comforted. Cindy experiences her world as very empty and lacking in any organization or any human relationships. It would appear from both her history and her responses to the tests that the only positive emotional experience she has found has been through genital stimulation.

SUMMARY IMPRESSION: Deprived of continued and stable relationships, particularly those which supply infantile needs for comfort and affection, Cindy continues the only kind of emotional stimulation she has known. Thus, she substitutes sexual stimulation for human love and affection, albeit on a childish level. The history given by Cindy's mother suggests that this pattern probably has existed in her family for several generations.

Because Cindy's pattern of behavior is so

much a part and parcel of the life led by her mother and her mother's family, it would seem extremely difficult to make much change in Cindy's behavior as long as she is part of the milieu. However, Mrs. K does show some signs of wanting to make changes in her own behavior. She experiences considerable depression regarding her own situation and, although her history and responses to the MMPI suggest considerable instability, she may be motivated to consider changes in her own ways of living.

These results were then discussed with Mrs. K in a follow-up interview. She very readily accepted the recommendation that she herself should enter into psychotherapy but asked that Cindy be seen at the same time. She accepted a referral to another psychologist for the psychotherapy, and the assessor continued to see Cindy in weekly play sessions. During the first several months, Cindy remained very guarded but seemed to be gradually edging into a relationship with the therapist. The two therapists held periodic collaborative discussions; Mrs. K's therapist reported that as she proceeded to explore her feelings, she was becoming more and more depressed whereupon she continued to "act out," for example, she frequently missed appointments with her therapist or would call desperately for extra appointments thereafter. Only twice did she fail to bring Cindy to her appointments. Six months after the assessment, Mrs. K was badly injured in an automobile accident which scarred her face and required the amputation of one arm. While recuperating from this accident, she became openly psychotic, made another attack on her mother's life, and was committed to a state hospital. At this point, Cindy's father, whom she had really never seen, reappeared and sued Cindy's grandmother for custody of both children. The court asked for the advice from the psychologist who suggested that the children be made wards of the court and that foster homes be found for them. At this point, Cindy had not seen her therapist for several months; when they met in the court antechambers, Cindy immediately rushed into his arms and wept. She could not say why she was crying but obviously saw the therapist as a comforting person.

CASE 50

Billy B., aged three years nine months, was referred for psychological assessment by a neurologist who had examined Billy on referral from the child's pediatrician. Billy had two defects at birth: a "clubfoot" and a mild "ptosis" or weakening of the eyelid muscles. The foot deformity necessitated a specially built shoe. The drooping of his eyelids did give Billy a look of being sleepy or possibly dull. Billy's mother had worried that his motor development might be slowed and that he might be retarded. She revealed to the neurologist her fears that defects might be signs of a trauma to the central nervous system. In referring Billy for psychological assessment, the neurologist reported that Billy's nervous system seemed quite intact, that there was no sign of any central nervous system disorder, nor of inadequate motor functioning. He also remarked that Mrs. B seemed unduly anxious about Billy's development in general, and that he had found it difficult to reassure her that in his opinion Billy's defects did not reflect any weakness of the brain. Because of this, the neurologist thought that further assessment of Billy's perceptual motor and intellectual functioning might be in order and that some assessment might be necessary of the role of Mrs. B's anxiety.

In making the appointment over the telephone, Mrs. B was full of questions and requests. She wanted to know what type of tests would be used, explaining that she was receiving training as a teacher of the mentally handicapped and was familiar with some of the tests. She wanted to be reassured that the complete examination would be given. She wanted to know from the first how many examinations would be necessary and was concerned that they be arranged at a time convenient to both her and her husband. She was very pleasant and courteous in all these questions, but her concern did confirm the neurologist's impression that she had considerable anxiety about the situation. She seemed a little surprised when the psychologist requested that she and her husband come in without Billy for the first appointment, until it was explained to her that the psychologist did need further information from them regarding Billy's development.

After this initial interview with the parents, Billy was seen in two subsequent one-hour sessions, accompanied first by his mother and then by his father. On each occasion each parent filled in the MMPI while waiting for the child. Both parents were then seen together in a follow-up interview. The Stanford-Binet Intelligence Test, Form LM, parts of the Merrill-Palmer Scale of Mental Tests, the Rorschach Technique, the Lynn Structured Doll Play Test, and the World Test were administered to Billy. During the initial interview with the parents, the Vineland Social Development Scale was filled out.

On the Binet, Billy passed all items at the III-6 level, five items at year IV, five items at IV-6, four items at year V, four items at VI, one item at VII, one item at VIII. Because Billy was getting somewhat restless and expressed some feelings of disinterest in items far beyond his ability, none of the items at year IX were administered. Thus, on the Binet he achieved a Mental Age of 5 years 4 months, IQ 138. On the Merrill-Palmer, Billy completed such perceptual items as tthe mannikin, the little pink tower, the picture puzzle, the Sequin Form Board, and the buttoning of two buttons at the 4½ year level. His only actual failure below the 5 year level was the six cube pyramids (which does not appear on this test before age 4).

In administering the Rorschach to Billy, the inquiry was conducted simultaneously with the free associations. His responses were as follows.

Card I 2″
It's a mountain (?) All of it, a big mountain. *W F N*
Here's a gun, here's a gun, and here's a gun. [indicates D5 and D8] (What makes them look like a gun?) They're pointing. *D Fm obj*

Card II 2″
It's got red and that makes it fire. *D CF Fire*
And here's another gun, it shoots. [indicates D3] *d Fm Obj*

Card III 2″
This doesn't have any gun. Here's a butterfly (D2) and dead (?). *D F A P*
It's dead, that red stuff is the blood (D3) *D CF Blood*

Card IV 4″
There's no red, it's not dead. It's a plant 'cause it has that [points to D1] (?) The leaves. *W F Pl*

Card V 3″
It's a butterfly. —Hey! It's both sides, both the same. (?) Big wings and those things [puts fingers over his forehead indicating antenna] *W F A P*

Card VI [Billy glances at the card and then looks at the ceiling] (What do you see on the card?) [still looking at the ceiling] 20″

It's spiderish, every part of it [looking again at the card and points to D3] It's too scary. *DW F A*

Card VII 5″
Too icky! Looks like some blood (?) All icky [rubs hand across card and slaps it]. *D c Blood*

Card VIII 3″
Goody, it has colors, blue, red, orange, pink, blue, and some green. *W C n Color*
Here's a stick, D1, or a fish, also D1. *D F Obj*
D F A

Card IX 7″
Yellow. Why is that broke (?) The yellow is broke [points to space between D23]. *D Cn, m Color*

Card X 6″
An octopus, D1. *D F A P*
And an archer. *D F H O*
And candles. *D F Obj O*

Billy was fascinated with the Structured Doll Play materials. In the first setting he decided that the child figure should sleep in a bed: "He's a bigger boy and doesn't have to be a baby no more" and thus not in the crib. He decided that a mother and father would have their own separate bedroom and that there was no place for either in the bed " 'cause the boy's sleeping in it." He also decided that the boy would drink from a glass and not a bottle and added that "he walks around the town with the boy; they've got to move to another house 'cause it's prettier than the one they have." (Later Mrs. B explained that the family had recently moved from an apartment to a home of their own.) On the peer choice, Billy decided that the boy should play with the boy and described the play as walking, kissing one another" 'cause they like to." Asked what else they do, he said, "They play and they fight and they open up wide." He decided that the boy would play similarly with the girl. In the fighting situation, Billy got very excited and did not at first want to join the assessor in making dolls fight, but then seemed to enjoy making a bigger fight than was illustrated to him. His verbalization at this point was a little difficult to understand: "The army check, one has to go to the army check and this boy doesn't, he's going off to his car." When the parent figures were introduced into the fighting scene, Billy had the mother say, "Why did you do that?" and then the mother doll spanked the little boy. He was less sure of what father would do and, when pressed,

RORSCHACH SUMMARY — CASE 50

Location		Determinants		Content	
W	$= 1$	M	$= 0$	H	$= 1$
DW	$= 1$	FM	$= 0$	Hd	$= 0$
D	$= 11$	m	$= 2 + 1$	A	$= 5$
d	$= 1$	F	$= 10$	Obj	$= 4$
R	$= 17$	c	$= 1$	N	$= 1$
		CF	$= 2$	$Fire$	$= 1$
		Cn	$= 2$	$Blood$	$= 1$
				Pl	$= 2$
P	$= 3$	$EB = 0.5 = 70E$		$Color$	$= 2$
O	$= 2$				

said, "Nothing." In the feeding scene, Billy chose the father to feed the boy figure and when asked how the boy liked the food, he remarked "He doesn't; he hates it and runs away." (What does the father do?) "He catches him; he comes back to eat." In the injury setting, Billy also selected the father to "come and take him on his arms" when the boy fell and hurt his leg. However, when the mother was introduced, Billy said in a high-pitched imitation of his own mother's voice, "I like you still but I don't like you falling," and Billy had the child reply, "I hooked you," and the mother, "I smacked you." (smacked?) "Not kissing," said Billy. In the pursuit scene, Billy chose first the mother and he had the mother and the child both fall down (?) "The mother didn't know what happened but there is a good elevator on the mommy and the boy came up," and Billy tried to place the boy doll in the mother doll's arms. When the father was introduced, the father continued to chase the boy with gales of laughter and when asked why the father was chasing the boy, he replied " 'cause he likes to." In the reprimand scene, he had the mother reprimand the child because "he fell and cried" and the father reprimand the child because "you hit." In the parental relationship scene, Billy had the parents face each other and decided they were going to change their clothes and go out and pick up the boy. Similarly, in the separation scene, he chose the mother and had her first put on a jacket and go pick up the daddy at school. This scene was repeated when the father was introduced, that is, the boy and father went

to pick up the mother at school. (Both parents were university graduate students and alternately cared for Billy while the other was in classes.) In the hospital scene, Billy decided that the doll boy was bad because he had cried about the shot. He had the father figure say, "You've been a bad boy at the hospital and you can hang up your jacket everyday." He had the mother doll take the boy out of the bed but remarked, "He did not get anything," indicating that the boy doll did not get any reward. In the toilet scene, Billy had the boy doll go to the toilet by himself and remarked with evident pride in his voice, "He used to go to the potty, now he goes here" (pointing to the toilet). In the bathing scene, Billy did not seem to perceive any difference or show any affect regarding placing of the girl and boy dolls in the same bathtub. Time prevented the administration of the nightmare scene. Using Lynn's preliminary standards, these results suggested that Billy was maturing fairly well in his personal and social relationships. He was evidently interested in developing independent need-gratification skills. It did appear that Billy was beginning to identify with his father, that is, he saw the father as a companion, who even fed him and controlled his eating habits. Quite noticeably, Billy thought of his mother as being threatened if he was hurt, injured, or cried. Most important, Billy thought that his mother equated being hurt with being "bad."

Billy was fascinated with the World Test materials and dug into the case with great glee, tossing objects out almost without glancing at them. After he had emptied most of the box, he set about arranging and rearranging them, stopping at various points to play with objects such as the cars, train, airplane, and soldiers. He lined up the buildings in several lines, asking the assessor to identify some of them. He selected some of the children and placed them around the school, and posted adult human figures at various points beside the buildings. He put the domestic and wild animals around the barn but put obviously aggressive animals such as the snake and dinosaur back in the chest. Although he played with the soldiers and some of the military equipment, he did not include these in his World but left them off to one side of his main scene. After constructing his World, he continued to move cars and the train and people up and down the streets of his village. He talked a great deal while he was working, identifying various pieces and remarking on them. He noted that the children were going to school; he had people going to the store, the hospital, and the church. He asked to have the jail identified and included it in the village, but seemed to pay very little attention to it. All in all, his play seemed quite spontaneous and happy.

In the initial interview, Mrs. B seemed quite tense. She was dressed rather plainly in dark clothes, wore little or no cosmetics, and her hair was tied together at the nape of her neck with a bun. She spoke rather rapidly and sharply, but nevertheless raising her voice at the end of the sentence as if asking a question. Her husband, although dressed in a suit and a tie, was so blonde and so slightly built that he appeared almost ten years younger than his stated age of 30. Although Mr. B was an elementary school principal, it would have been easier to imagine that he was a camp counselor. Neither parent spoke for a moment, but Mrs. B gave her husband a glance indicating that she wanted him to initiate the discussion. He remarked that "we" were worried when Billy's foot defect was discovered at birth and had become more disturbed when approximately three months later the eyelid ptosis was definitely established. He quickly added that he had not noticed any particular difficulties in Billy's development thereafter, but that he thought the complete assessments currently being conducted by the neurologist and the psychologist were quite necessary. Asked why he felt the examinations to be necessary, he indicated that he hoped that the examinations would end any further concerns; pressed further to voice his concerns, he shrugged and pointed at his wife.

Mrs. B's facial expression and gesture and tone of voice suggested that she was dissatisfied with her husband's statements. When the psychologist remarked on this, Mrs. B replied tartly that she thought her husband might not always observe some of Billy's difficulties, since he was not responsible for Billy's care as frequently as she. Moreover, she thought that her husband had a general tendency to brush aside and avoid anything unpleasant. Mr. B nodded in agreement, adding that he might be trying to gloss over things and that his wife did have more opportunity to observe Bill. (The assessor noted to himself that Mrs. B referred to her son with the diminutive *Billy,* while her husband referred to him as *Bill.*) When Mrs. B tried to describe her concerns about Billy's development, she was quite vague. She remarked that he seemed somewhat clumsy and then gave as evidence that he had not been successful in riding the two-wheeled bicycle which belonged to his six-year-old cousin. Billy was able to ride a tricycle and attempted to use skates (Mrs. B remarked on this with a note of horror in her voice) and loved to play on such equipment as slides and swings. His father quickly added that Bill enjoyed tossing and attempting to catch a ball which he thought was possibly above average for a child not yet four years old. Mrs. B agreed that Billy loved to try many activities and seemed relatively successful at them, but she explained that he was always falling or scratching or bruising himself. Asked how Billy reacted when he was hurt, she voiced the opinion that maybe he had something wrong with him, since he seldom complained of any pain. She remarked further that some of his bumps and bruises had caused him to limp further. Twice she felt that he had broken his arm, although when they went to the hospital emergency room, she was angered when the doctors informed her that the x-rays were negative and that he had merely a mild "contusion." Asked if Billy's club foot had proved to be of any great handicap to him, she remarked immediately that "of course, one worries more about a crippled child."

The psychologist then asked Mr. B specifically what he thought about this, and after some hesitation he replied that he did not see that Bill seemed particularly handicapped, but added quickly that he could understand his wife's concern. The parents were then interviewed regarding the specific items of the Vineland Social Development Scale. Both parents agreed that Billy could feed himself, dress himself, bathe himself, and tend to his needs at toilet with little or no supervision. They described him as exceedingly sociable, that he enjoyed showing off to adults, performing little tasks and household chores, and playing with peers, almost at the kindergarten level. They remarked that he particularly enjoyed being the company of adults, such as shopping with his parents or accompanying them on various errands. They were very proud of his behavior in public, remarking that they knew of no child who behaved himself as well as Billy did in restaurants or primarily adult settings.

As to Billy's developmental history, he was born when Mrs. B was 28 and her husband 26. They had been married approximately three years and had used birth control methods in order to avoid having children until after Mr. B completed his master's degree at the university and had obtained a job as a school vice principal. Until that time, Mrs. B had herself been employed as a school teacher, but once Mr. B was working she resigned with the purpose of having a child. Thus, Billy appeared to be both a planned and wanted child. Mrs. B reported that during her pregnancy she was frequently ill and had continued mild vaginal "spotting." Her labor pains began three days prior to Billy's birth although they were not continuous. Otherwise his birth was uneventful and initially he appeared to be a normal healthy neonate. His clubfoot was noticed several days after birth and Mrs B admitted that she was quite disappointed about this defect from the first and remarked that at the time she even found herself worrying that perhaps she had done something wrong in her dieting and exercise during her pregnancy which might have caused this defect. She breastfed Billy for approximately four months, but her breasts were exceedingly tender. Due to Billy's avid hunger, nursing him often was quite painful to her. Her obstetrician suggested that Billy be put on a bottle formula and that breast feeding did not seem necessary in view of the difficulty that she was experiencing. From the first, she was gratified that Billy seemed to be an alert and active baby, kicking and squirming, reaching and pulling, and attentive to any face that appeared over his crib or to footsteps that entered the room.

She had kept a baby book on his progress which she had brought with her. Her notes showed that in general Billy's motor development was at least normal, if not precocious. He was sitting up almost without support by age 3 months, pulling himself erect to his feet at 6 months, and attempting to walk holding onto things at approximately 10½ months. Her notes were not definite but as far as could be ascertained, he was walking by the time he was one year old. Since that time, "He has always been into things, and on the go." Her notes indicated that he had spoken his first words at age 8 months, but when questioned further she agreed that these were sounds such as "mamma," but that he seemed to understand both "go" and "come" and "potty" by the time he was walking. However, he first spoke words clearly somewhere between 18 and 24 months. By the time he was two, he was definitely speaking two and three word combinations. Mrs. B remarked very proudly that although she had feared that Billy might be difficult to toilet train, since he seemed to her so active and willful, it turned out that he almost toilet trained himself. He seemed to be a great imitator and had entered the bathroom and watched his father urinate whereupon he tried to ape him. He was then provided with a potty of his own and proceeded to use it almost exclusively for urination and a second potty was given him for defecation. She went on to remark that they did not realize how much children learn through imitation and that by and large Billy had acquired all his skills by observing and imitating them.

When the assessor remarked with some amazement on the rapidity of Billy's development of these motor and social skills, and particularly of his ability to imitate without much further training, Mrs. B quickly retracted her note of pride and remarked that she had observed similar abilities among retarded children whom she regarded also as "great imitators." Thus, she did not feel that Billy's development was any sign of intellectual development and she was still concerned lest he might turn out to be retarded.

Both parents readily accepted the assessor's request for information about their own background. Mrs. B was the oldest of five children born and reared in a rural village in a western desert state. Both of her parents were school teachers. Her next younger brother suffered a spasticity of his entire left side, probably from a birth injury. His care and management was of considerable concern to Mrs. B's mother, and Mrs. B was instructed by both parents to watch out for this brother at school. However, it turned out that her brother was quite capable of caring for himself in many ways. He was a bright boy who ultimately succeeded in completing a university education and at that time was employed as a geologist which entailed traveling over mountainous territory on horseback. One other younger brother was also frequently ill with asthma, and Mrs. B also helped her mother care for this brother as well as her baby sister who was 16 years her junior. Since both of Mrs. B's parents were employed full-time, a great deal of the care of the house and the younger children fell on Mrs. B's shoulders. She denied that she was at all concerned about this or ever resented it, but rather now regarded it as excellent training for becoming a mother. She added that she might have had more resentment about being tied down with home duties had it not been that she lived in a rural area where there were not as many places to go or things for a teenager to do. After she completed elementary school, she commuted to high school and then junior college in a nearby city, so that she did not actually leave home until age 19 when she decided to attend the university.

Mr. B was the youngest of three boys, born and reared in the city where the B's were currently living. His father also was a high school teacher and later a high school principal, but his mother did not work outside the home. As far as he could remember, his childhood was relatively uneventful. He remembered scrapping with his brothers but remarked that his two older brothers were more likely to fight among themselves than with him. He felt his mother was somewhat overprotective but that he and his brothers were able to avoid some of the mother's demand for cautiousness by obtaining their father's support. He remembered particularly that the mother was almost adamant that he should not play school football and was quite angry with his father who signed the permit without further discussion. Mr. B was active in sports, earning varsity letters in both swimming and football. He remarked that he did

not consider himself any great football player but that he had been quite obese and therefore had been a good block. In telling this, he seemed to enjoy this joke upon himself. He remained somewhat active in sports, although not going out for varsity teams in college. The B's had met while attending the university. Mrs. B remarked that she had first noticed him because he was an excellent dancer and she did not see how anyone as heavy set as he could dance so smoothly. In mentioning Mr. B's weight, he explained that he had at one time been seriously overweight but that in recent years he had been able to diet and lose weight to the point where his doctor felt he was at least within normal range for his height.

Following Billy's birth, Mrs. B had found herself bored and restless at home as Billy seemed to demand so little care. Thus, she began to look for extra things to do. She had volunteered to work with intellectually retarded children and finally decided that she would return to graduate school for some training in the special education of retarded children. She thus was attending two classes weekly. At approximately the same time, Mr. B received an inheritance which enabled him to take a leave of absence from his teaching position and return full-time to the university working toward a doctorate in education. He, too, was particularly interested in the education of handicapped children.

On the MMPI, two of Mrs. B's scale scores were above 70 (*D* and *Pd*) and two more were between 65 and 70 (*Hy* and *Pt*). The remainder of her scores were within the normal range. Her *K* score was 60, while *L* and *F* were both just below 50. This profile suggested that Mrs. B possibly had more rebellious and angry feelings and that there might be more dissension in the B's marriage than was indicated in this initial interview. It also suggested that she was an obsessive worrier, a person who is easily affected by guilt feelings, and that she tended to blame herself more than she blamed others.

In contrast, Mr. B's MMPI profile was almost unremarkable. His highest scale was at the *MA* which was at 55 and all other scales were close to 50.

The following report was sent to the neurologist:

In all areas of psychological development, Billy is markedly precocious. Intellectually, he is functioning at the 5 year 4 month level with an IQ of 138. Although the parents raised the question of a possible perceptual-motor defect, Billy's visual-motor development is actually advanced for his age. His social development is also more comparable to kindergarten than nursery school level. He feeds himself, dresses himself, is completely toilet trained, and plays with peers at the kindergarten level. Emotionally, also, Billy is developing very rapidly. He is already cognizant of the need for impulse control and shows signs of making efforts toward self-regulation of his impulses. He reflects his mother's anxiety over him in his doll play where his mother equates "getting hurt" with "being bad." His doll play further suggested that he is attempting to establish a masculine relationship with his father whom he also regards as a protector against injury. He playacted the busy schedule of his parents in which he is obviously involved, but showed little sign that any tension arises from these family activities. Billy's father raised little question about Billy's development and the concern was largely Mrs. B's. Her responses both to the MMPI and during the interview suggested that she worries excessively and is easily upset and made anxious. Her anxiety particularly concerning Billy's physical development is probably based in part on the fact that she was responsible for the care of ill and disabled siblings when she was younger, a concern which is still reflected in her interest in the education of the mentally retarded. This particular preoccupation may be associated with some of Mrs. B's feelings of guilt, particularly surrounding expressions of anger or of independence. Her current situation suggests that she might very well feel guilty about continuing her own education and her professional ambitions and might be using imagined difficulties in Billy as a rationale for such guilt. In discussing these findings with Mr. and Mrs. B, the disparity between Mrs. B's concerns about Billy and the findings of the test were noted directly with her and some of her overtly expressed feelings of tension and depression were remarked on further. She noted at this time that she had become so tense several months ago that she had requested her physician to give her a prescription for tranquilizers. He had recommended at the same time that she seek psychological consultation. This recommendation was reinforced at this courrent interview and Mrs. B seemed relatively accepting of it.

Part V

ASSESSMENT
AND RECOMMENDATIONS

Chapter 18

ASSESSMENT FOR PSYCHOTHERAPY

A. INTRODUCTION

As was stated in Chapter 1, the ultimate aim of any clinical assessment is to provide information about the child's ego development that may be useful in making decisions about the future of the child. It is in this sense that an assessment is a professional activity, similar to the legal investigations preceding judicial decisions, the medical diagnosis needed before prescription of treatment, or the geodetic survey preparatory to mining operations. As was also discussed in Chapter 1, the corollary of this practical aim of assessment is that there should be a potential choice of decisions. If every problem is handled with the same treatment, assessment is superfluous. On the other hand, assessment may be used not only to make decisions regarding the methods of changing the child's behavior or relieving his stress, but it also is usually necessary to plan the variations within the method of change as selected. Thus, for example, should one decide that psychoanalytically oriented therapy is the preferred method, the assessment data should also be used in planning this psychotherapy, for example, its frequency, the problems that should be explored first, the nature of the child's defenses, the degree of anxiety that might motivate—or overwhelm

—the child, etc. If one were planning to seek a foster home for a child, a survey of the child's ego functioning is essential in order to know what kind of home he might need or how he might adjust to a proposed home. Assessment thus implies that any treatment or change in the child's milieu should be planned to fit the needs of the child. Logically, this fitting of the treatment to the diagnosis has two requirements: (1) There should be a method of treatment possible for the problem, and (2) the treatment should be relatively specific as to that problem.

In practice, unfortunately, neither of these criteria is ever completely satisfied. There are major problems in child development for which no method of behavioral or environmental change has had notable success. For example, no single method of treatment or even combinations of methods has yet been found which makes any major changes in the ego functioning of a chronically retarded child—even where this failure to develop has little or no organic component and is demonstrably psychogenic and sociogenic. Similarly, that hypertrophied and distorted growth of the ego known as childhood schizophrenia seldom yields to the best planned and implemented treatment programs. These statements are not intended to discourage plans for treating childhood schizophrenia or functional retardation. On the contrary, when such major disturbances do severely limit the child's development, attempts to stimulate growth should be carefully planned. In fact, in the assessment of a severely disturbed or retarded child, the question is seldom merely one of diagnosis, but one in which the central concern is for signs of any potential growth or rehabilitation. A careful assessment often makes it possible to plan some practical relief for a child, even when his future looks entirely hopeless.

CASE 51

Sam, age 16, had been completely blind since birth and was considered to be severely retarded. For almost ten years he had been cared for in what was called a "school" but which was really a private nursing home. Neither of the parents could emotionally accept Sam's severe disabilities, but both felt guilty over having rejected him. Both attempted to maintain the delusion that Sam was not intellectually retarded, even though over the years several psychologists had previously advised them that his intellectual development was extremely slow and the prognosis very poor. The school provided excellent physical care and comforts, but such training program as was available was quite superficial. He had been taught to sing kindergarten songs in a childish voice—but at 16 he was not toilet trained and could not feed himself, nor find his way across a room he had lived in for ten years—much less go from one building to the next unguided, as one might expect. The attendants at this little institution waited on Sam hand and foot in a kindly, motherly fashion. In effect, they infantilized him.

As evidence of Sam's intelligence, his mother cited the fact that he remembered songs, remembered his parents (although they visited scarcely every 60 days), and even fantasied about his life prior to being at the school. When Sam was seen by the assessor, it seemed as if he did not recognize that anyone was in the room, even though spoken to several times. However, upon being touched, he did gradually begin to explore the assessor's arm and then his face. All the time he rocked back and forth in the chair, muttering something unintelligible or singing snatches of the songs he had learned. When objects were handed to him, he felt them momentarily and threw them on the floor.

However, when candy was handed to him, he recognized it and quickly popped it in his mouth, making noises of enjoyment. Obviously, the formal methods of testing intelligence were out of the question. The assessor continued to hand each of the inserts to the Seguin Form Board to Sam, to give him an opportunity to become familiar with their shape—even though they ended up on the floor. This process was repeated several times. Then the empty board was placed in front of Sam and his fingers were placed into the slots and run around their contours one at a time for several times. Then he was shown how an insert fitted into the slots, beginning with such simple forms as the circle, square, and triangle. Each time Sam succeeded in making a correct response, he was rewarded with candy. In approximately an hour and a half, Sam had learned to complete the entire Seguin without error. He seemed overjoyed with this new game and kept playing with it for another half hour. Each time he was successful, although he needed over five minutes for each completion. For each successive correct response, he was rewarded.

Although the only data that were available regarding Sam's intellectual functioning were the alleged facts that he "had a long-range memory" and that he could learn to perform very simple tasks, it did seem quite feasible that some attempt could be made to teach him a great deal more in the way of self-help skills. When this was discussed with the school, the director was pessimistic and quite defensive. Finally, she admitted that she and her elderly staff had no knowledge of or time for such methods of training. She felt that Sam had outgrown this school and was insistent that he be removed. Finally, she admitted with considerable embarrassment that since he had reached puberty, he occasionally masturbated in front of the other younger children.

Sam's parents were initially quite upset over the recommendation that he be put in a state hospital where there was a behavioral training program. To accept such a recommendation was an open admission of his severe retardation. Moreover, they could no longer merely assuage their guilt by the monthly payments to the school. However, the director readily agreed with this recommendation and insisted that the parents find some other living situation for Sam. Six months later he was admitted to the hospital for the retarded, and within the following year, according to his mother's report, Sam was toilet trained and was feeding himself. "The last time I saw him," she said with amazement, "he wouldn't even let me help him put on his coat!"

Even where a child's developmental problems do seem remediable, the fact remains that in many instances there is no treatment nor environmental treatment specifically designed for particular problems. Most psychotherapies, most environmental manipulation, and even most psychotropic drugs are not specific antedotes, but are rather general methods of attempting to ameliorate a wide variety of human problems. The adherents of most forms of treatment claim that their approach is applicable to many forms of behavioral disturbances. Moreover, therapists are inclined to try the form of treatment at which they are most skilled—even if there are indications that some other approach with which they are unfamiliar might be more effective. Although there are some indications that skill may be almost more important than the therapeutic theory (at least as regards treatment of adults with verbal interviews), such a viewpoint does discourage the introduction of and experimentation with new approaches. Of course, many of the disorders of development are fairly generalized, and most children present a variety of symptoms. Assessment usually reveals that although there may be a major disturbance of one function of the ego, other functions are consequently imbalanced. Thus, in many cases, the use of an approach which does seem to be effective with a wide variety of problems might be justified.

As will be discussed subsequently, it is possible to derive the general criteria for using each of the various therapeutic approaches. Far too often these criteria are stated only vaguely by the advocates of the particular approach, or have to be drawn from the literature. Even less frequently do the proponents of any particular method specify the contraindications for use of their approach. The fact that psychoanalytically oriented therapy proved not to be the complete and only possible treatment of emotional disturbances, as was once claimed by some of Freud's followers, led to the development of other methods of treatment, such as Client-Centered Counselling and Behavior Modification. Until more research is carried out on the specific processes and results of each of these various treatments, the most practical way of resolving the question of the treatment of choice is through a thorough assessment. Although each of these methods of therapy are based on somewhat different theories and deal with slightly different aspects of behavior, within their theoretical and practical limits, there is considerable variation in practice. Thus, it is quite possible to spell out from an assessment the needs and defenses of a child, so that direction may be given to any kind of treatment. The cases of two quite different "juvenile delinquents" may serve as examples of how assessment aids in selection of treatment.

CASE 52

The assessment indicated that Kevin was a bright, sensitive, and extremely angry 15 year old who seemed bent on destroying both himself and his family by his repeated clashes with the law. Like the hero of Lindner's *Rebel Without A Cause* (1944), this boy ached for a struggle with a male figure in order to free himself from the guilt aroused in his relationship with his overprotective, ill mother. These internal "dynamics" were so well defined in Kevin's responses that a psychoanalvtic approach seemed most applicable. (See discussion in paragraph D, this chapter.) Although the prognosis for a psychoanalytically oriented therapy seemed poor for any boy who had been on probation for numerous offenses for three years and who, at the point of the assessment, was being seriously considered by the Court of placement in a state reformatory, the assessor nevertheless recommended that such treatment be attempted with a therapist with whom the boy had made an initial contact and with whom he seemed to enjoy sparring. Further, the assessor suggested that there should be some limits on behavior agreed upon between the boy and therapist and that the therapist should be alert to warn Kevin against acting out when he felt threatened by depression or was angry at the therapist. Even so, it was predicted that the therapist probably would not be able to begin much uncovering of the boy's conflicts for quite some period until there was evidence that the boy felt comfortable and accepted by the therapist. Six months later, Kevin was still in twice weekly therapy sessions, and there had been only one critical incident; he had left the therapist one evening, depressed and angry because he thought the therapist had "made a crack about" his mother. At two A.M. the next morning, the patient called the therapist to announce he was going to commit suicide but allowed himself to be talked into meeting the therapist in his office. After 18 months, Kevin's rebellion seemed to slow down. He had had no further brushes with the law and was talking about going to college.

CASE 53

Stanley, who was about the same age as Kevin, and whose delinquencies were similar, proved—during the assessment—to be almost unapproachable through any verbal contacts. Although of at least average intelligence, he was almost retarded when he tried to verbalize his feelings or ideas and had equal difficulty in comprehending what others were trying to express. Unlike Kevin, Stanley was far less rebellious and much more amenable to the firm setting of limits and discipline. Unfortunately, these limits could not be set by his kindly but passive grandmother, who was responsible for his care. Based on this assessment, Stanley's probation officer was able to find a foster home which accepted the boy's needs and at the same time provided the regulation which he has sought. When limits were placed on him, he conformed without question.

Kevin would have attempted to disrupt any foster home in the same fashion in which he wreaked havoc in his own family. Stanley could have sat through endless hours of psychotherapy with negative results.

An individualized course of treatment planned for the specific needs of the child often entails the utilization of a mixture of methods. The needs of any one child are usually so complex that any one approach seldom suffices. Planning such treatment is not a simple task. Although it does require that a therapist be able to draw on a number of methods, his "eclecticism" cannot be based on a simple random sampling of possible approaches but should involve a knowledge of the various possibilities of each. The way in which such planning of treatment might operate is discussed at a later point in this chapter.

Another variable in the planning of therapy on the basis of assessment is the limited range of skills possessed by most therapists. Ethically, psychologists are required to limit their practice to the kinds of children's problems with which they are familiar and the methods of treatment in which they are trained. However, when a child's difficulties do not appear treatable by the methods immediately available, the child is often labeled "a bad risk" or "poor candidate" for psychotherapy. For example, those child guidance clinics whose staffs are psychoanalytically oriented often tend to reject children who are intellectually slow or brain damaged or who "act out." Little thought may be given to other kinds of remedial approaches which might help the poor candidate. There is the implication that "poor risk" means "untreatable." Similar attitudes may be found in agencies or hospitals with other orientations. However, the assessing psychologist cannot restrict his considerations to the range of therapies immediately available. Rather, he is ethically obligated to detail the needs of the child and make recommendations about possible methods of changing the child's behavior or environment without regard to the theoretical orientation or skills of the agency. When the child's needs cannot be met by the referrant, the assessor should recommend that the child be referred to a more appropriate agency.

Unfortunately, the kinds of treatment needed by children are not available at all in many instances. Child guidance clinics usually receive many more requests for assessment and treatment than they can possibly handle. Only a few families can afford private care. Residential treatment centers for children, public or private, are nonexistent in most communities, even in some metropolitan areas. Even the primarily custodial institutions for retarded or psychotic children have long waiting lists, dating back many months. Clinics and hospitals are likely to be located in large urban communities, and children who reside outside these areas must travel many miles if they are to receive treatment.

Thus, in recommending therapeutic or environmental interventions, the assessor has to consider this problem of the availability of resources. This "economic" question, as it may be called, may arise under several different conditions. When a clinic or hospital has a waiting list for admission, the assessor may be asked to state the urgency for treatment. Although some clinics consider each case in turn, first come, first served, most do attempt to give priority to those children who: (1) show most promise of being helped by the kinds of treatment available, (2) are most critically in need of the available treatment, and (3) cannot find treatment elsewhere. Quite often the data from an assessment can be helpful in considering each of these criteria for admission to a clinic or hospital. Whether a child's problems are "critical" or "more critical" than those of some other applicant for treatment is often a heart-rending question for which there are no really rational, satisfying criteria. Many clinics are prone to give priority to the child and family who are experiencing a crisis, chiefly because when under stress they are likely to be highly motivated and less resistant to change. On the other hand, the child whose problems are relatively static, who does not seem likely to deteriorate rapidly or become an immediate social problem, is more likely to wind up on the waiting list. Unfortunately, if such criteria are too rigidly applied, the waiting list may consist of children whose chronic problems become gradually more severe, and whose parents, despairing of help, become less motivated or become inured to the child's behavior.

The question of whether treatment is available elsewhere may seem more the province of the social worker than the psychologist. However, the psychologist should be familiar with other resources in the community and the possibility that the family might use them. For example, a psychoanalytically oriented clinic probably should not accept an intellectually retarded child, even on a waiting list, but should take time to carefully counsel the parents and encourage them to apply at a more appropriate agency. An agency designed for treatment of juvenile delinquents might well be justified in referring a psychotic child to another agency, even though the child be on probation from a court, because the agency's staff is sorely needed by children whose problems cannot be treated elsewhere. Similarly, children should not be placed in hospitals or residential treatment centers if their problems can be handled in outpatient facilities. Nor should they be kept in an inpatient facility any longer than is absolutely necessary. Careful and repeated assessment of children in inpatient centers is often a vital part of the information needed to decide whether hospitalization should be continued.

In most instances, the fact that parents accept a recommendation to seek psychological assessment does indicate that there is some crucial problem to be treated or that some change appears needed in the child's environment. Until recently, most parents did not accept the need for psychological help until the child's behavior became seriously unmanageable. However, over the past decade, an increasing number of parents have become aware of psychological aspects of child development through the educational programs of television, magazines, and other media. As a result, more parents are seeking psychological consultations about problems in child-rearing and child behavior which most parents formerly ignored. No doubt, if attention can be given to these relatively minor problems, it may be possible to prevent them from possibly becoming major deterrents to development. If treatment can be instituted early, it may be much more possible to help many children who might otherwise become so handicapped that no treatment would be effective. The assessment of these seemingly less severe behavioral complaints thus assumes considerable importance.

The consciousness of the public about psychological problems has also served to aggravate the difficulties of already overburdened facilities. When assessing a child whose immediate problems and development do not seem critical, the psychologist may be called upon to make some recommendation as to whether such a child should be put on a waiting list or whether the parents might be encouraged to undergo the expense of privately financed treatment. Many parents do struggle to meet such costs, curtailing family expenses, drawing on savings, or going into debt. Such a recommendation by the assessor should therefore not be made lightly or routinely. As public and private insurance coverage for "mental health" increases, very likely this question of the need for treatment will become even more crucial. With increasing frequency psychologists are asked the following types of questions: Does this child need any treatment at all? Will brief consultation with the parents suffice? Might brief treatment, perhaps combined with some environmental change, be enough? If the child changes schools (or makes some other environmental change), will his behavior change for the better? Should the parents be encouraged to invest considerable time and money in treatment for the child or themselves? The following case illustrates how these questions arise and how they may be handled.

CASE 54

Mrs. B had sought consultation regarding her son, Tony, age seven, from a public child guidance clinic but had been advised on the initial contact that the clinic served only those who could not afford private treatment. Since the B's income was over $10,000, the clinic referred her to a psychologist in private practice. Mrs. B was aware of the fees currently charged by private practtitioners in the community and when she contacted the psychologist, she mentioned—with some embarrassment—that she was afraid that the family might not be able to afford prolonged treatment. The psychologist invited Mrs. B and her husband to come in for a brief initial consultation at no fee, to discuss Tony's problems and the question of the cost of treatment.

In this 20-minute meeting, the psychologist learned that both Mr. and Mrs. B were quite worried because Tony was "acting up" at school and thus not achieving. They were also concerned because Tony was very resistant to accepting Mr. B, his stepfather, whom Mrs. B had married two years previously. Mr. B had completed law school just before his marriage, and although he was already becoming established in his legal practice, the family had incurred considerable expenses in purchasing a new home and furnishings. Mrs. B had quit the secretarial position that she had held before her marriage in order to devote her energies to caring for Tony and the home—and now her second child, Margie, born only two months previously. The psychologist informed the B's that he could not advise them about Tonly until he had an opportunity to assess Tony and the situation. This assessment, he estimated, would consist of one further discussion with them and two sessions with Tony, after which he would discuss his findings with them. The fee for this assessment was agreed upon at that time.

In the subsequent hour with Mrs. B, the psychologist inquired chiefly about the circumstances surrounding the complaint and

Tony's prior development. Tony was born when Mrs. B was 20, about 16 months after her marriage to her high school sweetheart. A year later, Tony's father, a fighter pilot, was killed in combat. Tony had barely seen his father and remembered him only as the hero in uniform in the picture on the living-room table—a picture Tony now kept in his room. Mrs. B's mother had died during Mrs. B's childhood, and she had not wanted to live with her alcoholic and dependent father, so she accepted an invitation from her husband's parents to reside with them. She had known them for many years, was fond of both of them, and was treated by them as a daughter. However, she was careful to emphasize, it had been mutually agreed that she was to have the major responsibility for Tony's care and discipline. In retrospect, she felt that they were respectful of her rights and duties as a mother. She had not gone to work until Tony was old enough to be in nursery school. She thus had taken the major responsibility for his care and training during his first three years. To the best of her memory, he was a cheerful, happy baby who developed rapidly without noticeable difficulty. Her in-laws encouraged her to date and seek a second husband. They liked Mr. B who visited the home many times before the B's were married. During their courtship, Tony once openly expressed a desire that Mr. B become his "Daddy," even before Mr. B had proposed to Mrs. B. The prospective marriage was discussed with Tony, and he seemed delighted. Yet, as the wedding date neared, Tony had become increasingly anxious, asking many questions but not waiting for answers. Several times he announced that he had decided to remain with his grandparents, but then quickly changed his mind. Initially, Tony liked his new home and was friendly with Mr. B, but soon it became evident that he held back when Mr. B attempted to be affectionate and completely ignored any discipline from him. He became furious when his mother insisted that he obey his stepfather. At these moments, Tony would demand that he return to his grandparents. Mr. B felt hurt and angry, and although the B's did not openly quarrel, there was considerable tension between them over Tony. During Mrs. B's pregnancy, Tony was so resistant that they did yield and frequently permitted him to visit the grandparents over the weekends. After such visits, Tony was usually well-behaved and congenial for several days. After Margie was born, even the visits to the grandparents did not help, and they also complained that Tony was surly and disobedient.

Tony proved to be an intellectually bright and talkative youngster, who openly discussed his family situation. Although he said he liked Mr. B, he admitted that he resented his stepfather's discipline. Repeatedly in his MAPS responses, the ghost was the hero, who rescued the boy character from an intruder; Superman prevented various villains from attacking female figures; a boy who had "lost his parents on the desert" was found and cared for by an elderly couple; finally, in the graveyard scene, a military figure came out of the tomb to rejoin a grieving woman and boy! Tony's drawing of his family did not include his sister, but he added in his grandparents to one side. On the Bene-Anthony, he did admit his sister into the family—but not the grandparents. He attributed most positive feelings, both incoming and outgoing, to his mother; only three responses were given to the father figure, whom Tony clearly identified as "stepfather"; two of these were "mildly negative, outgoing" responses and one related to "paternal indulgence." Almost all negative feelings in Tony's responses belonged to "Nobody." However, he did put most of the parental protection and indulgence items into the sister's box. This pattern of responses and his responses to the Rorschach did suggest that Tony tried to control his negative feelings. Very likely these negative feelings arose because Tony did not feel he was receiving his share of parental attention, although it was also possible that the overtly disdained such affection as babyish. Both of these attitudes appeared in his responses during the interviews: "Being kissed is for babies!" "They (his parents) always rush to see what *she* wants when *she* cries." There also was evidence in these and other data that Tony's struggle to hold back his anger resulted in his being at least mildly depressed. All in all, it did seem quite probable that unless Tony could resolve his confused feelings about his father's death and his new family situation, he might have continued and increasing difficulty in establishing affective controls during his latency years. Very likely these feelings of alienation would become more generalized, as was already evident in his peer relationships at school.

These results were discussed with the parents, who agreed that the psychologist's conclusions were consonant with their own observations. They also felt that Tony should have some help in resolving these conflicts but again raised the question of the cost. The psychologist admitted that it was difficult to predict precisely the extent of the treatment. However, since Tony's problems involved specific conflicts of fairly recent origin, it could be estimated that some resolution could be reached in approximately six to eight months of regular weekly sessions. Furthermore, the psychologist recommended that the parents meet with him every four weeks to review Tony's progress and discuss some of the things they might do to help him at home. The B's were relieved as they had heard of therapy which required daily sessions for several years. During the ensuing therapy, Tony worked through much of his anger and resentment over his mother's remarriage and the birth of his sister. At the end of six months, the B's reported that Tony was much more accepting of his stepfather and no longer as openly jealous of his sister. Most significantly, his mother reported Tony had put his father's photograph in a dresser drawer—without mentioning it to anyone. At school, Tony was working hard on his lessons and was no longer a discipline problem.

Once the decision has been made that a child does need psychotherapy, the next consideration is that the child comes to treatment. In many instances, even though the parents and child seem to accept the recommendation, the parents begin to have many excuses as to why the child cannot meet appointments. Studies of the rate of which adult patients continue in treatment (Sullivan, 1958) have shown that over half the adults in outpatient clinics do not attend more than ten interviews. Although there are no studies to indicate the rate at which children continue, it is this writer's impression that it is probably about the same. In many cases, perhaps as many as one out of three, treatment is broken off after two or three faltering sessions. Therapists often encourage those parents and children who show promise of continuing treatment and, for economical reasons, give less inducement to the family that is openly or even passively resistant. Special efforts are required to deal with these initial resistances. The child who is so anxious and guiltridden as to be unable to express anything, or the guarded and resentful child who sits pouting in anger, may not return easily for treatment even though he sorely needs help. Again, such children and their parents may not initially seem to be good candidates for psychotherapy, and the data from the assessment should be reviewed for the possibility of approaches other than purely verbal interactions.

Last, in these general considerations regarding assessment for psychotherapy, it is essential that the therapist be interested in and challenged by the child's problems. Often it is maintained that the therapist has to "like" his patient or that it is impossible to treat someone "you do not like." Theodore Reich once remarked (in a lecture attended by the writer) that this requisite that the therapist "love" his patients was an American myth. It does seem unreasonable to expect a therapist to "like" the child from the outset, or even feel friendly toward him. He may and probably should be relatively sympathetic with the child's problems, but it is also quite possible that he does not like the child's behavior. Therapists of children are often openly unsympathetic with the behavior of the parents, as discussed by Lovinger (1959). Although the therapist may be a conscientious, professional person, the child may be so full of resistances as to discourage him or so lackluster as to bore him. The therapist may be more challenged by these resistances or better able to discover the "spark" in the child if he can review the assessment protocols. These data may help the therapist to find the holes in the child's resistances or to promote the feelings which are nearest to the child's consciousness.

B. ASSESSMENT FOR DIRECTIVE COUNSELLING

For centuries past, the chief method for attempting to change individual behavior, other than through punishment, was direct advice. On the basis of magical divination or through a native intuitive knowledge of human behavior, witch doctors and wisemen counselled parents on how to rear or rule their children. Classic is the Biblical tale of Solomon, who tested the mother's love for her child—when the custody of the child was contested—by threatening to have the child cut in half. As scientific knowledge about child development began to accumulate, psychologists also attempted to inform and counsel parents what they should and should

not do about their children's behavior. Gradually psychologists began to realize that merely advising parents and children was not altogether effective. After Rogers (1942) introduced the concept and technique of client-centered counselling and demonstrated its effectiveness, direct advice giving became a bugaboo in many psychotherapeutic circles.

The chief arguments against direct counselling may be summarized as follows: (1) When the client receives and accepts advice, he is likely to become dependent on the therapist. Direct counselling thus may deter the development of independent decision making. (2) Many clients know what they *should* do but are unable to conduct their lives in a rational fashion because of their neurosis or because of limiting factors in their environmental circumstances. In most instances, the client cannot do what he knows he should do because to change his behavior would arouse overwhelming anxiety. His irrational behavior serves as a defense against this anxiety. Direct counselling in such cases is not only superfluous, but fails to assist the client in handling his anxieties. (3) Although the psychologist may be very knowledgeable about human behavior in general, it is often difficult to apply these generalities to specific instances. Psychologists are not able to "play God" and live other people's lives for them.

Nonetheless, direct counselling does have a place in the psychotherapeutic armamentarium and, in practice, is used far more often by skilled therapists than might be supposed. Some writers (Ellis, 1962) advocate this direct approach as an exclusive method of intervention for adults—although there is less indication of its applicability with children. That some advice giving creeps into the therapeutic work of nearly all therapists—except the most orthodox Rogerians—is evident in the samples of therapy that are submitted by candidates for the diplomate of the American Board of Examiners in Professional Psychology which this writer has reviewed as an examiner. Usually, however, such direct counselling enters as only one of a variety of interventions and plays a relatively minor role in the treatment. Moreover, it is usually modified to meet the above objections. Most psychologists are likely to "inform" the client or "point out" possible alternatives to his behavior—leaving the decision to the patient himself. Of course, such "informing" and "pointing out," coming as it does from a person in authority, may heavily influence the client's decisions. Psychotherapists are likely to combine direct counseling with reflection and recognition of the client's feelings and anxieties, using phrases such as, "Perhaps your anxiety has kept you from considering this alternative" or, "If you did stop what you are doing, then you might have to face some of your true feelings." Although such therapuetic remarks might more properly be labeled "confrontations" or "interpretations," the therapist is strongly and directly suggesting that the client consider the "alternative" or that he "face up to his true feelings." The skilled therapist also avoids "playing God" and does not try to give advice purely on his general knowledge of human behavior. His direct interventions are more likely to be derived from a thorough assessment followed by therapuetic investigation into the intimate details of the client's life and his behavior patterns.

Direct counselling in one form or another may be indicated under the following conditions: (1) When the client is uninformed about alternative patterns of behavior or about "facts." (2) When the client is unable to formulate or conceptualize his own behavior—as is done by the client himself in other forms of verbal therapy. (3) When the client is able to carry out the psychologist's advice without suffering undue hardships or anxieties, and (4) when such counselling does not interfere with the client's development of independent decision making.

Most children meet the first three criteria: they are often uninformed, they cannot easily conceptualize behavior, and they are suggestible. However, they are easily made anxious and have fewer and less well-formed defenses. Moreover, since they are not independent agents, they run realistic risks if they attempt to follow any advice which runs contrary to the dictum of their parents or other authorities. At times this writer has asked various adolescents, "Have you tried telling your father how you feel?" only to meet with the retort, "You don't know my old man; he'd murder me!" Helping the child face and deal with parental anger and anxiety is not easy. Most of all, independence of decision making, within the limits of the child's abilities and opportunities, needs to be fostered at each step whenever possible. This is especially true for the immature, passive, and dependent child, who is most likely to seek and be receptive to advice.

Directive counselling may be the preferred form of treatment when the chances for developing independent decision making are slim. For example, the mildly retarded adolescent often needs such direction because the chief problem for such adolescents is their inability to function independently. An assessor might recommend direct counselling when: (1) intellectual functioning is below average, especially when the child's thought processes are exceedingly concrete; (2) when, in addition, there is very little probability that the child's ability to develop independent decision making can be developed further; and (3) when the child is able to cope with stress by simple denial or through compulsive mechanisms. Directive counselling is most likely to be effective when the problems facing the child can be handled by concrete, explicit steps.

Various degrees of directive advice may also be in order in counselling some parents. Roughly the same criteria may be used. Parents who show little signs of insight or who are resistant to insight, parents who think concretely, and parents who are extremely passive but compulsive may need to be advised directly how to handle their children. The most important criterion for directive counselling with parents is that they be suggestible to advice from an authority. For example, it might be difficult to develop insight in an adult whose K and Hy scores on the MMPI are above 70. If these were the only significant peaks of the MMPI profile, directive counselling might be the treatment of choice. However, if there were strong signs of suspiciousness, rebellion, and confusion on the parents' MMPI, such as peaks on Pa, Pd, or Sc, the parent might be resistant and fail to carry out the therapist's recommendations.

C. ASSESSMENT FOR CLIENT-CENTERED COUNSELLING

Client-centered or nondirective counseling, a method introduced by Rogers (1942), operates chiefly through the reflections of the affective components of the client's responses. However, the reflection of feelings is a common component in all verbal and even nonverbal forms of altering behavior. Before Rogers called attention to the central importance of reflection of feelings, most skilled therapists who attempted either to advise or to condition their patients or to interpret their unconscious also attempted to understand the child's affect and to indicate their empathy to the child. Today nearly all therapists recognize that neither advice nor interpretation will be accepted unless the child realizes that the therapist understands his feelings, and unless some of these feelings are clarified. Roger's chief contribution (in these earlier works) was the recognition he gave to such reflection of feelings and his insistence that such reflection constitutes one of the primary therapeutic elements.

Originally Rogers introduced this reflection of feelings purely as a technique with little theoretical basis. Later, he introduced his general theory that continued emotional growth could be encouraged in the adult as well as in the child. He posited that growth was encouraged by the therapist's "warmth" which is expressed through a recognition of the client's feelings.

This particular approach to behavioral change proved not quite as simple as it first appeared. For one thing, most clients tend to express several and even contradictory feelings at the same time. Therapists found that it was not possible to reflect all feelings and, consciously or unconsciously, had to respond selectively to certain feelings. Roger's theory proved to be too vague to give precise guidance to the therapist about this necessary selection of feelings. The theory which Rogers finally propounded did include the feelings between client and therapist, but there was little indication as to whether or not this client-therapist relationship played any particular part toward changing the client's behavior.

As with any form of treatment which emphasizes one therapeutic technique exclusively, it gradually became clear that this was not equally successful with all clients. It did seem to be particularly applicable to the bright and verbal college students who came to Rogers' counselling centers. However, there were many adult patients who seemed to be either threatened or frustrated by the therapist's constant repetition and mirroring of their affect. Many clients had anger to express, including anger at the therapist, but felt stifled because Rogerian therapists responded only with "warmth."

Nondirective counselling appears to be used chiefly with adults. However, Axline (1947) reports on the use of this approach in treating adolescents and even younger children. There is some question whether children can assume the introspective attitude toward affect which client-centered counselling utilizes. Children do not verbalize their feelings in the same fashion as adults, but are more prone to act on them. However, reflection of feelings is very much a part of most psychotherapy with children; the therapist remarks on the child's feelings but does not expect the child himself to make the verbal recognition to the degree one might expect from adults. Children do listen to the reflections of the therapist. For example, this writer watched a nine-year-old-boy build a tomb of blocks in which he buried the mother doll and sealed it with clay. I remarked, "You must be very angry about something your mother has done." The child said nothing but continued with the funeral. A week later, he looked up from some other play and said, "You were wrong. I wasn't angry at nothing my mother *did*. I just hate her."

Although reflection of feelings is an important part of therapy with children, the fact that the child's affect is still in a stage of development does have to be taken into account. The preschool age child's affects are likely to be quite labile, momentary, and immediate responses to the environment. At this stage in life, the child figuratively wears his feelings on his sleeve, and his affect is short lived. As has been discussed at some length in prior chapters (see Chapters 4 and 13), the latency age child is engaged in developing control over his impulses and his affect and tries to mask them. The adolescent, facing surges of affect, also tries various controls but is easily aroused, moody, and "sensitive." Thus, reflections of feelings in the young child refer chiefly to feelings of the moment. Since the young child's affects are dominated by external stimuli, the therapist's reflections may determine, rather than clarify what the child feels. The latency child, although not unaffected by the therapist's remarks, may respond by tightening his defenses. Reflection of feelings of the child during this stage of development may result in silence and withdrawal rather than in opening up of feelings. Such children do need permission to express affect, but may not be able to be confronted with their feelings. Reflection of feelings to an adolescent requires considerable therapeutic sensitivity. The choice of which of an adolescent's affects to reflect and the phrasing of the reflection require all the skill a therapist can muster.

To the orthodox client-centered therapist, assessment was unnecessary since he believed that he merely had to await an expression of feeling from the client and reflect it. However, a thorough assessment, especially of affective development, is very necessary in preparation of the use of this technique in the treatment of children. Assessment can inform the therapist about: (1) the overall level of affective development in the child, (2) the degree of sensitivity to affect—and the defenses against such sensitivity, and (3) the kinds of feelings which it might be most important to reflect, that is, the question of selection.

Assessment of the overall level of affective development has already been discussed in Chapter 13. The degree of sensitivity and defensiveness against affect may be estimated from several sources of data. A classic sign of sensitivity to emotional nuances is the use of the texture of the inkblot on the Rorschach. More than one or two texture responses by a prepubescent child would suggest an unusual receptivity to affect. An absence of texturally determined responses before ages 12 to 13 is not unusual, but most prepubescent children are not "shocked" by the texture. They respond with some form-determined response to the textured card. They usually see the popular "bearskin" on Card VI, although without verbalizing any recognition of the texture. The child who retreats defensively from affect-creating stimuli is unable to responde effectively to the shaded cards; he either cannot respond at all, or he gives some evasive or confused response. Some children confuse sensitivity to affect with affective involvement; they equate *feeling with doing*. One sign of such confusion on the Rorschach is the response in which shading is interpreted as color by the child. For example, the child may see the top D (D3) of Card VI as "the sun . . . because it is red and flaming," pointing out the differences in shading as indicating color. The child who focuses his attention on the textural aspects of the colored cards without using the color is, inversely, attempting to avoid affective interaction by merely

recognizing affect without using it. He is what the layman designates as the "sensitive" child.

Sensitivity to feelings and conflicts over such sensitivity may also be indicated in responses to the TAT, MAPS, or the Sentence Completion. Again, it is unusual for the latency age child to remark extensively on the feelings of the characters in his fantasies, and it is more common for the child in this age group to shrug off any inquiry about the hero's feelings. The prepubescent child assumes that the hero's feelings are reflected in his actions and, if pressed, may retort, "Of course he's sad! What do you think? He'd be happy?" The child whose awareness of affect is unusually acute is likely to mention feelings in his stories or incomplete sentences, but with some hesitation or mild confusion. Frequently the latency age child mentions feeling at one moment and denies it at the next. Adolescent sensitivities and defenses are usually much more varied. After pubescence, the child cannot so easily blanket out his sensitivity to affect, and thus is more likely to comment voluntarily on the feelings of his TAT characters or to blurt out feelings on the Sentence Completion. However, his efforts to suppress or deflect such sensitivity is also likely to be more varied and more desperate. Confusion of feeling with action is more common in the adolescent years. If affect is attributed to the hero in an adolescent TAT story, then the hero is likely to be portrayed as taking some action to relieve the affect, often some illogical action. As noted in Chapter 13, shame and guilt are prominent affects in this age group.

Associative techniques also serve as the major instruments for assessment of the kinds of affect which are most important to the child. The affective content of the child's responses to the Rorschach, TAT, World Test, or Sentence Completion yield valuable information as to the kinds of affective conflicts which the therapist should be prepared to meet. These responses help to pinpoint the setting and nature of the affective conflict as well as identifying the affect per se. TAT stories reveal not only that the child feels hunger for love or is angry, but that these feelings are associated with certain figures in his life and in specific types of interaction with them. Thus, the therapist may be prepared to reflect the feelings of the child in respect to certain interactions. His "guesses" about affective aspects of the child's actions in the playroom will thus be more accurate.

D. ASSESSMENT FOR PSYCHOANALYTICALLY ORIENTED THERAPY

Admittedly, no brief account can possibly do justice to this complex therapy nor the theory on which it is based. This theory has already been discussed in previous chapters, chiefly in an attempt to relate it to other theories and to the practice of assessment of ego functioning. Moreover, psychoanalytic treatment, as Freud predicted, has been expanded and revised considerably since he propounded his original theses. Rather than review this theory and its changes, psychoanalytically based therapy will be considered as it is currently conceived and practiced. To relate this current therapeutic approach to assessment does require: (1) a summary of the general goals, (2) a brief overview of current practices—particularly as regard children, (3) some consideration of its limitations, and (4) a list of the general criteria which need to be considered when this approach is contemplated in the treatment of a child.

As to the goals of brief psychoanalytic treatment,* many people, including some psychologists, seem to view it mostly from second-hand summaries of Freud's earliest writings; they believe that this treatment consists chiefly of an uncovering of unconscious motivations. However, this is only one of the goals of psychoanalytic therapy, and in work with children, it is seldom the principal goal. Psychoanalytical theorists have come to recognize that these motivations are part of the ego and that this treatment therefore deals chiefly with ego functions. The main goal of psychoanalytically oriented treatment, particularly with children, is the *strengthening* of ego functions and their development. Such uncovering of unconscious motivations as may be attempted is to allow the child to recognize his needs and drives so that he may develop independent methods of need-gratification. Mere interpretation of drives has no purpose in itself. The second general goal of psychoanalytic treatment of children is to assist them in recognizing and coping with their impulses and needs. In strengthening ego development and assisting the child to cope with his impulses, psychoanalytic treatment has as its third and long-range goal the fostering of the child's sense of identity as a unique, independent, and worthwhile person.

The techniques used to achieve these goals have also been altered and vary considerably from setting to setting. The classic psychoanalysis, in which the patient—prone on the couch—free-associates and the analyst responds with interpretations, day after day over several years, may be the popular conception, but in actual practice, only a tiny percentage of adult patients receive this intensive treatment. Children are not treated in this manner; the analyst most often treats the child in a playroom setting. Far more commonly, psychoanalytic treatment of children consists of one or two sessions weekly over a period ranging from six to 20 months. It is this brief and less intensive form of psychoanalytic therapy with which this discussion is concerned.

Currently, psychoanalytic treatment of the child also includes the involvement of the parents in the therapy. There are some orthodox analysts who regard the parents somewhat as intruders, and interview them only occasionally to obtain information about the child's homelife or to instruct them about the care of the patient. Precedent for including the parents in the treatment of the child comes, of course, from Freud's (1909) classic case of a phobic boy, wherein he advised the father and actually saw the child only once or twice. Most psychoanalytic therapists today work very closely with the parents. Either they collaborate with colleagues who treat the parents separately or as a couple, or they themselves have regular personal interviews with the parents. Family group therapy (which will be discussed subsequently in this chapter) was developed by psychoanalytically oriented therapists (Ackerman, 1958; 1962). Of course, psychoanalytic concepts and techniques are often a part of any psychotherapy, even though they may not be labeled psychoanalytic. Such factors as defenses, resistances, and the relationship between the therapist and patient, all originating in psychoanalysis,

---

*Psychoanalytically oriented or brief psychoanalytic therapy is to be distinguished from the classic, long-term, and intensive treatment called psychoanalysis. Since psychoanalysis is not available to most children, it is not specifically considered here.

therapy and are necessary considerations in any form of treatment.

The techniques used in these psychoanalytically based therapies also have expanded far beyond the classic interpretation of free-association, fantasies, dreams, and slips of the tongue. In actual practice, psychoanalytic treatment begins with a great deal of reflection of feelings, very much like the client-centered therapy of Rogers, in what is known as the "cathartic" or "abreaction" stage. The child is encouraged to talk about his current life and relevant events leading up to his present situation. The therapist remarks on his affective reactions to these situations, especially regarding his parents, other important persons, and himself. Once the patient sees the therapist as a comforting and sympathetic person, it is possible to confront the patient with the irrational aspects of his behavior, both as the child reports it from his everyday life and as it occurs in the playroom. Gradually the therapist interrelates these feelings, motivations, and concrete behaviors into the generalizations called interpretations. Dreams, fantasies, and the child's play activities are an essential part of the data used by the psychoanalytic therapist, but they are not the only source of data. Increasingly, these therapists are concerned with the ongoing behavior of the child as well as with his past experiences. It should be emphasized that the only reason for considering these past experiences is to understand the present. As the treatment proceeds, these reflections, confrontations, and interpretations are repeated, each time with a slightly different reference and emphasis much like the theme and variation of a symphony. This repetition of the theme and its meanings is commonly referred to as "working through." Those who are more familiar with behavior modification therapy (see below) will recognize this "working through" as a complex form of verbal reinforcement.

The central element in psychoanalytic therapy with adults is the systematic use of the relationship between patient and therapist as an instrument to effect changes in the patient's behavior. In classical psychoanalysis, this core aspect of the treatment is known as the "transference." The analyst purposefully emphasizes those aspects of the adult patient's interactions with him which appear as a repetition and reformulation of prior relationships, in particular the patient's childhood relationships with his parents. Confronted with these infantile reactions which are inappropriate to the therapeutic situation and to the patient's current adult life, the adult becomes able to recognize the inconsistencies in his behavior and to seek more appropriate, independent, and self-satisfying modes. In working through the transference, the patient uses the therapist as a model on which to form an independent identity. To establish such an intimate relationship and to examine the transference in detail often requires considerable time, which is the chief reason that a complete psychoanalysis may continue for several years. This transference phenomenon is also used in brief psychoanalytic therapy of adults, but is not quite so intense or explored in as much detail.

In analytic treatment of children, the transference has had to be reconsidered and altered (A. Freud, 1946). The child has a relatively short past over which to build up relationships, and his memories are recent and brief. Most of all, he usually is still residing in the parental home. Thus, in contrast to the adult patient, it is realistic and appropriate for the child to react to the therapist as an adult authority and even to relate to him much as he relates to his parents. The child has an ongoing parental relationship which currently and continuously influences his relationships with other adults. The child thus transfers an ongoing parent-child relationship. The working through of this transference in psychoanalytic treatment of a child thus consists of an examination of current affects, motivations, coping techniques, and conflicts. Such working through of the transference is not aimed at the eradication of infantile relationships, but at the strengthening of effective coping mechanisms. The analyst seeks to help the child recognize and deal with his parents in as realistic a fashion as possible.

The remarkable insights which Freud possessed about human nature in general and human maladaptations in particular have led many people, including many analysts, to regard psychoanalysis as the ultimate and ideal therapy for all human ills. Moreover, there is a popular mythology which seems to equate the intensity or "depth" of treatment with the intensity of illness. Freud was more cautious. His original successes were with neurotic adults, especially those labeled hysterics. For many years he cautioned his followers that psychoanalytic treatment might not be as effective with other forms of maladaptive behavior, such as psychotic states or the so-called character neuroses. However, therapies based on psychoanalytic theory have been devised which have had at least moderate success with these other kinds of psychological disorders. This writer, in reading the psychoanalytic literature, and from his own experience as a therapist, has come to the conclusion that the applicability of psychoanalytic treatment depends not so much on the diagnosis of the patient as on the developmental stage and strength of the ego. The working through of feelings, motivations, and conflicts and the transference require a relatively intact ego. Thus, it is possible to treat a schizophrenic adult or adolescent, where the ego is at the moment severely disturbed or "shattered," if the patient at one time has been able to function relatively effectively. The acute or reactive schizophrenic patient may be a potentially fair candidate for psychoanalytic treatment but the chronic or progressive life-long schizoid character is less likely to respond. Psychoanalytic therapy is similarly more successful with those patients whose neurotic symptoms or characterological distortions, even though acute, do not affect the entire ego. On the other hand, the very immature and overly dependent adult may remain unaffected by psychoanalytic therapy. In fact, such adult patients may transfer all their dependency needs onto the therapist in what Freud (1937) called an "interminable analysis."

Psychoanalytic therapy involves considerable verbalization. It is an extremely wordy therapy. The patient must be able to put his feelings, experiences, and memories into words ad infinitum (and even ad nauseum!), until the full meaning is clear. Moreover, he must be able to comprehend the therapist's abstractions when the therapist interprets the relationships between these feelings and behavior. Psychoanalytic therapy thus requires a verbal sophistication and an ability to abstract and generalize. Therefore, it is not applicable to the intellectually dull patient, whether adult or child. In practice, psychoanalytic treatment is most often used with intellectually precocious children.

Because even brief psychoanalytic treatment often entails many hours over many months, the biggest practical limitation of this form of treatment is its cost in time and money. Privately purchased, it is so expensive that only the well-to-do person can afford it. Many public child guidance clinics attempt to provide this form of therapy for those whose incomes are below average. (It is almost unavailable to those of "average" income!) However, this treatment requires so much time for each child that with the limited personnel available in most clinics, only a small percentage of the large number of children who need treatment can receive it. If a clinic or private practitioner is to effectively serve the needs of the community, this treatment should be reserved for those who will benefit most, and other, more appropriate types of therapy should be used for other children. The selection of the children for whom this treatment is to be used is a frequent reason for assessment.

On the basis of the above discussion, the major criteria for the applicability of psychoanalytic therapy may be summarized as follows.

(a) The child's ego development should be past the earliest formative stage. He should be able to internalize some feelings and motivations and to be making some steps toward independent gratification.

(b) In particular, the child's intellectual development should be advanced, so that he verbalizes fluently and can understand simple abstractions and generalizations.

(c) Psychoanalytic treatment is more effective if the child resides with an intact family. Therapy is slowed or blocked if he tries to satisfy his natural dependency needs by using his therapist as a substitute for a missing parent.

(d) The time and money required for this treatment might best be invested in a child who shows more than an average potential for developing into a creative and productive adult.

When psychoanalytic therapy is being contemplated for a child, a thorough assessment of ego functioning is very necessary. Since assessment of ego functioning has been the major topic of the previous chapters, suffice it at this point to review briefly those assessment methods and data which are pertinent to the above criteria. First, as regards ego strength and internalization: The MMPI contains an "Ego Strength" scale, designed specifically to measure adaptability to psychoanalytic therapy (Barron, 1953). Although the norms on this scale were based on an adult sample, it would seem logical that an adolescent with a T-score above 50 could be considered as having ego strength equivalent to the average adult. Internalization is beginning in the child if the experience balance on the Rorschach is ambiequal or intratensive. The internal stirring indicated by the inanimate movement response to the Rorschach (*Fm, m*) is also a positive sign of nascent internalization. Ego strength can be seen in the everyday behavior of a child. For example, if a child is misbehaving at school and at home, one should try to discover in the interviews with the child and his parents the nature of such misbehavior. If this behavior proves to be chiefly regressive, that is, consists of an increasingly dependent demand-ingness and a retreat from growth, then it might be concluded that the child's ego development is being blocked. However, a child who is rebelling, who is rejecting parental demands in order to gain independence, or who is seeking to establish new methods of need-gratification, may be a "good candidate" for psychoanalytic treatment. The child's history should show some capacity for entering into human relationships. He should not be markedly withdrawn. If he does not get along with his peers, he should have at least one or two friends, peers or adults whom he half way trusts and enjoys. If he is rebelling against authority, he should have peer alies. Even if he is engaged in a vendetta with his parents and teachers, this can be a sign that he is able to engage in interpersonal relationships, albeit hostile ones. Strange as it might seem at first glance, the development of neurotic defenses in a child is a positive sign of ego development. For example, the ability to deny frustration, as might be measured on the P–F Study shows at least some tendency to withstand anxiety, as opposed to direct and aggressive attacks on the frustrating object. Children who give predominately need-persistent responses to the P–F are precocious in coping with frustration; they do seem ready at least in their attitudes to take responsibility for their own behavior.

As regards the second criterion, verbal intelligence may be measured by a number of standard techniques. Using the WISC, for example, the verbal IQ should be higher than the performance IQ if psychoanalytic treatment is to be favorably considered as the treatment of choice. The child should have an extensive and superior vocabulary. His Similarities and Comprehension subscale scores should also be above average. If weighted scores on these three tests were 13 or higher, it might not matter too much if the child stumbled on some other verbal scales, such as Arithmetic or Digit Span. It would seem unlikely that any child who is markedly deficient in his perceptual-motor development would be able to achieve an above-average verbal IQ. However, mildly retarded perceptual-motor development would not in itself seem a contraindication to analytic treatment of a child. The level of verbalization, sentence construction, and generalization may also be assessed from response to techniques such as the TAT and Sentence Completion. Some bright and verbal children react negatively to IQ scales but demonstrate their verbal competency on these other techniques.

Psychoanalytic therapy requires special investigation into family attitudes and habits regarding time and money. Many attempts at treatment of a child have been short lived because neither the parents nor the therapist were aware of the changes in the lives of the family demanded by the treatment. Moreover, very frequently part of the child's disturbance may be based on these factors. The parents, consciously or unconsciously, may be too busy for the child and unable themselves to decide clearly what the child needs, as opposed to their own needs. It is not necessary to "sell" the treatment to the parents nor to argue with them. Usually a review of their time schedules and their financial habits and problems will reveal to them the possibilities of working the treatment into their schedules and budgets. The "sacrifices" that the treatment of the child may mean to them should be recognized, if it seems to the assessor that they can realistically afford the time and money. In many instances this aspect of the assessment should be conducted by the prospective therapist, if the assessor is not to conduct the treatment. Even so, some investigation of this factor may be carried on as part of the assessment, at least to gather data for further consideration by the therapist.

As to the fourth criterion, much of the data necessary for assessmesnt of the other criteria can also be used to evaluate the creative potential of the child. His imaginative productivity on the associative techniques, his intellectual advancement, even his aggressive strivings for independence, are all signs of future productivity. It should be noted once more that precocity in itself can create problems and conflicts. Psychoanalytic therapy is particularly the treatment of choice for such children. As in the Biblical story of Jacob, they are ready to give up the potage of their childhood and wrestle with the angel. Often they need special help in this struggle.

E. ASSESSMENT AND BEHAVIOR MODIFICATION TECHNIQUES

To judge from current research (Gelfand and Hartmann, 1968), the various therapeutic techniques that are commonly labeled "behavior modification" open up the possibility of rapid relief for many childhood problems. These range from difficulties in child training to severe behavior disturbances which heretofore seemed implacable by any approach. Because of these possibilities, these methods have quickly attracted the attention of many clinical psychologists. However, Behavior Modification is such a recent innovation—in fact, it is often acknowledged to be as yet "experimental"—that there are as yet no well-established criteria nor techniques by which one may assess whether it is the treatment of choice for any particular child. The discussion which follows is therefore admittedly largely speculative. It may be justified, if for no other reason, on the grounds that methods of assessment appropriate to the treatment should be conceived or adapted as the therapeutic method develops—rather than as an afterthought as was the case with other therapies. It is to be hoped that this discussion will serve to stimulate further consideration of assessment methods for the behavior modification techniques.

Any innovation in methods of changing behavior seems bound to be not only fascinating but also challenging and controversial. Some of those most enthusiastic about the possibilities of behavior modification have been quick to contrast it with other therapies and to allege that the theoretical bases of other therapies are inadequate (Lovass, et al, 1965).* Still others are openly skeptical regarding what appears to be an overly simple

and as yet unproven approach. Such views make it difficult to discuss this therapy objectively. This writer must confess to two biases: first, I have not had an opportunity to experiment with this therapy myself; my information comes from the literature and the work of my colleagues and students. Second, it is only natural that this writer would attempt to relate behavior modification to the general framework of ego development used throughout this book. As will be seen, these two sets of concepts are not necessarily antithetical. Rather, it is hoped, both may be clarified by the attempt to relate them.

The theory of operant conditioning upon which most behavior modification is based* is not new, nor is its application in clinical approaches to behavioral change (Freud, 1909). As has been demonstrated repeatedly in prior chapters, social reinforcement is one —but only one—of the determinants of ego development. Verbal and nonverbal approval has been used—or withheld—in nearly every form of therapy, in order to influence the child's behavior, even though few therapists may have recognized and labeled their own behavior as operant conditioning. The innovation of behavior modification is the exclusive and systematic use of this one form of learning as a therapeutic technique, disregarding other theories, other forms of learning, or other techniques of behavior change.

This theory focuses on the child's immediate interactions with his environment, on the ways in which his physical and social environment affect him, rather than on past influences or the child's internal motivational and affective state. In this approach, it is the child's responses and their consequences which need to be changed. The etiology of the behavior is of little consequence to the behavior modification therapist. To quote Meyerson, Kerr, and Michael (in Bijou and Baer, 1967): "Most rehabilitation psychologists will accept the formula $B = f(P,E)$, or behavior is a function of a person's interaction with his environment. In concentrating on the P term in the formula, however, it is easy to neglect the fact that the formula has three terms and that B and E can be independent variables also." Behavior modification thus attempts to change B through altering E—but presumably without altering P. The alteration in E consists of changes of the reactions of E to the

---

*Lovass' comments refer to the treatment of childhood schizophrenia.

*Some work is also being attempted using respondent conditioning.

child's behavior. "Desired" behavior is rewarded; undesirable behavior is ignored or punished.

The typical childhood difficulties for which this therapy is used consist of simple behavioral acts, for example, speech patterns, motor habits, tantrums, fears and anxieties concerning specific objects or situations. As described by the users of behavior modification, the child is initially observed, through a one-way screen, in interaction with a parent or other caretaker. A baseline study of the patterns of rewards and punishments used to reenforce the child's pretreatment behavior is most essential since it is generally the behavior of the reenforcing parents which is to be altered. The parent, nurse, or teacher is then instructed how and when to reward, ignore, or punish the child regarding the act in question. The conditioning stimuli is often nonverbal, for example, candy, toys, or smiles of approval as rewards, and personal rejection, isolation, or even mild electric shock as punishment. However, these nonverbal operants may also be accompanied by verbalizations of approval or discouragement. Most behavior modification therapists seem to agree that if the newly acquired behavior is to be sustained, there must be continued intermittent reinforcement. Thus, the training of the parent, nurse, or teacher is frequently an important part of the therapy.

Although those experimenting with operant conditioning as a therapy have not as yet specified criteria for the types of childhood difficulties for which this therapy is most appropriate, some general criteria may be drawn from the above discussion.

1. The behavior to be changed should be primarily determined or influenced by reward and punishment from the environment. Because there is some reaction to external stress in nearly every act, and because these external stimuli are the most visible variable, it is often assumed that such stress is always the most important and the most dependent variable. However, as has been repeatedly argued and illustrated in this volume, not all stimuli come from the environment. Internalized memories, attitudes, fantasies, affects, and motivations (the "P" in the above formula) also stimulate the child's behavior.

This difference may be further understood by making a distinction between the terms "habit" and "symptom." A "habit" may be thought of as behavior which does arise primarily from operant conditioning, from the rewards and punishments of everyday life. They may become almost autonomous, or consist of circular reinforcements (as when the child's behavior invites more reward or punishment), but they may be extinguished at any time by a change in the environmental stress. Usually habits consist of rather simple acts, which are not generalized beyond the particular environmental system which stimulates them. In contrast, the term "symptom" suggests that the behavior arises principally from within "P." A symptom in a reaction to something else than the immediate environment, that is, to generalized internal states. Symptoms are inappropriate and unrealistic responses as regards the immediate environment. Symptoms are more likely to be relatively complex behaviors and to be generalized from situation to situation. On the basis of this distinction, behavior modification is most appropriately used and most effective in changing habits rather than symptoms.

2. The behavior in question must be susceptible to change through operant conditioning. As was discussed in Chapter 1, there are many kinds of learning, of which operant conditioning is only one. This is not to deny that operant conditioning is probably the most common nor that it is often very effective. Rather, the point is that not *all* behavior is learned via this method. For example, although in some instances a child may generalize from one operant situation to another, for the most part he is learning concrete acts. He does not learn to generalize or think abstractly through operant learning alone. Moreover, he remains dependent on the reward or punishment. Operant conditioning may free a child from an annoying or debilitating habit or help him to learn a specific skill which then makes it more possible for him to learn, via other methods, how to think abstractly or act independently.

3. The child in question must be susceptible to learning via operant conditioning. Because operant conditioning is so pervasive in the learning processes of most children, it might be assumed—as, indeed, the advocates of behavior modification appear to assume—that all children are equally affected by reward and punishment schedules. Unfortunately, little attention has been paid to individual differences in learning approaches. The concept of "cognitive styles" does suggest that

different children may have different and preferred styles of learning. That there are individual differences in response to operant conditioning by different children is evident from the research reports by experimenters using this technique. For example, many of the children in the studies collected by Bijou and Baer (1967) show marked response to this technique, but others show only a slight or even negative reaction.

It is also well recognized that adults differ widely as to suggestibility, dependency on their environment, or hypnotizability. Although children in general appear to be more suggestable and dependent on their environment than adults, there may well be differences among them in "conditionability." As might be expected, the subjects in reports on behavior modification with children are mostly under the age of seven, that is, in the age group in which children are most dependent on environmental guidance and support, and before children begin to internalize.

Behavior modification therapists do not seem to use the term "resistance" but they occasionally describe behavior in which the child is resistant to the treatment. Children occasionally reject the reward or ignore the punishment. For example, some autistic children drop anything placed in their hands or may even fail to swallow candy placed in their mouths. They are used to being isolated and even seem to prefer isolation. As Orlando and Bijou (1967) remark, anent operant conditioning of discrimination, "If an individual fails to show a discrimination . . . under these conditions, the question then becomes: What is unusual about this organism?" These authors then list some reasons why a child may not respond to their operant conditioning: "He may be color blind, he may not respond to the reinforcer in question as positive, he may be physically ill, or even emotionally upset (*sic!*), he may have a past history making extinction a condition in which he has often been reinforced for persevering long enough." To this list may be added the fact that some children, especially brighter and older children, may feel that they are being bribed or "taken in." Such children regard the reinforcement as an insult to their intelligence and independence. Assessment of all of these factors is necessary so that if behavior modification is to be used, the therapist will be prepared to meet the resistances.

4. The attainment of or elimination of the behavior should be desirable. Certainly the kinds of behavior to which operant conditioning is most commonly applied do seem to be most undesirable to the adult conducting the experiment, usually also to the parents, and very possibly to the child. It does seem hard to imagine that children do not desire to walk or talk or that they like injuring themselves. Most children will aver that they would like to stop stuttering or wetting the bed or losing their temper. Yet, it is often observable that such behaviors serve a definite purpose for the child in his interactions with the environment. For example, a child's stuttering may help him to keep from saying what he dare not say; another child may use his enuresis to disturb his parents; academic failure may serve the purpose of disappointing parents or of retaining the status of infancy. This is one reason why enuresis does not always respond to the variety of operant techniques specifically designed for this "habit." Martin and Kulby (1955), who followed up on the effects of one such technique, concluded: "The greater investment that the child has in the enuresis as an interpersonal expression—for example, as a passive way of expressing hostility and defiance toward the parents—the less likely that the habit training procedures will be effective."

The parents or caretakers should also desire that the child's behavior be changed. As illustrated in the cases of Eddie, Case 33, and Cindy, Case 49, the parents were willing to tolerate the child's behavior until the school or other community forces objected. In other instances, parents are also resistant to change in the child, particularly those parents who may unconsciously desire and foster the behavior. They may need to infantalize the child or otherwise use the child for their own neurotic ends.

5. Thus, the parents should be normal and cooperative. Operant conditioning techniques can be a boon to the well-meaning but inexperienced parent or to the caretaker of a mentally retarded or otherwise disabled child. However, if behavior modification techniques are to be successful, the parent or caretaker should not foster the undesirable behavior, either consciously or unconsciously. They should not find their own rewards in the child's failure. The child should not be playing the role of the "identified patient" (Satir, 1964), as will be discussed subsequently in

the section on family group therapy. For example, if a father finds his revenge against his wife when she is upset by their child's mannerisms, if the mother uses the child's behavior to try to involve the father in the discipline of the child, and if the siblings know how to instigate the child's disturbance for their advantage, then attempts at behavior modification will be rapidly sabotaged.

6. The behavior should have a rate that is frequent enough to allow opportunity for modification, that is, a sufficient number of pretreatment learning trials. If the behavior occurs, for example, only once a year (as in the case of fire-setting), it would be difficult to work with purely because there is little opportunity to observe and condition it.* Some other kind of therapy, which deals with incidental behaviors or with symptoms, might be in order.

7. In order for behavior modification to be effective, an exceedingly clear and precise description of the desired terminal behavior, as well as a careful description of the reinforcement contingencies that maintain the current undesired behavior, are essential. This requirement is one of the main advantages of the approach for the clinician. It requires a concise and communicable definition of the problem behavior and its antitheses at the outset. However, to arrive at such a definition, far more careful and detailed interviews with the parents or other authorities who are to follow the modification program are necessary than is usually illustrated in the literature. For example, Bernal (private communication) teaches her students to list the parents' complaints, obtaining if possible the order of importance the parents place on each complaint; these are then restated in *positive* terms, and are written down on a checklist sheet for the parents, who are asked to observe the frequency of the *positive* behavior daily during three-hour periods. For example, if the parents state that the child hits other children, the parent is asked to check those three-hour periods when the child plays quietly with sibs and peers. If the child wets the bed or refuses to go to bed, the parents are to note those nights when the child is dry or goes to bed without undue clamor. This procedure orients both parent and child toward the desired behavior, beginning in the assessment.

To summarize these criteria and counter-

indications: Behavior modification may well be the treatment of choice for altering simple habits or behavioral acts in very young or in retarded children. Through operant conditioning, it is possible to eradicate very disturbing and destructive behavior (Bernal et al, 1968). It also has inestimable promise in the training of retarded or physically handicapped children to perform simple but essential acts. The case of Sam, Case 51, illustrates how the lack of such training constituted severe disability in itself, and how after such training, this blind adolescent was beginning to take some responsibility for his own care. Through focusing attention on operant conditioning, it may be possible to modify considerably the lives of many children heretofore thought beyond any possible rehabilitation. Moreover, it is to be hoped, other types of treatment based on other learning theories can be developed.

Although behavior modification does appear to open new vistas in rehabilitation and training, it is not a substitute for other therapies which deal with other kinds of problems. It is unlikely to be the treatment of choice for those older and brighter children who are less susceptible to simple reward and punishment. Other kinds of treatment are needed when the child's behavior is a complex symptom of internalized conflicts, attitudes, and memories. Such symptoms may be eliminated by operant conditioning, but the child's general state of disturbance remains unchanged. Some reports on behavior modification (Yates, 1958) claim that following such elimination of a symptom, the disturbed child does not develop other symptoms, but a thorough follow-up is lacking. This writer observed one such child before and after treatment by operant conditioning. The child's tic was no longer present but he remained a severely anxious, withdrawn, and compulsive child, who walked, talked, and behaved in a machinelike fashion. However, his parents were satisfied with the eradication of the tic and sought no further treatment for several years thereafter, until he became almost psychotic and failed at school.

The assessment technique which behavior modification experimenters describe in their own procedures consists, as noted above, of a very thorough and systematic observation of the child, usually in interaction with a parent, caretaker, or even a peer. In these observations, the responses of the child are carefully counted and charted, sometimes

---

*The author is indebted to Dr. Martha Bernal for this point.

using special laboratory equipment or television tapes (Bernal et al, 1968). Since these therapists are interested primarily in the behavior per se, rather than causes, they often take little or no history—despite the above quoted remarks of Orlando and Bijou. Moreover, many behavior modification therapists see no utility in other kinds of assessment. Meyerson, Kerr, and Michael (op. cit.) argue that the other commonly used assessment techniques may possibly be misleading. It is understandable that in introducing a new and explicit therapeutic technique, it is tempting to disregard and even denounce those assessment techniques which, in the past, have been associated primarily with other therapies. As was noted above, such was also the case when Rogers introduced client-centered counselling. However, scientific clinicians must resist such a temptation, for the aim of science is the integration of knowledge, and science is weakened by the isolation of ideas.

Thus, a more varied assessment may be helpful and, in this writer's opinion, is necessary before behavior modification is selected as the treatment of choice. This assessment should be concerned with the immediate behavior at hand. As has been discussed at length in various points (see particularly Chapter 7), direct observation of the child — plus in interaction with a parent, or with peers on the playground or at school, or with his sibs in his home — all are extremely valuable sources of data and are used by behavior modification therapists. In any assessment for any therapy, it is necessary to observe the interactions between the child and his environment. However, direct observations in such settings are not the only assessment technique which provides data about interpersonal interactions. In fact, responses to most of the techniques discussed in this book can be viewed as behavioral operations, and data regarding interactions can be derived from them. Although many assessment techniques have long been used with children who were subsequently treated by psychoanalytic methods, and interpreted for that purpose in a psychoanalytic framework, assessment techniques and the data they provide are not in themselves psychoanalytic. The responses of the child to these assessment techniques are behaviors, and may be utilized and interpreted by advocates of any theoretical constructs. For example, several writers on the Rorschach Technique (Gibby, 1952; Gibby, Miller, and Walker, 1953) have established that this method, long considered the epitome of investigation into internalized attitudes, also can be viewed as an interaction process between assessor and subject. Moreover, the reliability and validity of direct observations of behavior when used exclusively as a method of assessment are quite doubtful as was pointed out in Chapter 7. As illustrated throughout this book, it is usually necessary to supplement such observations with other kinds of techniques.

The necessity for using a variety of assessment techniques prior to instituting behavior modification can be seen in the above criteria and contraindications. First, to establish that the behavior in question is in fact a habit or a response aroused primarily by the environment, it is necessary not only to discover the stimulus-response sequences, but also to investigate the degree to which the behavior may also be symptomatic of internalized conflict. This assumes that any behavior may have elements of either kind of responding. Further, data regarding the relation of the behavior in question to the environment might be derived, for example, from the World Test. Some children play by themselves, not involving the assessor. Others, especially younger children, ask for varying degrees of help and participation, which suggest they depend on others to structure the environment. As has been discussed in detail in prior chapters, the main purpose of the Rorschach Technique is the determination of the degree to which the child is responding in general to the environment or to his internalizations. A detailed history would be essential, with emphasis on the kinds of stimuli which have influenced the behavior in question. A model of such a history is presented by Bernal et al (1968). To assess the degree to which the behavior is embedded in the personality as a symptom, one might use the CAT or TAT. Lynn's Structured Doll Play (see Chapter 7) lends itself particularly well to assessment of parent-child interaction — as does the Bene-Anthony. As was noted, the child often remarks on and imitates parental stimuli and acts out his responses to the doll play situations.

Second, whether the behavior in question is susceptible to change through operant conditioning depends, in part, on how it was established. Thus, a history of the cause, in this sense, is necessary. Behavior modification is not necessarily limited to altering behavior previously established through operant conditioning, but it probably is most successful in readjusting such habits. However, other thepies might be more appropriate for other kinds of learned behavior. For example, a more verbal reflection of feelings and affective support might be the treatment of choice for a child reacting to grief, even though the reaction be a specific symptom. Assessment of a grief reaction may require more than simple observational techniques.

Third, the kinds of learning which the child prefers or responds to most easily may be assessed from both intelligence tests and from the Rorschach. From responses to these techniques, one can determine whether the child learns chiefly through one-to-one associations or whether he responds more easily to abstractions and generalizations. Operant conditioning deals chiefly with one-to-one responses. For example, one might not require the candidate for behavior modification to be able to verbalize a response to "What do you do when you are thirsty?" (Stanford Binet, Year III-6), but if he at least recognizes on the Seguin which forms belong in which inserts, the beginnings of such one-to-one associations are evidenced. Copying a block tower or "bridge," imitating a hand movement, and reproducing or attempting to reproduce the Bender drawings are all measurements of such learning. On the Rorschach, responses based on a simple and immediate reaction to the whole blot (as opposed to built-up or elaborated W responses), or those based on specific details, suggest that the child is using an immediate response to stimuli, without analysis or abstraction. On the other hand, the child who attempts to respond to the whole world at one moment, who gives markedly confused and contaminated responses to the Rorschach, might not respond easily to conditioning. Such contaminated or confabulated W responses are likely to come from children who experience a global, nonspecific set of stimuli, and extensive conditioning might be required to help them make meaningful discriminations.

Fourth, whether the contemplated change in the child's behavior is desirable also necessitates a more extensive assessment than described in most articles on behavior modification. The purposes, conscious and unconscious, of the child's acts may be assessed from interviews with the child and with the parents, from the child's interactions and "games" with the assessor, from TAT fantasies and Sentence Completion associations, and even from reactions to intelligence tests. Although both the parents and the child may be unable or unwilling in subjective interviews to state their respective purposes in maintaining the child's acts, they often reveal their motivations in slips of the tongue, in inconsistencies in their reports, and in the evasivenes and vaguenes of their statements. Such data may be obtained by asking the child or parent to give a blow-by-blow detailed description of a recent incident involving the behavior in question: What happened before it occurred? What happened next? When did the child demonstrate the act in this sequence of interchanges? How did the parent react? How did the child respond to the parents' reactions? CAT stories are often very revealing of the child's purposes in carrying out the act in question. The child may say directly that the CAT hero wanted to upset or destroy the parent figure or that the parent figure in the story permitted or encouraged the hero to misbehave.

Finally, assessment is necessary to determine whether the parent is "normal" and capable of carrying out the reinforcement. Most important here is the emotional stability of the parents. A psychotic parent or even a depressed parent may be so wound into their own affective states as to be unable to reinforce the child consistently. On the other hand, a highly suggestible but emotionally naïve parent, such as would be indicated by a high Hy score on the MMPI, might be most likely to comply. One might be reassured that the parent would carry out instructions if the MMPI profile "high points" were 3 and 7 — and if 8 and 2 were low. The Leary Interpersonal Check List would seem most applicable for assessing parental interpersonal reactions. A set of ICL profiles on each member of the family (including the child if he can read), and their projected attitudes toward other members (including the child), might serve to pinpoint those kinds of interactions between the parent and child which have to be modified and especially those which might be dealt with by behavior modification.

Further use of assessment techniques for planning behavior modification has been suggested by Greenspoon and Gersten (1967). According to these authors, assessment of four factors is required: "classes of contingent stimuli," "the selection of contingencies," "self-control," and "control by others." At least the last two are comparable to the criteria discussed above. These writers give examples of the techniques which might be used but insist that the relationships between test data and this therapy are yet to be established. They also emphasize that a shift in orientation about assessment for behavior modification is required.

F. ASSESSMENT AND GROUP THERAPIES

Of all the variations of group therapy, two forms are most commonly used with children: peer groups and conjoint family groups.

1. *Peer groups*

For those not familiar with this form of treatment, it should be emphasized that treating children in groups is distinctly different from individual therapy. It has a different purpose and is a different technique. The essential feature of group psychotherapy lies not in the behavior of single individuals within the group, but in the interaction between individuals and ultimately in the action of these group members as a group. Only the novice gathers together several people and attempts to conduct individual interviews with each person in front of the others. The therapeutic catalyst is the behavior of the group as a whole. In terms of behavior modification, it is the group who administers the rewards and punishments.

Thus, group psychotherapy is concerned with the dynamics of the individual only insofar as the individual's behavior affects others. As with behavior modification of an individual, group psychotherapy is less concerned with causes than with consequences. A group may be initially sympathetic with a member's problems and exchange support. Yet, after awhile, most groups become impatient with a member's explanations and excuses and demand change. Group therapy thus puts stress on the social functioning of the individual's ego. A group may accept and even support disability in other ego functions, but not in social behavior.

The general criteria for group psychotherapy may be summarized as follows.

1. The child's disturbance should in some way involve his social functioning. At first glance, this might seem true of every case. However, the degree of such social involvement does vary considerably. A large majority of children do manifest their disturbances in inadequate social relationships. Yet, some disturbed children are quite adept socially, so that their difficulties are not so obvious to others. Eventually, other children in a group may feel manipulated by or shown up by the child whose social development is hypertrophic, but such a child may not contribute much to a group of peers. Another type of child who may not overtly demonstrate social inadequacy is the one who suffers internally. He may not reach out to others or disturb others, and thus be a relatively passive, withdrawn or silent group member. He also may subsequently be drawn out by a group but contributes little initially.

2. The child should be susceptible to social pressure. Again, this criterion may appear to be universal, but there are also variations in the degree to which children do respond to groups. Some children are overwhelmed with anxiety in the presence of others. They are so easily embarrassed that they become mute. Other children have learned to inure themselves to group pressures. They shrug off what people say. At both extremes of this continuum of social involvement, children can ultimately be drawn into groups. The shy, embarrassed child can be made to feel accepted and the hard-shelled child can be opened up. Yet, such children do not make it easy to form a cohesive group.

3. The type of social pressure — the "contingent stimuli" (Greenspoon and Gersten, 1967) — should be appropriate to the child's needs. The group in which the child is to be placed should attract him and stimulate him to become involved. It is possible to bring together a miscellaneous set of children, but if they have little in common or too many antagonisms, they may never form a cohesive group. It is much more difficult to form and maintain a children's group than adult groups. The dropout rate is especially high in outpatient adolescent groups. Even in groups on a hospital ward, where attendance is nearly compulsory, adolescent or younger children find ways of escaping the group meetings. Thus, it becomes important to select group members who are halfway congenial, who have some problems in common, and who possibly will stimulate one another. However, it is also possible to have a group which is

too homogenous. If all members are depressed or all "act out," the group may fail to congeal or become so disruptive that no therapeutic work can be carried on. It is possible to mix neurotic and psychotic children in the same group, but a very psychotic child may disrupt a group or one neurotic child in a group of psychotic children may become more disturbed by the raw outpouring of psychotic feelings.

In peer groups, a relatively narrow age range is usually the rule, since the 16 year old has little in common with the 12 year old and vice versa. However, the age range may depend as much on mental, social, and emotional maturation as on chronological age. A socially precocious 14 year old may fit better into a group averaging age 16 than in one averaging 14. However, prepubescent children do not belong in adolescent groups. Sexually mixed groups of any age create special problems. Latency children and even junior high school children are much more compatible and open if grouped with the same sex. As was discussed at length in previous chapters, the latency age child is avoiding sexual stimulation. Mixed groups of boys and girls of high school age is somewhat more feasible, but embarrassment runs high even at this age.

If group therapy is to be the treatment of choice, then the child should be able to enter into peer relationships to at least a slight degree. The child who remains ensconced entirely in his family may need peer relationships but be unable to engage in them and be rejected by his peers. Such a child may need some individual or family group therapy before being put in a group. Often the parents are also treated in a concurrent group. However, the selection of the group should be based on the characteristics of the children, not of the parents. Some or all of the children in a group may also be in some form of individual therapy. This variable may have to be taken into account in forming the group. The child who has little or no prior therapeutic experience may seem naive to those who have "graduated" from individual therapy. Those in individual therapy may retreat from the group, or may use the group to act out their transference from the individual treatment. Although such differences in therapeutic experience may be worked through in the group sessions, it is usually wiser to avoid such extraneous problems by selecting group

members with roughly equal experience. For example, it is not wise to do a favor for a colleague and accept one of his long-term patients into an inexperienced group. Of course, the amount of time a child has spent in individual treatment is not in itself a reliable indication of the child's level of ego development. In the long run, groups should be equated on their level of ego development rather than on the basis of therapeutic experience, age, or even diagnosis.

In assessing a child for whom peer group therapy is considered, data collection should thus include information regarding his social functioning. In interviews with the child and with his parents, the assessor should be sure to inquire about his behavior with peers. For example, does he have friends? How old are they? Are they mostly acquaintances or are some close friends? How much time does he spend with them? What do they do together? Does he confide in them, telling them things he would not reveal to adults? Even if he has no close confidantes among his peers, does he try to conform to peer standards and join in the groups at school or in his neighborhood? If he is relatively socially isolated, is this by his choice, or is he kept out of peer groups by his mother or the fact that no schoolmates or children of his age live in the neighborhood? Some very lonely and isolated children desire peer group contacts even though they have little opportunity to engage in group activities.

CASE 55

Kurt R., age nine, was most obstreperous at school, playing the clown and disrupting the class. Although the children laughed at him, they had little to do with him. He neglected his schoolwork and was sullen and impudent to the teacher. The teacher, however, was sympathetic, noting that Kurt was rejected by other children. When the parents were called to the school they were most embarrassed. The teacher tried to convince Mr. R that whipping Kurt was not likely to be effective and that the R's should seek psychological consultation.

The R's complied with the teacher's advice, but it was evident that they had little faith in psychology. Both spoke with heavy European accents and began the interview by stating that they deplored the way Americans rear children, the 'lack of discipline" and "lack of respect" for authority. Yet, they admitted that Kurt behaved at home much as he did in the classroom. He was impudent to his father, called him names, made fun of his accent and foreign ideas and habits. Although Mr. R roared and made threats, he found himself impotent to carry out any form of discipline. Kurt was less hostile toward his mother, merely ignoring her plaintive urgings. Both parents were quite passive and dependent people. Neither had married until relatively late in life. Mr. R was 55, a short, plump, balding man who tried to earn a living as a cantor. He had fled Vienna when Hitler came into power. Prior to his emigration to the United States at age 30, he had lived with family and earned a living as a concert singer. After coming to the United States, he was often unemployed as he refused to do anything but sing, and would not sing popular music. Mrs. R, also a refugee from the Nazi regime, had remained with her family until age 35, when the marriage to Mr. R was "arranged." At home, the R's spoke only German and Kurt also had a German accent when he first started school. Sometimes when excited at school, he would burst out with German expletives, for which he was teased by his schoolmates. He often threw out the school lunch his mother packed for him — " 'cause it was only old black bread and cheese!" Despite Kurt's behavior at home, it was evident that these aging parents spoiled their only son and could not really bear to discipline him.

In the initial interview, Kurt was very careful not to criticize his parents in any way. "My parents are nice," he reported, evasively. He was much more open in his criticism of the teacher, but watered down his remarks by apologizing, "I should not say so, but . . . ." He excused his lack of friends by saying that his parents "didn't care for the type of children" who lived in the neighborhood, but denied that he disagreed with their judgments. He admitted that he did often play with one boy who lived nearby, whom his parents criticized but tolerated. Asked what he and his friend did together, he replied, "Oh, nothing much — just mess around and stuff — I like to go to his house 'cause they have such good stuff to eat." However, Kurt denied that the food his friend had was any better than at his own home—"Just different, you know." He did explain, "We have Jewish food at home. I like it but it's fun to have something different sometimes." Later, he revealed that

his friend's family were also Jewish, but not recent immigrants. He added that he and his "buddy" liked to talk "about stuff." Asked for an example, he shrugged and blushed, "Just kid stuff, you know!" He admitted that he would like to have more friends, but was quick to blame his schoolmates as forming "cliques." "They're a bunch of snobs and kooks."

Kurt possessed above average intelligence —IQ, 115. His Rorschach responses showed him to be more sensitive to environmental stimuli than most latency boys (three of his 14 responses contained references to the texture of the blot), but his actual involvement was rather restricted (two FC's). His psychogram was introversive ($M: C = 3:1$). There were no indications on these Rorschach responses of any gross perceptual difficulty ($F+ = 70\%$). Nor were there indications of excessive anxiety or depression. Kurt's TAT stories consisted of one fantasy after another in which "secret agents" succeeded in confusing and disrupting tyrannical authorities or in which the hero escaped punishment for some misdemeanor. For example, to Card 6BM, Kurt responded, "His grandmother caught him stealing some food from the icebox—but she probably won't do anything if he apologizes. So he apologizes. (Why did he steal?) Just for the fun of it. It wasn't serious or anything. (What will happen?) Oh, nothing. He just won't get caught next time, that's all"—and Kurt laughed.

Kurt eagerly accepted the invitation to join a male peer group which was just starting. Initially, he was the leader in disrupting the group, all of whom had difficulty in sitting still and talking. However, the group soon tired of his giggling, his faces, and his other antics and told him in no uncertain terms to "cool it." However, they were most sympathetic when he talked about his parents and home life. The group quickly saw through his difficulty and told him directly, "You just act up because you can't take it at home."

His parents, who attended a parent group, were much more silent and withdrawn. Finally, Mr. R grew irritated and shouted at another group member who kept pestering him and announced that she was determined to "open him up." In his anger, he revealed his feelings about "loud Americans who spoil their children." Accusations swung back and forth but quieted down when Mrs. R near tears, confessed that she was having as much trouble with Kurt as other mothers had mentioned they had with their children. Thereafter, the group was much more sympathetic and full of advice. In fact, they were most sympathetic as the R's story came out. Mr. R seemed to remain unmoved but Mrs. R seemed a bit more insightful as the parents compared notes. "Perhaps we have been mistaken and did not know what Kurt needed," she pleaded with her husband. Gradually, Mr. R decided that Kurt did need more play with his peers. He also was determined that Kurt "respect" him. With great reluctance, he accompanied Kurt to the Boy Scouts. He admitted that he was ignorant of baseball and embarrassed by Kurt's knowledge of American sports. However, he had been an expert skier and soccer player. He organized a soccer team among the Scouts, took Kurt to the professional games, and taught him to ski. He bought Kurt a set of drums (something Kurt had yearned for), and taught him rhythm, revealing that he had once played drums in a band. Kurt responded by dropping his disdain and insult, and Mr. R remarked ironically, "The trouble with being a father is that I enjoy it!"

2. Conjoint Family Therapy

This type of therapy is a relatively recent innovation. For many years, parents have been treated along with but separately from the child. Only rarely were interviews held with both parents and the child and seldom were other children or family members included. The concept of conjoint family therapy gained its impetus in the 1950's as an outgrowth of research on the family structure of young adult schizophrenics (Jackson and Weakland, 1961; Ackerman, 1958). Because the group in conjoint family therapy is a natural group with a historically determined structure with affective bonds, attitudes, and interests that have developed prior to treatment—in contrast to the peer groups who are strangers both before and after treatment—authorities on conjoint family therapy (Bell, 1961; Framo, 1965; Wynne, 1965) insist that it is quite distinct from peer group treatment. Granting the importance of this distinction, the main justification for discussing conjoint family therapy as a group therapy is that, like other group therapis, it focuses on the interactions between the group mem-

bers rather than on the intrapsychic conflicts of the individual. The fact that these interactions, or transactions, have been built up prior to the onset of therapy, and such transactions, hopefully revised, will continue in the family group thereafter does create a far different setting than in other kinds of groups. Nevertheless, most of the criteria for peer group treatment listed above also apply to family groups.

In refreshing contrast to most advocates of a particular form of therapy, Wynne (1965), in a chapter entitled "Some Indications and Contraindications for Exploratory Family Therapy," begins as follows (page 290):

"I approach this problem with an investigative spirit, not with the intent of making doctrinaire pronouncements or promulgating an ideological, family therapy party line. Let me state at the outset that I do not regard family therapy as a psychiatric panacea, but as a valuable addition to our psychiatric repertory. On the one hand, I consider family therapy as the treatment of choice which I shall attempt to specify. On the other hand, certain limitations, some of which are intrinsic to family therapy and others of which are imposed are imposed by external, practical considerations, restrict the range of problems for which this treatment approach is appropriate."

Subsequently, Wynne states as "a general indication for . . . family therapy: . . . the clarification and resolution of any structured intrafamilial relationship difficulty." As do other writers on this topic, Wynne advocates the use of another therapy for the intrapsychic problems of the individual—usually a psychoanalytic approach, since most writers on conjoint family therapy base their treatment on psychoanalytic theory. In fact, the use of conjoint family treatment in conjunction with individual psychoanalytic treatment, and the indications and contraindications for such combinations, form an important section of Wynne's article. Conjoint family therapy is viewed by the authors in Boszormenyi-Nagy and Framo (1965) as an extension of psychoanalysis, in which the patient's interactions with his family, usually reported in individual therapy by the patient from his memories, are actually demonstrated and resolved in vivo by treating the family rather than merely the patient. In fact, all authorities agree that it is the family and not any individual member which is disturbed and which is the object of treatment.

As a very specific form of group therapy, conjoint family therapy requires the following conditions.

1. The child's disturbance should be centered in a difficulty within a structured family relationship. As was pointed out in a discussion of some of the criteria for other therapies, this criterion seems applicable to nearly all children's problems. From the theoretical considerations of Section I, it is obvious that this writer thoroughly agrees with the proponents of conjoint family therapy that wherever a child lives in a family setting, the interactions and attitudes of the family toward the child and of the child toward his family, and in a third dimension (as Framo, 1965, indicates), the total pattern of family interactions and values constitute a major determinant of the degree and nature of children's disturbances—including intrapsychic physiological disturbances. Nevertheless, the fact that there are other determinants does have to be taken into account. Obviously a physiological disease or trauma requires medical attention, even though family counselling may well be in order just to maintain a medical regime. Learning problems, extrafamilial problems, developmental crisis, body image, and other identity problems, for example, all may require other therapeutic considerations in addition to the family interaction pattern. Most important is the distinction made by the advocates of family therapy themselves, that is, between family interaction difficulties and intrapsychic conflicts. Certainly in most instances, intrapsychic conflicts are associated with family conflicts; often they are an internalization of the family interaction patterns, albeit distorted and distilled. Yet, many family interaction difficulties also may be viewed as arising from the internalized, intrapsychic conflicts of one or more members of a family, as has been long recognized in the old concept of *folie à deux*. This distinction between intrapsychic and intrapersonal, familial disturbance is in fact usually a matter of degree. In most childhood problems, there is both family disturbance and an intrapsychic conflict within the child. The conjoint family therapists rightly do not regard the family disturbance as necessarily the cause of the child's intrapsychic conflicts, but rather use the disturbance within the family as a focal

point for the treatment. Assessment for this criterion thus should be centered about the questions: To what degree is the family interaction pattern disturbed? And, to what extent and in what ways do these family interaction patterns play a part in the child's internal conflicts?

2. The child should be susceptible to family pressures and be responding to family interaction patterns. Again, this may seem to be a universal condition. However, on even slight reflection, one may remember that many children today, especially adolescents for whom this treatment is particularly designed, are often influenced as much by their peers and other extrafamilial stress as they are by their parents. As was pointed out in Chapters 3 and 15, adolescents are very much a part of Reissman's *Lonely Crowd* (1950), perhaps even more so than their parents. Family ties and influences appear to be decreasing in strength with each generation. Although the proponents of conjoint family therapy do recognize that the kinship or family clan no longer exists in most cases, they do not seem to realize that the nuclear family also may be changing, and that the family's influence on the adolescent is much different than in the immediately preceding generations. Assessment should thus take into account the strength and influence of the family structure in question. The fact that an adolescent spends a great deal of his time outside the family or even that he no longer has strong affective and cognitive ties with his family may not necessarily indicate a disturbance of family interactions. In the rapid currents of today's society, social and emotional separations from the family occur much earlier than in prior generations. Such separations may disrupt the family but do not necessarily indicate that the family interaction patterns were disturbed prior to this separation. Some form of conjoint family therapy may aid in easing this separation, but it seems unreasonable to expect this or any therapy to stem a social tide.

3. In most instances, the social structure of the family should (if revised by treatment) serve the needs of the child. Dependent as he is on the family, it is this group to which he turns for nearly all his needs. However, as was pointed out in the preceding paragraphs, as the child enters adolescence, an increasing amount of his need-gratifications are obtained from extrafamilial sources. In fact, it is essential for the adolescent's devel-

opment into an independent adult that he learn to seek need-gratification on his own, outside of his childhood family. Again, conjoint family therapy may be needed to ease this separation—particularly in very tight-knit families—but the goal of this therapy should be to foster the eventual separation, not to maintain the nuclear childhood family structure.

Because a great deal of the impetus for conjoint family therapy originated in the treatment of young adult schizophrenics and with the separation problems of adolescence, there is little discussion of the use of this treatment with families in which the children are pubescent or prepubescent. In fact, writers on this therapy question whether such younger family members should be included in the group. However, since younger children are far more dependent on their families and thus far more under their influence than older adolescents, this would seem much more applicable to their families. Perhaps the emphasis on purely verbal treatment, utilizing psychoanalytic generalizations, etc. is the reason doubts are raised about treating younger children in family groups. However, this writer and several of his students and colleagues have had fairly successful experiences using conjoint family treatment with younger children. In fact, one such family* included an 11-month-old baby, whose presence and activities were very much a part of the family interactions and of the problems of the "identified" patient (age eight). It was the birth of this baby which disrupted the previously precarious balance of family interactions, a disruption which was manifested in the behavior of the eight-year-old brother, who had theretofore been the baby in the family, much to the disgust of his father and sister and the not-too-secret delight of his mother.

Wynne (op. cit.) lists four types of family patterns to which conjoint therapy is particularly applicable. They are: (1) "adolescent separation problems"; (2) "the trading of dissociations," that is, a mutual and interlocking set of projections of blame; (3) "collective cognitive chaos and erratic distancing"—in essence, a "schizophrenic" family; and (4) "amorphous communication" or a pattern of incomplete and vaguely implicit transactions. In treating families with

preadolescent children, one might add at least two further categories (which are not mutually exclusive): (5) the adulto-morphic family wherein all members of the family are expected to conduct transactions on an adult level, with little or no allowance for normal preadolescent communication, and (6) the infantilizing family, wherein all members of the family expect to be treated as children.

Despite his brave intentions, Wynne is much less specific regarding the contraindications for conjoint family therapy. He lists among "other factors affecting the indications": (1) "the family constellation available for therapy," that is, the question of precisely who constitutes the family group and who should be included in the treatment. He also discusses the important topic of the relative motivation of the various members of the family; (2) "phase of the psychotherapeutic process," that is, in regard to other aspects of psychoanalytic treatment of individual family members, and (3) "kind of available therapies" in which he discusses the behavior of the therapist. The most important contraindication, according to Wynne, is the inability of the therapist to control the "countertransference."

In addition to these considerations, there are some family patterns and some family problems which are not easily approachable by conjoint family therapy and for which family therapy may actually be contraindicated. First, as to what Wynne calls the family constellation available for therapy, there are many children whose disturbances arise chiefly from the lack of a definite family constellation. Most common of these are the children of divorced and remarried parents, who float between two antagonistic households and are unwelcome reminders or ghosts of the prior marriage for both of the original parents. This pattern is illustrated in the following case.

CASE 56

Marie, age eight, constantly demanded attention and rejected adult controls both at home and at school. She was born a year before her parents separated in what her mother openly admitted was an effort to force her husband to stay in the marriage. Thereafter, the mother withdrew from Marie, leaving her care to various maids and governesses and attempting to buy the child off with a constant flow of expensive presents and

---

*See Case 63 in Chapter 19.

clothes. Even after seven years of psychoanalysis, the mother remained a depressed and
schizoid woman. Marie's father was also
depressed and had little to do with this child
and her sibs for the next five years, until he
remarried. At the time treatment began,
Marie spent three days and four nights with
her father, stepmother, and their children and
four days and three nights with her mother
and adolescent sibs. Twice a week, one parent
delivered her to the therapist and the opposite
parent retrieved her. The fact that the therapist's playroom was in effect a passageway
between the two households was used to
assist Marie in attempting to handle the very
depressing fact that she had no real home.
Neither parent could be involved in this
treatment. Over a can of hot chicken soup,
which Marie purchased each therapy session
from a food dispenser, she worked through
the despair, anger, and depression of her
family situation. At first, she played out a
fantasied reunion of the parents, with fits of
rage at the therapist when this was identified
as fantasy. Then she spent months destroying
and reviving each parent in play. She demanded the therapist become a parent and,
failing in this fantasy, destroyed and revived
him. Finally but gradually she came to accept
the reality of her separation; she sought the
counsel and comfort of her young-adult
sister, who accepted her recognition that the
mother was depressed. In her own fashion,
Marie sought to comfort her mother and
received some comfort in return. At the
same time, Marie began to play the role of
oldest child in her father's family, as a help-
mate to her stepmother in the care of the
younger stepsibs, and thus found rewards
from her stepmother and her father. At this
time, her school problems disappeared and
her academic achievement rose to a superior
level. Despite her three years' diet of chicken
soup, Marie lost her excess weight and was developing into a lovely and charming pre-pubes-
cent girl when treatment was discontinued.

Perhaps Marie's father and stepmother
could have been involved in a conjoint family
therapy, but Marie's mother would certainly
have protested as she had adamantly refused
to permit the father to obtain custody of
Marie, and Marie's father was content with
the division of the child between two households. The mother's analyst, who was con-
sulted, advised that she was in no condition
to be involved in any other kind of treatment

at that time, although periodic conferences
were held with the mother.

In addition to considering the social membership of the family, one must assess its
affective and conative structure. It is not
enough to assume that consanguinal ties constitute an affective bond that motivates the
members of a family. Especially in disturbed
families, the nature of this bond needs close
examination and observation. Some families
are bound together by affection, others by a
mutual dependency, still others by almost
open erotic ties, by a common need achievement or need aggression, or even by mutual
hatreds. Perhaps all of these are elements
in most family ties, but the degree and nature
of these bonds should be assessed. Conjoint
family therapy may well be the treatment of
choice when these family ties are particularly
ambivalent. As the experts on family therapy
point out, an intense and prolonged marital
dissenion between the parents often underlies
the disturbed behavior of the child. If the
marriage does rest on the child's disturbance,
or if having attention focused on the child
masks the marital tension, then it may be
very difficult to treat the child separately
from the family. Every time the child im-
proves, such parents do something consciously
or unconsciously to reinstate the child's disturbance. A careful and thorough assessment
often serves to warn the therapist of such an
eventuality.

In this writer's experience, there is one
type of family bond or dynamics where conjoint therapy seems contraindicated, that is,
when the family seems held together primarily
by a sadomasochistic relationship; as Dr.
Walter Raine * states it: "when the hostility
in the family is highly eroticized." In such
families, each member is a whipping boy for
the other, and the passions aroused in these
mutual beatings, both physical and verbal,
are tinged with sexual arousal. In such marital battles, each marital partner may, for
example, accuse the other of impotency. Each
may fight to obtain demonstrations of affection
from the child. Often the battles are focused
on the adolescent's sexual behavior, real or
imagined, and each parent may vicariously
live out their sexual frustrations through the
child's behavior. Such families use conjoint
therapy as another battleground, often at-

---

*Personal communication.

tempting to involve the therapist or focus their erotic projections onto him. Usually this sadomasochistic relationship is the very basis of the marriage. In such instances, it is often better to try to get the parents to permit the placement of the child outside the home, in a foster home or a residential treatment center. Individual treatment of the child, if he remains with his parents, is usually constantly sabotaged by the parents. The chief exception is when the adolescent is nearly ready to leave the home on his own. If he can recognize the nature of his parents' relationship, it may be possible to help him recover from his depression and to separate himself from the family's sadomasochism. In such instances, assessment of the child's ego strength is most essential for if the child's identity has been overwhelmed by his family, it will be very difficult for him to withdraw on his own.

Most experts on conjoint family therapy agree that a thorough assessment is required. The usual techniques employed to assay ego-strength development in individuals are most helpful. However, the assessment of the individual members does not in itself provide the data needed to comprehend the interactions between members. It is possible to hypothesize about how one personality might interact with another on the basis of two sets of comparable protocols. However, the interactions within a whole family are so complex as to require a computer program— if a computer program could be formulated. The computer analysis of MMPI profiles, now being developed for individual profiles, might well be expanded in the future to allow for such prediction of family interactions. Even so, some tests of these hypothesis would be helpful before conjoint family therapy is instituted.

Considerable thought has been given to methods for assessing these family interaction patterns. Obviously, one of the most direct methods is to conduct one or more conjoint family interviews during the assessment. The case history material is often gathered in joint interviews with the parents in any case. If these data are gathered in a conjoint family interview, the exchange between parents and children about events in the family history may be very revealing. Not only may the memories of one member supplement those of another, but the conflicting memories and viewpoints which frequently come to the fore

reveal the dissonance in the family. It is a good idea in such conjoint assessment interviews to involve other siblings or important relatives in addition to the parents and the identified patient. Such initial involvement sets the stage for identifying the problem as a family interaction, rather than merely as the behavior of the child, and thus paves the way for conjoint treatment.

Other approaches to assessment of family interactions consist chiefly of involvement of the family in a common task (Hurwitz, Kaplan, and Kaiser, 1962; Elbert, Rosman, Minuchin, and Guerney, 1964). The latter authors also devised a method for having the family construct a common fantasy, comparable to the TAT. Levy and Epstein (1964) designed a method for a family Rorschach in which family decisions were required as to the possible interpretations of the inkblots. The use of Leary's Interpersonal Checklist has already been mentioned. Particularly informative in the study of interaction patterns are the descriptions each family member makes of each of the others on the ICL. In some instances, a family member may be assigned different roles by each member of the family and in other cases a family member may be assigned a common role by all. Whether the family member accepts these roles may be assessed from his description of himself on the ICL.

One of the problems commonly discussed by authorities on conjoint family treatment is the inclusion of "well" siblings. The question of how one child can develop schizophrenia while others do not appear to be disturbed has plagued those who maintain that this and similar patterns of behavioral disturbance arise from family interactions. Some authorities maintain, with some evidence, that the other siblings do manifest considerable disturbance, even though no immediate complaint is made about their behavior. In other instances, siblings do seem to escape with only mild disturbances at most. The practical import of this question is that very often neither the parents nor these siblings see any reason that anyone other than the identified patient should be included in the assessment. In settings where conjoint family therapy is employed, parents should be advised that assessment of all family members is routine. Furthermore, they may be informed that assessment of the parents and other siblings is necessary to understand the disturbances of the identified patient.

CASE 57

In discussing her 11-year-old daughter, Betsy, Mrs. S complained angrily that Betsy gave her "no satisfaction whatever. . . . She is always demanding, demanding, demanding, and never gives up," said Mrs. S wearily. For example, if she bought something for Betsy's sister, Adele, age 14, then Betsy would pout and whine endlessly unless she too was allowed a purchase. Every gift Betsy received was compared jealously with something Adele received—even though months had intervened. Betsy was resistant to any demands made on her. Mrs. S had to "nag" continuously to get Betsy to make her bed, take a bath, brush her teeth, and she was so slow in completing any household chores that Mrs. S had given up assigning them to her. Adele, however, was most cooperative. The biggest squabble between Betsy and her mother was over Betsy's schoolwork and behavior in the classroom. Betsy was barely making passing grades, yet she would claim that she had no homework. Subsequently Mrs. S would discover that Betsy was two weeks or more behind in her assignments. Betsy's behavior in the classroom was very similar to that at home. She was frequently at the teacher's desk for further help, even though the teacher had thought she had explained the work thoroughly moments before. She constantly complained about the behavior of other students, how they bothered her, got her in trouble, or tried to cheat. She talked out of turn constantly. If reprimanded, she burst into tears, denying her behavior and accusing other children, and claiming the teacher was unfair and biased against her. Several times after such an outburst, Betsy rushed from the classroom and telephoned her mother, who would panic at Betsy's incoherent tearful voice and come running to the school. Mrs. S was embarrassed by these disturbances at school and would blame variously Betsy, the teacher, the other children, and the educational system. Most of the children at school and in the neighborhood seemed to dislike Betsy and teased her unmercifully. Much larger than her peers, Betsy was known as "Betsy the Buffalo"—but even the boys respected her strength. She responded in kind, often with socially unacceptable language, tattling on the others, or kicking, jabbing, and pummeling them.

Mrs. S also complained about the strain of the routine in her home. Although she usually had household help, no domestic remained in her employ for more than a few months. Everything about the home seemed burdensome to her. The S's lived several miles from the school and shopping area; much of Mrs. S's time was consumed in driving the girls to and from different schools, music lessons, and other errands. Often she was exhausted or ill. An extremely obese woman, she had had several operations for varicose veins and had been advised that she might develop heart trouble. But when she tried to rest, Betsy would arouse her with some request or complaint, or the girls would begin to fight. All of these problems had been present for many years, but had come to a climax when the school authorities notified Mrs. S that Betsy might be held back a grade.

Mr. S had said little during this initial interview and, when asked to comment, he remarked that Betsy's insistence on buying things also bothered him and that he did not see why the girls always compared presents and clothes. "I can't afford this constant buying. I tell them they just have to be content with what they have." "You just don't know how much it costs to run a house or what girls need," Mrs. S retorted. She then complained that her husband seldom gave her any help in disciplining Betsy except when she pressured him or when he lost his temper. Mr. S, now aroused, replied that she would have much less trouble with the girls if she were more organized and budgeted her time and money more effectively. Mrs. S glared at him and pouted, but did not pursue the topic, nor did Mr. S elaborate at that time.

Neither parent mentioned the reason for which Betsy's pediatrician had referred them for psychological consultation, that is, her extreme obesity. When asked about Betsy's weight problem, each parent glanced at the other. Both of them were also obese. "I guess it's a family problem," Mr. S sighed. Mrs. S quickly explained that she had a "glandular problem" but Mr. S interrupted, "No! We're just fat. There's no physical problem. Our doctor has told us that many times." Again Mrs. S pouted angrily, "I've tried to diet but no one else tries." Only Adele had succeeded in reducing to within normal limits.

When asked what she had done to discipline Betsy, Mrs. S replied, "Everything!" She had shouted and screamed and nagged; she had restricted Betsy from such pleasures as TV or shut her in her room; she had promised rewards if Betsy obeyed, but Betsy seldom was able to please Mrs. S; she had even persuaded Mr. S to whip Betsy. All to no avail.

Betsy looked and acted very much like her mother. Her voice was equally shrill and she also frequently pouted, bit her lip, and gestured with her fist as she raged on about the injustices she endured at home and at school. Her chief complaints were that no one payed any attention to her needs or her feelings and that everyone expected too much of her. She regarded Adele as her chief enemy, as Adele was favored by "everyone." The present Adele received last year for her birthday was much nicer and more expensive than the one Betsy had received recently. Moreover, she did not really get what she wanted even though she had clearly specified it. Adele did not do her share of the work and Betsy was expected to do "everything." Her mother "always" screamed at her, but "never" at Adele. Her father whipped her "with a big belt" but "never touched" Adele. Adele "got away with everything," and Betsy always was blamed. The teachers at school blamed Betsy for "everything," and Betsy cited in detail incident after incident in which others started trouble but she was caught. She was bored with class assignments, "baby work" she called them—or they were too hard and the teacher never explained. Her mother took the teacher's side. The kids at school were all mean.

Since Betsy was so unsuccessful with her schoolwork, it was decided to assay her intellectual development with the WISC. Betsy made a sour face when the test was introduced and was resistant throughout. "That's too hard!" she would complain, or "How should I know!" With praise and encouragement, she often succeeded even when she had initially rejected a task. Her total IQ was 113, with a Verbal IQ of 115 and a Performance IQ of 110. She achieved scale scores of 12 on Similarities, Vocabulary, and Block Design, indicating that her reasoning and verbalization were more than adequate.

Her top score of 16 on the Picture Arrangement showed her acute perception of the social scene. In contrast, several of her responses to the Comprehension subtest were self-centered. She sputtered over the Arithmetic questions, asking for pencil and paper and to have the questions repeated, then claimed that she never had problems like that in school. She dawdled over the Digit Symbol subtest, biting her pencil and looking up at the examiner as if expecting some kind of help.

Similarly, on the Rorschach, she protested in helpless fashion that she could not tell what the blot was supposed to be or criticized the uneveness or incompleteness: Card I, "It couldn't be a butterfly, cause it's too big or a bird cause it's got those holes . . . I don't know . . . I can't tell." Most of her responses were vague and stereotyped reactions to the whole blot. She was irritated at having to explain her responses in the inquiry, and it was difficult to ascertain exactly what determinants she was using in several instances. She saw no human figures, and of the five animal responses, there were two which she indicated might be moving or at least alive. However, she was quite responsive to the color: 2 FC and 2 CF. Four of her 14 responses dealt with food: Card VII, "fried chicken," and Card VIII, "a banana split." This pattern of responses indicated that Betsy felt helpless and resentful when faced with making decisions on her own, that she had not as yet begun to internalize concepts upon which to make such judgments, and that she remained very dependent emotionally on others.

Betsy found the T.A.T. even more difficult. She described the cards, sometimes attributing some action or reactions to the characters but was seldom able to hazard a guess about the preceding events or the outcome. She rejected several of the pictures outright. After six attempts at story telling, she was given the MAPS as a substitute, but her reaction was the same. Her first MAPS story did seem significant: In the livingroom scene, she placed a maternal figure and two girls, all rushing to the door to meet the male figure carrying a present. "They want to see who it is for," she explained, but could not decide who did receive the present.

Betsy's feelings of being blamed and persecuted, her desires for retaliation, and her unwillingness to commit herself or take independent action all might be labeled "paranoia" if she were adult. However, it did appear that her mother fed Betsy's sense of being persecuted and, even more, that Betsy used her "paranoid" behavior as a means of manipulating her environment. Because Betsy did appear so dependent on her environment and because so many of Mrs. S's complaints involved family interactions, it was decided to continue the assessment with three family interviews, to explore the possibility of conjoint family therapy. It was carefully explained to Betsy and her parents that these meetings were a part of the assessment, that is, to understand more clearly the family interactions, and that Adele was to be included. However, Adele did not appear at the first session. Mrs. S had excused her so that she could attend a neighbor child's birthday party. Betsy immediately accused her mother of favoritism, pointing out that she also had been invited to the party. Mrs. S tried to calm her, saying that this meeting was to help *her,* not Adele, and that her father had taken time off from his business just because of her. "You hate me! You both hate me!" Betsy screamed. "That's why you brought me here. You think I'm crazy." Mrs. S shrugged and looked helplessly at the psychologist. Mr. S then attempted to reason with Betsy, assuring her that their concern for her indicated their love. Betsy then buried her head in her father's lap, sobbing loudly. Now Mr. S looked helpless. Asked how he felt about Betsy's feelings, Mr. S was puzzled. "I don't know how she can say we hate her. She gets everything she wants!" Betsy sat bolt upright and told him, "You didn't get the bike I wanted, and you promised!" "But you have a bike—two bikes," Mrs. S responded. "But not the one I wanted," Betsy sniffled. The hour continued much in the same vein, with Betsy complaining and the parents defending themselves. Neither parent seemed able to face Betsy with their complaints.

Adele appeared at the next session. Her face was tearstained and clouded with anger. The meeting began in silence, broken by the psychologist's inquiry into Adele's feelings about coming to this session. Mr. S chuckled, "She's playing the martyr." "She's a hellcat!" snapped Mrs. S. This remark brought forth an anguished scream from Adele: "You think you're so damn smart! Well! *I* don't have to come here. *I'm* not the one who needs to be psyched out. It's *her!* She's the

one who's failing at school. She's the one who causes all the trouble. I *hate* her!" Betsy stuck out her tongue, kicked Adele in the knee, and snuggled up to her father. Adele reached to grab Betsy, but her mother intervened. "You see! You see!" Mrs. S exclaimed, "That's what I have to put up with all the time!" Adele continued to attack Betsy verbally, repeating many of the complaints which Mrs. S had voiced in the initial interview. Betsy continued to ignore her, looking appealingly at her father. However, when Adele mentioned Betsy's behavior at school and her lack of friends, Betsy retorted, "That's none of your business!" and began to cry. Mrs. S scolded Adele, who continued, "I've got to be known as *her* sister!" and related more incidents at school in which Betsy allegedly attacked other children. Mrs. S tried to change the topic, saying, "We're here to talk about the family. Betsy's problems at school are a different thing. We can't all be smarties like you." "No they aren't!" Adele argued. "She behaves at school just like she does at home. Everything has to go her way or she acts like a baby and screams."

In the last session, Adele quickly sat herself between her father and mother, leaving Betsy to sit between her mother and the psychologist. Betsy began to demand "her chair." This time it was Mr. S who told her to "Shut up! I'm tired of your fighting—both of you!" "But you and mother fight all the time," Adele retorted. "That's none of your business, Miss Smarty," her mother responded. "You do! You do!" chimed in Betsy. Mrs. S glared at her husband who shifted uneasily in his chair. "She wanted to buy a new sofa." Adele went on, pointing at her mother, "And he wouldn't let her. He's such a tightwad." Mr. S then repeated his demand that Mrs. S stick to his budget before he would allow her to incur further debts. Mrs. S retorted that he was a poor businessman and that the reason the girls felt neglected was that she had to spend so much time at his office going over his accounts, trying to collect from his debtors. While the parents quarreled, the girls winked at each other, giggled, and yawned. Mrs. S suddenly noticed Betsy's derision and slapped her across the face. Both Betsy and her mother began to sob. Mr. S mopped his brow, and Adele smiled sweetly.

Sometimes, even after sessions similar to

he above, it is difficult to convince a family that the problem lies in their interactions rather than in the behavior of the identified patient. If television equipment is available, a family can often be helped to recognize the processes of their interaction when the video tape of such sessions is played back to them. In the case of the S family, the psychologist pointed out that all family members played a "game of accusation," and seldom communicated their feelings or responded to the feelings of others. Whether the S's understood or accepted this interpretation, they did seem to find some relief from these meetings and accepted the psychologist's offer to continue.

Although there were positive indications that conjoint family therapy might be the treatment of choice in this case, the decision was not clear cut. It might have been wiser, for example, to begin with a program of behavior modification in the hopes of retraining Betsy and thus easing some of the intensity of the family disruptions. However, Mrs. S appeared so overwrought and infantile herself that it seemed doubtful that she could carry out a reinforcement program in the home. Moreover, it did seem necessary to begin by relieving some of the emotional overtones before such a behavior modification could be instituted. The possibility of treating the parents separately and of individual treatment of Betsy was also considered, but it did not seem that the parents would accept the role of being patients for they continued to regard Betsy as the problem. As might be expected from the above, the course of family treatment for the S's did not go smoothly. After about four months, the marital dissension was so open and so intense that the parents were treated separately for a brief period and Betsy was treated by another therapist. Then the family group was reinstituted. Communication within the family gradually improved, and the parents were then able to conduct a program of behavior modification in the home encompassing both girls. This program was continually discussed in the family sessions.

G. INDIVIDUALIZED THERAPY — A SUMMARY

In the previous sections of this chapter, the question has been asked: Do the problems and needs of this child fit the goals and criteria of this form of treatment? However, only occasionally do the child's needs correspond to the stated goals and criteria of any one therapeutic approach. There are often as many contraindications as indications. Rather than ask whether the child fits any particular therapeutic mold, it would seem much more reasonable to use the data from the assessment to design an individualized program to fit the needs of the child. In this section, an attempt will be made to outline the ways in which therapy might be so programmed to the child.

To design such individualized treatment requires a careful and thorough assessment and thoughtful planning. Individualized therapy does not consist merely of a random sampling of therapeutic techniques, nor is it simply an electric approach. The design should systematically take into account the following factors.

(1) The needs and problems of the child.
(2) The basic principles common to all forms of therapy.
(3) The variations in techniques needed for the individual needs of the child.
(4) The time sequence of the therapy.
(5) The economic aspects of the therapy.
(6) Some difficulties in implementing a plan for therapy.

1. As was discussed in Chapter 1, the overall need of every child is growth, that is, the development of a unique identity with an ego which is capable of independent need-gratification. The raison d'être of any therapy is to promote such growth. Therapy, of course, does not create the urge to grow; this drive is a central aspect of the biological and social nature of the child. Rather, therapy is aimed at eliminating the obstacles and limitations to the child's growth, and thus deals with those specific behavioral stresses and conflicts which impede the child's development.

If therapy is to be planned to meet these impediments, then the first step is a comprehensive assessment. The assessment should not be limited to the questions asked by the referrant, but should explore in depth all ramifications of the child's ego development, and should contain a list of the various problems, that is, the manifest disturbing behaviors. Next, it should specify the different ways in which development is being impeded, the stresses and conflicts which underlie the disturbances. There should follow some reasonable hypotheses about the possible interrelationships of these factors, the dynamics or interacting forces. To plan therapy, an assessment should uncover and delineate the leitmotiv of the child's development, the core patterns of events and conflicts. These dynamics should be stated in terms of the child's stage of development. In particular, the assessment should specify the degree and nature of the child's dependency on others, and the process of internalization. The kinds of therapy to be used depend in part on the stage of development of the child's experience balance. The assessment should also contain a summary estimate of the overall ego strength of the child, again in terms of development, for the kinds of therapy and their implementation depend on the ability of the child to absorb and use the treatment.

2. As was repeatedly pointed out in the previous sections of this chapter, there are certain aspects of psychotherapy which all forms have in common and which appear to be fundamental to behavioral change. The therapeutic "couch" need not be a Procrustean bed, but even though it comes in various shapes and sizes and designs, there are some basic elements. Any therapy must include to some degree and fashion, the following.

(a) *A reflection or recognition of the child's affective states* or feelings. In behavior modification, which focuses on the environment, this recognition consists of the affective elements of the behavior of others in the environment and the affective responses of the child.

(b) *The relationships between these affects and the environment.*

(c) *The relationships between these affective states and the internal operations of the child.* In both client-centered therapy and behavior modification, this element of therapy is admittedly underestimated, since it is regarded as a constant.

(d) *The relationship of these affective states to the motivations of the child* and of his parents and other authorities. All therapies are concerned with what the child is trying to do, learn, achieve, or obtain. His affective states reflect the frustration of these goals.

(e) *The relationship between the child and the therapist.* In this relationship, the child both acts out the frustrations of his everyday life onto the therapist, and uses the therapist as a model.

(f) *All therapists repeatedly reinforce* various aspects of the child's behaviors, in a working-through process, sometimes using simple operant rewards and punishments, sometimes using very complex verbal and behavioral situations.

(g) Based chiefly on the therapeutic relationship, *all therapies use the therapeutic situation as a microcosm of everyday life.*

3. To design a therapeutic "couch" to fit the child, it is necessary to specify the variations needed in these basic dimensions of therapy. First, one needs to determine from the assessment which affective states need to be recognized and reflected. Which affective responses should be stressed? Which, possibly ignored? Which are closest to the child's consciousness and are thus most available for reflection? Which feelings does he hide at all costs? How much spontaneity and lability does he demonstrate? How much does he limit his affective awareness and expression? How sensitive is he? All these questions can and should be answered as best as possible if the reflection of affect is to planned.

Second, the assessment should specify the relationships between these affects and observable environmental stresses. Are these affects a response to the environment, and to what degree? What stimuli set off these affective reactions? What stimuli inhibit them? Third, the assessment should specify the degree to which these affective responses reflect the internal state of the child. What memories, fantasies, impulses, and drives trigger off these feelings? Are these generalized affective states, or are they specific to certain external or internal stimuli? Assessment of these factors are basic to planning the degree to which the external and internal facts of behaviors are to be manipulated. Fourth, the therapist needs to be advised of the specific motivational patterns which drive the child to act and feel as he does. Where and why is the child frustrated in meeting his need-gratifications? How does he react to deprivation of needs? With knowledge of these motivational patterns, the therapist can make plans to help the child cope with his frustrations and to find effective means of gaining need-satisfactions. Usually the behaviors which require altering are these coping mechanisms. In other instances, the child may be very adept at coping, but needs to redirect his efforts.

The kinds of interactions that the therapist may initially expect from the child are those which the child currently conducts with other adults. These interactions appear during assessment, directly with the assessor and indirectly in the child's responses to various techniques, and parents may openly or inadvertently mention them. From assessment of these patterns, the therapist may be able to predict how the child may react to him and his behavior. Finally, on the basis of the assessment, it is possible to plan out the kinds of reinforcements which may need to be used for the child under consideration. One may also estimate the frequency of these reinforcements and how they should be varied. With these variables in mind, the therapeutic situations or microcosms may be selected.

4. In all therapies, the timing and sequence of reinforcements are a major factor. Some learning has to be spaced; some consists of a rapid repetition of rewards and punishments. The question facing all therapists is: What is to be done first? Most often, therapy proceeds step by step from one element to the next, in the order listed above in paragraph 2: the therapist initially reflects the child's feelings, relating them to his environment and then to his own internal stresses. At the same time, the therapist begins to explore the child's motivations and their relationships to these affects. As these patterns of behavior are demonstrated in the therapy hour, the therapist uses his relationship with the child as a reinforcement. These and other reinforcements are repeated to obtain specific modifications of the child's behavior, externally and internally.

However, it is not possible to conduct all therapy in this exact order. Sometimes a program of operant conditioning has to be instituted before the child will respond to anything as, for example, in the case of so-called autistic children. With other children, for example, delinquent adolescents, a direct confrontation of motivations may be necessary, even before very much affect is dealt with. The planning of therapeutic strategy is made possible by the assessment of the child's modes of operation. If all of the child's functioning is overwhelmed by a habit, it may be necessary to begin with a program of behavior modification; thereafter, the feelings and motivations underlying the habit may be attacked. If the child has retreated to his daydream world, an exploration of that world may have to precede any alteration of his social environment, which then might be attacked through some form of group treatment. In other instances, it may be necessary to focus on the family and its interactions if that is where the child is operating, before turning to treatment of internal conflicts and affects.

5. The cost of the treatment in time and money also should be estimated. Unfortunately, there is no known basis for budgeting the cost of treatment. This important facet of treatment planning has yet to be studied. At best, one can make rough estimates of the number of sessions, the number of months over which these sessions will be spread, and the consequent cost in therapist's fees or salary. However, if the other aspects of treatment are systematically planned according to the assessment, and if these plans are effectively implemented, then it may be possible subsequently to determine the time and cost of various plans, much as the construction of buildings or highways are budgeted. The cost in terms of dropouts from treatment should decrease, and planned treatment should motivate more patients to remain. Conversely, the average length of treatment for those who do continue should also decrease. The number of wasted hours and misdirected efforts should be decreased by planning. The overall cost in terms of money spent on treatment may increase, but so should the number of successful outcomes.

6. *Difficulties and Objections.* If therapy is planned to meet the needs of the child, then there are no contraindications in the usual sense of the word. Each separate therapeutic endeavor is designed to be the indicated treatment of choice. However, this is not to deny that planning of therapy, in the present state of the scientific development, is often very difficult, if not nearly impossible. Admittedly, the above concepts of individually designed treatment are in many ways quite idealistic and only roughly outlined. Certainly, they are less specific than those proposed by advocates of other set plans, which do not take the variations of the individual into account. The only answer to this objection is that plans are necessary if treatment is not to be a hit-and-miss affair. Moreover, every expert in any kind of treatment

does attempt to plan his therapy to fit the exigencies of the individual child. This proposal is intended to broaden such planning, so that by using the assessment, these individual variations may be made more definite and the opportunities for varying treatment may thus also be widened.

A second objection is that such individually designed treatment is, in effect, no treatment at all, but a potpourri of therapies. It does not seem to allow any one therapeutic technique to be completed. Admittedly, any plan must run its course to be effective. One might hesitate to cut a course of behavior modification short to begin a peer group or drop an individual psychoanalytic treatment in midstream to begin a conjoint family treatment. Any planned treatment has to allow for a completion of any component approach. However, these approaches may be considerably shortened by the very fact that more than one is being employed. Very often, any one approach is prolonged by the fact that there are other problems which cannot be easily handled by this single one. Moreover, it is often possible to conduct several therapeutic approaches at once—especially if a program is planned in advance. Reductio ad absurdum, a child might come daily for a therapeutic hour, but instead of receiving psychoanalytic treatment only, he might have such treatment only on Mondays; Tuesdays, he and his mother might be engaged in a behavior modification session; Wednesdays, he might meet in a peer group; Thursdays might be parents' day, for separate or joint sessions; and on Fridays, the whole family might gather for exploration of the family interactions. Unlikely as it is that any child should need such a mixture of treatments all at once, there is no reason that several approaches might not be used at once or in overlapping sequence. Moreover, through such a multiplex of treatment, the total time needed might well be reduced.

Although some therapists are skilled at several different approaches, it is rare that any one therapist can treat all the problems of a child. When a therapist is practicing by himself, he usually uses the methods which he knows best, hoping they will make sufficient changes in the child's behavior. If the child needs other forms of treatment, he may refer him elsewhere. Sometimes a child may be receiving a psychoanalytic treatment plus a conjoint family therapy from one therapist, but be attending some school or institute for learning difficulties where some form of operant conditioning is used. Unfortunately, in private practice, these forms of treatment are rarely coordinated. As a result, both in private practice and in public agencies there is an increasing trend toward the use of multiple therapies. Private practice is now being conducted by groups of several therapists of diverse training. The private school attempts to have several kinds of therapy available or the individual practitioner is associated with several colleagues or a private clinic. The implementation of a plan of therapy calls not only for a variety of therapists, but for a continuous administration, supervision and direction. Any such five-ring circus needs some kind of ringmaster. On the hospital ward, where such multiple treatment programs have long been used, the administrative director, usually a psychiatrist, is responsible for coordination of these treatment programs. However, the coordination of the treatment program for the individual child, within this milieu of treatments, is usually delegated to the individual therapist, the person who is working individually with the child. It is he who determines, in consultation with the staff, which treatments the child needs. Outpatient clinics seldom coordinate their treatment programs quite as closely, and more responsibility is placed on the individual therapist. Far too often, even in the best of clinics, one therapist has only a slight idea of what is going on in other treatments of the child. Such miscellaneous uncoordinated treatment can be avoided if there is careful planning by the whole staff prior to instituting any therapy. The assessment should be available to the whole staff and be used by all in a coordinated plan.

Finally, it may be objected that no plan of treatment can possibly meet the many exigencies that arise. Even if one could detail all the current stresses and conflicts which the child is enduring, it can be predicted with a high level of certainty that other stresses will occur. For example, the therapist may leave the clinic; the groups will change in membership; the child may be expelled from school; one of his parents may leave the home; the child may fall ill or be injured. Often these emergencies call for a rapid change in plans. In many instances, such emergencies are visibly imminent and it may seem that no planning is possible. In fact some families present one crisis after another for the therapist to solve, playing a long-range game of family uproar, which in effect prevents therapy from ever beginning. However, treatment needs to be planned if only to prevent the therapy from being overwhelmed by crises. In a carefully outlined plan of treatment, it is possible to include these events as natural experiences to be worked through in treatment. Such treatment plans have to be flexible enough to allow for emergencies. Moreover, when the treatment is interrupted or disrupted by a crisis, there is no reason that the child's situation should not be reassessed. Case 19 illustrates such a reassessment when the delinquent adolescent suffered a head injury. If a family operates by creating one crisis after another, this fact usually is revealed in the assessment and plans can be made for approaching this mode of operations.

These modes of treatment do not exhaust all the possibilities of changing children's behaviors. Often it is necessary to make changes in the child's environment as well as in his actions and attitudes. The following chapter considers assessment for such environmental alterations and the manner in which they also may be integrated into an overall plan of behavioral change.

ASSESSMENT FOR PHYSIOLOGICAL AND ENVIRONMENTAL INTERVENTIONS

A. INTRODUCTION

Assessment can be extremely helpful when there are decisions to be made about possible changes in the child's environment or about proposed physiological interventions. In assessing the possible changes in the child's psychological functioning which might be affected either by changes in his environment or in medical or surgical interventions, there are at least four general considerations: (1) the nature and purposes of the proposed changes, (2) the attitudes of the child toward the change, (3) the child's ability to use the change for further growth, and (4) the need for someone to act as a "change agent" to assist the child in accepting and using the change.

1. The assessment of a child reveals only how the child views his social environment and his physical being. It does not usually provide much data about the realities of these environments unless home visits, and school and medical reports are included in the data. In order to make any estimate of the effects of possible environmental changes on the child, one needs to know the nature of the present environment and of the proposed alterations. One needs to know, for example, what the present school and new school are like, or what the current home situation is like and the nature of the proposed foster home, or the child's current physical condition and what kind of surgery, prosthetics, or drugs ar proposed, and the possible results thereof. When changes in the behavior of the child's parents are suggested through treatment of the mother or father, or both, the goals of this treatment should include consideration of the effects on the child. All in all, what needs to be done in the prediction of possible effects of such external changes is an assessment of the environment or of the proposed physiological change. Thus, before the assessment results can be viewed in the light of these proposed changes, it is necessary to have as precise data about them as possible.

Very often this assessment is accomplished by someone other than the psychologist. For example, if the psychologist works in collaboration with a social worker, it may be the social worker who visits the home or the school or the foster home. However, it is often very helpful for the psychologist also to join in such home or school visits. Where the question is of a proposed medical intervention, the psychologist should discuss the nature of this intervention with the physician so that data are obtained regarding the procedures the child will face and the nature of the expected physiological changes.

2. The second question to be asked is whether the proposed change is pertinent to the problems and needs of the child. In the referral, the parent, physician, teacher, or probation officer may propose major changes in the child's environment, but whether such changes really have any bearing on the child's problems is often questionable. For example, a parent may believe that the child's behavior arises from conflicts with his peers in a certain school or in a certain neighborhood; they may even be willing to go to the extent of selling their home and making a move in order to help the child. Or a physician may believe that surgical intervention, altering the child's physique, appearance, or muscular abilities might change the child's attitudes. The representative of a court may ask whether removing the child from the home and putting him in an institution would not change the child's behavior. Once one has investigated the nature of these proposed changes, then it is necessary to see in what way such changes would be pertinent.

Occasionally, as will be discussed below, the referrants's proposed change does fit very well with the child's needs, and thus is quite appropriate. Too frequently, the proposed change is actually an act of desperation which has little relevance to the child's needs. For example, parents frequently insist that the child be placed in a boarding school, but the assessment data may suggest that the child's problems have little to do with his school adjustment, but rather are the result of tensions within the family. In such instances, further investigation and discussion with the parents may reveal that they are attempting to avoid any recognition of the family tensions and are hoping secretly that, by further rejecting the child and expelling him from the home, their problems will be solved without any uncovering of their own behaviors. In other instances, where changes are proposed by physicians or by courts, one must take into account that the referrant may be proposing only those changes with which he is familiar. For example, it is quite understandable that a physician would propose physiological changes, such as the use of drugs or surgery. A teacher may be inclined to hope

for changes in the child through changes in the school or the teaching method. The court may be alarmed over a child's delinquency, but consider only the possibility of institutionalization or punitive measures.

If these proposed changes have little to do with the child's frustrations, then the results of the change will probably be negligible. In many instances, the child merely continues to be disturbed. Far too often, the change adds to the child's miseries. A foster home placement may actually increase the child's feeling of rejection rather than relieve it. Even physiologically successful surgery or quieting drugs may make little or no change in the child's behavior if his physiological condition was not the main problem in the first place. Most courts are now well aware that placing a retarded or psychotic child in a state institution for delinquents may be of little effect and possibly harmful.

3. Once it is determined that the proposed change may be relevant to the child's problems, the next question is whether he will accept and use the change. Where a change does seem pertinent, the hope is that the child's tensions will be relieved, since the environmental stresses are different. However, it is often true that there is a considerable lag between the shift in the tensions the child is experiencing and the hoped-for changes in his coping mechanisms. When a child is put in a new situation, he usually does not immediately give up his old, ineffective neurotic habits or psychotic behavior. He may not experience the situation as a change for some time and thus will continue these old behaviors. One needs to investigate whether the new environment will accept ineffective or disturbing behavior for at least a brief period. For example, a new school or a new foster home would need to be advised about the child's behavior and helped to recognize that there may not be an immediate change.

Furthermore, consideration should be given to the nature of the child's disturbing behavior. For example, in the treatment of the anorexia, the child's refusal to eat is not only a way of manipulating his parents, but usually also masks considerable depression. If the child is put in the hospital and his anorexic symptoms no longer make the authorities guilty and disturbed, it is very likely that the child will then be unable to hide his depression. Such depression following diets also is common. These problems are illustrated in the following case.

CASE 58

Between ages two and five, Allen gradually lost his vision as cataracts developed. The effect of their surgical removal on his behavior at age five was quite marked. Previously he had been a very dependent child who had been very well behaved. However, once he was able to see, he no longer could use his blindness for an excuse for being cared for. Furthermore, he now was able to do many things which were impossible before. As a result, he became very angry when people did not wait on him any longer. He also got into a lot more mischief than when he could not see. However, the surgeon had suspected that the child might be emotionally immature and had asked the psychological assessment before the surgery was instituted. Thus, the possibility of the child's reaction to the surgery was predicted and was discussed with the parents beforehand. They were therefore somewhat prepared for the change in the child's behavior. They were able to appreciate rather than to be thrown by his anger when they insisted that he could now care for himself in many ways. They were not shocked but were actually encouraged when they found him exploring and even damaging things that he had not been able to see or know about before.

4. The child's ability to accept and utilize a proposed change often requires that there be some person whose specific role is to help him during the period of change. It may be that the authorities in the new environment will play this role. If the new teacher or foster parent is advised of the child's behavior and the child's needs, he may be able to help the child accept and utilize the new environment. Sometimes if there is no one person in the environment who can do this, a child may need another person to act as counselor regarding the change.

CASE 59

Robert, age 12, had reacted in normal fashion with depression to the death of his father. However, the assessment revealed he had found the new relationship with his mother a very conflictual one. He shared her depression and became much closer to her, but at the same time this relationship threatened his approaching pubescence. He often reacted in negative fashion, especially to her offers of affection and succorance. He could not explain his behavior exactly, but did state with a burst of insight, "My mother and I are too close." The father's death had also necessitated that the mother take a job outside the home. Moreover, it was very likely that she would not be able to afford the home in which they had been living. Both for economic and psychological reasons, she was about to move in with her parents. She feared very much that Robert would not accept this change. Robert himself asked if it would not be possible that he go away to a boarding school. His grandfather offered to finance this schooling. Nevertheless, it was obvious that Robert was very ambivalent concerning this change. It did seem as though the proposed boarding school would offer Robert considerable support in his masculine development. It would also relieve him of the immediate strained relationships with his mother and his maternal grandparents. In order to make this change, several counselling interviews were conducted with Robert in which the nature of the change and the reasons for making it were discussed very openly with him. Robert was a fairly intelligent boy and able to explore his own feelings quite readily. He thus was much more prepared to meet the new school and saw it as a potential for relieving some of his depressed and angry feelings. He promised to write the psychologist about his feelings at the school. He sent several letters indicating that he was homesick but that he found many new attractions which kept him quite preoccupied. After about three months, no further letters were received from Robert but his mother reported that he seemed "a changed boy" when he came home on vacation.

B. ASSESSMENT OF POSSIBLE PHYSIOLOGICAL CHANGES

Although at one time there was little or no consideration given to the psychological effects of medical interventions, over the past several decades physicians have become increasingly aware that medical or surgical interventions, which might be considered routine, at times have marked effects on the child's behavior. For example, several decades ago tonsillectomies were performed fairly routinely, often in the physician's office. However, some children seemed to react very negatively to what might be considered a simple operation—not physiologically, but in their behavior. Sometimes children were discovered afterwards to be very depressed or to be quite phobic. Psychological assessment of such children even years after the surgery sometimes reveal that the child still fantasied that his life was threatened or that he had been "castrated." Physicians now know to prepare a child in advance for this and other surgery, advising him in very simple language of the nature of the operation, the reasons for it, and what is to be expected from it. Physicians are now more aware also of the possible negative effects of a surgical or medical intervention on an emotionally disturbed child. Thus, pediatricians or surgeons are increasingly prone to request psychological assessment of a child preoperatively when they feel that he will be so disturbed by the prospect or the results of an operation that it might be better if surgery were delayed.

Although it is known that surgical interventions of almost any kind do constitute a potential threat as well as a potential benefit, there is little or no research to indicate specific kinds of threats or hopes the children may have regarding a particular type of surgery. Of course, where a child has received some physiological trauma such as a broken bone, severe lacerations, or an injury, he is likely to see any type of surgical intervention as being beneficial and is not particularly threatened. However, where the proposed surgery may affect a part of the body about which the child has particular conflicts, repair of trauma might also require psychological assessment and assistance.

Case 60

Vincent, age 14, whose leg was badly smashed in an automobile accident, was advised by his surgeon that it probably would be necessary to amputate it. He was told that a prosthetic limb would make it possible for him to ambulate. The surgeon also told Vincent that if the leg were not amputated, he could walk with a crutch, but that there was danger of further complications or of possible infections. Upon receiving this advice, Vincent became markedly depressed and confused and was unable to make any kind of decision. His parents were also very

worried as Vincent tried to get the parents to decide for him. However, his father, realizing that this would affect a great deal of Vincent's future, insisted that the boy should be involved. Because of the boy's depression and confusion, psychological assessment was requested.

In brief, the results of the assessment showed that this boy was very motorically oriented, that he usually expressed his feelings in motor behavior and that he was far more dependent on doing things with his arms and legs than in verbalizing. Moreover, he was in the middle of pubescence when active sports and social activities such as dancing were most important to him. In Vincent's responses to the associative techniques, there was considerable evidence that the injury had rearoused old fears of castration and deprivation of masculinity, and that the prospect of amputation reactivated his childhood fears.

The nature of the boy's fears were then discussed with the surgeon and the boy's parents. Further consultation with the physiatrist and the rehabilitation department revealed that Vincent could be quite mobile when fitted with a prosthetic limb. The boy was advised of this, was taken to the prosthetics department where he saw people dancing on artificial limbs, and even watched a basketball game with young men in wheel chairs. He was then able to accept the probability that the amputation and prosthetic limb were the best possible choice. He remained somewhat depressed but a further consultation following the amputation and the fitting of the prosthesis showed that he was much less depressed and eager to try out his new limb.

Psychological assessment is even more called for when the proposed surgery is not an emergency for the child's life or immediate well being, but is "elective," for example, for "cosmetic purposes." For example, a pediatrician might advise a parent that the child needed a tonsillectomy but also recognize that the child seemed emotionally immature or otherwise emotionally disturbed and suggest that if necessary the proposed surgery would be delayed.

Case 61

Lisa, age four, had suffered from recurring bouts of tonsillitis with increasing frequency and severity. Both Lisa and her mother knew that a tonsillectomy seemed imminent. However, Lisa had also been showing many signs of behavioral disturbance which were in all probability associated with the recent divorce of her parents. The pediatrician therefore requested a psychological consultation. The assessment revealed that Lisa fantasied that she was the cause of her parents' separation and that she felt very guilty about it. Moreover, some of her fantasies suggested that she saw the impending operation as a punishment for her misbehavior. In consultation with the pediatrician, the psychologist decided that Lisa's infection might be controlled by medication for at least another year. A year and a half later, Lisa was again referred to the psychologist. At this time, the tonsillectomy no longer could be delayed. However, in the meantime Lisa's mother had remarried, and Lisa seemed less fearful and more at ease. The necessity of the operation and the nature of it were discussed very frankly with her by the pediatrician. Following the operation, the psychologist visited the child very briefly in the hospital and there was no indication that the surgery had in any way upset her. Several months later, the child was again brought to the psychologist by her mother as had been suggested by the pediatrician. The mother reported no untoward effects of the operation and Lisa seemed quite happy and voluntarily said she was glad to be relieved of her continual sore throat.

Cosmetic surgery for children as for adults has even more psychological implications. For example, it is sometimes proposed a child's big and flabby ears be altered or that a short limb or a disfigured face be repaired. Again, there is little or no research regarding the general psychological effects of such surgery on children. In each case it must be assessed separately. In these instances particularly, the psychologist should be aware of possible hidden motivations in the proposed surgery (Jacobson, 1961). Thus, a parent or even a child himself may look forward to the operation as a fantasied panacea for all anxieties. The bashful, withdrawn schizoid child whose face is disfigured or distorted may seek cosmetic surgery in the hope that then he will be welcomed among his peers or accepted by his parents. However, assessment quite frequently shows that the child's appearance is not the chief reason that he is rejected. In such instances, it is very often helpful to delay cosmetic surgery until other psychological interventions can be made, in order to make the psychological outcome of the surgery more realistic.

A prime example is Case 27 in Chapter 13. In this case, the child was born with one leg shorter than the other. There was no evidence that the child's disturbances at age 13 had any relation to this mild defect. The girl's mother, however, was firmly convinced that all the girl's behavioral difficulties arose from her reaction to this defect and ignored all of her psychological difficulties. Several surgeons advised the mother that surgical intervention at this late age might not necessarily be successful. It was pointed out to her that the child's bone growth was almost complete and that the possibility of lengthening the leg was not favorable. Nevertheless, the mother persisted until she found a surgeon who agreed to attempt the repair of the leg. The girl was unaware of the degree of pain involved in this surgery and the length of the rehabilitation. A total of four different surgical interventions proved to be necessary. Moreover, the child was in bed and out of school for almost two years. Further investigation revealed that the mother unconsciously was trying to separate the girl from peer activities and to keep this adolescent as a helpless child under her control. Although the child was able to walk more comfortably at the end of the rehabilitation period, she remained an excessively angry and rebellious child who blamed her mother for the loss of the years of her adolescence.

In most major rehabilitation centers, psychological assessment and consultation are considered an essential part of the total rehabilitation program for the child. Although the psychological aspects of the physiological rehabilitation of disabled children constitute a specialty within the field of clinical psychology, any psychologist should at least be aware of some of the problems involved. In the assessment of a disabled child, special attention needs to be given to the ways in which the child views the loss of a limb or a paralysis and how he handles the depression which accompanies such a loss. In this writer's experience, the "phantom limb" phenomenon noted among adult amputees (Roser, A. in Bellak 1952) is not quite as marked among children, although children also may refuse to recognize that the paralyzed or amputated member will not reappear or be repaired as "magically" as it was injured and lost. The adult who clings to this delusion is also likely to deny feelings of depression and pretend that everything is going to be all right. Such adult patients do very poorly in rehabilitation because of the lack of motivation. In general, children, whose defenses are less developed, are more apt to experience a normal grief reaction to the loss of a limb or to a paralysis. Once this grief has subsided, they are highly motivated toward rehabilitation. However, children are easily swayed by denying adults. The mother who bleats, "Don't worry dear, everything is going to be all right," convinces the child that some magic is going to happen and that he is not obligated to do anything about it. Thus, assessment of disabled children should include a careful study of the attitudes of the parents toward the disability, for example, the possibility that they may have hidden feelings of guilt regarding the cause of the child's loss, or unexpressed anger toward the child who is no longer "perfect." Where there are such attitudes on the part of the parent, the prosthesis itself becomes the magical answer. The parents, and consequently the child, come to regard the prosthesis as the total answer and fail to understand the necessity for learning to use the prosthesis and for continued physical and occupational therapy. In addition, when a child suffers a traumatic and disabling injury or disease, he is naturally more dependent on and demanding of the adult, and adults tend to become guilt-stricken and more likely to reinforce the child's dependency. In such instances, the prosthesis, rather than being regarded positively as an aid toward the further growth of the child, becomes a symbol in the eyes of both parent and child of the child's disability. Thus, in the assessment of a disabled child, special attention needs to be paid to his feelings of dependence and independence both in general and in relation to the prosthesis.

Assessment is rarely requested regarding the use of the much more common minor prosthesis such as glasses, hearing aids, or orthodentures. But such prostheses often arouse considerable social embarrassment and even feelings of self-doubt for a child. Although having braces on one's teeth is a very common event for the latency child or young adolescent, for the child who already may feel inadequate and socially on the outs, braces or spectacles may become just another sign that they are not considered adequate, beautiful, or even loved. The following case is an example.

CASE 62

Lana's schoolwork had been going downhill for almost two years. Although she had made above average grades during the first three years of elementary school, now in the sixth grade she was failing almost completely. Her parents were quite concerned, since Lana appeared to be studying quite hard, at least up until the current semester. Her teachers also reported that Lana was an attentive student and until recently there had been no behavior problems. In this first semester, Lana seemed excessively tense and nervous in the classroom, began to stutter and cry when she was called on to recite, and was extrasensitive to any teasing by her peers. She even began to complain that her teachers did not like her and, when corrected, she would run from the room in tears. She was defiant when the teachers tried to find out what was upsetting her, and her negativism got her more in trouble with school authorities. Moreover, Lana, although only 11, was at least a foot taller than any other child in her class, weighed nearly 150 pounds, and was beginning to develop breasts and hips. Her size and her behavior made her the target of other children, especially the boys who dubbed her "Lana the horse."

In considering the possible sources of Lana's difficulties, it did appear to both the parents and teachers that Lana might need glasses, since she did appear to squint at the blackboard and to hold books fairly close to her face. The teacher noted that if the instructions were given orally, Lana always understood but she did not seem to read rapidly. Thus, she was succeeding much better at oral arithmetic than in problems from the textbook. Prior to seeking psychological consultation, her parents had taken her to the opthalmalogist who examined her and who reported that her vision seemed within the normal limits.

During the psychological assessment, Lana was having obvious difficulties on such tests as the Bender-Gestalt and the visual items of the WISC, such as Picture Completion, Picture Assessment, and Block Design. Her verbal IQ was 117, but the Performance IQ was only 83. However, further qualitative analysis of both her Wechsler and Bender performance as well as her Draw-A-Person (which was, in contrast, quite adequate for her age) suggested that Lana did have a marked visual handicap. Her visual-motor coordination as such was not inadequate, and her high achievement on tests such as arithmetic appeared to contraindicate a possible brain damage. She went through the Rorschach peering closely at each card and the perceptual aspects of her responses were quite within normal limits. During the assessment, Lana became increasingly aware of her failures, biting her lips, making remarks like "Boy, am I stupid!"

After the assessment, the question of her "stupidity" was brought up with her. The assessor assured her that he did not see her as stupid, but guessed that she did have some kind of visual problem. Lana responded, "I hate *glasses*." When asked about the eye examination, Lana admitted to the assessor that she had failed to tell the opthalmologist how blurred her vision became and about her diplopia. Her eye muscles ached and she suffered headaches whenever she read even for brief periods. All of this she never told to her parents. Lana confessed further that she felt badly about the names which the boys called her, that she wished she were petite and pretty like the other girls. Although her friends were mostly 11 and 12, they were already fantasying boy-girl relationships. She harbored considerable fears that she would never be accepted by boys, and the threat that she may have to wear glasses only added to the apprehensions. After further discussion of this problem, Lana decided to repeat the ophthalmological consultation and her accomodation problem then became quite clear. The opthalmologist felt that contact lenses might be too painful for her at first and that it would be better for her to start off with regular glasses. However, at this time, Lana's mother was contemplating changing from glasses to contact lenses and it was agreed to let Lana try them at the same time that her mother did. The mother and daughter thus bore the difficulty of getting used to contact lenses together and, after a briefer period than usual, she had grown quite used to the discomfort of wearing them. Her school achievement rose markedly thereafter.

Another type of physiological intervention used chiefly to control behavior is the psychotropic drug or tranquilizer. When first discovered, just after World War II, these drugs seemed very promising. Through their use, many very disturbed hospitalized patients who theretofore had been completely out of contact were able to carry out their daily activities with minimum supervision, and thus were more amenable to care and treatment. Calmed by these drugs, no few chronically disturbed patients were able to enter into psychotherapy and begin to consider the reality of the world about them. This approach was so promising that an increasing number of new drugs were introduced and were prescribed for many different emotional conditions. Soon it became obvious that the reactions, and particularly the side effects, could not easily be predicted, since they often differed from person to person and the dosages had to be altered for each individual. The research on many of these drugs was often inadequate or entirely absent. Although these drugs continue to be used with both adults and children when they are very depressed or hyperactive, they are no longer regarded as a panacea. They have never been used as extensively with children as they are with adults. Moreover, there is even considerable controversy about the use of drugs with children. Redl, in his presidential address to the American Orthopsychiatric Association, lashed out against their use, labeling this practice "chemical warfare against children."* Nevertheless, proper use of these drugs can calm very psychotic children so that they do not pound their heads against walls, pull out their hair, or scratch themselves bloody. Antidepressant drugs may rouse the completely withdrawn and lethargic adolescent, so that he can be engaged in a rehabilitation program.

Although psychologists have participated in the research on the effects of these drugs, little or no relationship has been established between psychological assessment and the clinical use of drugs. Rarely if ever does a referrant request assessment for the use of this type of intervention. In some instances, the drugs are prescribed partly on the basis of an assessment, but for the most part, they are used as an emergency treatment. More-

---

*This remark was not included in the publication of this address.

over, since the effects are so variable, it is difficult to imagine how one might predict the possible outcome on the basis of the data of a psychological assessment.

However, psychological assessment is related to these drugs in at least two ways. First, if a child who is being medicated is referred for assessment, the psychologist needs to know about the possible effect of the drug on the child's behavior, particularly the possible effects of the drug on the child's performance on the techniques to be used in the assessment. Although these drugs generally slow down the child's reactions (except for antidepressants), there is no precise knowledge of how any one child may be affected. The best source of data is the nurse's notes, or if the child is not in the hospital, a report from the physician. The observations from the child's parents may also be helpful. When a child is known to be using such medication, the psychologist should be most observant of the child's behavior. It is wise to ask about the type of medication being used, the dosage, and how much time has elapsed between the most recent dose and the beginning of the assessment. Very often, a child who is using these drugs will be most drowsy for the first several hours after he has taken them and more alert just before the next dose is scheduled. This information is most important, since these drugs do temporarily affect the central nervous system and, as a result, the responses of a sedated child often correspond to those given by children who have some generalized brain damage. Thus, if the psychologist is not aware that the child is sedated, the child's responses may seem at least puzzling and the assessor may be misled into predicting the possibility of brain damage. The psychologist should also inquire whether the referrant needs a description of the child under the influence of the medication or when the child is least affected.

Second, psychologists may be requested to assess the effects of clinical use of these drugs on a particular child. Most commonly this request is made rather indirectly or implicitly. For example, a child may be very disturbed when admitted to a hospital, appearing severely psychotic and unmanageable. At that time, the child may be incapable of cooperating in an assessment. Or his responses may only mirror his psychotic affect and lack of contact with his immediate surroundings. After the child has been treated with drugs for a week or so, another assessment may be requested. By this time, the drug dosage may have been decreased and the child may be calmed down considerably. Although the referral may not directly request an evaluation of the effects of the drugs, in effect such a posttreatment assessment may reflect the results of the drug therapy. Usually the pretreatment psychotic state has been behaviorally ameliorated. However, the question arises: Are the child's thought processes and underlying affective states still very disturbed? Since the drug affects chiefly the child's motor functioning, it may be presumed that there is usually little effect on the ego as a whole. This presumption, however, needs to be assessed. Thus, the psychologist may be asked, "Now that the child is motorically calmed down, what is the rest of his ego functioning like? Is he still basically psychotic or was his psychotic behavior a temporary state?"

C. CHANGES WITHIN THE MILIEU

The central and most important environment of the child is, of course, his family. Any environmental change which removes him from that family setting is thus a very drastic and major alteration of his environment. Before any such major change in the child's environment is contemplated, one should consider the possibility of other changes within the child's milieu which do not remove him from the family circle. When a child is so emotionally disturbed that he is unable to function in his environment, changes within the family living structure and arrangements or in family living habits, a change of school, or even a move by the family to a new neighborhood are usually considered before removing the child from the home is contemplated. As mentioned above, very often such proposals are made out of desperation and with little relevance to the child's actual problems. However, in many instances the possibility that such a change would at least make life a little easier for the child should be seriously considered. Even where it is fairly obvious that such a move will not at all clear up the major problems facing the child and his family, there is often the possibility that the child may be much more able to work out the problems if the immediate stress of his environment is lessened. Thus, a child who has been failing badly in school and who has been a disrupting factor in the classroom might well be considered for a transfer to another school, even though his emotional disturbance is obviously a reflection of tensions within his home. Any such change would very likely require that the child and his family also begin some form of psychotherapy so as to work out these family tensions. Otherwise the child might very well repeat the same behavior in the new school and be threatened again with expulsion. As was noted above, some person should act as "change agent," that is, the parents, the therapist, or some representative of the clinic where the child is being seen should contact the school. Conferences should be held between the school authorities and this change agent so that the school might be better prepared to handle for at least awhile the child's continued disturbing effects. At the same time, as part of therapy with the child, the child should be helped to see the new school as an opportunity for a fresh start.

However, such changes are not easy to effect. In most school systems, the child's behavior as well as his scholastic achievement are recorded on an accumulated record and passed from school to school. Thus, the authorities at the new school are quite aware that they are receiving a difficult child. Sometimes it is almost impossible to negotiate and implement any kind of education rehabilitation program for an individual child in a new school once he has had an appreciable history of failures. Some parents and children are quite willing to receive the assistance of a psychologist in negotiating with the school, but others are very reluctant to admit to the public school that there is any emotional problem in the child or family, even though no specifics are given. Most school authorities welcome consultation with psychologists outside of their system. It should be remembered, however, that in an overcrowded and overburdened school system, it is often difficult to give special attention to the single child, even though he may sorely need it. This is not to say that a realistic and reasonable change of schools with the intervention of a change agent is impossible, but rather that the possibility that such a change can be carried out successfully, both by the child

and his parents, should be carefully assessed before any decision is made.

CASE 63

Larry, age 11, had a long history of a variety of school difficulties which had already resulted in two shifts in schools. A third change was now contemplated. Although IQ Tests at these schools had consistently indicated that he was of superior intelligence, his actual achievement had been extremely erratic. He would become fascinated for awhile with a subject and would do superior work, but for the most part he seemed to pay little attention to the assignments and dawdled over them. Sometimes when teachers recognized that he was bored and disinterested, they would try to give him extra projects and motivate him, often with fair success. The school Larry first attended was very overcrowded and there had been frequent changes of teachers, so that Larry's special needs were inadvertently neglected. Larry was an excessively restless child who amused and teased other children and often succeeded in getting the class into an uproar. He was angry, resentful, and impudent to school authorities when they attempted to correct him. After the first two years of school during which time his mother had had numerous conferences with the teachers, she decided to put him in a parochial school. His behavior continued much the same in the parochial school, and after less than a year and a half he was expelled because of his loud and vulgar language—specifically because he wrote sexual words on the school wall. He was then placed in another public school, a half-year below his normal grade level, since his record of achievement had been so poor. Again, his mother was frequently contacted by school authorities who complained of his classroom behavior, and his grades remained far below what might have been expected of him. During the most recent semester in the fifth grade, Larry had frequently wandered off the school grounds, without returning.

The assessment of Larry revealed that he was very angry and guilt-ridden and felt very rejected because his father had deserted his mother and himself five years previously. Moreover, his mother now had to work full-time to support the two of them and was often too tired and too depressed to deal effectively with Larry's emotional needs. She had not even been aware of his truancies because she had not been at home in the daytime. There were often indications in Larry's responses to the assessment that the bond between him and his mother was intensely conflictual and ambivalent. There were signs that he felt that his mother's anger at his father was also directed at him. At the same time, he felt pressured to take his father's place which was threatening to him. It was agreed that both Larry and his mother needed psychotherapeutic help, but there remained the immediate and acute problem of where Larry should attend school.

The school authorities were adamant that Larry be transferred to another school, and Larry himself was quite vehement that he would not return to this school. Although in most instances, the mother might have expected to conduct the negotiations with the school, she was extremely distraught and despaired of being able to communicate Larry's needs to the school authorities. The assessor, who was not the therapist for either Larry or his mother, agreed to assist her in negotiations with the school. A conference was then held between the psychologist, the mother, the principal, and the teacher at the school to which Larry was to be assigned. The exact nature of Larry's problems within his family were not discussed, although it was indicated that family circumstances were the source of Larry's behavioral difficulties. The teacher volunteered that he had a special interest in the motivation of bright boys and would consider the possibility of working out methods of dealing with Larry's boisterousness and other disrupting activities in a way which would not necessarily threaten Larry, but would nevertheless aid Larry in controlling himself. Larry was then brought into the conference also. The principal explained that he was aware of Larry's problems in the previous school—whereupon Larry made a sour face—but, the principal added, he also understood that Larry's behavior was to be helped by the clinic and that the new school thus hoped that they could offer Larry a fresh start. The teacher mentioned that he would help Larry with his classroom behavior if Larry so desired. Larry did seem genuinely pleased by this offer of help. The principal pointed out, however, that it would be necessary to limit this program to a single semester and that his mother would have to consider that this was a trial period.

For the following three months, the teacher conferred over the telephone with the psychologist almost biweekly. At first, it was necessary for the teacher to spend a considerable amount of time and energy with Larry, constantly warning him when his behavior started to get out of hand. Almost weekly Larry stayed after school to discuss his school behavior with the teacher. The teacher was able to work out a "warning signal" with Larry, which only he and Larry understood, as designating the times that Larry needed to exercise some control over himself. At the same time, Larry's mother received some extra help in the home from her mother. Although this created considerable conflict between the two women, it did mean that there was someone in the home when Larry arrived from school. At the end of three months, Larry's behavior at school had improved remarkably and Larry himself felt very encouraged.

Frequently there are possibilities of making changes within the milieu of the home or even the home structure which might relieve considerable pressure on the child. However, parents may be so upset by the child's behavior that they may fail to recognize these possibilities. Case 64 is one example.

CASE 64

Marty, who was eight, fussed constantly with his nine-year-old sister, whined about his mother's skirts, and annoyed his father by making many demands and failing to carry out his assigned household chores. He always wanted to be first at everything, monopolized the television, never seemed to want to go to bed, always forgot to brush his teeth, and so frequently disrupted family meals with his demanding and petulant behavior that he was often excluded from meals or other family activities. The list of complaints which his parents and sister had against Marty seemed inexhaustible. Marty himself complained that the family paid no attention to his needs, that his sister was always teasing him, that his mother was too busy for him, and that his father was too strict with him. In the initial two interviews which were held with these four members of the family, Marty would burst into tears and fling himself on the floor as his father pointed out that the family could never go anywhere because Marty was always late. It was only at the end of the second interview that it was discovered that there was another member of the family, namely, Marty's younger brother, age 11 months. As the assessment proceeded both in the family discussions and individually with Marty, it became increasingly apparent that no little of Marty's disturbances were associated with the birth of the younger brother. Marty himself voiced no complaint about the baby first. However, several of his TAT stories and other associative materials had strongly suggested that he felt very displaced and might be very resentful of the attention given to the new baby. The parents did date the onset of Marty's disturbing behavior as approximately a year ago, but failed to notice that this coincided with the mother's pregnancy and the birth of the baby. When this possibility was raised with Marty's mother, she seemed somewhat surprised, noting that Marty had seemed to look forward to a brother whom he envisioned as a potential companion and that he even at times seemed to enjoy playing with the baby. On further reflection, she remarked that he sometimes seemed annoyed because the baby got into his things. It was at this point that it was revealed that Marty was sharing a room with the baby. When Marty was asked about the baby, he readily volunteered that the baby messed his things up and kept him awake by his crying. He felt the baby had taken over his room. The fact that Marty had to share the room with the new baby brother seemed the crowning insult. This was clear enough evidence that Marty was no longer "the baby in the family," a remark his father frequently flung in his face when Marty failed to use the proper manners at the dinner table or to carry out the chores exactly as his father demanded. In pursuing this topic further in the family discussions, the father agreed that perhaps he had begun to expect more from Marty "since he is no longer the baby in the family."

Although there were several other aspects of this family which required further discussion, one possible change which struck everyone concerned as soon as the situation was clearly understood was that Marty needed a room that he could call his own. It seemed possible that such a change would restore Marty's position within his family. The parents had considered that their home would have to be expanded in the future but now realized how important this might be for Marty. Plans were then laid to convert the family garage into an extra room as soon as possible. In further discussion, it was revealed

that Marty had known that such plans were afoot and had felt very disappointed when he understood that they might be delayed, since his father wanted to spend the family savings on a new car instead of the new room. Marty's father was somewhat taken aback by this, and he volunteered that the baby should be moved immediately from Marty's room to the parents' room. Marty's behavior began to change almost as soon as a decision was made. The family continued in weekly discussions with the therapist for another six weeks, at which time Marty was moved into the new room. By this time a great deal of Marty's disturbing behavior had disappeared. The family feared that Marty would feel displaced by the fact that he would have to move from his room to another, and it was decided to give Marty a choice. Marty chose to exchange rooms. Although it is quite possible that the change of rooms in itself was not the main factor in Marty's change of behavior, at least it was a symbol to Marty that his parents were aware of his needs and would attempt to gratify them, "even though he was no longer the baby of the family."

Sometimes there are changes within the child's immediate family milieu which, although they do not mean that the child is actually removed from the family, do involve very major changes in the family constellation. Contemplated divorces are the most common instance. Children of parents who are contemplating separation and divorce are often referred for psychological assessment by marital counselors, attorneys, or court. In such instances, the question may be asked, "Should the couple be kept together for the 'good' of the child?" Although no assessment can answer this particular question phrased in this way, an assessment of the tensions within the family and the effect upon the child may be very helpful to the couple in making their decision about their marriage. The role of an assessment in such a case is illustrated by the following case.

Case 65

Mr. and Mrs. V, who were contemplating divorce, sought psychological consultation and assessment of their children Anna, age 14, and Don, age 12, on the recommendation of their attorney. The V's had been on the brink of divorce several times previously but had "stayed together for the sake of the children." Mrs. V felt that she no longer could stand the embarrassment and hurt of Mr. V's relations with other women, which he did not deny and which were common knowledge in the community. Mr. V complained bitterly that his wife was sexually frigid and neurotic, so that he no longer could live with her. Both of the V's had been previously married and divorced. Mr. V now age 50, had first married at age 25 and had a 23-year-old daughter by this marriage who was not living with the V's. He had divorced his first wife allegedly because of her alcoholism. He had married Mrs. V four years later, and their marriage had always been a stormy one. Mrs. V, who was 15 years younger than her husband, had married first at age 17 to a high school boyfriend by whom she was pregnant. However, she aborted this first child. Her first marriage ended in a divorce a year later and at age 20, she married Mr. V. Their daughter Anna was born a year later.

Although many of the disagreements had been building up over the entire 15 years, they had seldom quarreled openly in front of the children. They readily agreed, however, that the children were well aware of the general tension between them, especially in the more recent years. However, this tension was never discussed with the children. As far as they were aware, the children had no knowledge of Mr. V's extramarital affairs. They had not even told the children that a divorce was being contemplated. In spite of their intense differences, both the V's were quite concerned with the welfare of their children, and both stated that they would be willing to continue the marriage if they thought a divorce would markedly disturb the children.

They reported that Anna seemed particularly tense and sensitive, easily given to tears over even slight disappointments or failures, and recently seemed to have difficulty in sleeping. Don, they described as showing almost no disturbance. He seemed to be succeeding at school and continuing his daily activities and peer associations in a spontaneous and undisturbed fashion. Both parents agreed that there was a bond between Don and his father. For example, they were currently beginning golf lessons, and Don had participated in the selection of the new family car. Don also seemed to be somewhat sensitive for a 12-year-old boy; he had once or twice found his mother in tears and had attempted to comfort her without asking at all

about the source of her distress. Anna seemed particularly upset when her father criticized or disciplined her. Previously she had been very much "daddy's little girl," but over the past year had seemed to grow quite distant and aloof from him. Mr. V was quite hurt by her behavior. Anna also was much more apt to flare up against her mother than she had been in previous years.

One of the initial questions was what to tell the children about the purpose of the assessment. Both parents were adamant that the children should not be told about the contemplated divorce. The psychologist agreed that since the decision for the divorce was not yet completely made, it probably should not be mentioned to the children at this point, but that the fact of the family tension probably could not much longer be hidden from the children. The parents argued further that even if the children were told that the purpose of the assessment was to evaluate the effects of tension, they might immediately be threatened and that the assessment thus would be contaminated. Finally, the psychologist agreed to the suggestion that Anna be seen because of her recent emotional disturbances and that Don might come to an assessment just because his sister was coming.

Anna, a tall, slim girl whose feminine figure was rapidly developing, was dressed appropriately in the teenage fashion. She said that she understood that she had come to the psychologist because of her "nutty" behavior which she described as "easily flying off the handle" and "crying over nothing." She could not immediately think of any particular things that disturbed her, but remarked, "My whole family is nutty." She did complain mildly about Don whom she said teased occasionally or disregarded her rights in the family, but she did not seem particularly upset, adding with a laugh, "You're going to see him and you'll see what kind of nut he is." When reminded that she said her whole family was "nutty," Anna's demeanor became markedly depressed and she said "I know; I love them both and they both are swell to me, but something is wrong in my family but I don't know what it is." She seemed almost near tears and remarked very solemnly, "I think they are almost going to get a divorce." When asked what gave her that impression, she replied that they always talked as if they seemed quite angry with one another, that they seldom went anywhere together, that her father always seemed very busy at work and was away very frequently on weekends, and that her mother often referred to her father in a "sarcastic way." Anna, however, denied that she worried much about her parents but admitted that she had begun to think about this quite a bit when she knew she was coming to see the psychologist and was introspecting about her own behavior.

She said that she was worried about other things such as succeeding in school, a girlfriend with whom she had recently quarreled and stopped seeing, and a boyfriend whom she had hoped to attract, but who seemed to be paying little attention to her. Despite these things, Anna said she frequently felt quite happy and often had good times. She particularly enjoyed the activities in her girls' club, and she had recently become interested in sewing and, with her mother's help, had made the dress she was wearing. She usually went to the movies or other entertainment with her peers, but particularly enjoyed the occasional but recently rare attention she received from her father who would take her and her brother to a show and dinner—"but mother never comes along." She said she had been worried about her mother, since her mother seemed to have frequent sick headaches, especially when any family affair was planned. This, too, made Anna suspicious that all was not right between her parents.

The assessment revealed that Anna was intellectually very bright and emotionally quite sensitive. In general, Anna's ego functioning seemed to be developing quite normally and even slightly precociously. Her responses did confirm her mother's impression that Anna's sensitivity to the emotional nuances of her environment were at times slightly overwhelming to her, that she was aware of more emotional aspects of her environment than she was immediately able to cope with and understand. Although from Anna's responses one could not say that she was openly depressed, there was a depressive and dysphoric aspect to many of her responses. Her TAT's were filled with repeated themes of threatened separation. For example, on TAT Card 2, Anna thought the girl was afraid to leave home to go away to school because her home might no longer be there when she returned. However, Anna could not decide why the girl might think this. On Card 3GF, Anna thought the girl in the doorway had just discovered that her boy-

friend had just left her, "maybe because he saw some other girl who was prettier or maybe because she's a witch." On Card 4, Anna decided that the young man in the foreground was leaving for the army and that his wife was in despair. On Card 5, Anna saw the woman in the doorway as looking in on "her dead husband." She could not think how the husband died or what the woman might do next. Finally, she added with a laugh, "The old gal might commit suicide." She similarly saw the couple on Card 6GF as contemplating a separation and the two figures on Card 12 GF as mourning over the death of the father and husband.

In reviewing Anna's responses, the psychologist looked for any signs that Anna might feel involved or guilty over what she apparently realized as a near separation of her parents, but there was no evidence that there was anything more than a realistic and somewhat depressed appraisal of her family situation.

Don, a tall, husky lad, shrugged in noncommital fashion when asked why he thought he had been brought to see the psychologist. He admitted that he knew that psychologists "deal with people's problems," but added with a broad smile that he did not believe that he had any more problems "than any other kid." He said that he knew that his sister had also previously seen the psychologist and that he thought maybe she had some problems but could not say what they might be, or even why he suspected that she might have any emotional difficulty. In the discussion initiated by the psychologist about his general life pattern, Don talked freely and with enjoyment about his sport activities, mentioning the golf lessons with his dad. He claimed that he got along pretty well with Anna except that he too had noticed she seemed very "touchy." Asked next about his mother, Don paused briefly and added that she too seemed "touchy" but again could not describe what about his mother's behavior made him describe her with this term.

The assessment data showed that Don also was intellectually advanced for his age, but he showed little or none of Anna's emotional sensitivity. In fact, Don seemed particularly unaware either of emotional aspects of his environment, or of his own impulse life. His perception of the world was so very matter-of-fact that he seemed to be making extra efforts to neutralize and avoid any kind of emotional involvement. Whenever his own impulses began to play a part in his conceptualization of a situation, he quickly denied them. For example, on Card 5 of the Rorschach, he first described the "bat" as "flying" but then denied this, saying, "How could an inkblot fly?" Despite the fact that he was just passed 12 years old, Don showed no signs of internalization of any model for behavior. It seemed as though he made his judgments on the basis of what was immediately present. He blocked excessively on the TAT, apologizing that he had no imagination and could not think of stories. For example, he saw the boy with the violin, TAT Card 1, as wishing he could stop practice and go outside and play ball with the other fellows but could not say who required him to practice or how it would turn out. Pressed for a conclusion, he decided the boy would continue to "squeak away" until the assigned practice hour was finished. Similarly, he saw the figure on the Card 3BM as a guy who had fallen asleep on the edge of his bed. He could not think of why the figure had fallen asleep in this position except that "he must have been real tired." As for a conclusion, Don finally decided, "He'll wake up with a sore neck." As to the object in the left foreground of this card, Don studied it for a minute and decided that it was something that had dropped out of the boy's pocket. Only on Card 11 did Don become any more expansive. He groaned, "Oh boy! The whole world seems to be falling apart, and here's a dinosaur coming out of the cliff; he's been exposed by the earthquake, and this boy down here (pointing to a figure in the center) doesn't know what's going on at all. He's just knocked silly by a rock and he doesn't even see the dinosaur. The dinosaur will probably come down and kill this guy before he even knows what's happened." Thereafter Don's stories did become more morbid and depressive. He saw the standing figure in Card 12 BM as about to attack and murder the reclining figures. He decided that the murderer was a madman who had crept into the boy's bedroom and concluded the story by deciding it was all a dream. The boy would wake up and nothing would have happened. To 13B, Don responded that the boy was hungry and deserted by his parents, and that the boy was sad because "he didn't know what his parents were up to." Because the boy's surroundings looked so "poor," Don though maybe they

were on welfare and that the boy would be rescued by some welfare worker. Next, Don saw the silhouette figure in Card 14 as about to commit suicide, adding quickly, "I don't know why anybody would do that, maybe it's just that he's confused and doesn't know anything at all. I saw a TV story about that one time, but I don't remember it." Don claimed he couldn't think of any story to tell for the blank card, 16, and then added, "Oh yes, it must be a picture of that little kid story about Chicken Little, this is where the sky fell in." And finally, on Card 17, Don saw the figure climbing down a rope to escape a ship which was exploding and all on fire: "He'll have to swim through the oil and fire and all on the water; he may be all burned up if he's lucky—I mean if he's *un*lucky."

In reviewing Don's responses, it did seem as if he was relatively much less mature than his sister and much less prepared to meet a severe emotional trauma such as the threatened divorce. Nevertheless, there were hints in several of the TAT stories quoted above that Don, at least unconsciously, recognized some kind of impending doom. It was hypothesized that Don's emotional constriction might well be his defensive wall against this unconsciously recognized threat. While Anna was already almost aware of what was going on with her family consciously and might even be somewhat relieved if it should come out in the open, Don might be expected to avoid open recognition of the tension and attempt to guard himself even further against the feelings aroused by it.

These assessments were then discussed with the parents. Both agreed that the psychologist's appraisal was very consonant with what they themselves had thought. It was then planned to have a series of family meetings where at least some of the tensions between the parents might be gradually discussed with the children. Each family discussion was followed immediately by individual interviews with the children in which their feelings about their parents' dissension were explored further and where they were given further support. As was predicted, Anna cried openly during the first several family discussions, begging the parents not to get a divorce, but at the same time seemed somewhat relieved. She remarked during the individual hours with the psychologist that she felt better about the situation now that everybody knew what was going on, and that she guessed that she could "live" even if her parents decided to get a divorce.

Don, on the other hand, sat quite quietly during the initial family discussions responding very briefly only when a question was directed at him. He denied that he had had any indication that his parents were disagreeing so strongly and so frequently. When subsequently asked how he felt about it, he shrugged and said, "How is a fellow supposed to feel?" He tried at first to deny everything, claiming that whatever his parents did was "their business." However, he agreed that he would be very "sad" if they divorced. As the family discussions continued, Don became obviously more depressed. In the individual interviews, he became quite angry at the psychologist claiming that the psychologist was at fault for bringing him into the situation at all, and that the psychologist was "all wet." He remarked, "This might drive me bugs," whereupon he began to sob.

Thereafter Don and his sister both were able to express considerable anger toward both of their parents, blaming each of them for the tension within the family. Both parents expressed considerable guilt and depression and tried to reassure their children that their contemplated separation had nothing to do with them. "How can you say that?" exclaimed Anna. "It has to do with us because you are our parents and we need parents and you can't separate." However, in the final session, the parents informed the children that they had decided at least to live separately and that Mr. V would visit the home at least weekly. Although both children expressed some further sadness and anger regarding their parents' decision, they seemed markedly relieved that a decision had been made and everyone's feelings had been explored about it.

D. CHANGES WITHIN THE CHILD'S EDUCATIONAL MILIEU

Perhaps the most common question asked in a referral for assessment deals with the child's schooling. For example, a parent or pediatrician may ask whether the child needs some sort of remedial work at school, whether he should have a tutor, whether he should be placed in a special class or in a special school. These questions arise because very often a deterrent in the child's ego development is manifested in lowered academic achievement. The reasons for poor schoolwork, as they have been described throughout this volume, are varied and multiple. Whatever the cause, some decision usually has to be made regarding the possible remedial steps to be taken, for example, if the child is to need tutoring, special class assignments, or a special school. Thus, even if one does discover, for example, that the child is failing to read because of some emotional block, this finding in itself is only part of the step in making some decision of how the child may be taught to read.

Remedial education is a specialty that is usually beyond the knowledge of most clinical psychologists, and assessment to determine the specific *methods* of retraining or training lies in the purview of the educational psychologist. However, the data about ego development which the clinical psychologist gathers and analyzes are often very pertinent background to the specific decisions about the need for such educational remedial methods, the general effects of placing a child in a separate educational milieu, and the considerations which a remedial teacher might have to make about aspects of the child's ego functioning other than his intellectual advancement. Thus, a clinical assessment should provide data regarding the specific nature of the child's psychological disabilities, so that the remedial teacher will be able to estimate the limits of the child's abilities and recognize his special talents and interest. Moreover, as with any change of milieu, it is necessary to know how the child will react to the prospective change. In this instance, one needs to know how a child will feel if he is removed from a regular classroom and placed where children are receiving remedial aid—a situation which is often regarded by a child as indicating that he is inadequate and which socially isolates him or lowers his social status among his peers. Children who are in special classrooms and who are behind in their work are often referred to as "dummies" by their peers in regular classrooms. Perhaps the most important considerations for the remedial school teacher are the child's motivations and his affective responses, which must be considered before a teacher can approach any learning problem. This is especially true whenever the child has experienced failure and is discouraged and angry. It is in regard to these affective and social behavior problems of the child that the teacher turns to the clinical assessment.

One of the main difficulties in relating a psychological assessment of the child to educational needs is that educational philosophies as well as methods have been changing and developing rapidly over the past decade or more. The whole concept of special education programs for the educationally handicapped is relatively new. In some big cities there have been small, side programs for remedial work, but only in the past ten to 15 years have most school systems, large and small, begun to consider them as an essential part of their curricula. Educators vary considerably in their views on the content and even the aims and philosophies of such programs. Variations are almost as extensive as there are school systems.

One of the difficulties in relating the assessment of a child to such programs is the fact that in most instances educators think in terms of "programs," rather than the individual. The psychologist deals with one child at a time but the educator per force must deal with relatively large groups of children. There is no doubt that those responsible for the formation of educational programs do have "the individual child" in mind, but theirs is an average or idealized child, whereas the psychologist is dealing with an actual child's very specific needs. No few educators today do advocate that the "system" approach to education be scrapped, that such institutions as classes, grades, etc. be forgotten, and that an educational program be evolved for and tailored to the needs of each child. However, until such an ideal is realized, the clinical psychologist must attempt to fit his individual assessment to the realities of an educational system. Thus, a clinical psychologist should familiarize himself with the educational programs available in his immediate community. He should know what kinds of programs and classes are available, how they are constituted, and their aims. Many of the programs in larger areas are quite varied. It usually is possible in such centers to find a program which fits fairly closely the needs of the specific child. Usually, there are classes for children who are so disabled that they need to be separated entirely from those who are not disabled. However, there may be other situations where a disabled child can be accepted into a regular classroom. Most educational systems are flexible enough so that a child may attend one or two special classes or have some extra tutoring while attending a majority of the same classes as his other peers. However, even in large urban centers, it is rare to find special classes adapted to very special problems. In many systems, there are special classes for the educationally handicapped, which includes the emotionally disturbed child, the retarded child, and the physically or sensorily handicapped. Although at first glance, this throwing of all handicapped children into one group seems very unreasonable and possibly even undesirable, this writer has seen such classes, especially where they were fairly small, which have worked very well. There is at least the advantage that the source of the problem tends to be temporarily forgotten and the focus is on the immediate recovery of educational losses. There are, however, difficulties which sometimes outweigh this advantage; for example, in so mixing a variety of handicapped children together, it may be very difficult to meet the special needs of each child. Moreover, the child who has a severe motor handicap resents being put in a class with those who are retarded or with those who are "bad kids." Similarly, the emotionally disturbed child does not see himself as a "dummy" or a "spasz" which are common names for the retarded and the crippled child, respectively. Thus, wherever possible, school systems do at least try to separate these three groups.

The fact that the child is segregated at all from other children is one of the first considerations the assessor should take into account. Most children who have educational handicaps do not want to have this difference pointed up, especially to their peers. In fact, most of them are unwilling to admit to their handicap or difference to themselves. Thus, the assessor should look at the responses of the child to see whether he can accept and use this separation from the stresses of the normal classroom or whether it might be better to permit him at least to sit in the regular classroom and offer this remedial work to him on the side. Moreover, when treated in a special manner and put in a role of being inadequate, many disabled children quickly tend to become more dependent and less adequate. One of the very untoward results of the old special schools for the blind or the deaf or the retarded was that these very segregated schools created individuals who belonged, in effect, to a minority group. The graduates of many of these schools often continued to live together in little groups apart from the rest of society, communicating only with other deaf or blind people. In the past, the retarded adult, of course, continued to live in the institution. If disabled children are not to become a minority group based on physical and mental handicaps, then school programs need to be instituted which integrate these minorities into the school, similar to the integration of racial minorities. Although there are probably as many deaf and blind children or children with braces and wheelchairs as there are disabled adults, it is indeed amazing to find how many nondisabled children have never seen a disabled child, because they seldom meet them in the classroom.

These social and philosophical considerations aside, the practical problems of communication between the clinical psychologist and school authorities need to be considered. In the United States, the authorities who deal with the psychological problems of the child and those who are responsible for his education usually belong to two separate institutional systems. There are problems in communication for no other reason than that their schedules and paths do not adequately cross.* In addition, the psychologist has a telephone on his desk and someone to assist him in correspondence, whereas the school teacher has much more limited access to a telephone and very often little or no assistance with correspondence. This writer used to be very frustrated in attempting to contact the schools because it was difficult to get the child's teacher on the phone and weeks would go by before a letter written to a school would be answered. However, a message left for a teacher to return a phone call at her convenience usually brings results. A good example of communication between the clinical psychologist and the school system was given in Case 63 cited in this chapter. Since in most situations, the psychologist and teacher are not in a direct line of communication, the psychologist's written report assumes even greater importance. In writing reports for the school, the clinical psychologist should make extra efforts to state his results clearly and to make his findings relevant to the school situation.

---

*In the more closed society of the Soviet Union, clinics for children are part of the educational system.

There are, of course, quite a few similarities between the child's behavior in the classroom and in the assessment situation which help to make it possible to translate the psychologist's observations into statements which would be helpful to the teacher. As was mentioned above, the psychologist, like the teacher, is interested in the child's intellectual development, his motivations, and his ability to cope with stress and affect. In fact, children often are likely to see an assessment situation in terms of their school experience. Although the child may discover quite soon that the psychologist is not trying to teach him anything, the place where the child has experienced being tested before is usually in the classroom. Thus, it is very likely that the teacher has met with many of the same games that the child plays with the assessor, and the motivation and affect which the child displays during the assessment may not be far different from what he displays in the classroom when he is called upon to recite his lessons. Thus, the psychologist obtains a small sample in his office of how the child relates to teachers and educational authorities.

The psychologist, of course, has the skill and opportunity to observe what the teacher cannot, namely, the ego system behind the games and other manifest behavior of the child. The value of the assessment thus lies in the psychologist's ability to communicate his findings so that the teacher can utilize them in applying her special skills.

A brief example may be of help to illustrate this point.

CASE 66

Patty, age 15, presented several school difficulties which had accumulated over the years and which, by the time of her first year in high school, seemed almost insurmountable. Her school record showed that her intellectual functioning, while not grossly retarded, was, at best, at the lower edge of the normal range. Her academic achievement throughout elementary school had been mediocre. However, teachers had at least noted her "fair" effort and good "work habits and cooperation." There was no note prior to her entrance into junior high school of any kind of behavior problem. However, after she left the structured classroom environment of elementary school, Patty had an increasing number of difficulties. For the past four years, she had been just above the failing mark in all subjects. The school counselor now advised her father that there was serious question whether it was wise to attempt to keep Patty in school past the compulsory age of 16. Patty had become resistant to usual classroom routine and discipline. In junior high school she had been consistently difficult to handle because of her impudence and because she ignored the teachers' requests. During the tenth grade, Patty had become even more defiant of school rules and even somewhat disruptive in the classroom. She would outrage teachers by calmly and deliberately turning her back on them when they addressed her. If she did not care to do what they requested, she would rise and leave the classroom without any of the usual social amenities. She was frequently in conflict with the Dean of Women because of her dress and grooming. Her hair, which seemed untended, grew almost to her waist and she overused cosmetics in an amateurish fashion. She paid no attention to the rules for dress set down by the girls' student-body counsel and, instead, defiantly dressed in a teenage fashion which often appeared to be sexually provocative. The Dean of Women was particularly upset at one point when she discovered that although Patty had come to school fully dressed, by lunchtime she had taken off her underclothes and stuffed them in her purse. It was this total school problem that caused Patty's father to seek psychological consultation.

In the initial interview, Patty's father was most apologetic saying that he was afraid that it was his fault that the child's problems had gone so long unattended. He explained that his wife had died about four years previously and that he had found it very difficult to maintain communication with Patty's school, since he was employed full time. Moreover, he had four younger children who also made demands on his attention. He said that he thought he had particularly neglected Patty, since she presented no problem at home whatever, but actually had assumed a great deal of responsibility for the care of their home and of her younger brothers and sisters. He was quick to point out that there were no demands made on Patty to assume any of these obligations. He employed a full-time housekeeper. He was present in the home each evening and the entire weekend. Patty, however, delighted in helping to clean the house and

cook and to care for the little ones. He had attempted to correct her when he noticed that she left the house inappropriately dressed, but admitted that she always looked so crushed when he criticized her that often he did not have the heart to intervene. He had been more worried about Patty in recent months since she had seemed to be more sensitive, to "mope around the house," to avoid her friends, and to devote herself even more energetically to the household chores. He had recently taken her to the family doctor wondering if she might not be suffering from some kinds of "anemia," but had been advised by the physician that Patty was in good general health. He had tried to encourage her to "go places and do things," but to no avail. Until the beginning of this year, Patty had had many peer friends of both sexes who came to her home; she also frequently visited in the other children's homes. She had even been on a couple of "double dates," and during the ninth grade, he had made extra efforts to see that she went to the school dances. He wandered again if she might not be "mixed up over some boy" but when he tried to inquire about this, Patty assured him almost curtly that she was "not interested in boys now."

Patty's father was also concerned about Patty's situation, since he was planning to remarry in the very near future. He hoped that having a mother again in the home would be helpful to Patty, and that his new wife would not have to face the problems that Patty presented in regard to the school. Patty and his fiancé had met many times and they seemed to like one another a great deal. He noted as an example that Patty had urged him to redecorate his room and had suggested some feminine touches which he might not have thought of on his own. "You don't think she could be jealous?" he asked with a laugh.

When Patty's father brought her to the clinic, her appearance contrasted sharply with that described by the school. Her long black hair was the only bizarre feature. Otherwise, she was dressed very modestly in a simple but casual sheath dress and she wore no cosmetics whatever. A slim, slight built child, she showed few signs of secondary sexual development and might easily have been taken for three or four years younger than her stated age. She was quite tense and guarded, sitting upright in the chair and frequently wetting her lips. She volunteered little, and her responses were very terse. Yet, there was considerable and appropriate affect in what she did have to say. She sighed deeply as she admitted that she knew she had been brought to the psychologist "because I'm so stupid in school." Her eyes blazed as she stated that she did not care what anybody thought of her schoolwork, or what school authorities might do if she continued to dress and act as she pleased. She relaxed noticably and spoke spontaneously when talking about her home and her brothers and sisters. Her face froze again into a mask when the psychologist told her that he was interested in her school achievement among other things, and part of his job would be to help understand what these difficulties were in order that some further and more satisfying plans might be made for her. She remained quite tense throughout all the tests, but was cooperative.

Patty's Full Scale IQ of 81 was consistent with the scores obtained in previous years, and the school. Her difficulty in verbalizing was most acute (Verbal IQ 71) whereas she had somewhat greater degree of success on several of the Performance subtests of the Wechsler I (Performance IQ 98). Throughout the Wechsler, Patty did try to shrug off failure but it was obvious that she felt very badly about it, nor was she reassured by her successes. Qualitatively, Patty appeared to have a very practical mind; she did better on tasks where she did not have to think through abstractions but could go and do things, such as the Picture Completion, Digit Symbol, and Block Design. She did well on the Object Assembly Test also, except for the *Hand* which provides no immediate clues. Her intellectual functioning on the unstructured materials of the Rorschach and TAT were similarly rather simple and uncomplicated. She selected the large, usual details of the Rorschach inkblots, eliminating or ignoring those details of the test which did not fit precisely with her immediate impression. Her TAT plots consisted of a series of actions with little explanation of how one event led to another. When Patty had to explain or justify her percepts, she became uncomfortable and even resistant. Sometimes she would shrug and say, "I don't know," but there were occasions where she made no response at all when asked for further explanation. Patty's perceptual-motor development seemed quite normal for her age, and

there were no signs of any difficulty in this area. Affectively, Patty's responses suggested that she was severely constricted and considerably depressed. Her associations to both the Rorschach and TAT indicated that she was exceedingly cautious about allowing any emotional investment in her environment. Similarly, she attempted to block out or avoid any internal feelings. She was, however, somewhat more sensitive to other people's feelings and showed signs of being easily hurt. Her chief defense against affect seemed to be a mild but definite negativism. Patty almost seemed to be defending herself against her sensitivity by pretending that she did not care at all. By defying others and obstinately ignoring a situation, she could hide the fact that she felt hurt. Patty also used her "I don't care" negativism to hide her depression.

Her associations strongly suggested that she probably was still grieving over the loss of her mother and that she was trying very hard to suppress her longings for a dependent relationship with a maternal figure. In fact, at one point Patty did say very directly that she loved to care for her younger brothers and sisters because she knew how much they missed having a mother. Patty's feminine interests also suggested that her identification with her mother had been fairly strong. Nevertheless, several of Patty's TAT stories also indicated that while she might look forward to having a mother, it was very likely that she did not look forward to sharing her father's affections with anyone else. For example, she could not tell a story to Card 8GF, except to remark that the girl looked like she might be about to go to a wedding and, after a pause, Patty added, "She looks rather sad." On Card 18GF, Patty reversed the usual relationship attributed to the two women and described the "daughter as choking the stepmother." However, Patty could not expand on these remarks.

These results suggested that there were many problems with which Patty needed help and about which the school could do little. Yet, there were some features of these results that did seem particularly pertinent to the decision that would have to be made in the near future regarding Patty's attendance in school. For example, the school was apprised of not only Patty's slow intellectual development, but also of the nature of her intellectual functioning. It was suggested to the school that emphasis might be made on her practical interests and that further development of verbal skills or subjects involving abstract thinking might be relatively futile. The school was also advised of Patty's interest in home-making and feminine activities. It was suggested that any program in which she could be engaged in physical or manual activities would probably fascinate her. The school was not told of the sources of Patty's depression, but the fact that she was depressed and that a great deal of her negativism served to counteract her depression was made explicit. In discussing these results with Patty's counselor, it was discovered that the classes in which Patty's behavior was most disturbing were those which were least adapted to her abilities, such as history, mathematics, or English composition. Her "work habits and cooperation" were considered quite adequate in home economics, typing, and physical education. Unfortunately, the school which Patty was attending placed strong emphasis on preparing for college work and offered only a minimum program for anyone of Patty's particular needs. Taking these results into account, the high school counselor worked out a program with Patty as follows: since it seemed very likely that Patty would be finishing her education when she was graduated from high school, it was decided she could drop most of the "academic subjects" and emphasize the more practical courses in her curriculum. In addition to the home economics courses, Patty was enrolled in a special class for expressive dancing. Patty's situation was discussed with the teacher of drama who offered to try to interest Patty in costuming, stage designing, and makeup, since Patty's poor verbal ability did not give much promise to actual stage performances. Finally, Patty was enrolled in a practicum course two afternoons at another high school where the entire class time was spent in the care of nursery school children. The Dean of Women was involved in this planning, and it was readily agreed that further punitive action regarding Patty's dress and even her behavior might be of little avail. The Dean remembered that she had had some success the previous year with a girl very similar to Patty by assigning her duties in the office. The other girl had made extra efforts to conform with the school rules largely because of the special attention given her.

During the ensuing year, Patty was seen in weekly psychotherapy sessions by a woman therapist. These sessions were largely supportive, with a great deal of discussion about the day-to-day events about the home and school. A recheck with the school during this year showed that Patty responded well to this program and that there was every indication that in the following year she would receive a high school diploma.

E. MAJOR ENVIRONMENTAL CHANGES

When a change in the child's environment that involves removing him entirely from his family milieu appears necessary, a thorough assessment is in order. Such a complete change of environment is seldom contemplated unless the parental home contains so much stress and offers so little in the way of emotional support that the child's further development would be severely restricted. Usually in such instances, the child is already fairly disturbed and is likely to carry some of that disturbance with him to any new situation, at least temporarily. Moreover, the uprooting of the child from his home, however unstable, is likely to be a depressing event, adding to whatever feelings the child may already have of being rejected and guilty. Even where the child has shown no previous emotional disturbance and his separation from his family is caused by an event such as the parents' death, or their or his illness, the trauma of such a separation is not to be underestimated. The first step in the assessment of such a situation is a careful understanding of the exact circumstances which appear to necessitate a removal of the child from the home. In fact, the question of necessity itself should be considered.

For example, it appeared necessary for Jerry, age ten, and his brother Tim, age five, to move to another town to live with their grandparents when both of their parents were convicted of a felony and imprisoned. However, the grandparents, after consultation with the psychologist, spontaneously attempted to perserve the home structure by closing their own home and moving into the residence in which the boys had been living most of their lives. Thus, although the boys were rudely shocked by the separation of the parents from the home for reasons which they did not understand, their home routine could be maintained to a very large extent. In another instance, five children, including an adolescent girl, first lost their father who abandoned them and then their mother who had to be hospitalized for a psychotic breakdown. Rather than place the children in an institution or separate them out into foster homes, the County Welfare Office was able to use the same funds to pay a foster parent to live in the home during the six months of the mother's hospitalization; arrangements were even made for this foster mother to continue to be in the home when the mother returned from the hospital and was recuperating. Although several of the children did show signs of possible emotional disturbance and were having some difficulty in school, it appeared that this rather extraordinary and experimental move on the part of the Welfare Office prevented any of these children from suffering unduly because of this major disturbance in their lives, and the mother was subsequently able to work and care for her children without further assistance.

In other instances, a complete separation of the child from the family may be quite necessary if the chain of interactions within the family which brought about the child's disturbance is to be broken. For example, Bettelheim (1950) found such a separation necessary for the treatment of the schizophrenic children with whom he was working. In the experience of this author and his colleagues in the residential treatment of the severely anorexic child, it is often necessary to prohibit contact between the child and his parents for as long as three months. Such a separation almost inevitably results in the child becoming severely depressed, but since such children have previously sealed off all affective reactions, the appearance of this induced depression makes it possible to make contact with the child's affective life.

Where such a treatment plan does seem inevitable, the assessment usually proves to be invaluable, since it provides clues as to the nature of the child's possible reactions. Thus, in two of the three recent cases of anorexia admitted to the hospital to which this writer is attached, the assessment data strongly suggested the possibility of a psychotic reaction in addition to the usual depression and grief. The staff decided to proceed with the treatment but were prepared to handle the children's behavior and thought processes as well as the depression. Because the staff is aware of the fragility of the ego

of such children, they are able to offer special support and thus assuage the child's confusion, so that an open psychotic break is avoided. In one such case, there was some evidence in the child's history that she had at least come close to an open break with reality a year prior to the hospitalization. The staff was not surprised by her attempt to retreat to the corner of the ward in catatonic fashion; they supported all her efforts to maintain contact and were able to limit this behavior. After several weeks, the child's depression lifted entirely and she joined in ward activities.

Where the assessor does not work in a residential center or is otherwise not familiar with the kind of setting proposed for the child, the prediction of how the child will react to placement away from his parents is more difficult. As with other proposed environmental changes, the psychologist who hopes to make predictions about the child's reaction to changes needs to have some data concerning the possible foster home, residential institution, or boarding school. The data about such a placement of the child is most expertly gathered and analyzed by the psychiatric or medical social worker. However, whenever possible, the clinical psychologist should join the social worker in appraising these placement settings. Where such collaboration is not possible, the psychologist should make every effort to obtain as much evidence as possible about the situation. Very often, of course, no specific placement is as yet proposed, although the possibility of placement is being seriously considered. In these instances, the assessment data are usually very helpful in indicating the kinds of placements which might be preferable. Thus, the psychologist may be able to give some suggestions to his social work colleagues as to the type of foster home or placement that would be most likely to relieve the stresses which the child has experienced, and possibly promote his psychological growth. The same is true when a psychologist is advising a court which may have a choice of institutions or placements for a delinquent child. An example of such a study is given in the case of Tina, Case 15 in Chapter 10.

When the placement of the child outside the home is contemplated, information is needed at the outset of an assessment concerning the kinds of behavior on the part of the child which may have directly led to

such a consideration or at least be associated with it. In most instances, separation of the child from the home is not considered unless there is overwhelming evidence that the child is unable to live there. Sometimes the child's reaction to the environment might be considered a fairly effective method of coping, even though sociably unacceptable. For example, truancy is often the best possible choice a child may make to a very disruptive home. It certainly indicates less disturbance and a greater effort to deal realistically with the situation than such reactions as depressive withdrawal, somatic reactions, or suicide.*
Moreover, by frequent truancy, the child communicates to the society at large that all is not well in his family; even if the child does not otherwise state it, this possibility usually occurs to the most casual observer.

Quite often the immediate and manifest reason for considering the placement of a child outside the home is that his behavior is far too disturbing for the family, school, or the rest of society to endure. In such instances, the assessor should pay attention to the level of tolerance of the child's social environment as well as to the actual behavior of the child. Such acceptance or rejection of the child's behavior by his social milieu often has little to do with the actual degree of disturbance within the child. For example, surveys of public schools suggest that schools often tolerate very overt psychotic behavior on the part of children to the point that the child is learning absolutely nothing and is even a mild to moderate disturbance to the rest of the class, as long as the child's behavior does not openly violate the public mores of the classroom. On the other hand, most school systems are unable to tolerate continued asocial behavior on the part of a child even though such behavior be periodic, directed only against school authorities, and relatively nondisturbing to the classroom. Even a single public acting out of sexual conflicts may panic a school or a neighborhood to the point that expulsion of the child from his milieu is demanded by a band of voices.

For example, Roger, age ten, was so emotionally disturbed that he appeared almost unable to communicate; he sat in the back of the class making noises to himself or stood

gesturing on the playground, completely out of contact with his peers or the rest of his environment. Yet, he was permitted to return to the classroom year after year and was brought to the attention of the psychologist only on the pressure of the family's physician. Immediately across the street from Roger lived Anabelle, age 14, who had been a top student, very well behaved and liked by her teachers and peers, but whose immediate expulsion from school was demanded by all concerned when she became illegitimately pregnant. Anabelle's parents were able to use the school's rejection of her to aid in rationalizing their own anger at her and their need to reject her. The school and parents' acceptance of Roger's behavior, although it might well have contributed to his continued disturbance, did make it possible to involve both the school and the family in his treatment. On the other hand, the combined rejection of school, peers, and parents caused Anabelle to commit suicide before plans could be implemented for caring for her outside the home.

Quite often, once the child is removed from the environment, the social group becomes so relieved from the stresses caused by the child that even after his behavior changes, it becomes very difficult for the society to accept his return. A classic instance of such a problem is, of course, the law violator who, although he may be quite rehabilitated, often finds that he is not accepted back in the milieu from which he came. Similarly, once a family and a school has successfully expunged a disturbing child and have placed him in the role of being "sick," they are often unable to tolerate the child's return, even though the child's behavior may have become much less disturbing.

CASE 67

Dorcey, age 16, was remanded by the Juvenile Court for psychological assessment as the boy's mother had asked the Court to declare him "incorrigible" and "a ward of the Court," so that placement outside of the home could be considered. This move by the mother had been precipitated when Dorcey had fired a pistol several times at his mother's common-law husband. Investigation showed further that Dorcey was also not considered acceptable at school, for although his academic achievement had been fair, he often was openly resentful of school

---

*To remove a child from his home *only* because he is truant would seem to be reinforcing his behavior!

authorities, ignored school rules regarding behavior and dress, and it was suspected that he participated in the use of marijuana which was then widespread in the student body. Certainly, Dorcey's long hair, the dark glasses he constantly wore, and his unkempt clothes and boots all gave him a bizarre appearance. In the minds of a great many of the adults he met, including the Court, this appearance was associated with potential delinquency. Dorcey's mother said that she had barely been able to tolerate his appearance and attitudes prior to the shooting incident, and now she was frightened lest some further act of violence occur. Yet, she upheld Dorcey's story that he had fired the shots at her husband only because the man had been beating her and had dared Dorcey to defend her. This man had immediately left the home and had not returned. Dorcey said openly that he wondered if he would not be better off somewhere else since, in his words, his mother was a "stinking bitch." However, the very fact that he had tried to protect her did suggest that their relationship was at least ambivalent. Dorcey also regarded his school environment as barely tolerable, but said that he hoped to be able to graduate from school in another year and that he was depressed at the prospect of leaving his girl-friend and other peer companions.

The assessment revealed that Dorcey did seem to be attempting to resolve his conflicting relationship with his mother through the social acting out at school. Nevertheless, his abilities to appraise reality and even to control his own behavior were such that if the environment could continue to tolerate him, outpatient treatment seemed much more preferable than institutionalization. Upon receiving this report, the Court also took notice of the fact that Dorcey had no previous record of actual arrests. Since Dorcey was quite ready to accept the psychotherapy offered at the clinic, the Court accepted him as a ward, but decided to continue to place him with his mother. A transfer to another high school was arranged.

All these data about the circumstances leading to the consideration of placement of a child outside his home are necessary, so that in gathering and analyzing the data of the assessment it is possible to relate the child's level of ego development to his relationship to that specific environmental setting. By combining these environmental data with those obtained from the assessment proper, an estimate can be made of the degree to which the environment may be contributing to the child's disturbances. Thus, it becomes more possible to decide how much the interaction between the child and his environment does necessitate his being removed from it, and also the possibility of fostering those elements in this interaction which might make it possible for the child to remain. Moreover, a knowledge of the child's past and prospective environments provides the background for understanding the child's fantasies, coping mechanisms, and affective reactions.

Next, it is very important to be able to assess the child's reaction to the possibility of separation. Any assessment of such a case should be directed at the child's feelings about this separation, to see how the child perceives it, what tensions it arouses within him, and what possible coping mechanisms he may make in response to it. For some children, the removal from the scene of tension, although it may be accompanied by an almost inevitable feeling of depression, at the same time is experienced as a relief.

Moreover, it is common to find that the child also is experiencing no little amount of guilt. For most children, the fact that he is being removed from his home immediately suggests that he has done something awful to warrant such a rejection. These feelings of guilt are often present even when the actual reasons for considering removal have little to do with the child. For example, nearly every child whose family breaks up because of divorce feels at least some twinge of guilt, believing that in some way his behavior may have caused the parental separation. Fantasies that emphasize guilt feelings or feelings of being irresponsible also are quite common among children whose parents die quite suddenly. Sometimes even the display of depression and grief is inadmissable to a family or to the child. For example, a 40-year-old woman and her 15-year-old daughter endured the death, funeral, and social reception after the funeral of their 70-year-old husband and father, not only without tears but maintaining an outward show of social graciousness. Four months later, the girl, who had been a successful student, began failing at school and withdrew from her friends and social activities. It was only then that her depression was recognized. Assessment first of the girl and then of the mother revealed that they had readily accepted the supposed disapproval of their religion against any show of grief in order to hide their feelings of disappointment and even anger against the father because this aging man had been unable to satisfy their needs for almost a decade. The girl's subsequent tears were of anger as well as of grief.

The chief reason for paying special attention to the possible feelings of guilt involved in separation of the child from his family is that quite often this subsequent disturbing behavior turns out to be attempts to cope with guilt.

CASE 68

Ceila, age 11, was admitted to the residential treatment center after having failed to adjust in two different foster homes. She had originally been removed from her home the previous year after her father's death. Her mother, who was partially paralyzed from poliomyelitis, was unable to care for her as the mother's depression exacerbated her disability. In the foster homes, Ceila had run away several times, been very disobedient, fought with the other children, and started fires. It was evident from the assessment data that Ceila considered herself very inadequate and worthless. She openly called herself such names as "stupid" and "evil," but could not explain why she so derogated herself. Some of her remarks in the initial interviews openly suggested that she in some way felt responsible for both her father's death and her mother's polio, although she initially denied any such feelings. Strong feelings of guilt and depression pervaded her associations on the projective techniques. In a subsequent interview, Ceila did admit that her mother's polio was thought to be the result of an accidental use of a live serum used in the polio vaccine. Ceila believed if she had not taken these innoculations herself, her mother would not have done so either. Ceila's father, who was reputed to be a very emotionally distant man, had died of cirrhosis of the liver, probably as the result of a mild but lifelong alcoholism.

Ceila's TAT fantasies revealed ambivalent feelings toward father figures including both anger against being ignored and rejected by them and a guilt over the murderous wishes directed at them. In one story, the heroine committed suicide after the death of the father because she had been very angry at him. In another story, a witch was captured and killed by the community because she had caused the death of the community leader. The witch, Ceila explained, had caused the death of the man because he "didn't pay any attention to her." The fact that Ceila's responses to the Rorschach were replete with associations of explosive tension suggested she might well handle guilt feelings by acting out. Moreover, there were other associations on Ceila's TAT fantasies which suggested that she needed to continue to test whether people would accept her. The heroes of her TAT stories frequently initially escaped punishment for their crimes only to be apprehended and severely punished for much less minor infractions. For example, in Ceila's response to Card 3GF, the heroine was depicted as having just killed her unfaithful boyfriend but was subsequently arrested for crossing the street against the stop sign and was "thrown into jail for life."

On the basis of this assessment, it was decided to keep Ceila in the hospital until these guilt feelings could be ameliorated possibly through psychotherapy. A further search for a foster home was thus delayed.

Assessment was also made of Ceila's mother, and it was discovered that she, too, harbored intense feelings of anger and guilt. Not only did she feel rejected by and angry toward her deceased husband, but she had also been disappointed when she had tried to find support for her needs and affection in her relationship with Ceila. Her fantasies suggested that she saw her polio as a curse which had been inflicted upon her because of her previous anger toward her husband and daughter. She was so depressed that she had contemplated suicide. It seemed likely that no little of Ceila's depression was a reflection of her mother's attitudes. Ultimately, through psychotherapy with both Ceila and her mother, it was possible to reconstitute their relationship and to return Ceila to her own home.

Another case illustrates how the assessment may contribute to successful placement of the child outside his home.

CASE 69

Richard, age 12, had been suspended from junior high school after the school janitor had complained that Richard had threatened him with a knife. Richard was extremely defensive, charging that he thought the janitor was "after him," and that he needed to protect himself because the janitor was continually spying on him. Richard had made similar charges against several classmates, complaining that they had picked on him, threatened him with violence, and constantly called him names. The principal had been concerned because Richard seemed so withdrawn from his peers. The principal observed that Richard had in truth been the object of considerable teasing because he was quick to rise to the bait and because of his prissy ways. Richard was also liked to show up his teachers at any possible point, going to the extent of spending many hours in the library to prove that they were wrong about something they said in class. Richard was positive that the teachers and principal "have it in for me."

Richard was backed up in his feelings by his mother who hired an attorney to sue the school board. Even in the initial interview, it was evident that she was extremely suspicious and probably a paranoid woman. She had previously been involved in litiginous disputes with her neighbors. In front of Richard she openly referred to the peers at his school as "hoodlums" and hinted broadly that she thought the janitor was probably homosexual. Although she was adamant that Richard was purely as a victim of circumstances, with no emotional problems whatever, she did follow her attorney's advice to seek psychological consultation "if only to prove him innocent." In the same vein, she herself submitted to the assessment. Her responses supported the impression that she was a very paranoid, confused, angry and guilt-ridden woman. Although Richard's responses to the assessment suggested that he was experiencing many of the same feelings, it did appear that his disturbance was not nearly as extensive as his mother's. Thus, it seemed quite possible that he was echoing many of her concerns in a folie à deux.

Richard's father, an internationally famous scientist, had apparently extricated himself from the situation by devoting himself entirely to his work, which kept him away from the home much of the time. In fact, it appeared that the father's absence from the home served to reinforce the symbiotic bond between Richard and his mother. In an interview with the father, he openly admitted that his wife's paranoia had been evident even before their marriage, although he had not been aware of it at the time, and that her condition had grown steadily worse over the years. He had hoped that having a child would change his wife's attitude toward life, but when he found that this did not occur, he purposely avoided having any further children. He was conscious stricken and wept openly as he related how he felt he had badly neglected Richard in his absences from the home. Yet, he felt that if he had been forced to remain in the situation constantly, there would have been so much marital dissension that a divorce would have probably occurred. He had tried to "make up" for his absences from Richard by devoting as much time as possible with him on those weekend when he was at home and by taking the boy on camping trips and buying him presents, etc. However, his wife had been so full of precautions and fears that his efforts to be a companion to Richard often went awry. The previous summer he had taken Richard abroad with him, but their trip had been cut short when he was notified that his wife was ill in the hospital. Subsequently, her physician had advised him that his wife's illness was "imaginary," and that she had rejected his suggestion that she seek psychiatric help.

Despite strong objections from Richard's mother, his father accepted the staff's recommendation that Richard be temporarily hospitalized in a residential treatment center. Separated from his mother, Richard's symptoms abated very rapidly. In group therapy, his peers advised him that "we all have our hang-ups, and yours is your suspiciousness." Richard thus began to perceive his behavior as something that could be resolved just as the other children were attempting to resolve their conflicts. Furthermore, the other children and the staff noticed that Richard's symptoms were always strongest on Mondays after his mother had visited him over the weekend. Thus, they helped him to see the relationship between his symptoms and his mother's behavior. In individual interviews, Richard almost immediately revealed that he himself had been the subject of his mother's suspicions. When he heard other children talk about their relationships with their parents, he began to reveal how he had felt spied upon and unjustly accused of many things by his mother.

Richard's responses to the assessment also suggested that the bond with his mother severely threatened the development of his masculine identity. In part, such behavior as carrying a knife, quarreling with his peers, and his attempts to show up his teachers were Richard's way of asserting his virility and his independence from his mother. Although he was a sturdily built boy, he had never participated in athletics because of the over-protectiveness of his mother who constantly feared that he would be hurt. During his brief stay in the residential treatment center, Richard became skilled at basketball and spent many hours punching the punching bag. He became particularly close with one of the male attendants who was an expert at wrestling and judo, and he declared that he wished to take up judo when he left the hospital.

The staff gave serious consideration to the possibility that Richard should not be returned to live with his mother. These plans were discussed with Richard, who made only slight protest. Richard's father also readily agreed. Richard's mother was extremely upset by this suggestion and responded that she regarded the hospital as a collaborator with the school, her husband, and her attorney in a huge plot against her. The following week, after a violent quarrel with her husband, she attempted suicide and was subsequently hospitalized in a psychiatric hospital. Richard and his father were intensely guilt-ridden and some of Richard's symptoms returned. However, a week later, plans were reinstituted for Richard's discharge from the hospital. With his father's help, Richard was placed in a boarding school at quite a distance from his home, but close to the center of his father's work.

F. TREATMENT OF THE PARENTS

Last of the environmental changes to be considered is the possibility of relieving the stresses upon the child by assisting the parents in changing their attitudes and ameliorating their anxieties. Since simultaneous treatment of parents and the child in family group therapy has already been considered, the discussion here will be limited to treatment of the parents with little or no treatment of the child. There are several situations in which only the parents might be treated, among which are the following.

(1) The child's symptoms are temporary and mild, and the parents' emotional disturbances are quite open. Usually in such circumstances, the parents almost seem to forget about the child's behavior immediately and begin discussing their own anxieties and openly ask for help. In such instances, they are apparently using the child's behavior as an excuse to find help for themselves, as "their key to treatment," as it is commonly phrased.

(2) When a child is very young and relatively nonverbal, and when, as is usually the case, the child's symptoms are fairly obviously the result of the parents' anxieties, treatment of the parents may be the preferred approach, even though the child's disturbance may be fairly severe.

(3) Treatment of the parents or counseling them may be the chief possibility when the child is completely resistant to any treatment approach or is otherwise unavailable. Such an approach is almost necessitated when the child refuses to come to treatment, or becomes a captive audience. Again, it is usually found that the parents' reactions and fears have played a major part in the child's symptoms. Under these circumstances, it is often possible to involve the child in the treatment at a later point; the fact that his parents are attempting to make changes in themselves may motivate him to become more cooperative. Moreover, when the neurotic imbalance in the family shifts, the child frequently becomes so anxious as to be more motivated toward receiving help. For example, one 14-year-old girl who originally had stoutly declared that "there is nothing wrong with me except that my parents are nuts," and who absolutely refused to meet any further appointments with the psychiatrist, appeared three months later after her parents had been seen in weekly interviews and demanded to talk with the psychiatrist, to "find out what he's been telling my parents." She was extremely angered that her parents were beginning to deal with her in a more realistic manner, that they no longer ignored her poor achievement, that they were concerned about her social behavior, and even that they were less threatened by some of her somatic symptoms. She continued to make appointments with the psychiatrist, even appeared without an appointment on occasion, almost weekly for the following year.

(4) Counselling with parents may be the preferred approach when dealing with the

behavior and learning problems of retarded or other disabled children. As was noted previously, such counselling is often needed to clarify the attitudes and reactions of the parents.

The assumption in all of the above conditions is that in some way the disturbing behavior in the child is related fairly directly to the parents' anxieties, fears, and attitudes. Such a relationship is present so very frequently that many mental health workers presume that it is the core to all psychological disturbance in children. Although it is probable that the parents' anxieties do play some part, it certainly is not true that it is always the central factor. As has been illustrated in many cases throughout this book, there are many other factors that play a part in disturbances of development. Not infrequently the parents' behavior is found to be a reaction to the child's behavior or to the circumstances which are beyond the immediate power of the parent to alter. Moreover, as was pointed out in family group therapy in Chapter 18, even where the child's disturbance is probably based primarily on the interaction between the child and his parent, there are many instances where separate treatment of the child is very much in order—particularly when these family interactions have begun to be internalized as part of the child's identity and are intermingled with and confused with the child's developmental struggles. In such instances, treatment of the parents without treatment of the child might be a very prolonged, if not unsuccessful, approach.

Obviously, when treatment of the parents with or without parallel treatment of the child is to be considered, assessment of the parents is in order. As indicated above, the first reason for such an assessment is to determine whether treatment of the parents will be of a major assistance in relieving the child's disturbances. It is quite possible, for example, that the parents may need treatment for their own neuroses, but that the child's problems are relatively separate from those of the parents and that thus parallel treatment is in order. Second, the assessment of the parents may assist in answering the question whether the treatment of the parents should be oriented chiefly toward resolution of their own problems, or it should consist of counselling oriented chiefly to their attitudes to and care of the child. Even where the child does

appear to be "the parents' key" to treatment the parent may be so defensive in the begin ning that they can be led into consideration of their own problems only by a discussion of their child-rearing practices. In other instances, assessment may reveal that the parents' compulsive introspection may be a mask for their refusal to consider their interactions with the child. Other parents may be puzzled and even irritated by questions about the child's behavior, since they are motivated chiefly to resolve some of their own conflicts. Such assessment of the parents is, of course, a prerequisite to the further planning of their treatment.

Although many of the principles and techniques for assessment which have been discussed in this book for children are also applied in the assessment of adults' problems, the assessment of the adult does have many other aspects to it which are beyond our purview and have been discussed elsewhere (Pope, 1967). The aspect which is peculiar to this situation is that the assessment includes both parent and child and a comparison of these results. Several illustrations of how such comparisons are made have already been given in previous chapters and a brief additional illustration may suffice.

CASE 70

Mrs. R, age 40, brought her five-year-old daughter Julie to the clinic because Julie was unable to separate from her mother and thus would not attend kindergarten. At the suggestion of the teacher, Mrs. R had tried remaining on the school grounds for brief periods and leaving a few minutes earlier each day, but Julie continued to scream in terror if she discovered her mother was not nearby. Julie also stayed close at home when playing and would not allow her mother to leave the house unless Julie accompanied her.

Julie's responses to the assessment indicated that she was an intellectually precocious child and also considerably emotionally sensitive. She did appear to have a few more fears than the usual five year old; witches and monsters permeated her Rorschach associations, all in humanlike movement. Her drawing of a person was a "big, big, big, mother" which finally occupied three pages of paper. Julie's responses to the CAT also indicated that she perceived her environment as dominated by her mother; the infant figures in her stories "got lost" or otherwise became unhappy without the mother's constant protection.

In the initial interview with Mrs. R, she began by announcing brightly that she was well aware that Julie's symptom was probably related to her own "neurosis." She went on immediately to describe her "migraine headaches," her inability to sleep, her feelings of restlessness and boredom in the home, her guarrels with her own mother, and a recent anxiety dream she had experienced—almost in breathless sequence. Subsequently, while Julie was being assessed, the MMPI, a Sentence Completion Test, and Drawing of a Person Test were administered to Mrs. R. Her responses to the initial assessment techniques did confirm the initial impression from the interview that she was obsessively concerned with many of her own anxieties, that she tried to defend herself by a great deal of rationalization and intellectualization, but nonetheless was experiencing considerable free-floating anxiety.

During the subsequent interview with Mrs. R, while she was conducting a monologue about her relationships with her mother, the assessor glanced down at the drawing she had made, a very artistic sketch of a young and voluptuous woman in a seductive pose, and then glanced up at Mrs. R, an obese gray-haired, drab-looking woman and wondered to himself the relationship between the drawing and Mrs. R's appearance. Mrs. R noticed the assessor looking at the drawing and suddenly burst into tears. She revealed that on the completion of high school, she had won a scholarship to a well-known institute of art, but her family had been unable to supply the needed additional financial assistance because their funds were then tied up in the medical education of her older brother. Later she had earned her own way through college, including a Master's Degree in social work and had been employed as a medical social worker for three years subsequently to support her husband while he finished his doctorate. After her husband had obtained his present teaching position, she stopped work and had devoted all her energies to the rearing of three children of whom Julie was the youngest. The personal isolation of this intellectually bright and artistically talented woman was extreme. She had no social life whatever and devoted herself almost entirely to the care of her home and children. Her sons, ages 14 and 13, had separated themselves from her several years ago by forming a close association with their father, who had repeatedly made it clear that they were not to be "mama's boys." She had almost consciously decided to have a third child when she found the boys separating from her. For almost a year prior to her pregnancy with Julie, she had been quite depressed. Now, she admitted she had conflictual feelings about Julie, since "I had hoped that when I became 40 I could begin to live a life of my own." On the basis of the assessment, it was decided to treat Mrs. R without seeing Julie. Julie was pressed to attend kindergarten for the subsequent three weeks of the semester. The following fall, the relationship between Julie and her mother had relaxed sufficiently to the point that Julie began the first grade with no disturbance whatever.

Chapter 20

ERGO SUM—AN EPILOGUE

As has been discussed throughout this book, one of the chief problems facing the clinical psychologist in this, the latter half of the twentieth century, is that he exists in a rapidly changing society. The children whom psychologists attempt to help live in an exploding and mobile population, where the technology is capable of relieving many of the major stresses of past centuries while also creating new social pressures. The turmoil throughout this changing society is nowhere better illustrated than in the problems in the rearing and educating of children. In fact, the "youth" problem is a central issue in all nations at this time. These social evolutions and revolutions are creating intense conflicts between parents, teachers, and other adult authorities and the generation whom they are attempting to rear and educate. These conflicts are popularly termed "the generation gap." Some such gap has always existed between generations; as Margaret Mead (1942) has so cogently pointed out, this has been fostered in American ideals and values. Yet at no time has this gap of understanding between adult and child seemed so strikingly apparent and so intensely conflictual.

Even the basic psychological problems of children are different than those of a generation ago. The question of identity, the "Who am I?" was voiced by a few literati in the beginning of the century, but has now become a central issue for the current generation. Moreover, it is a question poorly understood, and almost inconceivable, to many parents and teachers.

Clinical psychologists may attempt to take an unbiased perspective of their society, but their values, attitudes, methods, and training often are embedded in their social milieu. These social changes also create a generation gap in the training of clinical psychologists, stemming from the fact that the current generation has to deal with problems that were unknown to their teachers. "Identity crisis," for example, is as new a concept to the professors of psychology as it is to the other parent figures of the current generation. To students, the concepts and techniques now being taught often appear to have little bearing on these new social and personal problems. Certainly the concepts and research developed in scientific psychology in its first hundred years were not aimed at the solution of the unforeseeable problems of the upcoming century. Nevertheless, as will be discussed below, the concerns of scientific psychology have too often been rooted in the past rather than in the present or future. Teachers are inclined to teach what they have been taught or are interested in and, too often, they are less concerned with or are even unable to instruct and guide the student in attempting to solve current or future social problems. As in society at large, the generation gap in the rearing and educating of psychologists is more acute than ever before. Many of the current differences between teacher and student appear to be magnifications of the unresolved problems of the teacher's own generation. The concepts of 1920–1940 had little bearing on the new field of clinical psychology in 1940–1970. Clinical and academic scientists both attempted to salvage what they could of the ideas and methods of the previous 50 years in order to understand and solve the human problems of today. Because they found the previous theories inadequate, they created new ones, as witness the dynamic personality theories and projective techniques, and the interest of psychologists in psychotherapy both as a practical solution to the problems of their clients and as a naturalistic scientific exploration into unknown territory. Yet these had scarcely been introduced, let alone tested, before new demands were presented by both clients and students for new theories and techniques to solve new problems. For example, the effects of current social problems on individual behavior are now recognized to be so extensive that the approach of individual psychotherapy often appears to be analogous to attempting to build a dam with a teaspoon. Projective techniques may reveal a great deal about the inner experiences of the individual child, but seem hopelessly inadequate in the study of interpersonal interactions.

As is probably true of any text, this book has dealt with established practice, that is, with the theory and practice of assessment as it has been developed since 1940. Admittedly, some of the recent innovations have not been discussed, either because they are as yet purely exploratory or because this writer is not fully acquainted with them. Yet the problems currently facing psychologists urgently require rethinking of theory and revision and innovation in technique and practice. Considering the discontent which many young psychologists currently express with the state of their science, it is relatively safe to predict that there will be at least attempts at major changes both in research and practice. Some of the techniques described herein should be thoroughly revised, if not altogether scrapped. Moreover, the personal and social problems of the upcoming generation may so overshadow the concerns of the past generation that the many approaches described in this book may prove no longer applicable and new forms of assessment and treatment will be needed for a wholly new set of conflicts.

Although these changes may need to be radical in order to meet the social upheavals, neither the human scene nor the scientific study of behavior is likely to be altered so extensively that all previous knowledge and skills will be discarded. Such revolutions in theory and practice as will occur may appear to erase prior concepts and to change the focus of scientific interests, but the history of scientific change suggests that revolutions usually are only an extruding crisis in a more gradual, on-going evolution of thought. Thus, in part, the new psychology of the latter half of the twentieth century is being influenced by and even generated out of extant approaches. The extent to which this book may serve the student and contribute toward the expansion and change of psychology depends on the nature of these changes and their relationship to current theory and practice. Although the exact nature of these changes cannot be predicted precisely, some general trends may be foreseen by reviewing in broad outline the ways in which the psychologists have met the problems of their generation— and have mirrored their times. Such a historical perspective has been interjected in prior chapters, but may bear some restatement at this time.

Developing out of philosophy and as a part of education, psychology has long been associated with the climate and thought of the university. Franklin Murphy (1968)* designated three trends of thought in the development of the modern university, which also seem to be appropriate in considering the development of the study of the behavioral sciences and of particular import to the current question of identity formation. The modern university, according to Murphy, developed under the influence of the Cartesian dictum *"cognito ego sum"*—"I think, therefore I am." University life up until the middle of the nineteenth century was dominated by the search for knowledge per se, with little concern about its practical application. However, Murphy pointed out, with

---

*In his farewell address on his resignation as chancellor of the University of California at Los Angeles.

the advent of the industrial revolution and the flowering of capitalism, there was an increasing demand for technical knowledge with practical applications, as witness the establishment of teachers' colleges and agricultural colleges under governmental sponsorship. This change in the philosophy of the university, he called *"facere ego sum"* — "I do, therefore I am." Finally, Murphy viewed the changes now going on within the society as creating a new set of values, also pressing on the university. This new set of values Murphy epitomized as *"sentio ergo sum"* — "I feel, therefore I am." This new philosophical motto is at the heart of the current student revolution throughout the world, which in turn is part of a widespread expression of many people for a new sense of personal worth and dignity. Although a great deal of this social revolution is concerned with political rights and power, embedded in it is the cry for recognition of personal feelings. Hubert Humphrey (1968) states this demand for personal recognition as follows: "And what's really being said by the student protester, surely by the poor and surely by the Negro is: 'Establishment here I am! Don't card-index me. My name is Joe Jones. Joe L. Jones.' They even give the middle initial. And, they say, 'I count. Don't take me for granted. I'm not to be had.'" In race relations, there is as much focus on prejudice as on discrimination, for the acts of discrimination reflect these prejudices. Similarly, the students are as concerned with the attitudes of the university and with the social "establishment" as they are with the actual practice of education. Moreover, the philosophy, music, and art of the current student generation reveal their concern with feeling and experiencing life, rather than with either knowledge-seeking or achievement. Instead of dulling weary senses with alcohol, young people exhilerate them with psychedelic drugs, music, and lights. Murphy gives a pungent example of this change in attitude in the definition of obscenity: for the parent generation, obscenity has referred to the bathroom or brothel; for students, obscenity has to do with senseless hatred and violence. Youth would define as obscene, for example, the statement of the American military officer in Vietnam that he had to "destroy the village in order to save it."

These changes in the university and the world in which it exists may also be seen in the science of human behavior. A concern with cognition and the nature of thought dominated the metaphysics and epistemology of prescientific psychology and has continued, quite appropriately, to be a central area of theory and research throughout the past century. Most of the major psychological treatises, other than in psychoanalysis, have been based on the assumption that man is essentially a rational being and that the chief, if not the exclusive, subject of psychology should be the nature of this rationality. Moreover, prior to World War I—and even thereafter—the application of psychological research to human problems was considered beneath the dignity of the scholar and antithetical to the purposes of scientific psychology. Prior to World War II, chairs in industrial psychology existed chiefly at the major universities, but the subject of clinical psychology was rarely taught. Among psychologists, knowledge was sought for its own sake, and the problems of the individual were left by default to medicine (see Chapter 1).

Nevertheless, even before psychology had much opportunity to establish itself as a pure science, there existed increasing pressure from the society outside of the academic halls for a more practical orientation. For example, in the land grant colleges, "child welfare" institutes or "stations" were established, very comparable to the agricultural or business administration centers. Although these child welfare institutes were altogether research oriented and not clinics, their studies dealt with the practical problems of nuturing, disciplining, and educating of the child (often they were part of a school of education). They were concerned only peripherally with the nature of the child's thought, and seldom with the child's feelings. During the first half of this twentieth century, the dictum *"facere ergo sum"* became a part of the identity of most scientists, including the psychologist. Being a wise teacher or an understanding counselor meant little toward promotion on the academic ladder or even in the eyes of one's colleagues. Psychologists, like other scientists, were valued according to their research productivity, often with little regard for the contribution of this research toward knowledge in the field. Covertly, many psychologists began to recognize that such forced productivity too often led to little or no real knowledge. Even today, the focus of psychological research remains on method rather than results, as any Ph.D. candidate can testify. Only those behaviors which can be measured are considered *de rigueur* in psychological research, and descriptive or explorative investigations into such unknown territory as human motivations or emotions are usually avoided or ignored as if outside the pale of science. For example, although Freud, at the beginning of the century, introduced the topic of dreams as a fascinating phenomenon wherein one might possibly understand the nature of man's motivations, feelings, and even cognitive processes, to date there has been almost no other significant study of this common human behavior. Even at this writing, the chief approach in dream research is essentially methodological and physiological, that is, the rapid-eye-movement sleep studies.

Although *"facere ergo sum"* continues to be the most widespread identity among psychologists, the concern for men's sensibilities and motivations has not been entirely ignored and has gradually increased. In 1905, some American scholars were interested enough in the ideas of Freud and Jung to invite them to Clark University. Yet the Victorian mores of those times did not allow American psychologists to consider the tabooed topics of sex, love, anger, or other private thoughts of individual men. Nevertheless, not *all* American psychologists limited themselves to studies of sensation, perception, learning, intelligence, and the central nervous system. They did invent paper-and-pencil questionnaires on "temperament," or observed children at play, for example. Perhaps the major breakthrough in the study of human emotions was the Harvard studies in the 1930's which resulted in the classic, *The Exploration of Personality* (Murray et al, 1938), and in such techniques as the TAT and later the P-F. Outside university halls, clinical attention to the social and emotional problems of children also dates back to the beginning of the century, as, for example, Healy's clinic in Chicago and the first juvenile courts. A few of the "schools" for the "feeble-minded" employed psychologists, but psychologists were seldom on the staff of mental hospitals, Wooster State Hospital and St. Elizabeth's in Washington, D.C. being notable exceptions. However, prior to World War II, the involvement of psychologists in such activities was negligible. In such clinics for children as did exist, the psychologist "tested" and "diagnosed" with a label, but the child's problems were seldom investigated in the manner described in this book.

Since World War II, the number of psychologists who are interested primarily in affective and social behavior has increased enormously. For example, the membership of Division 12, The Division of Clinical Psychology, of The American Psychological Association increased over 250% between 1950 and 1965, (from 1148 to 2899).* Members calling themselves counselling psychologists have also increased in number, as have those interested in the "Society for the Psychological Study of Social Issues" (SPSSI). New divisions of the APA have been added for those interested in rehabilitation and in psychotherapy. Psychologists have become integral staff members in every major hospital and clinic in the United States. In metropolitan centers, there is an increasing number of psychologists in private practice of assessment and psychotherapy.

This marked increase in the interest of psychologists in the social and emotional aspects of behavior and their involvement in clinical practice are often attributed to the fact that World War II created a demand for understanding and treating the cataclysmic injuries to the sensibilities of those who participated in that human holocaust. The Veterans Administration helped to train many of the current generation of psychologists and channeled their research interests into unexplored fields. Yet the war alone cannot account for the continued and expanding concentration by psychologists in the study of conative, affective, and social aspects of behavior and in creating methods of altering such behavior. Their focus on human problems has been sustained and fostered by the growing demands of society for such understanding and for methods of relieving conflicts. The nature of these social and individual conflicts has been discussed at length in the introductory chapters. The chief aspect of this social change of pertinence here is the growing awareness that society is made up of individuals, as expressed so pungently in the above quotation from Hubert Humphrey.

---

*During this period, the total membership of APA increased from approximately 7300 to 23,500, according to the membership directories for these respective years. The proportion in Division 12 remained the same. However, fewer APA members were affiliating with divisions, and Division 12 had special membership requirements. Therefore, many younger clinicians did not join.

Although psychologists, like other members of society, are becoming aware of the importance of human sensibilities and human experience, the youth and the racial minorities who are speaking most cogently and forcefully of these topics and of the values of *"sentio ergo sum"* did not learn them from professors of psychology. Indeed, the psychologists are learning from their students and clients, and from excursions into the community.

Although there exists this everincreasing adaptation of psychologists to the demands by their society, it cannot be said that the majority has changed their identity to Murphy's *"sentio ergo sum."* Perhaps it is too much to expect that matured scientists or even a majority of their students would alter their identities altogether, especially toward a set of values and attitudes which are as yet being defined and which remain foreign to the white middle class to which most psychologists belong. Yet many do recognize that these changes in values are going on around them, and they seek to learn more about them. Some psychologists do appear to be adapting these values personally, and they participate as faculty members in the unrest and change in the university and as citizens in the public protest movements. Within psychological circles there are developments such as "sensitivity training" and a philosophic approach labeled "humanistic" psychology (Bugental 1965; Jouard 1968; Watts 1966). Yet others appear to be retrenching, to demand even stricter adherence to scientific rigor both in theory and research. For example, the increasing interest in such topics as brain research and in conditioning approaches to child behavior problems—both undoubtedly worthy topics—does not seem to fall under the rubric of *"sentio ergo sum."* In fact, during the past 25 years, there has developed a sharp division of opinion among psychologists as to the directions to which their science and practice should turn. This division has been marked by an intensely emotional rather than rational argument. Some psychologists whose identities are almost exclusively *cognito* or *facere* have been so disturbed by the growth of clinical psychology and other groups interested in the human scene that they have threatened to leave the APA. In many universities, the clinical and social psychologists appear to live separate lives, scientifically and personally, from the other psychologists who are engaged in nonclinical research and teaching. In some universities, clinical training has been sharply curtailed, while in others, new and expanded clinical training facilities and staff are being built. Even within clinical psychology there exists a highly emotionally charged divisiveness between those who advocate behavior modification and those who seek to develop a humanistic approach. All in all, there appears to be an identity crisis within the body of psychology, very comparable to that experienced by other social groups and individuals.

As was discussed previously (see Chapter 5), these identity conflicts had their beginnings early in the century, but have only come to the forefront of social consciousness currently. The generation gap is the more acute because the upcoming generation makes obvious the problems denied and avoided by their parents and teachers. Of particular import to psychologists is the fact that both generations, parents and their offspring, recognize as never before that these conflicts are psychological. The immediately prior generations were preoccupied with developing technology and with war. Personal and social psychological problems were sloughed aside; one could not waste time with "silly" psychological problems when there were "things to be done," that is, *"facere ergo sum."* Moreover, recognition of psychological conflicts involved for prior generations an admission of weakness and consequently of shame and guilt. Even though psychologists themselves were actually identified with the *facere* values, laymen generally were suspicious that psychologists were going to uncover the *sentio* in them. The shift in emphasis toward the *sentio* now going on in society is already putting considerable pressure on psychologists to reconsider their attitudes and values. Since there is a growing recognition of the psychological aspects of the human scene, more and more is being expected of psychologists. Whereas psychology in the past has been regarded as a relatively minor science, the study of human behavior is increasingly being considered as possibly the most necessary. This historically youthful science is being thrust into the limelight, with expectations and responsibilities it is often not prepared to meet.

These social and personal conflicts in society will undoubtedly require further major changes both in the attitudes of psychologists toward their science and in the focus of their interests and concerns. First and foremost, the affective and motivational aspects of human behavior, the *sentio,* can no longer be pushed aside, ignored, or denied. Any research study which fails to mention or take into account these aspects should be considered incomplete. *Sentio* will have to be recognized and, for awhile, be given primary consideration by psychologists. A psychology of *persons* (not merely *personality*) needs to be developed, in which methods of describing and even measuring the behavior of an *individual* are constructed, so that predictions about that *individual* can be made lawfully. Such predictions may or may not apply to any other individual. Such a psychology of persons would be in contrast to the more traditional psychology of individual differences. This latter field, although labeled "individual," has actually been concerned with differences between groups, in which the individual is considered an "error" variable. These group differences have been emphasized almost in the same manner that the society in which it flourished emphasized group differences. This psychology of individual differences can be useful in the study of the person when it is used in a profile analysis of the individual's behavior, that is, to mark the variations in an individual's functioning. However, even this approach is at most a beginning step in the study of a person.

One of the chief objections made against the development of a scientific study of the individual has been that there were no methods. Since the psychology of individual differences depended chiefly if not exclusively on actuarial (statistical) methods, other possible technicians of analyzing data have seemed unacceptable. Imagine, if you can, a doctoral committee accepting a dissertation in psychology which did not contain any statistics. Strangely, many psychologists who have sought to study persons have ignored the fact that the experimental approach often deals with trials rather than subjects, with results expressed in curves or graphs about that subject or even statistical analysis of the trials (not the individuals).

Nor are psychologists lacking in tools and techniques for assessing the affective behavior of the person. One reason that so much attention was given to projective techniques in this book is the fact that, however primitive, they do represent a step away from the group difference techniques into the study of individual affects and motives. Moreover, the rejection of the study of *sentio* has been epitomized in the fact that these projective techniques remain outside the pale of the psychological establishment. The theory represented by them has not been integrated into the body of psychological knowledge. Now that psychologists are turning to the study of human experience, that is, of emotional perception, the theoretical concepts of Herman Rorschach may acquire renewed importance, even if his technique be limited.

Such a psychology of individual sentiments and experiencing will not, however, meet the expectations of society unless it is accompanied by another allied field of study of interindividual relationships. In fact, many psychologists have already become cognizant that the functioning of the individual is interdependent with his relationships with other individuals. Again, this fact has been a major theme throughout this book. However, scientific research on interindividual relationships is only beginning. The recognition of this factor has come chiefly from the practice of psychotherapy, particularly the group therapies, and has been represented in research in the last decade in the studies of family relationships. In social psychology, these interindividual relationships have been partly recognized—but only partly—in the studies of role playing or in the theories of social learning. However, social psychology has tended to emphasize the nature of groups and group interactions, that is, the place of the individual within a group, rather than the ways in which one person communicates and interacts with another.

The development of a science of interindividual behavior will require even greater integration of the fields of social and clinical psychology. This alliance is the more necessary because of yet another expectancy of society. Even though primary emphasis is being given to the status of the individual, there is simultaneously a demand for study of and intervention in the emotional conflicts of groups of individuals, often fairly sizeable groups such as communities. The problem is not merely the general question of how groups behave, but the specific question of how affects and motivations shared by a group can be expressed and satisfied without sacrificing the needs of individuals within the group. Equally critical is the question of how emotional conflicts between groups can be resolved. As noted above, psychologists have been awed by the seeming enormity of these problems, but, even though they have only scraps of theory and research regarding them, they are responding and engaging in these clinical-social tasks.

The fact that psychologists are taking action in unexplored fields with ill-defined problems and using untried tools again reflects the nature of the times. Action *now,* epitomized in "Freedom *Now,*" is the temper of the youthful society and the socially deprived. Murphy noted that *sentio* calls for immediate satisfaction. When students or minority groups confront a governmental body, they disdain "another survey." They see no need to be studied and seek immediate redress or resolution. Psychologists are learning that they must combine action and research. Just as the clinical psychologist has learned about individual functioning through the practice of assessment and psychotherapy, so the psychologist involved in community problems can learn from the processes and results of his efforts. Later, the psychologist may conduct more traditional research studies, bringing back some of their findings into the laboratory for further verification and analytic refinement, as has now been started with hypotheses formulated in clinical practice.

Murphy, in concluding his address to his students, expressed the hope that in emphasizing *sentio,* they would not exclude *cognito* and *facere* in their *ergo sum.* Even though it is time that the *sentio* be recognized, he advised that *sentio* without rational practice results in social chaos. Certainly an individual who operates on affect alone, disregarding reason or the effects of his behavior, also is chaotic. Nor, as Murphy also pointed out, can affective needs always be satisfied immediately, for either individuals or groups. As Jung reasoned, in his *Modern Man in Search of a Soul* (1947), a modicum of dissatisfaction, even anxiety, serves as a ferment of life for both the individual and society.

Some psychologists behave as if they feared that by studying *sentio,* they would in some way have to lose their traditional *cognito* and *facere* identities. The affective side of human behavior threatens them, as if they could not know about it or deal with it without being overwhelmed by it. At the same time, some younger psychologists have proclaimed that all one has to do is be "sensitive" and "feel" and that cognitive comprehension and planned action somehow destroy pure "experience" of the individual or interpersonal emotional involvements. Since the tradition of cognitive comprehension and the practical application of knowledge are so entrenched in the identities of psychologists, it seems highly improbable that they would either entirely lose or abandon these aspects of their functioning when they become engaged in the study of *sentio.* Rather, as was noted above, it seems both probable and possible that psychologists would and could maintain these traditional identities as they add in the *sentio* values. This does not mean that affective behavior can be reduced to or explained in terms of intellectual functioning or by sets of "facts." *Sentio* requires experiencing, becoming involved, and interacting. The psychologist cannot study it or do anything about it unless he comes out from behind the laboratory screen and the clinical couch. It is through such "gut-level" interaction with the subject, patient, group, or community that the psychologist can begin to comprehend and deal with the affective side of behavior.

BIBLIOGRAPHY

Ackerman, N. W., 1958, *The Psychodynamics of Family Life: Diagnosis and Treatment of Family Relationships.* New York: Basic Books.

Ackerman, N. W., 1962, Family psychotherapy and psychoanalysis: The implications of difference. *Family Process, 1,* 30-43.

Albee, G. W., 1966, The dark at the top of the agenda. *The Clinical Psychologist, 20,* 7-9.

Allport, G. W., 1948, *Personality: A Psychological Interpretation.* New York: W. W. Norton and Co.

Altus, W. and Thompson, G., 1949, The Rorschach as a measure of intelligence. *J. consult. Psychol., 13,* 341-347.

The American Psychiatric Association Mental Hospital Service, 1952, *Diagnostic and Statistical Manual of Mental Disorders.* Washington, D.C.: A.P.A.

Ames, L. B., Learned, J., Métraux, R., and Walker, R. N., 1952, *Child Rorschach Responses.* New York: Hoeber-Harper.

Ames, L. B., Métraux, Z. W., and Walker, R. N., 1959, *Adolescent Rorschach Responses.* New York: Hoeber.

Andrew, G., Hartwell, S. W., Hutt, M. L., and Walton, R. E., 1953, *The Michigan Picture Test.* Science Research Associates.

Arbit, J., Lakin, M., and Mathis, A., 1959, Clinical psychologists diagnostic utilization of human figure drawings. *J. clin. Psychol., 15,* 325-327.

Arthur, G., 1947, *A Point Scale of Performance Tests. Revised Form II.* New York: Psychology Corp.

Axline, V., 1947, *Play Therapy.* Boston: Houghton-Mifflin.

Barron, F., 1953, An ego-strength scale which predicts response to psychotherapy. *J. consult. Psychol., 17,* 327-333.

Baughman, E. E., 1965, The role of the stimulus in Rorschach responses. In Murstein, B. I. (Ed.), *Handbook of Projective Techniques.* New York: Basic Books, Inc., 221-255.

Bell, J. E., 1961, *Family Group Therapy.* Washington, D. C.: Public Health Monogr. #64.

Bellak, L., 1952, *Psychology of Physical Illness.* New York: Grune and Stratton.

Bellak, L. and Bellak, S. S., 1949, *Manual of Instruction for the Children's Apperception Test.* New York: C.P.S. Co.

Bender, L., 1938, *A Visual Motor Gestalt Test and its Clinical Use.* New York: The American Orthopsychiatric Association.

Bene, E. and Anthony, J., 1957, *Manual for the Family Relations Test.* London: National Foundation for Educational Research in England and Wales.

Benedict, P. R. and Jacks, I., 1954, Mental illness in primitive societies. *Psychiatry, 17,* 379-390.

Bernal, M. E., Duryee, J. S., Pruett, H. L., and Burns, B. J., 1968, Behavior modification and the brat syndrome. *J. clin. consult. Psychol., 32,* 447-455.

Berne, E., 1964, *Games People Play.* New York: Grove Press, Inc.

Bettelheim, B., 1950, *Love is Not Enough.* Ill.: Free Press.

Bijou, S. W. and Baer, D. M., 1967, *Child Development: Readings in Experimental Analysis.* New York: Appleton-Century-Crofts.

Blum, G., 1949, A study of the psychoanalytic theory of psychosexual development. *Genet. psychol. Monogr., 39,* 3-99.

Blum, G., 1950, *The Blacky Pictures: A Technique for Exploration of Personality Development.* New York: Psychological Corporation.

Blum, G., 1953, *Psychoanalytic Theories of Personality.* New York: McGraw-Hill.

Blum, G. and Hunt, H., 1952, The validity of the Blacky Pictures. *Psychol. Bull., 49,* 238-250.

Boszormenyi-Nagi, I., and Framo, J. L., (Eds.), 1965, *Intensive Family Therapy.* New York: Harper and Row.

Bruner, J. S., 1950, *Symposium on Personal and Social Factors in Perception.* Denver, 1949, Durham, N.C.: Duke University Press.

Buck, J. N., 1948, The H-T-P technique: A quantitative and qualitative scoring manual. *J. clin. Psychol. Monogr. Suppl., No. 5.*

Bugental, J., 1965, *The Search for Authenticity.* New York: Holt-Rinehart-Winston.

Buhler, C., Lumry, B. K., and Carrole, J. S., 1951, World Test standardization studies. *J. child Psychiat.,* **2**, 1-81.

Burgemeister, B. L., Blum, L. H., and Lorge, I., 1954, *Columbia Mental Maturity Scale.* New York: World Book. Co.

Byrd, E., 1965, The clinical validity of the Bender-Gestalt Test with children: A developmental comparison of children in need of psychotherapy and children judged well-adjusted. In Murstein, B. I., (Ed.), *Handbook of Projective Techniques.* New York: Basic Books, Inc., 751-765.

Cain, L. F., and Levine, S., 1961, A study of the effects of community and institutional school classes for trainable mentally retarded children. San Francisco State College, Mimeo.

Caldwell, B., 1964, The effects of infant care. In Hoffman, M. L. and Hoffman, L. W. (Eds.), *Review of Child Development Research.* Vol. 1., New York: Russell Sage Foundation, 9-87.

Call, J. D., 1964, Newborn approach behavior and early ego development. *Int. J. Psycho-Anal.,* **45**, 2-3.

Call, J. D., 1967, Lap and finger play in infancy, implications for ego development, *Intern. J. Psa.* (in press).

Cattell, P., 1940, *The Measurement of Intelligence of Infants and Young Children.* New York: The Psychological Corporation (Rev. 1960).

Claussen, A., 1962, *The Bender Visual Motor Gestalt Test for Children: A Manual.* Beverly Hills: Western Psychological Services.

Cronbach, L. and Meehl, P. E., 1955, Construct validity in psychological tests. *Psychol. Bull.,* **52**, 281-302.

Darwin, C., 1887, A biographical sketch of an infant. *Mind,* **11**, 286-294.

Derner, G. F., Aborn, M., and Canter, A. H., 1950, The reliability of the Wechsler-Bellevue subtests and scales. *J. consult. Psychol.,* **14**, 172-179.

Dewey, J., 1938, *Experience and Education.* New York: MacMillan.

Doll, 1947, *Vineland Social Maturity Scale.* Minneapolis: Educational Test Bureau, Educational Publishers, Inc.

Dollard, J., Doob, L. W., et al, 1939, *Frustration and Aggression.* New Haven: Yale University Press.

Dollard, J. and Mowrer, O. H., 1947, A method of measuring tension in written documents. *J. Abnorm. and Soc. Psychol.,* **42**, 3-32.

Dos Passos, J., 1938, *U.S.A.* New York: Harcourt, Brace and Co.

Dunn, L. N., 1965, *Expanded Manual for the Peabody Picture Vocabulary Test.* Minnesota: American Guidance Service, Inc.

Edwards, A. L., 1957, *The Social Desirability Variable in Personality Assessment and Research.* New York: Dryden Press.

Edwards, A. L., 1959, *Edwards Personal Preference Schedule.* New York: The Psychological Corporation.

Eisenberg, L. and Kanner, L., 1956, Early infantile autism. *J. Amer. Orthopsychiat.,* **26**, 556-566.

Elbert S., Rosman, B., Minnchin, S. and Guerney, F., 1964, A method for the clinical study of family interaction. *Amer. J. Orthopsych.,* **34**, 885-894.

Ellis, A., 1962, *Reason and Emotion in Psychotherapy,* New York: Stuart.

Erickson, E. H., 1950, *Childhood and Society.* New York: W. W. Norton and Co., Inc.

Eron, L. D., 1950, A normative study of the Thematic Apperception Test. *Psychol. Monogr.,* No. 315, Vol. 64, No. 9.

Ervin-Tripp, S., 1966, Language development. In Hoffman, M. L., and Hoffman, L. W. (Eds.), *Child Development Research,* Vol. II. New York: Russell Sage Foundation, 55-105.

Estes, B. W., Curtin, M. E., DeBurger, R. A., and Denny, C., 1961, Relationships between 1960 Stanford-Binet, 1937 Stanford-Binet, WISC, Raven, and Draw-A-Man. *J. consult. Psychol.,* **25**, 388-391.

Fenichel, O., 1945, *The Psychoanalytic Theory of Neuroses.* New York: W. W. Norton and Co., Inc.

Fisher, J., 1959, The twisted pear and the prediction of behavior. *J. consult. Psychol.,* **23**, 400-405.

Fitzgerald, F. S., 1925, *The Great Gatsby.* New York: Scribner.

Fonda, C. P., 1960, The white-space response. In Rickers-Ovsiankina, M. A. (Ed.), *Rorschach Psychology.* New York: John Wiley and Sons, Inc., 80-105.

Forer, B. R., 1950, A structured sentence completion test. *J. proj. Tech.,* **14**, 15-29.

Framo, J. L., 1965, Rationale and techniques of intensive family therapy. In Boszormeny-Nagy, I., and Framo, J. L. (Eds.), *Intensive Family Therapy.* New York: Harper and Row, 143-212.

Frenkel-Brunswik, E., 1948, Tolerance toward ambiguity. *Amer. Psychologist,* **3**, 268 (abstract).

Frenkel-Brunswik, E., 1951, Patterns of social and cognitive outlook in children and parents. *Amer. J. Orthopsychiat.,* **21**, 543-558.

Freud, A., 1946, *The Ego and Mechanisms of Defence.* New York: International Universities Press, Inc.

Freud, A. and Burlingham, D., 1944, *Infants Without Families.* New York: International University Press.

Freud, S., 1909, Analysis of a phobia in a five year old boy. In *Collected Papers,* Vol. III, 1948, London: Hogarth Press, 149-289.

Freud, S., 1937, Analysis terminable and interminable. In *Collected Papers,* Vol. V, 1950. London: Hogarth Press, 316-357.

Friedan, B., 1963, *The Feminine Mystique.* New York: Norton.

Fromm, E., 1947, *Escape from Freedom.* New York: Farrar and Rinehart.

Frostig, M., 1961, *Developmental Test of Visual Perception.* Los Angeles, privately printed.

Gelfand, D. and Hartmann, D., 1968, Behavior therapy with children: a review and evaluation of research methodology. *Psychol. Bull.,* **69,** 204-215.

Gesell, A., Halverson, H. M., Thompson, H., Ilg, F. L., Castner, B. M., Ames, L. B., and Amatruda, C. S., 1940, *The First Five Years of Life: A Guide to the Study of the Preschool Child.* New York: Harper and Brothers.

Gibby, R. G., 1952, Examiner influence on the Rorschach inquiry, *J. consult. Psychol.,* **16,** 449-455.

Gibby, R. G., Miller, D. R., and Walker, E. L., 1953, The examiner's influence on the Rorschach. *J. consult. Psychol.,* **17,** 425-428.

Gibson, R. W., 1958, The family background and early life experience of the manic-depressive patient: a comparison with the schizophrenic patient. *Psychiatry,* **21,** 71-90.

Goldberg, L. R., 1965, The effectiveness of clinicians' judgments: the diagnosis of organic brain damage from the Bender-Gestalt Test. In Murstein, B. I. (Ed.), *Handbook of Projective Techniques.* New York: Basic Books, Inc., 727-740.

Goldberg, P. A., 1965, A review of sentence completion methods in personality assessment. In Murstein, B. I. (Ed.), *Handbook of Projective Techniques.* New York: Basic Books, Inc., 777-821.

Goldfarb, W., 1955, Emotional and intellectual consequences of psychologic deprivation in infancy: a re-evaluation. In Hoch, P., and Zubin, J. (Eds.), *Psychopathology of Childhood.* New York: Grune and Stratton, 105-119.

Goldstein, K. and Scheerer, M., 1945, *Goldstein-Scheerer Cube Test.* New York: Psychological Corp.

Goldstein, M. J. and Palmer, J. O., 1963, *The Experience of Anxiety.* New York: Oxford Univ. Press.

Goodenough, F. L., 1926, *Measurement of Intelligence by Drawings.* Chicago: World Book Co.

Graham, F. K. and Kendall, B. S., 1948, Further standardization of the Memory-for-Designs Test. *J. consult. Psychol.,* **12,** 349-354.

Greenspoon, J. and Gersten, C. D., 1967, A new look at psychological testing: Psychological testing from the point of view of a behaviorist. *Amer. Psychol.,* **22,** 848-853.

Hammer, E. F., 1958, *The Clinical Application of Projective Drawings.* Springfield, Ill.: Charles C. Thomas.

Hammond, K. R. and Allen, J. M., 1953, *Writing Clinical Reports.* New York: Prentice-Hall.

Harlow, H. F., 1958, The nature of love. *Amer. Psychologist,* **13,** 673-685.

Harlow, H. F. and Zimmerman, R. R., 1958, Affectional responses in the infant monkey. *Science,* **130** (3373), 421-432.

Hathaway, S. R., 1940, A multiphasic personality schedule (Minnesota): I Construction of the Schedule. *J. Psychol.,* **10,** 240-254.

Hathaway, S. R. and Meehl, P. E., 1951, *An Atlas for the Clinical Use of the MMPI.* Minneapolis: The University of Minnesota Press.

Hathaway, S. R., and Monachesi, E. D., 1963, *Adolescent Personality and Behavior: MMPI Patterns.* Minneapolis: University of Minnesota Press.

Hathaway, S. R. and Monachesi, E. D., 1961, *An Atlas of Juvenile MMPI Profiles.* Minneapolis: University of Minnesota Press.

Haworth, M. R., 1966, *The CAT: Facts About Fantasy.* New York: Grune and Stratton.

Hayakawa, S. I., 1957, Sexual fantasy and the 1957 car. *Etc. Rev. gen. Semant.,* **14,** 163-168.

Hertz, M. R., 1934, The reliability of the Rorschach Ink-Blot Test. *J. appl. Psychol.,* **18,** 461-477.

Hertz, M. R., 1943, Personality patterns in adolescence as portrayed by the Rorschach Ink-blot Method: III. The "Erlebnistypus" (a typological study). *J. gen. Psychol.,* **29,** 3-45.

Hertz, M. R., 1943, Personality patterns in adolescence as portrayed by the Rorschach Ink-blot Method: IV: The "Erlebnistypus" (a normative study). *J. gen. Psychol.,* **28,** 225-276.

Holsopple, J. Q. and Miale, F. R., 1954, *Sentence Completion: A Projective Method for the Study of Personality.* Springfield, Ill.: Charles C. Thomas.

Holtzman, W., Thorpe, J., Swartz, J., and Herron, E. W., 1961, *Inkblot Perception and Personality.* Austin, Texas: University of Texas Press.

Humphrey, H., 1968, This process of growth and freedom. *Sat. Rev.,* **51,** 22-25, 69-70.

Hurwitz, S. I., Kaplan, D. M., and Kaiser, E., 1962, Designing an instrument to assess parental coping mechanisms. *Soc. Casewk.,* **43,** 527-532.

Hutt, M., and Briskin, G. J., 1960, *The Clinical Use of the Revised Bender-Gestalt Test.* New York: Grune and Stratton, Inc.

Huxley, A. L., 1946, *Brave New World.* New York: Harper.

Jacobsen, W., 1961, Screening of rhinoplastic patients from the psychologic point of view. *Plastic and reconstr. Surg., 28,* 279-281.

Jackson, D. D., 1961, Family therapy in the family of the schizophrenic. In Stein, M. I. (Ed.), *Contemporary Psychotherapeutic.* New York: Free Press of Glencoe, 272-287.

Jackson, D. D., 1964, *Myths of Madness.* New York: Macmillan Co.

Jackson, D. D. and Weakland, J. H., 1961, Conjoint family therapy: some considerations on theory, technique, and results. *Psychiatry, 24,* 30-45.

Jastak, J., 1950, An item analysis of the Wechsler-Bellevue Tests. *J. consult. Psychol., 14,* 88-94.

Jenkins, J. G., 1946, Validity for What? *J. consult, Psychol., 10,* 93-98.

Jones, H. E., 1949, *Motor Performance and Growth.* Berkeley: University of California Press.

Jourard, S., 1968, *Disclosing Man to Himself.* New York: Van Nostrand.

Jung, C., 1947, *Modern Man in Search of a Soul.* New York: Harcourt-Brace.

Kanner, L., 1962, Emotionally disturbed children: a historical review. *Child Develpm., 33,* 97-102.

Kardiner, A., 1939, *The Individual and His Society.* New York: Columbia University Press.

Kinsey, A. C. et al, 1948, *Sexual Behavior in the Human Male.* Philadelphia: Saunders.

Klein, M., 1932, *The Psychoanalysis of Children.* London: Hogarth Press and the Institute of Psychoanalysis.

Klett, C. J., 1957, Performance of high school students on the Edwards Personal Preference Schedule. *J. consult. Psychol., 21,* 68-72.

Klopfer, B. et al., 1956, *Developments in the Rorschach Technique.* Vols. I and II, New York: Harcourt, Brace and World, Inc.

Klopfer, B. and Kelly, D., 1942, *The Rorschach Technique.* New York: World Book Company.

Klopfer, W. G., 1960, *The Psychological Report.* New York: Grune and Stratton.

Koppitz, E., 1963, *The Bender-Gestalt Test for Young Children.* New York: Grune and Stratton, Inc.

Lamke, T. A. and Nelson, M. J., 1958, *The Henmon-Nelson Tests of Mental Ability.* New York: Houghton Mifflin Co.

Lazarus, R. S., 1965, Ambiguity and nonambiguity in projective testing. In Murstein, B. I. (Ed.), *Handbook of Projective Techniques.* New York: Basic Books, Inc., 89-93.

Leary, T., 1957, *Interpersonal Diagnosis of Personality.* New York: Ronald Press Co.

Lebowitz, M. H., Colbert, E. G., and Palmer, J. O., 1961, Schizophrenia in children. *Amer. J. Dis. Child., 102,* 25-27.

Leiter, R. G., 1948, *Leiter International Performance Scale.* Chicago: C. H. Stoelting Co.

Levitt, E., and Lyle, W. H., Jr., 1955, Evidence for the validity of the children's form of the Picture-Frustration Study. *J. consult. Psychol. 19,* 381-386.

Levy, J. and Epstein, W. B., 1964, An application of the Rorschach Test in family investigation. *Family Process, 3,* 344-376.

Lewin, K., 1936, *Principles of Topological Psychology.* New York: McGraw-Hill.

Linder, R. M., 1944, *Rebel Without a Cause.* New York: Grune and Stratton.

Linton, R., 1945, *The Cultural Background of Personality.* New York: Appleton-Century-Crofts.

Liverant, S., 1960, Intelligence: a concept in need of re-examination. *J. consult. Psychol., 24,*(2), 101-110.

Loevinger, J., 1959, Patterns of parenthood as theories of learning. *J. abnorm. and soc. Psychol., 59,* 148-150.

Loosli-Usteri, M., 1931, La notion du hazard chez l'enfant. *Arch. Psychol. Genève, 23,* 45-66.

Lovaas, O. I., Simmons, J. Q., and Schaeffer, B., 1965, Building social behavior in autistic children by use of electric shock. *Journal of Experimental Research in Personality, 1,* 99-109.

Lynn, D. B., 1959, *Structured Doll Play Test (SOP) Manual of Instructions.* Colorado: Test Developments.

McClelland, D. C., Atkinson, J. W., Clark, R. A., and Lowell, E. L., 1953, *The Achievement Motive.* New York: Appleton-Century Crofts.

McKinley, J. C., and Hathaway, S. R., 1943, The identification and measurement of the psychoneuroses in medical practice. *J. Amer. Med. Assoc., 122,* 161-167.

Machover, K., 1949, *Personality Projection in the Drawing of a Human Figure.* Illinois: Charles C. Thomas.

Mainord, F. P., 1956, *Parental Attitudes in Schizophrenia.* Unpublished doctoral dissertation, University of Washington.

Marks, P. A., 1961, An assessment of the diagnostic process in a child guidance setting. *Psychol. Monogr., 75,* (3) (whole No. 507).

Martin, B. and Kirbly, D., 1955, Results of treatment of enuresis by a conditional response method. *J. consult. Psychol., 19,* 71-73.

Maslow, A., 1950, Self-actualizing people: a study of psychological health. *Personality Symposia,* No. 1, 11-34, New York: Grune and Stratton.

Mead, M., 1942, *And Keep Your Powder Dry.* New York: Morrow.

Mead, G. H., 1932, *The Philosophy of the Present.* Chicago: Open Court.

Meltzoff, J., Singer, J. L., and Korchin, S. J., 1953, Motor inhibition and Rorschach movement responses: a test of the Sensory-Tonic theory. *J. Pers., 21,* 400-410.

Menninger, K., 1962, *A Manual for Psychiatric Case Study.* New York: Grune and Stratton.

Meyer, A., 1948, *Commonsense Psychiatry.* Lief, A. (Ed.). New York: McGraw-Hill Book Co., Inc.

Mowrer, O. H., 1950, *Learning Theory and Personality Dynamics.* New York: The Ronald Press Co.

Mowrer, O. H., 1960, *Learning Theory and the Symbolic Processes.* New York: John Wiley and Sons.

Mullahy, P., 1948, *Oedipus, Myth and Complex.* New York: Grove Press.

Murphy, F., 1968, The state of the university. *UCLA—From the Chancellor's Desk,* **10,** 2-4.

Murray, H. A., 1938, *Explorations in Personality.* New York: Oxford University Press.

Murray, H. A., 1943, *Thematic Apperception Test Manual.* Harvard College

Murray, H. A., 1965, Uses of the thematic apperception test. In Murstein, B. I. (Ed.), *Handbook of Projective Techniques.* New York: Basic Books, Inc., 425-432.

Murstein, B. I. (Ed.), 1965, *Handbook of Projective Techniques.* New York: Basic Books, Inc.

Ochs, E., 1960, Changes in Goodenough Drawings associated with changes in social adjustment, *J. clin. Psychol.,* **6,** 282-284.

Oppenheimer, R., 1956, Analogy in science. *Amer. Psychologist,* **11,** 127-135.

Orlando, R. and Bijou, S. W., 1967, Rapid acquisition of multiple-schedule discrimination performance in a single response free-operant situation with retardates. In Bijou, S. W. and Baer, D. M. (Eds.), *Child Development: Readings in Experimental Analysis.* New York: Appleton-Century-Crofts, 81-92.

Orwell, G., 1950, *Nineteen Eighty-Four.* London: Secker and Warburg.

Palmer, J. O., 1952, A note on the intercard reliability of the Thematic Apperception Test. *J. consult. Psychol.,* **16,** 473-474.

Palmer, J. O., 1955, Rorschach's experience balance: the concept, general population characteristics and intellectual correlations. *J. proj. Tech.,* **19,** 138-145.

Palmer, J. O., 1956, Attitudinal correlates of Rorschach's experience balance. *J. proj. Tech.,* **20,** 207-211.

Palmer, J. O., 1957. *A Survey of Staffing Needs in Psychology Departments of the State Hospitals for the Mentally Ill in California.* A report of the Ad Hoc Committee on Psychology Staff, Department of Mental Hygiene, State of California. Sacramento: unpublished mimeo, Department of Mental Hygiene, State of California.

Palmer, J. O., 1957, Some relationships between Rorschach's experience balance and Rosenzweig's frustration aggression patterns. *J. proj. Tech.,* **21,** 137-141.

Palmer, J. O., 1964, A restandardization of adolescent norms for the Shipley-Hartford. *J. clin. Psychol.,* **20,** 492-495.

Palmer, J. O. and Lustgarten, B. J., 1962, The prediction of TAT structure as a test of Rorschach's experience-balance. *J. proj. Tech.,* **26,** 212-220.

Piaget, J., 1954, *The Construction of Reality in the Child.* New York: Basic Books.

Pope, B., 1967, *Psychological Diagnosis in Clinical Practice.* New York: Oxford University Press.

Preyer, W., 1881, *Die Seele des Kindes* (translated as *Mind of the Child,* 1889). New York: Appleton.

Rabin, A. I. and Haworth, M. R. (Eds.), 1960, *Projective Techniques with Children.* New York: Grune and Stratton.

Ramzy, I. and Picard, P. M., 1949, A study in the reliability of scoring the Rorschach Inkblot Test. *J. gen. Psychol.,* **40,** 3-10.

Raven, J. C., 1956, *Coloured Progressive Matrices.* London: H. K. Lewis and Co., Ltd.

Redl, F. and Wineman, D., 1951, *Children Who Hate.* Glencoe, Ill.: Free Press.

Reissman, D., Glazer, N., and Denney, R., 1950, *The Lonely Crowd.* New Haven: Yale University Press.

Rickers-Ovsiankina, M. A., 1961, *Rorschach Psychology.* New York: John Wiley and Sons, Inc.

Rogers, C. R., 1931, *A Test of Personality Adjustment.* New York: Association Press.

Rogers, C. R., 1942, *Counseling and Psychotherapy.* Mass.: Houghton Mifflin Company.

Rogers, C. R., 1951, *Client-Centered Therapy.* Mass.: Houghton Mifflin Company.

Rohde, A. R., 1957, *The Sentence Completion Method: Its Diagnostic and Clinical Application to Mental Disorders.* New York: Ronald.

Rorschach, H., 1921, *Psychodiagnostik, Methodik und Ergebnisse eines wahrnehmungs diagnostische Experiments.* Bern: Bircher (Translation: *Psychodiagnostics.* New York: Grune and Stratton, 1951.)

Rosenzweig, S., 1950, Levels of behavior in psychodiagnosis with special reference to the picture-frustration study. *Amer. J. Orthopsychiat.,* **20**, 63-72.

Rosenzweig, S., Fleming, R., and Rosenzweig, B., 1948, The Children's Form of the Rosenzweig Picture-Frustration Study. *J. Psychol.,* **26**, 141-191.

Rosenthal, M. J., 1952, Psychosomatic study of infantile eczema. I. Mother-child relationship. *Pediatrics,* **10**, 581-592.

Rotter, J. B., Rafferty, J. E., and Schachtitz, E., 1965, Validation of the Rotter Incomplete Sentence Test for College Screening. In Murstein, B. I. (Ed.), *Handbook of Projective Techniques.* New York: Basic Books, Inc., 859-872.

Rotter, J. B., and Willerman, B., 1947, The incomplete sentence test as a method of studying personality. *J. consult. Psychol.,* **11**, 43-48.

Samuels, H., 1965, The validity of personality-trait ratings based on projective techniques. In Murstein, B. I. (Ed.), *Handbook of Projective Techniques.* New York: Basic Books, Inc., 163-187.

Sanford, R. N., 1936, The effect of abstinence from food upon imaginal processes. *J. Psychol.,* **2**, 129-136.

Sargent, H. D., 1951, Psychological test reporting: an experiment in communication. *Bull. Menninger Clin.,* **15**, 175-186.

Satir, V., 1964, *Conjoint Family Therapy.* California: Science and Behavior Books, Inc.

Schafer, R., 1954, *Psychoanalytic Interpretation in Rorschach Testing: Theory and Applications.* New York: Grune and Stratton, Inc.

Schwebel, M., 1963, Studies of children's reactions to the atomic threat. *Amer. J. Orthopsychiat.,* **33**, 202.

Seeley, J. R., Sim, R. A., and Loosley, E. W., 1956, *Crestwood Heights.* New York: Basic Books, Inc.

Shneidman, E. S., 1952, *Manual for the Make-A-Picture Story Method.* Projective Techniques Monographs, No. 2, The Society for Projective Techniques and Rorschach Institute, Inc.

Shuttleworth, F. K., 1949, The adolescent period: a pictorial atlas. *Monogr. S.R.C.D.,* **50**, (2).

Spitz, R. A., 1946, Anaclitic depression: An inquiry into the genesis of psychiatric condition in early childhood. *Psychoanal. Stud. Child.,* **2**, 313-342.

Spock, B., 1946, *Baby and Child Care.* New York: Duell, Sloan and Pearce.

Start, K. B., 1961, The relationship between the games performance of a grammar school boy and his intelligence and streaming. *Brit. J. educ. Psychol.,* **31**, 208-211.

Stein, M. I., 1948, *The Thematic Apperception Test.* Cambridge: Addison-Wesley.

Stoltz, R. and Smith, M., 1959, Some effects of socio-economic age and sex factors on children's responses to the Rosenzweig Picture Frustration Study, *J. Clin. Psychol.,* **15**, 200-203.

Storms, L. H., 1960, Rationales for the "twisted pear." *J. consult. Psychol.,* **24**, 552-553.

Stutzman, R., 1931, *Guide for Administering the Merrill-Palmer Scale of Mental Tests.* New York: Harcourt, Brace & World.

Sullivan, P. L., Miller, C., and Smelser, W., 1958, Factors in length of stay and progress in psychotherapy. *J. consult. Psychol.,* **22**, 1-9.

Symonds, P. M., 1949, *Adolescent Fantasy: An Investigation of the Picture Story Method of Personality Study.* New York: Columbia University Press.

Symonds, P. M., 1949, Unpublished comments at Amer. Psychol. Assn. Meetings.

Szass, T., 1961, *The Myth of Mental Illness.* New York: Hoeber-Harper.

Tamkin, A. S., 1965, The effectiveness of the Bender-Gestalt Test in differential diagnosis. In Murstein, B. I. (Ed.), *Handbook of Projective Techniques.* New York: Basic Books, Inc. 741-745.

Tolman, E. C., 1952, A cognition motivation model. *Psychol. Review,* **59**, 5, 389-400.

Trager, H. and Yarrow, M. R., 1952, *They Learn What They Live; Prejudice in Young Children.* New York: Harper Brothers.

Tucker, J., 1950, Rorschach human movement responses in relation to intelligence. *J. consult. Psychol.,* **14**, 283-286.

Ulett, G. and Gleser, G., 1952, The effect of experimental stress on photically activated EEG. *Science,* **115**, 678-682.

Vernon, M. D., 1961, The relation of perception to personality factors. *Brit. J. Psychol.,* **52**, 205-217.

Watts, A., 1966, *The Book: On the Taboo Against Knowing Who You Are.* New York: Pantheon.

Wechsler, D., 1944, *The Measurement of Adult Intelligence.* Baltimore: The Williams and Wilkins Company.

Wechsler, D., 1949, *Wechsler Intelligence Scale for Children.* New York: Psychology Corp.

Wenar, C., 1961, The reliability of mothers' histories. *Child Developm.,* 32, 491-500.

Wenar, C., Handlon, M., and Garner, A., 1959-60, Patterns of mothering in psychosomatic disorders and severe emotional disturbances. *Merrill-Palmer Quart. of Behavior and Development,* **6**, 165-170.

Whyte, W. H., 1956, *The Organization Man.* New York: Simon and Schuster.

Wildman, R. W. and Wildman, R. W., Jr., 1967, The practice of clinical psychology in the United States. *J. clin. Psychol.*, **23**, 292-295.

Wilson, S., 1955, *The Man in the Gray Flannel Suit.* New York: Simon and Schuster.

Winnicott, D. W., 1953, Transitional objects and transitional phenomena. *Internat. J. Psychoanal.*, **34**, 89-97.

Work, H. H., and Call, J., 1965, *A Guide to Preventive Child Psychiatry: The Art of Parenthood.* New York: McGraw Hill Book Co.

Wynne, L., 1965, Some indications and counterindications for exploratory family therapy. In Boszormenyi-Nagy, I. and Framo, T. L. (Eds.), *Intensive Family Therapy.* New York: Harper and Row, 289-322.

Yarrow, L. J., 1964, Separation from parents during early childhood. In Hoffman, M. L. and Hoffman, L. W. (Eds.), *Review of Child Development Research.* Vol. 1, New York: Russell Sage Foundation, 89-137.

Yates, A. J., 1958, The application of learning theory to the treatment of tics. *J. abn. soc. Psychol.*, **56**, 75-182.

Zemlich, M. and Watson, R. I., 1953, Maternal attitudes of acceptance and rejection during and after pregnancy. *Amer. J. Orthopsychiat.*, **23**, 570-584.

AUTHOR INDEX

SUBJECT INDEX

o

WITHDRAWN